Expedited Debt Restructuring
An International Comparative Analysis

Expedited Debt Restructuring

An International Comparative Analysis

Edited by

Rodrigo Olivares-Caminal

Published by:
Kluwer Law International
P.O. Box 316
2400 AH Alphen aan den Rijn
The Netherlands
E-mail: sales@kluwerlaw.com
Website: http://www.kluwerlaw.com

Sold and distributed in North, Central and South America by:
Aspen Publishers, Inc.
7201 Mc Kinney Circle
Frederick, MD 21704
United States of America

Sold and distributed in all other countries by:
Turpin Distribution Services Ltd.
Stratton Business Park
Pegasus Drive, Biggleswade
Bedfordshire SG18 8TQ
United Kingdom

ISBN 978-90-411-2485-2

© 2007 Kluwer Law International BV, The Netherlands

All rights reserved. No part of this publication may be reproduced, stored in a retrieval system, or transmitted in any form or by any means, mechanical, photocopying, recording or otherwise, without prior written permission of the publishers.

Permission to use this content must be obtained from the copyright owner. Please apply to: Permissions Department, Wolters Kluwar Legal, 76 Ninth Avenue, 7th floor, New York, NY 10011, United States of America. E-mail: permissions@kluwerlaw.com.

Summary of Contents

Foreword
About the Authors
Preface

Chapter 1 Introduction
Formal Processes and Alternative Mechanisms of Reorganization in
International Initiatives on Insolvency   1
Adolfo Rouillon

Chapter 2 Argentina
Expedited Debt Restructuring Under Argentine Law: Acuerdo
Preventivo Extrajudicial (APE)   19
Rodrigo Olivares-Caminal

Chapter 3 Australia
Voluntary Administration Leading to a Deed of Company
Arrangement   55
Ian Walker

Chapter 4 Brazil
Brazil's Two New Mechanisms for Out-Of-Court Reorganizations:
'Homologation Of Consensus' and 'Enforcement Of Agreement'   97
Luiz Fernando Valente-de-Paiva

Chapter 5 Canada
Canada's Expedited Debt Restructuring   129
Kevin P. McElcheran

Chapter 6 England & Wales
Schemes of Arrangement and Company Voluntary Arrangements 157
Samantha Bewick, Mark Fennessy and David Marks

Chapter 7 France
The Idiosyncrasy of the French Judicial System and its Preventive Procedures for Expedited Debt Restructurings 257
Isabelle Didier

Chapter 8 Hong Kong
Corporate Rescue in Hong Kong 297
Charles D. Booth, Stephen Briscoe and Philip Smart

Chapter 9 India
The Corporate Debt Restructuring Mechanisms in India 323
Rajiv Luthra

Chapter 10 Italy
Article 182bis of Law 80/2005 and the Code of Conduct to Restructure Debt Issued by the Italian Bank Association 357
Antonio Auricchio

Chapter 11 Japan
Expedited Corporate Debt Restructuring in Japan 377
Shinjiro Takagi

Chapter 12 Poland
Out-of-Court Debt Restructuring in Poland 405
Lech Giliciński

Chapter 13 Turkey
Pre-packaged Corporate Restructuring Mechanism Under the Turkish Execution and Bankruptcy Law 419
Sevi Simavi

Chapter 14A USA (theory)
The United States Expedited Proceedings: 'Pre-Packaged' Chapter 11 Plans 437
Lindsee P. Granfield and Andrés de la Cruz

Summary of Contents

Chapter 14B USA (practice)
American Bankruptcy Reform and Creativity Prompt the
***In re Blue Bird Body Company* One-Day Pre-packaged Plan of**
Reorganization 457
Jay M. Goffman, Mark A. McDermott, and Kurt Ramlo

Chapter 15
Private International Law Implications of Expedited
Corporate Debt Restructurings 477
Gerald Arends

Chapter 16
The Tax Consequences of Corporate Debt Restructuring 509
Daniel Dürrschmidt

Chapter 17
Implications of Merger Legislation for Corporate Restructuring 543
Ioannis Kokkoris

Table of Contents

Foreword	xxxi
About the Authors	xxxiii
Preface	xliii

Chapter 1
Introduction   1

Formal Processes and Alternative Mechanisms of Reorganization in International Initiatives on Insolvency
Adolfo Rouillon

I.	Introduction		3
	A.	Preliminary Explanation	3
	B.	Forms of Reorganization of Insolvent Companies	3
	C.	Reorganization as an Objective of the Insolvency Legislation	4
II.	Reorganization Proceedings		4
	A.	'Formal' or 'Full' Reorganization Proceeding	4
	B.	Dual and Unitary Insolvency Systems	7
	C.	Reorganization in Liquidation	8
III.	Voluntary Restructuring Negotiations		8
	A.	Introduction to Voluntary Restructuring Negotiations	8
	B.	Voluntary Restructuring Negotiations in the Principles	8
	C.	Voluntary Restructuring Negotiations in the Guide	12
	D.	Those Bound by Voluntary Restructuring Agreements	13
IV.	Introduction to Expedited Reorganization Proceedings		13
V.	Conclusions		17

Chapter 2
Argentina 19

Expedited Debt Restructuring Under Argentine Law: Acuerdo Preventivo Extrajudicial (APE)
Rodrigo Olivares-Caminal

I.	Introduction	21
II.	The Argentine Crisis	22
III.	Pre-Packaged Reorganization Plans under Argentine Law	24
IV.	The APE: A Workable Solution. Two Case Studies	27
	A. The Multicanal Case	28
	1. Litigation in Argentina	28
	2. Litigation in the US	31
	3. Concluding Remarks In Re the Multicanal Case	41
	4. New Chapter 15. A Brief Explanatory Note.	42
	B. The Telecom Case	43
	1. Facts and Litigation in the US	43
	2. Concluding remarks re the Telecom case	49
V.	Concluding Remarks	50
ANNEX: KEY LEGISLATION		52

Chapter 3
Australia 55

Voluntary Administration Leading to a Deed of Company Arrangement
Ian Walker

I.	Introduction	57
	A. Purpose of Chapter	57
	B. Corporate Restructuring using Voluntary Administration	57
II.	Voluntary Administration	58
	A. Workings of Voluntary Administration	58
	1. Introduction to the Framework of Administration under Part 5.3A	58
	2. Timeframe of Voluntary Administration	58
	a. First meeting of creditors	59
	b. Second Meeting of Creditors	60
	B. Operative Elements of Part 5.3A Administration	61
	1. Objects of Part 5.3A	61
	2. Statutory Moratorium	61

Table of Contents xi

		3.	Voting at Creditors Meetings	63
			a. Casting Vote	63
			b. Secured Creditors	64
		4.	Powers, duties and liabilities of Administrators	65
		5.	Statutory Indemnity and Lien	66
			a. Nature and Extent of Statutory Lien	67
			b. Equitable Lien	67
		6.	Role of the Court in Part 5.3A Administrations	68
			a. Court's Power to Alter Operation of Part 5.3A	69
			b. Extension of convening period	70
			c. Directions to Administrators	72
			d. Borrowing by Administrators	72
			e. Limitation of Personal Liability of Administrator	74
III.	Restructuring under Part 5.3A			75
	A.	Deeds of Company Arrangement		76
		1.	Types of Deed	76
		2.	Format of Deeds	77
	B.	Creditors' Trusts		77
	C.	Courts and the Restructure		78
		1.	Section 447A again	79
		2.	Post restructure insolvency–the role of the court	80
	D.	Shares in companies under administration		81
IV.	A Case Study in Expedited Corporate Restructuring: The Pasminco Group—an administration under Part 5.3A of the Corporations Act			83
	A.	Background		83
	B.	The Administration and Restructure Planning Phase		84
	C.	The Restructure		85
V.	An Afterword on Schemes of Arrangement			87
ANNEX: KEY LEGISLATION				88

Chapter 4
Brazil   97

Brazil's Two New Mechanisms for Out-Of-Court Reorganizations: 'Homologation Of Consensus' and 'Enforcement Of Agreement'
Luiz Fernando Valente-de-Paiva

I.	Introduction. The Pervious Legislation and its Limitations	99
II.	The Two Types of Out-of-Court Reorganization Procedures: (1) Reorganization by Homologation of Consensus; and, (2) Reorganization by Enforcement of Agreement	102

	A.	Preliminary Concepts	103
		1. Reorganization by Homologation of Consensus	103
		2. The Enforcement of Agreement Procedure	103
	B.	Who May Apply	105
	C.	Requirements to be Complied With for Use of the Out-of-Court Reorganizations	105
		1. The General Requirements	106
		2. Requirements for Each Type of Procedure	106
		3. Impediments	107
III.	Preparation of an Out-of-Court Reorganization Plan		109
	A.	Creditors Not Subject to the Effects of Out-of-court Reorganization	110
	B.	Treatment of Creditors in Bankruptcy Proceedings	111
	C.	Limitations Applicable to the Out-of-court Reorganization Plan	113
		1. Selection of Creditors for Homologation of Consensus	114
		2. Selection of Creditors to be Subject to Enforcement of Agreement	114
IV.	Restrictions and Effects of the Plan		115
	A.	Restrictions of Treatment to Creditors. Acts Subject to Review	115
	B.	Effects Caused by Signature and Homologation of the Plan. Bankruptcy Related Crimes	115
	C.	Effects Arising from the Homologation by Consensus or Enforcement of Agreement	116
		1. Administration of the Debtor. Disposal of Assets	116
		2. Individual Rights and Actions	117
V.	The Procedure		118
	A.	Competent Court	118
	B.	The Petition and its Instruction	118
	C.	Summon of Creditors	119
	D.	Oppositions to the Application. Obstacles in the Homologation Process	120
	E.	Role of the Judge. Judgments of Homologation and Judgments of Refusal	120
VI.	Conclusions		121
VII.	Review of the First out-of-Court Case (Enforcement of Agreement)		121
	A.	Debtor	121
	B.	*Preventive Concordata*	122

Table of Contents xiii

    C. Out-of-Court Reorganization Plan   122
    D. Reorganization by Enforcement of Agreement   123
ANNEX: KEY LEGISLATION   125

Chapter 5
Canada   129

Canada's Expedited Debt Restructuring
Kevin P. McElcheran

I.	Introduction	131
II.	Formal Insolvency Proceedings in Canada	131
	A. Restructuring Proceedings	132
	B. Sale Proceedings	133
	1. Court Supervised Sale Proceedings	133
	2. Private Sale Proceedings	135
III.	The Basic Requirements of an Expedited Process	137
	A. Expedited creditor compromises	138
	1. Private debt restructuring	138
	a. Bilateral Settlements	138
	b. Multilateral Settlements	140
	i. Common Benefit Restructuring	140
	ii. Delegated Settlement Authority	141
	c. Disclosure and Confidentiality	142
	d. Conclusions on the Subject of Private Restructuring	142
IV.	Efficient and Effective Court Supervised Reorganization Procedures	143
	A. The Focused Plan	143
	B. Six Steps to Implementing a Focused Restructuring Plan	144
	1. Step One: Identify the Business Problem and Form a Responsive Business Plan	144
	2. Step Two: Identify the Stakeholders who Must Compromise their Claims	145
	3. Step Three: Sell the Fairness of the Restructuring Plan to the Trustee/Monitor	146
	4. Step Four: Communicate the Plan Clearly and Fairly	147
	5. Step Five: Develop Consensus Support Among the Key Constituents of the Plan	147
	6. Step Six: Deliver a Simple, Effective and Focused Restructuring Plan	149

V.	Governance, Using Professional Advisors Effectively and Directors Liability Issues	149
VI.	Accelerated Sale Proceedings	151
	A. Underwater Security	153
	B. Pre-filing Marketing	154
	C. Failed Restructuring	155
VII.	Concluding Comments	155

Chapter 6
England & Wales 157

Schemes of Arrangement and Company Voluntary Arrangements
Samantha Bewick, Mark Fennessy and David Marks

I.	Introduction	161
	A. The Value and the Risks of Schemes	162
	B. The Merits and Demerits of CVAs	164
	C. Schemes: The Cross-Border Advantages	166
	D. Protocols	169
	E. The UNCITRAL Model Law	170
	F. Conclusion	171
II.	Schemes of Arrangement	171
	A. General: Section 425 of the Companies Act 1985	171
	B. Schemes of Arrangement and Insurance	174
	C. Section 425 of the Companies Act 1985: The Key Concepts	174
	D. Insurance Companies	176
	E. Members' Rights	177
	F. What Constitutes a Class of Members?	177
	G. Who is a Creditor?	178
	H. What Constitutes a 'Class' of Creditors?	179
	I. Estimate of Debts	183
	J. The Conduct of Class Meetings	183
	K. Notice of Meetings	185
	L. Sanction	186
	M. Meetings and Sanction: A Recent Example	189
	N. Costs	191
	O. The Effect of Liquidation	191
	P. Appeal	192
	Q. Particular Issues: Debenture Deeds	192
	R. Section 426 of the Companies Act 1985: General	193
	S. Section 427 of the Companies Act 1985: The Facilitation of a Company Reconstruction or Amalgamation	194

III.	Company Voluntary Arrangements		195
	A. General		195
	B. Composition or Scheme of Arrangement?		196
	C. Nature of a CVA		196
	D. Procedure: The Basic Steps		197
	E. Practical Factors		197
	F. The Role of the Court		197
	G. Members' Involvement		198
	H. Procedure		198
		1. The Proposal	198
		2. The Moratorium	199
		3. Effect of the Moratorium	201
		4. Post-Moratorium Procedure	202
		5. Role of the Nominee. The Nominee's Report	202
		6. The Nominee's Costs	205
	I. The Proposal: Contents		205
	J. Creditors		208
		1. Preferential Debts	209
		2. Secured Creditors	210
		3. Unsecured Creditors	211
		4. Future and Uncertain Claims	212
		5. Creditors with Rights of Set-Off	214
		6. Connected Creditors	214
		7. Guarantors	215
		8. Creditors' Committees	216
		9. Creditors' Meetings	216
		10. Creditors Not In Receipt of Notice	218
		11. The Chair of the Creditors' Meeting	220
		12. Adjournments of Creditors' Meetings	220
		13. Attendance by Directors to the Creditors' Meetings	221
		14. Proxies	221
		15. Modifications and Adjournments	222
		16. Creditors' and Members' Meetings: The Chairman's Report	223
	K. Members' Meetings: General		223
	L. CVAs: Implementation		226
		1. Publicity	226
		2. Formal Considerations: Complaints, Replacements, More Than One Supervisor and Notifications	226
		3. Report of the Meetings and other Reports	227
		4. Accounts and Records	228
		5. Fees and Remuneration	228

		6.	Completion of the Arrangement	228
		7.	Payments of Dividend	229
		8.	Challenge of Directors' Actions	229
		9.	Variation	230
		10.	CVA Following a Liquidation	231
		11.	Change of Supervisor	232
		12.	Implementation and Termination	232
	M.	Default and Failure		233
		1.	Supervisor's Liability	234
		2.	Liability of Directors	235
		3.	Certificate of Non-compliance	235
	N.	The Effect on the Underlying Trust		236
	O.	Default and Subsequent Liquidation		237
	P.	The Supervisor as Liquidator		237
IV.	Schemes and CVAs Case Studies			238
	A.	Schemes Case Study: The Marconi plc and Marconi Corporation plc		238
		1.	Introduction	238
		2.	Background	238
		3.	The terms of the restructuring	239
		4.	Scheme creditors	239
			a. Identification of Creditors	239
			b. Notification	241
			c. Classes	242
		5.	Key Features of the Schemes	243
			a. Shareholder Issues	243
			b. Proposals	243
			c. Information	244
			d. Operative Provisions	244
			e. Other Key Items	244
			f. Other Key Documents	245
			g. Separate Documents	245
			h. Effective Date	245
		6.	Consideration and Distributions	246
			a. Consideration	246
			b. Funds Flows	246
			c. First Day Distributions	246
		7.	Conclusion	247
	B.	CVA Case Study: TXU Europe group		247
		1.	Introduction	247
		2.	Background to the CVAs	247
		3.	Ability to Bind Third Parties	249

Table of Contents xvii

		4.	Creditor Issues	249
			a. Notification of Creditors	249
			b. Identification of Creditors	250
		5.	Class Issues	252
		6.	The US Angle and the Need for Section 304 Bankruptcy Code Relief	252
		7.	Is There a Requirement for Sanction by the Liquidation Committee?	252
		8.	Challenges to the Compromise	254
		9.	Conclusions	255

Chapter 7 257
France

The Idiosyncrasy of the French Judicial System and its Preventive Procedures for Expedited Debt Restructurings
Isabelle Didier

I.	Introduction	259
	A. Overview	259
	B. Legal framework	260
	1. The Commercial Courts	260
	2. The Public Prosecutor's Office	261
	3. The Judicial Auxiliary Officers	261
	C. The Alert Process	262
	1. Sounding the Alarm	262
	2. The Role of the President of the Commercial Court and/or Civil Court	263
	3. Roles of Advisors. Other Parties to the Process	264
II.	Preventive Procedures	264
	A. Mandat ad hoc	264
	1. Definition	264
	2. Main Characteristics	265
	3. Conditions for Opening	265
	a. Scope of Application	265
	b. Who May Initiate Mandat ad hoc Proceedings?	266
	c. Eligibility Criteria for Opening of the Mandat ad hoc Proceeding	266
	d. Participants to the Process	266
	e. Mission and Remuneration of the Ad Hoc Receiver	266
	4. The Procedure Illustrated in Steps	267
	5. Potential Outcomes of the Proceedings	267

		6.	Advantages and Inconveniences of the Mandat ad hoc	267
			a. Disadvantages	268
			b. General comments	268
	B.	Conciliation Procedure		268
		1.	Definition	268
		2.	Main Characteristics	268
		3.	Conditions for Opening the Proceeding (L.611–4 and 5 of the Commercial Code)	269
			a. Scope of Application	269
			b. Who May Initiate the Conciliation Proceedings?	269
			c. Eligibility Criteria for Opening the Procedure	269
			d. Participants to the Process	269
			i. The Debtor	269
			ii. The Conciliator	270
			iii. The Expert Appraiser	270
			iv. The President of the Commercial Court	270
			v. The Public Prosecutor s Office	270
			e. Mission and Remuneration of the Conciliator	270
		4.	The procedure Illustrated in Steps	271
		5.	During Conciliation	271
		6.	Potential Outcomes of the Conciliation Procedure (Art. L611–7, 8, 9 and 10 of the Commercial Code)	272
			a. Conciliator-terminated	272
			b. No Agreement. Failure	272
			c. Successful Conciliation and Conclusion of Agreement/s. Two options: President-approved or Court-registered	272
			i. President-approved (no publicity)	272
			ii. Court-registered (officially advertised)	273
			d. Termination of the Agreement	273
		7.	Advantages/Disadvantages of Conciliation	274
			a. For all Conciliation Agreements Whether President-approved or Court-registered	274
			i. Advantages	274
			ii. Disadvantages	275
			b. Exclusive to Conciliation Agreements which are President-approved:	275
			i. Advantages	275
			c. Exclusive to Conciliation Agreements which are Court-registered:	276
			i. Advantages	276

Table of Contents xix

			ii.	Disadvantages	277
			iii.	General comments	277
C.	Rescue				277
	1.	Definition			277
	2.	Main Characteristics			277
		a.	Debtor initiates Rescue		277
		b.	Automatic suspension of payments upon opening of Rescue proceedings		277
		c.	New payment schedules possible with banks and main suppliers		278
		d.	Debtor remains in control, but under supervision of court		278
	3.	Some Notes on the Rescue Proceeding			278
		a.	Scope of Application		278
		b.	Who May Initiate Rescue Proceedings?		278
		c.	Eligibility Criteria for Opening		278
		d.	Participants to the Process		279
			i.	The Debtor	279
			ii.	The Bankruptcy Judge/s	279
			iii.	The Judicial Administrator	279
			iv.	The Judicial Liquidator	279
			v.	The Creditor Committees	279
			vi.	Staff-representative Bodies	279
			vii.	Bailiff or Auctioneer	280
			viii.	Controllers	280
		f.	Mission and Remuneration of Insolvency Professionals		280
			i.	The Liquidator	280
			ii.	The Judicial Administrator	280
			iii.	Their Remuneration	280
			iv.	Pay Scales for Administrators and Liquidators	280
	4.	The Procedure Illustrated in Steps			281
		a.	Major Steps		281
		b.	Certain Steps of the Procedure. Further Discussion		282
		c.	During the Observation Period		283
		d.	End of the Difficulties		283
	5.	Potential Outcomes of the Rescue Proceeding			283
	6.	Advantages and Disadvantages of the Rescue proceedings			283
		a.	Advantages		283
		b.	Disadvantages		284
		c.	General Comments		284

	D. Progress Report on New Legislation	285
	E. Best Practices	287
III.	Case Studies	288
	A. Case Study No. 1 : The JRH File: A Successful Deployment of the Mandat Ad Hoc Process	289
	1. Executive Summary of the JRH Group of Companies	289
	2. 2052: the JRH Group Begins Experiencing Diffic	290
	3. The 30 August 1993 Memorandum of Agreement	290
	4. Conciliation Begins (7 September 1993)	290
	5. The JRH Group Was Placed in Court-ordered Receivership (27 February 1995)	291
	6. Management of the JRH Liquidation Proceedings	291
	7. Author's Comments	292
	B. Case Study No. 2: Pax Hotel	293
IV.	Concluding Words	295

Chapter 8
Hong Kong

297

Corporate Rescue in Hong Kong
Charles D. Booth, Stephen Briscoe and Philip Smart

I.	Introduction	299
II.	Schemes of Arrangement	299
	A. Overview	299
	B. Difficulties	300
III.	Proposed Provisional Supervision Procedure	301
	A. Legislative Background	301
	B. Overview of the Provisional Supervision Procedure	302
	C. The Problem–Workers' Wages	303
IV.	Provisional Liquidation	305
V.	Out-of-Court Workouts and the *HKAB/HKMA Guidelines*	309
VI.	An Example of the Use of a Scheme of Arrangement and Provisional Liquidation to Rescue an Insolvent Construction Company in Hong Kong	311
	A. Introduction	311
	B. Recognition of the Problem	313
	C. Background to the Problem	314
	D. Options Available	315
	E. Ongoing Contracts	316
	F. Classes	317

Table of Contents

	G.	Meeting of Creditors	318
	H.	Sanction Hearing	319
	I.	Role of the Provisional Liquidator	319
	J.	Success Achieved?	320
VII.	Conclusion		321
ANNEX: KEY LEGISLATION			322

Chapter 9
India
323

The Corporate Debt Restructuring Mechanisms in India
Rajiv Luthra

I.	Introduction: South East Asian Crisis and Adoption of the Corporate Debt Restructuring Mechanism in India	325
II.	Background to the Crisis in the Indian Financial System	326
III.	Limitations of the Indian Legal System for Recovering the Debt Due From Debtors	328
	A. Sick Industrial Companies Act	328
	B. Indian Companies Act, 1956 ('Companies Act')	329
IV.	Developments in the Nineties	330
V.	Corporate Debt Restructuring	333
	A. Structure of the Corporate Debt Restructuring Mechanism	333
	B. Operation of the Corporate Debt Restructuring Mechanism	335
	C. Various restructuring options/methods employed in Corporate Debt Restructuring System	336
	D. Legal Aspects of the Corporate Debt Restructuring Mechanism	339
VI.	Conclusion	340
ANNEX: KEY LEGISLATION		342

Chapter 10
Italy
357

Article 182bis of Law 80/2005 and the Code of Conduct to Restructure Debt Issued by the Italian Bank Association
Antonio Auricchio

I.	Background	359
II.	The Code	361

	A.	Main Provisions.	361
	B.	The Implementation of the Code.	363
III.	182BIS DRA		363
	A.	Main steps of 182bis DRA	363
	B.	Legal requirements	364
	C.	The content and filing of 182bis DRA	365
	D.	The expert	366
	E.	The judicial phase	367
	F.	The approval by the Court	368
	G.	Dissolution and avoidance of the 182bis DRA	369
	H.	182bis DRA main and debatable issues	369
		1. Claw-back action exemption rule	369
		2. DIP Financing	371
IV.	Case Study		371
V.	Conclusions		373
ANNEX: KEY LEGISLATION			375

Chapter 11
Japan 377

Expedited Corporate Debt Restructuring in Japan
Shinjiro Takagi

I.	Overview of Expedited Corporate Debt Restructuring Procedures in Japan	379
	A. Out-of-Court Workout	379
	B. Statutory Reorganization Proceedings	380
	C. Civil Rehabilitation and Corporate Reorganization Proceedings	380
	D. The Resolution & Collection Corporation	381
	E. The Industrial Revitalization Corporation	381
	F. The Small and Medium-sized Enterprises Turnaround Committees	382
	G. Private Equity Funds	382
	H. Resolved Non-Performing Loans Problem	382
II.	Out-of-Court Workout Restructuring	383
	A. Establishment of the Guideline for Out-of-Court Workout	383
	B. Process of Out-of-Court Workout Based on the Guideline	383
	C. Requirements for a Reorganization Plan	384
	D. Out-of-Court Workouts for Small and Medium Sized Enterprises	385

Table of Contents xxiii

	E.	Necessity of a New Statute to Facilitate an Out-of-Court Workout	385
	F.	New Company Law Enables 100 per cent Wipe-Out of Existing Stocks in an Out-of-Court Workout Process	386
III.		Civil Rehabilitation Proceeding Based on Civil Rehabilitation Law	387
	A.	Court should Commence the Proceeding Unless Exceptional	387
	B.	Debtor can Sell its Business with Court Permission during the Early Stage without Shareholders' Consent	388
	C.	DIP in Normal Cases	388
	D.	Summarized Proceedings to Verify Claims, Avoid Preferential and Fraudulent Transfers and Assess Damages of Responsible Managers	388
	E.	Some Restrictions on Secured Rights	389
	F.	Rehabilitation Plan	390
	G.	Closing the Case	390
IV.		Corporate Reorganization Proceeding under Corporate Reorganization Law	392
	A.	Eligibility	392
	B.	Stronger Weapons than Civil Rehabilitation	392
	C.	Change of Owners and Managers	393
V.		Case Study: the 'X Construction Corporation Case' (A Hypothetical Out-of-Court Workout Case Based on the Guideline)	395
ANNEX: KEY LEGISLATION			398

Chapter 12 405
Poland

Out-of-Court Debt Restructuring in Poland
Lech Giliciński

I.	Introduction	407
II.	Selected Major Restructurings in Poland To Date.	408
III.	Restructuring Pursuant to the Restructuring Chapter	409
	A. Who can Restructure	409
	B. Commencement of Proceedings and Judicial Control.	409
	C. Repercussions of the Commencement of Restructuring.	410
	D. Role of Creditors in the Process of Conclusion of an Arrangement	411

	E.	Court Approval of the Arrangement		412
		1. Lack of Legal Basis to Conduct Restructuring Proceedings		412
		2. Lack of Filing of All Relevant Documents Required in the Proceedings		413
		3. Inaccuracy of the Data in the Documents and Statements Made by the Entrepreneur		413
		4. Lack of Notifications to All Known Creditors about the Dates of the Creditors' Meeting		413
		5. Inability of the Court Supervisor to Exercise Supervision		414
		6. Infringements of Provisions of Law which could be Relevant to the Outcome of the Voting		414
		7. Siphoning of Assets by the Entrepreneur or Granting Certain Creditors Greater Benefits in Violation of the Provisions of the Insolvency and Restructuring Law		414
		8. Lack of Prospects for the Performance of an Arrangement		415
		9. Detriment to Creditors who Raised Objections or Lack of a Guarantee that the Restructuring Plan will Enable the Entrepreneur to Compete in the Market		415
	F.	The Consequences of an Arrangement		415
	G.	Setting Aside an Arrangement		416
	H.	Discontinuation		416
IV.	Conclusions			416
V.	Proposed Amendments to the Restructuring Chapter			417

Chapter 13
Turkey   419

Pre-packaged Corporate Restructuring Mechanism Under the Turkish Execution and Bankruptcy Law
Sevi Simavi

I.	Introduction			421
II.	Brief History and the Case for Reform			421
III.	'Restructuring of Corporations and Cooperatives Via Reconciliation'–Pre-Packaged Restructuring			423
	A.	An Overview		423
	B.	The Process		424
		1. Eligibility for Application and the Test for Insolvency		424
		2. Out of Court Negotiation Process		425
			a. Identification of Affected Creditors	425
			b. Classification of Claims	426

			c.	The Restructuring Plan	427
			d.	Preparing Disclosure Documents, Financial Statements, Feasibility and Liquidation Analysis	428
			e.	Vote Solicitation and Voting Process	429
		3.		Application to the Court for Approval	431
			a.	Application, Procedure and Measures Taken During the Hearing	431
			b.	Effects of the Plan and Appeals	432
		4.		Implementation of the Plan	433
			a.	Amendments	434
			b.	Partial Termination of the Plan	434
			c.	Full Termination of the Plan	434
IV.	Conclusion				435

Chapter 14A
USA (Theory) 437

The United States Expedited Proceedings: 'Pre-Packaged' Chapter 11 Plans
Lindsee P. Granfield and Andrés de la Cruz

I.	General Background: Plenary Bankruptcy Proceedings under the US Bankruptcy Code for Business Organizations		439
	A.	Chapter 7 and Chapter 11 in General Entities That Can file these Cases in the US	439
	B.	The Main Differences between Chapter 7 and Chapter 11 for Business Entities	440
	C.	General Provisions Relating to US Chapter 11 Plans (Non-Pre-Packaged Plans)	442
II.	Speedy Pre-Packaged Chapter 11 Plans		444
	A.	Pre-Bankruptcy Solicitation and Streamlined Post-Bankruptcy Procedures are Key Elements	444
III.	The Predicates of a Successful Pre-Packaged Plan		447
	A.	Only A Well-Defined Group of Creditors with Common Interests Are Being Affected by the Plan	447
	B.	The Plan is Negotiated With A Group of Creditors Whose Acceptance Gets Close to the Amount Needed for Bankruptcy Acceptance	448
	C.	Achieving a Consensus Will Lead to the Most Streamlined Cases	448

	D. The Company in Financial Difficulty Can Be 'Fixed' by Simply Restructuring or Reducing Its Debt Load	449
IV.	Conclusion	449
ANNEX: KEY LEGISLATION		450

Chapter 14B
USA (Practice) 457

American Bankruptcy Reform and Creativity Prompt the *In re Blue Bird Body Company* One-Day Pre-packaged Plan of Reorganization
Jay M. Goffman, Mark A. McDermott, and Kurt Ramlo

I.	Introduction	459
II.	Blue Bird Body Company	460
III.	A One-Day Prepackaged Case	462
IV.	Bankruptcy Abuse Prevention and Consumer Protection Act of 2005	463
V.	Continuing Limitations on Prepetition Solicitation	465
VI.	Lessons From Blue Bird–Process	466
VII.	Conclusion	468
ANNEX: KEY LEGISLATION		469

Chapter 15
Private International Law Implications of Expedited Corporate Debt Restructurings 477
Gerald Arends

I.	International Jurisdiction to Administer ECDR			479
	A.	International Jurisdiction		479
		1.	Qualification of ECDRs	479
		2.	International Jurisdiction in Insolvency Matters	481
			a. Winding-up Jurisdiction	482
			b. Restructuring Jurisdiction	484
			c. Policy Considerations	485
	B.	Refusing Jurisdiction		487
	C.	Restraining Foreign Proceedings		489
II.	Applicable Law			490
	A.	Lex Fori Concursus		490
	B.	Choice of Forum–Choice of Law?		494
III.	Recognition of Foreign ECDR			496
	A.	Multicanal		496
	B.	Recognition of Foreign ECDRs in a Model Law Country		498

Table of Contents

		1.	Foreign Proceeding	499
		2.	Foreign Representative	502
	C.	Recognition of Foreign ECDRs in a Civil Law Country		504
IV.	Conclusion			506

Chapter 16   509
The Tax Consequences of Corporate Debt Restructuring
Daniel Dürrschmidt

I.	Introduction				511
II.	General Comments				513
	A.	Relationship between Insolvency Laws and Tax Laws			513
	B.	Connecting Factors of Tax Laws Regarding Corporate Debt Restructurings			514
III.	Issues Regarding Direct Taxes (Income and Corporation Tax)				516
	A.	Debtor			516
		1.	General Comments		516
		2.	Cancellation of Indebtedness Intended to Rescue the Debtor		517
			a.	Cancellation of Indebtedness Income	517
			b.	Relief	519
				i. General Comments	519
				ii. General Exemption	519
				iii. Exemption on a Case-By-Case Basis	521
				iv. Alternative Forms of Relief	525
		3.	Cancellation of Indebtedness by a Related Person		526
			a.	General Comments	526
			b.	Creditor Shareholder of the Debtor	526
			c.	Debtor Shareholder of the Creditor	527
		4.	Alternative Forms of Debt Restructuring		527
			a.	Modification of Debts	527
			b.	Subordination of Debts	528
			c.	Debt-for-Debt and Debt-for-Equity Transactions	529
			d.	Transfer of Assets	530
		5.	Debts Resulting from Delivery of Goods		531
	B.	Creditor			531
		1.	General Comments		531
		2.	Cancellation of Indebtedness Intended to Rescue the Debtor		531
		3.	Cancellation of Indebtedness by a Related Person		532
			a.	General Comments	532

		b.	Creditor Shareholder of the Debtor	532
		c.	Debtor Shareholder of the Creditor	533
		4.	Alternative Forms of Debt Restructuring	534
			a. Modification of Debts	534
			b. Subordination of Debts	534
			c. Debt-for-Debt and Debt-for-Equity Transactions	535
			d. Transfer of Assets	535
		5.	Debts Resulting from Delivery of Goods	535
	C.	International Aspects		535
IV.	Issues Regarding Indirect Taxes			536
	A.	General Comments		536
	B.	Value Added Tax (VAT)		536
		1.	Debtor	536
		2.	Creditor	537
	C.	Transfer Taxes		538
V.	Tax Liabilities Subject to Debt Restructuring Agreements			539
	A.	General Comments		539
	B.	Tax Liabilities and Corporate Debt Restructuring Procedures		540
	C.	Requirements for the Participation of Tax Authorities in Corporate Debt Restructuring Procedures		540
	D.	Effects of Corporate Debt Restructuring Procedures on Tax Liabilities		541
	E.	Collection and Execution of Tax Liabilities		542
VI.	Conclusion			542

Chapter 17
Implications of Merger Legislation for Corporate Restructuring   543
Ioannis Kokkoris

I.	Introduction			547
II.	Corporate Debt Restructuring			550
III.	Failing Firm Defence			552
IV.	The European Union Perspective			554
	A.	Legislation		554
		1.	The European Community Merger Regulation	554
		2.	The Horizontal Merger Guidelines	559
	B.	Application of the Failing Firm Defence		563
		1.	Aerospatiale-Alenia/de Havilland	563
		2.	Kali und Salz	564
		3.	Saint Gobain	567
		4.	Blokker/Toys 'R' Us	568

		5.	Boeing	569
		6.	Bertelsmann	570
		7.	Rewe/Meinl	571
		8.	BASF	572
		9.	The Arthur Andersen Cases	575
		10.	Newscorp	576
		11.	Kelt	578
IV.	United States of America			579
	A.	Legislation		579
	B.	Application of the Failing Firm Defence		587
		1.	International Shoe	587
		2.	*United States v. General Dynamics Corp*	589
		3.	*Citizen Publishing Co. v. United States*	590
		4.	Other Cases	591
V.	Reflections from Theory and Practice			592
VI.	Concluding Remarks			598
ANNEX				600

Foreword

The recent two decades have witnessed a proliferation of insolvency and related debt restructuring cases worldwide. Among other things, speed is of the essence in the debt solution as quick corrective steps can minimize losses to creditors, especially for financial creditors whose problems will worsen rather than disappear with the passage of time. This accounts for the fact that expedited debt restructuring has been given more and more importance by the international insolvency community. In particular, the technique of taking an out of court agreement and making it binding on creditors in court, generally referred to as 'pre-arranged' or 'pre-packaged' restructuring plans, is of paramount significance for those jurisdictions suffering from a systemic crisis.

While in some countries it is popular to accommodate pre-packaged or pre-negotiated plans in their insolvency legislation, in China it is more complicated due to a variety of reasons, such as a lack of understanding of the insolvency system in tradition and other institutional drawbacks, which create many difficulties when proposing a plan immediately after the commencement of proceedings. Although it was a good opportunity to establish such schemes in China's new Enterprises Bankruptcy Law passed on 27 August 2006 and effective as of 1 July 2007, there is no provision for expedited debt restructuring in the new law. Also, when it comes to the Chinese practice in this respect, I should say it is very limited and in its infancy stage.

In practice, considering that some key issues such as (1) State Owned Enterprises' bankruptcy and (2) employees' rearrangement in the Chinese bankruptcy legislation, have been addressed by China's new Enterprises Bankruptcy Law, it may be fair to state that there were other driving reasons why China has not included expedited debt restructuring procedures on the agenda at this point. Despite a pressing need to adopt a bankruptcy law which suits a market economy, the fact that China has been long dominated by a centrally planned economy means that it will take more time for China to adjust its bankruptcy law to internationally recognized principles. In any event, it can be expected that China will adopt – sooner or later – the best accepted practices in the bankruptcy field to match its new role in the global economy.

Taking a broader perspective, international cooperation may be essential for developing a successful expedited debt restructuring. In the context of complicated cross-border cases, it is apparently hard to obtain agreement from all relevant parties. This problem is magnified when creditors come from many divergent jurisdictions which foster divergent commercial cultures. Accordingly, in order to facilitate expedited debt restructurings, it is necessary to set up a legal mechanism which binds the dissenting minority with the precondition that a threshold standard of treatment that appropriately protects their interests is achieved by such plan. Although this currently can – in a certain way – be achieved by means of the expedited debt restructurings, creditors in different jurisdictions can question the validity of said procedures (e.g. the Multicanal case, an Argentine pre-pack that has been extensively litigated under New York law). In other words, although such mechanisms are established within many countries' insolvency laws, they are not readily applied to cross-border cases. Therefore, we may expect such initiatives as the Model Law on Expedited Debt Restructuring which would provide with a standardized procedure for adoption by different jurisdictions in the near future.

I think that this book is quite meaningful as the expedited restructuring processes become more and more practical and significant in dealing with the insolvency cases. In addition, I trust that this book will keep the audience up-to-date with respect to the most meaningful legal issues arising in expedited debt restructurings in key jurisdictions across the globe.

Jingxia Shi
New Haven – Beijing
November 2006

About the Authors

GERALD ARENDS, Dipl.-Jur. Univ. (Bayreuth, Germany), LL.M. (Warwick), PgDL (London), PgLP (Oxford). He is a Solicitor (England & Wales). He works as an Associate in the London office of Ashurst and is due to move to the Athens office of Thomas Cooper. He is a Visiting Fellow of the School of Law of the University of Warwick and has taught and published in the field of international commercial litigation.

ANTONIO AURICCHIO, J.D. (Naples, Italy), Postgraduate Degree at the Academy of American and International Law (University of Texas). He is a partner in the Litigation area and Restructuring & Insolvency Department of the Rome office of Gianni, Origoni, Grippo & Partners. His areas of particular experience are insolvency law, restructuring and reorganizations, as well as commercial and corporate matters and arbitration. His practice includes both litigation and the provision of commercial/transactional advice to banks and domestic and multinational corporations in these areas. He publishes regularly on topics related to insolvency law.

SAMANTHA BEWICK, BA (Hons) (Oxford). She is a Fellow of the Institute of Chartered Accountants in England and Wales and a Licensed Insolvency Practitioner (England and Wales). She is a Director in the London office of the Restructuring practice of KPMG LLP. Her areas of practice primarily include complex cross-border restructuring and insolvency. She has worked on Barings plc, Marconi plc, TXU (Europe), Schefenackerplc and similar cases which are not in the public domain. She regularly writes on matters related to restructuring. She is a member of the Institute of Chartered Accountants' Insolvency Committee, a sub-committee of the financial Markets Law Committee and sits on the Editorial Board of International Corporate Rescue.

CHARLES D. BOOTH, B.A. (Yale); J.D. (Harvard). He is an Associate Professor of Law and the Director of the Institute of Asian-Pacific Business Law at the William S. Richardson School of Law at the University of Hawaii. He previously taught for $16\frac{1}{2}$ years at the University of Hong Kong, where he was also the Director of the Asian Institute of International Financial Law. His expertise is in comparative and cross-border insolvency law, Hong Kong and Chinese insolvency law reform, and the development of insolvency and commercial law infrastructures in Asia in the aftermath of the financial crisis. He has more than 50 publications that have appeared in eight jurisdictions, including the *Hong Kong Personal Insolvency Manual* (2003, 392 pp.) (co-author with Philip Smart and Stephen Briscoe) and the *Hong Kong Corporate Insolvency Manual* (2002, 245 pp.) (co-editor with Philip Smart and Stephen Briscoe). He is a Fellow in the American College of Bankruptcy, a Founding Member of the International Insolvency Institute, and a member of the International Academy of Commercial and Consumer Law. He has served as a consultant on insolvency and commercial law reform projects in China, Vietnam and Asia generally for the World Bank, the Asian Development Bank and other organizations. This most recent insolvency law reform project was in Vanuata.

STEPHEN BRISCOE. He has worked full-time on corporate recovery and insolvency assignments since 1973. He worked for 11 years for the Official Receiver in the United Kingdom before moving into private practice. He has considerable experience in both personal and corporate insolvency, and in particular, investigations, liquidations, and trading receiverships particularly in the manufacturing and leisure industries. He has practiced in Hong Kong since 1997 where he has acted as liquidator or receiver of several hundred insolvent companies in a variety of industry sectors including construction, property, manufacturing, import and export and various service industries. Many corporate recovery assignments in Hong Kong have a China element and he has had notable success in creating value for foreign investors through the disposal of investments by foreign companies in the Joint Ventures or Wholly Foreign Owned Enterprises in PRC. His team has also acted as members of the Liquidation Committees of PRC registered companies on behalf of foreign investors to assist in maximising recoveries for foreign creditors. He is the co-editor of the Hong Kong Corporate Insolvency Manual and co-author of the Hong Kong Personal Insolvency Manual and has written a number of articles on various aspects of insolvency. He is also actively involved in steps to promote and improve the quality of education for insolvency practitioners in Hong Kong as one of course directors of the Hong Kong Insolvency Diploma, run jointly by the HKICPA and Hong Kong University. He is also a member of the Insolvency Practitioners Committee of the HKICPA. He is responsible for the corporate recovery and insolvency operations team of RSM Nelson Wheeler in Hong Kong, including the construction related corporate recovery team, which has an unrivalled level of experience in the construction industry in Hong Kong.

About the Authors

ANDRÉS DE LA CRUZ, LL.B. (Buenos Aires), LL.M. (Michigan), Dipl. (Johns Hopkins Advanced International Studies). He is a partner currently based in the Frankfurt office of Cleary Gottlieb Steen & Hamilton LLP. His practice focuses on corporate and financial matters, including securities offerings, structured financing and debt restructurings, as well as mergers and acquisitions and joint ventures, for private and public sector clients. His experience in the restructuring field covers sovereign as well as private sector restructurings. In 2003, he advised the Republic of Uruguay in the reprofiling of its financial indebtedness, which resulted in the introduction of collective action clauses with aggregation provisions for sovereign debtors. Ranked by Chambers for two years consecutively (2005 and 2006) within the first tier of Corporate and Finance Lawyers in Latin America. He is admitted to practice in Buenos Aires, Madrid and New York.

ISABELLE DIDIER, Business law studies (Paris X). A leading French Insolvency Practitioner regularly appointed by civil and commercial courts in both amicable and typical liquidations, as well as by banks or foreign investors with interests in France. She lectures regularly on English, French and US insolvency proceedings and participates in courses for training judges or professionals internationally (e.g. France, Madagascar, Poland, etc.). She is an active member of INSOL International having been the President of INSOL Europe in 2000. She also is a member of the International Insolvency Institute, the International Bar Association, the *Union Internationale des Avocats* and the president of GRIP 21. She is regularly invited to participate in the working groups of UNCITRAL (UNO). Since 2000 she has been nominated in the 'Who's Who legal' as a prominent French practitioner.

DANIEL DÜRRSCHMIDT, Ass. jur. (Bavaria, Germany), Dipl.-Jur., Wirtschaftsjurist (both Bayreuth, Germany), LL.M. (Sydney, Australia), admitted to practice law in Germany (Rechtsanwalt). After the completion of his doctoral thesis, he joined the Munich office of Linklaters as a tax specialist. Before that, he has completed his practical legal training (Referendariat) with stages in Munich and London and he joined the University of Erlangen-Nuremberg (Germany) as a researcher on legal issues of taxation. He regularly publishes in international tax law journals.

MARK J. FENNESSY, BSc (Hons) (UCL,London), LLDip (City,London). He is a partner in the London office of Hunton & Williams. He has experience in acting for banks, financial institutions, corporates and officeholders on all aspects of formal and informal restructurings. He has particular strengths in dealing with multi-faceted group collapses, particularly involving cross-border issues. In the UK, he is a licensed Insolvency Practitioner and an authorized Fixed Charge Receiver, as well as a Fellow and Council Member of the Non-Administrative Receivership Association and Fellow of the Association of Business Recovery Professionals. He is the Editor-in-Chief of International Corporate Rescue published by Chase

Cambria, a Board member of the Commercial Law Centre at UCL in London and has been recognized by Chambers & Partners Global 2007 and Chambers & Partners UK 2007, as a 'Leader In Their Field' for Restructuring/ Insolvency.

LECH GILICIŃSKI, Magister Iuris summa cum laude (Adam Mickiewicz University in Poznań, Poland); Certificate of Studies (Oxford); LL.M. (University of Connecticut School of Law); PhD (Adam Mickiewicz University in Poznań, Poland). He is a partner in the banking and restructuring department of the Warsaw office of White & Case and has a broad range of experience in assisting Polish and multinational clients in corporate and financial restructurings, as well as banking and finance matters. He was the head of legal team advising the Minister of Justice and the European Bank for Reconstruction and Development (EBRD) in the process of implementing a new Law on Insolvency and Restructuring. He is also World Bank's country partner in Poland in the area of insolvency.

JAY M. GOFFMAN, B.S. (State University of New York), J.D. (University of North Carolina) with Honors. He is a senior partner in the Corporate Restructuring Group of the New York Office of Skadden, Arps, Slate, Meagher & Flom LLP. He has represented numerous public and private corporations in out-of-court restructurings and prepackaged Chapter 11 cases, as well as traditional Chapter 11 cases. He has also represented financial institutions, creditor committees, bank groups, bondholders, equity holders, investment funds and investors in all types of distressed investments. He was a pioneer in the use of prepackaged and prearranged restructuring and is widely regarded as one of the leaders in the field. His recent one-day prepack for Blue Bird Corporation has set a new standard for prepackaged restructurings. He is regularly selected as one of the leading restructuring lawyers in the US and/or the world by various corporate restructuring and/or legal organizations including Turnarounds & Workouts (top 10 U.S. Bankruptcy attorneys), Chambers Global: The World's Leading Lawyer, The K&A Restructuring Register, a listing of the top corporate restructuring attorneys and financial advisors in the United States, The Best Lawyers in America, New York Times' Super Lawyers, The Law Dragon 3000: Leading Lawyers in America, Madison's Who's Who and The Deal: Top Bankruptcy Lawyers. The Wall Street Journal noted his talents when it profiled in a cover page story his innovative and highly successful out-of-court restructuring for Evergreen International Aviation. He frequently lectures and writes a variety of restructuring topics, including prepacks, mergers and acquisitions in distressed situations, fiduciary duties of board of directors, 'zone of insolvency' issues and basic bankruptcy analysis. In addition, he has assisted the National Bankruptcy Review Commission with respect to potential legislative amendments regarding prepacks and co-chaired a committee of premier bankruptcy lawyers addressing potential bankruptcy legislation. He has led or played a major role in numerous major restructurings over the past twenty-five years including America West Airlines, Ameriserve Corp., Blue Bird Corporation, Bridge Information Systems, Eastern Airlines, Evergreen International Aviation, Focal Corporation, Globix, Grove Worldwide, Harvest Foods, In-Store Advertising, Memorex Telex, NTL,

Offshore Logistics, Olympia & York World Financial Center, Pocket Communications, Portland Trail Blazers, RCN, Saxon Industries, Specialty Foods, Allegheny/Sunbeam, U.S. Food Service and XO Corporation.

LINDSEE P. GRANFIELD, J.D. (University of California at Berkeley). She is a partner based in the New York office of Cleary Gottlieb Steen & Hamilton LLP. Her practice focuses on restructuring, insolvency, bankruptcy and commercial litigation matters. She has extensive experience in representing creditors and debtors in bankruptcy and insolvency matters throughout the United States and in international restructurings. She has participated in Chapter 11 cases in the U.S. Bankruptcy and District Courts in New York, Delaware, California, Texas, Illinois, Ohio, Florida, Arizona, Nevada, Maryland and Washington, DC. Some of the countries with which she has been involved for cross-border insolvency issues include, Argentina, Chile, Mexico, France, Italy, The Netherlands, The Cayman Islands, Bermuda, Canada and The United Kingdom. She has also represented clients in many domestic and international out-of-court restructurings. She is distinguished as one of the leading bankruptcy and restructuring lawyers by *Chambers USA America's Leading Lawyers for Business* (2006).

IOANNIS KOKKORIS, B.A. in Economics (Essex, UK), LL.M. with Distinction (Warwick, UK), MPhil in Economics (Cambridge, UK), PhD in Law (King's College, UK). He is a Principal Case Officer Economist in the Mergers branch of the Office of Fair Trading. He also holds a visiting lecturer position at City University and a Visiting Fellow position at Durham University in the UK. Prior to that he worked in the Merger Task Force of the Competition Directorate of the European Commission, and as an economist at the Inland Revenue. He is the General Editor of a forthcoming book on competition case law by Sweet and Maxwell and has co-authored a book on competition law in Greece titled Ελεύθερος Ανταγωνσμός ('Free Competition'). He has published extensively in leading journals in Europe (ECLR, World Competition, ICCLR, etc.) and is the co-founder of the *Institute for Studies in Competition Law and Policy (IMEDIPA)*. He is member of the Advisory Board of the Journal of Business and Company Law (in Greece), as well as co-Editor in Chief of International Finance and Banking Law Online (www.ifblonline.com).

RAJIV K. LUTHRA, LLB (India), specialization courses on corporate structuring and negotiations (Harvard). He is the Founder & Managing Partner of Luthra & Luthra Law Offices – one of the largest law firms in India. He has over 25 years of experience in advising clients on a vast range of complex commercial transactions including infrastructure projects in India, Sri Lanka, Bangladesh, People's Republic of China, Nepal and Nigeria. He has successfully handled various disinvestment, privatization and restructuring assignments and has worked on some of the largest mergers in Indian corporate history. He has been appointed by the Government of India on the drafting of several rules and regulations. He has been ranked amongst the 'Leading Individuals' in Banking & Finance by The Asia Pacific Legal 500 and has also featured in the 'Leaders' Profiles – India – Project Finance' of the

Chambers Global – The World's Leading Lawyers, a Chambers & Partners' publication. Further, he has to his credit, a number of publications in various national and international professional journals and magazines'.

DAVID MARKS, M.A. (Oxon) B.C.L. He is a senior barrister who practices at what is generally regarded as the leading set of barristers' chambers dealing with insolvency related matters, 3-4 South Square, Gray's Inn, London. He has acted for various parties over many years in most of the major well known insolvencies and has appeared in many important decisions in the field of insolvency and banking related law. In addition he is a well known writer and lecturer on those topics, currently co-editing a leading loose leaf work on Insolvency as well as the leading practitioners' book on the law of guarantees known as Rowlatt on Principal and Surety. He also contributes to many leading works on insolvency related topics including the leading English text book published by the Oxford University Press on the EC Insolvency Regulation. He sits as a part time Bankruptcy Registrar in the High Court in London and is also a part time Deputy Chairman of the Information Tribunal which deals with freedom of information and data protection matters. He is listed as a Legal Expert in the Legal Business Report published in 2006 in relation to insolvency related matters. He is a member of the Editorial Board of International Corporate Rescue.

MARK McDERMOTT, B.S. (Iowa State University), J.D. (Northwestern University) *cum laude*. He is a partner in the New York office of the Corporate Restructuring Group of Skadden, Arps, Slate, Meagher & Flom LLP. He represents corporations and their principal constituencies in troubled company restructuring, M&A and financing situations. He has represented debtors, lenders, creditors and purchasers in all stages of complex restructuring transactions throughout the United States, and recently was named one of America's 'Outstanding Young Restructuring Lawyers' by *Turnarounds & Workouts* magazine. He was responsible for the legal coordination of the Chapter 11 case activity for Kmart Corporation, the largest retail business reorganization in history, entailing the restructuring of approximately USD 11 billion of debt obligations and a portfolio of approximately 5,000 leases and subleases. He represented Blue Bird Bus Company in the fastest prepackaged Chapter 11 reorganization case in history, with the company's stay in bankruptcy lasting approximately 32 hours. Other representative company engagements have included Amkor Technology, Inc., Eagle Finance, Inc., Friedman's, Inc., Goss Graphics, Inc., Master Graphics, Inc., McLeod, Inc., Outboard Marine Corporation, RCN Corporation, Refco, Inc., SourceOne Wireless, Inc., and numerous real estate development projects.

KEVIN P. McELCHERAN, B.A. (Hon.) (University of Toronto, Canada), LL.B. (Queen's University, Canada), Certified Specialist in Bankruptcy and Insolvency Law (The Law Society of Upper Canada). He is a Partner in the Toronto office of McCarthy Tétrault LLP. He uses commercial expertise and strong advocacy skills to advance the interests of debtors, creditors and other stakeholders in large restructuring and insolvency cases. In the academic field, he

About the Authors xxxix

has lectured extensively on matters of insolvency law at programs sponsored by The Law Society of Upper Canada, the Ontario Bar Association, Canadian Institute and Insight International and has published papers on a variety of topics related to insolvency law. He is the author of *Commercial Insolvency in Canada*, published by LexisNexis Butterworths in 2005. He is recognized in many publications as a leading insolvency and corporate restructuring lawyer including: *IFLR1000: The Guide to the World's Leading Financial Law Firms – 2007 Edition*, *The Canadian Legal Lexpert Directory* 2006 as 'most frequently' recommended for insolvency litigation and 'consistently' recommended for corporate restructuring, *Chambers Global: The World's Leading Lawyers for Business*, 2007, *The International Who's Who of Insolvency & Restructuring Lawyers 2007*, and The International Who's Who of Business Lawyers, and PLC Which Lawyer? Yearbook 2007.

RODRIGO OLIVARES-CAMINAL, LLB (Buenos Aires), LLM with distinction (Warwick), PhD (cand) at the University of London, College of Queen Mary. He is an Assistant Professor at the University of Warwick and has taught in undergraduate and postgraduate courses in various Schools of Law and Business Schools in Argentina and in the United Kingdom as well as in professional courses provided by Euromoney. He has researched at the Centre for Commercial Law Studies in London; and, the Ambrosio L. Gioja Academic Institute in Buenos Aires. He specializes in insolvency and law having acted in several international transactions. He is the co-Editor in Chief of International Finance and Banking Law Online, the associate Editor-in-Chief of International Corporate Rescue and is a member of the Advisory Board of the NAFTA Law and Business Review of the Americas. He has many articles published in some of the leading peer-reviewed legal journals in the UK, the US and Argentina. He is a member of national and international institutes and associations specialized on comparative commercial and insolvency law, including American Bankruptcy Institute, INSOL International and the London Forum for Economic Law & Development.

KURT RAMLO, B.M. (California State University, Northridge), J.D. (University of California, Davis). He is a Counsel in the Corporate Restructuring Group of the Los Angeles Office of Skadden, Arps, Slate, Meagher & Flom LLP. He has represented debtors, creditors' committees, creditors, stockholders, plan sponsors and purchasers in traditional and prepackaged chapter 11 cases throughout the US. He has been a former Assistant United States Attorney and also has extensive experience representing litigants in complex commercial matters before federal courts. In addition to representing Blue Bird Bus Company in its one-day prepack, he has been part of the legal teams restructuring Dephi Corporation, Refco Inc., Friedman's Inc., Airwalk, The Clift Hotel, Kmart Corporation, and Washington Group.

ADOLFO ROUILLON, LL.B. (Rosario, Argentina), Ph.D. with the highest of distinctions–summa cum laudae (Catholic University of Argentina). He is a Senior Counsel in the Finance, Private Sector & Infrastructure practice group of the World Bank's Legal Vice-Presidency. He has served more than 25 years as a civil and commercial judge in Rosario, Argentina, presiding over the Court of Appeal in 1992. He was also President of the Santa Fe Judges' Association and member of the Board of Directors of the Argentine Judiciary Federation. In the academic field, he Rouillon taught insolvency and commercial law in various universities in Argentina, and was Director of the Law Department of the Faculty of Business Studies in the Austral University. He is the author of seven books on bankruptcy law, and has published 150 articles on bankruptcy and commercial law. He has attended numerous conferences and seminars, in most of which he has delivered papers or served on panels. He is the Editor-in-Chief of two Argentine law journals ('La Ley Litoral' and 'Derecho y Empresa'). He is a member of the Argentine National Academy of Law and Social Sciences in Buenos Aires, and a member of national and international institutes and associations specialized on comparative, commercial and insolvency law, including INSOL International, American Bankruptcy Institute, International Insolvency Institute, American College of Bankruptcy, Argentine Association of Comparative Law.

JINGXIA SHI, LL.B. and Ph.D. (Wuhan University, China). She is a Professor in the Law School, China University of International Business & Economics (UIBE) and a research fellow at the China National Institute of WTO Studies. She was a visiting scholar at the Center for Commercial Law Studies (CCLS), University of London, College of Queen Mary (2000) and a Global Research Fellow in New York University Law School (2003-2004). She has been one of members in the Drafting Committee of the Enterprise Bankruptcy of the People's Republic of China (organized by Fiscal and Economic Committee of NPC), which was adopted on August 27, 2006 and became effective as of June 1, 2007. She also practices law at Beijing Junzhi Law Firm as a part-time lawyer. Her research interests focus on various aspects of international trade of services, cross-border insolvency, and international investment. She has published extensively in international peer reviewed journals in China and abroad. She was awarded the 'National Prize for 100 Excellent Ph.D. Dissertations' (the only such prize in the legal subject) jointly by The Ministry of Education and The Degree Committee of State Council of China for her Ph.D. dissertation entitled 'Legal Issues in Cross-border Insolvency' in 2000. She will receive her LL.M degree from Yale Law School in June 2007 and currently is J.S.D Candidate at Yale Law School.

SEVI SIMAVI, LL.B. (Marmara, Turkey), LL.M. (Georgetown). She is a fully qualified lawyer, currently working as Investment Policy Specialist at the Financial and Private Sector Development Vice Presidency of the World Bank Group. She is specialized in creditor rights, insolvency and secured transactions law and policy. She has lead or contributed to several research and legal reform projects in emerging markets such as in Armenia, China, Mauritius, Romania, Turkey and Vietnam as well as regional and global initiatives, including the 'World Bank Principles and Guidelines on Creditor Rights and Insolvency'. Between 2002-2004 she was a member of the World Bank team of legal experts providing advice to the Turkish government in development of the country's new bankruptcy law. Before joining the World Bank Group, she practiced business law at Arthur Andersen LLP in Istanbul.

PHILIP SMART, LLB (Lond), LLM (Lond), Hardwicke Scholar of Lincoln's Inn, Barrister (England and Wales and Hong Kong). He is the Harold Hsiao-Wo Lee Professor in Corporate Law at the University of Hong Kong. His particular area of interest and expert*ize* is Cross Border Insolvency, a field in which he has been active since his time at the British Institute of International & Comparative Law in London in the mid-1980s. He is the author of *Cross-Border Insolvency* (2nd ed, 1998, Butterworths, London, 420 pp.), a co-author of the *Hong Kong Personal Insolvency Manual* (2003, 392 pp.) (with Charles D. Booth & Stephen Briscoe) and a co-editor of the *Hong Kong Corporate Insolvency Manual* (2002, 245 pp.) (with Charles D. Booth & Stephen Briscoe). He is a Founding Member of the International Insolvency Institute.

SHINJIRO TAKAGI, LLB (Chuo University), PhD (Toyo University). He is an advisor for Nomura Security Co. Ltd. After being in private practice for 25 five years, he was appointed to the Judge of Tokyo District Court. In 1995 he became the President and Chief Judge of Yamagata District & Family Court and in 1997 appointed to the President and Chief Judge of Niigata District Court. From 1998, he was the Judge of Tokyo High Court (Court of Appeal) and retired the judgeship in 2000. After resuming private practice, he successfully reorganized several big corporations including Kyo-ei Life Insurance which was the biggest insurance bankruptcy case ever happened all over the world. He was the chairperson of the Committee for Guidelines of Multi-Creditors Out of Court Workout organized by the Japanese National Bank Association, Federation of Economic Organizations and other organization in 2001. He also the chairperson of the Advisory Committees regarding Reformation of Corporate Reorganization Law and the Drafting Committee of Guidelines to reorganize troubled business at early stages and speed up the reorganization for Ministry of Economy Industry and Trade from 2001 to 2003. He established Japanese Association of Business Recovery, National Network of Bankruptcy Lawyers, Education Center of Business Restructuring and Japanese Association of Turnaround Professionals in 2002 and 2003 and is the Chairperson, President or Advisor of these organizations. He was the Professor of Law at Dokkyo University (2000 to 2003) and at Chuo University Law School (2003-2006). He was Chair of the IRC Commission for Industrial Revitalization Corporation of Japan (2003 to 2007). He is a fellow of American College of Bankruptcy and member of Board of Governers of International Insolvency Institute. He wrote numerous books and articles regarding Japanese and foreign insolvency and other related matters including 'An Overview of United States Bankruptcy Laws'.

LUIZ FERNANDO VALENTE DE PAIVA, LL.B. (São Paulo Catholic University, Brazil), Graduate Studies at the São Paulo Catholic University School of Law (currently preparing his thesis). He is a Partner in the bankruptcy and restructuring practice of the São Paulo office of Pinheiro Neto Advogados. He is a member of the Joint Ministerial Committee that drafted the final wording of the New Brazilian Bankruptcy Law, the American Bankruptcy Institute, INSOL International, the Committee on Bankruptcy Law and Business Restructuring of the São Paulo Lawyers Institute. He is the coordinator of courses offered by the Getúlio Vargas Foundation (FGV-SP) on the New Bankruptcy Law for members of the Judiciary Branch throughout Brazil and members of the Attorney General Offices in São Paulo and Rio de Janeiro; and, of the bankruptcy committee on the Brazilian Institute of Corporate Law (Ibrademp). He also is a lecturer on a course on *'Business Restructuring and Bankruptcy under the New Bankruptcy Law'* offered by FGV-SP. He has edited the book 'Direito *Falimentar e a Nova Lei de Falências e Recuperação de Empresas'* – *Editora Quartier Latin 2005*. He is the author of several chapters for books and articles about the New Brazilian Bankruptcy Law published in Brazil and abroad and a speaker at several events on the New Bankruptcy Law in Brazil and abroad.

IAN WALKER, BComm (Melbourne) LL.B.(Melbourne) He is a partner, in the Insolvency and Reconstruction and Commercial Disputes groups of the Melbourne office of Minter Ellison. He has more than 20 years' experience and comments regularly on insolvency law reform issues. He is a member of the Law Council of Australia's Insolvency and Reconstruction sub-committee and one of the vice chairs of the Insolvency Legislation and Legislative Reform and Harmon*ization* Sub-committee, International Bar Associations of Section on Insolvency Reconstructing and Creditors Rights of the International Bar Association. In 2002, Ian was listed among the world's leading insolvency and reconstruction lawyers by *EuroMoney Legal Media Group's Expert Guide to Insolvency and Reconstruction*. The 2003/2004 edition of *Global Counsel 3000* identified him as a highly recommended restructuring and insolvency practitioner in Australia. The 2004 *Chambers Legal Dictionary* ranked him as one of the world's leading lawyers and in 2007 Chambers Global 2007 as a leading individual in Restructing/Insolvency. He was recommended as one of Australia's leading restructuring and insolvency lawyers in the PLC Cross-Border Restructuring and Insolvency Handbook 2005/06 2006/07 and Asialaw Leading Lawyers 2005 Guide. He has presented on many topics including Administration under Part 5.3A, Mortgagees Powers of Sale, The administration of Complex corporate groups, Insolvency Law Reform.

Preface

Upon reviewing trends in domestic insolvency law regimes around the world, one point is strikingly clear: many insolvency laws have recently been amended or are currently under review. One reason is a political reaction to address–for the interests of various parties–the financial and economic cycles which gave rise to some unforgettable crises (e.g. the Asian crisis of 1997 or Argentina's external debt default in 2001 and its banking crisis in 2002). It is also a response to a global impetus focused on avoiding liquidation of troubled companies as well as to the adoption of UNCITRAL's cross border insolvency Model Law.

As stated by Stone, corporate restructuring on a large scale is usually made necessary by a systemic financial crisis, i.e. a severe disruption of financial markets that by impairing their ability to function, has large and adverse effects on the economy.[1] The episodes of Enron, Parmalat, Yukos and Worldcom are helpful to remind us that developed countries are not strangers to the need of restructuring. However, restructurings are more frequent in developing states due to systemic financial crises.[2] What are some of the key characteristics of recent legislation?

Time is Money: 'Expedited' Insolvency Laws

Since corporations doing business in countries undergoing crises are not exempt from the turmoil, it can be argued that recently amended insolvency laws are aiming for expedited debt restructuring procedures. Clear examples are the

---

1. Mark Stone, *Corporate Sector Restructuring: The Role of Government in Times of Crisis*, International Monetary Fund, Economic Issues No. 31, June 2002.
2. A 2003 report on Argentine corporations after the 2001–2002 crises stated that over USD 31.5 billion were restructured including 95 per cent of the stock of corporate bonds (Deutsche Bank, *Compañías Argentinas: de las Cenizas a los APEs*, November 2003).

recently amended laws of Argentina (2002), Turkey (2004) and Brazil (2005), all of which streamlined or included an expedited debt restructuring procedure similar to the US Chapter 11 pre-packaged deals. Also, e.g., Peru (2002) or Bolivia (2003) adopted pre-negotiated plans as a restructuring option. The difference between the pre-packaged deals and pre-negotiated plans is the moment of solicitation of the creditor's consent. As clearly stated by Jacoby,[3] the difference lies in if it is 'pre-voted' or 'post-voted', assessed as of the moment that a court approval (homologation) is requested by the debtor. The key element of these expedited mechanisms is that by giving limited intervention to the court the debtor has the chance to 'cramdown' the dissenting minorities thereby solving the ever feared problem of the holdout creditors.

The intervention of the court is limited in the sense that its role would be limited to: (1) ensure that certain principles (equity, fairness, etc.) have not been violated by the debtor and that the required restructuring threshold has been achieved; and, (2) to homologate the approved plan/agreement making it mandatory to the dissenting minority. If we are facing a pre-negotiated plan, the court will also have to summon creditors to vote the plan under the auspices of the court. However, it is worth noting that the debtor would not request the court's approval if it has not– as its name indicates–pre-negotiated the creditor's consent yet. It is worth noting, that there are some countries where such proceedings do not even involve a court and where the overseeing authority is an administrative entity (e.g. Peru or Bolivia).

Other countries, like Japan or Malaysia, have created specific bodies to deal with the restructuring of their corporations on an expedited basis. These restructuring bodies have their own budget to acquire the debt of distressed companies. More examples of the expedited trend in restructuring can be exemplified by soft law or codes of conduct for certain types of debt as is the case in India, Italy or Japan as well (e.g. the Revised Guidelines on Corporate Debt Restructuring (CDR) Mechanism issued by the reserve Bank of India in 2001 as amended and restated in 2005, the *Codice di Comportamento tra Banche per Affrontare i Processi di Ristrutturazione atti a Superare le Crisi di Impresa* issued by the Italian Banking Association in 2000; or the Guideline for Multi-Creditor Out Of Court Workouts established by the Japanese National Bankers' Association and other relevant organizations in 2001). The initiative of codes of conduct is no other that the well known London approach coined in 1976 as result of Zaire's payment problems to its creditors (mostly banks).

Importantly, the substance of the new 'expedited' bankruptcy laws is that they provide a signal to creditors that they may be better off engaging in swift, voluntary and less cumbersome restructurings than actual insolvency proceedings.

During the economic stability periods corporations invest and try to expand. During recessive periods, corporations try to maintain their market share and develop new lines of business. In both cases, corporations recourse to different financing techniques to raise the required capital to achieve their objectives.

---

3. Melissa B. Jacoby, *Prepacks and the Deal-litigation Tension*, March 2004, 23–2 ABIJ 34.

Preface xlv

Subject to their debt-to-equity ratio, corporations have to decide if they are going to finance themselves with debt or equity.[4]

All time low default rates in the past couple of years have pushed non-bank financial institutions into new areas in order to extract value during a period of excess cash and low returns which in turn has enabled arranging banks to structure ever bigger and more complicated debt packages comprising tranches of senior debt, second lien, mezzanine and sometimes junior mezzanine.[5] This de-equitization trend based upon the lower cost of debt, excess liquidity in banks due to their tradability in the secondary debt market and collateralized debt obligations (CDOs) repackaging has made bond debt (as well as loan debt) relatively more attractive in certain markets vis-à-vis equity.

Role of Converging Investment Funds

It is also important to refer to Hedge Funds and Private Equity Firms, two very important financial players, since the line dividing their activities is blurring. Hedge Funds are typically active in the distressed debt market acting on a short-term basis and providing important returns to their clients. On the other hand, Private Equity Firms operate on a long term basis obtaining loans and buying companies to turn them into profitable entities and sell them for a difference in the acquisition price.[6]

In booming periods, Hedge Funds and Private Equity Firms co-exist peacefully but the negotiation skills or aggressiveness (depending your view) of certain Hedge Funds and the fact that they started overlapping in the same business opportunities (although on different sides of the negotiation table) have made them recourse to new techniques. Some Private Equity Firms have requested their lending bank to have the right to know the holder of the loans on a name-by-name basis aiming to avoid being faced with Hedge Funds; and others, by means of side letters, have even barred certain Hedge Funds from voting in the event that the latter have acquired the debt in the secondary market.[7]

Debt grants their holders a right to collect monies. Therefore, the corporation is obliged to repay the agreed sums of money and the fulfilment of this obligation can be enforced by courts, eventually leading to insolvency. In the case of equity, technically there is no liability. Holders of equity have a residual right over the assets of the company.

---

4. See Jack S. Levin, *Structuring Venture Capital, Private Equity and Entrepreneurial Transaction*, Aspen Publisher, 2000.
5. See S. Patel and M. Fennessy, The Changing Nature of Stakeholders in Restructurings, International Corporate Rescue, Volume 3, Issue 5, 2006, page 266.
6. There is some criticism that private equity firms are now more focused on getting their risk-free adjusted returns up front in the way of fees, and not waiting for the back end so much, but this is another tale, beyond the scope of this piece.
7. See Henny Sender, Debt Buyers vs. The Indebted–Showdown Between Hedge Funds and Private Equity May Be Inevitable, The Wall Street Journal, 17 October 2006.

Opportunities for International Arbitrage

Since corporations usually have an international presence in different markets, they are able to take advantage of obtaining financing from other financial markets in a foreign currency with better terms, resulting in lower costs. On the other hand, if a corporation does not have international presence and it tries to obtain financing abroad, which–in the case of developing countries and some developed countries as well–the debt would be denominated in a strong foreign currency in order to avoid risks (financial, currency, political, etc.). In both cases, corporations will end up being indebted in a foreign currency while its income is normally denominated in the local currency of the country of said corporation's place of business.

When the economies of the countries of these indebted corporations are going through a recessive period, they are faced with low rates of return. Upon a crisis, currencies of legal tender are usually devaluated resulting in even lower rates of return. While the income of corporations is reduced, the burden to pay principal and/or interests of the corporation's indebtedness in a foreign and 'strong' currency increases. This mismatch, in many cases has ended in restructuring episodes. As Rieffel stated, a sharp depreciation of the domestic currency in the course of a crisis causes companies to default on their loans from domestic banks as well as from foreign creditors, rendering a large segment of the corporate sector insolvent.[8]

The use of expedited debt restructuring episodes–a debtor driven approach– allows debtor and creditors to negotiate the terms of an agreement in a shorter period of time than traditional reorganization procedures avoiding the problem of hold-out creditors, long and costly procedures, full disclosure of information, bad press, etc.

As the recent Argentine crisis has proven–not only with the sounded Multicanal case trialed in New York but with many other Argentine companies that recently had restructured their debts[9]–expedited debt restructuring episodes were essential in facilitating reorganization procedures. Highly indebted corporations have been able to 'wash' their balances over a short period of time with the collaboration of their creditors gaining a solid credit ratio. Although we would expect, as it is common, increased business activity in the debt market, that may not be the case since trying to block a restructuring to obtain better terms might become too risky.[10] *In lieu*, buying shares of a distressed company upon an event of default (when non-qualified investors usually try to get rid of their shareholding or qualified investors sell their shareholdings due to a liquidity

---

8. Lex Rieffel, *Restructuring Sovereign Debt: The Case for Ad-hoc Machinery*, Brookings Institution Press, 2003, pages 43–44.
9. Among others, Acindar S.A., Autopistas del Sol S.A., CTI Holdings S.A., Metrogas S.A., Química Estrella S.A.C.I, Sideco S.A., and, Telecom Argentina S.A.
10. Moreover, it should also be borne in mind that most of the companies undergoing reorganizations–at least from the Argentine experience–are utilities companies or service providers which in the case of liquidation do not have many assets to liquidate.

problem as result from the crisis) might provide the possibility to buy shares of a highly indebted company at low cost. Actually, this is what Hedge Funds are doing: trading. Hedge Funds have the added value of their expertise in the distressed debt market.

Thus–over a short period of time–by means of an expedited debt restructuring procedure, the default would be cured and a big portion of the company's liabilities would have disappeared from the balance sheet. Consequently, an expedited debt restructuring procedure contributes to the viability of the company and could increase the value of the shares that were bought at steep discount after an event of default. The example of Telecom Argentina S.A. (see the Argentine chapter in this volume) can be used to demonstrate the decrease experienced in the price of share receipts (ADRs) of a highly indebted company upon financial distress and its increase upon achieving a successful restructuring.

In summary, it is my opinion that we are heading towards an environment where (1) traditional players (e.g. Investment Banks) are losing terrain with Hedge Funds (e.g. Silver Point represented the creditors in the Chapter 11 restructuring proceeding of Tower Automotive in *lieu* of the investment bank involved, i.e. Morgan Stanley); (2) Hedge Funds and Private Equity Firms are starting to face each other on opposite sides of the table; (3) the use of expedited debt restructuring mechanisms, as the codification of private workouts would start to be seen more often (the term codification is used as the mechanism of becoming part of the norms of each jurisdiction); (4) a much more complex restructuring environment will arise as result of the sophistication of international financing and globalization.

Therefore, this volume focuses on a comparative analysis of expedited corporate debt restructuring procedures in different jurisdictions across the globe, particularly on the so-called 'out-of-court' restructurings.[11] By means of the use of these techniques, a debt restructuring can be achieved expeditiously avoiding the inconveniences of a 'full-blown' court proceeding and obtaining a similar outcome. This successful use of these procedures can be relevant in certain jurisdictions where resorting to the courts is time consuming, expensive and might lack of legal certainty.

Rodrigo Olivares-Caminal
London, April 2007

---

11. However, it is worth stressing that the term 'out-of-court' is technically incorrect since–as you will see–the court involvement's is necessary (and therefore it is not an 'out-of-court' procedure as commonly denominated).

Chapter 1
Introduction

Formal Processes and Alternative Mechanisms of Reorganization in International Initiatives on Insolvency

Adolfo Rouillon

ACRONYMS, ABBREVIATIONS & DEFINED TERMS

UNCITRAL	United Nations Commission for International Trade Law
Principles	The World Bank 'Principles and Guidelines for Effective Insolvency and Creditor Rights Systems' 2001 and the amended and restated 2005 version.
Guide	The United Nations Commission for International Trade Law (UNCITRAL) 'Legislative Guide on Insolvency Law'
Standstill Period	A period in which all relevant creditors should agree to refrain from taking any steps to enforce their claims against or (otherwise than by disposal of their debt to a third party) to reduce their exposure to the debtor but are entitled to expect that during said period their position relative to other creditors and each other will not be prejudiced.

I. INTRODUCTION

A. PRELIMINARY EXPLANATION

This chapter summarizes the several variants of reorganization, briefly analyzing two documents that are the result of initiatives of the international community: (1) the World Bank 'Principles and Guidelines for Effective Insolvency and Creditor Rights Systems' (the 'Principles')[1] and the United Nations Commission for International Trade Law (UNCITRAL) 'Legislative Guide on Insolvency Law' (the 'Guide').[2]

B. FORMS OF REORGANIZATION OF INSOLVENT COMPANIES

In various countries, the dual procedural outline as regards insolvency was consolidated during the second half of the 20th century; that is to say: an insolvency liquidation proceeding and other insolvency proceeding designed to prevent liquidation.

In turn, modern insolvency legislations are focusing their concern on the reorganization of viable companies rather than in punishing or rewarding the conduct of a businessman. This is due to the spreading of the system for the mass production of assets and services, in charge of corporate units of great magnitude, when deciding whether an insolvent company should be liquidated or not. Therefore, the insolvency proceeding aimed at preventing the liquidation is no longer a concession granted to the businessman who acted with good faith (as it used to happen in most legislations during the first half of the 20th century). Currently, insolvency proceedings not favouring liquidation are mechanisms that provide viable insolvent companies the opportunity to survive; usually, this is achieved through the reorganization of such company. Hence, the term 'reorganization' has been increasingly used to identify the objective of an insolvency proceeding – or the proceeding itself – when besides aiming at remedying the causes of the crisis or the insolvency of the company; its purpose is the payment of obligations.

The reorganization of insolvent companies can take different forms. In other words, the reorganization can be achieved not only through a 'formal' insolvency proceeding: there are other alternative mechanisms whereby companies can achieve, by negotiating with creditors, the restructuring of debts or the reorganization of the corporate activity to rehabilitate the financial or commercial health of the company. These reorganization mechanisms (which have been called

---

1. The complete text of "Principles and Guidelines for Effective Insolvency and Creditor Rights Systems", World Bank, April 2001, can be found at: <http://siteresources.worldbank.org/GILD/PrinciplesAndGuidelines/20773844/Principles (Spanish2001).pdf>. The complete text of the 2005 updated version can be found at: <http://web.worldbank.org/WBSITE/EXTERNAL/TOPICS/LAWANDJUSTICE/GILD/0,,contentMDK:20774194~pagePK:64065425~piPK:162156~theSitePK:215006,00.html>.
2. *See* the 'Legislative Guide on Insolvency Law', UNCITRAL, 2004, at: <www.uncitral.org>.

'alternative' as opposed to the 'full' or 'formal' reorganization proceeding) have been the focal point of various international insolvency initiatives to be discussed later on.

C.   Reorganization as an Objective of the Insolvency Legislation

The Principles and the Guide regard the reorganization of an insolvent company as a desirable objective that should be considered by any insolvency legislation.

According to the Principles, 'the modern trend supporting rehabilitation or rescue is an extension of the goal to maximize value'. It is predicated on the idea that the value of the whole is greater than the value of parts. In other words, an enterprise is more valuable as a going concern rather than liquidated. This approach also reflects other objectives, such as preserving jobs.[3]

Similarly, the Guide states that 'the insolvency law should include the possibility of reorganization of the debtor as an alternative to liquidation. In reorganization, creditors would not involuntarily receive less than in liquidation and the value of the debtor to society and to creditors may be maximized by allowing it to continue its activities. This is predicated on the basic economic theory whereby greater value may be obtained from keeping the essential components of a business together, rather than breaking them up and disposing of them in fragments'.[4]

II.   REORGANIZATION PROCEEDINGS

A.   'Formal' or 'Full' Reorganization Proceeding

Not so long ago, there was no need of labelling reorganization proceedings as 'formal' or 'full', for there was virtually no other mechanism aside from the traditional proceeding filed before a court, with different stages: the negotiation of the reorganization plan and its approval by creditors; and, generally, also by the court. Currently, the expression 'formal' or 'full' reorganization proceeding is used to differ the traditional reorganization proceeding from the new pre-packaged or expedited reorganization versions. Admittedly, most of the Principles and the Guide are devoted to the traditional reorganization, within a 'formal' or 'full' proceeding.

The term reorganization is used in the Guide 'in a broad sense to refer to the type of proceeding whose ultimate purpose is to allow the debtor to overcome its financial difficulties and resume or continue normal commercial operations (even though in some cases it may include a reduction in the scope of the business, its sale as a going concern to another company or its eventual liquidation)'.[5]

---

3. Principles (April 2001) number 70.
4. Legislative Guide on Insolvency Law, UNCITRAL, Part One, I, B, number 6.
5. Guide, Part One, II, C, number 23.

Introduction 5

This proceeding is designed 'to give a debtor some breathing space to recover from its temporary liquidity difficulties or more permanent over indebtedness and, where necessary, provide it with an opportunity to restructure its debt and its relations with creditors'.[6]

Regardless of the insolvency system to be adopted, there are certain 'key or essential elements' to be considered in every reorganization proceeding or in a proceeding aimed at its achievement.

Regarding reorganization proceedings, the Principles describe the following characteristic guidelines: (1) the quick and easy access to the process; (2) the continuation of the corporate activity; (3) its financing and the administration system during the insolvency proceeding; (4) the stay of actions of creditors against the debtor's assets during a certain period; and, (5) aspects related to the formulation, consideration, approval and implementation of the reorganization plan.[7] While considering these essential elements, the Principles develop a series of standards whose performance should result in the effective operation of insolvency systems.[8]

Similarly, the Guide[9] sets out the following key elements related to reorganization proceedings. The recommendations[10] provided by the Guide are based on these elements:

(1) the submission of the debtor to the proceedings (whether on its own application or on the basis of an application by creditors), which may or may not involve judicial control or supervision;

---

6. Guide, Part One, II, C, number 24.
7. 'To be commercially and economically effective, the law should establish rehabilitation procedures that permit quick and easy access to the process, provide sufficient protection for all those involved in the process, provide a structure that permits the negotiation of a commercial plan, enable a majority of creditors in favor of a plan or other course of action to bind all other creditors by the democratic exercise of voting rights (subject to appropriate minority protections and the protection of class rights) and provide for judicial or other supervision to ensure that the process is not subject to manipulation or abuse.' (Principles and Guidelines for Effective Insolvency and Creditor Rights Systems, World Bank, April 2001, Principle 17, number 159. *See:* <www.worldbank.org/gild>.
8. Principles 17 to 23 in the April 2001 version, and Principles C.14.1 to C.14.6 in the updated 2005 version.
9. Guide, Part One, II, C, number 28.
10. In order to direct the reader when using the Guide, it is advisable to bear in mind that the recommendations that implement the key elements of the insolvency reorganization proceeding are not centered in a special chapter, except for those related to the reorganization plan. Consequently, consultation on key subjects should be done resorting to the sections of the Guide indicated *below*, according to the following order: (1) Submission of the debtor to the proceeding: *Part Two, I. Application and commencement of the insolvency proceeding (Recommendations 8 to 29);* (2) Stay or suspension of actions against the debtor's assets: *Part Two, II. Treatment of assets on commencement of the insolvency proceeding. B. Protection and preservation of the insolvency estate (Recommendations 39 to 51);* (3) Continuation of the business of the debtor and management regime: *Part Two, II. Treatment of assets on commencement of the insolvency proceeding. C. Use and disposal of assets. D. Post-commencement finance. (Recommendations 52 to 68)* and *Part Two, III. Participants. A. The debtor (Recommendation 112)*; and, (4) Reorganization plan: *Part Two, IV. Reorganization. (Recommendations 139 to 159).*

(2) the automatic and mandatory stay or suspension of actions and proceedings against the assets of the debtor affecting all creditors for a limited period of time;
(3) the continuation of the business of the debtor, either by existing management, an independent manager or a combination of both;
(4) the formulation of a plan that proposes the manner in which creditors, equity holders and the debtor itself will be treated;
(5) the consideration of, and voting on, acceptance of the plan by creditors;
(6) possibly, the judicial approval or confirmation of an accepted plan; and
(7) the implementation of the plan.

The reorganization should be procured with flexibility; therefore, different forms – more or less complex – can be adopted. The Guide mentions, on one hand, a simple agreement concerning debts whereby the creditors 'agree to receive a certain percentage of the debts owed to them in full, complete and final satisfaction of their claims against the debtor'. It may also include an assumption of complex reorganization under which, for example, some debt may be converted to equity; the non-core assets may be sold or unprofitable business activities closed. The choice of the way in which reorganization is carried out is typically a response 'to the size of the business and the degree of complexity of the debtor's specific situation'.[11]

The Principles point out that a reorganization can still produce one, more or all of the following results:

(1) A liquidation or sale of some or all of the enterprise's assets to third parties, including an income – producing business – bearing in mind that the rescue regime creates a more appropriate market in which to obtain the best value for such an asset.
(2) The ultimate termination of the life of the corporation, which may come about through a later formal liquidation of the corporation.
(3) The total cancellation of owner equity. This interest should be secondary to the interests of creditors unless the owners are prepared to support the preservation of their interests in the corporation by injecting further capital or debt funding.
(4) The removal of power from and the possible replacement or dismissal of some or all of the corporation's management.
(5) The retrieval of rights of various classes of creditors – particularly creditors who hold security over the corporation's assets – which may have been suspended or curtailed as a result of the formal rescue process.
(6) A compromise or composition of debt owed to creditors. It will be rare that even a rescue that might be described as successful will result in full payment of debt. Instead, rescue may result in the transfer of ownership from the previous equity holders to creditors.[12]

---

11. Guide, Part One, II, C, number 27.
12. Principles (April 2001) number 158.

B.   DUAL AND UNITARY INSOLVENCY SYSTEMS

It is frequent for countries to organize their insolvency systems on the basis of two formal insolvency proceedings: liquidation and reorganization. Under the so-called dual systems, the latter proceeding can be generally used provided the liquidation proceeding has not commenced, except the respective legislation provides for the possibility of the conversion of a liquidation recently filed into a reorganization proceeding. The possibility of converting a reorganization proceeding in liquidation is frequent, while 'most insolvency systems do not allow reconversion to reorganization once conversion of reorganization to liquidation has already occurred'.[13] The need to follow, or not, a certain sequence between both proceedings is another difference that characterizes dual systems. Thus, while some regimes allow the debtor or creditors to choose between the filing of the reorganization or liquidation proceeding, other systems require such proceedings to be carried out 'sequentially; that is, liquidation proceedings will only run their course if reorganization is unlikely to be successful or if reorganization efforts have failed. In some insolvency systems, the general presumption is that a business should be reorganized and liquidation proceedings may be commenced only when all attempts to reorganize the entity have failed'.[14]

Under the name 'unitary insolvency system' we do not refer to regimes that provide for just one insolvency liquidation proceeding and exclude reorganization as an alternative. The modern unitary system is the one followed by countries adopting an insolvency proceeding with a 'single or common entry', which may subsequently tend towards reorganization or liquidation as alternative ways.[15]

Though less frequent than the dual system, some regimes adopt 'a unitary, flexible insolvency proceedings with a single commencement requirement alternatively resulting in reorganization or liquidation, depending on the circumstances of the case'.[16] Under the 'unitary' approach there is commonly 'an initial period (usually referred to as an 'observation period', which in existing examples of unitary laws may last up to three months) during which no presumption is made as to whether the business will be eventually reorganized or liquidated. The choice between reorganization and liquidation proceedings only occurs once the financial situation of the debtor has been assessed and a determination made as to whether reorganization is actually possible'.[17]

---

13. Guide, Part One, I, D, number 24.
14. Guide, Part One, I, D, number 24.
15. E.g.: Germany, Mexico and Spain.
16. Guide, Part One, I, D, number 21.
17. Guide, Part One, I, D, number 25.

C. REORGANIZATION IN LIQUIDATION

In some situations reorganization and liquidation are not incompatible; the insolvency law provides for the case when liquidation should be carried out by transferring the company as a going concern to another entity. In these cases, there is a real liquidation in the sense that the assets (i.e. the establishment as a going concern) of the insolvent debtor are transferred to a third party and the creditors' claims are collected on a pro rata basis over the price of such sale. But such mechanism, in fact, facilitates the company reorganization, for when it is transferred as a going concern it is actually exempted from the liabilities that hindered its operation.[18]

Admittedly, the aim of reorganization can be achieved through flexible criteria and even within a liquidation proceeding or a proceeding tending to its achievement.

III. VOLUNTARY RESTRUCTURING NEGOTIATIONS

A. INTRODUCTION TO VOLUNTARY RESTRUCTURING NEGOTIATIONS

The reorganization of a distressed or insolvent company can be achieved through a formal insolvency proceeding or else, more informally, through negotiations to be carried out between the debtor and all or some of the creditors – an informal (as opposed to formal) reorganization proceeding is filed in these cases. The result of these informal or voluntary restructuring negotiations shall be the approval and implementation of a reorganization plan attempting to put an end to the difficulties or to the company insolvency.

This sort of voluntary negotiations has been generally boosted by the banking sector as a rapid, discrete and cost-effective means of corporate reorganization. As a business practice, in some jurisdictions the repeated use of these mechanisms has enabled the preparation of a series of guidelines resulting from different experiences. They are not formal legal rules – not even a custom with force of law – rather, they are 'standard practices' that should facilitate restructuring through voluntary negotiations.

B. VOLUNTARY RESTRUCTURING NEGOTIATIONS IN THE PRINCIPLES

The Principles attach great importance to the voluntary restructuring negotiations.[19] In the preparation of the Principles and comments to the April 2001 version, there is a recognition for the significant role played by the publication of the

---

18. These are the cases mentioned in the Guide as 'difficult to classify', where the term reorganization is used to refer to a particular way of ensuring preservation and possible enhancement of the value of the insolvency estate in the context of liquidation proceedings, such as where the law provides for liquidation to be carried out by transferring the business as a going concern (Guide, Part One, II., C., number 20).
19. Principles 25 and 26 in the April 2001 version; Principles B.3 to B.5 in the 2005 updated version.

'Statement of Principles for a Global Approach to Multi-Creditor Workouts' by INSOL International,[20] that states the following eight best practices or principles for such workouts:

(1) Where a debtor is found to be in financial difficulties, all relevant creditors should be prepared to co-operate with each other to give sufficient (though limited) time (a 'Standstill Period') to the debtor for information about the debtor to be obtained and evaluated and for proposals for resolving the debtor's financial difficulties to be formulated and assessed, unless such a course is inappropriate in a particular case.

(2) During the Standstill Period, all relevant creditors should agree to refrain from taking any steps to enforce their claims against or (otherwise than by disposal of their debt to a third party) to reduce their exposure to the debtor but are entitled to expect that during the Standstill Period their position relative to other creditors and each other will not be prejudiced.

(3) During the Standstill Period, the debtor should not take any action which might adversely affect the prospective return to relevant creditors (either collectively or individually) as compared with the position at the Standstill Commencement Date.

(4) The interests of relevant creditors are best served by coordinating their response to a debtor in financial difficulty. Such co-ordination will be facilitated by the selection of one or more representative co-ordination committees and by the appointment of professional advisers to advise and assist such committees and, where appropriate, the relevant creditors participating in the process as a whole.

(5) During the Standstill Period, the debtor should provide, and allow relevant creditors and/or their professional advisers reasonable and timely access to, all relevant information relating to its assets, liabilities, business and prospects, in order to enable proper evaluation to be made of its financial position and any proposals to be made to relevant creditors.

(6) Proposals for resolving the financial difficulties of the debtor and, so far as practicable, arrangements between relevant creditors relating to any standstill should reflect applicable law and the relative positions of relevant creditors at the Standstill Commencement Date.

(7) Information obtained for the purposes of the process concerning the assets, liabilities and business of the debtor and any proposals for resolving its difficulties should be made available to all relevant creditors and should, unless already publicly available, be treated as confidential.

(8) If additional funding is provided during the Standstill Period or under any rescue or restructuring proposals, the repayment of such additional funding should, so far as practicable, be accorded priority status as compared to other indebtedness or claims of relevant creditors.

---

20. The complete text of *Statement of Principles for a Global Approach to Multi-Creditor Workouts* can be found in <www.insol.org>.

The Principles (April 2001) identified the conditions to be met to attempt an informal agreement, namely:

(1) A significant amount of debt owed to a number of main bank or financial institution creditors.
(2) The inability of the debtor to service that debt.
(3) The attitude that it may be preferable to negotiate an arrangement for the financial difficulties of the debtor – not only between the debtor and the creditors but also among the creditors.
(4) The availability of relatively sophisticated refinancing, security and other commercial techniques that might be used to alter, rearrange or restructure the debts of the debtor or the debtor itself.
(5) The sanction that if the negotiation process cannot be started or breaks down there can be a swift and effective resort to the insolvency law.
(6) The prospect that there may be more benefit for all parties through the negotiation process than through direct and immediate resort to the insolvency law (in part because the outcome is subject to the control of the negotiating parties and the process is less expensive and can be accomplished more quickly without disrupting the business).
(7) The debtor does not need relief from trade debt, or the benefits of formal insolvency, such as the automatic stay or the ability to reject burdensome contracts.
(8) Favourable or neutral tax treatment for restructuring both, in the debtor's jurisdiction and the jurisdictions of foreign creditors.

However, the most important condition is the presence of the 'shadow' of a legislation establishing effective formal insolvency proceedings and individual enforcement of debts. On the one hand, this statement emphasizes that informal or alternative reorganization mechanisms work, or work better, in countries where the formal system is a credible threat. On the other hand, it is stressed that informal or alternative mechanisms do not substitute; they rather supplement formal or full insolvency proceedings.

The Principles (April 2001) also discussed the following main aspects of the workouts: (1) commencing the process; (2) engaging advisers; (3) coordinating participants; (4) stabilizing the business; (5) ensuring adequate cash flow and liquidity during negotiations and restructuring; (6) access to complete, accurate information on the debtor's business; (7) negotiating, agreeing and implementing the restructuring plan; (8) dealing with outside and dissenting creditors; and, (9) the restructuring agreement must be legally binding on all affected creditors.

Lastly, in 2005 an updated version of the Principles was adopted; they are related to the voluntary restructuring negotiations and are transcribed *below*:

Principle B3: Enabling Legislative Framework

Corporate workouts and restructurings should be supported by an enabling environment that encourages participants to engage in consensual arrangements designed to restore an enterprise to financial viability. An environment that enables debt and enterprise restructuring includes laws and procedures that:

1. Require disclosure of or ensure access to timely, reliable and accurate financial information on the distressed enterprise;
2. Encourage lending to, investment in or recapitalization of viable financially distressed enterprises;
3. Flexibly accommodate a broad range of restructuring activities, involving asset sales, discounted debt sales, debt write-offs, debt reschedulings, debt and enterprise restructurings and exchange offerings (debt-to-debt and debt-to-equity exchanges);
4. Provide favourable or neutral tax treatment with respect to losses or write-offs that are necessary to achieve a debt restructuring based on the real market value of the assets subject to the transaction;
5. Address regulatory impediments that may affect enterprise reorganizations;
6. Give creditors reliable recourse to enforcement as outlined in Section A and to liquidation and/or reorganization proceedings as outlined in Section C of these Principles.

Principle B4: Informal Workout Procedures

1. An informal workout process may work better if it enables creditors and debtors to use informal techniques, such as voluntary negotiation or mediation or informal dispute resolution. While a reliable method for timely resolution of inter-creditor differences is important, the financial supervisor should play a facilitating role consistent with its regulatory duties as opposed to actively participating in the resolution of inter-creditor differences.
2. Where the informal procedure relies on a formal reorganization, the formal proceeding should be able to quickly process the informal, pre-negotiated agreement.
3. In the context of a systemic crisis or where levels of corporate insolvency have reached systemic levels, informal rules and procedures may need to be supplemented by interim framework enhancement measures to address the special needs and circumstances encountered with a view to encouraging restructuring. Such measures are typically of an interim nature designed to cover the crisis and resolution period, without undermining the conventional proceedings and systems.

Principle B5: Regulation of Workout and Risk Management

(1) A country's financial sector (possibly with the informal endorsement and assistance of the central bank, finance ministry or bankers' association) should promote the development of a code of conduct on a voluntary, consensual procedure for dealing with cases of corporate financial difficulty in which banks and other financial institutions have a significant exposure, especially in markets where corporate insolvency has reached systemic levels.

(2) In addition, good risk management practices should be encouraged by regulators of financial institutions and supported by norms that facilitate effective internal procedures and practices that support prompt and efficient recovery and resolution of non-performing loans and distressed assets.

C. VOLUNTARY RESTRUCTURING NEGOTIATIONS IN THE GUIDE

The Guide takes elements of the voluntary restructuring negotiations, though it does not draw up particular recommendations to be included in an insolvency law. This is due to the fact that generally such voluntary negotiations are not a matter of an insolvency law regulating formal insolvency proceedings. Insofar as the aforementioned negotiations end in an agreement between the debtor and his creditors, the rules regulating the contracts of the respective country shall apply.

The comments of the Guide on the voluntary negotiations are consistent with the comments of the Principles (April 2001) as regards the premises that should be considered before deciding whether those mechanisms are to be used or not. They should also serve to get an idea about measures to be adopted and techniques to be applied in the negotiation process.

According to the Guide, the *abovementioned* premises or necessary requirements to effectively approach voluntary restructuring negotiations[21] are, not restrictively, the following:

(1) a significant amount of debt owed to a number of main banks or financial institution creditors;
(2) the present or imminent inability of the debtor to service that debt;
(3) acceptance of the view that it may be preferable to negotiate an arrangement, as between the debtor and the financiers and also between the financiers themselves, to resolve the financial difficulties of the debtor;
(4) the use of relatively sophisticated refinancing, security and other commercial techniques that might be employed to alter, rearrange or restructure the debts of the debtor or the debtor itself;
(5) the sanction that if the negotiation process cannot be started or breaks down there can be swift and effective resort to the insolvency law;
(6) the prospect that there may be a greater benefit for all parties through the negotiation process than by directing and immediate resorting to the insolvency law (in part because the outcome is subject to the control of the negotiating parties and the process is less expensive and can be accomplished quickly without disrupting the debtor's business);
(7) the debtor does not need relief from trade debts, or the benefits of formal insolvency, such as the automatic stay or the ability to reject burdensome debts; and,
(8) favourable or neutral tax treatment for reorganization both in the debtor's jurisdiction and the jurisdictions of foreign creditors.

---

21. Guide, Part One, II, B., number 5.

As regards the techniques and measures to be adopted in the negotiation process, the Guide develops a number of valuable tips on: (1) the commencement of negotiations; (2) the participants and appointment of one or several creditors to coordinate the negotiations; (3) the initial signing of an agreement to suspend actions against the debtor for a defined short period; (4) the involvement of independent experts and advisors from various disciplines to ensure an independent professional information, essential to the success of these negotiations; (5) the implementation of agreements whereby creditors participating in the negotiation subordinate their claims to the creditor who provides fresh credit to the distressed company; (6) the access to information on the debtor; and, (7) agreements to be reached as a result of the voluntary negotiation.[22]

D. THOSE BOUND BY VOLUNTARY RESTRUCTURING AGREEMENTS

The achievement of a restructuring agreement in a voluntary negotiation is often insufficient for the reorganization objective, since such agreement exclusively binds signatory creditors.[23] The creditor who does not grant his consent is not bound because such agreements – as previously mentioned – are regulated by contract law. Thus, voluntary restructuring agreements have the advantage of being obtained in a rapid, discrete and inexpensive manner through informal negotiations between the debtor and all or part of his creditors. Nevertheless, they lack the inherent advantage of the agreement or plan achieved through the formal reorganization proceeding, binding even dissenting creditors.

In order to combine the advantages of the voluntary restructuring negotiation with the benefit of the obligatory force of the agreement or plan obtained through a formal proceeding, some laws have been gradually implementing certain pre-packaged or expedited mechanisms for reorganization. We are going to refer now to the treatment given to this subject in the international documents we are discussing.

IV. INTRODUCTION TO EXPEDITED REORGANIZATION PROCEEDINGS

A reorganization agreement obtained through a voluntary negotiation, outside a formal insolvency proceeding, can be binding even with respect to non-signatory creditors provided the law establishes a procedure to give such effect to these agreements. In the Guide, this sort of proceeding is called 'expedited reorganization proceeding', as opposed to the traditional or 'full' reorganization proceeding.

As indicated by its name, the expedited reorganization proceeding is characterized by brevity. Alternatives for reorganization have been discussed and agreed prior and outside the proceeding; therefore, this is not its core objective. It rather aims at ensuring information to creditors – who should be reached by the agreed

---

22. Guide, Part One, B., numbers 6 to 15.
23. Guide, Part One, B., number 31.

plan – so that they can raise objections prior to the decision of the court on whether to confirm or reject the plan.

Once this procedure is achieved and the plan is confirmed by the court, minority creditors (those opposing or dissenting) of each category of creditors affected by the plan shall be bound as if such plan had been approved in a 'formal' or 'full' insolvency reorganization proceeding.

Thus, the advantages of the voluntary negotiations can be preserved through the expedited reorganization proceeding, whereby the significant majority of creditors (though not all of them), belonging to categories of creditors affected by a plan, give their consent. Such procedure reduces to a minimum the delays and costs. It avoids, in turn, the possible failure of a plan reached through voluntary restructuring negotiations, owing to enforcement actions filed by opposing or dissenting minority creditors.

The Principles consider that formal insolvency proceedings should be capable of processing rapidly a pre-packaged agreement (in voluntary negotiations) so that such agreement can be turned into a formal reorganization plan (binding also dissenting creditors pertaining to the class or classes affected by the plan). Accordingly, the insolvency legislation would allow to combine the benefits of voluntary restructuring negotiations with the advantages of the reorganization plan achieved in a formal insolvency proceeding. In this way, the main weakness of agreements achieved in purely voluntary negotiations can be remedied; that is to say, the lack of binding effects as regards those who did not sign such agreements.

The Guide also has a favourable view on this type of procedure,[24] drawing up a considerable number of recommendations[25] for its legislative establishment, which are transcribed *below*.

B. EXPEDITED REORGANIZATION PROCEEDINGS[26]

Recommendations 160–168. Contents of legislative provisions

160. The insolvency law should specify that expedited proceedings can be commenced on the application of any debtor that:

(a) Is or is likely to be generally unable to pay its debts as they mature;
(b) Has negotiated a reorganization plan and had it accepted by each affected class of creditors; and
(c) Satisfies the jurisdictional requirements for commencement of full reorganization proceedings under the insolvency law.

161. The insolvency law may additionally specify that an expedited proceeding can be commenced on the application of any debtor if:

---

24. Guide, Part One, II., C., number 31, and Part Two, IV., B., numbers 76 to 94.
25. Guide, Recommendations 160 to 168.
26. Because these proceedings are based on the agreement achieved in voluntary restructuring negotiations, this section should be read in conjunction with part one, chapter II, paras. 2–18 of the Guide.

(a) The debtor's liabilities exceed or are likely to exceed its assets; and
(b) The requirements of recommendation 160, subparagraphs (b) and (c), are satisfied.

Application requirements (para. 89)

162. The insolvency law should specify that the following additional materials should accompany an application for commencement of expedited reorganization proceedings:

(a) The reorganization plan and disclosure statement;
(b) A description of the voluntary restructuring negotiations that preceded the making of the application for commencement, including the information provided to affected creditors to enable them to make an informed decision about the plan;
(c) Certification that unaffected creditors are being paid in the ordinary course of business and that the plan does not modify or affect the rights or claims of unaffected creditors without their agreement;
(d) A report of the votes of affected classes of creditors demonstrating that those classes have accepted the plan by the majorities specified in the insolvency law;
(e) A financial analysis or other evidence that demonstrates that the plan satisfies all applicable requirements for reorganization; and
(f) A list of the members of any creditor committee formed during the course of the voluntary restructuring negotiations.

Commencement

163. The insolvency law should specify that the application for commencement will automatically commence the proceedings or that the court will be required to promptly determine whether the debtor satisfies the requirements of recommendations 160 or 161 and if so, commence proceedings.

Effects of commencement (para. 90)

164. The insolvency law should specify that:

(a) Provisions of the insolvency law that apply to full reorganization proceedings will also apply to expedited proceedings unless specified as modified or not applicable;[27]

---

27. Provisions of the insolvency law that generally would not be applicable or that could be modified would include: (1) full claim filing; (2) notice and time periods for plan approval; (3) the post-commencement mechanics of providing the plan and disclosure statement to creditors and other interested parties and for solicitation of votes and voting on the plan; (4) appointment of an insolvency representative (who generally would not be appointed unless required by the plan); and, (5) provisions on amendment of the plan after confirmation. An exception to the provisions of the insolvency law applicable to full reorganization proceedings would be that creditors not affected by the plan would be paid in the ordinary course of business during the implementation of the plan.

(b) Unless otherwise determined by the court, the effects of commencement should be limited to the debtor, individual creditors and classes of creditors and equity holders whose rights are modified or affected by the plan;
(c) Any creditor committee formed during the course of the voluntary restructuring negotiations should be treated as a creditor committee appointed under the insolvency law; and
(d) A hearing on the confirmation of the plan by the court should be held as expeditiously as possible.

Notice of commencement (para. 87 and chapter I, paras. 64–71 and recommendations 22–25)

165. The insolvency law should specify that notice of the commencement of expedited proceedings is to be given to affected creditors and affected equity holders. The notice should specify:

(a) The amount of each affected creditor's claim according to the debtor;
(b) The time period for submitting a claim in a different amount if the affected creditor disagrees with the debtor's statement of the claim and the place where the claim can be submitted;
(c) The time and procedure for challenging claims submitted by other parties;
(d) The time and place for the hearing on confirmation of the plan and for the submission of any objection to confirmation; and
(e) The impact of the plan on equity holders.

Confirmation of the plan (paras. 60–63 and 88 and recommendation 152)

166. The insolvency law should specify that the court will confirm the plan if:

(a) The plan satisfies the substantive requirements for confirmation of a plan in full reorganization proceedings, in so far as those requirements apply to affected creditors and affected equity holders;
(b) The notice given and the information provided to affected creditors and affected equity holders during the voluntary restructuring negotiations was sufficient to enable them to make an informed decision about the plan and any pre-commencement solicitation of acceptances to the plan complied with applicable law;
(c) Unaffected creditors are being paid in the ordinary course of business and the plan does not modify or affect the rights or claims of unaffected creditors without their agreement; and
(d) The financial analysis submitted with the application demonstrates that the plan satisfies all applicable requirements for reorganization.

Effect of a confirmed plan (para. 64)

167. The insolvency law should specify that the effect of a plan confirmed by the court should be limited to the debtor and those creditors and equity holders affected by the plan.

Introduction 17

Failure of implementation of a confirmed plan (paras. 70, 71and 91)

168. The insolvency law may specify that where there is a substantial breach by the debtor of the terms of the plan or an inability to implement the plan, the court may close the judicial proceedings and parties in interest may exercise their rights at law.

V. CONCLUSIONS

The main documents on insolvency, prepared by the international community in recent years, recognize the importance of reorganization mechanisms so that 'the possible eventual return to creditors is maximized, providing a better result than if the debtor were to be liquidated in order to preserve viable businesses as a means of preserving jobs for employees and trade for suppliers'.[28]

The aforementioned documents have a favourable view and provide recommendations on: (1) practices used in various countries for the achievement of restructuring agreements in voluntary negotiations; and, (2) legislations establishing the possibility of turning, rapidly, pre-packaged agreements into reorganization plans to bind creditors in the same way as in the plans achieved through the most traditional 'formal' reorganization proceedings.

In countries adopting modern and effective insolvency systems, the reorganization of insolvent companies is not currently limited to the traditional judicial reorganization proceeding. At present, reorganization mechanisms have been broadened and can cover the following alternatives:

1. Reorganization through purely voluntary negotiations, governed by the ordinary contract law.
2. Reorganization resulting from the voluntary negotiation, whose plan is subject to an expedited proceeding that can reach the advantages of a plan approved through a traditional or 'full' insolvency proceeding.
3. Reorganization achieved in a 'formal' or 'full' proceeding, whether: (a) in a 'unitary' insolvency system (sole insolvency proceeding, turned subsequently to reorganization or liquidation); (b) in a 'dual' system (different insolvency proceedings for reorganization and liquidation); and/or (c) even within liquidation, mainly through the sale and transfer of the company as a going concern.

---

28. Guide, Part Two, IV, A., number 3.

Chapter 2
Argentina

Expedited Debt Restructuring Under Argentine Law: Acuerdo Preventivo Extrajudicial (APE)

by Rodrigo Olivares-Caminal

ACRONYMS, ABBREVIATIONS & DEFINED TERMS

ABL	Argentine Bankruptcy law No. 24.522, as amended and restated by Laws No. 25,563 and 25,589
APE	*Acuerdo Preventivo Extrajudicial* or 'extrajudicial preventive agreement', Argentina's expedited debt restructuring procedure under the auspices of the Argentine bankruptcy law
appellants	Argentinian Recovery Company LLC; W.R. Huff Asset Management Co., LLC; The Huff Alternative Income Fund, L.P.; WRH Partners Global Securities LP; Willard Alexander; and, WRH Global Securities Pooled Trust
ARC	Argentinian Recovery Company LLC
Argo	The Argo Fund Ltd
ARP	Argentine Peso
BAPCPA	Bankruptcy Abuse Prevention and Consumer Protection Act of 2005, Pub. L. No. 109–8, 119 Stat. 23 (2005).
Chapter 11	US reorganization procedure under the auspices of §§ 1101 to 1146 of the US Bankruptcy law (11 U.S.C.)
EUR	Euro
GDP	Gross Domestic Product
ITL	Italian Lira (the currency of Italy between 1861 and 1999)
JPY	Japanese Yen
Multicanal	Multicanal S.A.
Non-QIBs	Non-Qualified Investor Buyers
QIBs	Qualified Investor Buyers
SEC	US Securities and Exchange Commission
Telecom	Telecom Argentina S.A.
TIA	Trust Indenture Act of 1939, 15 U.S.C. § 77aaa to § 77bbbb
UNCITRAL	United Nations Commission for International Trade Law
US Bankruptcy Code	11 U.S.C. § 101 et seq.
US Securities Act	US Securities Act of 1933
USD	United States Dollar
WRH	WRH Partners Global Securities L.P.
WRH-ARC	WRH Partners Global Securities L.P. jointly with Argentinian Recovery Company LLC

I. INTRODUCTION

This chapter will provide an analysis of the expedited debt restructuring mechanism contemplated in the Argentine Bankruptcy law No. 24.522, as amended and restated by Laws No. 25,563 and 25,589 (ABL). The expedited debt restructuring mechanism is provided in sections 69 to 76 and is known by its acronym 'APE', which stands for *Acuerdo Preventivo Extrajudicial* or 'extrajudicial preventive agreement' (APE). The Argentine APE is very similar to the pre-packaged plan under § 1125(g) of the US Bankruptcy Code.[1] The APE reached international notoriety as result of the 2001–2002 Argentine crisis that resulted in USD 31.5 billion being restructured including 95 per cent of the stock of corporate bonds.[2] In addition, as result of the Multicanal case litigated in the jurisdiction of the State of New York, the APE gained international notoriety.[3]

The analysis will commence with a brief description of the legal and economic consequences of the 2001–2002 Argentine crisis in order to understand why many Argentine companies were faced either with a complete restructuring of their outstanding debts or with the declaration of their bankruptcy and the subsequent liquidation of their assets.

Secondly, the chapter will address the legal framework of the Argentine APE, providing a theoretical analysis.

Thirdly, the analysis of the restructuring of Multicanal S.A. (Multicanal) will be provided. Its relevance lies on the facts that: (1) it was litigated in the US Bankruptcy Court for the Southern District of New York where recognition was granted to the APE as an international insolvency reorganization proceeding under US law; and, (2) majorities were hardly reached and it clearly illustrates how an expedited debt restructuring procedure with scarce involvement of a court could have been used to cram-down the dissenting minorities or the holdout creditors. However, it is worth stressing that as result of the continuous litigation in the US this case has not been successful in achieving an expedited debt restructuring. Therefore, this case study is used to illustrate what are the things that need to

---

1. 11 USC § 1125(g).
2. *See* A. Milne, A. Panton and B. Saez, 'Argentina Corporates 2003–2004: From Ashes to APEs' Deutsche Bank, 10 November 2003.
3. The case under study includes the *following* cases or filings: (1) In re: Board of Directors of Multicanal S.A., Debtor in Foreign Proceeding. In a Proceeding Under § 304 of the US bankruptcy Code, Case No. 04–10280 (ALG), 307 B.R. 384 (Bankr. S.D.N.Y., 12 March 2004); (2) In re: Board of Directors of Multicanal S.A., Debtor in Foreign Proceeding. In re Multicanal S.A., Alleged Debtor (in a proceeding under § 304 of the Bankruptcy Code, Case No. 04–10280 (ALG), Involuntary Chapter 11, Case No. 04–10523 (ALG)), 314 B.R. 486 (Bankr. S.D.N.Y., 27 August 2004); (3) order dated 6 January 2005 in Cases No. 04–10280 (ALG) and 04–10523 (ALG). *See* <www.nysb.usCourts.gov>; (4) *Argentinian Recovery Company LLC v. Board of Directors of Multicanal S.A.,* 331 B.R. 537, Fed. Sec. L. Rep. P 93,584; and, (5) In re Board of Directors of Multicanal S.A., 340 B.R. 154.

be avoided and which are the key elements that should be taken into account when proposing a pre-packaged deal under an APE.

Fourthly, the restructuring of Telecom Argentina S.A. (Telecom) will be provided as a second case study. This case is important in relation to the fast recovery of a troubled company. Its real value lies in the fact that since it was a listed company – which was not the case of Multicanal at the time of the filing of its APE restructuring – it can be used to demonstrate the financial impact of an expedited debt restructuring on the value of the company. In addition, the degree of creditors' participation can also be used to illustrate how a well drafted plan reflecting creditors' needs and a continuous and fluent communication with them can facilitate a restructuring.

Finally, some concluding remarks will be made summarizing the features included in the chapter and stressing the key issues under Argentine law and the lessons that can be drawn from the two case studies.

II. THE ARGENTINE CRISIS

As per Law 23,928 of 1991, Argentina's currency – the Argentine Peso (ARP) – was pegged to the United States dollar (USD) at a 1:1 rate.

In 2001 – the forth recessive year in a row – after a series of policy blunders and tax increases/creation, the rating agencies downgraded the Argentine debt twice and the market reacted by withdrawing vast amounts of money from the banking system fearing that the scenario would get even worse.[4] Some US academics stated that the way out of the acute situation of Argentina was by means of a default.[5]

On 1 December 2001, in an attempt to avoid a bank run, a Presidential Decree was enacted to temporarily limit further withdrawals of deposits from the financial system and to set forth regulatory requirements for money transfers abroad.[6] The measure was known as '*corralito*' (little corral) because it was a sort of fence put around bank deposits to avoid money from escaping the banking system. Unfortunately, it triggered a series of violent acts. Supermarkets were sacked, general strikes were called and finally riots on the streets forced President De la

---

4. The withdrawal of bank deposits amounted USD 5.5 billion in March, USD 5.2 billion in July, USD 2 billion in August, USD 0.6 billion in September and USD 2.9 billion in November 2001.
5. *See* the article published on May 2001 by Adam Lerrick and Allan H. Meltzer in the *Carnegie Mellon Gailliot Center for Public Policy's Quarterly International Economics Report, titled 'Beyond IMF Bailouts: Default without Disruption'*, where these authors considered that the only way to supersede Argentina's crisis was by defaulting on its debt.
6. Presidencial Decree No. 1,570/01 was originally going to be in full force for the term of 90 days which was the required time to perform a complete debt restructuring of the international bonds. Since the bond swap did not take place in the 90 days period, the effects of the Decree were extended by Resolution No. 6/02 of the Argentine Ministry of Economy until Resolution No. 668/02 – issued on 21 November 2002 and entered into force on 2 December 2002 – put an end to the cash withdrawal limits established by the '*corralito*'.

Argentina 23

Rua to resign to his office on 20 December 2001 after 35 people died in the whole country as the result of clashes between demonstrators and the police.

Following De la Rúa's resignation, Argentina had five different presidents in less than 15 days.[7] On 1 January 2002, Eduardo Duhalde – the last president of this saga of appointments – devaluated the ARP. The framework to solve the crisis was mainly construed by: (1) Law 25,561 that overruled the 1:1 parity between the ARP and the USD; (2) Decree 71/2002 that established two exchange rates, an official one at a USD 1:1.4 ARP rate ('asymmetry pesofication') and a free market exchange rate that at the moment of the devaluation climbed to USD 1:3.6 ARP; and, (3) Decree 214/2002 that established a mandatory conversion of all credits and debts at a USD 1:1 ARP rate except for Bank deposits that were converted at a USD 1:1.4 ARP rate; and, suspended judicial claims for a period of 180 days.

The main consequences of the devaluation were: (1) a nominal devaluation of the ARP up to USD 0.25, finally stabilized at approximately USD 0.33; (2) an inflationary impact that resulted in a 30 per cent shrunk of real salaries; (3) a domestic redistribution of wealth in the order of USD 30 billion which were diverted from savers' bank deposits and pension funds to private-sector debtors and Provincial Governments;[8] (4) in USD terms, 2003's GDP was less than 50 per cent of 2001's GDP; and, (5) as a result of the *corralito* and the mandatory

---

7. According to section 88 of the Argentine Constitution, upon the resignation of the President, the Vice President should take office. Since the Vice President elected together with De la Rúa (Carlos Alvarez) had resigned on 6 October 2000, according to Law 20,972 the following persons should act as President: (1) upon the resignation of the Vice President, the President of the Senate is the head of the country; (2) in any event, the President of the Senate should be replaced by the President of the Chamber of Deputies; and lastly, (3) the latter should be replaced by the President of the Supreme Court. The temporary appointment of the President of either the Senate, Chamber of Deputies or the Supreme Court is temporary and up to a maximum of 48 hours, term in which the Congress in full (both chambers) should appoint a Senator, Deputy or Governor to substitute the President until a new general election takes place.

   Fernando De la Rúa resigned from his office on 20 December 2001. Since the Vice President had resigned to his office on 6 October 2000, Ramón Puerta in his capacity of President of the Senate was appointed temporarily as President. On 23 December 2001, Adolfo Rodríguez Saa was appointed by a general assembly of the Congress (Senates and Deputies all together) the as interim President. On 30 December 2001, Rodríguez Saa resigned to his office due to the lack of political support. Although he was supposed to be replaced by the President of the Senate again (Ramón Puerta), since he also resigned from his office, Eduardo Caamaño (President of the Chamber of Deputies) was appointed as temporary President. Another general assembly was summoned and Eduardo Duhalde was appointed as President to complete De la Rúa's original mandate until December 2003. This resolution was in breach of section 88 of the Argentine Constitution and Law 20,972 that establishes that the appointed of the president will be temporary until a general election takes place and not to complete the mandate of the resigning President.

8. For (a), (b) and (c) *see* Domingo F. Cavallo, *How did the foreign debt triggered the Argentine Crisis (or the new 'Washington Consensus' that triggered the Argentine Crisis)*, conference delivered at the Real Instituto Elcano, Madrid, Spain, 11–12 December 2003 during the series '*La Seguridad Jurídica y las Inversiones Extranjeras en América Latina – El Caso Argentino*', available at <www.cavallo.com.ar/papers/Elcanodic03ingles.html>, (last visited 5 March 2006).

conversion of USD bank deposits into ARP at a exchange rate different to the free market rate, this mandatory practice resolved by the Government can be understood as a seizing of property that ended in a crisis of the Judicial System due to the lack of an apolitical response.[9] According to US courts entertaining claims against the Argentine government stated that Argentina suffered *'the worst economic crisis in its history'*.[10]

Given this framework, on 15 May 2002, Law No. 25,589 was passed to amend the ABL. Among other things, the provisions of the pre-packaged reorganization plans were amended.

III. PRE-PACKAGED REORGANIZATION PLANS UNDER ARGENTINE LAW

In May 2002, the Argentine Congress passed Law No. 25,589[11] which particularly amended the bankruptcy law in relation to pre-packs in an intend to boost its use as the result of the combination of both, the devaluation of the ARP and the high rate of USD highly indebted corporations.

In accordance to the ABL,[12] a debtor[13] who suspends his payments or has general economic or financial difficulties may reach an agreement[14] with his creditors and submit it for judicial homologation. The terms of the agreement may consist of a write-off, extension in maturity dates or both; the delivery of assets to the creditors; the organization of a company with the general creditors in which the latter shall be partners; reorganization of the debtor company; management of all or part of the assets for the creditors' benefit; issue of negotiable obligations or debentures; issue of bonds convertible into shares; creation of guarantees on third-party assets; assignment of stock in other companies; capitalization of claims, including labour creditors, into shares, or in stock ownership programs; or, in any other understanding which were to obtain sufficient acceptance within each category over the aggregate number

---

9. *See* La Nación Newspaper, *Por una Mayor Transparencia Judicial*, 27 February 2005, available at <http://www.lanacion.com.ar/herramientas/printfriendly/printfriendly.asp?origen=3ra&nota_id=683190>, (last visited 27 February 2006).
10. *See* Applestein TTEE FBO D.C.A. *Grantor Trust v. Republic of Arg.*, 2003 US Dist. LEXIS 20922, No. 02 Civ. 4124, 2003 WL 22743762, (S.D.N.Y. 2003). *Also Lightwater Corp. v. Republic of Argentina*, 2003 US Dist. LEXIS 6156, No. 02 Civ. 3804, 2003 WL 1878420, (S.D.N.Y. 2003).
11. A Spanish version of this law is available at <http://infoleg.mecon.gov.ar/txtnorma/74331.htm>, (last visited 27 November 2006).
12. *See* Section 69 of the ABL.
13. According to section 2 of the ABL the debtor is meant to be either: (1) individuals, (2) private corporate entities and corporations in which the National, Provincial or Municipal Government may have an interest – whatever its percentage may be –, (3) in the deceased's estate while it is separate from the heirs' estate; and (4) debtors domiciled abroad with respect to assets existing within the country. The entities excluded are banks, insurance companies, mutual and pension funds, and any other excluded by special laws.
14. *See* section 43 of the ABL.

of creditors to whom the proposal is made. The parties may include in the agreement those matters they deem advisable according to their interests and such agreement shall be binding upon them even when legal homologation has not been granted, unless expressly agreed otherwise by the parties.[15]

The agreement mentioned in the previous paragraph is known as APE and is an alternative mechanism provided by the ABL similar to the US pre-packaged deals to avoid initiating a full court-supervised reorganization procedure (*concurso preventivo*, comparable to the US' Chapter 11).[16] The agreement may be executed by means of a private instrument, with the signature of the parties and the representations invoked attested to by a notary public.[17]

Once an agreement has been reached with the creditors, said agreement can be filed with a bankruptcy court for homologation to make it binding to all creditors subject to it.[18] In order to request the judicial homologation of the agreement the

---

15. *See* section 71 of the ABL. Except that the proposal is abusive or contrary to the law, the debtor and creditor can reach an agreement without a substantial supervision of the terms by the court. It is worth mentioning that prior to the amendment of law 25,589, agreements that implied a write-off of more than 60 per cent of the credit were not permitted. In a court supervised reorganization procedure (*concurso preventivo*), the National Commercial Court of Appeals stated that an agreement to pay only a net present value of 12.39 per cent of the liabilities was abusive if an irregular proceeding was used to obtain the required majorities (*See* National Commercial Court of Appeals, Chamber 'A' in re '*Arcangel Maggio S.A. s/ Concurso Preventivo*').
16. *See* 11 U.S.C. § § 1101 to 1146.
17. *See* section 70 of the ABL. Original or authenticated copies of the documents evidencing the capacity of the parties to the agreement should be attached to the agreement. If the agreement is signed abroad or the power of attorney to sign the agreement is granted abroad the document should then be legalized following the procedure established by the Hague Convention on the 'Abolition of Legalization of Documents' of 5 October 1961, or at the nearest Argentine consulate if the country where the document was signed has not ratified said convention.
18. According to section 72 of the ABL, the following documents – duly certified by a chartered accountant – shall be filed with the competent court, together with the agreement: (1) financial statements updated as of the date of the APE, expressly indicating the valuation standards used for its preparation; (2) a list of creditors indicating their domiciles, amount of their credit, origin of claim, maturities, co-debtors, guarantors or third party obligors and payers; the accountant's certification shall state that there are no other creditors recorded and shall detail the accounting and documentary evidence supporting his statement; (3) a list of lawsuits or administrative proceedings pending or with un-enforced judgment, specifying the Court or agency hearing same; (4) a list of the accounting books and other records kept by the debtor, indicating the number of the last page used as of the date of the 'agreement'; and, (5) the capital amount represented by the creditors who signed the agreement, and the percentage that they represent over the total creditors recorded by the debtor. Although section 72 of the ABL does not clarify whether it refers to the date of the agreement reached with the debtors or the date of the filing with the court, a reasonable interpretation indicates that it should be the date of the agreement. This notwithstanding, it might be possible that different creditors signed the agreement on different dates. Even, the required majorities for the court approval could have been achieved on one date but a greater percentage of acceptances obtained at a later stage. Therefore, considering that the updated financial statements have to be prepared as of the date of the agreement we might be facing two different dates: (1) the date that the required majorities were achieved; or, (2) the date that the agreement was signed by all the agreeing parties. So far, as to my knowledge, this issue has not come up in a proceeding.

ABL states that it is necessary to obtain a double majority threshold: (1) an absolute majority (more than 50 per cent) of unsecured creditors on a head-count basis, i.e, numerosity; and, (2) at least two thirds (66⅔ per cent) of the aggregate amount of unsecured liabilities.[19] Upon the filing with the court to obtain the judicial approval or homologation and as of that date, all actions against the debtor involving monetary claims are stayed.[20]

So far, Argentine courts have applied by analogy certain provisions of the reorganization procedure (*concurso preventivo*) which is also similar to US' Chapter 11 to clarify or fill in certain gaps in the APE regime. The most relevant provision is section 45bis of the ABL that rules the voting system for securities issued in series (e.g. notes or bonds). Section 45bis of the ABL, applicable to the APE, provides that: (1) a meeting summoned by the trustee, or when pertinent by the court, shall be held; (2) at the meeting, the creditors who attended will approve or reject the proposed agreement (in the event there are different options and the proposal is approved, each creditor shall state which alternative they support); and, (3) the consent shall be calculated by the capital representing all those who have accepted the proposal and as though granted by one single person; rejections shall also be calculated as one single person.[21] Each series is counted as a single person and if there are votes in favour and against it will be considered as tendered twice, one in favour and one against, representing the amount of capital in favour and against the proposal. In a hypothetical situation, if for example there were five banks and five bond series, there are going to be ten votes, five for each bank and five for each bond series. However, if there is any bond series voting against the proposal, there should be a vote for each one of them as well. Therefore, there is a chance to have a maximum of 15 votes: (1) five from each bank; (2) five in favour of the proposal from each bond series; and, (3) five against the proposal from each bond series.

The submission of the agreement for its homologation must be made publicly known by: (1) legal notices published during five working days in the official gazette within the court jurisdiction; and, (2) in one leading newspaper in the area.[22]

---

19. The double threshold requirement of the APE is set-forth in section 73 of the ABL, which refers to section 45 of same. In the case of corporations, partners, managers and creditors that also are in connection to the debtor (spouse; relatives within the fourth degree of consanguinity, second of affinity or adoptive relatives; and, assignees within the year prior to the filing) are excluded from the calculation. This prohibition is not applicable to those creditors who are shareholders in the debtor company, except in the event that they were to control same. *See* section 45 of the ABL.
20. Litigation as to condemnation matters and actions based on family relationships are exempt from the stay. *See* section 21, par. 2 of the ABL. Additionally, no new actions involving monetary issues against the debtor on account of any cause or title prior to the filing shall be brought. *See* section 21, par. 3, of the ABL.
21. *See* section 45bis of the ABL.
22. Should the debtor have establishments in other jurisdictions, the legal notices must be published during the same period in each one of them. *See* section 74 of the ABL.

Creditors listed by the debtor or other creditors who prove – by way of a summary proceeding[23] – that they were omitted may file oppositions against the agreement. These oppositions shall be filed within ten days following the latest publication of notices, and may be grounded only on: (1) omissions of assets or liabilities and/or if the company has understated or overstated the value of said assets or liabilities; or, (2) on the failure to obtain the required majorities.[24]

If the legal requirements have been met and no objections are pending, the judge shall homologate the agreement. The main effects of the homologation are: (1) the novation of all the obligations having an origin or cause prior to the agreement;[25] and, (2) the homologated agreement produces effects with respect to all general creditors whose claims had been included in the agreement, even if they have not participated in the restructuring agreement or if they have opposed it.[26]

The homologated composition may be declared null at the request of any creditor subject to it – within six months of its homologation – on the existence of fraud used to exaggerate the liabilities, simulation of non-existing or fraudulently created preferences and conceal or exaggerate assets.[27] The judgment declaring the nullity of the APE must contain the declaration of bankruptcy against the debtor and the adoption of measures to protect the assets of the company.[28] No court shall homologate an agreement which is fraudulent or abusive.[29]

If the debtor were not to fulfil the composition, either totally or partially a judge must declare the bankruptcy at the request of an interested creditor, or of the overseer of the composition.[30]

IV. THE APE: A WORKABLE SOLUTION.
     TWO CASE STUDIES.

This section of the chapter will provide an analysis of two very interesting case studies which reflect some of the pros and cons on the use of the APE as an expedited debt restructuring tool. The case studies are also very useful to illustrate in practice how the APE can creatively be used to achieve a successful

---

23. If necessary, a term of ten days shall be established for the production of evidence, and the judge shall adopt a decision within ten days following the expiration of the trial period.
24. *See* section 75 of the ABL.
25. *See* section 55 of the ABL. According to Grispo, the homologation of the agreement does not implies the novation of the obligations unless the parties have expressly agreed so (Daniel Grispo, *Acuerdo Preventivo Extrajudicial Según Ley 25,589*), available at <http://www.infobaeprofesional.com/adjuntos/documentos/09/0000927.pdf>, last visited 27 November 2006.
26. *See* section 56 of the ABL.
27. Section 60 of the ABL.
28. Section 61 of the ABL.
29. *See* section 52(4) of the ABL. Moreover, section 1,071 of the Argentine Civil Code defines an 'abusive exercise of rights' as that which 'contravenes the aim of the law that acknowledged those rights or that which exceeds the limits imposed by good faith, morals and generally accepted good practices'.
30. Section 63 of the ABL.

restructuring. The cases to be analyzed are: Multicanal and Telecom. These two argentine companies, as result of the 2001–2002 crisis, were forced to restructure their outstanding debt, particularly due to the steep devaluation of the ARP and the fact that their indebtedness was expressed in hard currencies while their income in a soft currency (i.e. the ARP). The difference in these two cases lies in the fact that (1) although Multicanal reached an APE agreement on 14 April 2004 with the majorities required by the ABL as of 2006 it was still litigating in New York courts with holdout creditors without being able to settle the restructuring; and, (2) Telecom successfully achieved a debt restructuring on an expedited basis as result of the fairness of its proposal, the full disclosure of its financial condition and carefully making all the required filings on time.

The Multicanal case was litigated in Argentina and in the jurisdiction of the State of New York. Its relevance lies on the facts that: (1) a New York court granted recognition to the APE as an international insolvency reorganization proceeding under US law; and, (2) majorities were hardly reached and it clearly illustrates how an expedited debt restructuring procedure with scarce involvement of a court can be used to cram-down the dissenting minorities or the holdout creditors. This notwithstanding, the lack of equal alternatives to different creditors resulted in lengthy litigation in New York and ended converting what was supposed to be an expedited debt restructuring in a lengthy procedure with an uncertain outcome. This is an excellent example to demonstrate how things can get spiteful and risk the whole restructuring. It also provides different lessons as to what are the issues that should be borne in mind to plan and obtain a successful restructuring.

The Telecom case is important to illustrate the fast recovery of a troubled company by means of the financial impact of an expedited debt restructuring on the value of its shares. In addition, the degree of creditors' participation in this particular APE is useful to reflect that a well drafted plan including/reflecting creditors' needs and the continuous and fluent communications with them can facilitate an expeditious restructuring.

A.   THE MULTICANAL CASE

1.   Litigation in Argentina

Multicanal is a cable company with its headquarters in Argentina and with a 10 per cent of its total business in Uruguay and Paraguay. Multicanal is a wholly-owned subsidiary of Grupo Clarin SA, owner of the largest circulation newspaper in Argentina between 1997 and 2001. Multicanal issued five series of unsecured notes governed by the law of the State of New York according to the following details: (1) USD 97 million in principal amount of 9.25 per cent notes due 2002; (2) USD 99 million in principal amount of 10.5 per cent notes due 2007; (3) USD 131 million in principal amount of Series E 13.125 per cent notes due 2009; (4) USD 38 million in principal amount of Series C 10.5 per cent notes due 2018; and (5) USD 144 million in outstanding principal Series J Floating Rate Notes due 2003. These notes are registered with the US Securities and Exchange Commission (SEC)[31] and were issued under indentures qualified under the US Trust Indenture Act of 1939 (TIA).[32]

The aggregate principal amount corresponding to the notes of Multicanal is USD 509 million which together with the banks' debt represents 97 per cent of Multicanal's total outstanding debt. Due to the Argentine crisis that resulted in the devaluation of the ARP abandoning the 1:1 pegged rate with the USD, Multicanal's debt service became more difficult and the acquisition of programming from the US became much more expensive. On 1 February 2002, Multicanal defaulted on one of the notes, defaulting on payments due on all series of notes by April 2002. In order to solve its financial situation, Multicanal formed an informal negotiating group with creditors holding 25 per cent approximately of the outstanding debt.[33] On 31 January 2003, Multicanal announced a restructuring proposal, which was later amended on 25 July 2003.[34] The terms of the amended proposal can be summarized as follows:

(1) *Cash Option*: a cash tender offer to purchase USD 100 million of its outstanding debt at a price of USD 300 per USD 1,000 (30 per cent) of principal amount tendered plus a 2 per cent interest per annum from the date on which the APE was approved to the date on which noteholders receive payment. Non-qualified investors (non-QIBs)[35] were able to accept only this offer.

(2) *Par Option*: an exchange offer of USD 1,050 principal amount of Multicanal's 10-year notes bearing interest at rates that would increase over time from 2.5 per cent to 4.5 per cent for each USD 1,000 of existing debt tendered. And,

(3) *Combined Option*: a combination of USD 440 principal amount of Multicanal's 7-year notes bearing interest at a fixed 7 per cent annual rate or an economically equivalent floating rate, as elected by the holder, and 641 of Multicanal's Class C shares of common stock for each USD 1,000 of existing debt tendered. This option had a 35 per cent cap out of the total outstanding shares of Multicanal.

---

31. Originally, the notes were not registered but upon a commitment taken by Multicanal at the moment of issuance, they were registered in 1997.
32. 15 U.S.C. § 77aaa to § 77bbbb.
33. This creditors' informal negotiating group included Deutsche Bank, Credit Suisse First Boston, Credit Lyonnais, Toronto Dominion, TIAA-CREF, Fintech Advisory Ltd., Orix Capital Markets LLC, Dolphin Fund Management, Argentinian Recovery Company LLC and WRH Partners Global Securities L.P.
34. Multicanal requested a signed support agreement to vote in favour of the proposal from some members of the negotiating group in order to amend the proposal.
35. In the US, non qualified investors or non-QIBs, as opposed to qualified investors buyers or QIBs, is an institution that in the aggregate owns and invests on a discretionary basis at least USD100 million in securities of issuers that are not affiliated with the entity (17 CFR 230.144A).

The Cash Option was only available to non-QIBs as result of the effect of US securities law. On the other hand, the Par Option and the Combined Option were available to institutional holders in the US since the offering of securities would be exempt as a private resale to qualified investors buyers (QIBs) under Rule 144A.[36]

On 12 August 2003, Multicanal filed with an Argentine commercial court the APE for homologation in order to make it binding to all creditors. Multicanal requested the court to summon a noteholders' meeting. The meeting was held on 10 December 2003, with 94 per cent participation. Holders of USD 318,599,001 aggregate principal amount of notes and USD 18,542,827 principal amount of bank debt voted in favour of the APE (i.e. 68 per cent), while holders of USD 159,083,024 principal amount of notes voted against (i.e. 32 per cent). As previously mentioned, Argentine law requires a double threshold: at least two thirds (66⅔ per cent) of the aggregate amount of unsecured liabilities – which was obtained – and also, an absolute majority (more than 50 per cent) of unsecured creditors on numerosity. As described *above*, according to Argentine law, the numerosity of those who granted their vote is calculated by the capital representing all those who have accepted the proposal and as though granted by one single person. Rejections are also calculated as one single person. That means that since holders of all the series were present at the meeting and votes for and against the APE were granted, following the Argentine voting system for securities issued in series there were five votes in favour and five votes against the proposal. Moreover, considering that five banks were also

Votes Tendered in the Multicanal Case					
Aggregate Amount of Unsecured Liabilities			**Numerosity**		
Type of Creditor	**In Favour**	**Against**	**Type of Creditor**	**In Favour**	**Against**
Noteholders	USD 318,599,001	USD 159,083,024	**Noteholders**	5	5
Bank Loans	USD 18,542,827	—	**Bank Loans**	5	—
Total	USD 337,141,828	USD 159,083,024	**Total**	10	5
Percentage	68 per cent	32 per cent	**Percentage**	66⅔ per cent	33⅓ per cent
ABL Requirement	66⅔ per cent	n.a.	**ABL Requirement**	>50 per cent	n.a.

---

36. 17 C.F.R. § 230.144A

present and voted in favour of the APE, on a head-count basis the result was ten votes in favour (i.e. five banks and the five votes representing the noteholders that voted in favour of the proposal) and five against the proposal (i.e. the five votes representing the noteholders that voted against the proposal). Since the numerosity threshold was also achieved, the requirements set-forth in the ABL were fulfilled. Therefore, the court issued a resolution stating that *prima facie* the requirements were fulfilled ordering to proceed with the publicity required by law. After the last day of publications and during a 10-day period, creditors were allowed to file observations. In this case, six observations were filed.

On 14 April 2004, the Argentine judge issued a resolution going through the six observations filed. The judge overruled all the observations but one. The observation in question stated that creditors who rejected or abstained should be given some time to opt among one of the three options. The judge's resolution granted a 30-day term to those creditors who voted against or abstained to vote to choose one of the alternatives proposed by Multicanal.

Two creditors appealed the judge's resolution confirming the APE and granting the 30-day term to certain creditors to elect one of the alternatives. On 15 December 2004, Multicanal was notified that the Argentine Commercial Court of Appeals confirmed the ruling of the lower court. This resolution was appealed to the Argentine Supreme Court.

2. Litigation in the US

On 19 December 2003, WRH Partners Global Securities L.P. (WRH) and Argentinian Recovery Company LLC (ARC, and jointly with WRH referred as WRH-ARC), commenced two lawsuits in the Supreme Court of the State of New York to obtain a judgment on their overdue amount on the notes and an injunctive relief that Multicanal could not restructure WRH-ARC's debt in the Argentine pre-pack, i.e. the APE, based on provisions of the TIA.

Multicanal's reply did not take long since on 16 January 2004: (1) filed a petition under § 304 of the US Bankruptcy Code[37] seeking recognition in the US of

---

37. § 304 of the 11 USC has been repelled by the Bankruptcy Abuse Prevention and Consumer Protectors Act 2005. Before being repelled it, read as follows:
    '*Cases ancillary to foreign proceedings.*
    (a) *A case ancillary to a foreign proceeding is commenced by the filing with the bankruptcy Court of a petition under this section by a foreign representative.*
    (b) *Subject to the provisions of subsection (c) of this section, if a party in interest does not timely controvert the petition, or after trial, the Court may:*
        (1) *enjoin the commencement or continuation of:*
            (A) *any action against:*
                (i) *a debtor with respect to property involved in such foreign proceeding; or*
                (ii) *such property; or*
            (B) *the enforcement of any judgment against the debtor with respect to such property, or any act or the commencement or continuation of any judicial proceeding to create or enforce a lien against the property of such estate;*

the APE which was taking place in an Argentine court; and, (2) moved to enjoin WRH-ARC from continuing to pursue lawsuits to obtain a judgment on the overdue amount on the notes. On the same date, the United States Bankruptcy Court for the Southern District of New York granted a temporary restraining order enjoining WRH-ARC, '*from prosecuting or taking action in furtherance of the State Court lawsuits, taking action in the US interfering with the administration of the Argentine restructuring proceedings, or commencing or continuing any other action against Multicanal or its property outside the Bankruptcy Court relating to any bond, note or bank debt owed by Multicanal.*'[38]

ARC, WRH Global Securities Pooled Trust and Mr. Willard Alexander filed on 28 January 2004, an involuntary Chapter 11 petition against Multicanal under § 303 of the US Bankruptcy Code.[39]

On 12 March 2004, the Court granted a resolution stating that rights under the TIA do not preclude the granting of relief to Multicanal under § 304 of the Bankruptcy Code in spite of WRH-ARC's argument that a § 304 proceeding recognizing a foreign procedure cannot impair its rights as noteholder[40]. WRH-ARC appealed.

At that date – 12 March 2004 – the Bankruptcy Court did not consider the issue whether the APE proceeding satisfied the requirement of § 304 because according

---

  (2) *order turnover of the property of such estate, or the proceeds of such property, to such foreign representative; or*
  (3) *order other appropriate relief.*
 (c) *In determining whether to grant relief under subsection (b) of this section, the Court shall be guided by what will best assure an economical and expeditious administration of such estate, consistent with:*
  (1) *just treatment of all holders of claims against or interests in such estate;*
  (2) *protection of claim holders in the United States against prejudice and inconvenience in the processing of claims in such foreign proceeding;*
  (3) *prevention of preferential or fraudulent dispositions of property of such estate;*
  (4) *distribution of proceeds of such estate substantially in accordance with the order prescribed by this title;*
  (5) *comity; and*
  (6) *if appropriate, the provision of an opportunity for a fresh start for the individual that such foreign proceeding concerns'.*
38. 2004 Bankr. LEXIS 356.
39. It is worth mentioning that according to the Court, Multicanal purchases goods and materials from the US but it has no ongoing business in that country. As of the date of the involuntary reorganization petition, Multicanal's assets in the US were three bank accounts totalizing USD 9,500 (*See* 2004 Bankr. LEXIS 356). Additionally, according to § 303 (a), an involuntary liquidation or reorganization case may be commenced only under chapter 7 (liquidation) or 11 (reorganization) of the Bankruptcy Code by three or more entities against a person – except a farmer, family farmer, or a corporation that is not a moneyed, business, or commercial corporation – that may be a debtor.
40. According to § 101 (23) of the US Bankruptcy Code, 'foreign proceeding' is defined as a proceeding, whether judicial or administrative and whether or not under bankruptcy law, in a foreign country in which the debtor's domicile, residence, principal place of business, or principal assets were located at the commencement of such proceeding, for the purpose of liquidating an estate, adjusting debts by composition, extension, or discharge, or effecting a reorganization.

to § 304(b), if a party in interest does not timely controvert the petition it should be determined *'after trial'*.[41]

As stated by the intervening court, WRH-ARC has opposed recognition of Multicanal's APE under § 304 of the US Bankruptcy Code as prejudicial and unfair to US creditors on three principal grounds: (1) that the APE is a form of private insolvency regime not subject to adequate judicial control and not entitled to recognition under the general standards of § 304(c); (2) that the vote taken in favour of the APE was coerced and unfair, and that a lack of judicial oversight (among other things) led Multicanal to engage in abusive practices that created an atmosphere of coercion and intimidation; and, (3) that Multicanal discriminated against US retail investors in its restructuring.[42]

In regard to the first issue under consideration, after a detailed comparison between the APE and the US pre-packaged Chapter 11 proceeding, the Bankruptcy Court stated that the APE *'is the type of reorganization proceeding that, in principle, is subject to recognition under § 304'*.[43]

Regarding the second *thema decidendum*, WRH-ARC argued that the voting was coercive and unlawful and that the court should withhold recognition of the APE or require a new vote. Since the coercive aspect of the claim lacks of legal entity, reference would only be made to the analysis of whether the vote was unlawful. In this regard, the Bankruptcy Court considered that the way in which the votes were calculated is in accordance with the ABL. Also, it referred to the fact that the method for *'calculation of majorities is exactly the same in a* [US] *Chapter 11 case, where those who do not vote are not included in the numerator or denominator'*.[44] As regards the method for calculation of numerosity, although it is not the same as in the US *'there is no basis for rejecting the entire APE because the Courts in Argentina applied Argentine law in accordance with determinable standards'*.[45]

Finally, in connection to the third issue, i.e. the allegations of discrimination against US noteholders, the Bankruptcy Court found that the APE discriminated against the US non-qualified investor noteholders and that such discrimination must be remedied if to receive recognition under § 304 of the US Bankruptcy Code.

According to US securities laws, the new securities to be offered in any restructuring – even if the securities were issued abroad under an exemption from US registration – cannot be offered without either registration or an exception from registration because those new securities can end in the hands of non-QIBs. It is worth to note that Multicanal registered the securities in 1997 to access the US retail market; and, that from the documentation filed in the case under study, the Bankruptcy Court established that 80 per cent of all of the noteholders were located in the US and 5 per cent or more were non-QIBs. If Multicanal was going to offer

---

41. See 11 USC. § 304(b). Also see 307 B.R. 384; 2004 Bankr. LEXIS 308.
42. 2004 Bankr. LEXIS 356.
43. 2004 Bankr. LEXIS 356.
44. 11 USC. § 1126(c).
45. 2004 Bankr. LEXIS 356.

securities to the non-QIBs it was obliged either to register the securities or to fall within one of the exceptions of registration. The exceptions available to Multicanal were: (1) issuance of securities in exchange of other securities;[46] or, (2) issuance of securities in connection with a judicial proceeding 'after a hearing upon the fairness of such terms and conditions at which all persons to whom it is proposed to issue securities in such exchange shall have the right to appear'.[47] As regard the first possibility, it was not available because said exception does not permit the exchange agent to receive an incentive compensation and JP Morgan Securities Inc. who was acting as Exchange Agent had an agreed success fee. The second possibility neither applies because it requires that the securities issued in exchange under the US Bankruptcy Code, be issued, 'after a hearing upon the fairness of such terms and conditions at which all persons to whom it is proposed to issue securities in such exchange shall have the right to appear, by any Court, or by any official or agency of the United States, or by any State or Territorial banking or insurance commission or other governmental authority expressly authorized by law to grant such approval'.[48]

Since Multicanal was not able to qualify to any exception and was not willing to register the securities under US law, it decided not to offer securities to the non-QIBs in the exchange offer and limit their choice to the cash alternative only (Cash Option).

US retail holders received a different treatment from other noteholders because they were only able to accept the Cash Option and have been excluded from the Par and the Combined Options. Likewise, by means of the amendment to the terms of the proposal – since it was originally proposed to creditors and it was finally drafted – the securities options were significantly improved. According to the Court, the amendment to the initial APE proposal seems to have been negotiated with the large noteholders who signed support agreements. This resulted in the Cash Option remaining at 30 per cent and was only marginally improved by the addition of 2 per cent interest applicable from the date of approval of the APE through the date of distribution to noteholders. In concluding that the Par and Combined Options were significantly improved, it is worthy of note that: (1) Deutsche Bank's Head of Loan Products testified before the Bankruptcy Court that the Bank valued the Cash Option at substantially less than the Combined Option; and, (2) there was disproportionate number of noteholders who elected the Par Option and Combined Option over the Cash Option.[49]

---

46. § 3(a)(9) of the Securities Act of 1933 (15 U.S.C. § 77c(a)(9)
47. § 3(a)(10) of the Securities Act of 1933 (15 U.S.C. § 77c(a)(10)
48. See § 3(a)(10) of the Securities Act of 1933 (15 U.S.C. § 77c(a)(10). Moreover, the court expressly stated in a footnote quoting Mendales that the Securities and Exchange Commission has construed the fairness exemption narrowly (*See* Richard E. Mendales, *We Can Work It Out: The Interaction of Bankruptcy and Securities Regulation in the Workout Context*, 46 Rutgers L. Rev. 1213, 1270 (1994)).
49. As stated in the Court's resolution, '*[t]he Cash Option was oversubscribed in the initial tender. However, following the amendment and change in the terms of the APE, there was a large flow*

Therefore, this raised the question whether the admitted discrimination against the creditors is inconsistent with the recognition of the APE under § 304 of the US Bankruptcy Code since: (1) § 304(c)(1) requires the '*just treatment of all holders of claims*'; (2) § 304(c)(2) provides for the '*protection of claim holders in the United States against prejudice and inconvenience in the processing of claims in such foreign proceeding*'; and, (3) § 304(c)(4) requires '*distribution of proceeds of such estate substantially in accordance with the order prescribed by* [title 11]'.

The court considered that Multicanal had at least four alternatives to offer the same treatment to non-QIBs: (1) to restrict the 'success fee' for soliciting votes of its exchange agent; (2) to register the new securities in the US; (3) to file for reorganization under Chapter 11 and make available the exemption to the securities laws found in § 1145 of the US Bankruptcy Code;[50] and, (4) to restrict the participation of non-QIBs in the US in the Par Option and the Combined Option and ensure that the Cash Option had a value equivalent to the other options.

On 27 August 2004, in the Memorandum of Decision, the Bankruptcy Court stated that the APE may be recognized and enforced in the US pursuant to § 304 of the US Bankruptcy Code subject to the elimination of the discrimination. In the meantime, the temporary restraining order entered on 16 January 2004 would remain in full force and effect as a preliminary injunction. Moreover, the involuntary Chapter 11 was dismissed.

Multicanal cured the discrimination against US retail holders (non-QIBs) by offering them the same alternatives originally offered to sophisticated QIBs, i.e. any of the three alternatives (Cash, Par and Combined Options). On 6 January 2005, the Bankruptcy Court ordered the granting of § 304 petition and the issue of a permanent injunction as well as dismissing the involuntary petition.[51] It is worth stressing that the Bankruptcy Court did not rule whether the cure was lawful under § 3(a)(9) or § 3(a)(10) of the US Securities Act of 1933 (Securities Act)[52] since at that time it was premature (no option was exercised yet) and due to the fact that Multicanal reasonably believed that it would be able to comply with § 3(a)(9).[53]

An appeal was filed in Argentina with the Commercial Court based on the fact that the cure offered amended the APE. The appeal was dismissed on 16 May 2005.

---

from the Cash Option to the securities alternatives. The figures that Multicanal provided to the Argentine Court in April 2004 indicate that $ 44.1 million was tendered for the Cash Option ($ 37.7 million of which was tendered through Morgan), while $ 116.9 million and $ 181.6 million were tendered for the Par and Combined Options, respectively. A significant amount of the Notes tendered for the Cash Option was ostensibly held by US retail holders. These figures lead to the conclusion that, although the US retail holders held the same Notes as the QIBs and were placed in the same class by Multicanal for APE voting purposes, they were provided with a distribution of significantly lesser value'.

50. 11 U.S.C. § 1145.
51. A copy of this resolution is available at <http://www.multicanal.com.ar/inversores/eng/Multicanal103.pdf> (last visited 27 July 2006).
52. 15 U.S.C. § 77c(a)(9) and § 77c(a)(10).
53. See *Argentinean Recovery Company LLC v. Board of Directors of Multicanal S.A.* 331 B.R. 537, Fed. Sec. L. Rep. P 93,584 at 543).

In addition, the resolution issued by the US Bankruptcy court was also appealed to the District Court.

According to § 5 of the US Securities Act[54] it is unlawful to sell securities if they are not registered. Moreover, § 12 of the US Securities Act[55] provides civil liability to those who offer or sale securities in violation of § 5. Therefore, the offering of securities to non-QIBs by Multicanal must: (1) be registered with the SEC; (2) fall within an available exception (§ 3(a)(9) or § 3(a)(10)); or (3) the SEC staff should issue a no-action letter.[56] If Multicanal does not comply with one of these requisites it would not be able to effectively cure the discrimination against non-QIBs and the approval under § 304 of the US Bankruptcy Code will fall as result of the appeal.

Multicanal reasonably believed that it would be able to comply with § 3(a)(9) arguing that the commission paid to its agent relates to the solicitation of votes prior to the 10 December 2003 meeting held by the noteholders to approve the plan and that such compensation was separate and distinct from the exchange of securities now to be offered to noteholders upon exercising their options.[57] Multicanal argued – following the criteria set forth by Rule 502(a) of Regulation D[58] – that since more than six months elapsed as of the commissioned solicitation of votes, the issue of registered securities to non-QIBs and opposing or abstaining creditors should be treated as a separate one. In addition, Multicanal also relied on Rule 155.[59] Rule 155 is intended to provide clarity and certainty to issuers to enhance their ability to switch from a private offering to a registered offering, or vice-versa. However, Rule 155 does not modify or rescind the traditional five-factor test[60] used to determine if multiple offerings are to be integrated.[61]

On 5 April 2005, Multicanal applied to the SEC for a no-action letter based on the exception provided by § 3(a) (9) of the Securities Act. A strong argument in favour of Multicanal was the fact that the SEC staff *'traditionally looks to the six-month non-integration safe harbour of Regulation D even if the private offering*

---

54. 15 U.S.C. § 77e(a).
55. 15 U.S.C. § 77l.
56. A no-action letter is a letter granted by the SEC staff where it concludes that would not recommend to take enforcement action against the requester in re a violation of the federal securities law based on the facts and representations described in the individual's or entity's original letter submitted with the SEC to obtain their opinion on whether a given situation violates the federal securities law, see <http://www.sec.gov/answers/noaction.htm>.
57. See *Argentinean Recovery Company LLC v. Board of Directors of Multicanal S.A.* 331 B.R. 537, Fed. Sec. L. Rep. P 93,584 at 546).
58. 17 CFR 230.502(a).
59. 17 CFR 230.155.
60. See Securities and Exchange Commission, Release No. 33–4434 (6 December 1961) [26 FR 11896], and Release No. 33–4552 (6 November 1962) [27 FR 11316). Also see Rule 502(a) of Regulation D [17 CFR 230.502(a)]. The 'five factor test' will be analyzed *below*.
61. Securities and Exchange Commission, 'Final Rule: Integration of Abandoned Offerings' 17 CFR Part 230, [Release No. 33–7943; File No. S7–30–98], RIN 3235–AG83, available at http://www.sec.gov/rules/final/33–7943.htm#P54_11624.

does not rely on Regulation D for an exemption'[62]. However, the application was declined. The District court sustained that '*there is no safe harbour provided for, or directly associated with, section 3(a) (9)*' and that '*[t]here are simply too many tangled facts at play ... to defer to the mere lapse of more than six months since the December 2003 vote of creditors, or otherwise to persuade me that the SEC would apply a six-month safe harbour to the facts of this case*'.[63] The court also stressed the fact that the SEC staff was unwilling to give Multicanal the no-action letter.

Since the no-action letter was declined, the District Court entertaining the appeal turned to consider the traditional five-factor test for determining if multiple offerings are integrated. The five factors identified as relevant to the question of integration are as follows:

1. Are the offerings part of a single plan of financing?
2. Do the offerings have the same general purpose?
3. Are the offerings of the same class of security?
4. Are the offerings made at or about the same time?
5. Are the securities sold for the same type of consideration?

The District Court considered that the answer to these five questions favours integration. Question No. 4 could be the one that will struck as not being so clear if someone considers the time elapsed between the APE approval and the moment that securities are to be offered to non-QIBs. However, the finding of the court was that the offering post-cure necessarily followed and was dependant on the pre-cure offering approved by creditors on 10 December 2003.[64] Therefore, since the offering of securities to cure the discrimination of non-QIBs is integrated to the previous offering of securities where a commission was paid to the agent for soliciting votes, the exception provided in § 3(a)(9) of the Securities Act does not apply. Consequently, Multicanal options were reduced to either the exception included in § 3(a)(10) of the US Securities Act or to comply with registration requirements.

Section 3(a)(10) of the US Securities Act provides that any security issued in exchange for one or more bona fide outstanding securities after a hearing upon the fairness of their terms and conditions at which all persons to whom it is proposed to issue securities in such exchange shall have the right to appear, by any court, or by any official or agency of the United States, or by any State or Territorial banking or insurance commission or other governmental authority expressly authorized by law to grant such approval can be issued without being registered. According to

---

62. Securities and Exchange Commission, 'Final Rule: Integration Of Abandoned Offerings', 17 CFR Part 230, [Release No. 33–7943; File No. S7–30–98], RIN 3235–AG83, available at <http://www.sec.gov/rules/final/33-7943.htm#P127_28264>.
63. See *Argentinean Recovery Company LLC v. Board of Directors of Multicanal S.A.* 331 B.R. 537, Fed. Sec. L. Rep. P 93,584 at 547.
64. See *Argentinean Recovery Company LLC v. Board of Directors of Multicanal S.A.* 331 B.R. 537, Fed. Sec. L. Rep. P 93,584 at 548.

different no-action letters issued by the SEC, the scope of the term 'any court' in § 3(a)(10) of the US Securities Act embraces a foreign court.[65] Another issue worth stressing is the fact that the intervening court shall be advised before hand that it will conduct a fairness hearing under § 3(a)(10) of the US Securities Act.[66]

Multicanal's arguments to benefit from the exception in § 3(a)(10) of the US Securities Act were summarized by the District court as follows: (1) the securities are to be issued 'in exchange for one or more bona fide outstanding securities'; (2) the Argentine and US courts have approved 'the terms and conditions of such issuance and exchange'; (3) the issuance comes after an adequate 'hearing upon the fairness of such terms and conditions' by both courts (Argentine and US); (4) all persons concerned have had the right to appear; and, (5) the Argentine and US courts who have ruled on the issues have had the requisite authority to do so.[67] Based on section 75 of the ABL, the appellants[68] argued that the capacity of the Argentine courts is limited to conduct a fairness hearing since they can only review: (1) omissions and exactness of assets or liabilities; and, (2) if the required majorities have been obtained.

In addition, on 6 September 2005, Multicanal filed a registration form with the SEC to register the securities being offered to non-QIBs and stated that these securities would also be available to those creditors that voted against the plan or abstained from voting. The aim of this filing was to avoid the potential expense

---

65. See AngloGold Ltd., SEC No-Action Letter, 2003–2004 Fed. Sec. L. Rep. (CCH), 78,641 (15 January 2004) (High Court of Ghana), 2004 WL 111629 (S.E.C. No - Action Letter); Canadian Pacific Ltd., SEC No-Action Letter, 2001 Fed. Sec. L. Rep. (CCH), 78,146 (15 August 2001) (Alberta Queen's Bench); 2001 WL 945405 (S.E.C. No - Action Letter); Mechala Group Jamaica Ltd. and Industrial Commercial Developments Ltd., SEC No-Action Letter, 2000 Fed. Sec. L. Rep. (CCH), 77,823 (24 February 2000) (Jamaica); 2000 WL 250120 (S.E.C. No - Action Letter).
66. The SEC issued the Revised Staff Legal Bulletin No. 3 (CF) (20 October 1999), where the following conditions that must be satisfied before reliance may be made upon the exemption provided in Section 3(a)(10) where identified: (1) The securities must be issued in exchange for securities, claims or property interests; they cannot be offered for cash; (2) A court or authorized governmental entity must approve the fairness of the terms and conditions of the exchange; (3) The reviewing court or authorized governmental entity must (a) find, before approving the transaction, that the terms and conditions of the exchange are fair to those to whom securities will be issued, and (b) be advised before the hearing that the issuer will rely upon the Section 3(a)(10) exemption based on the court's or authorized governmental entity's approval of the transaction; (4) The court or authorized governmental entity must hold a hearing before approving the fairness of the terms and conditions of the transaction; (5) A governmental entity must be expressly authorized by law to hold the hearing, although it is not necessary that the law require the hearing; (6) The fairness hearing must be open to everyone to whom securities would be issued in the proposed exchange; (7) Adequate notice of the hearing must be given to all those persons; and, (8) There cannot be any improper impediments to the appearance by those persons at the hearing. Special attention should be paid to No. 3(b) *above*.
67. See *Argentinean Recovery Company LLC v. Board of Directors of Multicanal S.A.* 331 B.R. 537, Fed. Sec. L. Rep. P 93,584 at 549.
68. The appellants are Argentinian Recovery Company LLC; W.R. Huff Asset Management Co., LLC; The Huff Alternative Income Fund, L.P.; WRH Partners Global Securities LP; Mr. Willard Alexander; and, WRH Global Securities Pooled Trust (appellants).

Argentina 39

and delay that could result from further litigation regarding the availability of § 3(a)(9) and § 3(a)(10) exceptions.[69] The appellants argued that the fact that only the securities to be offered to non-QIBs (who will also be available to the opposing or abstaining creditors) would be discriminatory to those who previously voted in the APE since securities offered via an exception are less valuable that registered securities.[70]

The District Court affirmed the decision of the Bankruptcy Court in all respects but resolved to remand the proceedings to the Bankruptcy Court for further proceedings regarding the compliance of the proposed cure with § 304 of the US Bankruptcy Code and the availability of the exception provided by § 3(a) (10) and Rule 152[71] of the US Securities Act.

Therefore, the Bankruptcy Court acting due to the remission of the District Court to analyze if the exception provided by § 3(a)(10) of the US Securities Act applies and to conclude if the fairness hearing therein provided has taken place either in Argentina or with that court, summarized the statutory pre-requisites as follows: (1) an exchange of securities, claims or property interests; (2) a hearing on the fairness of the exchange at which all persons to whom the securities will be issued pursuant to such exchange may appear and be heard; and (3) a finding of fairness and consequent approval by a court or other governmental authority of the terms and conditions of the exchange.[72]

As to the first pre-requisite, it is clear that there is an exchange of securities as result of the APE accepted proposal in Argentina. Therefore, although the APE has received recognition under § 304 of the US Bankruptcy Code (it is an ancillary proceeding, as opposed to a full fledged bankruptcy case and does not create a bankruptcy state) it is not entitled to the registration exception of securities provided by § 1145 of the US Bankruptcy Code.

In order to consider the second pre-requisite, the first thing to establish is the jurisdiction of the court over the subject matter of the hearing. After reviewing the history of the US Securities Act, the opinion of different scholars and the only no-action letter that stated that a Chapter 11 judge or referee did not have jurisdiction to held a § 3(a)(10) fairness hearing,[73] the Bankruptcy Court concluded that a bankruptcy court has jurisdiction to do so – either in the US or Argentina.[74] In the analysis of the second pre-requisite the Bankruptcy Court also considered: (1) notice and due process considerations (i.e. a hearing open to everyone to whom securities are being offered, adequate notice must be given, there cannot be improper impediments of appearance and the court should be aware that the debtor

---

69. See *Argentinean Recovery Company LLC v. Board of Directors of Multicanal S.A.* 331 B.R. 537, Fed. Sec. L. Rep. P 93,584 at 551.
70. See *Argentinean Recovery Company LLC v. Board of Directors of Multicanal S.A.* 331 B.R. 537, Fed. Sec. L. Rep. P 93,584 at 544.
71. 17 C.F.R. § 230.152.
72. See In re Board of Directors of Multicanal SA, Bankruptcy SDNY, 2006, 340 B.R. 154 at 162.
73. See O'Neill Bondholders Committee, 18 June 1974, 1974 WL 10005 (S.E.C. No - Action Letter).
74. See In re Board of Directors of Multicanal SA, Bankruptcy SDNY, 2006, 340 B.R. 154 at 167.

will rely on § 3(a)(10) of the US Securities Act); and, (2) findings of substantive fairness. As to 'notice and due process considerations', the Bankruptcy Court considered that all issues were met but making the court aware that Multicanal will rely on § 3(a)(10) of the US Securities Act.[75] The Bankruptcy Court expressly referred to *Merger Mines Corp. v. Grismer* which held that a proceeding cannot be turned into a § 3(a)(10) fairness hearing without prior notice.[76]

Finally, in regard to the third pre-requisite the Bankruptcy Court expressly stated that '[t]*he record is clear that neither the Court in Argentina nor this Court has expressly found that the Multicanal APE was fair, within with meaning of § 3(a)(10) ... [and] no express finding was made ... that the APE met even the 'best interest of creditors' test'*.[77] In arriving to this conclusion, the Bankruptcy Court also referred to the fact that it previously considered some aspects of a hypothetical liquidation in findings related to § 304 of the US Bankruptcy Code and the fact that the Argentine Court rejected a claim on fairness by the appellants but with a very narrow scope of action based on section 75 of the ABL.

The other main issue considered by the Bankruptcy Court is the applicability of Rule 152 of the US Securities Law. Rule 152 reads as follows:

> [t]he phrase 'transactions by an issuer not involving any public offering' in Section 4(2) shall be deemed to apply to transactions not involving any public offering at the time of said transactions although subsequently thereto the issuer decides to make a public offering and/or files a registration statement.

The SEC stated that Rule 152 provides that Section 4(2) of the US Securities Act[78] is available for a transaction not involving any public offering at the time of the transaction although the issuer later decides to make a public offering and/or files a registration statement.[79] The Bankruptcy Court contends that Rule 152 has been described as an exception to the SEC's 'integration doctrine', which provides that an issuer cannot use two or more exemptions to avoid registration of what is in reality a single transaction and determines what constitutes a single offering for purposes of registration.[80]

The Bankruptcy Court – based on Lander's opinion that the Securities Act '*does not permit a transaction commenced as a private placement to be completed*

---

75. See In re Board of Directors of Multicanal SA, Bankruptcy SDNY, 2006, 340 B.R. 154 at 168–169.
76. *Merger Mines Corp. v. Grismer*, 137 F.2d 335, 341 (9th Circuit, 1943).
77. See In re Board of Directors of Multicanal SA, Bankruptcy SDNY, 2006, 340 B.R. 154 at 172–173. The 'best interests of creditors' test refers to the fact that the plan must be better than other alternatives to creditors (U.S.C. 11 § 1129(a)7).
78. 15 U.S.C. § 77d(2).
79. Securities and Exchange Commission, 'Final Rule: Integration of Abandoned Offerings', 17 CFR Part 230, [Release No. 33–7943; File No. S7–30–98], available at <http://www.sec.gov/rules/final/33-7943.htm#P34_3639>.
80. See In re Board of Directors of Multicanal SA, Bankruptcy SDNY, 2006, 340 B.R. 154 at 174.

as a registered offering of those same securities to the same investors'[81] – concluded that: (1) Multicanal is arguing for a construction of Rule 152 that would permit a subsequent registration and sale of securities to offerees who were solicited in the earlier private placement and rejected it; (2) Multicanal is proposing to register not only the securities to be offered to US retail holders, who were never offered a security in the earlier APE, but the securities to be issued to those who were already offered the same package but voted 'no' or abstained; (3) Multicanal initially determined not to register any securities in its offering, but its change of mind creates classifications that are fundamentally at odds with the basic purposes of the integration doctrine; (4) if Multicanal is permitted to offer unregistered securities to certain holders of debt and then offer registered securities to those who did not accept the offer would go beyond the existing no-action letters and contravene a basic goal of the securities laws, which is to assure the widest availability of information to potential investors before they make an investment decision; and, (5) Multicanal's registration of securities for the benefit of the 'no' voters and the US retail holders creates its own form of reverse discrimination against the 'yes' voters since a registered security is generally more valuable than an unregistered security.[82]

In summary, the Bankruptcy court concluded that the safe harbour of Rule 152 is not available and restated what the district said in regard to § 3(a)(10) of the US Securities Act, i.e. that the fairness hearing has not been held. However, it stated the fact that the fairness hearing can be held although it posed the fact that due to the elapsed time a new vote might be required. The Bankruptcy Court also stressed the fact that both US courts are concerned over the passage of time and stated that certainly the Argentine court must be concerned as well.[83]

3. Concluding Remarks In Re the Multicanal Case

As it has been the case of Multicanal, a US court can, by means of the ancillary proceeding, provide an eligible debtor with any appropriate relief (including orders to enjoin the commencement or continuation of actions).[84] The Multicanal case has proved that a restructuring procedure in Latin America, particularly in Argentina, can be recognized under the US Bankruptcy Code.

As result of the amendment of the original proposal and the terms offered to creditors, which in turn resulted from the litigation initiated in New York against Multicanal,[85] Multicanal is (1) forced to register the new securities that

---

81. Guy P. Lander, 'U.S. Securities Law for International Financial Transactions and Capital Markets' § 5:42 (2d ed.2005).
82. See In re Board of Directors of Multicanal SA, Bankruptcy SDNY, 2006, 340 B.R. 154 at 176–177.
83. See In re Board of Directors of Multicanal SA, Bankruptcy SDNY 2006, 340 B.R. 154 at 179–180.
84. See U.S.C. 11, § 304 (b).
85. See *In re: Board of Directors of Multicanal S.A., Debtor in Foreign Proceeding. In re Multicanal S.A., Alleged Debtor (in a proceeding under § 304 of the Bankruptcy Code, Case*

are to be issued to the unsophisticated creditors; and (2) therefore will discriminate QIBs, i.e. the debt instruments to be offered to unsophisticated creditors will be registered and would end up giving them a preferential status. Moreover, if the original terms of the APE need to be amended as result of the registration of the securities and the new terms to be offered, a new vote might be requested by the Argentine court which might end up being tragic to Multicanal since it would be hardly probable that the required threshold to approve the plan can be reached on a second voting.[86] According to the Bankruptcy Court, it seems that those that originally opposed to the APE have acquired what seems to be a blocking holding.[87]

4. New Chapter 15. A Brief Explanatory Note

It is relevant in the analysis of the case studies provided to mention that § 304 of the US Bankruptcy Code – as referred in the Multicanal case and as it is going to be referred in the Telecom case *below* – has been repelled by the enactment of the Bankruptcy Abuse Prevention and Consumer Protection Act of 2005 (BAPCPA).[88]

The BAPCPA became law on 20 April 2005 and will apply to bankruptcy cases filed on or after 17 October 2005. One of the most relevant features of the BAPCPA is that it has replaced § 304 of the US Bankruptcy Code by a new Chapter 15 titled 'Ancillary and other Cross-Border Cases' which incorporates the Model Law on Cross Border Insolvency of the United Nations Commission for International Trade Law (UNCITRAL). The aim of the new Chapter 15 – besides incorporating UNCITRAL's Model Law on Cross-Border Insolvency – is to provide: (1) effective mechanisms for dealing with cases of cross-border insolvency with the objectives of cooperation between different courts; (2) greater legal certainty for trade and investment; (3) fair and efficient administration of cross-border insolvencies that protects the interests of all creditors, and other interested entities, including the debtor; (4) protection and maximization of the value of the debtor's assets; and, (5) facilitation of the rescue of financially troubled businesses, thereby protecting investment and preserving employment.[89]

No. 04–10280 (ALG), Involuntary Chapter 11, Case No. 04–10523 (ALG)), 314 B.R. 486 (Bankr. S.D.N.Y., 27 August 2004)

86. It is worth noting that at the moment of writing this chapter, no press releases where made by Multicanal in relation to the issues at stake as result of the ruling by the Bankruptcy Court for the Southern District of New York dated 29 March 2006 (In re. Board of Directors of Multicanal S.A. No. 04–10280 (ALG), 340 B.R. 154).
87. See In re Board of Directors of Multicanal SA, Bankruptcy SDNY 2006, 340 B.R. 154 at 159. Also note that the Bankruptcy court mentions that two parties that originally voted in favor of the APE, i.e. Robert Tractman (a non QIB) and Deutsche Bank (a QIB), appeared before the court in support of the appellants' position which can be interpreted that if a new vote has to be tendered on the APE it is almost certain that they will vote for the 'no' (*See* In re Board of Directors of Multicanal SA, Bankruptcy SDNY 2006, 340 B.R. at 179).
88. Bankruptcy Abuse Prevention and Consumer Protection Act of 2005, Pub. L. No. 109–8, 119 Stat. 23 (2005).
89. See 11 U.S.C. § 1501.

Although § 304 of the US Bankruptcy Code is not in effect anymore, the analysis provided in both cases is relevant to comprehend how ancillary cases work. Now, with the new Chapter 15, the outcome of ancillary cases would be more predictable and – in theory – contradictory rulings would be avoided.

B.   THE TELECOM CASE

1.   Facts and Litigation in the US

Telecom is a corporation organized under Argentine law which provides public telecommunications services in Argentina. Its services include fixed-line local, national and international long distance calls; data transmission; internet services; publication of telephone directories; and, mobile telecommunications through a subsidiary. The latter service is also provided in Paraguay.

As previously mentioned, before the crisis, the ARP was pegged to the USD at a 1:1 rate. Among the array of measures put in place by the Argentine Government as result of the crisis: (1) the ARP was de-pegged from the USD and devaluated in a 400 per cent – levelling at approximately 300 per cent; (2) it was prohibited to index tariff *vis á vis* foreign currencies; and, (3) a prohibition on increases to public services rates was put in place.

This is a typical case study of a corporation of a developing country that either due to lack of resources on its local market or as result of better comparative financial terms in the international capital markets it is indebted in 'hard' currencies while their income is denominated in a 'soft' currency. When the developing economy of its country is going through a recessive period, they are faced with low rates of return. Upon a crisis, the currency of legal tender is (usually) devaluated resulting in even lower rates of return (in USD values). While its income is reduced, the burden to pay principal and/or interests of the corporation's indebtedness in a foreign and 'strong' currency increases. This mismatch, in many cases has ended in restructuring episodes. As Rieffel stated, a sharp depreciation of the domestic currency in the course of a crisis causes companies to default on their loans from domestic banks as well as from foreign creditors, rendering a large segment of the corporate sector insolvent.[90]

Telecom was faced with a steep depreciation in its income as a result of the conversion of rates into ARP without the possibility of increasing and/or indexing them. Since its income was reduced from 400 per cent to 300 per cent, the servicing of its debt denominated in foreign currency become extremely burdensome. It was so burdensome that it produced a mismatch that led into a liquidity crisis that resulted in a default episode.

---

90. Lex Rieffel, *Restructuring Sovereign Debt: The Case for Ad-hoc Machinery*, Brookings Institution Press, 2003, pages 43–44.

On 27 February 2002 – before disclosing any financial difficulties – Telecom hired Morgan Stanley & Co. and MBA Banco de Inversiones S.A. as its financial advisors to develop a comprehensive plan to restructure its outstanding debt.[91]

On 2 April 2002 Telecom publicly announced the need to suspend payments on principal. An ad hoc creditor committee was formed and on 4 June 2002 it contacted Telecom requesting negotiations regarding the restructuring. Subsequently, on 24 June 2002 Telecom announced the suspension of interest payments.

At the beginning of the month of October 2002, Telecom posed its initial proposal and disclosed information on its business plan and financial condition. On 5 February 2003, Telecom presented a revised restructuring proposal.

Telecom launched a tender offer between 16 April and 2 June 2003 that enabled it to purchase and retire the equivalent of approximately USD 208 million of debt for USD 115 at a 45 per cent discount.

As of 31 December 2003, Telecom had the following unconsolidated outstanding debt (calculated in USD equivalents): (1) approximately USD 1.677 billion aggregate principal face amount of outstanding notes issued under medium term note programmes in Europe and the US;[92] (2) approximately USD 876 million aggregate principal face amount of outstanding loans owed to financial institutions relating to working capital loans, debt issuances and trade financings; and, (3) approximately USD 248 million in accrued but unpaid interest (including penalties and post-default interest rate increases) on outstanding notes and loans.[93] In addition, there were some other commercial obligations (accounts payable, intercompany and related party accounts payable, tax obligations, salaries and social security payments, agency fees under outstanding syndicated loans. The total outstanding debt including unconsolidated debt and other commercial obligations amounted USD 3.3 billion.

On 9 January 2004, Telecom announced its restructuring proposal pursuant the APE included in the ABL. Moreover, since Telecom decided to conduct its solicitation of consents pursuant to the applicable public offering regulations it filed a registration statement with the regulatory authorities of Argentina, Italy and the US. On 11 May, 22 June and 9 July 2004 Telecom amended the proposal to reflect the concerns and interests of its creditors. Each of these amendments followed a filing with the regulation authorities of each jurisdiction.

---

91. In re Board of Directors of Telecom Argentina SA, not reported in B.R., 2006 WL 686867 (Bankruptcy SDNY).
92. These include: Series C Medium Term Notes Due 2002 (ISIN No. US879273AE01, CUSIP No. 879273AE0); Series E Medium Term Notes Due 2005 (ISIN No. XS0076226942); Series 1 Medium Term Notes Due 2003 (ISIN No. XS0109260686); Series 2 Medium Term Notes Due 2004 (ISIN No. XS0131485624); Series I Medium Term Notes Due 2004 (ISIN No. XS0096148779); Series K Medium Term Notes Due 2002 (ISIN No. XS0099123712); Series F Medium Term Notes Due 2007 (ISIN No. XS0076689024); and Series H Medium Term Notes Due 2008 (ISIN No. XS0084707313).
93. Telecom Argentina S.A. Registration statement for certain foreign private issuers dated 18 June 2004, No. 333–111790 (Acc-no: 0001193125–04–002312) at page 21.

In the aim of avoiding any misunderstanding and facilitating the restructuring Telecom entered in road shows, meetings with its creditors, distributed the solicitation statement to its creditors through holders of record and clearing systems, issued press releases and hired a proxy service.

If the APE was executed and subsequently homologated, each consenting holder of 1,058[94] of Telecom's outstanding debt including principal face amount adjustment denominated in USD (in the case of Option A only, in USD, EUR, JPY or ARP) – subject to proration (in the case of Option B and Option C) – was able to select one of the following options:[95]

1. *Option A*: 1,058 principal amount of series A notes due 2014.
2. *Option B*: USD 1,000 principal amount of series B notes due 2011 (except that holders of outstanding debt denominated in EUR, ARP and JPY who select Option B will receive an amount of series B notes equal to the USD equivalent of 94.5 per cent of their principal and principal face amount adjustment).

    Combination of Option B with 37.5 per cent Participation in Option C – If Option C is undersubscribed, holders who elect to receive Option B will have up to 37.5 per cent of their principal face amount and principal face amount adjustment of outstanding debt allocated to Option C. In addition, if Option C is undersubscribed, holders who select Option B will receive at least 625 principal amount of series B notes, and up to 319 of cash consideration, which will vary based on the applicable currency as described *above*.

3. *Option C*: cash consideration at a price not greater than 850 nor less than 740, to be determined pursuant to a 'Modified Dutch Auction', i.e. the single lowest purchase price based on the prices specified by holders, within the range of 740 to 850 per 1,058 of principal face amount and principal face amount adjustment of outstanding debt will be selected, that will enable Telecom to purchase an aggregate of the equivalent of up to USD 825 million principal face amount and principal face amount adjustment of outstanding debt.

Depending on their selections, creditors would be paid amounts ranging from 80.3 per cent to 100 per cent, which according to an expert is the best consideration offered to creditors under an APE.[96]

---

94. This adjustment amount of 1,058 represents an amount equal to LIBOR plus 3 per cent on the aggregate principal face amount of our outstanding debt, less the aggregate amount of the partial payment of past due interest paid to holders of Telecom's outstanding debt in June 2003 for the period beginning on 25 June 2002 and ending on 31 December 2002.
95. See Telecom Argentina S.A. Registration statement for certain foreign private issuers dated 18 June 2004, No. 333–111790 (Acc-no: 0001193125–04–002312) at page 175 et seq.
96. See In re Board of Directors of Telecom Argentina SA, not reported in B.R., 2006 WL 686867 (Bankruptcy SDNY) at 5.

On 23 August 2004, Telecom announced that it had achieved a 94.4 per cent participation of its outstanding debt in the solicitation process.[97] Three days later, Telecom executed the APE agreement. On 21 October 2004, Telecom filed its APE with the Argentine courts for homologation. The 94.4 per cent of debt participation represents 82.35 per cent of the total number of creditors subject to the APE.[98]

According to the terms of the debt restructuring proposal, 37.5 per cent of the creditors selecting Option B (approximately USD 631.3 million) will be allocated from Option B to C on a pro-rata basis, being the purchase price for Option C 850 per 1,058 of principal amount of outstanding debt.[99] The following table reflects the consideration that each participating holder will receive as result of the exchange offer/APE.

Consideration Received by Participating Noteholders

Options	Series A Notes	Series B Notes	Cash	Total
Participating holder selecting Option A[1]	1,058	n.a.	n.a.	1,058
Participating holder selecting Option B[2]	n.a.	625	319	944
Participating holder selecting Option C[2]	n.a.	n.a.	850	850

[1] In USD, EURO, ARP, JPY
[2] In equivalent USD
Source: Press Release, 'Telecom Argentina Files APE with Argentine Court', 21 October 2004

Upon the filing of the APE, the Argentine Court ordered Telecom to convene a noteholders meeting to cast their votes in re the APE and, if applicable, to select a consideration option. The noteholders meeting was held on 4 February 2005 and all participating noteholders – in person or represented by proxy – voted in favour of the APE.

On 25 February 2005 the Argentine Court completed the examination of the documentation filed with the APE, its fairness and the accuracy of the calculations of the required majorities. It issued an order stating that the APE was approved and that Telecom should publish notices to comply with the right of creditors to file objections to the APE.

---

97. See Telecom Press Release, 'Telecom Argentina Updated participation in its APE Solicitation', 23 August 2004.
98. See Telecom Press Release, 'Telecom Argentina Files APE with Argentine Court', 21 October 2004.
99. See Telecom Press Release, 'Telecom Argentina Updated participation in its APE Solicitation', 23 August 2004.

On 7 April 2005 the period to file objections to the APE expired. A total of four objections were filed: (1) two objections were filed by the Argentine tax authorities stating that the amount of their credit was greater than the one reported by Telecom; (2) an objection was filed by one creditor stating that non-consenting creditors and absent creditors should be permitted to elect the form of consideration to be paid; and, (3) the last objection was filed by a creditor claiming that the consideration to be paid to creditors was less than the liquidation value of Telecom.[100]

On 26 May 2005 the Argentine Court overruled the objections filed and homologated the APE agreement stating that it was not abusive, fraudulent or discriminatory and making it mandatory to all the parties included. The court also ordered to grant the right to select a consideration to non-consenting creditors or those who were absent.

While creditors were still able to file objections, Telecom started discussing the procedures for completing the APE with the Bank of New York (settlement agent), the US Bank National Association (indenture trustee) and the clearing systems. Completing the APE implied the cancellation of the 'old' debt instruments that were tendered as result of the APE.

The US Bank National Association informed that they would not proceed with the cancellation of the 'old' notes held by creditors that have not consented to the APE or the cancellation of said notes in the absence of an order from a US court.[101]

On 31 August 2005 the closing took place whereby Telecom paid or made available the consideration offered to its creditors as result of the APE and the original notes were cancelled. Since US Bank National Association did not cancelled the notes of non-consenting creditors Telecom ended tangled with pre and post reorganization notes and being deprived from the benefits of the APE. Therefore, on 13 September 2005 Telecom decided to file a case ancillary to a foreign procedure under § 304 of the US Bankruptcy Code.

As result Telecom's filing, on 11 October 2005: (1) US Bank National Association filed a limited objection to Telecom's § 304 petition requesting the inclusion of certain language protective of the indenture trustee in any order granting the requested relief; (2) The Argo Fund Ltd. (Argo) filed a motion to withdraw the reference of the § 304 petition in a US District Court on the grounds that consideration of Telecom's petition would require substantial and material consideration of the TIA; and, (3) Argo also filed a purported answer to the § 304 petition.[102] Argo is an emerging markets fund based in the Cayman Islands. In its

---

100. This objection was rejected because it was not filed on time. However, a valid point was made since the fact that Telecom was paying its creditors less than its liquidation value might have been considered as an abusive practice.
101. See In re Board of Directors of Telecom Argentina SA, not reported in B.R., 2006 WL 686867 (Bankruptcy SDNY) at 9.
102. See In re Board of Directors of Telecom Argentina SA, not reported in B.R., 2006 WL 686867 (Bankruptcy SDNY) at 11.

own name or through affiliated entities owned over USD 35 million in notes of Telecom, which were purchased after Telecom's default.[103]

On 18 November 2005, the US District Court denied Argo's motion. Based on the Multicanal decision, the District Court held that: (1) *'there is no real conflict between the TIA and § 304'* of the US Bankruptcy Code; (2) *'[i]f a foreign insolvency proceeding is entitled to comity under § 304, there is no principled basis for concluding that a noteholder's rights under the TIA should trump that proceeding'*; and, (3) *'[f]oreign debtors need not grant recalcitrant minority noteholders absolute rights under the TIA that those noteholders would not have in a bankruptcy case in the United States'*.[104]

Argo challenged with the Bankruptcy Court the fact that the APE violates the 'best interest of creditors test' and the 'absolute priority' right of bondholders as result of the increase in the price of the shares of Telecom. According to Argo, the APE together with the raise in the price of the shares implies stripping bondholders' value and redistributing it to the shareholders.[105] It is worth noting that Argo did not file any objection with the Argentine Court regarding the fairness or abusiveness of the substantive provisions. The Bankruptcy Court understood that what Argo is doing is attacking Argentine Court's finding collaterally in a different forum.[106] On 24 February 2006, in its conclusions of law, the Bankruptcy Court stated that the APE qualifies for recognition under § 304 of the US Bankruptcy Code and that:[107]

(1) just treatment of foreign creditors was provided (notices, due process and an opportunity to participate in the negotiations and voting of the APE were provided as well as a court supervised approval procedure);
(2) US creditors were not prejudiced or inconvenienced (notices were numerous, filings were made, a proxy agent was appointed, etc.);
(3) the ABL provides procedures for the prevention of preferential or fraudulent distributions of estate property (sections 75 and 52(4) of the ABL);

---

103. The following is the detail of Argo's purchases: (1) on 29 October 2003 and 8 January 2004, EUR 560,000; (2) on 9 January 2004, EUR 5,000,000; (3) between 9 January 2004 and 26 August 2004, Argo had purchased EUR 14,010,000 Euro, ITL 13,535,000,000 and USD 1,000,000; (4) 27 August 2004 ITL 2,755,000,000 and EUR 615,000; (5) between 27 August 2004 and 21 October 2004, EUR 2,296,000, ITL 2,755,000,000 and USD 120,000; (6) on 10 November 2004, EUR 66,000; (7) on 6 July 2005, ITL 400,000,000; and, (8) on 31 August 2005, EUR 319,000. Also, it is worth noting that on 9 September 2005 Argo: (1) purchased USD 1,640,625 of the new notes issued under the APE; and, (2) attempted to purchase USD386,657.01 of the old notes but was prevented from doing so by the terms of the APE, which blocked the purchase of old notes after the closing (31 August 2005).
104. See In re Board of Directors of Telecom Argentina SA, not reported in F. Supp. 2d. 2005 WL 3098934 (SDNY), 55 Collier Bankr. Cas. Sd 178 at page 2.
105. See In re Board of Directors of Telecom Argentina SA, not reported in B.R., 2006 WL 686867 (Bankruptcy SDNY) at 7.
106. See In re Board of Directors of Telecom Argentina SA, not reported in B.R., 2006 WL 686867 (Bankruptcy SDNY) at 18.
107. See In re Board of Directors of Telecom Argentina SA, not reported in B.R., 2006 WL 686867 (Bankruptcy SDNY) at 21–29.

Argentina 49

(4) the APE provides for distribution substantially in accordance with the US Bankruptcy Code (all creditors were provided with the same consideration options – different to what occurred in the Multicanal case – which is in line with the ABL that states that all unsecured creditors should be treated alike and no discriminatory treatment should be given to creditors in the same situation);
(5) comity should be granted (§ 304 petition, the Bankruptcy Court found that the APE is a foreign proceeding under the US Bankruptcy Code, it fulfils the requirements set forth in § 101(23) of same and is substantially in accordance with US bankruptcy law); and,
(6) Argo and the US Bank National Association are bound by the approval order of the Argentine Court which is entitled to *res judicata*.

Argo appealed this resolution of the Bankruptcy Court claiming that it made four principal errors: (1) *res judicata* should not have barred consideration of Argo's objections to the petition; (2) comity should not have been afforded because the APE approval order violated the laws and public policies of the US; (3) the APE order does not provide just treatment to creditors; and, (4) the Bankruptcy Court's exclusion of expert witness testimony and denial of discovery constituted an abuse of discretion.[108] The intervening District Court denied the appeal and affirmed the order of the Bankruptcy Court of February 2006.[109]

2. Concluding remarks re the Telecom case

Telecom maintained formal and informal fluent and continuous communications with its creditors. Also, in its aim to resolve the financial difficulties in an orderly fashion and taking into account creditors' interests, an ad hoc creditors' committee was set up to facilitate dialogue. Moreover, evidencing its *bona fide* in the restructuring process, Telecom paid for the expenses and legal fees of the committee.

The high participation rate (in aggregate amount and numerosity) is the result of the dialogue among debtor and creditors which produced a well structured plan.

Telecom did not discriminate its creditors and posed a fair proposal to achieve its restructuring. The fact that the liquidation value of Telecom might have been higher than the proposal should not be an obstacle in the restructuring since creditors always have the last word in a restructuring thereby being able to oppose to the plan and making it fail.

Finally, the table *below* is very helpful to demonstrate how a company can be re-valorized over a short period of time upon the completion of a successful restructuring and a good business plan put into place.

---

108. See In re Board of Directors of Telecom Argentina S.A., Slip Copy, 2006 WL 3378687 (SDNY).
109. See In re Board of Directors of Telecom Argentina S.A., Slip Copy, 2006 WL 3378687 (SDNY).

Fluctuation of the Price of Shares (ADRs) of a Telecom Argentina S.A. undergoing a pre-pack deal

Date (dd/mm/yy)	Status of the Restructuring	Value of the ASRs (USD)[1]
02/10/2001	Six months prior to default	1.60
02/04/2002	Announcement of the need to suspend payments on principal	1.40
24/06/2002	Announcement of moratorium on interests	0.61
03/10/2002	Initial restructuring proposal	0.87
09/01/2004	Announcement of APE proposal	11.05
23/08/2004	Announcement of the results of the solicitation process	8.60
21/10/2004	Filing of the pre-pack with the court for homologation	6.18
04/02/2005	Noteholders' meeting endorsing the pre-pack	7.05
04/03/2005	One month after achieving the restructuring	8.42

[1] There are other factors besides the APE restructuring that might also have an impact on the price of the share (i.e. country risk, company's performance, etc.). Due to the scope of this article, no further analysis is provided on this regard.

Telecom is a restructuring case study to be followed. However, it might be said that although Telecom achieved a successful restructuring it had to litigate in the US. This is a fact that every company fears with rogue creditors or vulture funds. Filing a § 304 petition in the US prior to the challenge of any creditor might have been over cautious and unnecessary since at that moment no claims were filed in the US.

In summary, despite the brief US litigation, the restructuring was expedited and successful. The figures in the table *above* reflect the fast recovery in the value of a troubled company.

V. CONCLUDING REMARKS

The ABL provides the elements to achieve an expedited debt restructuring with scarce involvement of a court by means of an APE.

An APE enables the debtor to restructure its debts and recover from a distressed situation of financial difficulties by means of an agreement with the majority of its creditors. If the majorities required by the ABL are achieved, said agreement becomes mandatory to all unsecured creditors included in the agreement even if they have not been present or voted against it. By means of a successful APE, a debtor can achieve a sustainable debt reduction.

While Multicanal illustrates what not to do in an APE restructuring, Telecom shows what are the key elements to be borne in mind. If a proposal is fair and result from a fluent dialogue with creditors it is highly probable that the required threshold would be achieved. Moreover, if the debtor has provided sufficient and truthful information to its creditors and made the necessary disclosure to the regulatory agencies (e.g. stock exchanges, etc.) there should not be any impediment in achieving a fast recovery by means of an APE.

ANNEX: KEY LEGISLATION

Provisions on the APE included in the Argentine Bankruptcy Law: Sections 69 to 76

Section 69 [Eligibility]: A debtor who is in a state of cessation of payments or undergoing economic or financial difficulties of a general nature may enter into a composition with its creditors and submit it to the court for approval.

Section 70 [Form]: The composition may be executed in the form of a private instrument, with the signatures of the parties and capacities invoked certified by a notary public. The signatories' qualifying documents, or authenticated copies thereof, shall be attached to the instrument. Creditors need not affix their signatures on the instrument on the same day.

Section 71 [Freedom of contents]: The parties may give to the composition such content as deemed most suitable to their interests, and it shall be binding on them even if it is not approved by the court, unless otherwise expressly agreed upon.

Section 72 [Approval requirements]: In order to obtain judicial approval, the following documents, duly certified by a chartered accountant, shall be filed with the competent judge together with the composition:

1. An asset and liability statement updated as of the date of the instrument, expressly indicating the valuation standards used for its preparation.
2. A list of creditors, specifying domicile, claimed amounts, origin of claim, maturities, co-debtors, guarantors or third party obligors and payors; the accountant's certification shall state that there are no other creditors recorded and shall detail the accounting and documentary evidence supporting his statement.
3. A list of lawsuits or administrative proceedings pending or with unenforced judgment, specifying the court or agency hearing same.
4. An accurate list of the accounting books and other records kept by the debtor, indicating the number of the last page used as of the date of execution of the private instrument.
5. The capital amount represented by the creditors who signed the composition, and the percentage they represent over the total creditors recorded by the debtor.

Filing effects. As from the filing of the request for judicial approval of the out-of-court composition all actions against the debtor involving monetary claims are stayed, under the terms set forth in Section 21, subsections 2 and 3.

Section 73 [Majorities]: In order for the composition to obtain judicial approval, the absolute majority of unsecured creditors representing two thirds of the total unsecured liabilities shall have expressed their consent thereto, excluding from the computation the creditors falling within the scope of the provisions of Section 45.

Section 74 [Publicity]: The filing of the composition for judicial approval shall be made known by the publication of notices for five (5) days in the legal publications newspaper of the place where the court has jurisdiction and in one (1) newspaper of wide circulation within the location of the debtor. If the debtor has establishments in a different judicial jurisdiction, it shall publish notices for like term in the location of each of such establishments and, if applicable, in the relevant official publications newspaper.

Section 75 [Objections]: Reported creditors and creditors who prove by way of a summary proceeding that they were omitted from the list set forth in subsection 2 of Section 72, may file objections to the composition. Objections shall be filed within ten (10) days following the latest publication of notices, and may be grounded only on omissions or misrepresentation of assets or liabilities or on the failure to obtain the majority required under Section 73. If necessary, a term of ten (10) days shall be established for the production of evidence, and the judge shall adopt a decision within ten (10) days following the expiration of the trial period. If the legal requirements have been met and no objections are pending, the judge shall approve the composition. The assessment of fees, in case challenges have been raised, shall be made by the judge taking into account only the magnitude and merit of the tasks carried out by the professionals involved in the case, without regard to the monetary value or committed amounts included in the composition, or the amount of the challenging creditor's claim.

Section 76 [Effects of judicial approval]: The composition, once judicially approved in accordance with the provisions of this chapter, has the effects set forth in Section 56 and becomes subject to the provisions of Sections III, IV and V of Chapter V, Title II of this law.

Chapter 3
Australia

Voluntary Administration Leading to a Deed of Company Arrangement

Ian Walker

ACRONYMS, ABBREVIATIONS & DEFINED TERMS

ASIC	Australian Securities and Investments Commission
CA2001	Australia's Corporations Act 2001
Corporations Act	Australia's Corporations Act 2001
CAB 2007	Corporations Amendment (Insolvency) Bill 2007
IPO	Initial Public Offering
Part 5.3A	Part5.3A of Australia's Corporations Act 2001 titled Administration of a Company's Affairs with a View to Executing a Deed of Company Arrangement

I. INTRODUCTION

A. Purpose of Chapter

This chapter will identify the elements of the Australian voluntary administration regime which lends itself to expedited corporate debt restructuring. The restructure of the Pasminco Group will be examined as it serves to illustrate a successful reconstruction of the publicly listed mining and smelting group through a Part 5.3A administration, concluding with the subsequent float of Zinifex Limited on the Australian Stock Exchange.

B. Corporate Restructuring using Voluntary Administration

The opportunity in Australia for expedited corporate restructuring was substantially enhanced in 1993 following the implementation of aspects of what had become known as the Harmer Report.[1] The Harmer Report was originally published in 1988 and its recommendations led the Government to introduce amendments to the corporations law of Australia by introducing a new part entitled 'Part 5.3A – Administration of a company's affairs with a view to executing a deed of company arrangement'.

The Harmer Report recommended a new voluntary procedure for insolvent companies designed to integrate the procedures for voluntary winding up and a scheme of arrangement in the so called voluntary administration regime. The procedure proposed was intended to be capable of swift implementation, as uncomplicated and inexpensive as possible, and flexible, providing alternative forms of dealing with the financial affairs of the company.[2]

The Harmer Report considered that even if voluntary administration was introduced there was still a place for schemes of arrangement for larger private or public companies.[3] The reality of corporate restructuring in Australia today, however, is that Part 5.3A administrations are the method of choice in the formal restructuring of insolvent companies. Schemes of arrangement have diminished as a viable method of restructuring insolvent companies.

While the impact of Part 5.3A is difficult to measure qualitatively, there seems to be little doubt that the administration regime provided by Part 5.3A is increasingly used by insolvent companies and those advising them as an entry point into a restructuring process. Administration under Part 5.3A can lead to a restructuring of the insolvent company through a deed of company arrangement, or alternatively if

---

1. Named after the Commissioner in Charge Ronald Harmer. This report was the outcome of a reference to the Law Reform Commission, of the law and practice relating to the insolvency of both individuals and bodies corporate. ALRC 45 p2.
2. ALRC 45 at 29.
3. ALRC 45, 57. Schemes of arrangement are governed by Part 5.1 of the Corporations Act 2001 (Cth) (CA 2001).

it cannot be restructured but its business is viable, sees that business continue in existence through a sale.

Among the reasons for the increasing use of voluntary administration and deeds of company arrangement is the encouragement given to directors of a company that is insolvent, or likely to become insolvent, to place the company into administration. This stems from the imposition of a duty on directors to prevent insolvent trading and consequent personal liability for a breach of that duty.[4] Under Australian tax legislation, where a company does not pay to the Australian Tax Office income tax deducted by it from employees' wages and salaries, directors can in certain circumstances have a personal liability to pay those deductions.[5] The piercing of the corporate veil achieved by these provisions has contributed to use of the Part 5.3A administration regime by directors and those advising them.

II. VOLUNTARY ADMINISTRATION

A. WORKINGS OF VOLUNTARY ADMINISTRATION

1. Introduction to the Framework of Administration under Part 5.3A

An understanding of the operative elements of Part 5.3A and how it works is essential to any appreciation of the use of Part 5.3A administrations in insolvent restructuring.

Administration under Part 5.3A aims to strike a balance between creating an opportunity for the best return to creditors, whilst minimizing the interference with third party rights such as those of secured creditors, owners or lessors of property used by the company. To achieve this aim, administration under Part 5.3A provides for a very short time-frame for events to occur. A moratorium on actions against the company and enforcement of security is imposed for the period of the administration.[6] Creditors will determine the outcome that is acceptable to them, based on reports provided to them by the administrator. The creditors' wishes will determine whether the company is returned to the control of the directors, wound up or enters into a deed of company arrangement.

2. Timeframe of Voluntary Administration

Much of the ready appeal of voluntary administration under Part 5.3A stems from the ease with which it can be commenced and the control that the creditors can, and do, exercise over the process.

---

4. Leading to a personal liability on the directors to pay the debts incurred when the company was insolvent; CA2001 s588G.
5. *Income Tax Assessment Act 1936* (Cth) s222A & B.
6. CA2001 s440D and s440B.

Australia 59

Voluntary administration is most commonly commenced by the company itself. All that is required is a resolution of the board to the effect that, in the opinion of the directors voting for the resolution, the company is insolvent, or is likely to become insolvent at some future time and that an administrator should be appointed.[7] The proposed appointee must have consented in writing to be appointed as administrator of the company[8] and must be a registered liquidator to be appointed.[9] The company then appoints the administrator in writing and the administration commences.[10]

Other persons can commence a Part 5.3A administration, such as where a company in liquidation, through its liquidator, appoints an administrator.[11] A creditor holding an enforceable charge over the whole or substantially whole of the company's property, can also appoint an administrator.[12] The administrator when appointed is however an agent of the company and is to be treated as such when performing a function or exercising a power.[13] Despite this agency capacity the administrator is given personal liability as a principal in certain circumstances.[14]

The *Corporations Act* provides a number of specific disqualifications for persons connected with the company which would preclude such a person from taking office as administrator.[15] These include a former auditor of the company, or a creditor of the company for more than Australian dollars (AUD) 5,000, or a debtor of the company for more than AUD 5,000.

The court can be asked to rule on whether the appointment of a person as an administrator of a company is valid.[16] It is relatively rare for a court challenge to be launched against an administrator at this stage of the administration. More commonly, the wishes of creditors regarding the choice of administrator will be reflected in a vote at the first meeting of creditors which might result in the removal of the incumbent administrator.

a.   *First Meeting of Creditors*

Once an administrator is appointed events must move quickly. The administrator is forced to call two meetings of creditors, the first of which is to be held within five business days after the administration begins.[17] The first meeting has limited

---

7. CA2001 s436A(1).
8. CA2001 S448A.
9. CA2001 s448B(2).
10. CA2001 s435C(1)(a).
11. CA2001 s436B(1) and see at III.A (3.2) *below* for the consequence where a company in liquidation appoints an administrator and the company enters a deed which terminates.
12. CA2001 s436C(1).
13. CA2001 s437B.
14. post p8 and CA2001 s443A.
15. CA2001 s448C(1).
16. CA2001 s447C(2).
17. CA2001 s436E(2). This period will be increased to eight business days after the administration begins as a result of amendments provided for in CAB 2007.

purposes. It can only determine to appoint a committee of creditors and replace the administrator by appointing someone else.[18]

The committee of creditors, if appointed, is a consultative body only. It is however entitled to receive and consider reports by the administrator. The committee acting reasonably can require an administrator to report to it about matters relating to the administration.[19] The committee cannot however, give directions to the administrator.[20]

b. Second Meeting of Creditors

Once the administrator is appointed, time starts to run towards the second meeting of creditors, which must be convened within a period of 21 days, beginning on the day when the administration begins (or 28 days if the administration begins in December or 28 days prior to Good Friday).[21] The meeting must be held within five business days after the end of the convening period.[22] Creditors therefore have a week within which to consider the report and the administrator's opinion on the options facing the company before having to vote on them.

The purpose of the second meeting is to enable the creditors to determine the company's future. At the second meeting of creditors, the creditors can resolve that:

1. the company execute a deed of company arrangement; or
2. the administration should end; or
3. the company be wound up.

In order to enable creditors to form a view on these matters, the law requires that the administrator give creditors a report at the time of giving notice of the second meeting.[23] To assist with preparation of this report, upon appointment, the administrator is given a statutory mandate to investigate the company's business, property affairs, and financial circumstances.[24] The company's directors are required to give the administrator a statement about the company's business, property, affairs and financial circumstances.[25] The administrator is also entitled to call on the directors to attend and give him information on the matters about which he is required to report.[26] The administrator is required to report on the company's business, property, affairs and financial circumstances and express an opinion on whether it would be in the creditors' interests for the company to execute a deed of company

---

18. CA2001 s436E(4).
19. CA2001 s436F(3).
20. CA2001 s436F(2).
21. CA2001 s439A(1) and (5). This period is to be extended to 20 business days and time will not start running until the day after the administrator is appointed. CAB 2007.
22. CA2001 s439A(2).
23. CA2001 s439A(4).
24. CA2001 s438A.
25. CA2001 s438B(2).
26. CA2001 s438B(3) Failure to do so is an offence of strict liability. CA s438B(5) which means there are no fault elements to be established to prove the offence. A reasonable excuse will be a defence. See *Criminal Code Act* 1995 s6.1(I)(a).

arrangement, or for the administration to end or for the company to be wound up. The report is required to contain the reasons for the administrator's opinion and if a deed of company arrangement is proposed, then the administrator is required to provide a statement setting out the details of the proposed deed.[27]

It is possible for the second meeting of creditors, to be adjourned but for no more than 60 days.[28] The 60 day period cannot be extended except with leave of the court. A consequence of the second meeting of creditors concluding without a resolution as to the affairs of the company, is that the administration ends automatically as a result of the operation of the law.[29]

In theory, a voluntary administration can be brought to a conclusion within 28 days of the commencement of the administration. The statutory minimum timeframe is, however, practically impossible to achieve in larger administrations where an administrator, because of the independence requirements imposed and the sheer size of the task will largely be still coming to grips with the company's operations at the end of the 21 day convening period. The reality is that in the more complex restructures of an insolvent company through a Part 5.3A administration the statutory minimum timeframe is not achievable and extensions of time will be required.

B.   OPERATIVE ELEMENTS OF PART 5.3A ADMINISTRATION

1. **Objects of Part 5.3A**

The introductory words of Part 5.3A are found in section 435A of the *Corporations Act* which defines the objects of the Part as being to:

> provide for the business, property and affairs of an insolvent company to be administered in a way that:
>
> (a) maximizes the chances of the company, or as much as possible of its business, continuing in existence; or
> (b) if it is not possible for the company or its business to continue in existence – results in a better return for the company's creditors and members than would result from an immediate winding up of the company.

These objectives are important when considering the operation of Part 5.3A and the procedures under it. They also inform the courts and their approach when interpretation of the legislation is required.

2. **Statutory Moratorium**

In recommending the introduction of voluntary administration the Law Reform Commission considered that a stay or a moratorium was necessary for the orderly

---

27. CA2001 s439A(4)(c).
28. CA2001 s439B(2).
29. CA2001 s435C(3)(e).

dealing with the company's affairs and that the moratorium should extend to secured creditors, as well as other creditors who own property used by the company.[30] Once administration commences under Part 5.3A a statutory moratorium operates to provide a breathing space to give an opportunity for the company's administrator to assess the prospects of the company surviving and the appropriate method for that to be achieved.

During the administration period a company in administration cannot be wound up.[31] If a winding up application is on foot the court is required to adjourn the application if it is satisfied that it is in the creditors' interests for a company to continue in administration rather than be wound up.[32] There are also blanket prohibitions that operate subject to the administrator's written consent, or with leave of the court, to prohibit a person from enforcing a charge on property of the company,[33] or the owner or lessor of property used or occupied by the company from taking possession of it.[34] Proceedings against the company are stayed. Again the administrator may consent in writing to the action continuing or leave of the court may be sought.[35] Enforcement of a judgment by an unsecured creditor in relation to property of the company that started prior to the administration cannot be started or continued.[36] The moratorium also extends to present creditors enforcing guarantees of the company's debts against a director of the company or a spouse or relative of such a director.[37]

Despite provisions which expressly prohibit chargees or owners of property from acting during the administration period, there are exceptions which permit them to do so as of right without the need for a court or the administrator to give permission. For example, a charge holder who has a charge over the whole or substantially the whole, of a property of a company who has either commenced enforcement before the appointment of the administrator or does so in the ten business days after the administrator's appointment, can continue.[38]

Associated with the moratorium is the opportunity, for the first seven days of the administration, given to the administrator to consider whether or not the administration requires continued use of property owned by another party but used by or in the company's possession. If within this seven day period the administrator gives notice to an owner or lessor in respect of the property that the company does not intend to exercise any rights in relation to that property, then the administrator will not have any

---

30. ALRC 45 at 49.
31. CA2001 s440A(1).
32. CA2001 s440A(2).
33. CA2001 s440B.
34. CA2001 s440C.
35. CA2001 s440D.
36. CA2001 s440F.
37. CA2001 s440J(1).
38. CA2001 s441A(1) as far as owners or lessors of property owned by the company are concerned see CA2001 s441F.

Australia

personal liability for the rent payable under the lease.[39] Otherwise, the administrator will have a personal liability for the rental payable under the lease.[40]

The features of the statutory moratorium are often continued into the next phase of the company's restructure when a deed of company arrangement is introduced. The deed of company arrangement operates as a contract that is given statutory recognition, although the law does not provide for the automatic continuation of the statutory moratorium during the period of the deed of company arrangement.[41]

3. Voting at Creditors Meetings

As in any restructure, where creditors must be consulted and their wishes determine the outcome, voting mechanisms and the thresholds for the passing of resolutions at meetings are important. Part 5.3A uses different thresholds to those applicable in schemes of arrangement where, for a compromise or arrangement to be passed requires a 75 per cent vote in favour by the creditors voting[42] is required. There is no requirement under Part 5.3A for creditors to vote in classes, as is required in schemes of arrangement. The voting thresholds applicable to creditors meetings under Part 5.3A of the Corporations Act are contained in the regulations which are made under Chapter 5 of the Corporations Act.[43]

a. Casting Vote

In voluntary administration, voting on resolutions at meetings of creditors is decided in the first instance on the voices, unless a poll is demanded before or on the declaration of the result of the votes.[44] A bare majority is sufficient to carry the vote.[45] When a poll has been called for a resolution is carried if the majority of the creditors in both number and value, vote in favour of the resolution.[46] If there is no result on the poll, either because the majority in number vote in favour of the resolution, while the majority in value vote against the resolution, or vice versa, then a deadlock occurs. If a deadlock occurs then a casting vote is provided for by the law to break the deadlock.[47] The casting vote is given to the administrator as the person who presides at the creditors' meeting.[48] The administrator is given the freedom to exercise a casting vote in the case of a deadlock between the majority in number and the majority in value. Depending on which way the administrator votes will determine whether the resolution is carried or not.

---

39. CA2001 s443B.
40. CA2001 s443A(c).
41. CA2001 s444D and s444G.
42. CA2001 s411(4).
43. *Corporations Regulations 2001* Reg 5.6.12 to 5.6.36A.
44. *Corporations Regulations 2001* Reg 5.6.19(1).
45. *Corporations Regulations 2001* Reg 5.6.19(1) and (2).
46. *Corporations Regulations 2001* Reg 5.6.21(2).
47. *Corporations Regulations 2001* Reg 5.6.21(4).
48. *Corporations Regulations 2001* Reg 5.6.17(1), 5.6.22(3) and CA2001 s439B(1).

Use by administrators of the casting vote at creditors' meeting has, as might be expected, generated some controversy. The Insolvency Practitioners Association of Australia[49] has published a Statement of Best Practice dealing with calling and conducting creditors' meetings.[50] The Statement of Best Practice requires administrators to weigh up all relevant factors in making a decision on whether to exercise the casting vote and requires an administrator to exercise it in good faith for proper purposes and in the best interests of the creditors as a whole.[51]

One writer considers the fact that the casting vote can be exercised in favour of a resolution, even if a creditor with the majority in value of the company's debts votes against it, as an extraordinary interference with the rights of the creditors and a gross distortion of the general conception of a casting vote as it is normally used to resolve deadlocks.[52]

The court is empowered to review a chairperson's exercise of a casting vote at a creditors meeting.[53] Only a person who voted against the resolution can apply for an order under the provision and if the application is granted the court has power to set aside or vary the resolution.[54] Likewise, a refusal or failure to exercise a casting vote which causes a proposed resolution to be lost can be reviewed.[55] The threshold for standing to make the application is that the person voted for the proposed resolution.[56] The court is empowered to review a resolution passed on the vote of related creditors.[57]

b. *Secured Creditors*

During administration, a secured creditor voting at creditors' meetings is treated no differently to an unsecured creditor and can vote for the full extent of its debt. The secured creditor is not obliged to vote only for the balance due after deducting the value of security, as would apply in winding up.[58]

Unless a secured creditor votes in favour of a deed of company arrangement, it will not be bound by it, so as to prevent it from realizing or otherwise dealing with

---

49. Australia's Professional Association for specialists practising in corporate and personal insolvency.
50. Insolvency Practitioners Association of Australia: Statement of Best Practice Calling and Conducting Creditors Meetings, Effective 1 July 2005.
51. The Statement of Best Practice currently does no more than reflect the law; see *Kirwan v. Cresvale Far East Ltd (in liq)* (2002) 44 ACSR 21; Re *Coaleen Pty Ltd (Admin Appointed)* [2000] 1 Qd R 245; Re *Martco Engineering Pty Ltd* (1999) 32 ACSR 487; Re *Ansett Australia Limited (ACN 004 209 410)* (2006) 56 ACSR 718; [2006] FCA 277 BC 2006 01460.
52. J O'Donovan, 'Company receivers and administrators' (Sydney, Law Book Company, 2000) [17.1810], 17–6129.
53. CA2001 s600B.
54. CA2001 s600B(3).
55. CA2001 s600C.
56. CA2001 s600C(2).
57. CA2001 s600A.
58. *Corporations Regulations 2001* Reg 5.6.24.

Australia

its security.[59] It will be bound by a deed to the extent of any unsecured shortfall, whether it votes against the deed or not. A court may order a secured creditor of the company not to realize or otherwise deal with its security where a deed of company arrangement is proposed and the creditor's action in enforcing its security would have a material adverse effect on achieving the purposes of the deed.[60] A court can only make this order, however, having regard to the terms of the deed if it is satisfied that the creditor's interests will be adequately protected.[61] The same order can be made in respect of the rights of an owner or lessor of property in the possession of or used by the company where a deed is proposed.[62]

4. Powers, Duties and Liabilities of Administrators

The powers of an administrator are conferred to ensure that the administrator is in a position to either continue the business of the company while the restructure is implemented, or, alternatively, preside over its wind-up if the business cannot be saved.

Once the company is under administration, the administrator assumes control of the company's affairs to the exclusion of the directors and officers.[63] Despite the suspension of powers that affects directors and officers or executive management they remain in office. Where a liquidator appoints an administrator as permitted by section 436B of the *Corporations Act* then the liquidator's powers are suspended but the liquidator remains in office.[64]

The administrator has:

1. control of the company's business, property and affairs;
2. the capacity to carry on the business and manage its property and affairs;
3. power to terminate or dispose of all or part of the business and any of its property;

---

59. CA2001 s444D(2).
60. CA2001 s444F(1).
61. CA2001 s444F(3).
62. CA2001 s444F(5).
63. CA2001 s437C(1): Definition of 'Officer' in s.9 CA2001 includes:

    'A person:
    (i) who makes, or participates in making, decisions that affect the whole, or a substantial part of the business of the corporation; or
    (ii) who has the capacity to effect significantly the corporation's financial standing; or
    (iii) in accordance with whose instructions or wishes the directors of the corporation are accustomed to act (it excludes advice given by a professional person giving advice in their professional capacity to the company).

64. *Re Nardell Coal* (2004) 40 ACSR 110 at 121; see also pp. 15-16 post for the impact of termination of a deed of company arrangement where the company was in liquidation before the administration commenced.

4. power to perform any function and exercise any power that the company or any of its officers could perform or exercise if the company were not under administration.[65]

The administrator is also expressly empowered to:

(a) remove a director from office;
(b) appoint a director whether to fill a vacancy or not;
(c) execute a document, bring or defend proceedings or do anything else in the company's name and on its behalf;
(d) do whatever else is necessary for the purposes of Part 5.3A.[66]

The administrator cannot, currently affect the position of shareholders. In future the administrator of a deed of company arrangement may transfer shares in the company with consent of the owner or leave of the court. The court is only to give leave if it is satisfied that the transfer would not unfairly prejudice the interests of members of the company.[67] The administrator has an ability to dispose of encumbered property, despite the fact that a floating charge has crystallized over the property.[68] Disposal of encumbered property the subject of a floating charge can still occur in the ordinary course of a company's business during administration.[69]

In order to encourage creditors to continue to deal with a company in administration, the law provides that the administrator will be personally liable for certain debts incurred in the performance or exercise of any functions and powers as administrator.[70] This personal liability attaches despite the fact that the administrator is the agent of the company.[71] The debts for which specific liability exists in this regard are for services rendered, goods bought, or property hired leased used or occupied by the company.[72]

5. Statutory Indemnity and Lien

In order to balance the potentially draconian imposition of personal liability on the administrator, Part 5.3A provides the administrator with a statutory right of indemnity out of the company's property for these debts for which personal liability exists and for the remuneration of those administrator once it is fixed.[73] The right of indemnity is given priority over unsecured debts and debts secured by a floating charge[74], although this priority will not apply if the floating charge holder has

---

65. CA2001 s437A(1).
66. CA2001 s442A.
67. CBA 2007. s2g, New s444GA.
68. CA2001 s442B.
69. CA2001 s442C(2)(a).
70. CA2001 s443A(1).
71. CA2001 s437B.
72. CA2001 s443A.
73. CA2001 s443D, certain taxation payments required to be made by the administrator are also covered by this indemnity.
74. CA2001 s443E(1).

Australia

moved to enforce its charge before the beginning of the administration.[75] The right of indemnity will also cease to have priority for debts and remuneration incurred after the date of enforcement where the secured creditor moves to enforce the charge during the administration.[76]

a. *Nature and Extent of Statutory Lien*

As security for the right of indemnity the administrator is given a statutory lien on the company's property.[77]

The administrator's lien will, subject to some qualifications, have priority over all the company's unsecured debts and the debt secured by a floating charge.[78] If enforcement of the security has occurred prior to the appointment of the administrator, or occurs during the decision period generally the first ten business days of the decision period, then the priority for the administrator's lien will cease.[79] If an enforcement by a charge holder permitted under Part 5.3A occurs during the administration period then the administrator's functions and powers are subject to the functions and powers of the chargee or receiver appointed by the charge holder to enforce the security.[80] The same applies to property where steps have been taken to enforce the right of the owner or the lessor of the property to possession or recovery of the property prior to the administrator's appointment.[81] There are similar carve outs and limitations in relation to perishable property.[82] On the assumption no enforcement by a secured creditor occurs to postpone the administrator's indemnity then the indemnity will have priority.[83] The scope of the priority is limited however by the property that the administrator actually recovers during the course of the administration. Additional assets recovered by a subsequently appointed provisional liquidator or liquidator will not be subject to the administrator's lien as a first priority.[84]

b. *Equitable Lien*

In addition to the statutory lien, the administrator will also have an equitable lien.[85] This lien has its genesis in Australia in the liquidator's lien for the actual costs of realization of assets where those assets are subject to a security.[86] These costs

---

75. CA2001 s443E(2).
76. CA2001 s443E(3).
77. CA2001 s443F(1).
78. CA2001 s443E(1).
79. CA2001 s443E(2) and (3).
80. CA2001 s442D(1).
81. CA2001 s442D(3).
82. CA2001 s441G, s442D(2).
83. CA2001 s443E(1).
84. *Weston & Anor v. Carling Constructions Pty Ltd (in prov. liq) & Anor* (2000) 35 ACSR 100.
85. *Weston & Anor v. Carling Constructions Pty Ltd (in prov. liq) & Anor* (2000) 35 ACSR 100, 105.
86. Re *Universal Distributing Co Ltd* (1933) 48 CLR 171.

when incurred by the liquidator constitute an equitable lien on the proceeds of realization.[87] However if an expense is not incurred for the sole purpose of preserving or realizing the property then it will not form part of the expenses protected by the equitable lien.

While the existence of the lien is clear enough, what is difficult is actually determining what is covered by the lien.[88] The consequence of the administrator not having an equitable lien with priority ahead of unsecured creditors and ahead of the priorities that operate in a winding up, means that the administrator's right of recoupment in respect of a particular debt or liability can drop down the priority hierarchy. Under section 556(1) of the *Corporations Act* an expense incurred by an administrator can drop from first ranking down to eighth ranking, depending on the nature of the expense.

The administrator's equitable lien has been held to cover an administrator acting in good faith in selling property, who commits an innocent conversion and sells property owned by a third party. The reasonable costs and expenses of the administrator in resisting the conversion claim and the cost of settling it or meeting will be covered by the equitable lien. The principle seems to be that an administrator should be indemnified against whatever liabilities the administrator becomes liable to in a fair discharge of duty in respect of the management of the assets, in priority to unsecured creditors.[89]

The full scope of the equitable lien is uncertain however, and there will be legislative reform to ensure that the right of indemnity will cover personal liabilities of an administrator incurred in the due performance of the administrator's duties including other debts or liabilities damages or losses sustained in good faith without negligence.[90]

6. Role of the Court in Part 5.3A Administrations

Jurisdiction in corporations matters is given to State Supreme Courts and the Federal Court of Australia. There is no mandatory role for a court in an administration under Part 5.3A of the *Corporations Act*. In theory, it is possible for an administration to commence, for a deed of company arrangement to be passed by the creditors, implemented and performed on its terms so that the deed comes to an end, and for the company to be returned to the control of its directors, without any participation by the court at all.

There are, however, many situations where the court can be approached by either the administrator or a creditor. A creditor may attempt to avoid the full force of the statutory moratorium that applies during the administration period.[91] A creditor may apply to the court for an order to protect its interests while the

---

87. Re *Universal Distributing Co Ltd* (1933) 48 CLR 171.
88. *Commonwealth Bank of Australia v. Butterell* (1994) 14 ACSR 343, 349.
89. *Commonwealth Bank of Australia v. Butterell* (1994) 14 ACSR 343 349–350.
90. CBA. 2007. New paragraph 443D(2).
91. CA2001 s440B, 440C, 440D, 440F.

Australia

company is under administration[92] or where the conduct of an administration is prejudicial to the interests of some or all of the company's creditors.[93] Most commonly, the assistance of the court is sought by administrators, who require the assistance of the court to extend the short time frames that the *Corporations Act* imposes for the completion by them of new various statutory obligations or to seek directions.[94]

Inevitably the court will have a role to play in a complex corporate restructure. The court's role in a Part 5.3A administration is partly supervisory when its jurisdiction is invoked. Its role, where it is called upon, is to ensure that secured creditors are not prejudiced and to use its powers to tailor make a procedure for each company to ensure the implementation of the aims and objectives of Part 5.3A can be realized.[95]

a.   *Court's Power to Alter Operation of Part 5.3A*

Section 447A(1) is a unique provision which enables a court to in effect re-write the operation of Part 5.3A to suit the particular needs of a corporation that is subject to the Part. On its terms section 447A(1) enables the court to *'make such order as it thinks fit about how ... Part (5.3A) is to operate in relation to a particular company'*. It has been used to authorize borrowings by administrators by removing doubts about the administrator's personal liability.[96] It has also been used to declare valid an appointment that had not been fully effectuated on the instructions of a sole director prior to his death.[97]

The High Court originally considered the operation of section 447A(1) in the context of an attempt to overturn an administration where the second meeting of creditors had not been held strictly in accordance with the provisions of the law.[98] The second creditors meeting, instead of being held within five business days after the end of the convening period, was held eight days too early. The High Court considered section 447A(1) was broad enough to confer power to make orders which had prospective effect, but which arose as a result of something that had been done or not done under the other provisions of Part 5.3A before the application was made. The High Court held the section was not limited in terms of a power to make orders to cure defects or to remedy some breach of Part 5.3A.

---

92. CA2001 s447B(2).
93. CA2001 s447E(1)(a).
94. CA2001 s447D(1).
95. *Cawthorn v. Keira Constructions Pty Ltd* (1994) 33 NSWLR 607,611; (1994) 13 ACSR 337; (1994) 12 ACLC 396.
96. *Spyglass Management Group Pty Ltd (admins appointed) Martha and Anor* (as jointed several admins of Spyglass Management Group Pty Ltd admins appointed) (2004) 51 ACSR 432; [2004] FCA 1469.
97. Re *Pasdonnay Pty Ltd (ACN 009 131 622) (Admins Appointed); McDonald & Anor* 53 ACSR 717.
98. *Australasian Memory Pty Ltd & Anor v. Brien & Anor*, (2000) 172 ALR 28, 33 (2000) 200 CLR 270; (2000 ALJR 94.

Orders under section 447A(1) may alter the operation of other provisions of Part 5.3A. The provision can be used even if an administration under Part 5.3A has come to an end.[99]

b.   *Extension of Convening Period*

Upon the administrator's appointment the convening period, what is in effect a 21-day investigation period, commences. This period culminates in the preparation and despatch of reports prepared by the administrator to creditors prior to the second meeting of creditors. The consequence for an administrator who fails to meet the statutory time frames in convening the second meeting of creditors is quite draconian. The administration of a company will end if the convening period ends without a meeting having been convened in accordance with the law.[100] The court is given a power to extend the convening period if the application is made during the convening period itself.[101] Notwithstanding the clear words of section 439A(6) of the *Corporations Act*, conferring jurisdiction on a court only during the convening period to extend the convening period, courts have extended the convening period outside the convening period.[102]

In a large and complex administration where restructuring is essential, an extension of a convening period will almost certainly be required, given that a 21 or 28 day period (depending on what time of year the administration commences) is unlikely to be adequate to enable an administrator to conduct the investigations required in order to prepare the report to accompany the notice of meeting given to the creditors and express the requisite opinion on the three statutory options that face creditors at the second creditors meeting.[103]

It is unlikely that the reforms to be introduce in the Corporations Amendment (Insolvency) Bill 2007 will make much difference to the need to obtain extensions of the convening period in a larger more complicated corporate restructuring. The reforms announced will have the effect of extending the reporting phase to 20 or 25 business days, increasing that period from three or four weeks to four or five weeks, but will not change matters dramatically.[104]

The extent to which the administrator can be expected to have fulfilled the task prescribed by the law can only be assessed realistically in the light of the time

---

99. *Australasian Memory Pty Ltd v. Anor & Brien*, (2000) 172 ALR 28 , 33 (2000) 200 CLR 270; (2000) ALJR 94.
100. CA2001 s435C(3)(b)(i).
101. CA2001 s439A(6).
102. Re *V.anfox Pty Ltd* [1995] 2 Qd R 445; (1994) 13 ACSR 209; Re *Ricon Constructions Pty Ltd* (in liq); ex parte McDonald (1997) 43 NSWLR 174; (1997) 26 ACSR 655; Re *V.ouris; EPromotions Australia Pty Ltd v. Relectronic-Remech Pty Ltd* (in liq) (2003) 47 ACSR 155; (2003) 177 FLR 289.
103. 28 days is the convening period where the administration begins in December or less than 28 days before Good Friday, CA2001 s439A(5).
104. CBA 2007. 514-516.

allowed by the law for the performance of those duties.[105] The independence of the administrator comes at a price, measured in terms of the time taken by an administrator to effectively start from scratch and become familiar with the company's financial affairs, business and accounting systems, and perhaps most importantly, to determine the future prospects of the company and its chances of reconstruction. In some of the less complicated administrations, a lower level of investigation is required of an administrator given the time available to gather information, prepare a report and send it to creditors.[106] Some latitude will be allowed to an administrator in the extent and scope of investigations due to the shortness of time available if the statutory minimum periods are to be observed. The same latitude will not be extended to an administrator faced with a complex restructure who needs and obtains further time from the court to complete the statutory prescribed tasks of investigating the company's affairs and commenting on the options available to creditors.

Once the court is approached for an extension of time to convene a creditors' meeting the court will consider what the administrator has done, but also what is proposed to be done. The court's function is to strike an appropriate balance between, on the one hand, the expectation that the administration will be a relatively speedy and summary process, and on the other, the requirement that undue speed should not be allowed to prejudice sensible and constructive actions directed towards maximizing the return for creditors and any return for shareholders.[107] An application for an extension of the convening period will also be assessed by reference to whether the extension is necessary to enable the administrator to provide the report and statements on the three options available to creditors, in order to inform creditors adequately so that the creditors are in a position to choose one of the three options identified by the statute.[108]

The convening period can be extended for reasons as diverse as a need to value the company's assets,[109] to allow a dispute regarding the original appointment of the administrators to be resolved,[110] to enable the administrators to prepare an adequate report,[111] to obtain access to company's books and records held by a receiver and manager,[112] or to enable a large business to be sold.[113]

---

105. *McVeigh & Anor v. Linen House Pty Ltd & Anor No. 2* [2000] VR 31 (Phillips JA) at 46.
106. *Hagenvale v. Depela* (1995) 17 ACSR 139, 145 and 149; (1995) 13 ACLC 885.
107. Re *Diamond Press Pty Ltd* [2001] NSWSC 313; BC200101857 [10].
108. Re *Pan Pharmaceuticals Ltd* (2003) 46 ACSR 77; (2003) 21 ACLC 1144.
109. Re *South Burnett Wines Limited* (2004) 52 ACSR 298; [2004] NSWSC 1239; BC200408905.
110. *Albaren v. Prescription Healthcare Limited* [2005] NSWSC 347; BC200502349.
111. Re *Henry Walker Eltin Group Limited* [2005] FCA 316; BC200501553.
112. Re *New Horizons Corp (Receivers and Managers Appointed) (Administrators Appointed)*; ex parte Devries [2004] NSWSC 455; BC200403290.
113. Re *WC Penfold Limited*; ex parte Lombe (as administrator of WC Penfold Limited) (Administrators Appointed) [2004] NSWSC 248; BC200401499.

While generally courts prefer to give short extensions of the convening period, they have been granted for periods of up to four[114] and five months[115] on a single application and cumulatively, on a number of separate applications to court in the one matter for longer periods than that. The size and complexity of the administration may dictate that more than one extension of the convening period is required. In the Pasminco Group, for example, the original appointment of administrators occurred on 19 September 2001. The convening period was extended on three occasions for a total of nine months. The final creditors meeting was held on 30 August 2002. In support of each application, however, the administrators were required to submit substantial affidavits, which explained to the court the work that had been done and the work that remained to be done in order to enable the administrators to properly report to creditors as required by the law.

c.   *Directions to Administrators*

There are restrictions on the court's powers to give assistance to administrators. The basic power is found in section 447D(1) where an administrator can apply to the court for directions about a matter arising in connection with the performance or exercise of any of the administrators' functions and powers. The court's power, however, is not unlimited and will not extend to giving an administrator a direction as to a decision which is of a wholly business or commercial nature. There must be some issue calling for the exercise of legal judgment before the court can be asked to give directions. It is not enough for the administrator to feel apprehensive or uneasy about a business decision made or to be made and to seek reassurance.[116]

The court can give directions where the propriety or reasonableness of conduct undertaken or a decision made by an administrator is called into question.[117]

d.   *Borrowing by Administrators*

Most, if not all, insolvent reconstructions require some form of working capital arrangements to ensure operations can continue during the restructure. In administration under Part 5.3A the administrator has complete control of the company's business and its property. The administrator has the power to perform any functions that the company can perform if the company were not under administration. This

---

114. *Gympie Gold Limited (Administrators Appointed) (Receivers and Managers Appointed)* [2004] NSWSC 11.
115. Re *AFG Insurances Limited (Voluntary Administrators Appointed)* [2002] NSWSC 803; *Cawthorn v. Kiera Constructions Pty Ltd* (1994) 33 NSWLR 607.
116. Re *Ansett Australia Limited & Korda (No 3)* (2002) 115 FCR 409 at 428 (2002) 40 ACSR 433.
117. Re *Ansett Australia Limited and Ors (all subject to deed of company arrangement) and Mentha and Anor (as deed administrators and former administrators)* (2002) 41 ACSR 605 at 616; (2002) 120 FCR 310; (2002) 20. ACLC 833.

would extend to borrowing and express authority exists for an administrator to sign documents on behalf of the company.[118] The difficulty with a borrowing by the company in administration entered into with the administrator's approval is that any security given by the company would, if it is a floating charge, rank behind the deed administrator's unregistered statutory lien.[119] In practice therefore, the risk for the lender providing working capital to the company in administration is that its security would be postponed to the administrator's statutory and equitable liens.

Borrowing of money does not fall squarely within any of the categories of debts for which an administrator has personal liability under section 443A of the *Corporations Act*. The closest head of possible personal liability under s443A is as a debt for services rendered, but the Federal Court has held that the lending of money does not constitute the rendering of services in the context of an administration under Part 5.3A.[120]

During the Pasminco administration within days of the administration commencing the administrators required a substantial working capital facility to ensure the Group could continue to trade normally while the administration ran its course. Financiers were prepared to provide facilities totalling up to AUD 300 million, on condition the administrators were personally liable for them. At the time the borrowing in Pasminco was to be made, the decision in the *Ansett* case referred to *above* had not been given, accordingly, there was still some doubt that the administrators would be personally liable for these borrowings.[121] Once the administrators were personally liable this would entitle them to secure their indemnity out of the assets by way of a lien over the assets of the Pasminco Group in respect of the indebtedness. The security achieved through this process was paramount as there were no secured creditors in the Pasminco Group. It was also relatively simple as there is no formal registration required as for many other types of security.[122]

The solution in Pasminco was to render the administrators personally liable for the borrowing. Orders were applied for under section 447A of the *Corporations Act* to alter the specific operation of section 443A which imposed personal liability for debts on the administrators. Section 447A can be utilized by a court to change the strict operation of Part 5.3A to suit the circumstances of an individual company.[123] As a result of the orders of the court in Pasminco, by entering into the financial lending facilities with lenders and incurring indebtedness under them, the administrators incurred a debt in the performance or exercise of their functions and

---

118. CA2001 s442A(c).
119. Re *Spyglass Management Group Pty Ltd (Admin Appointed); Mentha & Anor (as joint and several administrators of Spyglass Management Group Pty Ltd (Admin Appointed)* (2004) 51 ACSR 432; (2004) 23 ACLC 28.
120. Re *Ansett Australia Limited & Ors (All Administrators Appointed) and Mentha & Anor (As Administrators)* (2001) 40 ACSR 389; (2001) 115 FCR 376.
121. Re *Ansett Australia Limited & Ors (All Administrators Appointed) and Mentha & Anor (As Administrators)* (2001) 40 ACSR 389; (2001) 115 FCR 376.
122. CA2001 s262(2)(a).
123. *Australasian Memory Pty Ltd & Anor v. Brien & Anor* (2000) 200 CLR 270; (2000) 172 ALR 28; (2000). 74 ALJR 94.

powers as administrators for services rendered within the meaning of section 443A.[124] This in turn entitled them to a statutory right of indemnity out of the assets and the statutory lien to secure that right of indemnity.

At an operational level, prior to the administrators' appointment, the Pasminco Group was structured so that one company provided treasury facilities to other companies in the Group. The treasury company was used by the administrators as the borrower from the financiers. It was also used as the conduit for the transmission of working capital within the Group during the administration. Accordingly, there was also a need to ensure that any on-lending by the administrators by them in their capacity as administrators of the treasury company to other companies in the Group was also secured. Accordingly, orders were obtained such that when the administrators were lending within the corporate group for working capital purposes, they were simultaneously incurring an indebtedness for which they had a personal liability as the administrators of the borrowing company and in turn had a right of indemnity out of the assets of the particular borrowing company for that borrowing.

e. *Limitation of Personal Liability of Administrator*

It is not possible for an administrator and/or the company to contract out of the personal liability imposed by section 443A.[125] Where the court considers it is justified, it is possible to relieve the administrator from a personal liability to ameliorate the operation of section 443A(2). In Pasminco the original facilities obtained by the administrators were rolled over into the period of the deed of company arrangement. This was done due to accomodate the financiers' preference to continue to rely on the 'super priority' constituted by the administrators' personal statutory lien. The administrators were keen to avoid the continuance of the personal liability for those debts, given that the imposition on the administrators of a personal liability under s443A ceases (except for already incurred debts) when the company enters into a deed of company arrangement. In practice it would have been possible for them to arrange for the repayment of the administration period borrowing.

In Pasminco, relief was provided to the administrators by rendering the loan non-recourse. Section 447A(1) was used by the court, such that if the administrators' indemnity out of the assets of the companies in the Group was insufficient to meet the debts concerned, then the administrators were not to be personally liable to repay them to the extent of the insufficiency. Similar orders have been made subsequently in other matters.[126]

---

124. CA2001 s443A(1).
125. CA2001 s443A(2).
126. Re *Spyglass Management Group Pty Ltd (Administrator Appointed); Mentha & Anor (As Joint and Several Administrators of Spyglass Management Group Pty Ltd (Administrator Appointed)* (2004) 51 ACSR 432; (2004) 23 ACLC 28.

III. RESTRUCTURING UNDER PART 5.3A

Restructuring under Part 5.3A is in the control of the creditors who with the administrator's guidance determine the future of the company.

The first objective of Part 5.3A of the *Corporations Act* is to provide for the insolvent company's business, property and affairs to be administered so as to maximize the chances of the company, or as much as possible of its business, continuing in existence.[127] Implicit in this provision is the possibility of a divestment of the company's business as a going concern. If that divestment is to occur with the business as a going concern and liquidation is to be avoided, then a deed of company arrangement will be necessary, given that there is no mechanism under Part 5.3A for the distribution to creditors of the proceeds of sale of a business sold by an administrator. A distribution of proceeds can only occur via a deed of company arrangement with appropriate provisions or through a liquidation, if the administration ends without a deed of company arrangement.

There is no dictate which prescribes or limits who may promote a deed of company arrangement for consideration by the creditors. The genesis of a deed of company arrangement will often be the administrator's analysis of the company's affairs and the options for its survival. Given the professional expertise of the administrator, it is not uncommon for the administrator, with the support of creditors, equally, a tested by consultation with the committee of creditors, to fashion a reconstruction proposal. Deed may be promoted by the directors, who have a vested interest in preventing the company going into liquidation, which in turn exposes them to the risk of a breach of their duty to prevent insolvent trading.[128] The directors may procure related or third parties to propose arrangements for the introduction of fresh capital to the company in order to achieve a compromise of its debts. A deed could be promoted by the holding company of an insolvent subsidiary, where the holding company is anxious to mitigate the risk of liability for its insolvent subsidiary's insolvent trading.[129]

Whatever the source of the restructuring proposal, the administrator has an obligation to assess the proposal by reference to the objectives of Part 5.3A and express a view on whether it is in the creditors' interests for the suggested restructuring to proceed. This has to be done in the context of the administrator also expressing an opinion on the other options that face the creditors under the Part when considering the affairs of a company. The other options are the administration ending and the company returning to the control of the directors, or the company being wound up and placed in liquidation. The latter is a process which is facilitated under Part 5.3A by an automatic transition to a creditors' voluntary winding up,

---

127. CA2001 s435A.
128. CA2001 s588G; it seems however that putting the company into administration does not entirely remove the risk as ASIC has in a rare case prosecuted directors for breach of their duty to prevent insolvent trading despite the company entering into a deed of company arrangement where debts were compromised, see *Elliot v.. ASIC & Anor* (2004) 10 VR 369; (2004) 205 ALR 594; (2004) 185 FLR 265; (2004) 48 ACSR 621.
129. CA2001 s588V.

which is an insolvent winding up initiated by the creditors without the intervention of the court, where the administrator becomes the liquidator.[130]

A. DEEDS OF COMPANY ARRANGEMENT

The manner and form of the restructure of an illiquid or insolvent company through a deed of company arrangement will be a matter for the creditors guided by the administrator.

1. Types of Deed

The permutations and combinations of deeds of company arrangement that can be entered into under Part 5.3A are as wide and varied as the companies that find themselves subject to administration under Part 5.3A. The types of deeds of company arrangement can range from a straight moratorium type deed, where the company is in a position to trade on, but needs breathing space to deal with its creditors, to more complicated deeds that provide for the restructure of a complex corporate group.

The Ansett group initially entered into moratorium deeds with the added element that they required the deed administrators to put a pooling arrangement to the creditors. Deeds of company arrangement may provide for a de facto winding up, and providing for the orderly realization of the company's assets followed by the distribution of the proceeds of sale of those assets to the creditors.[131] A deed of company arrangement can provide for a composition or compromise of creditors' debts, in return for payment out of a fund created through the sale of assets, or alternatively from a third party source. The deed will only operate to release a company's debts if it specifically provides to that effect and the creditor concerned is bound by the deed.[132]

While in general, the principle of equal distribution or *pari passu* distribution amongst all creditors is most often observed in deeds of company arrangement, it is not the case that equal distribution amongst the creditors is essential. For example, where an unprofitable part of the business is to be closed down, but a profitable part of the business is to continue, there may be some discrimination in favour of those creditors whose ongoing support is necessary for the continued operation of the business.[133] Discrimination in favour of employees and subcontractors over unsecured creditors has been permitted.[134]

Part 5.3A is sufficiently broad to permit an arrangement for the consolidation of assets and liabilities of two insolvent companies.[135]

---

130. CA2001 s446A.
131. *Commonwealth of Australia v. Rocklea Spinning Wheels Pty Ltd (Receivers and Managers Appointed)* (Subject to Deed of Company Arrangement) (2005) 145 FCR 220; (2005) 23 ACLC 1328 [2005] FCA 902 BC200504584.
132. CA2001 s444H.
133. *Lam Son Australia Pty Ltd (Admin Apptd) v. Molit (No. 55) Pty Ltd* (1996) 22 ACSR 169.
134. *Hagenv.ale Pty Ltd v. Depela Pty Ltd & Another* (1995) 17 ACSR 139.
135. *Mentha & Ors v. GE Capital Limited* (1997) 154 ALR 565, 571 (1997) 27 ACSR 696; (1997) 16 ACLC 1032.

Mention has been made of pooling. Pooling can be provided for in a deed of company arrangement where suitable creditor approval is given. The deeds of company arrangement in the Pasminco Group are pooling deeds, where one company in the group holds all the proceeds of sale of the assets of the other companies in the group and undertakes itself to receive and accept proofs from all creditors, not just its own direct creditors, but creditors of all other companies in the group.

2. Format of Deeds

Where a deed of company arrangement is proposed, the administrator of the company will be the administrator of the deed unless the creditors appoint someone else to be deed administrator[136]. The administrator of the deed must prepare the deed which must contain certain specified matters including:[137]

1. the property of the company that is available to pay creditors' claims;
2. the nature and duration of any moratorium;
3. to what extent the company is to be released from its debts;
4. the conditions precedent for the deed to come into operation and the conditions subsequent for the deed to continue in operation;
5. the circumstances in which the deed terminates;
6. the order of distribution of the proceeds of realization of the property amongst creditors;
7. the day on or before which claims must have arisen if they are to be admissible under the deed.

The law also provides for a series of prescribed provisions which are contained in the *Corporations Regulations*.[138] The deed will contain those provisions unless they are expressly excluded.

B.   CREDITORS' TRUSTS

A device which is sometimes used for ending deeds of company arrangement, is a creditors' trust. A creditors' trust is a mechanism which is used to accelerate a company's exit from a deed of company arrangement. Its use has been particularly associated with companies originally listed on the stock exchange, but whose trading has been suspended as a result of insolvency.

The process will involve the creation of a trust, often administered by the deed administrator, of all the property that is the subject of the deed of company arrangement that would otherwise be available to creditors. Under the terms of the deed,

---

136. CA2001 s444A(2).
137. CA2001 s444A.
138. Corporations Regulations 2001 Schedule 8A. Reg 5.3A.06 and Deed of Company Arrangement – Prescribed Provisions.

creditors' claims are compromised as against the company and transferred to the trust which then assumes the liability for them.

The terms of the trust then provide for the management of creditor claims in much the same way as a deed of company arrangement would, with the exception that the entity responsible is the new trust administered by the new trustee, rather than the administrator under the deed of company arrangement.

Once the creditors' trust is created, usually through a variation of an existing deed of company arrangement voted on by the creditors at a specially convened meeting, and the trust is implemented then the deed of company arrangement can be brought to an end. Once a creditors' trust is created and the deed of company arrangement is terminated, the company is restored to solvency. The delisted company is often used as a vehicle to take a transfer of a business into the company structure which can then be re-listed and returned to trading on the stock exchange.

Creditors' trusts are an example of the flexibility that exists in the area, where the termination of the administration is in the interests of creditors and shareholders, but the actual realization of assets that are to be available to meet creditors' claims will take some time to achieve. The consideration for the transfer to the creditors' trust sometimes includes shares in the relisted company which, assuming the restructure is a success will have a value that can be realized through an on market sale.

Australia's corporate regulator, the Australian Securities and Investments Commission (ASIC) has expressed some concerns about the use of these devices. From the regulator's perspective, it seems that what is of concern is that creditors lose the benefit of regulation of the administrator under the Corporations Act and substitute that for a regime which operates in respect of trusts where creditors as beneficiaries have different, possibly higher thresholds to overcome before complaints can be mounted regarding the conduct of trustees. ASIC has released a discussion paper providing guidance to potential administrators regarding the operation of this area of the law.[139]

C. COURTS AND THE RESTRUCTURE

The court has no role in relation to a deed proposal. It is not required to give its approval to the nature and concept of the deed, be it a compromise or a 'liquidation' deed. The court does not, in anticipation, vet materials to be sent to creditors by administrators prior to their despatch. Nor does ASIC have any role to play in vetting the material sent to creditors prior to its despatch. The process is self administered with the administrators required to determine what is relevant to creditors and an obligation to provide creditors with sufficient information to enable the creditors to make an informed decision on the options facing the company. The process is one where the wishes of creditors will determine the outcome. It is for the creditors to decide upon the reasonableness or otherwise of a proposed deed.[140]

---

139. External administration: deeds of company arrangement involving creditors trusts – An ASIC Guide for Registered Liquidators Appointed Under Part 5.3A, May 2005.
140. *Mentha & Ors v. GE Capital Limited & Anor* (1997) 154 ALR 565, 570.

In one case an administrator sought to gain a court's imprimatur for the manner and form of a reconstruction through a deed of company arrangement. This was rejected by the court which was prepared to assist with directions regarding the ancillary documents required to give effect to the restructure but did not see the need to give an administrator approval to enter into a deed of company arrangement where the creditors had voted for it and the law required the administrator to execute it.[141]

If a creditor complains about the information supplied to it for decision-making purposes and the court finds that it was false or misleading or contained a material omission, and was material to creditors in deciding to vote for the deed of company arrangement then the court can terminate the deed of company arrangement.[142] The court also has jurisdiction to terminate a deed which is oppressive, or unfairly prejudicial, or discriminatory against one or more creditors, or is simply contrary to their interests.[143]

1. Section 447A Again

Section 447A of the *Corporations Act* is available to administrators and deed administrators alike and it is regularly called in aid by them to deal with situations which can arise in a particular restructure as a result of the nature of the restructure and the particular circumstances of the company concerned.

Recently the deed administrators of the Ansett Group sought directions from the court on voting at meetings of creditors to be held to approve the pooling of the assets and liabilities of the Ansett group of companies in one company.[144] Because of intercompany debts and trusts which existed in respect of some of the assets under their control, the administrators perceived that they were at risk of a conflict of interest if they voted for pooling. Some of the companies had substantial assets and in voting for pooling in those companies the administrators would be voting contrary to the interests of their creditors who would be disadvantaged, as they would receive a distribution lower than was likely if there were no pooling.

The administrators sought a declaration from the court that they were entitled to vote in favour of pooling in all the companies including those where creditors would be disadvantaged, and if necessary to exercise their casting vote to break any deadlock at the creditors meetings.

Section 447A of the *Corporations Act* enables the court to fashion directions in a particular case to suit the administration of the company concerned.[145] Inevitably, however, the court's general power under section 447A, which is extremely broad, is limited by the requirement that orders made and directions

---

141. *Mentha & Ors v. GE Capital Limited & Anor* (1997) 154 ALR 565
142. CA2001 s445D(1).
143. CA2001 s445D(1).
144. Re *Ansett Australia Ltd* (2006) 56 ACSR 718; (2006) 24 ACLC 386.
145. Re *Ansett Australia Limited and Mentha* (2002) 41 ACSR 605, 615–616; (2002) 120 FCR 310; (2002) 20 ACLC 833.

given must be designed to achieve the objects of Part 5.3A. This includes bringing about a better return for the particular creditors than would result from a liquidation.[146] The Ansett administrators sought a direction as to how they might vote on the question of pooling relying on section 447A to enhance the directions power.[147] The court was not prepared to countenance the use of its power under section 447A without regard to the interests of the particular company and its creditors.[148] Likewise, section 447A could not be used to direct the administrators in their capacity as trustees to act otherwise than in the interests of the beneficiaries under the trusts which attached to certain assets. The court held that Section 447A has no operation where the deed administrators are acting in a specific and discrete trustee capacity.[149]

In the context of a group situation, the court will not exercise a power under section 447A without regard to the interests of the particular company and its creditors. Accordingly, if there is a proposal which while it is substantially advantageous to the majority of the creditors, but is disadvantageous to a minority of creditors, the court will be most reluctant to exercise its section 447A power in a manner which will disadvantage that minority.

2. Post Restructure Insolvency – the Role of the Court

Sometimes the court is given an opportunity to scrutinize a deed of company arrangement. One opportunity that regularly arises is where a company originally in liquidation enters into a deed of company arrangement which is subsequently terminated because the deed has been performed on its terms. In that event the original liquidation remains on foot, having been suspended during the deed period[150] and can only be terminated through an order of the court. In considering whether to terminate the winding up, the court will consider the terms and operation of the deed of company arrangement as part of the issues that go to its discretion on the question of the termination of a winding up. The court will consider the interests of the creditors of the company including future creditors, the liquidator, the contributories and the public, the public interest in matters of commercial morality and particularly the public interest that insolvent companies should be wound up.[151]

Where it is not apparent that a company will be solvent once the performance of the deed is completed, courts have refused to terminate the winding up. For

---

146. Re *Ansett Australia Ltd (ACN 004 209 410)* (2006) 56 ACSR 718 at 738; [2006] FCA 277 BC 200601460.
147. CA2001 s447E(1).
148. Re *Ansett Australia Ltd* (2006) 56 ACSR 718, 746; (2006) 24 ACLC 386.
149. Re *Ansett Australia Ltd* (2006) 56 ACSR 718, 739; (2006) 24 ACLC 386.
150. *Mercy & Sons Pty Ltd v. Wanari Pty Ltd* (2000) 157 FLR; 35 ACSR 70; *Re Nardell Coal Corporation Pty Ltd* (2004) 182 FLR 290; 49 ACSR 110; *Sutherland v. Rahme Enterprises Pty Ltd* (2003) 46 ACSR 458.
151. Vero Workers Compensation (NSW) Ltd v Ferretti Pty Ltd (in liq) (2006) 57 ACSR 104.

example, where directors have purported to subordinate very large claims held by them personally via a deed of company arrangement, the court was unwilling to relaunch the company with a significant debt hangover as the director's subordinated claims would impact on the company's dealings with its new trade creditors and dilute their claims to any assets in the event of a future insolvency.[152] Accordingly, postponement of related party or directors' claims may not be sufficient to convince a court that the future interests of creditors are protected in all circumstances from the postponed claim being revived.

D.   SHARES IN COMPANIES UNDER ADMINISTRATION

Under Australian takeover law, a person is prevented from acquiring a relevant interest in the issued voting shares in a listed company or if it is unlisted, a company with more than 50 members, where the acquirer's voting power in the company increases from 20 per cent or below to more than 20 per cent, or if the starting point is below 20 per cent to anywhere below 90 per cent.[153] While insolvency of a company might render the shareholders' shares of little value, the Corporations Act does not contain any exemptions from the takeovers provisions for dealings in shares in a company under administration under Part 5.3A that would otherwise attract the operation of the takeovers provisions.

The takeover provisions exempt an acquisition if it results from a compromise or scheme of arrangement approved by the court under Part 5.1 of the *Corporations Act*. This part deals with schemes of arrangement and is rarely today used in insolvent reconstruction.[154] Other methods of avoiding the operation of the takeovers provision include a full takeover, an onmarket purchase during a bid period or a meeting of the members approving the acquisition.[155] It is also possible for the ASIC to provide an exemption in respect of the application of the takeovers provision in any particular case.[156]

During the reconstruction phase of the Pasminco administration, one of the options actively considered for the restructure was a partial debt for equity swap, whereby creditors would be issued with fresh shares in Pasminco in exchange for cancellation of a certain portion of their debt. This would be accompanied by a moratorium on claims. The new shares were to constitute between 95–97 per cent of the shares in Pasminco on a fully diluted basis.

Given the size of some of the major finance creditors, it was likely that the issue to them of any shares would result in a breach of the takeovers provisions, as they would as a group control voting power exceeding 20 per cent, as defined in the takeovers provisions, because they would be associated by virtue of being parties to

---

152. *Vero Workers Compensation (NSW) Limited v. Ferretti Pty Ltd (in liquidation)* (2006) 57 ACSR 104.
153. CA2001 s606(1).
154. CA 2001 s611, item 17, table.
155. CA2001 s611 items 1, 2 and 7 table.
156. CA2001 s655A.

relevant agreements over the control of Pasminco and the conduct of its affairs. This arose as the creditors would have been required to collectively enter into agreements controlling disposal of the shares issued for the period of the workout. This meant that each creditor would have relevant interests in the shares of each other creditor in contravention of the takeovers provisions, unless it was exempt or relief was granted as Pasminco was suspended and there was no market in its shares, putting any debt for equity swap to the members for approval ran the clear risk of giving the members a right of veto over a transaction in which they had no true economic justification for participation, having regard to the impact of the insolvency on their shares.

These considerations prompted the administrators to seek an exemption from the ASIC from the takeovers provisions of the Corporations Act of the partial debt for equity swap in Pasminco. The ASIC refused to grant that relief. This led the administrators to apply to the Takeovers Panel for a review of the ASIC's decision.

The Takeovers Panel reviewed the ASIC decision in Pasminco and reversed it by a majority of 2 to 1. Accordingly, the proposed debt for equity swap was exempt from the takeovers provisions of the *Corporations Act*. The majority decision reflects what might be described as a conventional view of the position of shareholders in an insolvent company. In essence, the Takeovers Panel was unwilling to see the members controlling and possibly being given a right of veto in respect of a restructure at a time when their shares were worthless.[157] Eventually the restructure did not proceed based on this relief.

While the company is in administration, prior to entry into a deed of company arrangement, there is no clear mandate to an administrator to issue or allot shares. It is conceivable that it would be a proper exercise of the administrators' powers under section 437A to allot shares, but unless the allotment could be said to be for a purpose associated with the continuance of the company's business or the maximizing of a return to creditors over that which might be obtained if the company were wound up, then it is unlikely that this power would be normally exercisable. It cannot be ruled out, however.

A more common scenario is that as part of the reconstruction under a deed of company arrangement fresh capital is required and steps may need to be taken for the issue and allotment of shares to subscribers for that capital. The fact that a placement of shares to the new shareholders would have the effect of diluting existing shareholders is not itself a ground for objection and there seems to be no reason in principle why a placement cannot occur under the terms of an appropriately drafted deed of company arrangement.[158]

However, unless the deed administrator is given specific powers by the deed of company arrangement to allot shares, there may be no power to do so. It seems that the power of the company to allot and issue shares and the authority of the directors

---

157. *Re Pasminco Ltd (Administrators appointed)* 41 ACSR 511.
158. *Cresvale Far East Limited (in liq) v. Cresvale Securities Limited & Ors* (2001) 37 ACSR 394, 431; (2001) 19 ACLC 659.

to exercise that power to do so under the constitution of a company is not suspended or extinguished when the company is subject to deed of company arrangement. Austin J in *Cresvale v. Cresvale* considered the power remained vested in the directors, subject to an obligation on the directors not to use it inconsistently with the terms of the deed and the arrangement which it reflects.[159]

It is likely that amendments will be introduced into Part 5.3A to give the administrator a power of sale of the shares in a company under administration with the consent of shareholders, or absent that with the approval of the court.[160]

IV. A CASE STUDY IN EXPEDITED CORPORATE RESTRUCTURING: THE PASMINCO GROUP—AN ADMINISTRATION UNDER PART 5.3A OF THE CORPORATIONS ACT

A. BACKGROUND

The Pasminco Group of companies went into administration on 19 September 2001 when the companies appointed administrators. At the time of the administrators' appointment, Pasminco was publicly listed on the Australian Stock Exchange with approximately 60,000 shareholders. It employed 3,500 staff across 11 operating sites in Australia, the Netherlands and the United States. It was at the time of the administrators' appointment the largest integrated zinc and lead producer in the world. Its annual turnover was in excess of AUD 2 billion. It had 1,200 customers in 30 different countries.

Pasminco was originally formed in July 1988 as a merger of the zinc-lead-silver mining smelting and international marketing activities of CRA Limited and North Broken Hill Peko Limited. Its original operating smelters were at Cockle Creek near Newcastle in New South Wales, Hobart in Tasmania, Port Pirie in South Australia, together with a 50 per cent share in the Budel smelter in The Netherlands. Its mining activities had been conducted at Broken Hill and Elura in New South Wales and Rosebery in Tasmania. In the period from 1997 to 1999 Pasminco expanded its operation through the acquisition and development of Century Mine in Queensland and the takeover of Savage Resources.[161]

Pasminco failed because of a combination of a number of factors according to the administrators.[162] One of these was declining zinc prices. A decline in zinc

---

159. *Cresvale Far East Limited (in liq) v. Cresvale Securities Limited & Ors* (2001) 37 ACSR 394, 435.
160. CBA 2007, 529 New S444 GA.
161. Pasminco Group Administrators' Report pursuant to section 439A of the *Corporations Act 2001*, 1 July 2002.
162. Pasminco Group Administrators' Report pursuant to section 439A of the *Corporations Act 2001*, 1 July 2002 p. 91.

price by USD 100 per tonne was broadly approximate to a decline in Pasminco's gross revenue by AUD 150 million. In the 12 months prior to the administrators' appointment, zinc price had actually dropped from a peak of USD 1,206 per tonne to USD 801 per tonne as at the date of the appointment of the administrators.[163] This was a drop of USD 405 per tonne which translated to a drop in revenue of approximately AUD 600 million.

Falling revenues were compounded by high debt levels which faced Pasminco at the date of the administrators' appointment. These came about as a result of the acquisition of Savage Resources for AUD 457 million in early 1999 and the acquisition and development costs in respect of Century Mine, totalling approximately AUD 1.3 billion. By mid 2001, Pasminco was facing the impact of the declining zinc price on its revenue and cash flow, and was in breach of certain debt covenants as at June 2001, although it had not formally defaulted on payment to any of its financiers when the administrators were appointed.[164]

Among the other problems that contributed substantially to the collapse of Pasminco was its takeover of Savage, a takeover that never truly delivered real value to Pasminco, and the inheritance from Savage of a substantial hedge book which suffered greatly as a result of the devaluation of the Australian dollar[165]. Inadequate management information systems, particularly lack of reliable cash flow data, were also contributing factors, in the administrators' view, to the failure of the company.[166]

Pasminco had operated under a provision of the corporations legislation which permitted it to avoid filing audited accounts for each of its subsidiaries on the basis of relief granted by the corporate regulator, ASIC.[167] In practice, the conditions of granting relief required that each company in the Group guaranteed to each creditor of any company in the Group payment of any debt due to that creditor by any other group company.

B. THE ADMINISTRATION AND RESTRUCTURE PLANNING PHASE

Pasminco did not cease trading following the appointment of the administrators on 19 September 2001, indeed it was business as usual – essential to maintaining as much value as possible in the business. A large funding facility for AUD 300 million was obtained to enable all of the Pasminco businesses to continue to trade normally whilst options for Pasminco's future were considered and

---

163. Pasminco Group Administrators' Report pursuant to section 439A of the *Corporations Act 2001*, 1 July 2002 p. 92.
164. Pasminco Group Administrators' Report pursuant to section 439A of the *Corporations Act 2001*, 1 July 2002 p 93.
165. Pasminco Group Administrators' Report pursuant to section 439A of the *Corporations Act 2001*, 1 July 2002 pp. 93–98.
166. Pasminco Group Administrators' Report pursuant to section 439A of the *Corporations Act 2001*, 1 July 2002 p. 99.
167. CA2001 s313(6) Corporations Law.

restructure options formulated. Sales processes already in train in respect of businesses that had been up for sale prior to the administrators' appointment, such as Century Mine and Broken Hill Mine were continued.

The first meeting of creditors was held on 26 September 2001 when a committee of creditors was appointed comprising representatives of Pasminco's financiers and the employees through their unions. Given the size of the task associated with the planning for a restructure, it was necessary for the second creditors' meeting to be adjourned and this was done following an application to court on 5 October 2001, which extended the time for a period of 90 days to 7 January 2002.

The court was also approached on 10 October 2001 for orders that the original funding facility was to be classified as a personal liability of the administrators using the powers under section 447A.[168]

In December 2001, the court granted a further extension of the convening period for the second meeting of creditors. This provided an additional 90 days to 8 April 2002 to enable continued consideration of proposals for the restructure of Pasminco. Broken Hill Mine was sold on 8 March 2002 and on 19 March 2002 the administrators commenced the sale process for Elura Mine which was in turn sold.

A final order for an extension of the second meeting of creditors was obtained on 27 March 2002. Under this order the second meeting of creditors was to be held by no later than 15 July 2002. The meeting was held and adjourned. Finally, on 30 August 2002, the creditors met and accepted the administrators' recommendation that the Group should enter into deeds of company arrangement that provided for the restructure of the Group.

Eventually, and only after additional time was taken for the negotiation of financing facilities associated with the deed period, the company and its administrators signed deeds of company arrangement on 4 October 2002 and entered into a range of associated financing documents.

C. THE RESTRUCTURE

The final outcome of the restructure was still to be determined dependent as it was on zinc prices and the market's appetite for Pasminco assets, but the deeds of company arrangement entered into on 4 October 2002 and the associated documents contained all the mechanisms required to achieve the restructure.

The creditors had voted on a general proposal for restructure the effect of which was to split the group into two. These were the Ongoing Group, comprising the entities that were capable of operating on an ongoing basis which included the more attractive assets and entities of the Pasminco Group. The remaining entities, to be combined in what was known as the Residual Group, were those entities that were to be sold during the course of the reconstruction or that would otherwise not form part of the Ongoing Group, such as the holding company Pasminco Ltd and the former treasury company.

---

168. See above II.B(6.4).

The aim of the restructure was that under the provisions of the deeds of company arrangement, the Ongoing Group companies were released from any claims of creditors that existed at the date of the appointment of the administrators, so that those companies could continue to trade freed from their liabilities that had existed as at the appointment of the administrators.

Once restructured, equity in the Ongoing Group was to be partially sold. Initially, it was anticipated that creditors would be issued with shares in consideration of the compromise of the debts owed to them. This did not eventuate, largely as a result of the final pricing and the need for 100 per cent of the Ongoing Group to be sold to achieve an acceptable outcome from the restructure.

Initially, it was proposed that the restructured Pasminco would start trading in November 2002. However, world zinc prices and the poorly performing Australian dollar at that time meant that this was not achievable and the IPO was postponed. Eventually the restructure was not achieved until April 2004 with the float of Zinifex.

The final restructure of the Pasminco Group was achieved by a combination of transactions. These included: (1) the acquisition by Zinifex of shares in the Ongoing Group entities from Pasminco; and, (2) the acquisition by Zinifex of shares in certain special purpose entities associated with parts of the infrastructure associated with the Century Mine. Zinifex issued shares in consideration for these to Pasminco Holdings, a wholly owned subsidiary of Pasminco Limited. Pasminco Holdings then offered these shares to the market under terms of an IPO. The sale price of the shares was AUD 1.95 per share which had been determined by the Pricing Committee, comprised of creditors with claims of more than AUD 5 million.

Under the terms of the offering, there was an offering of 500,000,000 Zinifex shares to the market less shares taken up pursuant to an employee gift offering and shares issued to the company's Managing Director. The offering comprised two parts: a global institutional offering and an Australian retail offering. The Australian retail offering opened on 15 March 2004 and closed on 30 March. The global institutional book build opened on 31 March and closed on 2 April. Under the terms of the deeds of company arrangement, once the Pricing Committee had approved the aggregate price achieved under the book build and the administrators were satisfied that the offering was able to proceed through the sale and transfer of shares to investors as contemplated by the deeds of company arrangement, then the administrators were required to give their final approval for the implementation of the restructuring. This approval was given.

Ultimately, the consideration received from the restructure of the Pasminco Group through the IPO was AUD 960,000,000.

Total debt of Pasminco Group compromised through this restructure was approximately AUD 2.8 billion. Today, Zinifex is trading successfully on the Australian Stock Exchange. It has ridden the commodities price boom and its share price has risen from a low of AUD 1.46 after the IPO to a recent high of AUD19.62.

V. AN AFTERWORD ON SCHEMES OF ARRANGEMENT

Schemes of arrangement under Chapter 5.1 of the *Corporations Act* are not commonly used in insolvent restructuring in Australia today. The inherent nature of a scheme of arrangement contains within it many of the factors that render a scheme of arrangement less likely to be used to achieve a corporate restructure in the case of insolvency. Schemes of arrangement are still regularly used in corporate restructures, but by and large these are solvent restructurings where the company's ability to pay its debts as and when they fall due is not in question.

A recent example serves to illustrate the difficulties faced in practice by those promoting a scheme of arrangement in insolvency. The liquidators of the HIH Group of eight companies recently sought and obtained approval in both Australia and the United Kingdom for the holding of creditors' meetings to consider schemes of arrangement to operate in both countries in relation to all the companies in the HIH Group. The schemes were seen as a more efficient way of concluding the winding up of the companies than if the winding up continued in the normal course. Despite the requisite special resolutions being passed at all the creditors' meetings, a small group of creditors identified a possible unfairness in the way the scheme would affect them as compared to the statutory scheme that would apply to them in the winding up. This unfairness which lead to the identification of another class of creditors that had not separately voted on the scheme, lead the court initially to refuse the final approval necessary for the implementation of the schemes.[169] This occurred despite the fact the liquidators had been to court to obtain approval for despatch of the scheme documents[170] and overcome a previously failed attempt to gain approval for the holding of scheme meetings.[171] Eventually, the liquidators were successful in gaining court approval but only after an alteration to the scheme to bring it into line with what had been contained in the original explanatory statement.[172]

---

169. Re *HIH Casualty and General Insurance Ltd* (2006) 57 ACSR 791; (2006) 24 ACLC 545; [2006] NSWSC 485.
170. *HIH Casualty and General Insurance Ltd* (2005) 56 ACSR 295; [2005] NSWC 1180 and [2006] NSWSC 6; BC200600160.
171. Re *HIH Casualty and General Insurance Ltd* (2005) 215 ALR 562; 53 ACSR 12; [2005] NSWSC 240.
172. Re *HIH Casualty and General Insurance Ltd* (2006) 58 ACSR 1; (2006) 24 ACLC 564; [2006] NSWSC504.

ANNEX: KEY LEGISLATION

Part 5.3A Administration of a company's affairs with a view to executing a deed of company arrangement

Division 1 Preliminary

435A.   *Object of Part*

The object of this Part is to provide for the business, property and affairs of an insolvent company to be administered in a way that:
  (a) maximizes the chances of the company, or as much as possible of its business, continuing in existence; or
  (b) if it is not possible for the company or its business to continue in existence – results in a better return for the company's creditors and members than would result from an immediate winding up of the company.

Division 4 Administrator Investigates Company's Affairs Administrator to Investigate Affairs and Consider Possible Courses of Action

438A.   *Administrator to Investigate Affairs and Consider Possible Courses of Action*

As soon as practicable after the administration of a company begins, the administrator must:
  (a) investigate the company's business, property, affairs and financial circumstances; and
  (b) form an opinion about each of the following matters:
      (i) whether it would be in the interests of the company's creditors for the company to execute a deed of company arrangement;
      (ii) whether it would be in the creditors' interests for the administration to end;
      (iii) whether it would be in the creditors' interests for the company to be wound up.

438B.   *Directors to Help Administrator*

(1) As soon as practicable after the administration of a company begins, each director must:
  (a) deliver to the administrator all books in the director's possession that relate to the company, other than books that the director is entitled, as against the company and the administrator, to retain; and
  (b) if the director knows where other books relating to the company are—tell the administrator where those books are.

Australia

(2) Within 7 days after the administration of a company begins or such longer period as the administrator allows, the directors must give to the administrator a statement about the company's business, property, affairs and financial circumstances.

(3) A director of a company under administration must:

(a) attend on the administrator at such times; and
(b) give the administrator such information about the company's business, property, affairs and financial circumstances;

as the administrator reasonably requires.

(4) A person must not fail to comply with subsection (1), (2) or (3).

(5) An offence based on subsection (4) is an offence of strict liability.

Note: For **strict liability**, see section 6.1 of the *Criminal Code*.

(6) Subsection (4) does not apply to the extent that the person has a reasonable excuse.

Note: A defendant bears an evidential burden in relation to the matter in subsection (6), see subsection 13.3(3) of the *Criminal Code*.

Division 9 Administrator's Liability and Indemnity for Debts of Administration

Subdivision A Liability

443A.   General Debts

(1) The administrator of a company under administration is liable for debts he or she incurs, in the performance or exercise, or purported performance or exercise, of any of his or her functions and powers as administrator, for:

(a) services rendered; or
(b) goods bought; or
(c) property hired, leased, used or occupied.

(2) Subsection (1) has effect despite any agreement to the contrary, but without prejudice to the administrator's rights against the company or anyone else.

Subdivision B – Indemnity

443D.   Right of Indemnity

The administrator of a company under administration is entitled to be indemnified out of the company's property for:

(a) debts for which the administrator is liable under Subdivision A or a remittance provision as defined in subsection 443BA(3); and
(b) his or her remuneration as fixed under section 449E.

443E.   *Right of Indemnity has Priority over other Debts*

(1)   Priority over debts unsecured or secured by floating charge
Subject to section 556, a right of indemnity under section 443D has priority over:

   (a) all the company's unsecured debts; and
   (b) subject to subsections (2) and (3) of this section, debts of the company secured by a floating charge on property of the company.

(2)   No priority where floating chargeholder already moved to enforce charge

Where:

   (a) debts of a company under administration are secured by a floating charge on property of the company; and
   (b) before the beginning of the administration, the chargee:
      (i) appointed a receiver of property of the company under a power contained in an instrument relating to the charge; or
      (ii) obtained an order for the appointment of a receiver of property of the company for the purpose of enforcing the charge; or
      (iii) entered into possession, or assumed control, of property of the company for that purpose; or
      (iv) appointed a person so to enter into possession or assume control (whether as agent for the chargee or for the company); and
   (c) the receiver or person is still in office, or the chargee is still in possession or control of the property;

the right of indemnity of the administrator under section 443D does not have priority over those debts, except so far as the chargee agrees.

(3)   Priority where floating charge fixes during administration

Where:

   (a) debts of a company under administration are secured by a floating charge on property of the company; and
   (b) during the administration, the chargee, consistently with this Part:
      (i) appoints a receiver of property of the company under a power contained in an instrument relating to the charge; or
      (ii) obtains an order for the appointment of a receiver of property of the company for the purpose of enforcing the charge; or
      (iii) enters into possession, or assumes control, of property of the company for that purpose; or
      (iv) appoints a person so to enter into possession or assume control (whether as agent for the chargee or for the company); and

the right of indemnity of the administrator under section 443D has priority over those debts only in so far as it is a right of indemnity for debts incurred, or

Australia

remuneration accruing, before written notice of the appointment, or of the entering into possession or assuming of control, as the case may be, was given to the administrator.

443F.   Lien to Secure Indemnity

(1)   Administrator's lien
To secure a right of indemnity under section 443D, the administrator has a lien on the company's property.

(2)   Priority over charge
A lien under subsection (1) has priority over a charge only in so far as the right of indemnity under section 443D has priority over debts secured by the charge.

Division 11 Variation, Termination and Avoidance of Deed

445D.   When Court may Terminate Deed

(1)   Grounds for termination by court
The Court may make an order terminating a deed of company arrangement if satisfied that:

  (a) information about the company's business, property, affairs or financial circumstances that:
       (i) was false or misleading; and
       (ii) can reasonably be expected to have been material to creditors of the company in deciding whether to vote in favour of the resolution that the company execute the deed;
was given to the administrator of the company or to such creditors; or

  (b) such information was contained in a report or statement under subsection 439A(4) that accompanied a notice of the meeting at which the resolution was passed; or
  (c) there was an omission from such a report or statement and the omission can reasonably be expected to have been material to such creditors in so deciding; or
  (d) there has been a material contravention of the deed by a person bound by the deed; or
  (e) effect cannot be given to the deed without injustice or undue delay; or
  (f) the deed or a provision of it is, an act or omission done or made under the deed was, or an act or omission proposed to be so done or made would be:
       (i) oppressive or unfairly prejudicial to, or unfairly discriminatory against, one or more such creditors; or

(ii) contrary to the interests of the creditors of the company as a whole; or

(g) the deed should be terminated for some other reason.

(2) Who may apply for order
An order may be made on the application of:

(a) a creditor of the company; or
(b) the company; or
(c) any other interested person.

Division 13 Powers of Court

447A.   *A General Power to make Orders*

(1) The Court may make such order as it thinks appropriate about how this Part is to operate in relation to a particular company.

(2) For example, if the Court is satisfied that the administration of a company should end:

(a) because the company is solvent; or
(b) because provisions of this Part are being abused; or
(c) for some other reason;

the Court may order under subsection (1) that the administration is to end.

(3) An order may be made subject to conditions.

(4) An order may be made on the application of:

(a) the company; or
(b) a creditor of the company; or
(c) in the case of a company under administration – the administrator of the company; or
(d) in the case of a company that has executed a deed of company arrangement – the deed's administrator; or
(e) ASIC; or
(f) any other interested person.

447E.   *Supervision of Administrator of Company or Deed*

(1) Power where management prejudicial to creditors
Where the Court is satisfied that the administrator of a company under administration, or of a deed of company arrangement:

(a) has managed, or is managing, the company's business, property or affairs in a way that is prejudicial to the interests of some or all of the company's creditors or members; or

Australia

(b) has done an act, or made an omission, or proposes to do an act, or to make an omission, that is or would be prejudicial to such interests;

the Court may make such order as it thinks just.

(3) Who may apply for order
An order may only be made on the application of ASIC or of a creditor or member of the company.

PART 5.7B RECOVERING PROPERTY OR COMPENSATION FOR THE BENEFIT OF CREDITORS OF INSOLVENT COMPANY

Division 3 Directors Duty to Prevent Insolvent Trading

588G.   Director's Duty to Prevent Insolvent Trading by Company

(1) This section applies if:

(a) a person is a director of a company at the time when the company incurs a debt; and
(b) the company is insolvent at that time, or becomes insolvent by incurring that debt, or by incurring at that time debts including that debt; and
(c) at that time, there are reasonable grounds for suspecting that the company is insolvent, or would so become insolvent, as the case may be; and
(d) that time is at or after the commencement of this Act.

(1A) For the purposes of this section, if a company takes action set out in column 2 of the following table, it incurs a debt at the time set out in column 3.

When debts are incurred	*[operative table]*
Action of company	*When debt is incurred*
1 Paying a dividend	when the dividend is paid or, if the company has a constitution that provides for the declaration of dividends, when the dividend is declared
2 making a reduction of share capital to which Division 1 of Part 2J.1 applies (other than a reduction that consists only of the cancellation of a share or shares for no consideration)	when the reduction takes effect

When debts are incurred [*operative table*]

	Action of company	When debt is incurred
3	buying back shares (even if the consideration is not a sum certain in money)	when the buy-back agreement is entered into
4	redeeming redeemable preference shares that are redeemable at its option	when the company exercizes the option
5	issuing redeemable preference shares that are redeemable otherwise than at its option	when the shares are issued
6	financially assisting a person to acquire shares (or units of shares) in itself or a holding company	when the agreement to provide the assistance is entered into or, if there is no agreement, when the assistance is provided
7	entering into an uncommercial transaction (within the meaning of section 588FB) other than one that a court orders, or a prescribed agency directs, the company to enter into	when the transaction is entered into

(2) By failing to prevent the company from incurring the debt, the person contravenes this section if:

(a) the person is aware at that time that there are such grounds for so suspecting; or
(b) a reasonable person in a like position in a company in the company's circumstances would be so aware.

Note: This subsection is a civil penalty provision (see subsection 1317E(1)).

(3) A person commits an offence if:

(a) a company incurs a debt at a particular time; and
(aa) at that time, a person is a director of the company; and
(b) the company is insolvent at that time, or becomes insolvent by incurring that debt, or by incurring at that time debts including that debt; and
(c) the person suspected at the time when the company incurred the debt that the company was insolvent or would become insolvent as a result of incurring that debt or other debts (as in paragraph (1)(b)); and

(d) the person's failure to prevent the company incurring the debt was dishonest.

(3A) For the purposes of an offence based on subsection (3), absolute liability applies to paragraph (3)(a).

Note: For *absolute liability*, see section 6.2 of the *Criminal Code*.

(3B) For the purposes of an offence based on subsection (3), strict liability applies to paragraphs (3)(aa) and (b).

Note: For *strict liability*, see section 6.1 of the *Criminal Code*.

(4) The provisions of Division 4 of this Part are additional to, and do not derogate from, Part 9.4B as it applies in relation to a contravention of this section.

Chapter 4
Brazil

Brazil's Two New Mechanisms for Out-Of-Court Reorganizations: 'Homologation Of Consensus' and 'Enforcement Of Agreement'[1]

Luiz Fernando Valente-de-Paiva

---

1. The opinions expressed here are those of the author, not of Pinheiro Neto Advogados. This chapter partially reproduce the author's views already expressed in other articles, specially in the chapter 'Out-of-court Reorganization' included in the book edited by him, titled *Direito Falimentar e a Nova Lei de Falências e Recuperação de Empresas* (São Paulo, Editora Quartier Latin, 2005), page 561 *et seq.*

ACRONYMS, ABBREVIATIONS & DEFINED TERMS

NBLR	New Bankruptcy and Reorganization Law (*Nova Lei de Falências e Recuperação de Empresas*), which came into effect on 9 June 2005
Previous Law	Decree-Law 7661
Homologation of Consensus	Expedited debt restructuring procedure under the auspices of the Brazilian insolvency law whereby an a plan signed by all the creditors subject to it, i.e. 100 per cent, is filed with the competent court for homologation.
Enforcement of Agreement	Expedited debt restructuring procedure under the auspices of the Brazilian insolvency law whereby a plan submitted by the debtor and accepted by creditors representing at least 3/5 (60 per cent) of the total amount of the credits affected by the plan in each class is homologated by the competent court becoming mandatory to all creditors affected by it even though they have participated or opposed to it.
Out-of-court Reorganization	Expedited Debt Restructuring procedures under the auspices of the Brazilian Insolvency law
US Code	Chapter 11, Title 11 of the United States Bankruptcy Code
Prolan	Prolan Soluções Integradas S.A.
BRL	Brazilian Real

I. INTRODUCTION. THE PERVIOUS LEGISLATION AND ITS LIMITATIONS

On 9 February 2005 the government of Brazil enacted Law No. 11,101, referred to as the New Bankruptcy and Reorganization Law (*Nova Lei de Falências e Recuperação de Empresas*, or 'NBRL'), which came into effect on 9 June 2005. It is the first major overhaul of Brazil's corporate insolvency laws in more than half a century. The NBLR replaced the previous bankruptcy law, i.e. Decree-Law 7661 ('the Previous Law'), which had been in force since 1945. The NBLR represents a significant change in the principles and the form of activity of the various players involved in bankruptcy and reorganization processes in Brazil. Older practices are now abandoned in a process of adaptation of society to the new stimuli incorporated into the Brazilian legal system by the NBRL.

One of the primary aims of the NBRL is to provide financially distressed, but economically viable companies with the opportunity to restructure their operations through market-based solutions directly negotiated with creditors. The NBRL is guided by the basic principle that debtors generally have greater *social value* as going concerns than they would from a piecemeal sale of their assets through a forced liquidation. However, for this principle to be generally adopted and effective, it is necessary that the parties involved change their behaviour from the practice of the last 60 years. This is the first challenge for full and successful application of the NBRL, especially in the use of the two newly incorporated expedited debt restructuring procedures, so-called out-of-court reorganizations: (1) 'Homologation of Consensus', and (2) 'Enforcement of Agreement'.

The challenge arises from one of the major deficiencies of the Previous Law which prohibited debtors from negotiating reorganization schemes with creditors. Under the Previous Law a negotiation could be sanctioned with what was referred to as an 'act of bankruptcy'.[2] These acts automatically opened the door to a bankruptcy petition against the debtor, which could be decreed independently of the debtor's economic situation, that is to say, even if it were solvent. The only reorganization structure provided for in the Previous Law that is now repealed was the application for the so-called 'preventive *concordata*', which was no more than a moratorium imposed by the debtor on those unsecured creditors. This is why this stance of imposition by the debtor is so rooted in Brazilian life, and constitutes one of the main difficulties for the

---

2. Despite this prohibition, the attempt to prevent negotiation between debtors and creditors, as introduced in the Brazilian legal system by the Previous Law did not work out since debtors frequently negotiated through fronting parties the assignment of credits at a discount that were not always the same for all creditors. This means that there have always been negotiations between debtors and creditors, albeit outside the realm of the law.

implementation of a new type of behaviour that is necessary for the use of the new mechanisms provided by the NBRL.

Discharge of debt in a *concordata* was restricted to a statutorily prescribed percentage of the debtor's unsecured claims, and since the *concordata* was based on the principle of *pars conditio creditorum*, a debtor was required to provide identical treatment to all interests of different creditors. Consequently, few debtors were able to shed sufficient amounts of debt to restructure their operations successfully, and the vast majority of '*preventive concordata*' proceedings under the Previous Law would end with its conversion into liquidation under a bankruptcy proceeding.

Over the past decade Brazilian legal scholars have increasingly criticized the prohibition on the debtors' possibility of renegotiating with creditors and the fact that reorganization mechanisms were limited to '*preventive concordata*'. They argued that Brazil's corporate insolvency laws should provide debtors and creditors with appropriate legal tools to achieve market-based solutions in distress situations.[3]

In response to these criticisms, Brazilian lawmakers created the concept and procedure of the Out-of-court Reorganization (which had no equivalent in the Previous Law), and Judicial Reorganization (taking the place of the previous *preventive concordata*). Both reorganization procedures authorize debtors to seek court confirmation of reorganization plans negotiated directly with creditors. The introduction of these two new reorganization options is an acknowledgement in Brazil that the role of the courts in overseeing corporate insolvency proceedings should be limited to clearing the obstacles that prevent debtors from achieving market solutions to financial and economic crises. In other words, the NBRL recognizes that the judiciary is not the best body to find the *means* of reorganization for a company that is in crisis, and limits its role (in a comparison with the Previous Law) to conducting the process of negotiation between debtors and creditors, on the basis of application of the law and the limits that it imposes.

Several factors have contributed to the difficulties that arise in this initial period of application of the NBRL, generating uncertainties: (1) the scarcity of understanding of the new role by the judiciary; (2) the fact that few judges are specialized with bankruptcy, reorganization practices and with the economic aspects involved in insolvency proceedings; and, (3) the fact that, since the bankruptcy law is federal, its application is a duty and a function of the courts of the states (Brazilian political subdivisions), which results in the judges of small legal districts having to apply it. Within the Brazilian territory these uncertainties will undoubtedly be overcome as these new legal tools and regimes are used repeatedly.

---

3. Bankruptcy legislation enacted before the recently repealed Previous Law included the possibility of out-of-court settlements. However, given the system then in force, these were usually used as a means to defraud creditors.

Brazil

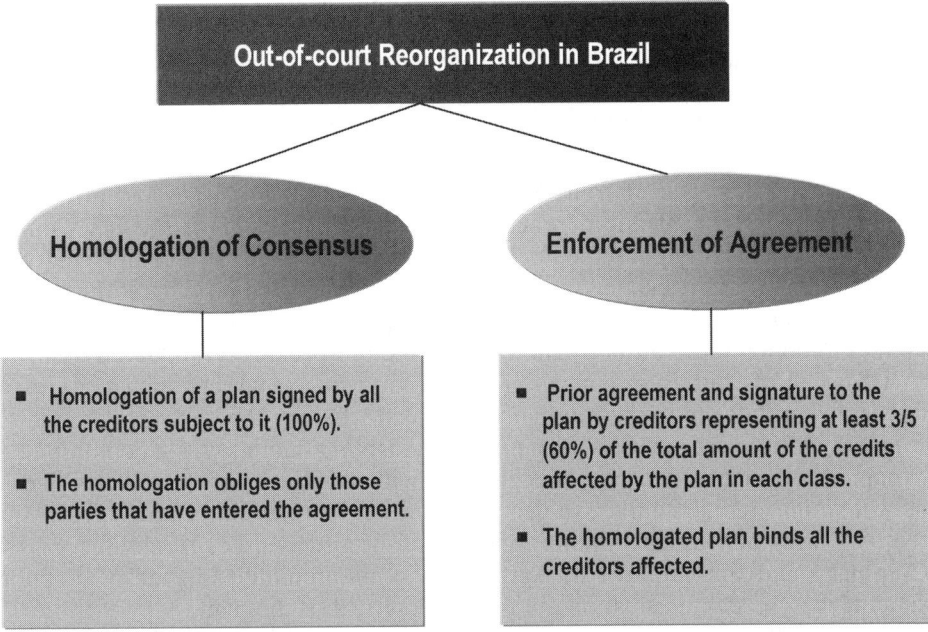

As mentioned, a key component of the NBRL is the creation of two new legal proceedings, Judicial Reorganization (*Recuperação Judicial*), which is similar to the traditional Chapter 11 procedure under the United States Bankruptcy Code (the 'US Code'),[4] and Out-of-court Reorganization (*Recuperação Extrajudicial*) which is analogous to 'pre-packaged' reorganization under the US Code.[5]

In this chapter, the legal requirements for the use of these Out-of-court Reorganization procedures will be analyzed. There are two types of Out-of-court Reorganizations:

1. Homologation of Consensus (*Recuperação Homologatória*): simple homologation by the court of an agreement plan reached between debtor and all creditors; and,
2. Enforcement of Agreement (*Recuperação Impositiva*): imposition by the court of a plan agreed by a required majority to all creditors.

Also, the following sections will also deal with the treatment given to creditors by the NBRL in relation to bankruptcy proceedings; the parameters and limits for the preparation of an Out-of-court Reorganization Plan; the applicable procedural rules; the various stages that have to be completed for achieving the homologation of an Out-of-court Reorganization Plan. In addition, a brief recount on the first Out-of-court Reorganization filed after the enactment of the NBRL came into force will also be provided.

---

4. Chapter 11, Title 11 of the US Code.
5. 11 USC. § 1126 et seq.

II. THE TWO TYPES OF OUT-OF-COURT REORGANIZATION PROCEDURES: (1) REORGANIZATION BY HOMOLOGATION OF CONSENSUS; AND, (2) REORGANIZATION BY ENFORCEMENT OF AGREEMENT[6]

The new Brazilian Out-of-court Reorganization is in many aspects similar to a 'pre-packaged reorganization' proceeding under Chapter 11 of the US Code.[7] Under it, a financially distressed debtor negotiates the terms of a plan of reorganization (i.e., a 'pre-packaged plan'), privately, with its creditors. After the debtor obtains the required creditors' support for such plan, it will start a legal proceeding aiming to obtain ratification by the court of the pre-packaged (approved) plan.

The Out-of-court Reorganization has the nature of a contract,[8] so that it is up to the debtor to indicate in the reorganization plan what are the contracts or credits whose conditions for payment it intends to change.[9] In summary, the debtor is free to negotiate the terms of a pre-packaged plan with all or some of its creditors and to choose which creditors will be subject to its terms. The primary difference between the two types of Out-of-court Reorganization procedures, i.e. Homologation of Consensus and Enforcement of Agreement, is the minimum degree of creditor support that the debtor must obtain for the approval of the plan.

In brief, the new mechanisms offer the possibility of obtaining a homologation of the plan entered by the debtor and its creditors by a court, offering the debtor the possibility to reorganize its debts. These new alternative tends to be on the one hand efficacious and fast, and on the other, less expensive, complex and traumatic.

---

6. The NBRL Bill contemplated only Reorganization by Homologation of Consensus. Reorganization by Enforcement of Agreement was included in the bill by an amendment by the Senate. In other words, the Out-of-Court Reorganization chapter was structured to include only the first procedure. The second procedure was created at the end of the legislative process, when there was no longer the possibility of introducing extensive changes in the bill. Thus, the entire procedure for Reorganization by Enforcement of Agreement was inserted in four articles of the law, which explains in part certain criticisms regarding technical aspects of this type of procedure. Despite its limitations and the criticisms, creation of the Reorganization by Enforcement of Agreement constitutes an enormous contribution of NBRL towards modernization of the Brazilian bankruptcy system, as demonstrated in this work.
7. Although certain authors point out certain similarities with the concept of *'Acuerdo Preventivo Extrajudicial*' or 'APE' as set out in the Argentinean Law, Francisco Satiro de Souza Jr. states in the book that he edited, that '[Brazilian] out-of-court reorganization is much closer to the repealed concept that originated the APE, i.e. the *acuerdo preconcursal*, which, neither prevented the individual action of creditors during its performance nor ensured the validity and effectiveness of the acts performed under it should the debtor be declared bankrupt', in: Souza Júnior, Francisco Satiro de, *Comentários à Lei de Recuperação de Empresas e Falência* (São Paulo, Editora Revista dos Tribunais, 2005), p. 514.
8. This is the main feature of the Out-of-court Reorganization and one of the main changes introduced by NBRL in relation to the repealed law. Whereas the NBRL has a contractual nature and, consequently, renders relative the mandatory imposition of the principle of *pars conditio creditorium*, the repealed law was imposed on creditors, which should receive identical treatment.
9. Subject to the restrictions in relation to the credits which may not be renegotiated in these types of reorganizations.

Brazil

In practical terms, Out-of-court Reorganization is likely to be used effectively as a mechanism to accelerate financial restructurings. It is probable that debtors will conduct their initial negotiations with their creditors in a manner already oriented by the requirements of an Out-of-court Reorganization, so that *Judicial* Reorganization would only be used in cases where: (1) the Out-of-court attempt has not been successful, especially, for example, when the minimum required percentage of acceptances has not been obtained; (2) the profile of the debt is not appropriate for the use of Out-of-court Reorganization procedures; (3) the debtor has to request and obtain a re-profiling of its tax debts; (4) the debtor needs the protection of a *stay* order to avoid the commencement or continuance of enforcement and/or collection proceedings; (5) the plan includes the sale of assets and there is interest in avoiding the risks of succession caused by tax and social security debts; (6) the plan contemplates acts capable of being considered ineffective in the event of adjudication of debtor's bankruptcy (i.e. liquidation) and the creditors are interested in having specific protections against future claw back/revocatory claims concerning such acts; and, (7) when the plan includes adjustments of an operational nature that call for more specific monitoring or supervision.

A.   Preliminary Concepts

1.   Reorganization by Homologation of Consensus

Homologation of Consensus can be conceptualized as a procedure by which the debtor file with the courts for homologation an Out-of-court Reorganization plan signed by all the creditors subject to it. The homologation of the plan obliges only those parties that have entered the agreement. A study and understanding of the relationship of forces between debtors and creditors, or between the various creditors, becomes irrelevant for this procedure, since all creditors who will have their credits altered have to agree previously and voluntarily to the plan, and sign it.

The main advantage of this first type of proceeding was in fact withdrawn from the Bill of the NBRL in its final phase of debate in the Senate, i.e. protection of any agreement homologated by the court against any claw back/revocatory actions seeking to declare the inefficacy of the acts included in the plan. This protection was expected to give more security to legal agreements entered by debtors in financial difficulties, stimulating the creation of agreements that would eventually avoid the slow and costly proceedings of judicial reorganizations or bankruptcies.

In the renegotiation of debt the creditor often agrees to grant new payment terms and conditions only if it obtains certain guarantees in exchange. Additionally, debtors not infrequently offer goods and/or assets as payments in kind to creditors, especially when they are having difficulties in monetizing fixed assets. Often when these possibilities are raised, the agreements do not materialize due to creditors' unwillingness to accept the risk of future claw back actions. Other countries such as Argentina have this protection against claw back actions in their analogous proceedings, and it would be an important improvement, in Brazil,[10] in the cases where the agreement involves: (1) granting of additional guarantees for existing obligations; or (2) payment of obligations in a form other than originally agreed – a factor which would certainly contribute to a solution for many company crises.

With that protection withdrawn from the text that was approved (and is now in force), the only benefit of the Homologation of Consensus procedure, in relation to other private agreements, resides in the fact that the homologatory order of the court constitutes and enforcement instrument, which can be enforced pursuant through a 'fast track' procedure. This does reduce the number of points in an agreement that are susceptible to challenge in the future enforcement proceedings, in the event that the plan is not honoured, but this benefit appears to be a very small stimulus for the Homologation of Consensus type of reorganization to be used widely. Indeed, this appears, together with the reasons that are common to the Enforcement of Agreement procedure (*given below*), to be the reason why, almost one year and a half after the NBRL came into effect, there is no known case of any application for Homologation of Consensus having been presented to the Brazilian courts.

2. The Enforcement of Agreement Procedure

The second type of Out-of-court Reorganization, which in this chapter is referred as Enforcement of Agreement procedure, calls for prior agreement and signature to the plan by creditors representing at least three-fifths of the credits of each class, type or group of creditors subject to such plan.[11] The substantial difference from the Homologation of Consensus procedure is that in the Enforcement of Agreement procedure the plan homologated by the court binds all the creditors affected by the plan, whether or not they have expressly and previously agreed with it, or even manifestly expressed opposition to it. Although the Enforcement of Agreement procedure has a contractual nature, as mentioned *above*, the conditions of the contract may be altered without the express agreement of the other party, or even against its will.

Provided the minimum percentage level of agreement has been met, the conditions specified in the plan are imposed on the creditors who did not sign it, and indeed on those who expressly rejected it. In other words, the NBRL provides for a form of cram-down system. This is certainly one of the greatest advances contained in the NBRL, and possibly the most significant contribution of Out-of-court Reorganization to solve financial crises and impasses in collective negotiations – and what truly makes the break with the old pattern of behaviour adopted by debtors and creditors involved in collective processes of debt renegotiations. This has already been seen in some private negotiations.

---

10. This protection already existed in the Brazilian bankruptcy law before the Previous Law.
11. This percentage is calculated on the total amount of the credits affected by the plan and not on the number of affected creditors.

Brazil

B. WHO MAY APPLY

The standing to apply for both types of Out-of-court Reorganization procedures (Homologation of Consensus or Enforcement of Agreement), is exclusively that of the debtor, whether it be a company or an individual businessman.

The creditors – regardless of their concern about the debtor's need to submit to a process of reorganization – continue to be at the mercy of any initiative taken by the debtor.[12] This was also the case for preventive *concordata*. It is worth noting, however, that if there is evidence of any unequivocal act by the debtor to delay or try to delay payments, or to sell part or all of its establishment for the purpose of frustrating the payment of creditors, the creditors may apply for bankruptcy (i.e. liquidation) of the debtor to preserve its assets and guarantee the application of the principle of equality of treatment.[13]

C. REQUIREMENTS TO BE COMPLIED WITH FOR USE OF THE OUT-OF-COURT REORGANIZATIONS

The NBRL eliminated some of the requirements previously required from the debtor who wished to apply for preventive *concordata*. The legislator's decision to reduce the requirements necessary for filing applications for an Out-of-court Reorganization is clearly expressed in the objectives that are stated as justifying the creation of the new mechanism – and which can thus be considered as being the principles that guide the new system. These are stated as: '*preservation of the source of production, of the employment of the workers and the interests of the creditors, in such a way as to preserve the company and the fulfilment of its social and economic function*'. In this context it should be noted that for several years Brazilian courts have been granting preventive *concordata* proceedings for debtors who did not meet certain formal requirements, and thus in a certain sense anticipating and applying the spirit of the NBRL.

In the case of Out-of-court Reorganizations, the legislator's decision to eliminate some requirements that were required for a preventive *concordata* appears to be correct. This is so because Out-of-court Reorganizations can only be applied for after the debtor obtains the agreement of either the totality (for Homologation of Consensus) or at least three-fifths (for Enforcement of Agreement) of the credits pertaining to creditors affected by the plan.[14] In other words, the creditors may, for example, accept a plan presented by a debtor that has a negative net worth, that is,

---

12. At one stage, while the bill was in Congress, the draft contained the right for creditors to call for the reorganization of the debtor as in the US Bankruptcy Code.
13. This principle, although limited in the out-of-court reorganization and judicial reorganization, continued to be fully applicable in the event of bankruptcy.
14. The obtaining of a minimum percentage of signatures, i.e. consent, in favour of the plan is a formality to be complied with before.

which is technically insolvent; what is important in the new mechanism is the assessment (and acceptance) by the creditors of the debtor's capacity[15] to pay.[16]

Summing up, with both types of reorganization (Homologation of Consensus and Enforcement of Agreement), the parties have more flexibility to find ways of leading the debtor company into recovery and making the payment of its debts viable. It is now up to the creditors, as a last resort, to verify whether or not restrictions on certain factors that were prohibitive to have access to the preventive *concordata* under the Previous Law are indeed factors that recommend refusal of the proposed reorganization plan.

1. The General Requirements

To apply for either type of Out-of-Court reorganization (Homologation of Consensus and Enforcement of Agreement) the debtor has to fulfil three requirements: (1) it must be carrying a business activity; (2) it must prove that it has done so regularly, for at least two years; and, (3) it must have obtained the minimum required percentage of creditors' consent of those that are affected by the Out-of-court Reorganization plan.

In relation to the exercise of business activity, the NBRL does not make any substantial change from the requirements of the Previous Law. The use of the mechanism is still denied to a company or individual businessman that it is not regularly established – i.e. does not have its acts of constitution or association and its books duly registered with the competent Commercial Registry, although in fact, it is regularly exercising the activity.[17] The 'de facto entrepreneur' may have its bankruptcy declared, but cannot apply for Out-of-court Reorganization.

2. Requirements for Each Type of Procedure

Besides the three general requirements listed *above*, a debtor applying for Out-of-court Reorganization by Homologation of Consensus must obtain the prior agreement of all the creditors that such debtor has chosen and that are subject to the plan. The NBRL does not prevent the plan from covering creditors of different types, nor, for example, various creditors of one type and a single creditor of another type.

The positive requirement demanded for Homologation of Consensus is that the totality of the creditors chosen by the debtor shall have expressly agreed with the proposed plan. Fulfilment of this condition needs to be demonstrated by

---

15. To apply for *preventive concordata*, the debtor was required to evidence that it had assets, after deduction of those necessary to pay creditors holding claims with priorities or claims with a security interest, sufficient to pay at least 50 per cent of the unsecured credits.
16. The supremacy of the will of the creditors was already recognized when the Previous Law was in force. As mentioned *above*, this law considered the calling of the creditors, by the debtor, for an extension of payment period to be an act of bankruptcy. In this respect, the consensus of legal scholars was that the acceptance of the plan for renegotiation by the totality of the creditors was sufficient grounds for not declaring the bankruptcy of the debtor.
17. This restriction was already imposed by the previous law on a *de facto*, or irregular, businessman who wished to use the previous mechanism of *preventive concordata*.

Brazil

attachment to the case records, at the time of application, of a plan containing the signature of all the creditors that are affected by the plan.

Enforcement of Agreement, on the other hand, requires: (1) the three general requirements listed *above*; and, (2) the signature of creditors representing at least three-fifths of all credits of each type of credit covered by the plan. As shown *below*, the debtor may indicate in the plan the different types, type or even group of creditors subject to the plan, and must prove, at the moment of applying for the relief, that the minimum percentage of acceptance has been obtained in each class, type or in the group of creditors affected by the plan.

It is possible, although unnecessary, for the debtor to obtain during the proceedings the agreement of all or of some of the remaining (dissident) creditors, defined as those who have not subscribed to the plan before it was submitted to the courts or have expressly rejected it.

To be noted, in any event, that a debtor who has not obtained the necessary agreements (totality, for Homologation by Consensus; or at least three-fifths of the credits of each class, type or group affected by the plan, for Enforcement of Agreement) is allowed to apply for a judicial reorganization, in which it will have the opportunity to continue to negotiate with all of its creditors and obtain their approval during the proceedings (achieving a lower percentage of credits agreement than that required for the Out-of-court Reorganization).

In the calculation of whether the minimum percentage required for homologation of the plan has been achieved, credits not included and not affected by the plan are disregarded; as also are credits subject to the plan, but held by: (1) the debtor's stockholders or partners; (2) affiliated companies, parent companies, subsidiaries or those which have a partner or stockholder that holds more than 10 per cent of the registered capital of the debtor, or in which the debtor or one of its partners has more than 10 per cent of the registered capital; (3) a wife or relative by marriage or blood up to second degree upward or downward in parentship of the debtor, a manager, controlling partner, stockholder or a member of the consultative, audit or similar Boards of the debtor company or of a company in which any of these persons exercise those functions.

In calculation of the qualifying percentage, credits in foreign currency are converted into Brazilian currency at the exchange rate of the day prior to the signature of the plan.

3. Impediments

The NBRL eliminated the requirement of the inexistence of commercial protests'[18] filed against the debtor which under the Previous Law was a condition for application for *preventive concordata*. Under the Previous Law, any debtor against

---

18. In Brazil, the process of commercial protest is a formality by which the creditor officially presents the credit instrument to the debtor for payment. This procedure is only necessary if the debtor does not make the payment of such credit instrument voluntarily within the period agreed. In the event that payment does not take place, the protest is formalized and constitutes, for bankruptcy purposes, a proof of the insolvency of the debtor and authorizes the creditor to apply for, and the Judge to decree, the bankruptcy of the debtor.

which commercial protests had been lodged had no alternative but to apply for *preventive concordata* and rely on the goodwill of the courts to reduce the importance of this impediment and avoid its bankruptcy being decreed. Demonstration of the existence of any commercial protest led automatically to filing of *concordatas* which could have been avoided. The elimination of this impediment for debtors to access the procedures of Out-of-court or Judicial Reorganization results in an improvement in debtors' possibilities.

The debtor would not be able to resort to an Out-of-court Reorganization and its judicial homologation if: (1) it has been declared bankrupt and its liabilities in a bankruptcy have not been declared extinct by a court ruling against which no further appeal lies; (2) it has been, or has as a manager or controlling stockholder who has been judged for one of the bankruptcy crimes specified in the NBRL;[19] and, (3) 'if any application for Judicial Reorganization is pending, or if the debtor has obtained a judicial reorganization or homologation of another plan for Out-of-court Reorganization within the last 2 (two) years or less.[20] In relation to the latter prong, the choice made by the Legislator differs from the modern legislations. The time limit for applying for a new Out-of-court Reorganization goes against the very principle of maintaining productive activity, which is the main aim of the NBRL. It seems possible that a debtor who has renegotiated its debts based on cash flow planned under an economic reality may have to propose a new agreement to its creditors if some unexpected external factor occurs that affects its cash flow forecasts.

If the NBRL has as a fundamental precept the preservation of productive activity, it does not seem to be reasonable to prohibit application for a renewed Out-of-court Reorganization procedure if the debtor happens to suffer another blow within a period of less than two years. The agreement of all, or at least three-fifths of the creditors, is already a condition for applying for an Out-of-court Reorganization – so there is no reason why the legislator should prevent a new Out-of-court Reorganization if the majority of creditors agree to it. In practice, a debtor facing this situation will now have, in principle, to use other amicable alternatives, facing the same difficulties that he would have encountered prior to the NBRL, especially the lack of existence of protection against opportunistic creditors. During this 'blackout' period, the debtor will have as an alternative the possibility of applying for Judicial Reorganization, with all the costs and difficulties inherent to this type of complex proceeding.

On the other hand and for the same reasons, after the lapse of the minimum two-year period mentioned *above*, the debtor may file again for an Out-of-court Reorganization, even if it has not properly complied with the obligations assumed

---

19. Chapter VII of the NBLR, i.e. articles 168–178 include a list of different crimes contemplated under the bankruptcy law.
20. According to article 161, paragraph 3 of the NBRL, the debtor shall not file for a homologation of an Out-of-court plan if a petition for judicial reorganization is pending or if he has been granted a judicial reorganization or another out-of-court reorganization plan has been homologated within the last two (2) years.

in the previous reorganization plan. Strictly speaking, in this new proceeding the debtor may reschedule the obligations set out in the previously ratified plan, upon the minimum consent of its creditors.

III. PREPARATION OF AN OUT-OF-COURT REORGANIZATION PLAN

The reorganization plan is a document that is essential to the initial application for an Out-of-court Reorganization, and must contain the terms and conditions of the agreement entered into between the debtor and creditors, as well as specifying the means of reorganization that will be used.[21] Hence, the plan must indicate what the obligations that will be changed are: the list of creditors embraced by the plan, the payment type and its schedule.

The NBRL contains a list of at least 16 reorganization mechanisms that the debtor can use in both types of reorganization.[22] The plan may, for example, propose a write-off, a conversion of debt into equity, payment in goods, discounts or extension of the debt period. The purpose is to give the debtor enough flexibility to prepare a plan that is appropriate for both the actual scenario and the possibilities of payment, and also acceptable to the majority of its creditors.

In preparing its Out-of-court Reorganization plan the debtor must ascertain whether it meets the legal requirements qualifying it to apply. Also, it should analyze which are the creditors that can be included in or compelled to accept the plan, and assess the probabilities of the creditors accepting the conditions of the plan that is being prepared. This requires (1) the debtor to ascertain what treatment these creditors would receive in a process of bankruptcy or reorganization, either Out-of-court or Judicial, so as to assess whether the creditor is likely to accept the

---

21. For the preparation of the Out-of-court reorganization plan, the debtor may use one, or more than one, of the methods specified in Article 50 of the NBRL, or any others accepted by the creditors, provided the relevant legislation is obeyed.
22. Article 50 of the NBLR states that a judicial reorganization may be performed – among others – by any of the following alternatives: (1) granting of special terms and conditions for repayment of maturing or matured obligations; (2) spin-off, merger, consolidation or change of corporate type, opening of a wholly-owned subsidiary or assignment of shares or units, with due regard for the partners' rights and pursuant to applicable law; (3) change in the corporate control; (4) full or partial replacement of the debtor's senior management or change in its management bodies; (5) creditors' entitlement to a separate election of senior managers and to veto powers on certain matters specified in the plan; (6) capital increase; (7) disposal or lease of an establishment, including a company formed by the employees themselves; (8) salaries reduction, offsetting working hours and workday reductions either by a collective bargaining agreement or a labour convention; (9) payment in kind or novation of outstanding debts, with or without offering own or third-party guarantees; (10) incorporation of a company by the creditors; (11) partial sale of assets; (12) equalization of financial charges relating to debts of any kind, being the initial term the date on which the petition for judicial reorganization is filed and also applying to rural credit contracts without impairment to the provisions of a specific law; (13) right of enjoyment of the company; (14) shared management; (15) issuance of securities; and, (16) formation of a special purpose company to adjudicate the debtor's assets in payment of the claims.

proposal or, e.g. to prefer to subject the debtor to bankruptcy; and, (2) what are the limits that the law imposes in regard to which creditors can be subject to the plan. The debtor also has to analyze the limitations provided by law, if any, for a differentiated treatment among the creditors.

A. CREDITORS NOT SUBJECT TO THE EFFECTS OF OUT-OF-COURT REORGANIZATION

An Out-of-court Reorganization plan cannot impose new terms on the following types of credit: (1) credits of a tax nature; (2) labour-related credits; (3) credits of the owner or committing vendor of a real property, in which the respective contract contains an irrevocable clause related to a real estate development structure; (4) credits of the owner in a sale contract with title retention; (5) credits arising from advances of money on foreign exchange contracts; (6) credits of the owner of chattel mortgages on movable or immovable goods (*alienação ou cessão fiduciária*); and, (7) credits arising from leasing contracts.

This means that the conditions of these credits or contracts may not be affected compulsorily by plans presented in Out-of-court Reorganization proceedings, and these obligations must be paid regularly by the debtor. Upon a default in payments the creditor can exercise its rights, including, when applicable, the right for repossession of assets (i.e. under chattel mortgage or leasing). The application for Out-of-court Reorganizations does not prevent the right of repossession of assets in these two latter types of contracts since there is no stay period in Out-of-court Reorganization.

It is, thus, essential that the debtors, on the one hand, voluntarily re-negotiate with the creditors who hold this type of credits, the conditions for their payments and, on the other hand, include the amounts necessary for the payment of these contracts in their forecasts for cash flow to be presented to the creditors that are affected by the Out-of-court Reorganizations.

The NBRL maintained the privileged treatment for credits arising from foreign exchange contracts in the case of bankruptcy of the debtor, making it possible for the creditor to file an application for restitution. Thus, if on the one hand the law eliminates the possibility of requesting an application for restitution of advances on exchange agreements in the process of reorganization, on the other hand it now demands that the debtor should perform the contract, facing the risks that the financial institution carried out the process of collection, or even applied for the bankruptcy of the debtor.[23]

Finally, although the NBRL excludes the credits listed *above* from the process of Out-of-court Reorganization, it is possible for the debtor to include them – even labour law credits – in the out-of-court reorganization plan, provided that the respective creditor agrees with the terms of the plan and the novation that the homologation of the plan will cause.

---

23. This condition is subject to the verification that one of the cases specified in Article 94 of the NBRL is in fact present.

Brazil

B. TREATMENT OF CREDITORS IN BANKRUPTCY PROCEEDINGS

One of the challenges faced by the Brazilian legislator in preparing the NBRL was the substantial modification of the basic principles of the bankruptcy system, i.e. altering the treatment and the privileges given to various creditors involved in the process, while at the same time maintaining a certain balance of forces between the debtor and creditors.

The implementation and the efficacy of the mechanisms of Judicial and Out-of-court Reorganizations introduced by the NBRL are intrinsically related to a process of cultural change. Before the NBRL there were very few successful cases of collective debt re-negotiations in Brazil. In the preparation of reorganization plans (both Judicial and Out-of-court), the black-and-white dualism in negotiation that prevailed under the Previous Law will tend to disappear, as efforts are made to adapt the multiple interests involved, through the use of creative proposals and solutions that aim to maximize satisfaction of the interests of all parties.[24]

In tune with this statement, it can be said that under the NBRL, all those involved have both lost and gained. The debtor ceases to have absolute control over the process of reorganization, since the NBRL eliminated the *preventive concordata* and the related possibility of imposing it on unsecured creditors. In contrast, for example, the NBRL gives the creditors the right whether or not to accept the payment plan proposed by the debtor, for a Judicial Reorganization. At the same time, the new procedures of judicial and Out-of-court Reorganization are very flexible and allow the debtor to present a payment plan that is appropriate to its cash flow capacity, making possible the reorganization of its economic-financial equilibrium, in such a way as to avoid its failure.

In the preparation of the Out-of-court Reorganization plan, the debtor should be aware not only to the multiple interests involved. Also, special attention should be given to the fact that other creditors may be stimulated to refuse the plan, with the purpose of causing the bankruptcy and preventing filing an Out-of-court Reorganization plan with the court, if the conditions presented for payment of its credit in the plan are worse than their collection expectations under bankruptcy (i.e. liquidation).

In this respect, it is important to note that the order of payment and the privileges of the creditors in the bankruptcy (i.e. liquidation) process were also modified by the NBRL.

Labour-law credits, for example, were kept in first place in the ranking of credits in a bankruptcy proceeding, but with their privilege limited to 150 times the minimum wage per employee, which means that any credit which exceeds this amount is considered to be unsecured. As a counterpart, in a Judicial Reorganization, credits arising from the labour legislation or from

---

24. 'Integrative strategies require that the members of the group discover what are the preferences of the other members of the negotiation to expand the range of resources so as to accommodate the questions rationally'. Max H. Bazerman and Margaret A. Neale, *Negociando Racionalmente* (2rd edn, São Paulo, Altas, 1998), p. 154.

work accidents which are due up to the date of the application must be paid within a maximum period of one year. Credits of a strictly salary nature that have become due during the three months prior to the distribution of the Judicial Reorganization (limited to five times the minimum wage per employee) must be paid in within 30 days.[25]

Financial institutions find themselves with a higher credit risk in transactions in which they are holders of *in rem* guarantees (i.e. pledge or mortgage), since this type of credit (previously not subject to *preventive concordata*) is subject to the procedures for Judicial and Out-of-court Reorganizations.[26] In the Judicial Reorganization, provided that certain requirements are met, at least in theory there is the possibility of cram down of a plan into different classes of creditors (i.e. the creditors may impose the reorganization plan on the creditors who have *in rem* guarantees if they obtain the approval of at least one-third of said creditors). Conversely, in Out-of-court Reorganizations, it is not possible for creditors of one specific type, class or group to cram-down the proposed plan on creditors pertaining to other types, class or groups.

On the other hand, creditors with *in rem* guarantees are benefited in the event of bankruptcy (i.e. liquidation) of the debtor. The NBRL eliminates the risks of labour-law, tax and social security succession for parties acquiring assets from the bankrupt estate and accelerates the process of sale of the debtor's assets. Sale of assets immediately after an adjudication of bankruptcy without the risk of succession tends to maximize the value received in payment for such assets and therefore acts in favour of the sale of the business while still operating, so as to preserve the going concern and the employment of its workers. These changes started to encourage investments in distressed companies in Brazil, attracting new investors to this particular market, increasing the raising of funds by insolvent/illiquid companies and consequently, the capacity for payment to creditors, notably those creditors with *in rem* guarantees[27] – who have been moved into second place in the order of classification of credits, inverting the order with tax credits, which are now third in the classification.[28]

Thus, now that the value of the privilege of the first class of creditors in bankruptcy has been limited, the creditors with *in rem* rights being in second

---

25. However, there is no legal obstacle to labour-law creditors entering into individual agreements to accept a longer payment period. Nevertheless, this condition, even if accepted by the majority of the class of creditors (labour credits), cannot be imposed on those labour-law creditors who have not expressly stated their acceptance.
26. After the NBRL came into force, financial institutions have preferred to enter into agreements secured by fiduciary ownership rights (and, as such, not compulsorily affected by judicial or out-of-court reorganization proceedings) instead of executing agreements secured by mortgages or pledges.
27. In Brazil, the proceeds from the sale of an asset secured by collateral in a bankruptcy proceeding do not go to the respective creditor, but rather to the bankruptcy estate for payment of creditors, subject to the priority ranking set out in law.
28. Under the Previous Law, tax related credits would be paid with priority over secured creditors (i.e. creditors with *in rem* guarantees).

place in the order of payment in the event of bankruptcy, and considering that the possibility of generation of funds for the company in bankruptcy have increased, it is possible to say that the secured creditors (i.e. with *in rem* guarantees) will have real expectations of collecting their credits, or at least part of them, in the event of the bankruptcy of the debtor. Thus, it seems reasonable to imagine that such secured creditor will look at the possibility of (and the time necessary for) payment of its credit in a bankruptcy, comparing it with the proposal presented by the debtor in an Out-of-court Reorganization plan.

C. LIMITATIONS APPLICABLE TO THE OUT-OF-COURT REORGANIZATION PLAN

Under the previous Law, a debtor that applied for a *preventive concordata* in many cases found itself obliged to pay debts already due under the same conditions as debts that would ordinarily mature only years later. The debtor was also prevented from paying in full suppliers whose receivables were small in value (sometimes even when they were less than 1 per cent of the value of the credits subject to the *concordata*).[29]

At the same time it is also true that creditors have different interests. Some, for example, prefer to accept a reduction in their credit rather than an extension on the payments. Others may prefer to convert their credit into equity in the debtor's company.

The Brazilian legislator recognized that creditors' interests are asymmetrical and that a proposal of identical payment terms for all of them might not satisfy all creditors (in the case of Homologation of Consensus), or the required majority (for Enforcement of Agreement). It therefore made the procedures for both Out-of-court and Judicial Reorganization more flexible so that the debtor might be able to propose a plan molded on its own reality and which may be feasible for the reorganization of its business.

Thus, although the legislator has eliminated the requirement for parity of treatment between all creditors, by granting some flexibility for the debtor in the preparation of its plan, the NBRL does not contain highly specific parameters for the segregation of creditors into classes or sub-groups for the purposes of payment, as is the case in other foreign legislations. In this aspect, the Brazilian legislator has pointed in the correct direction, by restricting the application of the principle of parity, on the basis that legal scholars and case law[30] should give their contribution to the setting of the criteria for segregation of the creditors.

---

29. The prohibition on payment of the small supplier produced no relief in terms of the debtor's cash flow – whilst causing immense damage to small creditors, often micro-companies whose owners depended on these revenues to support their families.
30. Or a future amendment in legislation to improve this aspect.

However, the fact that the principle of parity of treatment should be applied to those creditors whose credits have the same origin, nature and profile it is possible in the Out-of-court Reorganization procedure, for a creditor to opt for the payment conditions of another group of creditors. This notwithstanding, such choice does not have to be an unfavourable treatment to creditors in a similar situation.

Thus, the debtor, as well as assessing its capacity for payment and the structure of its assets, should identify the individual expectations and interests of each group of creditors. As mentioned *above*, the debtor should analyze the probability of succeeding in obtaining the minimum required consent for each type of credits included in the plan (100 per cent for Homologation of Consensus; and, at least 3/5 for Enforcement of Agreement).

1. Selection of Creditors for Homologation of Consensus

As indicated *above*, the Homologation of Consensus procedure requires prior agreement by the totality of the creditors affected by the plan. The debtor can negotiate freely with those creditors that it selects, just as it would do in any private negotiation not subject to judicial homologation. There is nothing in the NBRL that prevents the plan catering for different types of creditors, or even various creditors of one type and one single creditor of another type.[31]

Differentiated treatment for creditors of the same type does not create any difficulty in the case of Homologation of Consensus, since all the creditors have to sign the plan and agree with it. The only restriction relates to the contents of the plan which, as will be shown *below*, cannot contain any provision that results in unfavourable treatment for the creditors *not* affected by the plan.

2 Selection of Creditors to be Subject to Enforcement of Agreement

The NBRL allows the debtor to prepare a plan for Enforcement of Agreement which covers: (1) one or more types or classes of creditors; or, (2) a group of creditors of the same nature subject to similar payment conditions.

A debtor who decides to prepare a plan segregating its creditors by type must obligatorily provide for the payment of the totality of the creditors of the type or types selected. The types are: (1) secured creditors, i.e. those with *in rem* guarantees; (2) creditors with special privilege; (3) creditors with general privilege; (4) unsecured creditors; and, (5) subordinated creditors. The plan binds all the creditors of the type or types covered by the plan, which exist up to the date of the debtor's Out-of-court Reorganization.

---

31. The prerequisite is that the creditor should be fully and freely in a position to administer his or its own assets and be represented by a party holding power to dispose of rights, freely agree to accept the plan, and accept the renegotiation conditions proposed by the debtor.

Brazil 115

Thus, if the debtor intends to renegotiate the debt with a certain secured creditor, i.e. a creditor that has an *in rem* guarantee and wishes to include it in the plan for Enforcement of Agreement, it must: (1) include in the plan all the creditors of that type (i.e. creditors with an *in rem* guarantee), obtaining the prior agreement of at least three-fifths of the totality of credits of that type; or (2) include it in a group of creditors, subject to the requirements shown *below*.

Additionally, the Debtor may segregate its creditors for the purposes of an Out-of-court Reorganization plan into one or more groups of creditors (as necessary), which would have the same nature and similar payment conditions under their respective original obligations. While such division would provide the Debtor with more flexibility to compose the different groups of creditors, generally one should expect such divisions to be more strict than a qualification dividing creditors by types or classes.

As well as the division by *type*, the debtor may also prepare a plan by *class* of creditors in the manner specified in the NBLR in respect to the chapter on Judicial Reorganization.

IV. RESTRICTIONS AND EFFECTS OF THE PLAN

A. RESTRICTIONS OF TREATMENT TO CREDITORS. ACTS SUBJECT TO REVIEW

The plan may not impose unfavourable treatment for the creditors which are not subject to it. The legal system continues to provide protection against any connivance between a debtor and a group of creditors,[32] such as, for example, transfer of the debtor's business establishment, resulting in insufficient assets – for payment to the other creditors who have not agreed to the plan.

The judge – in principle – will not homologate a plan that included the possibility of executing of the so-called 'acts of bankruptcy'[33] (Sub-item III, Article 94, of the NBRL), or acts which aim to cause an impairment on the creditors.

B. EFFECTS CAUSED BY SIGNATURE AND HOMOLOGATION OF THE PLAN. BANKRUPTCY RELATED CRIMES

Under the NBRL, the plan produces effects in relation to the debtor, and creditors that are subject to it only after it has been homologated by the court. However,

---

32. The absence of effective fraud protection provisions in previous laws led to a lack of any kind of out-of-court preventive agreement for over sixty years in Brazil.
33. 'Acts of Bankruptcy' are acts specified by law which when practiced by the debtor characterize his condition of bankruptcy, and authorize the judge to decree that bankruptcy, regardless of the asset or equity situation of the debtor.

since the nature of an Out-of-court Reorganization is contractual, the signatories to the plan may agree differently in a case of Homologation of Consensus, so that the plan produces effects before its homologation in relation to the clauses that change the amount of the debt or the payment method. Nothing prevents such effects from being provided for, even in an Enforcement of Agreement. However, such a provision can only bind creditors who are signatories of the plan, since in the case of Enforcement of Agreement it will only produce effects after the homologation by the court for all the non-signatory creditors to the plan.

The plan does not bind the parties if it is not homologated, and in this case the creditors resume the right to demand and enforce their respective credits and claims on the original conditions. However, any release of the creditors in the event of the plan not being homologated in court seems to be a contractual issue and would need to be reviewed on a case-by-case basis. Thus, the parties may define in the instrument of agreement – which is, of course, the plan: (1) whether the homologation is or is not a condition for cancellation, that is to say, whether certain effects will not occur if the plan is not homologated; (2) whether by mere signing the plan it entails the novation of the credit obligations; and whether, (3) the novation will be conditional to the homologation of the plan or adherence to it by the minimal percentage of the credits involved.

The plan binds the parties, and signatory creditors do not have the possibility of withdrawing from that commitment,[34] other than in the event of express consent by the other signatories. This prohibition aims to avoid any creditor using its 'inclination to withdraw' as a means of taking additional advantages by threatening to withdraw from the plan and thus breaking the overall agreement entered into by the group as a whole.

Finally, the plan may not provide for the sale of an asset that is under mortgage or pledge. Also, the plan cannot suppress or substitute the guarantee, nor may convert credits in foreign currencies into the Brazilian currency, without express consent by the respective creditor.

The homologation of the Out-of-court Reorganization plan is an objective criminal condition in relation to certain types of economic crimes included in the NBRL. The NBLR increased the number of bankruptcy crimes to cover certain conducts that can be exercized before or after an Out-of-court Reorganization.

C. Effects Arising from the Homologation by Consensus or Enforcement of Agreement

1.   Administration of the Debtor. Disposal of Assets

The debtor maintains the free administration of its assets during the process of Out-of-court Reorganization, and is not subject to any restrictions imposed on the

---

34. Paragraph 5, Article 161 of the NBRL.

Brazil 117

debtor in the judicial reorganization. Thus there is no legal basis, nor any practical reason to appoint a court administrator.

The NBRL does not prevent the debtor from the acts of placing a charge on or disposing of its assets, and thus it is lawful to give assets in payment in kind of debts that are subject to the plan. In this respect, it should once again be highlighted that the acts practiced in the course of an Out-of-court Reorganization may be considered ineffective (i.e. clawed back) in the event of declaration of bankruptcy of the debtor, if the act is related to Article 129 of the NBRL[35] and was practiced within the period specified for each of the acts indicated in the subparagraphs of said article.

If, on the other hand, the plan involves legal disposal of branches or isolated production units, its realization must obey the rules for disposal of assets in a bankruptcy,[36] and take place by auction, either in the form of closed bids or open outcry.

2. Individual Rights and Actions

The filing of the plan of an Out-of-court Reorganization plan does not produce the suspension of individual rights, actions or executions of those creditors who have not subscribed to the plan. The suspension or extinction of actions is a consequence of novation of the obligations that are the subject of the restrictive actions. Thus, as a general rule, only the homologation of the plan will cause suspension or extinction of actions, and only in relation to those creditors who are affected (whether by consent or by enforcement) by the plan that is homologated.

Actions brought by creditors who have subscribed to the plan may be suspended or extinguish even before the respective homologation, depending on the

---

35. Article 129 of the NBLR reads as follows: *'The following acts are ineffective with regard to the bankruptcy estate, whether or not the contracting party was aware of the debtor's economic and financial distress and whether or not the debtor intended to defraud creditors: (I) payment by the debtor within the legal term of debts not yet fallen due, by any means of extinguishment of the credit right, including by discount of the respective instrument; (II) payment made within the legal term of debts fallen due and enforceable, in any way other than as provided for in the respective contract; (III) creation of a security interest, including lien, within the legal term, in the case of a debt contracted previously; if the mortgaged assets are given in subsequent mortgage, the bankruptcy estate shall receive the portion otherwise applying to the creditor of the revoked mortgage; (IV) acts performed free of charge during the two (2) years preceding the decree of bankruptcy; (V) waiver of inheritance or legacy during the two (2) years preceding the decree of bankruptcy; (VI) sale or transfer of an establishment without the express consent of or payment to all creditors existing at the time, if the debtor has not kept sufficient assets to settle his liabilities, unless, within thirty (30) days, there is no opposition by creditors after being duly notified by a court clerk or by an officer of the registry of deeds and documents; (VII) registration of in rem rights and of property transfer inter vivos, for a consideration or free of charge, or an annotation of real property made after the decree of bankruptcy, unless there is a previous annotation thereof.*

    Ineffectiveness may be declared by the judge on his own initiative, alleged in defence or claimed under a specific action or incidentally during the proceedings'.
36. Article 142 of the NBRL.

terms agreed between the parties. Thus, if the plan stipulates that the novation of the obligations take effect by the mere signature of the document, independently of the respective homologation, and if any creditor who has subscribed is the plaintiff in a court claim based on a credit subject to the plan, such obligation will have been novated and the action will lose its object and be dismissed.

The existence of a bankruptcy petition in progress against the debtor does not prevent the debtor from applying to the court for an Out-of-court Reorganization. In the same sense, applying for an Out-of-court Reorganization does not bar a bankruptcy request, nor prevent those creditors who have not subscribed to the plan, or who are not affected by it, from filing a bankruptcy petition against the debtor. However, as previously mentioned, the homologation of an Out-of-court Reorganization, which needs to be examined by the Judge before passing a judgment on the bankruptcy petition will entail the novation of the credits affected by the plan and will result in the dismissal of the petitions for bankruptcy that are based on credits that were subject to novation.

Finally, all creditors that are not affected by the plan may exercise their rights regularly as if the Out-of-court Reorganization did not exist. They can apply for, and obtain, a decree of bankruptcy of the debtor, even if the reorganization plan has been homologated.

V. THE PROCEDURE

The procedure, common to both types of Out-of-court Reorganization, is very simple and tends to be expedited since no interlocutory decisions are allowed during the process. Disputes should be limited only to the formal aspects of the plan since once the parties have reached an agreement no minority is allowed to make any application to challenge or modify the conditions or the means of payment contemplated in the plan.

A. COMPETENT COURT

The judge that is competent to homologate an Out-of-court Reorganization is the judge of the domicile of the debtor's principal place of business or of a branch of a company that has been incorporated outside the Brazilian territory. The allocation of the competent court in an Out-of-court Reorganization must be made by a draw among the different competent courts within the jurisdiction.

B. THE PETITION AND ITS INSTRUCTION

The initial petition for an Out-of-court Reorganization must contain the reasons that demonstrate and justify the need for the petition, and also be accompanied by the reorganization plan with indication of the terms, conditions and means of payment to be used by the debtor.

Brazil

The debtor must also provide: (1) a standing certificate from the Public Register of Companies, an updated version of the act of incorporation, copies of the minutes of the appointment of the managers/directors and copies of the minutes of the meeting of the board of directors and/or of the general meeting of stockholders authorizing the filing of the petition; and, (2) a certificate from the assigning body of the courts stating where the principal place of business of the debtor is located and the non-existence of impediments to file the petition.

The debtor must present a series of additional documents in an Enforcement of Agreement process since there is not prior express agreement by the creditors subject to the plan. The aim of this additional request is to provide more transparency to the process. The additional requirements are:

1. a detailed description of the equity and the status of the assets of the debtor;
2. the financial statements of the previous fiscal year and those prepared especially to be filed with the petition ;
3. documentation evidencing the faculties of the signatories to novate or accept changes on the terms of their obligations; and,
4. a complete list of the creditors,[37] their address, nature of their business, classification and present value of their respective credits (broken down by origin, maturity and indication of the accounting records of each pending transaction).

C.   SUMMON OF CREDITORS

Once the application has been properly filed, the judge will order the publication of a notice in the official gazette and in a massive-circulation newspaper, or in newspapers that circulate in the jurisdictions of the head office and branch offices of the debtor. The purpose of this add is to summon all debtor's creditors, whether or not subject to the Out-of-court Reorganization plan, to present oppositions, if any.

Those creditors that are affected by the plan and domiciled (or have their head office) in Brazil shall also be summoned to a meeting by a letter sent by the debtor. The letter should indicate which is the court dealing with the application and contain the terms and conditions of the plan, instructions on procedure and timeframe in which the creditor may contest the application. The debtor must produce in court the evidence that the said letters have been sent to its creditors.

It is important to note that there is no differentiation of treatment between Brazilian and foreign creditors in relation to the right to contest the plan. However, it is possible that foreign creditors are unlikely to become aware of the application, since the debtor is not obliged to notify them[38] of the filing of the petition for

---

37. Some scholars argue that the debtor should submit only the list of creditors affected by the plan. I disagree with this interpretation, since the requirement that the complete list of creditors be submitted seeks to allow all creditors, whether or not affected by the plan, to check whether the debtor violated the rules on creditors' protection when preparing its plan, i.e., whether the debtor granted privileged treatment to a creditor that, for instance, were excluded of the plan.
38. In this respect, Paulo Penalva Santos, in the book he edited *A Nova Lei de Falências e de Recuperação de Empresas – Lei n. 11.101/05* (Editora Forense, 2006), p. 386, states that despite

Out-of-court Reorganization and the publication of the announcements relating to the proceedings is mandatory only in Brazilian newspapers.

D. OPPOSITIONS TO THE APPLICATION. OBSTACLES IN THE HOMOLOGATION PROCESS

Any creditor may oppose to the plan within 30 days as of from the publication of the creditor's summon notice. A creditor may not, in its opposition, apply for changes in the conditions proposed, since the matter to be discussed in the opposition should be restricted to the following matters:

1. unfavourable treatment of creditors that are not subject to the plan;
2. early payment of debt;
3. non-compliance with the minimum percentage specified for Enforcement of Agreement;
4. the existence of any of the 'acts of bankruptcy' specified in sub-clause III of Article 94 of the NBRL;
5. the exercise of any act with the intention of harming creditors' interests;
6. non-compliance with any requirements specified in the NBRL or any other legal provision;
7. simulation of credits;
8. misrepresentation of the creditors that have subscribed to the plan.

E. ROLE OF THE JUDGE. JUDGMENTS OF HOMOLOGATION AND JUDGMENTS OF REFUSAL

The judge shall not homologate an Out-of-court Reorganization Plan if he or she believes that there are good grounds to one or more of the contestations or, in the absence thereof, if he or she finds that: (1) the plan provides for the practice of an act or acts which aim to cause an impairment on creditors' interests and are subject to repeal under Article 130 of the NBRL; (2) there is a misrepresentation of one or more creditors who have subscribed the plan;[39] or (3) there is proof of simulation of credits.

In the event that the plan is not homologated, the debtor may propose a new Out-of-court Reorganization plan after having corrected the mistake pointed out, or file a petition for a judicial reorganization. If the homologation takes place, the Out-of-court Reorganization plan then produces effects on all creditors covered by it, whether or not they have subscribed to the plan. As shown *above*, the signatories may stipulate that the plan shall produce effects as of the moment of its signature.

---

the legislative flaw that omitted the requirement that all foreign creditors be notified by letter, the judge should demand such action from the debtor.
39. Provided that such defect is not cured and changes the minimum adhesion percentage applying to the judicial reorganization mode then chosen.

Appeal lies against a judgment that gives or denies homologation of an Out-of-court Reorganization plan.

VI. CONCLUSIONS

The reintroduction of out-of-court reorganization alternatives in the Brazilian bankruptcy system, after more than 60 years, is one of the major breakthroughs of the NBRL. Despite criticisms about certain specific issues, the Out-of-court Reorganization offers much expedited and less costly alternatives than judicial reorganization (particularly, the Reorganization by Enforcement of Agreement), creating proper mechanisms to stimulate a better environment for collective negotiation (its effects is already being seen in practice) and to provide a rapid solution for distressed companies.

Therefore, out-of-court proceedings are expected to be used more frequently, particularly in the events in which it is impossible to obtain the agreement of all the creditors affected by a reorganization plan, rapidly resolving deadlocks in negotiations and allowing debtors to turn around its business more quickly. All this is targeted at reaching the objectives of the NBRL, *i.e.* to preserve the production process, jobs, tax revenues, etc. while increasing the debtor's ability to honour its obligations.

VII. REVIEW OF THE FIRST OUT-OF-COURT CASE (ENFORCEMENT OF AGREEMENT)

After more than one year since the NBRL came into force, no reorganization by homologation of consensus was actually filed, whereas very few reorganization proceedings by enforcement of agreement were filed.

The first reorganization by enforcement of agreement was filed by Prolan Soluções Integradas S.A. (Prolan), underway at the 2nd Lower Bankruptcy and Reorganization Court in São Paulo. The Prolan case, as well as other judicial reorganization proceedings that have hit the headlines such as the Varig and Parmalat cases, have atypical features and depart – in certain extent – from the NBRL.

A. DEBTOR

Prolan was founded in 1990 and operates in the communication and information technology market. The company benefited from the market reserve introduced by the Brazilian government for companies engaging in such kind of activities, and achieved a steady growth. Subsequently, with the opening of the market to foreign competitors, most Brazilian companies engaged in these activities were closed or declared bankrupt. Prolan, however, succeeded in maintaining its activities, as its clients included large companies of the telecom and bank sectors and government agencies.

As a consequence of the worldwide crisis that hit the information technology segment, particularly the telecom sector, preceded by the enormous devaluation of Brazilian currency in 1999, Prolan was faced with serious financial reverses.

B. *Preventive Concordata*

To avoid being declared bankrupt, Prolan filed for *preventive concordata (concordata preventiva)* at the Second Lower Civil Court in São Paulo before the NBRL became effective. Prolan was supposed to pay its unsecured creditors within two years, but this proved to be unfeasible and the company would have its bankruptcy adjudicated. After the entry into force of the NBRL, Prolan attempted to sign a collective agreement with all its creditors with a view to putting an end to its preventive concordata, but it did not succeed in obtaining the adhesion of all its creditors affected by the plan. As a result, Prolan was unable to file a petition for voluntary discontinuance of its preventive concordata. Therefore, on the verge of being declared bankrupt because of a merely procedural matter, despite having obtained the agreement of a significant portion of its creditors, Prolan elected to avail itself of the benefits of the NBRL.

C. Out-of-Court Reorganization Plan

Prolan, with the intention of availing itself to the Out-of-Court Reorganization by Enforcement of Agreement to implement new payment terms on all its creditors, called a General Meeting of Creditors.[40] At this meeting, Prolan provided its creditors with its business plan, cash flow projection as well as with a new proposal for payment to its creditors. The new proposal basically consisted of a payment of an equal sum to each creditor, so that at the end of the first year 36 per cent of its creditors would have been fully paid at the end of the second year other 33 per cent of its creditors would have been paid and thus successively in a manner that all credits would have been settled in 2010. The value of the annual payment increased in the same proportion as the projected growth of the Prolan business. If Prolan generated a cash surplus, this would be used to accelerate payment of creditors in accordance with the criteria set out in the plan.

This plan relied on the adhesion of 92 per cent of the unsecured claims out of a total debt of approximately BRL 33 million. It also provided for the possibility of the voluntary adhesion of labour creditors, which hold claims of approximately BRL 3 million.[41]

---

40. This meeting of creditors was held prior to filing of the Out-of-court Reorganization, but it is not required and would suffice for creditors to ratify their attendance in writing. On the other hand, at least in theory, no meeting of creditors may be held after distribution of the petition.
41. In an Out-of-court reorganization by enforcement of agreement, the reorganization plan cannot be imposed on creditors holding labour-related claims. The adhesion of such creditors must be voluntary.

D. REORGANIZATION BY ENFORCEMENT OF AGREEMENT

On 3 April 2006, Prolan filed its Out-of-court Reorganization along with its initial petition, all documents prescribed by the NBRL including the reorganization plan with the adhesion of 92 per cent of the credits affected by the plan. Prolan also evidenced that there was no prior reorganization petition and, therefore, no hindrance to the distribution of the reorganization petition.[42]

Subsequently, Prolan provided proof of the notice sent to all its creditors with respect to the Out-of-court Reorganization petition and to the term for oppositions, and published the mandatory notices in the official gazette and newspapers.

Some creditors opposed the plan, alleging that their credits included in the plan were accounted/registered at a lower value. Prolan admitted its error as to the opposed credits and rectified the reorganization plan to state the correct values.[43]

Moreover, one of the creditors alleged that a document submitted by the debtor was not consistent with the applicable legal formalities. The debtor clarified that there was no formal mistake or omission in such contested document.

The Public Attorney's Office[44] has not been offered the opportunity to render its opinion on the case. However, the Second Lower Bankruptcy and Reorganization Court rendered a decision ultimately homologating the plan proposed at the very first Reorganization by Enforcement of Agreement filed in São Paulo.

Nevertheless, two creditors filed motions for clarifications against the court decision which homologated the plan. The first creditor alleged the existence of a material error concerning the amount attributed to its credit. The second creditor claimed that the decision should be clarified to note that its credit is not subject to the effects of the plan.

On 19 October 2006, another decision was rendered by the court according to which: (1) the motion for clarification filed by the first creditor was granted, essentially to ratify the amount of its claim, as requested; and, (2) the motion for clarification filed by the second creditor was rejected, noted that the debtor

---

42. In this respect, judicial reorganization is the procedure that replaced the former *preventive concordata*. Therefore, in my opinion, the legal provision that prevents the debtor from resorting to an Out-of-court Reorganization when it has a 'pending' judicial reorganization would apply to the case. In other words, while under *preventive concordata*, Prolan or any other debtor could not, in principle, resort to an Out-of-court Reorganization to impose its plan on the creditors that did not sign the plan, leading to dismissal of the preventive *concordata* proceeding. However, the trend of the Brazilian Judiciary when the Previous Law was still in force was to relax the law's formal requirements if – in the case at hand – the solution found better met the law's purpose, which seems to be the case of Prolan.
43. There is no legal provision allowing for adjustments and/or rectifications of the plan by the debtor. However, considering that the debtor could propose another plan if that one was not ratified, and in light of the principle of procedural economy and less burdensome conditions, it seems reasonable that the solution given by Prolan be accepted.
44. There is no legal provision determining that the Public Attorney's Office issue its opinion, and legal writings are highly controversial when it comes to the need of granting the Public Attorney's Office access to the case docket so that it express itself on the reorganization plan and any oppositions filed against it.

had obtained the prior approval and confirmation of more than ⅗ of the creditors[45] affected by the plan which would bind all creditors. It was additionally noted that the interested creditor did not manage to demonstrate that the plan was not homogenous.[46] On 10 November 2006, Prolan filed a motion recognizing the material error in the amount of the credit attributed to the first creditor, as it had previously assigned 40 per cent of the respective claim to a third party.

Considering that all the procedural stages were already conducted, it is expected that in the next days the aforementioned second creditor will file the appropriate appeal against the decision that homologated the plan or such decision will become final and unappealable.

As a final remark, it is worth noting and stressing that the simplicity of the procedural rules governing the Reorganization by Enforcement of Agreement proceeding – in part explained because of the legislative moment in which they were introduced to the bill of law that eventually became the NBRL – did not prevent the judge from entertaining certain requests whose terms were not expressly provided for in the NBRL. More significantly, it did not prevent the judge from – in a judicious manner and heeding to the principles of procedural economy and the dictates of the NBRL – authorizing the debtor to make the necessary adjustments to the proposed plan, which ultimately culminated with the homologation of the plan by the court.

In one hand, one should note that with such a sensitive approach and determination of the case, the liquidation of a company – whose activities were considered viable by more than 90 per cent of its credits – was avoided. In the other hand, the Reorganization by Enforcement of Agreement mechanism prove to be an efficient alternative to the debtor in financial distress, allowing such debtor, jointly with a qualified majority of creditors, to impose a plan to the entire community of creditors, reducing the period of uncertainties concerning the debtor and the related procedural costs (especially when compared with the costs inherent to the judicial reorganization), all in benefit of the creditors, the debtor, its employees and the State.

---

45. Although the wording of the decision clearly used the expression 'creditors', consistently to the provisions of the NBRL it should have noted that the plan was approved and confirmed by three-fifths of the credits (instead of creditors).
46. In this respect, to be noted that even if the plan was to contemplate a non homogeneous treatment with respect to groups of creditors, there is no legal provision impeding the plan to provide such a different treatment, provided the parameters *indicated above* are observed.

Brazil

ANNEX: KEY LEGISLATION

Out-of-Court Reorganization

Article 161. A debtor who meets the requirements set forth in article 48 hereof may propose and negotiate an out-of-court reorganization plan with his creditors.

> **Paragraph 1.** The provisions of this chapter do not apply to the holders of tax or labour-related claims or to occupational accident claims, nor to those under article 49, paragraph 3, and article 86, main section, II hereof.
> **Paragraph 2.** The plan shall not contemplate accelerated maturity of debts or an unfavourable treatment of the creditors not subject to the plan.
> **Paragraph 3.** The debtor shall not file for ratification of an out-of-court plan if a petition for judicial reorganization is pending or if he has been granted judicial reorganization or ratification of another out-of-court reorganization plan within the last two (2) years.
> **Paragraph 4.** The petition for ratification of the out-of-court reorganization plan shall not entail a stay of rights, actions or enforcement proceedings, nor shall it prevent the creditors not subject to the out-of-court reorganization plan from filing for a decree of bankruptcy.
> **Paragraph 5.** After distribution of the petition for ratification, creditors cannot withdraw from being bound to the plan, unless with the express consent of the other signatories.
> **Paragraph 6.** The decision ratifying an out-of-court reorganization plan shall constitute a judicial enforcement instrument, pursuant to article 584, main section, III of Law No. 5869 of 11 January 1973 (Code of Civil Procedure).

Article 162. The debtor may file for court ratification of an out-of-court reorganization plan, attaching his reasons and a document stating the terms and conditions of said plan, signed by the creditors adhering thereto.

Article 163. The debtor may further file for ratification of an out-of-court reorganization plan that is binding on all creditors encompassed therein, provided that such plan has been signed by creditors representing over three-fifths (3/5) of all claims of each kind encompassed therein.

> **Paragraph 1.** The plan may encompass all of one or more kinds of claims provided for in article 83, main section, II, IV, V, VI and VIII hereof, or a group of creditors of the same kind and subject to similar payment conditions; once this plan is ratified, it shall be binding on all creditors of the kinds encompassed therein, solely with respect to claims constituted up to the date of the petition for ratification.
> **Paragraph 2.** For purposes of ascertaining the percentage provided for in the main section of this article, claims not included in the out-of-court reorganization plan shall not be taken into consideration, and their amount and original conditions of payment shall not be altered.

Paragraph 3. For exclusive purposes of ascertaining the percentage provided for in the main section of this article:

I. foreign currency-denominated claims shall be converted into domestic currency at the exchange rate prevailing on the day before plan is signed; and
II. claims held by the persons listed in article 43 hereof shall not be computed.

Paragraph 4. Upon disposal of an asset given as collateral, the end or replacement of said guarantee shall only be permissible upon the express approval of the creditor holding the respective guarantee.

Paragraph 5. In foreign currency-denominated claims, the exchange variation may only be ruled out if the creditor holding the respective claim expressly approves a different provision in the out-of-court reorganization plan.

Paragraph 6. For ratification of the plan under this article, in addition to the documents provided for in article 162, main section hereof, the debtor shall attach:

I. a statement of the debtor's equity condition;
II. accounting statements for the last financial year and those drawn up especially to support the petition, pursuant to article 51, main section, II hereof; and
III. documents evidencing the powers of the respective signatories to novate or compromise, coupled with a full nominal list of creditors stating their addresses, the kind, rating and updated amount of the claim, and specifying its origin, the system of the respective maturity dates and the accounting records of each pending transaction.

Article 164. Upon receipt of the petition for ratification of an out-of-court reorganization plan under articles 162 and 163 hereof, the judge shall order the publication of a notice in the official press and in a newspaper circulated nationwide or in the localities of the debtor's headquarters and branches, calling all of the debtor's creditors to challenge the out-of-court reorganization plan, with due regard for paragraph 3 of this article.

Paragraph 1. During the public notice period, the debtor shall evidence that a letter was sent to all creditors domiciled or headquartered in Brazil and subject to the plan, informing of distribution of the petition, the conditions of the plan, and the term for opposition.

Paragraph 2. Creditors shall have thirty (30) days from publication of the notice to challenge the plan, attaching the proof of their claims.

Paragraph 3. To oppose ratification of the plan in their statement, creditors may only allege:

1. failure to meet the minimum percentage requirement established in article 163, main section hereof;
2. performance of any of the acts under article 94, III, or article 130 hereof, or non-compliance with any requirement hereunder;
3. non-compliance with any other requirement of law.

Paragraph 4. Opposition being filed, a term of five (5) days shall start for the debtor to answer.

Paragraph 5. Upon elapse of the period set forth in paragraph 4 of this article, the case record shall be promptly concluded and sent to the judge for examination of any oppositions and for a decision within five (5) days on the out-of-court reorganization plan, ratifying it by judgment if he considers it does not entail the performance of acts under article 130 hereof and that there are no other irregularities to make its rejection advisable.

Paragraph 6. If there is evidence of simulation of claims or defective representation of the creditors who adhere the plan, ratification thereof shall be denied.

Paragraph 7. The decision may be appealed without stay of proceedings.

Paragraph 8. If the plan is not ratified, the debtor may, after the formalities have been performed, file a new petition for ratification of an out-of-court reorganization plan.

Article 165. The out-of-court reorganization plan is effective after its judicial ratification.

Paragraph 1. A plan may lawfully establish effects prior to ratification, provided that they solely relate to a change in the amount or conditions of payment of the signatory creditors.

Paragraph 2. In the event under paragraph 1 of this article, if the judge later rejects the plan, the signatory creditors regain the right to enforce their claims on the original terms, less any amounts actually paid.

Article 166. If the ratified out-of-court reorganization plan involves judicial sale of branches or separate business units of the debtor, the judge shall order that this be performed, with due regard, as applicable, for the provisions of article 142 hereof.

Article 167. The provisions of this Chapter do not rule out other types of private settlement between the debtor and his creditors.

Chapter 5
Canada

Canada's Expedited Debt Restructuring

Kevin P. McElcheran

ACRONYMS, ABBREVIATIONS & DEFINED TERMS

BIA	Bankruptcy and Insolvency Act (R.S., 1985, c. B-3)
CAD	Canadian Dollar
CCAA	*Companies' Creditors Arrangement Act* (R.S., 1985, c. C-36).
Monitor	The 'supervisor' appointed by the court in a proceeding under the *Companies' Creditors Arrangement Act*. The CCAA sets out minimum obligations of the Monitor but the court can and usually does supplement the minimum powers.
PPSA legislation	*Personal Property Securities Acts* of different Canadian provinces
Receiver	An officer appointed by the court with the power to operate the debtor's business and to offer the assets of the debtor for sale. A Receiver can also be appointed privately with the aim of achieving a restructuring.
Soundair case	*Royal Bank v. Soundair Corp.*, (1991), 4 O.R. (3d) 1 (C.A.).
Trustee	The 'supervisor' appointed by the court in a proceeding under the *Bankruptcy and Insolvency Act*. Its powers and responsibilities are set out in the BIA itself.
US	United States
Vesting Order	Orders that the purchaser will acquire the assets free and clear of the claims of creditors of the debtor in a court supervised receiverships' or CCAA proceedings sale approved by the court
Wise case	*Peoples Department Stores Inc. (Trustee of) v. Wise*, 2004 SCC 68, [2004] 3 S.C.R. 461

I. INTRODUCTION

Before Air Canada's insolvency filing in 2003, formal Canadian insolvency proceedings were straightforward, practical and expeditious, particularly when compared to formal insolvency proceedings under Chapter 11 of the US Bankruptcy Code.[1] Even large companies substantially completed a restructuring or sale of the business as a going concern in six to eight months from the date of filing. Any case that approached its first anniversary without resolution was exceptional.

This practical and expeditious Canadian approach to fixing troubled companies, even in formal proceedings, somehow lost its influence with the filing of Air Canada under the *Companies' Creditors Arrangement Act* ('CCAA')[2] on April fool's day in 2003. After a number of 'near death' experiences and countless court appearances to resolve even mundane issues, Air Canada emerged from CCAA proceedings 18 months after its filing date. Not to be outdone, Stelco, Canada' largest steel company, took 27 months (from January 2004 until March 2006) to exit from its CCAA proceedings.

The professional fees incurred by all parties involved in the CCAA proceedings of each of Air Canada and Stelco were measured in hundreds of millions of dollars, but professional fees were only a fraction of the social and economic cost of these mammoth and unwieldy restructuring cases.

Notwithstanding the immense cost, both cases yielded limited success. Instead of renewing and revitalizing these icons of Canadian business, the bitter multi-party conflicts that characterized the formal insolvency proceedings spread like a pall over all of their business activities. The stench of acrimony that permeated the insolvency process, particularly in relation to their employees, continues to pervade their businesses operations, even after emergence from the formal process.

These recent experiences have reminded Canadian insolvency practitioners of the many benefits of less formal and expedited restructuring processes. A number of alternative methods of restructuring financially distressed businesses expeditiously and efficiently will be described in this chapter. A number of the methods discussed will include court proceedings or expedited formal proceedings. Accordingly, the discussion will begin with a description of the various formal proceedings that are available in Canada.

II. FORMAL INSOLVENCY PROCEEDINGS IN CANADA

Canadian insolvency proceedings can be divided into two categories. The first category is restructuring proceedings. The second category is sale proceedings, including receivership and bankruptcy.

---

1. 11 USC.
2. An Act to facilitate compromises and arrangements between companies and their creditors (R.S., 1985, c. C-36).

A.   RESTRUCTURING PROCEEDINGS

Restructuring proceedings are commonly initiated under either the Proposal provisions[3] of the *Bankruptcy and Insolvency Act* ('BIA')[4] or the CCAA. These statutes are similar in that they both provide a mechanism by which a debtor can compromise the obligations owing to all members of affected classes of creditors by a favourable creditor vote in each class and court approval. Once approved by the court, the proposal or plan of arrangement binds all members of the affected classes including those class members who did not vote or voted against the proposal or plan of arrangement. However, they are dissimilar in many other respects which may affect the implementation of 'expeditious' restructuring processes.

The BIA and the CCAA differ fundamentally in the degree to which judicial discretion impacts the conduct of restructuring processes under each such statute. Judicial discretion plays a minor role in BIA restructuring proceedings as the BIA provides for an automatic statutory stay of all proceedings against the debtor. The initial stay of 30 days is obtained as a matter of right by the filing of a statutory notice of the debtor's intention to file a proposal to its creditors. That stay can be extended by court order for up to five additional months or replaced with a new stay by the filing of a proposal on which the creditors may vote.

A debtor wishing to restructure under the CCAA is not entitled to an automatic statutory stay. It must have debt exceeding CAD 5 million to qualify and must apply to the court for an 'Initial Order' that will contain stay provisions to protect the debtor's business while it develops a plan. Because the CCAA stay is a discretionary order of a judge rather than the application of a statutory provision, it is more case specific and flexible in its terms. The stay may also be combined with injunctive relief that may enhance the protections that would be available under the statutory BIA stay and, although the initial stay is limited to 30 days, it can be extended indefinitely. Because of this flexibility of the CCAA stay protections, the CCAA is the formal procedure of choice for insolvent Canadian companies seeking to restructure their debt.

Both the CCAA and the BIA require approval of the proposal or plan of arrangement by all affected classes of creditors and the approval or 'sanction' of the court. No affected class of creditors can be 'crammed down' although, within classes, dissenting creditors are 'crammed' in the sense that they may be outvoted.

The vote required to pass the plan in each class is more than 50 per cent in number and 66⅔ per cent in value of proven claims voting in the class. The voting rules may provide a strategic opportunity for large creditors to assert negative control over the plan approval process. Any creditor in a class containing only two or fewer creditors and any creditor controlling more than 33.3 per cent of a class by value has a veto over the plan and may use the veto power to insist on favourable terms for the class.

In Canadian restructuring proceedings, the classification of creditors has key strategic significance to the success or failure of the plan. The courts apply a

---

3. Part III, Section 50 et seq. of the *Bankruptcy and Insolvency Act* (R.S., 1985, c. B-3).
4. An Act respecting bankruptcy and insolvency (R.S., 1985, c. B-3).

'commonality of interest' test, which classifies secured creditors having regard to such matters as the similarity of the legal remedies available to them and the proposed treatment of these claims under the debtor's restructuring plan or proposal. Thinking practically, courts have been reluctant to permit the creation of too many classes because class fragmentation makes the restructuring process difficult to manage. Consequently, all unsecured creditors will be included in the same class in restructuring cases under the CCAA. However, secured creditors will often have unique elements to their claims and relative priorities that often provide the basis for a separate class.

B.   SALE PROCEEDINGS

Sale proceedings are often supervised and implemented by the court but may sometimes be effected by secured creditors enforcing their private security rights. They result in the transfer of the debtor's business assets to a purchaser either on a going concern or liquidation basis. Whether the sale results in the continuation of the business by the purchaser or its liquidation, the proceeds of the sale will be distributed among the creditors in accordance with the priority of their claims.

1.   Court Supervised Sale Proceedings

Court supervised receivership proceedings are a common alternative insolvency process to restructuring proceedings. Canadian courts have jurisdiction under local provincial laws and under the Canada-wide BIA to appoint a receiver and manager with the power to operate the debtor's business and to offer the assets of the debtor for sale ('Receiver'). The Receiver appointed by the court is an officer of the court and is not the agent or representative of any party or affected stakeholder. As a court officer, the Receiver has a duty to balance the interests of parties affected by the performance of its duties. Almost universally, Receivers appointed by courts are accredited insolvency professionals associated with an accounting firm.

The sale methodology adopted by the Receiver will vary from case to case depending on the nature of the business or assets. The Receiver will consult with significant stakeholders such as secured creditors and employee representatives before it implements a sale process. In large or difficult cases, Receivers often retain professional advisors such as investment bankers and seek advice from the court on notice to the key stakeholders before marketing the debtor's assets and business for sale.

Court receivership sale processes typically adopt a four stage approach. In the first stage, the Receiver will prepare an initial marketing document or 'teaser' describing the assets and business available for sale which it will distribute widely. In the second stage, the Receiver will prepare a confidential information memorandum which it will make available to interested purchasers who are prepared to sign a confidentiality agreement. At the end of the second stage, interested purchasers are required to submit a non-binding letter of intent. In the third stage, the Receiver will select a short list of candidates who will undertake more extensive due diligence and will prepare to submit an offer to the Receiver. In the fourth stage, the Receiver will select leading candidates and negotiate a final agreement that it will recommend to the court for approval.

In most respects, the sale process that a Receiver would undertake resembles a sales process that any company would undertake if it were interested in selling its own business. The differences arise from the circumstances of the sale. Because of the financial distress of the debtor it is often difficult to maintain going concern value while the business is being operated by the Receiver. As a result, Receivership sale processes often run on a tight timetable. Additionally, the Receiver has fewer options than a normal seller. The 'must sell' atmosphere that is an inevitable companion of a Receivership sale process tends to favour buyers at the expense of value for creditors.

The typical Canadian sale process does not generally permit overbids and in that sense it differs from a typical sale under section 363 of the US Bankruptcy Code.[5] In the US, unlike in Canada, courts usually require that any offer made to purchase business assets be subject to higher and better bids. As a result, the court approval stage of a US process often includes an auction. Because of the risk that an interested purchaser may lose the auction after 'making the market' with its initial bid, agreements to purchase businesses in US bankruptcy sale processes usually include 'bid protections' including break fees payable to the purchaser if they are over-bid, reimbursement of costs incurred in due diligence and documentation of the deal and minimum over-bid requirements.

As will be discussed in more detail in this chapter, one important reason that Canadian court supervised sale procedures have not included a court auction has been the time and care taken in the marketing of the business by the Receiver. Canadian courts have permitted the Receiver to design and conduct a marketing process which, in the view of the Receiver, is appropriate for the specific business and to negotiate a sale that is commercially reasonable. Canadian courts concluded that permitting overbids after the Receiver had conducted a comprehensive marketing process and negotiated an acceptable offer would undermine the Receiver's position in such negotiations.

The essential principle accepted by Canadian courts has been that the Receiver will be able to achieve better results through an extended sale process designed to generate competitive bids and a private negotiation of the final business terms than could be achieved through a court auction. As will be discussed *below*, when restructuring or sale proceedings are expedited, the time for conducting an extended sale process under court supervision in an insolvency proceeding is sacrificed in the interests of efficiency. Accordingly, if an expedited sale process is to be approved by the court, it becomes necessary to find other ways to establish the value of the assets included in the sale. Consequently, in an expedited sale process, a court may be more inclined to order a court supervised auction, similar to a typical auction under section 363 of the US *Bankruptcy Code* to demonstrate that the expedited sale has generated the best value available.

---

5. 11 U.S.C. § 363.

In most Canadian provinces (the sole exception being Alberta), Canadian courts supervising CCAA restructuring proceedings also have the jurisdiction to approve sales of all or substantially all of the debtor's business. The courts in Alberta have been reluctant to approve such sales because, in their view, CCAA proceedings should be limited to restructuring proceedings. Notwithstanding the misgivings of the Alberta Court of Appeal, court supervised sales in CCAA proceedings are common in Canada.

The legal principles that apply to sales by court appointed Receivers are the same for sales by debtors who are in CCAA proceedings. The principal differences are in the context of the sale and the involvement of the debtor company in the sale process. In Receivership proceedings, the sale is conducted by the Receiver as the Receiver displaces the debtor company's directors and officers. In Canadian restructuring proceedings the directors and officers of the debtor company continue to manage the business under supervision of the court and its representative, a Trustee,[6] in a BIA Proposal proceeding, or a Monitor,[7] in a CCAA proceeding (universally, an accredited insolvency professional with an accounting background).

If the debtor is seeking to sell any significant portion of its business, the Trustee/Monitor will be required by the court to take an active role to ensure that the sale is conducted in a fair and effective manner according to the principles set out in the leading case *Royal Bank v. Soundair Corp.* ('Soundair case').[8] Those principles, which apply to any Canadian court approved sale process established that the intervening court should consider:

(1) whether the Receiver (or debtor) has made a sufficient effort to get the best price and has not acted improvidently;
(2) the interests of all parties affected by the sale;
(3) the efficacy and integrity of the process by which offers were obtained; and
(4) whether there was any unfairness in the working out of the process.

Sales in court supervised receiverships or CCAA proceedings must be approved by the court on notice to affected creditors and stakeholders, including all secured creditors. When the court approves the sale, it also orders that the purchaser will acquire the assets free and clear of the claims of creditors of the debtor. Such an order is called a 'Approval and Vesting Order' or simply a 'Vesting Order'. The Vesting Order converts creditors' claims from claims to the assets included in the sale to claims on the proceeds of the sale which will rank in the same priority of distribution as the corresponding claims on the assets.

2. Private Sale Proceedings

A secured party or a private Receiver has the right to dispose of collateral that is moveable property upon the default of the debtor in compliance with the

---

6. The 'supervisor' appointed by the court in a proceeding under the BIA ('Trustee'). Its powers and responsibilities are set out in the BIA itself.
7. The 'supervisor' appointed by the court in a proceeding under the CCAA ('Monitor'). The CCAA sets out minimum obligations of the Monitor but the court can and usually does supplement the minimum powers.
8. (1991), 4 O.R. (3d) 1 (C.A.).

mandatory requirements of provincial legislation governing such security rights ('PPSA legislation').[9] Similarly, with respect to real or immoveable property, the mortgagee or its Receiver may dispose of the charged property in compliance with provincial legislation in respect of the enforcement of mortgages. In Ontario this may be achieved through a private sale in accordance with the *Mortgages Act*.[10] In most other provinces, court proceedings will be necessary to complete a sale of real property.

Through the effect of PPSA legislation and, in Ontario, the *Mortgages Act*, the sale by the private Receiver discharges the interest of the debtor and the security interest of the secured party making the sale and, where the buyer of the collateral buys in good faith for value, any security interests subordinate to that of the secured party making the sale. Of course, any such sale by the Receiver will be subject to any interest which ranks as a prior encumbrance on the property.

The proceeds of disposition are to be applied first against the reasonable expenses of the private Receiver in making the disposition and preparing the collateral for disposition, and then against the obligation owed to the secured party. While the disposition of collateral pursuant to security discharges the interest of the debtor and all subsequent security interests in the collateral, such interests continue in the proceeds of the sale pursuant to PPSA legislation and the *Mortgages Act*. Accordingly, any surplus after satisfaction of the entitlements of the appointing secured creditor must be paid to parties with subordinate interests in the collateral in order of the priority of their claims.

Both PPSA legislation and the mortgage enforcement legislation contain mandatory statutory procedures for the realization of security in personal property and real estate, respectively. In Ontario, where private mortgage sales are permitted, both the Ontario PPSA legislation and the *Mortgages Act* require the secured creditor to send written notice to subordinate creditors with registered security, as well as the debtor and any guarantors, that the secured creditor intends to dispose of the assets subject to the security unless the secured debt is redeemed within the period of notice provided in the statute.

However, PPSA legislation does not always require notice. For example (1) where the collateral is perishable; (2) where the collateral is of a type customarily sold on a recognized market; (3) where the cost of storage of the collateral is disproportionately high relative to its value; or (4) where the disposition is made by a Receiver and manager in the ordinary course of the debtor's business, notice can be foregone. In the case of PPSA security, the notice period may be waived by the parties entitled to the notice after the security becomes enforceable. In the case of mortgage security, the *Mortgages Act* sets out a procedure for obtaining an order abbreviating or dispensing with the notice requirements in appropriate cases.

PPSA legislation affords the private Receiver a considerable degree of latitude in how it disposes of the collateral, provided that every aspect of the disposition

---

9. PPSA stands for *Personal Property Security Act*. There are different provincial PPSAs in Canada.
10. R.S.O. 1990, Chapter M.40.

is commercially reasonable. What is commercially reasonable is to be determined objectively. In the context of marketing the assets for sale, the Receiver must conduct the sale in a manner that is consistent with the nature of the collateral. The Receiver must be able to demonstrate that it has reasonably canvassed the marketplace and has attempted to maximize the sale proceeds. In considering what is reasonable in the circumstances, the court may take into account that a receivership implies distress sale conditions. Therefore, the Receiver would not necessarily be expected to sell the assets for what could be obtained in a normal market and the Receiver is not required to hold the assets until the market for them improves.

III. THE BASIC REQUIREMENTS OF AN EXPEDITED PROCESS

Insolvency proceedings shake a business and its stakeholders to the core. The stakes are high. Financial creditors face substantial losses of their financial investments in the debtor. Trade creditors may lose a valued customer. Employees face job loss and personal financial distress. Pensioners may lose health benefits and pension entitlements. Because of these dire implications of commercial insolvency, Canadian lawmakers have enacted formal insolvency and security enforcement legislation that emphasizes participation and procedural fairness.

Participation requires that everyone who may be affected by the restructuring or sale be given notice and an opportunity to participate in the proceedings. Procedural fairness requires information flow to participants and time to assess and respond to such information so that they can be in a position to vote on a plan or proposal or attend court and oppose or support the sale or restructuring. Procedural fairness takes time to allow participants in the process to take a meaningful role.

Although a fair process takes time to unfold, the amount of time the business must remain embroiled in the formal insolvency process may eliminate opportunities to revitalize the business. Time spent embroiled in the formal insolvency process may harm the business through the loss of key customers and employees who choose not to wait and see whether the debtor will be able to restructure and continue its business. Time spent embroiled in litigation and controversy in formal insolvency proceedings increases professional costs that must ultimately be borne by the debtor and its stakeholders.

This conflict between principle, requiring participation and procedural fairness to ensure that important creditor interests are taken into account, and the very practical risk that those same interests will be prejudiced by the delay and cost of the fair process, defines the challenge. An 'expedited insolvency process' must be effective and efficient but also fairly balance legitimate creditor interests. Defining the challenge in this way, however, assists us in designing efficient insolvency processes that are fair to the constituents of each case. In Canada, we are fortunate in having relatively flexible insolvency laws that allow the key participants to do just that.

Because the principle that affected stakeholders must have notice and fair opportunity to participate is fundamental to the insolvency process, there is a direct correlation between the number of parties affected by the insolvency process and the procedural complexity that will be a necessary element of the restructuring process. Accordingly, designing an expedited and efficient insolvency process appropriate for any particular business must start with a clear understanding of the restructuring objectives of the business. From that starting point, the leaders of the restructuring must identify the stakeholders in the business who will be most affected by the restructuring (given the restructuring objectives). Because the more stakeholders that are affected, the more complex and potentially time consuming the process will become, it may be necessary to re-evaluate some less essential restructuring objectives if too many stakeholders will be affected.

In the balance of this chapter, specific alternative processes that may be available to restructure a Canadian business on an expedited basis will be considered. The formal restructuring processes available in Canada provide the framework for expedited restructuring alternatives. Like formal restructuring processes, expedited restructuring processes fall into two categories, legally enforceable compromises of creditor claims and sales of continuing businesses.

A. EXPEDITED CREDITOR COMPROMISES

1. Private debt restructuring

a. *Bilateral Settlements*

The simplest form of debt restructuring is a contractual settlement of debts owed by the debtor company to one or more of its creditors. In a restructuring settlement, the creditor agrees to accept less than it thinks it is legally entitled to recover from the defendant because the creditor believes that the debtor may become insolvent and its business may fail if the creditor insists on payment of its full legal entitlement.

Imbedded in the decision of a creditor to settle its claim on a bilateral basis, in part because of the debtor's potential insolvency, is the acceptance that other creditors will receive payment in full and may not suffer the same 'insolvency discount' in the payment of their claims. The motivation of the creditor accepting less than it believes it is owed is to achieve an expeditious and efficient resolution of its claim; to solve the problem now and move on. The creditor accepting the settlement makes the judgment that any increased settlement payment that could theoretically be achieved by insisting that other creditors also accept an insolvency discount would be lost in the extra time and complexity that would result from expanding the number of participants. Either the extra costs would eliminate the benefit or the settlement itself would be lost because other creditors may not agree.

Bilateral settlements with insolvent debtors run the risk of challenge by other creditors if the debtor subsequently becomes subject to formal insolvency proceedings under the BIA or the *Winding-up and Restructuring Act*.[11] Both statutes permit the Trustee in bankruptcy or liquidator, as the case may be, to seek a declaration that a payment (or grant of security) by the debtor, when insolvent, to a creditor less than three months prior to the bankruptcy or winding-up, is void as a 'fraudulent preference' and must be repaid to the Trustee or liquidator. The review period for preferential transactions is one year if the recipient is related to the debtor. The intended effect of preference provisions of Canadian insolvency law is to ensure that the debtor's assets are fairly distributed among its creditors.

While a bilateral settlement may be attacked as preferential, defences may be available to the recipient if it gives consideration for the payment. Under Canadian insolvency law, a fraudulent preference must be 'intentional'. That is, the debtor must intend to give the creditor preferential treatment. Such intention is presumed, if the effect of the transaction is 'to give the creditor a preference over other creditors'. However, the presumption can be rebutted by evidence of another intention such as to compromise a debt that is due and owing and to continue in business.

In order to further mitigate concerns about preference risk, a creditor considering a bilateral settlement may insist on structuring adjustments that reduce or eliminate such risk, although care must be taken that the structuring alternative does not create different risks. Strategies that address preference risk begin with a careful examination of the elements of a preference.

First, a preference must be a transaction between the debtor and a creditor. Accordingly, a payment from someone other than the debtor cannot be a preference over the claims of other creditors of that debtor. However, if payment or security is accepted from a person other than the debtor, a creditor accepting the payment must investigate the impact of the payment on the constituents of the payor. If the payment or security renders the payor insolvent, its creditors may attack the payment.

Second, a transaction is a preference only if it is granted or made less than three months prior to the bankruptcy or winding-up. Although the creditor cannot control the timing of a bankruptcy or winding-up, it should provide itself some protection from a later challenge by making any compromise it gives in the transaction conditional on the payments or other consideration given by the debtor being 'irreversible'. Such a provision cannot protect the transaction from attack but will permit the creditor to assert the full amount of its original claim in the event that it is ordered to return any consideration it received in return for a compromise of the debt.

Third, preferences are limited to transactions that relate to obligations outstanding at the time of the payment or grant of security. It is not a preference to receive security or immediate payment for new supply. Accordingly, creditors

---

11. An Act respecting the winding-up and restructuring of companies (R.S., 1985, c. W-11).

should structure any settlement with an ongoing customer to ensure that any on-going supply is paid or secured.

b. *Multilateral Settlements*

If, instead of accepting that other creditors will be paid in full, creditors asked to compromise their claims insist that other creditors must also compromise their claims, the negotiation of the required multi-party settlement will necessarily become more complex. Further, the restructuring effort will fail unless the debtor is able to achieve settlements that are binding on all affected creditors.

Because every participating creditor has a veto and can stymie any private restructuring initiative, multilateral private restructuring agreements are rarely viable unless a compelling economic reason forces all affected creditors to work together. Two situations that sometimes offer an opportunity to restructure a debtor privately are situations in which (1) the number of participating creditors is relatively small and those that are participating expect a common benefit from participation or (2) the participants have contractual arrangements among them that permit acceptance of the settlement without unanimous agreement among the creditors.

i. Common Benefit Restructuring

An example of the first type of restructuring is a settlement between a contractor and its subcontractors on a construction project. Each of the subcontractors has a common interest in the completion of the project by the contractor because their best source of payment of their claims is the payment of the contract price by the owner on the completion of the job. If they terminate the supply of services to the project, the owner may terminate the contract and hire a new contractor, setting off the additional cost against the contract price payable to the first contractor.

In this example, all of the participants in the settlement have a common interest in the preservation of the asset they all share, the contract price payable by the owner to their debtor, the contractor. Also, the completion of the contract may require their continued efforts and cooperation with each other and the contractor. Their mutual interest and the economic benefits of cooperation may motivate them to participate in a multilateral settlement designed to preserve the shared asset and to allow the contractor, the common debtor, to continue as a viable business to contribute to the preservation of that shared asset.

The mechanics of completion of such a settlement may be simple and straightforward. In essence, each supplier would agree to complete its subcontract and the debtor/contractor would ensure that the contract price payable by the owner, together with an additional contribution by the contractor that is acceptable to the creditors, will be shared on an agreed basis among the suppliers.

Under Canadian construction law the sub-contractors of an insolvent contractor have a statutory trust interest in the contract price payable to the contractor on completion that ranks in priority to the claims of secured creditors. Obviously, the situation illustrated by the example could be reproduced in many other commercial situations in which cooperation is necessary to the completion of a project by the granting of a security interest in the contract price to secure performance of the settlement. However, in non-construction situations, it will be necessary to also obtain the support and cooperation of any secured creditor that has a prior secured interest in the contract price.

A variation on the same theme would be a multiparty settlement between suppliers and a customer that is a single source supplier to the auto industry. As the end user requires price reductions and other concessions that put its single source (and single customer) supplier in financial distress, the single source supplier may seek to restructure its relationships with the next tier of suppliers through a multiparty adjustment of its contractual rights and obligations.

The common theme of these examples are the relatively small number of participants who must agree to adjust or compromise their legal rights and a common objective among the debtor and the participants that focuses their attention on a concrete goal that is in their mutual best interest to achieve. Additionally, the fruit of the common endeavour must be available solely to the participants in the settlement. In the construction example, the subcontractors are protected by a statutory trust in most jurisdictions in Canada. However, in a non-construction context, without the benefit of statutory priority, even these simple 'common objective' restructuring arrangements would be impossible without the consent of any secured creditor with a priority claim over the consideration offered to the participating creditors.

ii. Delegated Settlement Authority

An example of the second type of private multilateral restructuring would be a settlement with a lender syndicate that has delegated decision making authority or has agreed among themselves that the syndicate members' common legal rights may be compromised or adjusted through a lender vote or the actions of a 'steering committee' or agent.

Private restructuring of syndicated loans are very common. However, they are only manageable if the syndicate is small and cohesive or if the compromise itself does not require unanimous approval of the lenders. The terms of each syndicated loan are somewhat unique but follow a familiar pattern. In most cases, any compromise of the principal amount or reduction of interest will require unanimous approval of the lenders. Other compromises that may be of assistance to the debtor and may be approved by majority vote include waivers of some covenants and, in some cases, deferrals of enforcement steps.

Because the powers of the agent or steering committee of syndicated loans to compromise the legal rights of the lenders are limited, any private restructuring with a lender syndicate will be similarly limited in scope. If the amount of the debt cannot be reduced or converted to another form, such as equity, without unanimous approval, private restructuring will be difficult to achieve for those debtors that need to reduce the leverage in their businesses. As a result, private restructurings with syndicated lenders are permanent solutions only for businesses that are suffering temporary set backs but will ultimately satisfy all creditor claims.

Otherwise, deferrals and standstills that may be negotiated with the agent or steering committee of a syndicate will be temporary steps on the path to a more substantive restructuring under a formal process which facilitates principal reduction or conversion through a special majority vote or permits the sale of the business free and clear of creditor claims.

c. *Disclosure and Confidentiality*

Essential to any compromise based on the inability of the debtor to pay the full amount of the debt is the disclosure of intimate financial information about the business of the debtor. A creditor cannot be expected to compromise the amount it will receive unless it is able to confirm by due diligence that the debtor is, in fact, unable to pay the full amount of the debt.

In bilateral settlement agreements, disclosure of financial information by the debtor to the creditor can be protected by appropriate confidentiality agreements which may include a covenant by the creditor not to commence insolvency proceedings against the debtor. However, disclosure of financial information to larger groups of creditors, that may include competitors, can be harmful to the debtor and its business. As a practical matter, confidentiality agreements will be difficult to negotiate and, if negotiated, virtually impossible to enforce.

In Canada, the disclosure of financial information by the debtor, even in the context of settlement discussions, has very direct implications. It is an 'act of bankruptcy' and therefore, the basis of bankruptcy order for a debtor to exhibit 'to any meeting of his creditors any statement of assets and liabilities that shows he is insolvent, or presents or causes to be presented to any such meeting a written admission of his inability to pay his debts.

In a very real way, because the disclosure of financial information that is necessary to any compromise of debt is an act of bankruptcy in itself, the direct effect of attempting and failing to achieve a private restructuring may well be a creditor initiated formal insolvency process under the BIA. Through the appointment of a Trustee in bankruptcy in such informal proceedings, the debtor can lose control of its business and the insolvency process. If that happens, it will not matter if the majority of creditors would have accepted the private settlement that was proposed.

d. *Conclusions on the Subject of Private Restructuring*

In summary, private restructuring in Canada, is a fragile process. The reasons for this fragility are: (1) preference concerns if the restructuring is not successful in saving the business, participating creditors cannot be certain that they will be able to retain the benefits they receive in return for compromising their legal rights; (2) private compromises only affect participating creditors, even in successful restructuring arrangements, the compromises of some creditors will benefit others who do not contribute; (3) assets that must be available to offer in settlement may be subject to claims of secured creditors, the debtor may not be able to deliver when called upon to perform the settlement; (4) all creditors necessary for the settlement must agree to be bound, one holdout can frustrate the process; and (5) disclosure of financial information is a necessary part of the process, attempting to achieve a private restructuring exposes a debtor to the loss of control of its business through involuntary proceedings.

Despite these impediments and risks, all debtors should seriously consider initial settlement discussions with key creditor groups for two reasons. First, if successful and sufficiently complete, private, unanimous restructuring is the most effective and constructive resolution of a debtor's insolvency. Second, if a formal restructuring process is necessary, controlled communication and discussion with key creditors groups, even if unsuccessful in achieving a private restructuring, are critical steps toward the completion of an expedited formal proceeding in Canada.

IV. EFFICIENT AND EFFECTIVE COURT SUPERVISED REORGANIZATION PROCEDURES

A. THE FOCUSED PLAN

As outlined *above*, Canadian insolvency legislation provides the debtor with an opportunity to extricate itself from its insolvency through a court supervised and statutorily mandated restructuring process in which the debtor remains in possession of its assets, and control of the business enterprise. The most commonly used statutory restructuring vehicles of the CCAA and the BIA proposal provisions facilitate reorganization as an alternative to the liquidation of assets of business enterprises.

Plans of arrangement or compromise under the CCAA and proposals under the BIA are similar to private restructuring settlements in the sense that they are legally effective agreements between the insolvent debtor and its affected creditors that compromise the obligations owed by the debtor to the affected creditors. However, they differ from private restructuring settlements in the sense that the plan or proposal under the CCAA or BIA is binding on all affected creditors, even those that voted against its acceptance, if the required double majority (two-third in value and a majority in number of creditors who vote) accepts the plan or proposal and the plan or proposal is approved by the court.

Because the special majority of creditors within the class can impose the compromise on all members of the class with the result that the former obligations are replaced by the obligations undertaken under the plan or proposal, the BIA and the CCAA provide mechanisms to successfully restructure a business when a private restructuring would fail.

The statutory ability to impose a settlement on unwilling creditors is a powerful right. In order to insure that such a powerful right is not abused or misused, the BIA and the CCAA contain procedural safeguards that must be observed in all cases.

In order to ensure fair, but not necessarily equal, treatment of creditors by the plan or proposal, the restructuring statutes provide for the classification of creditor claims for the purposes of voting and distribution of the value offered in the plan or proposal using the principle of 'commonality of interest'. All affected classes must vote in favour of the plan or proposal.

In order to determine the identity and amount of the claims of all affected creditors, the restructuring statutes or orders made in restructuring proceedings provide procedures requiring all affected creditors to prove their claims against the debtor.

In order to ensure the fairness of the restructuring process, the dissemination of financial information necessary to permit the creditors to assess and vote for or against the plan or proposal and to assist the debtor and its creditors in the development of the plan, the restructuring statutes provide for the appointment of a Monitor in CCAA cases and a Trustee in proposals under the BIA. The Monitor or Trustee, as the case may be, is a court officer with broad and, in the case of the Monitor particularly, flexible powers and responsibilities which they must exercise for the benefit of all stakeholders of the debtor.

These principal elements of restructuring proceedings, the stay of creditor remedies, the classification and proof of creditor claims, the acceptance of the plan or proposal by a double majority vote, the supervision of the court, both through orders and the day to day supervision and guidance of the Monitor or Trustee, and the final sanction or approval by the court, form the framework of all restructuring proceedings of commercial enterprises in Canada.

Accepting and working with these basic elements, the embodiment of procedural and substantive fairness in any restructuring process, does not doom a Canadian restructuring proceeding to waste and delay. Canadian debtors can use Canada's insolvency laws to facilitate an effective and efficient restructuring process if the debtor and its key stakeholders focus on the real problems impeding the business and avoid battles that cannot be won or can only be won at a prohibitive cost. The key is to conceive and implement a **focused** restructuring plan.

B.   Six Steps to Implementing a Focused Restructuring Plan

1. Step One: Identify the Business Problem and Form a Responsive Business Plan

Because insolvency is a business problem, the return to viability of the business must start with a business plan that is responsive to the causes of the debtor's financial distress and, if effected, would return the debtor to viability.

Therefore, the management leaders of the debtor company must first engage in deep introspection, usually aided by a fresh set of eyes in the form of a turnaround professional, to discover the problems affecting the business and realistic business solutions to those problems. Both the problems and the solutions should be articulated in a business plan that is focused on the implementation of the business solution.

Beginning with a focused business plan, management and its advisors must then plan a restructuring process that is responsive to the business issues impacting the debtor's business and effectively implements solutions.

2. Step Two: Identify the Stakeholders who Must Compromise their Claims

The second step is identifying the constituents of the business who must contribute to the solution by compromising their legal rights in order to accomplish the business plan. Not every case requires all creditors to accept a compromise. When selecting which constituencies must contribute by compromising their rights, the debtor must bear in mind that the greater the number of creditors who are affected by the plan, the more complicated and time consuming the plan formation and approval processes will be.

In a focused and efficient plan, a debtor must find the right balance between sharing the pain of compromise fairly and minimizing complexity and its accompanying cost and delay. Extended insolvency proceedings are costly in the sense that professional and other expenditures are an added burden that grows with complexity and time. However, they also harm the business by undermining customer and supplier confidence. Given these costs, the obvious and the more subtle, the debtor should attempt to compromise only those creditor constituents who **must** compromise their claims if the restructured business is going to be viable.

The debtor should avoid costly and destructive confrontations with creditor constituents that are better left unaffected by the plan. The initiation of the second step of identifying the classes of constituents that must compromise their claims, is often complicated by the lack of any obvious spokesperson for some classes. For many companies, the unsecured creditor class is disparate and unfocused. It includes small suppliers whose financial health depends on the continuation of the debtor's business. It includes large suppliers who may not care whether the debtor is successful in restructuring. In large companies, the unsecured class sometimes includes holders of public securities such as bonds or debentures. It also may include employees whose employment with the debtor may be terminated as part of a downsizing of the debtor's business.

In many cases, the treatment of the unsecured creditor class cannot be negotiated with representatives of that class before a formal filing because, as a practical matter, no one representative of the class has a mandate to negotiate on behalf of any significant creditor group. Even after a formal filing, in the absence of a creditor committee in most Canadian insolvency cases, the unsecured class often persists as an amorphous mass of undifferentiated debt.

In a focused restructuring process, the debtor does not wait for representatives of the unsecured class to come forward on their own timetable. Rather, it pursues two basic strategies to ensure that a plan or proposal with a good chance of success is presented to creditors on an expedited timetable. First, before any formal filing, in its discussions with creditor groups that are effectively represented, it negotiates enough room to offer generous consideration, relative to expected liquidation results, to the unsecured creditor class. Second, it actively facilitates the organization of creditor spokespeople for the unsecured class to provide a sounding board for reorganization ideas that may be reflected in the plan.

3. **Step Three: Sell the Fairness of the Restructuring Plan to the Trustee/Monitor**

The third step is gaining the support of the Trustee to be appointed in any proposal filing or the Monitor to be appointed in any CCAA filing for the proposed plan outline.

As indicated earlier in this chapter, every formal restructuring process in Canada is supervised by an officer of the court. In BIA proposals, the 'supervisor' is called a Trustee and its powers and responsibilities are set out in the BIA itself. In CCAA restructuring cases, the court appoints a Monitor. The CCAA sets out the minimum obligations of the Monitor but the court can and usually does supplement the minimum powers. Monitors and Trustees are almost always firms of accountants who have special training and experience in insolvency and restructuring.

The Trustee/Monitor will be entitled to full disclosure of all information of the debtor that may be relevant to its financial situation and its restructuring effort. The Trustee/Monitor has obligations to inform the court and the creditors of the debtor of any financial data that may relevant to debtor's operations and to the fairness of its plan or proposal.

The Trustee/Monitor is said to be a 'fiduciary' for all participants in the insolvency process. Although often called a fiduciary, the Trustee/Monitor is not an advocate for any one constituent group. It is more accurate to describe it as the court's emissary within the plan process. Like the court, the Trustee/Monitor has a duty to be fair and impartial while it facilitates the process of development, acceptance or rejection and implementation of the plan or proposal if accepted.

Although the Trustee/Monitor is not formally appointed until the initial insolvency filing, a debtor seeking to implement a focused plan will engage a prospective Trustee/Monitor either before or immediately after it has developed its business and restructuring plan outline. Further, the debtor must recognize that any successful restructuring plan is dependent on Trustee/Monitor support, both because creditors who must accept the plan or proposal will rely on the opinion of the Trustee/Monitor as to its fairness and because the court, when considering whether the plan or proposal should be approve, will also rely on the Trustee/Monitor's opinion of the fairness of the plan to all of its constituents.

In a focused plan, the only way to convince the Trustee/Monitor of the fairness of the plan in an expedited time frame is to involve the prospective Trustee/Monitor in the development stage of the plan before it has received any formal appointment in the initial filing. Further, the prospective Trustee/Monitor must be given complete access to all information that it may consider necessary in order to evaluate the fairness and appropriateness of the plan. To the extent that the Trustee/Monitor has full access to information and involvement in the pre-filing development stage, it will have no hesitation in recommending the restructuring plan to creditors and the court when it is formally appointed as the court's advisor and watchdog in its role as Trustee/Monitor.

4. Step Four: Communicate the Plan Clearly and Fairly

The fourth step is developing the 'story' of the plan. The plan's story must explain why the business is in distress, what company management proposes to do to fix the problems that caused the distress and why the compromises reflected in the plan outline are responsive to the problems, fit with a rational business plan and are fair among all classes of affected creditors and between affected creditors and unaffected creditors.

The plan's story must ring true and must be transparent in the sense that everyone who hears the story must be convinced that all stakeholders will hear the same story and must be satisfied that the treatment of everyone affected by the plan is disclosed. Finally, like the plan or proposal itself, the story must have the support of a Trustee/Monitor who affected constituents believe to be knowledgeable, capable, impartial and fair.

5. Step Five: Develop Consensus Support Among the Key Constituents of the Plan

The fifth step is developing a consensus among the key affected constituents about the basic elements of the plan outline. The leaders of the debtor company must develop a strategy for canvassing key creditor constituencies about the plan outline. While the debtor may believe that the plan outline is fair to all constituents, it must be open to legitimate input from each constituent group.

Building consensus is an iterative process. It builds from the core and spreads to the periphery of affected creditor groups. Most companies that are successful in restructuring their businesses approach creditor groups in order of their relative strength and influence over the plan. Often the debtor will leave the least organized group, usually the unsecured creditor class, to the end as the result in that class will likely be determined by a vote.

Both the CCAA and the BIA require that the plan or proposal be accepted by more than 50 per cent in number representing more than two-third in value of the votes cast in each affected class. Accordingly, in order to reach consensus, the debtor must identify any creditors who have enough votes to veto any plan or proposal and negotiate the consideration to be offered in that class directly with such creditors. In negotiations with veto creditors, no additional benefits can be offered to any individual creditor outside the plan or proposal to induce it to vote in favour of a plan or proposal. In a focused restructuring, these negotiations would be held in advance of any formal filing and would be reflected in the plan or proposal presented to creditors immediately after the plan filing.

In many cases, the debtor's restructuring plan will depend on the acceptance of a large unorganized group of stakeholders. In order to develop a consensus of support in such classes, the debtor may pursue two basic strategies. It can help those stakeholders organize so that the debtor can effectively communicate the plan and advocate its acceptance to the stakeholders' representatives, or, in other cases, the debtor may have to accept that the large unorganized class cannot be organized and simply take the risk that the offer made to the class will be acceptable. In such cases, a debtor may have to rely on the advice of its professional advisors in determining the appropriate consideration to offer the class. Also, the debtor may accept input from the Trustee or Monitor concerning the appropriate level of consideration to be offered in any large and unorganized class, such as, for example, the general unsecured creditor class.

If the business plan requires the termination of employees and the plan or proposal must compromise the employee claims arising from the terminations, the debtor should seek input from employee representatives to avoid unnecessary controversy and ill feeling surrounding plan acceptance, approval and implementation. If the employees are unionized, the union will be involved in the negotiation of the treatment of union claims in the plan or proposal. Non-union employees, on the other hand, do not have an obvious representative with a mandate to negotiate with the debtor company. In some cases, it will be sufficient for the debtor to discuss the treatment of employee claims in the plan with the union on the theory that the treatment of non-unionized employees will be the same. In other cases, when that theory does not apply, the debtor should take positive steps to generate feedback through employee representatives.

In any restructuring plan or proposal, the debtor should treat small unsecured creditors as a 'convenience class' by offering them better treatment than is offered other unsecured creditors. Canada's insolvency legislation provides for only one unsecured class of creditors. However, Canadian courts have been prepared to approve plans that offer smaller unsecured creditors greater proportionate recovery within the unsecured class. Accordingly, a typical Canadian plan would offer 100 per cent of every claim up to CAD 1,000 and say 15 per cent of every claim to the extent that it exceeds CAD 1,000. The result of this treatment, that notionally applies to every claim but favours small claims, is that small creditors are induced to vote in favour of the plan. Since small claims vastly outnumber large claims in any restructuring process, this technique virtually assures that the restructuring plan or proposal passes the headcount test in the unsecured class by receiving the favourable vote of more than 50 per cent in number of unsecured creditors.

6. Step Six: Deliver a Simple, Effective and Focused Restructuring Plan

The business plan should be directed to objectives that the debtor sets to re-establish itself as a viable economic entity. The restructuring plan must be designed to distribute the value of that newly viable business to the debtor's creditors fairly and simply. Fairness requires that the compromise requested of each affected creditor class must be an improvement over the recovery that they could reasonably have achieved through the exercise of their legal rights.

Simplicity requires that the consideration offered in each class be easy to understand and useful to the recipient. If the focused restructuring plan includes an offer to a large general unsecured creditor class, the offer should include cash. If cash cannot be offered for a technical or structural reason, the debtor should find a financial partner who will acquire unsecured claims or otherwise sponsor the plan so that cash can be offered to unsecured creditors. The success of a focused restructuring depends on accurately setting the consideration offered in each class such that each affected creditor class votes in favour of the plan or proposal.

Simplicity also requires the debtor to resolve contingencies such as the securing of necessary consents or governmental approvals prior to any vote or court approval of the plan or proposal. The focused restructuring plan must seem like a sure thing that can be delivered faster than any other solution can be found or implemented. Highly contingent plans invite constituents to make contingency plans and to discount the value of the plan.

V. GOVERNANCE, USING PROFESSIONAL ADVISORS EFFECTIVELY AND DIRECTORS LIABILITY ISSUES

Key to all of these steps is the right professional input. Very few company managers have the skill sets, experience or objectivity about the business to enable them to identify the key business problems that must be addressed, create a business plan to return the company to viability, develop a plan outline that is fair to all constituents and fits the business plan and build consensus in support of the plan. For businesses of any size, at a very early stage, the board of directors of the debtor should establish a 'restructuring committee' of the board, retain a financial advisor and insolvency counsel and seriously consider hiring a 'chief restructuring officer' to lead the company through the process.

A focused restructuring process must begin before any formal proceedings are filed. The need to plan for an insolvency restructuring process before any stay protection has been obtained raises the difficult issues of the directors' potential duties and liabilities to creditors who may be adversely affected, particularly if the restructuring attempt fails. Implicit in the conclusion that the business must undergo a financial restructuring is the recognition that the debtor may not be able to meet all of the obligations it has incurred or will incur prior to the commencement of insolvency proceedings. Inevitably, directors and officers of the debtor must know of this risk and that creditors may be adversely impacted by the continuation of the business.

In the US and in other common law jurisdictions, courts have concluded that directors have primary duties to shareholders but once a corporation enters the 'vicinity of insolvency', the directors' fiduciary responsibilities shift so that their duties are owed to the corporation's creditors. The basis of this theory is the proposition that once a corporation is near insolvency, its primary economic stakeholders are its creditors and therefore, directors should exercise business judgment in a way that safeguards the interests of creditors. As appealing as this logic may be, it assumes that directors can and should shift allegiances depending on whether or not the company is in the nebulous and ill-defined state, the 'vicinity of insolvency'.

The Supreme Court of Canada rejected this theory, deciding that directors do not change allegiances when the corporation comes under financial pressure. Rather, in *Peoples Department Stores Inc. (Trustee of) v. Wise* ('Wise case')[12] Canada's highest court stated that there is only one beneficiary of the directors' fiduciary duties, the corporation itself, stating '[a]t all times, directors and officers owe their fiduciary obligation to the corporation'.

Describing 'fiduciary duty' as equivalent to a 'duty of loyalty', directors are required to act with a view to the best interests of the corporation. Instead of favouring the interests of any stakeholder group or another, Canadian corporate law requires directors to consider and balance the interests of many stakeholder groups, including shareholders, employees, suppliers, creditors, consumers, governments and the environment.

The implication of this decision, and the result in the particular case, is that directors of corporations incorporated under the laws of Canada (federal corporations) are not subject to being sued by creditors for failing to put creditors' interests first when the debtor is in financial difficulties. However, in drawing this conclusion, the Supreme Court relied heavily on the sufficiency and appropriateness of other statutory obligations that may subject the directors to legal liability at the suit of creditors.

In the exercise of their powers, directors have two classes of statutory duties. They have a duty not to take actions that are oppressive, unfairly prejudicial or that unfairly disregard the interests of creditors and other stakeholders. Put positively, they have a duty to balance the interests of their stakeholders, including creditors. Second, they have a duty to exercise reasonable care and skill. Put another way, they have a duty of competence. In its decision in the *Wise* case, the Supreme Court suggested that this statutory duty of competence may be owed directly to creditors harmed by the failure to meet the duty.

The *Wise* case suggests a liberal consideration of the oppression remedy that, rather than placing the heavy onus on the plaintiff of proving bad faith on the part of the directors, imposes a positive duty on directors to balance the interests of all

---

12. 2004 SCC 68, [2004] 3 S.C.R. 461.

stakeholders of the company to pursue a result that makes the corporation 'better' in all circumstances. In postulating this duty, the court recognizes and endorses the 'business judgment rule' articulated in previous decisions.

Rather than second-guess the decisions of directors with the wisdom of hindsight and with the benefit of knowing the results of such decisions, the court endorses a *process* of decision-making. If the directors take the appropriate steps to gather information necessary for the decision, retain advisors to assist them in the decision-making process and take into account the circumstance of the corporation at the time it makes its decision bearing in mind the interests of all its stakeholders, their judgment will be respected.

While endorsing the business judgment rule as a defence for directors, the Supreme Court's ruling in the *Wise* case is far from certain protection for directors. The pursuit of the 'better corporation' in the context of the exigencies created by financial difficulties that threaten the life of the business enterprise is by its nature the pursuit of an uncertain objective. The difficulties faced by directors are further complicated by the urgency of the crisis that may make it impossible for the directors to initiate the appropriate process (or one that would stand up to scrutiny in litigation). As a consequence, real world directors must make decisions that have far-reaching impacts without an opportunity to obtain the assistance of professional advisors and take other steps that they can later use to demonstrate that they exercised their business judgment appropriately.

It is fair and appropriate that directors must approach their obligations and their duties responsibly and take into account the interests of all stakeholder groups that are affected by their actions or face legal liability. The *Wise* case sets reasonable standards and articulates them in a general way because every case must be considered on its own facts. The many issues that face boards of directors through the daily conduct of the business of Canadian corporations cannot be anticipated. However, the uncertainty faced by directors and officers in continuing their role of guiding the corporation through the sometimes treacherous waters of insolvency, outside of formal proceedings, can become intolerable. In such circumstances, a formal insolvency filing under the CCAA can create a forum in which difficult business judgments can be addressed by the supervising court.

VI. ACCELERATED SALE PROCEEDINGS

Restructuring, focused or not, is about the resurrection of the debtor itself through compromise. The underlying business provides the impetuous for the restructuring process. It provides the value and the compromises of creditors, as approved by the supervising court, is the methodology of distribution of the value that resides in the business to the creditors.

Sometimes, the underlying business of an insolvent debtor is viable. However, for a variety of reasons, it is impossible for the creditors of the insolvent debtor to achieve a compromise to distribute the value in the business through a consensual restructuring plan or proposal. In such cases, the viability of the business can only be preserved if it is sold as a going concern to a purchaser who will carry on the business, leaving the proceeds of the sale to be distributed in accordance with the legal entitlements of the creditors.

As is discussed earlier in this chapter, Canadian courts have two mechanisms for the supervision of court ordered sale proceedings. Canadian courts will authorize a debtor who is subject to CCAA or proposal proceedings to conduct a sale under the guidance of a Monitor/Trustee or it can appoint a Receiver to conduct the sale process. In either case, the court must approve the ultimate sale and, in reviewing the sale process, will require that the sale process be fair, conducted with integrity and appropriate to generate the best value available for the assets of the debtor.

Also, as discussed earlier in this chapter, sale processes take time: time to identify potential bidders; time to prepare information packages; time for due diligence; time to negotiate an agreement of purchase and sale; and time for court approval motions and appeal periods. During this time, the debtor's business must be continued on a business as usual basis.

In most cases, Canadian courts will insist that the sale process follow the usual process described in the *Soundair* case and summarized earlier in this chapter. Allowing the sale process to unfold over two or three months viewed by Canadian courts as assisting the debtor or Receiver in encouraging competition and permitting interested purchasers a fair chance for due diligence. Accordingly, before approving a sale of assets of an insolvent debtor, a Canadian court will usually require the debtor or the Receiver to widely market such assets, inviting many potential purchasers to consider the opportunity, and to permit extensive due diligence reviews by anyone willing to incur the time and expense for due diligence.

While time spent marketing an insolvent debtor's business may increase the court's confidence that all potential purchasers have been made aware of the opportunity, the business itself may suffer because of the uncertainties and risks that are inherent in the insolvency process itself. The risks of continuing in business during an extended insolvency marketing process are particularly difficult if the business must be operated by a Receiver. In a number of recent cases, Canadian courts have held that, although receivers appointed by the court are court officers, the court does not have the jurisdiction to protect receivers from liabilities that may be imposed on them as 'successor employers' by provincial and federal legislation protecting unionized employees. Consequently, inherited risks arising from continued operation of the business while it is offered for sale by the Receiver impose a practical restraint on court supervised sale processes of insolvent but viable businesses.

An expedited sale procedure may be the only option available to preserve the business and generate a 'going concern' premium for distribution to creditors. Notwithstanding the need in any particular case for the sale processes to be expedited, the court approving any such sale must be satisfied that the requirements of the *Soundair* case have been met (see II.B.1 *above*). While the *Soundair* tests are flexible and case specific, they still require time. The degree to which that time can be accelerated in individual cases will depend on the specific exigencies of such cases. However, they typically involve one of three fact patterns.

A. UNDERWATER SECURITY

In Canada, no plan or proposal can be approved by the court unless all of the creditor classes have voted in favour of the plan or proposal. Consequently, no plan or proposal can succeed in Canada unless consideration is offered in all classes sufficient to induce that class to vote in favour of the plan or proposal in the requisite majorities.

If the value of the business assets of the debtor is less than the value of its secured claims, no value is available to compromise the claims of subordinate classes of creditors and any plan to restructure the debtor will fail unless priority classes are prepared to effectively subordinate their claims to permit distributions in subordinate classes. In many cases, secured creditors will agree to accept less than full recovery in order to facilitate a plan that, overall, will provide them with a superior recovery than would liquidation. In some cases, the affected secured creditor will not agree to permit recovery for subordinate creditor classes and will veto any plan that would be supported by the subordinate classes.

Notwithstanding that the restructuring process may be doomed to failure, because of secured creditor opposition courts have been prepared to approve sales of the assets on an accelerated time table if the secured creditor consents to the proposed sale and the court is satisfied from objective sources that no other creditor has an economic stake. In such cases, courts have been prepared to approve sales on a 'quick flip' basis without extensive marketing.

As a practical matter, secured lenders will not support a quick flip sale of their collateral unless they are satisfied that no better deal would be available if the assets were broadly marketed. Accordingly, the court will often take comfort from the consent of the secured lender provided that the court is satisfied that the secured lender's security is valid, effective and enforceable as a first lien on all of the affected collateral and that the value of the assets are clearly less than the amount of the debt owed to the secured lender. Evidence of the legal effectiveness and priority of the security is usually addressed by search evidence together with an independent legal review of the security documentation relating to the secured lender. Evidence of value is usually obtained through appraisals or valuations of the business. The greater the apparent discrepancy between the value of the collateral and the debt, the less judicial scrutiny will be applied to the proposed sale.

Even if the court is satisfied that the secured creditor is the only party with an economic interest, the court is reluctant to approve a quick sale of the debtor's assets, without full marketing, unless there is also evidence that other benefits of the transaction will be realized by the completion of the accelerated sale that may be lost in the event of any delay. Accordingly, 'quick flip' sales are usually accompanied by evidence of continued employment and other benefits for non-financial creditors and the broader community.

B.   PRE-FILING MARKETING

A formal filing under Canada's insolvency laws should be the last resort for the leaders of the debtor's management team. Before filing for protection from creditors, debtors attempt informal solutions for the underlying business problems facing the business, usually including a sale of the business as a going concern.

If the debtor's business is under financial or operational distress when it is being marketed by the management group, the offers may reflect that distress through reduced price. If the price available in the market after a comprehensive marketing effort is insufficient to satisfy all creditor claims, it may be impossible for the debtor to complete the sale without some form of court approval.

Court approval may be obtained for the completion of a sale by an insolvent company through three procedural vehicles. First, the debtor may apply for protection from its creditors under the CCAA and in the CCAA proceedings seek authority from the court to sell part or all of its business as a going concern. Second, the debtor may file a notice of intention to file a proposal under the BIA and, in the proposal proceedings seek similar relief. Third, a creditor could apply for the appointment of a Receiver by the court to enter into the sale agreement and complete the sale.

Regardless of the procedural context, the court will only approve the sale without any further marketing if it is satisfied that the marketing conducted by the debtor was consistent with and met the standards of a court supervised marketing process. Accordingly, the debtor would have to submit evidence that all potential purchasers had been offered a fair opportunity to participate as a potential bidder and that the process had been conducted thoroughly and with integrity.

Each of these procedures involves the appointment of a court officer, a Monitor, Trustee or Receiver. The success of any expedited sale based on the debtor's previous marketing of its business will depend on the recommendation of the court officer after reviewing the marketing programme conducted by the debtor. As a practical matter, it will be easier for the court officer to give such a recommendation if it has been involved in the marketing process and had an opportunity to observe the process first hand.

Obviously, since the court officer does not receive its formal appointment until the CCAA, proposal or receivership proceedings are commenced, the pre-filing involvement of the prospective Monitor, Trustee or Receiver must be under a private engagement by the debtor or another interested party such as a secured creditor. Accordingly, the pre-filing engagement of the prospective court officer is something of a double-edged sword. The court and other parties may be concerned that its recommendation given after its formal appointment may be tainted by its previous 'private' engagement. For this reason, the appointing party should seek to preserve the independence of the proposed court officer through the appointment itself. This might be achieved through provisions of the appointment that state that the proposed court officer is not an agent or advocate of the appointing party and that it is to act with the same impartiality and with similar powers relative to the debtor as it would have as a court officer.

C. FAILED RESTRUCTURING

Many restructuring plans are sponsored by the investment of a party who will become the owner of the business through the restructuring plan. Sponsors may have agreed to subscribe for new equity of the debtor which would be injected if the plan is approved. In such cases, the consideration offered to the creditors and other stakeholders is made available through the new investment.

As discussed *above*, Canada's restructuring laws require that any plan of arrangement or proposal receive the affirmative vote of all classes of creditors. There is no class cramdown in Canada. As a result, an otherwise viable restructuring plan or proposal may be frustrated by the exercise of a 'veto' by a subordinate creditor group. In such cases, the sponsor may wish to reformulate its offer to acquire the business through a plan or proposal instead as an offer to purchase the business assets of the debtor as a going concern. If the offer is acceptable to the debtor and its stakeholders (other than the veto creditor), the court may approve the sale either under an existing CCAA/BIA process or under a new receivership process. The success of such an application for court approval will inevitably depend on the court being satisfied that the proposed sale transaction is fair and reasonable and, consequently, that the veto creditor's opposition to the transaction was an unreasonable attempt to lever its veto position into an unfair economic benefit.

VII. CONCLUDING COMMENTS

Canada's multifaceted insolvency laws provide parties seeking to complete an efficient and effective restructuring process with a number of options. Although informal compromises are possible in Canada, the parties to informal restructurings incur legal risk and potential complexity that can be avoided or reduced by expedited formal proceedings, either through a focused restructuring plan or through an accelerated sale. Canadian courts are receptive to efficient and expedited restructuring processes provided that the court is satisfied that the affected parties have been involved in the process at least on a representative basis, that the debtor has been forthright and fair in all aspects of the proposed transaction, that critical affected parties are consenting or not opposing and that the Monitor/Trustee/Receiver appointed by the court recommends that the transaction (plan, proposal or sale) be approved and completed.

Chapter 6
England & Wales

Schemes of Arrangement and Company Voluntary Arrangements

Samantha Bewick, Mark Fennessy and David Marks

Rodrigo Olivares-Caminal, *Expedited Debt Restructuring: An International Comparative Analysis*, pp. 157–255.
©2007, Kluwer Law International BV, The Netherlands.

ACRONYMS, ABBREVIATIONS & DEFINED TERMS

2002 Practice Statement	Practice Statement of 15 April 2002 issued by the Companies Court in the wake of the *Re Hawk* decision
Account Holder	The financial institution in the Marconi schemes of arrangement which held an account with the depositories, being DTC, Clearstream and Euroclear
Chapter 11	A US chapter 11 is a court supervised reorganization of an insolvent or near insolvent business while continuing with its day to day operations.
COMI	Centre of Main Interests
Companies Act 1985	UK Companies Act 1985
Core Companies	Six TXU Europe group companies through which there were material flow of funds, had significant external creditors, and from which TXU Corporation (the ultimate holding company of the group) required releases.
Corp	Marconi Corporation plc
Corp settlement	A settlement of potential litigation against the directors and the ultimate holding company of the TXU Europe group (i.e. TXU Corporation) valued at some USD 220 million
Cross Border Regulations	Cross-Border Insolvency Regulations 2006
CVA/s	Company Voluntary Arrangement/s
DTI	Department of Trade and Industry
EC	European Community
EC Council Regulation Directive on the reorganization and winding-up of insurance undertakings	Directive 2001/17/EC of the European Parliament and of the European Council of 19 March 2001 on the reorganization and winding-up of insurance undertakings
EC Insolvency Regulation	Council Regulation (EC) No. 1346/2000 of 29 May 2000 on Insolvency Proceedings
EC Judgments Regulation	Council Regulation (EC) No. 44/2001, of 22 December 2000 on jurisdiction and the recognition and enforcement of judgments in civil and commercial matters

England & Wales 159

ECHR	European Convention on Human Rights
EEA	European Economic Area
Enterprise Act 2002	UK Enterprise Act 2002
EU	European Union
EUR	Euro
FSMA	Financial Services and Markets Act 2000
GBP	Great Britain Sterling Pound
Holding Companies	The holding companies of the TXU Europe Power Group, with assets of GBP 0.6 billion and liabilities of GBP 2.5 billion.
Insolvency Act 1986	UK Insolvency Act 1986
Insolvency Act 2000	UK Insolvency Act 2000
Insolvency Rules	UK Insolvency Rules
IVA	Individual Voluntary Arrangement
Marconi	Marconi Corporation plc and Marconi plc
Model	An extremely complex computer program to model outcomes and distributions on an entity priority basis as result of the complex inter-company balances, which gave rise to a circular flow of funds within the TXU Europe group.
Official Receiver	A civil servant in The Insolvency Service and an officer of the court
Operating Companies	The operating companies of the TXU Europe Power Group, with assets of some GBP 2.1 billion and liabilities of some GBP 2.3 billion
plc	Marconi plc
Registrar of Companies	English Registrar of Companies
Scheme/s	Scheme/s of Arrangement
SI	Statutory Instrument
SIP	Statement of Insolvency Practice
TXU Europe group	TXU Europe Power Group

UK	United Kingdom
UNCITRAL Model Law	United Nations Commission on International Trade Law Model Law on Cross-Border Insolvency
US	United States of America
US Bankruptcy Code	Title 11 of the United States Code which governs bankruptcy cases.
USD	United States Dollar
VAT	Value Added Tax

England & Wales

I. INTRODUCTION

The use of section 425 of the UK Companies Act 1985 Schemes of Arrangement (Schemes) and Company Voluntary Arrangements, (CVAs) both of which techniques will be described in further detail in the following sections, have in the former case, a relatively long legal pedigree and in the second case, a more recent but fairly settled jurisprudence, at least in English law. However, as techniques in the practical world of corporate restructurings, their use has increased markedly in the last decade or so in order to tackle and implement complex and often internationally affected corporate reorganizations.

Schemes are now commonly used in relation to all forms of commercial and business restructurings. In particular, there has been an enormous growth in the areas of insurance companies and finance related business, e.g. with regard to formal schemes of arrangement. The probable reason for such a return to Schemes, fundamentally a court-driven process, is to ensure that in cases where there may be a risk of dissent to any proposal, the court's sanction will in effect bar for all time any subsequent attack upon the validity and efficacy of the Scheme.

A word should be said about the general requirements of both Schemes and CVAs. Before turning to consider the key principles behind a CVA, it is perhaps useful to stress the essential features of Schemes under the UK Companies Act 1985 (Companies Act 1985). A Scheme is formally described as a composition or arrangement between a company and its members, or a class of members or its creditors or a class of creditors. If the relevant proposal is approved by a majority in number representing not less than 75 per cent in value of those who, being entitled to do so, attend and vote at a meeting convened under court direction and the court then sanctions it, the Scheme becomes binding on all affected parties whether or not they voted or even if they voted against the Scheme.

There is therefore a three stage process and each stage fulfils a distinct purpose. At the first stage, the court must consider whether it is appropriate to convene meetings to consider and vote on the Scheme. Secondly, the creditors must meet and vote. If the requisite majority is achieved, the third stage will involve the court deciding whether to sanction their Scheme.

The function of the court in the third and final stage involves both procedural and substantive considerations. The court must see whether all the procedural requirements have been complied with: but equally, it must also ensure that all decisions were taken in a *bona fide* manner, and perhaps most importantly, it must consider whether in all the circumstances the Scheme is a fair one. This last requirement involves an objective analysis of whether an honest and intelligent member of the relevant class or classes would view the Scheme as fair.

As will be seen in the detailed section dealing with the legal aspects of Schemes, there has been an ongoing judicial examination of the constituent parts of the regime, in particular with regard to the manner in which it is regarded as appropriate to convene and constitute meetings of the various classes of creditors and members otherwise affected by the Scheme.

There is little doubt that the complexity of the law regarding schemes led to a formal review of the way in which a more informal restructuring technique could be initiated. The UK Insolvency Act 1986 (Insolvency Act 1986) gave rise to a mode of personal insolvency known as the Individual Voluntary Arrangement (IVA). There is little doubt that IVAs as an informal means of avoiding the rigours of formal bankruptcy have proved to be a great success. The hopes and expectations of creditors in an IVA are usually fulfilled in the sense that they receive a higher dividend than they otherwise would do in a formal insolvency. In the case of an IVA there is little formal contact with the judicial process. In theory and in practice, it is and remains the insolvency practitioner (as distinct from the court) who is normally responsible for drafting the IVA and who manages the process from the initial proposal right through to the decision of the creditors' meetings. In essence, the court merely monitors the process.

Prior to the recent UK Enterprise Act 2002 (Enterprise Act 2002), the UK Government declared its resolve to promote what it called the 'rescue culture' and in particular to ensure that that culture extended to corporate as well as to individual business failures. The manifestation of this resolve took the form of the UK Insolvency Act 2000 (Insolvency Act 2000) which came into force on 1 January 2003 and the new Enterprise Act 2002 was then subsumed into the principal Act, namely the Insolvency Act 1986.

It might be thought that the success of CVAs which had been introduced in the original 1986 Act does not quite reflect the marked success of IVAs and such a contention is perhaps debatable. The Insolvency Act 2000 Act introduced for the first time the concept of a moratorium in an effort to reflect the statutory moratorium already in place with regard to administrations which, prior to the Enterprise Act, were all instituted by a court order. The introduction of the moratorium in the CVA however, also built on the example provided by IVA being a process which required no direct court involvement. Equally significantly, but somewhat outside the scope of this work, the voluntary arrangement procedure now extends to partnerships, many of which operate on a scale equal to if not greater than that witnessed in the case of limited companies.

A. THE VALUE AND THE RISKS OF SCHEMES

For many years, Schemes have been used in relation to insurance insolvencies principally because the approval of a Scheme virtually guarantees that an orderly reorganization can be imposed on the creditors. More recently, their use has grown in relation to solvent as distinct from insolvent insurers. There is no doubt that in this particular context, Schemes are regarded as sufficiently flexible to allow insurance companies with discontinued lines of business to set up compromises which enable the company in effect to draw a line under all or part of its business, utilizing suitable systems in order to estimate and pay ultimate claims fixed at what is called a 'bar date'. On the other hand, it is fair to say that there do remain difficulties in identifying liabilities which are the subject of solvent schemes, particularly where the Scheme deals with specific portfolios, rather than the entire business of the company. This has not stopped the successful prosecution of a number of significant Schemes over the past few years, many which have found their way into the law reports. This in turn has led to an even greater scrutiny of the Scheme process as a whole as well as greater concentration on the way in which Scheme documents are prepared. Policyholders' support has on occasion been problematic, resulting in the regular adjournment of creditors' meetings in order to deal with policyholder related issues. Litigation involving a Scheme relating to the British Aviation Insurance Company scheme in the event resulted in failure to obtain sanction from the English High Court. This was in the face of opposition from a number of US based creditors.

An abiding query about the real value of Schemes, even in the case of insurance insolvencies, relates to the extent to which Scheme companies go to ensure that proper notice is given to all creditors and potential creditors who may, or will be, affected by the Scheme. One might expect that companies such as insurance companies, would in reality readily have available the correct address and contact names to be able to reach policyholders, but such is frequently not the case, if nothing else, given the lengthy periods of time over which the relationships may have endured. The English courts have in fairness recognized that underlying reality, namely that all that can be reasonably ensured is that proper endeavours have been conducted by the Scheme companies to identify potential creditors. In practice, many forms of advertisement and communications are used apart from the usual forms of press advertisement.

A further perceived drawback relating to the use of Schemes relates to the applicable timeframe, in particular, the period available in which to submit claims for voting purposes as well as the time available to meet the 'bar date' already referred to, namely the time at which claims are valued. There is little doubt that the relatively short time limits, together with the apathy normally attributable to most creditors, account for the relatively low number of votes which are in fact submitted in relation to Schemes. In the British Aviation Insurance Company scheme, it appears that only just over 70 creditors voted, as against the fact that over 17,000 notifications were sent out. This may be because the primary, if not sole motivation of a creditor is to ensure that his or its claim is lodged prior to the bar date, and not be too concerned about any preliminary issues.

The above considerations lead in turn to another attendant risk with regard to Schemes which relates to the sheer administrative burden borne by those behind the Scheme, invariably the firm of insolvency practitioners who have been brought in to prepare and administer the Scheme to collate all the relevant claims as well as in the case of insurance insolvencies, the actuarial information regarding contractual exchanges going back in most cases over many years. In the case of insurers, it is invariably the case that they will not have provided policy dates to creditors: rather, in practical terms, the onus has been placed on the creditor to supply details of his or its dealings which often may prove if not impossible, at least time consuming and expensive.

Another source of difficulty, if not frustration, is the frequent complaint expressed by policyholders in an insurance related Scheme that they find it difficult to identify with any degree of precision which part of the business is in fact included as part of the proposed Scheme. This may well be based on mis-descriptions or inaccuracies in the Scheme documentation. If there is a perceived lack of clarity, a frequent consequence of this is for the creditors, and in particular policyholders, to submit details of claims and policies which go well beyond the ambit of the relevant part of the business or portfolio forming the subject matter of the Scheme.

Overall therefore, it could be said that many refinements can still be made as to the practical way in which Schemes are prepared and administered. These stem from many of the points which are made in the preceding paragraphs. Although these items are not necessarily limited to insurance related Schemes, it is in that area that the need for reform is perhaps most noticeable. The matters which are arguably in some immediate need of care and attention are: (1) the need to provide greater details of claims and policy information on all claims and voting forms; next, the need to provide longer periods for voting purposes with at least a six month period for bar dates; (2) the increased use of some form of formal adjudication process to deal with contested claims, particularly overseas disputes where ideally a panel of adjudicators who are duly qualified should be established and set up under the scheme documentation; (3) the need to provide a full set of financial data regarding those parts of a company's business which are to be the subject of the Scheme; and, (4) the setting up of some form of centralized information or data bank which records the progress of the Scheme as a whole. This list is by no means exhaustive.

B. THE MERITS AND DEMERITS OF CVAS

There are admittedly many reasons why a contemplated compromise or series of compromises should not be regulated under the umbrellas of either a Scheme or a CVA, even in the case of a complex and interlocking series of compromises. The ability to elect for either procedure arises frequently in practice and can perhaps best be illustrated by means of an example drawn from the recent collapse of a major energy supplier described more fully in the practical example section of this chapter. The principal issue involved a settlement of potential litigation against the directors of a group of companies which for present purposes can be called the 'holding companies'. In addition, there was a substantial claim against the ultimate holding company. The terms of this latter settlement, in effect provided a long stop date prior to which it was necessary to hold meetings to approve the compromises. The same settlement also mandated that any challenge to the compromise had to be disposed of before the end of a stated period failing which the settlement would no longer be binding. The settlement also entailed the need for releases by key members of the 'holding companies' and finally sanction needed to be obtained from the US Bankruptcy Court to certain aspects of the overall settlements.

The 'holding companies' themselves had assets which comprised principally the proceeds of swaps transactions which were encashed prior to those companies' insolvencies, receipts from certain subsidiary companies which were already undertaking CVAs, certain guarantee claims, significant amounts of debt and inter-company balances.

Pausing here, none of the *above* elements militated particularly one way or the other in favour of either a CVA or a Scheme, nor was it particularly significant in that respect that the affected companies had to enter the same procedures at the same time. In the event, 16 interlocking CVAs were proposed, each on the same terms, to settle all the relevant matters, in particular the need to ensure that there were valid releases between the 'holding companies' and the ultimate holding company and that the funds representing the inter-company balances were properly distributed to all affected companies, which in turn entirely depended on a number of key companies known as the 'core companies' entering into the contemplated distribution process. The 'core companies' were in effect those companies through which all the relevant funds would flow, as well as those companies which had significant external creditors.

The primary reason for resorting to CVAs was that it was considered that the relevant rules regarding CVAs would mean that every creditor otherwise entitled to vote at the creditors' meeting would be bound provided due notification was made. In addition, use of the CVA procedure removed the need to resort to both court procedure and court approval. In particular, it was important to avoid those procedural requirements which would have compelled physical notification to all creditors. In general terms, a CVA requires that all notices relating to CVA meetings should be in writing and should be sent by post. However, this is always subject to specific direction from the court in this regard, and in fact a direction was sought and made to the effect that a variety of forms of notification and procedures could be employed.

What is perhaps of greater significance in the present example for illustrating the possible greater benefits of a CVA relates to the question of class issues. In a Scheme, there are frequently serious and complex disputes over the proper constitution of classes of creditors, even as between unsecured creditors. The test in relation to a Scheme as distinct from a CVA is whether the rights of particular groups of creditors, albeit of the same degree, are sufficiently similar for them to consult together. No such difficulties apply in the case of a CVA. Failure to establish the appropriate classes of creditors in a Scheme will invariably lead to its collapse. Again, no such principle applies to a CVA, although it is perhaps fair to say that complaints about the constitution of classes may well be relevant to any claim that the CVA is unfair, i.e. a claim for so-called unfair prejudice. All those considerations therefore rendered the employment of the CVA potentially a more attractive option, quite apart from the cost and time advantages which militated against the use of a Scheme. In addition, a CVA is generally regarded as a much more flexible tool with which to exit from a formal insolvency such as administration and liquidation, and in the case just described, the CVAs were proposed by the various Companies' Administrators.

As will be seen in the section dealing in greater detail with the CVAs, as long as the CVA is not unfair, no creditor can block a CVA proposal on the basis that the classes of creditors have been improperly constituted. The voting rules concerning CVAs are perhaps more favourable than those affecting a Scheme. In a CVA it is sufficient if at least half of the creditors who are not connected with the company vote in favour. In a Scheme, any creditor who is seen to have a collateral interest will generally be disenfranchised: no such principle applies in the case of CVAs.

What may, however, be critical in arriving at a considered decision as to whether to employ a CVA or a Scheme is the need to seek assistance or approval from a foreign court. Insofar as a proposal whose question concerns foreign assets or related following proceedings, sanction of a foreign arrangements may well be indispensable. In the example given, it was thought appropriate to enter into CVAs in the wake of pre-existing administrations since it was felt that the foreign court in question, namely the US Bankruptcy Court, would look more favourably on the arrangements in fact embodied in the CVAs given the provision then reflected in section 304 of Title 11 of the US Code which governs bankruptcy cases (US Bankruptcy Code).[1] This will be explained in a little further detail *below*. US law has recently introduced a new Chapter 15[2] proceeding where again it is likely, though for the moment by no means certain, that the US courts will be amenable to the view that there is no reason not to recognize a CVA as an exit from administration wherever US interests are concerned. The position, however, for the moment is still uncertain.

However, against many of the virtues which could be said to be inherent in the CVA process, there is no doubt that there is no cast-iron guarantee, such as that afforded by a court sanction in respect of a Scheme that no aggrieved creditor will not seek to upset a CVA by a claim that he or others have been unfairly prejudiced by the terms of the CVA or that there has been a material irregularity at the meetings. Any such attack will necessarily delay implementation of the CVA, quite possibly for an inordinate period until the challenge is resolved, sometimes by a full court hearing which may last for several days. This may be the case despite the desire of those otherwise behind the Scheme to seek expedition of the challenge: the fact remains that the implementation of the CVA will remain in abeyance until the challenge is resolved.

C.   Schemes: The Cross-Border Advantages

It might readily be inferred from what this section has already suggested that Schemes are complicated, cumbersome and expensive and therefore should rarely, if ever, be used. Against this, however, two particular benefits suggest themselves as to why Schemes nonetheless remain valuable tools available for a restructuring, both of which reasons having already been alluded to. First, but by no means conclusively, complex financial restructurings tend to be achieved by means of Schemes, such as the recent Marconi, Telewest and My Travel Schemes testify. Secondly, as noted *above*, solvent insurance companies have increasingly resulted to solvent schemes as a quick exit strategy to finalize run-offs.

This section however deals with an additional virtue attributable to the use of Schemes in the context of cross-border restructuring. The underlying potential

---

1. 11 U.S.C. § 304.
2. 11 U.S.C. §§ 1501 to 1532.

difficulty with all Schemes involving an international element is that at first glance, a section 425 of the Companies Act 1985 Scheme will not be binding on a foreign creditor in the sense that such a creditor is one whose claim is governed by a foreign law, since despite the approval and implementation of the Scheme, that creditor may still be entitled to enforce his or its claim against the company in a foreign courts. There are however two methods which have been increasingly deployed in practice to overcome this particular problem. The first concerns the US. Under what was formerly section 304 of the US Bankruptcy Code, the court could seek permanent injunctive relief in order to protect its assets, including those in the US. Secondly, in cases in which there were assets in jurisdictions other than the US and where there existed equivalent restructuring regimes, parallel schemes can be put forward in the appropriate jurisdiction or jurisdictions. In addition, in certain jurisdictions such as Canada, steps can be taken to enforce the English Scheme overseas as a judgment.

An example can again be drawn from insurance. An English insurance company is registered in Ontario to accept property and casualty reinsurance business. It claims to do active business and consequently goes into run-off as to risks written in the UK, and generated through its overseas branches. A solvent Scheme is proposed under which the present and future claims of insurance creditors are to be valued at a certain date and are to be paid in full at value to be agreed or determined in accordance with the Scheme at the earliest possible date.

In due course, the English High Court formally grants leave for the convening of meetings and shortly thereafter, indeed as soon as the following day, the company applies to the Ontario Court for an order recognizing the English court's order and staying all proceedings against the company in Canada. In such a case, there are two jurisdictional bases for the court's ruling in upholding the stay. First, reliance is placed on the appropriate Canada-United Kingdom Civil and Commercial Judgments Convention Act,[3] and secondly the court relies on its own inherent jurisdiction. More specifically, the English judgment is entitled to recognition in Canada because, at the very least, there is a real and substantial connection as to the subject matter of the English court's order and as to the jurisdiction of the English court. In addition, and in accordance with the requirements of comity, the court exercises its inherent jurisdiction to recognize the English order. Exercise of the inherent jurisdiction is facilitated by the realization expressed in terms by the Canadian court that the Canadian insurance companies must be taken to have known that they could be subject to a United Kingdom plan of compromise or arrangement. Next, the Canadian court stresses that English law was well used to sanctioning such schemes which in many cases have seen complementary orders being made in the US, and finally the court notes that such Schemes were not in any way repugnant to Canadian law and practice.

It is to be noted that the order which was recognized in the above example drawn from the case of the Cavel Insurance restructuring was an order granting

---

3. An Act to implement a convention between Canada and the UK providing for the reciprocal recognition and enforcement of judgments in civil and commercial matters.

leave to convene creditors' meetings. It might be said to follow that similar recognition should be accorded to a formal court sanction. Such a course would preempt the need for parallel Schemes. It is however not entirely clear that even an order granting sanction is necessarily tantamount to a judgment, despite the holding of the Canadian case. This is only because a Scheme as such is not solely the product of a court order. It has been judicially confirmed (as if it was really necessary to do so) that the court cannot alter the substance of the Scheme and impose on creditors an arrangement to which they did not agree. Against that, however, it is equally clear that court sanction is not merely a formality and, as has already been seen at the outset of this section, the role fulfilled by the court at the sanction stage involves a judicial consideration of whether in all the circumstances the Scheme is a fair one. There is therefore, on balance, a strong argument for characterizing a sanction order as a judgment capable at least of recognition according to general principles of private international law. Such support for such a view can be drawn from the Council Regulation (EC) No. 1346/2000 of 29 May 2000 on Insolvency Proceedings (EC Insolvency Regulation), Article 25, which treats 'compositions' albeit court approved ones, as judgments to which the EC Judgments Regulation will apply. It could with some force be said that such compositions may well include a section 425 of the Companies Act 1985 Scheme.

The irony is that if the roles are reversed, a court order sanctioning a Scheme made in at least one Commonwealth jurisdiction, apart from Canada, would not necessarily be recognized by an English court. This is principally because one of the preconditions to recognition is that the defendant in the relevant proceedings must have resided in the jurisdiction at the time of the proceedings, or have submitted to a foreign jurisdiction, or had a place or business within the foreign jurisdiction. Clearly, in some cases the last two considerations may be capable of being invoked, but the English court would lack the inherent jurisdiction which was capable of being invoked in the Canadian example.

If an English court order sanctioning a scheme does constitute a judgment within the Council Regulation (EC) No. 44/2001, of 22 December 2000 on jurisdiction and the recognition and enforcement of judgments in civil and commercial matters (EC Judgments Regulation),[4] this would of course greatly facilitate European cross-border restructurings. The alternative is undoubtedly a much more cumbersome process of seeking, at the very least, parallel Schemes. However, the Canadian example represents perhaps a boon to the insurers, at least to the insurance run-off industry. The recent UK Insurers (Reorganization and Winding-Up) Regulations 2004, which implement the Directive 2001/17/EC of the European Parliament and of the European Council of 19 March 2001 on the reorganization and winding-up of insurance undertakings.(EC Council Regulation Directive on the reorganization and winding-up of insurance undertakings),[5] does not view a Scheme of arrangement as a reorganization measure within the directive. In practice, this means that increasingly European insurance companies

---

4. Official Journal L 12 of 16.01.2001.
5. Official Journal L 110 , 20/04/2001 P. 0028–0039.

in run-off will be able to use English solvent schemes. It is true that the EC Judgments Regulation does not deal with insolvency matters. However, an insolvent Scheme sheltering behind an English insolvency procedure such as administration, should be freely enforceable throughout the EU.

Reference has already been made to the possible impact of the new Chapter 15 within the US Bankruptcy Code. Its predecessor, namely section 304, defined a 'foreign proceeding' in wide terms specifically addressing compositions and reorganizations. Chapter 15 talks of 'collective judicial or administrative proceeding(s)' in which proceedings, assets are subject to a foreign court's control 'for the purposes of reorganization or liquidation'. With many debt obligations which are to be restructured under an English scheme subject to, say, New York law, it is clearly vital that such restructurings be binding in the US. It remains to be seen however, whether schemes as well as CVAs which are in principle generated by a company's directors will fall within the description of 'foreign proceeding'. It seems difficult at first blush to regard such Schemes, let alone CVAs as being subject to 'control or supervision' by a court, particularly when compared to the US Chapter 11 proceedings.[6] However, the point is clearly arguable. The position however appears to be different when a UK insolvency office-holder proposes a scheme or a CVA, but such is not always the case.

Even were the US courts now to regard director-driven proposed schemes of arrangement or CVAs as falling within Chapter 15, this might in turn lead to an invidious decision which will then need to be made in the US as to whether the reorganization proceedings were the principal, or as it is called, the 'main proceedings' while other proceedings should be regarded as secondary or 'non-main'. This in turn will involve a consideration of where a debtor's centre of main interests (COMI) resides. The recent Eurofoods litigation in the European Court of Justice[7] which has been widely discussed has demonstrated the difficulties necessarily inherent in this exercise.

On the other hand, there can be no doubt that under Chapter 15, recognition is infinitely easier to obtain than it previously was. A foreign representative need only provide a certified copy of the order commencing the foreign proceedings and the order appointing him, together with a certificate from the foreign court confirming the commencement of the proceeding and his appointment in relation to the proceeding. The relief will include an automatic stay.

D.   PROTOCOLS

Finally, in the realm of cross-border restructuring, reference should perhaps be made to the development that is sometimes particularly key in promoting judicial or operation in relation to jurisdictional differences between the regimes that are controlling or overseeing any particular form of restructure. Ever since the collapse

---

6. A chapter 11 proceeding is a court supervised reorganization of an insolvent or near insolvent business while continuing with its day to day operations.
7. Eurofood IFSC, OJ C143 of 17 June 2006, page 11.

of the Maxwell group of companies in the 1990's, courts, particularly in the US and the UK, have utilized judicial protocols in order to regulate the interaction of related proceedings in their respective jurisdictions. The jurisprudential basis for such protocols is not as yet entirely clear, but sections 1525[8] and 1527[9] of the new Chapter 15 of the US Bankruptcy Code permit the Bankruptcy Court to enter into.

E.   THE UNCITRAL MODEL LAW

Great Britain has finally implemented its version of Chapter 15 being the United Nations Commission on International Trade Law Model Law on Cross-Border Insolvency (UNCITRAL Model Law) on 4 April 2006 by virtue of the Cross-Border Insolvency Regulations 2006 (Cross Border Regulations). This chapter is not the occasion to review the Model Law in any detail. As indicated *above*, it is not at present clear whether a European Scheme under section 425 of the Companies Act 1985 will necessarily and in all cases be recognized in other jurisdictions, in particular, those jurisdictions which have adopted the Model Law, given that it is arguably part of corporate law and not an insolvency proceeding, nor indeed is it clear whether an equivalent foreign proceeding will necessarily be recognized in Great Britain, in particular proceedings commenced out of court such as the foreign equivalent of a CVA. This is largely on the basis that a foreign court is defined in general terms as a judicial or other authority competent to control or supervise a foreign proceeding: it remains to be seen whether this will extend to what would be largely out of court insolvency arrangements.

It should also be remembered that despite similarities in terminology between the new Cross-Border Regulations which implement the UNCITRAL Model Law and the EC Insolvency Regulation, the way in which both instruments approach cross-border insolvency issues is quite different. The latter applies directly to all EU Member States so that it is able to regulate which Member State will open the so-called main proceedings, and in effect, dictate that in large measure the law of that Member State will govern the insolvency ramifications stemming from a debtor's insolvency. By comparison, the UNCITRAL Model Law is a voluntary code, and must necessarily operate on a request basis if anything in a manner analogous to a formal judicial request for assistance made to a relatively small number of designated countries for English purposes set out under section 426 of the Insolvency Act 1986. The main differences with section 426 of the Insolvency Act 1986 however is the imposition of an automatic stay imposed on recognition to go with the fact that any country in the world may see recognition under the new Cross-Border Regulations. As the Cross Border Regulations confirm, that in the case of a conflict with the EC Insolvency Regulation, the latter will prevail.

---

8.   11 U.S.C. § 1525.
9.   11 U.S.C. § 1527.

England & Wales

F. CONCLUSION

Both schemes and CVAs have their place in the armoury of debt restructuring techniques. It cannot be said that one is invariably superior to the other, and different situations demand different approaches. It is clear from this part that either, or both, can be used in large and complex cases although due to the time and cost of a scheme a CVA may be more appropriate for smaller restructurings.

II. SCHEMES OF ARRANGEMENT

A. GENERAL: SECTION 425 OF THE COMPANIES ACT 1985

Schemes have long been a feature of English company law having been introduced under the Companies Act 1948. They represent a flexible method of a company entering into a restructuring process to avoid the relatively rigid network of rules which accompany a formal insolvency, in particular liquidations, in order to achieve a consensus between the company and its creditors as well as its members. This consensus addresses not only the manner in which existing liabilities can be addressed but also a method by which a new corporate structure can be promoted within which the previous business or assets of the company can be recognized. It has been observed that a court would be unlikely to sanction a Scheme that was an alternative to winding-up and that was likely to result in creditors receiving less than they would in a winding-up.[10]

Section 425 of the Companies Act 1985 provides as follows:

(1) *Where a compromise or arrangement is proposed between a company and its creditors, or any class of them, or between the company and its members, or any class of them, the court may on the application of the company or any creditor or member of it, or in the case of a company being wound up or in administration, of the liquidator or administrator, order a meeting of the creditors or class of creditors, or of the members of the company or class of members (as the case may be), to be summoned in such manner as the court directs.*

(2) *If a majority in number representing three-fourths in value of the creditors or class of creditors or members or class of members (as the case may be), present and voting either in person or by proxy at the meeting, agree to any compromise or arrangement, the compromise or arrangement, if sanctioned by the court, is binding on all creditors or the class of creditors or on the members or class of members (as the case may be), and also on the company or, in the case of a company in the course of being wound up, on the liquidator and contributories of the company.*

(3) *The court's order under sub-section (2) has no effect until an office copy of it has been delivered to the registrar of companies for registration and*

---

10. *Re T&N Limited* [2005] 2 BCLC 488.

a copy of every such order shall be annexed to every copy of the companies memorandum issued after the order has been made or, in the case of a company not having a memorandum, of every copy so issued of the instrument constituting the company or defining its constitution.

(4) If a company makes default in complying with sub section (3), the company and every officer of it who is in default is liable to a fine.

(5) In this section and the next -
  (a) 'company' means any company liable to be wound up under this Act, and
  (b) 'arrangement' includes a reorganization of the Companies' share capital by the consolidation of shares of different classes or by the division of shares and of shares of different classes, or by both of those methods.

Many of the expressions used in section 425 of the Companies Act 1985 are defined elsewhere in the said Act as well as in the Insolvency Act 1986. For present purposes perhaps the most significant expressions are the terms 'member' which is defined by section 22 of the Companies Act 1985 as the subscriber to a companies' memorandum as well as every other person who agrees to become a member and whose name is entered on the register of members, as well as the term 'contributory' which is defined by the Insolvency Act 1986 as every person liable to contribute to the assets of a company in the event of its being wound up.

Insofar as section 425 sub section (6) of the Companies Act 1985 is concerned, the expression 'any company liable to be wound up under this Act' imports within the meaning of the term 'the Act' the Insolvency Act 1986 by virtue of section 735A of the Companies Act 1985. Since Part V of the Insolvency Act 1986 provides for the winding up of so called 'unregistered companies' being companies which are not registered in the UK, it means that foreign companies will be unregistered companies for this purpose.

In *Re Drax Holdings Limited*[11] it was held that foreign companies and unregistered companies which could be wound up under the Insolvency Act 1986 could therefore be the subject of an order under section 425. However, the relevant creditors which had to be satisfied were similar to those which were engaged when a court had to consider whether a winding up order should be made against such a company. These were matters which it was held went to discretion and principally concerned whether it could be shown that the company had a sufficient connection with England.

A company which carries on business in the UK and countries such as the US outside the ambit of the EC Insolvency Regulation referred to *below* and which in due course is subject to a winding-up in the US, can be the proper subject of a Scheme under section 425 of the Companies Act 1985 where not only the procedural requirements of an English Scheme have been fulfilled but also where the terms of the Scheme will not affect the conduct of the US or overseas liquidation.[12]

---

11. [2004] 1 BCLC 10. See also *Re La Mutuelle du Mans Insurance* [2005] EWHC 1599 where the *Drax* decision was applied.
12. *Re Home Insurance Co* (2006) BCC 164.

The EC Insolvency Regulation regulates companies which have their COMI or an establishment in England and Wales as those respective terms are applied under the EC Insolvency Regulation. Any such company can be the subject of a Scheme. Section 225 of the Insolvency Act 1986 specifically confirms the rule that where a company incorporated outside Great Britain but carrying on business in Great Britain ceased to carry on business as such, it may be wound up as an unregistered company under the Insolvency Act 1986 notwithstanding that it has been dissolved or otherwise ceased to exist as a company under its laws of incorporation. In *Re Dap Holding NV*[13] it was confirmed that there was nothing in the EC Insolvency Regulation which precluded the courts in England and Wales from finding that a foreign company with neither its COMI nor an establishment in England and Wales was liable to be wound up provided a sufficient connection or series of connections existed with jurisdiction.

The *Drax* decision has been applied in *Re Sovereign Marine & General Insurance Co*[14] to the effect that a foreign company apart from insurers in the EU and EEA dealt with *below*, may promote a Scheme under section 425 of the Companies Act 1985, provided there exists a sufficient connection with England and Wales. However, the decision also involved two EU insurers, one in England and one in France raising further considerations, in particular the EC Council Regulation Directive on the reorganization and winding-up of insurance undertakings, and the appropriate English regulations, namely the Insurers (Reorganization and Winding-up) Regulations 2004, which implement the directive in the UK. The court confirmed that the Directive contains the entire code for the determination or jurisdiction in relation to the winding-up of insurance undertaking.[15] The EC Council Regulation Directive on the reorganization and winding-up of insurance undertakings specifically provides that liquidation proceedings and reorganization measures may take place only in the Member States in which the relevant insurer is regulated. Regulation 4(1) of the Insurers (Reorganization and Winding-up) Regulations 2004 provides that a court in the UK may not make a winding-up order or an administration order in relation to the European Economic Area (EEA) insurer or a branch of such an insurer whilst regulation 5(1) provides that for the purposes of section 425(6)(a) of the Companies Act 1985[16] an EEA insurer or one of its branches is to be treated as a company liable to be wound up under the Insolvency Act 1986 if it would be liable to be so wound up under that Act but for the prohibition in regulations 4(1).

Solvent Schemes are not within the scope of the EC Council Regulation Directive on the reorganization and winding-up of insurance undertakings. In consequence of the matters set out in the preceding paragraph, the test of an EU/EEA insurer is the same as the test for a non-EU/EEA insurer. In short, the correct interpretation of 'a

---

13. (2006) BCC 49.
14. Reported: 9 June 2006
15. i.e. those insurers authorized to write direct insurance business in the EEA excluding pure insurance, being those who write only reinsurer business.
16. *See above* at II.A..

company liable to be wound up' as that expression is used in section 425(6) of the Companies Act 1985, is whether the company is the kind of company capable of being wound up under the Insolvency Act 1986: the question of whether there exists a sufficient connection relates to discretion and not to jurisdiction.[17]

B.   SCHEMES OF ARRANGEMENT AND INSURANCE

At or before the time of the EC Council Regulation Directive on the reorganization and winding-up of insurance undertakings, the UK formed the view that Schemes under section 425 of the Companies Act 1985 did not fall within the scope of said Directive. However, such schemes will be effective albeit indirectly by the provisions prescribed by the Insurers (Reorganization and Winding-up) Regulations 2004 introduced in the wake of and in compliance with the Directive and by certain restrictions imposed in order to protect the position of the Home Member State in which the insurance undertaking is based.

The relevant Regulations are effectively the Insurers (Reorganization and Winding up) Regulations 2004[18] subject to minor amendments in SI 2004 No. 546. The scope of the Insurers (Reorganization and Winding-up) Regulations 2004 are properly beyond the scope of this chapter. It follows that an EEA insurer being an undertaking other than UK insurers carrying on the activity of direct insurance with authorization received from its home Member State regulator can be subject to an English Scheme even though there may be no corresponding jurisdiction to wind it up.[19]

C.   SECTION 425 OF THE COMPANIES ACT 1985: THE KEY CONCEPTS

For a Scheme to become binding by virtue of section 425 of the Companies Act 1985 there are five distinct stages in the process. First, as the section suggests there has to be a compromise or arrangement between the company and its members or creditors or a class of either of those groups. Secondly, there has to be an application made to the court for a meeting or meetings of those groups or classes within those groups to be summoned. Thirdly, there has to be approval of the compromise or arrangement by the majority required by section 425(2) of the Companies Act 1985 at a suitable meeting. Fourthly, the court must sanction the Scheme. And, fifthly and finally and largely as a formality, the order of the court must be delivered for registration with the English Registrar of Companies[20] in accordance with section 425(3)) of the Companies Act 1985.

---

17. *See also Re DAP Holdings NV* (2006) BCC 48 which dealt with the sanction of schemes in respect of Dutch insurers and a reinsurer, non of which had its COMI or establishment in England and Wales under the EC Insolvency Regulation and where *Re Drax* supra was again applied.
18. SI 2004 No. 253.
19. *See* generally *Re Sovereign Marine & General Insurance Co* [2006] EWHC 1335.
20. The Registrar of Companies deals with the incorporation and dissolution of limited companies; examine and store company information delivered under the Companies Act 1985 and related legislation; and makes this information available to the public.

The question of what constitutes a compromise or arrangement is not straight forward. The notion of the compromise necessarily suggests there must be a pre-existing underlying dispute which has to be resolved.[21] The word 'arrangement' is wider in its scope[22], saves for example in *In Re Guardian Assurance Co,*[23] it was held that an arrangement was not necessarily analogous to a compromise. However, an extinction of rights which is in effect tantamount to an expropriation will qualify neither as a compromise nor as an arrangement since it is implicit in both ideas that there must be an element of give and take.[24]

In a Scheme which catered for the asbestos claims of employees and former employees as well as their dependants against a company and its associated companies and which also involved the compromise of claims against insurers, it was confirmed that the settlement of the litigation was in substance a tripartite matter involving the employees.[25] In the circumstances, there was therefore an 'arrangement'. However, it was not a necessary element of an arrangement under section 425 of the Companies Act 1985 that it should alter the rights existing between the company and its creditors or members, though in most cases it would probably do so. Provided the context and content of the scheme were such as to constitute an arrangement between the company and its members or creditors it would fall within section 425 of the Companies Act 1985. An arrangement was not necessarily outside section 425 of the Companies Act 1985 because its effect was to alter the rights of creditors against another party or because any such alteration could be achieved by a scheme with the other party.

On account of the width of the notion of an arrangement, it can cover not only a reduction or reorganization of share capital but also a case in which the company's business or even the business of a number of companies can be transferred to a new company.[26] Indeed the split of one company into two or more companies can itself constitute an arrangement.[27] It might be thought that a take over would inevitably fall to be dealt with by section 425 of the Companies Act 1985 but as indicated *above* the critical question is whether there is an arrangement between the company and its creditors or members.[28] Section 425 of the Companies Act 1985 applies both to companies which operate as going concerns as well as those which are in winding up. As indicated *above*[29] in addition section 425 of

---

21. See e.g. *Mercantile Investment and General Trust Company v. International Company of Mexico (1891)* [1893] 1 Ch 484.
22. See *Mercantile Investment and General Trust Company v. International Company of Mexico supra* and *see also Mercantile Investment and General Trust Co v. River Plate Trust* [1894] 1 Ch 578.
23. [1917] 1 Ch 431 and *see also Re Odhams Press* [1925] WN10.
24. *Re NFU Development Trust Limited* [1972] 1 WLR 1548: *see also Re Equitable Life Assurance* [2002] 2 BCLC 510, *cf IRC v. Adam* [2001] 1 BCLC 222.
25. *Re T&N Limited* (2007) 1 All ER 85.
26. This particular form of restructuring is also addressed by section 110 of the Insolvency Act 1986 which applies only in the case of a liquidation. The provisions of section 110 are outside the scope of this chapter.
27. Public companies are dealt with by section 427A of the Companies Act 1985.
28. See e.g. *Re Savoy Hotel Limited* [1985] Ch 351 (offer or shares to be registered as shareholder in place of existing shareholders).
29. See II.A *above*.

the Companies Act 1985 applies to companies which are registered under the Companies Act as well as unregistered companies such as foreign companies provided in the case of the latter that sufficient connection can be made with England and Wales. In *Re St James' Court Estate Limited*[30] it was held that the conversion of issued preference shares into redeemable preference shares could not be sanctioned since a specific statutory rule would otherwise be infringed. Equally, if the Scheme entails the commission of an act which is *ultra vires* the company, the court will not have jurisdiction to sanction it.[31] In *British and Commonwealth Holdings Plc v. Barclays Bank Plc*,[32] however, and pursuant to a sanctioned scheme, the company issued redeemable preference shares in satisfaction for ordinary stock units held by the company and another company. Although the arrangement was considered as constituting an *ultra vires* act committed by the company, the result of the court's sanction was that the act could not be challenged.

D.   INSURANCE COMPANIES

Insurance companies are obliged to abide by the provisions of the UK Financial Services and Markets Act 2000 (FSMA), Part VII. In *Re AXA Equity and Law Life Assurance Society Plc*,[33] the court dealt with the relevant principles to be applied when considering whether to sanction a Scheme of insurance companies. It was held that the UK Insurance Companies Act 1982 conferred an absolute discretion on the court as to whether such a Scheme should be sanctioned but the discretion needed to be exercised by giving due recognition to the commercial judgment entrusted by the company's constitution to its directors. In particular the court was concerned with whether a policy holder, employee or other interested party or any group of those parties would be adversely affected by the Scheme. This was in turn primarily a matter of actuarial judgment and for the purposes of comparing the security with the reasonable expectations of the policyholders at the time the Scheme was proposed, the 1982 Act assigned an important role to the independent actuary whose report was to be provided to the court. The court had also to pay close attention to the views of the Financial Services Authority. Overall the critical question was whether the Scheme as a whole was fair as between the interests of the different classes of persons affected: this did not mean that the court had to consider whether the scheme was the best Scheme possible. Ultimately, it was the directors who make the appropriate choice.

If the party objects to a Scheme for the transfer of an insurance business under Part VII of the FSMA, but then withdraws its objections prior to the hearing for sanction, it would generally not be entitled to a costs order in its favour.[34]

---

30. [1944] Ch 6
31. *In Re Oceanic Steam Navigation Company Limited* [1939] Ch 41. See also *Brady v. Brady* [1988] BCLC 20 CA reversed on other grounds [1989] AC 755.
32. [1996] 1 WLR 1 the trial judge considered that sanction could also cure the granting of unlawful financial assistance otherwise created by the scheme: *see* [1996] 1 BCLC 1.
33. [2001] 2 BCLC 447. See also *Re Equitable Life Assurance Society* (2007) EWHC 229 (Ch).
34. *Re Alliance Assurance Co Limited* ([2006] EWHC 3947 (Ch). unreported: 17 October 2006).

E. MEMBERS' RIGHTS

It has been held that any form of share reorganization can be the subject of a Scheme under section 425 of the Companies Act 1985. Consequently, even if preference or special rights are attached to shares in accordance with the company's memorandum of incorporation, those shares can be altered under a Scheme[35]. The most important qualification to this principle is in the case of a reduction of capital which is largely regulated by section 135 of the Companies Act 1985 and where certain formalities are required.[36] In *Re St James' Court Estate Limited*[37] it was held that for issued shares to be converted to redeemable preference shares in the Scheme there had to be a reduction of capital involving cancellation of the issued shares and the creation of the latter type of shares in an equivalent amount. In practice this reduction will be reflected in the terms of the Scheme.[38]

As referred to in the terms of section 425 of the Companies Act 1985 itself, a Scheme can be in respect of a company which is being wound up and can even cover the case of such a company transferring its undertaking to a foreign company in exchange for shares to be distributed to the former company's members.[39] In *Re BTR Plc*[40] it was considered that even if the scheme involved what is in essence a necessary transfer of the undertaking of a company in winding up to a transferee company in exchange for the shares which would otherwise be the proper subject matter of court sanction under section 110 of the Insolvency Act 1986 such an arrangement still would constitute a Scheme which could be sanctioned under section 425 of the Companies Act 1985 although the court should have regard to the specific provisions contained in section 110 of the Insolvency Act 1986.

F. WHAT CONSTITUTES A CLASS OF MEMBERS?

In *Re Heron International NV*[41] it was stated that whether members form a class for the purposes of section 425 of the Companies Act 1985 depended on whether there existed a sufficient community of interest between them, and the issue was finally a matter of degree. The classic discussion of this issue is found in *Sovereign Life Assurance Co v. Dodd*[42] where the term 'class' was said to be

---

35. See e.g. *Re Schweppes Limited* [1914] 1 Ch 323.
36. *Re Cooper, Cooper & Johnson* [1902] WN 199: see also *Re Glendale Land Development Limited (No. 2)* (1982) 7 ACLR 171 and compare *British & Commonwealth Holdings Plc v. Barclays Bank Plc* [1996] 1 WLR 1.
37. [1944] Ch 6.
38. See *Re Robert Stephen Holdings Limited* [1968] 1 WLR 522.
39. e.g. *Re Anglo-Continental Supply Co* [1922] 2 Ch 723; *Re Canning Jarrah Timber Co* [1900] 1 Ch 708; *Re Tea Corporation* [1904] 1 Ch 12.
40. [1999] 2 BCLC 675 especially at 684.
41. [1994] 1 BCLC 667.
42. [1892] 2 QB 573 at 583 per Bowen LJ. See also *Re Osiris Insurance Limited* [1999] 1 BCLC 182; *Re BTR Plc* [1999] 2 BCLC 675, 682, [2001] 1 BCLC 740; *Re Hawk Insurance Co Limited* [2001] 2 BCLC 480, [2001] BCLC 57; *Re Equitable Life Assurance Society* [2002] 2 BCLC 510.

confined to those persons 'whose rights are not so dissimilar as to make it impossible for them to consult together with a view to their common interest'. An obvious exception to this definition would be where different amounts are to be paid for shares.[43] In *Re Hellenic & General Trust Limited*[44] all the company's issued and fully paid up share capital was to be cancelled. New ordinary shares of the same amount and value were to be issued and credited as fully paid to a third party which would then pay the ordinary shareholders a higher value per share than the former ordinary shares' value. The third party already owned over 53 per cent of the ordinary shares through the medium of a wholly owned subsidiary. The court held that the interests of a subsidiary as an entity owned by an intended purchaser were sufficiently different from those of the other ordinary shareholders. Consequently, different considerations applied in deciding whether to approve the scheme. It followed that the subsidiary constituted a different class of members from the other ordinary shareholders and sanction was refused. Although it might be said that there appeared to be no difference in the rights attaching to the shares such as to justify separate meetings, it now seems to be the view that if there is a difference of interest which was argued in the case in the *Hellenic* case, that issue can be properly dealt with at the sanction stage even though no separate class of meetings have been held.[45] Although further reference will be made to the procedure concerning the means by which the applicant, usually the company, is responsible for determining whether different classes exist and if so how many classes should be determined,[46] failure properly to constitute class meetings will generally lead to the court not approving the Scheme. However, it must also be shown that if the meetings had been properly constituted, they would not have produced the necessary consents.[47] Section 425(6)(b) of the Companies Act 1985 defines an 'arrangement' as including a reorganization of the company's share capital by the 'consolidation of shares of different classes or by the division of shares into shares of different classes, or by both such methods'. The term arrangement would include not only the conversion of two distinct forms of shares in e.g. ordinary and preference shares albeit with different rights into a single class of shares with the same rights but also the sub division of the same class of shares into sub divisions of differing types of shares.

G.   WHO IS A CREDITOR?

For the purposes of Section 425 of the Companies Act 1985, a creditor is any person who has a pecuniary claim against the company whether actual or

---

43. *See* e.g. *Re United Provident Assurance Co Limited* [1910] 2 Ch 477.
44. [1976] 1 WLR 123.
45. *See* now *Re BTR Plc* [2000] 1 BCLC 740, *Re Hawk Insurance Co Limited* [2001] 2 BCLC 480 (where the Court of Appeal emphasized that it was the difference in rights rather than interests which determined whether creditors fell into different classes; see also *Re Equitable Life Assurance* decided [2002] 2 BCLC 510 and *Re UDL Holdings Limited* [2002] 1 HKC 172 especially at 184 per Lord Millett.
46. *See below* at II.H.
47. At this points *see* generally Practice Statement [2002] 1 WLR1345 and generally *Re Hellenic and General Trust Limited* supra.

contingent.[48] The definition is sufficiently wide to cover option holders,[49] life assurance policy holders,[50] and debenture holders.[51] It has been confirmed that present tort claimants who enjoy only contingent rights as well as those who might have similar claims against the company in the future might constitute creditors both for the purposes of section 425 of the Companies Act 1985 as well as for the purposes of Part I of the Insolvency Act 1986 which regulates Company Voluntary Arrangements.[52] This is so even though the latter type of class would not constitute a provable debt for the purposes of a formal winding-up.

The width and flexibility of section 425 of the Companies Act 1985 means that subject to the court's sanction, not only debenture holders but secured creditors as a whole can be compelled to take shares instead of their security,[53] just as an appropriate majority of a company's secured creditors can force a minority to relinquish their security interest on receipt of payment of less than the amount due to them.[54] Special attention should be paid to the case of foreign creditors, i.e. those creditors whose obligations are governed by contract where the proper law is one other than English law. In general, such creditors, even though bound by a Scheme under section 425 of the Companies Act 1985 will remain able to enforce their rights under the appropriate foreign contract.[55] To ensure that such creditors are fully bound by an English Scheme, the Scheme must be treated as binding under the law of the place where any assets are located. Clearly the presence of assets within the jurisdiction of the English court will mean those creditors will be fully bound by the Scheme. If assets are present outside the jurisdiction of the English court, the probability is that despite any apparent similarity with the rights afforded to other creditors, such creditors will form a separate class.[56] There is no restriction on where class meetings can be held so that in an appropriate case the court can direct that a meeting can be held abroad.[57]

H.   WHAT CONSTITUTES A 'CLASS' OF CREDITORS?

In accordance with the principles discussed above,[58] whether a group of creditors constitutes a specific and distinct class depends upon whether their rights are not so dissimilar as to make it impossible for them to consult together with a view to

---

48. See *Re Cancol Limited* [1996] 1 All ER 37 especially at 45 per Knox J.
49. *Re Compania de Electridad de la Provincia de Buenos Aires Limited* [1980] Ch 146 especially at 179 to 183.
50. *Re Equitable Life Assurance Society* [2002] 2 BCLC 510.
51. *Re Alabama New Orleans, Texas and Pacific Junction Railway Co* [1891] 1 Ch 213.
52. *Re T&N Limited* [2006] 1 WLR 1728.
53. See e.g. *Shaw v. Royle* [1911] 1 Ch 138.
54. See *Re Madras Irrigation Co (1882)* [1891] 2 Ch 228.
55. *Ellis v. McHenry* (1871) LR 6 CP 228; *Wight v. Eckhardt Marine GmBH* [2004] 1 AC 147.
56. In *Quincy Mutual Fire Insurance Co* [2004] EWHC 1594 it was confirmed that if a group of creditors have contracts governed by different laws this may be relevant when the applicant is determining whether there is a single class of creditors or not.
57. *Re RMCA Reinsurance Ltd* [1994] BCC 378.
58. See *above* at II.F.

determining their common interest.[59] Reference to the rights of creditors refers both to the rights which are to be released, varied or affected under the Scheme as well as any new rights which come into existence.[60] Where rights are not sufficiently similar there has to be a separate meeting for each distinct class of creditors even where only one creditor constitutes the class.[61] In *Re Hawk Insurance Co*[62] the principle was rephrased in the following manner, namely whether the rights of those creditors who are to be affected by the proposed Scheme are such that the Scheme can be seen to be a single arrangement or whether the Scheme should instead be regarded as a number of linked arrangements. In the case of the latter it will be necessary to identify the different classes of creditors who are affected by the linked arrangements. There is, perhaps contrary to the formulation set out at the beginning of this section no need therefore to consider whether consultation is in fact feasible. As was also stated *above* in the case of classes of members, whether there is a sufficient community of interest is a matter of degree. In *Re Hawk Insurance*[63] which involved an insurance company there were non-insurance creditors as well as insurance creditors, some of whom had unsettled paid claims whilst others had outstanding loses, either certain or uncertain. The Scheme proposed that each of these types of creditors would be paid a proportion of their valid claims, as a means of winding up the company. They were treated differently for distribution purposes but the court held that together they constituted a single class, principally because they had the same rights on a winding up and also showed a common interest, namely the desire to achieve an orderly and efficient winding up of the company and its affairs[64]. The court also stressed that taking a broad view of what constituted a class would generally help reduce costs. The fact remains that the court ultimately retains a discretion whether or not to approve the Scheme, especially where there is evidence of majority oppression.

The approach exemplified by *Re Hawk Insurance Co* can perhaps be subject to the observation that it fails properly to take into account the particular economic reality the different creditor groups have by way of differing interests, especially when it comes to the valuation of their claims. It might also be said that to allow the possible over-enlargement of groups may not provide sufficient protection to minority interests. However, for the moment the *Hawk*-type approach has been adopted in subsequent decisions.[65] In the particular case of a life assurance

---

59. *Sovereign Life Assurance Co v. Dodd* [1892] 2 QB 573 especially at 582 confirmed in *Re Hawk Insurance Co Ltd* [2001] 2 BCLC 480 at para 31; see also *Re Osiris Insurance Limited* [1999] 1 BCLC 180 and 188; *Sea Assets Limited v. Perasahaan* [2001] EWCA 1696 where it was observed that the key element was similarity in the rights which the creditors had so that not all those creditors with a similar interest needed necessarily to be members of the same class. See also *Re Equitable Life Assurance Society* [2002] 2 BCLC 510.
60. *Re Hawk Insurance Co Limited* supra at para. 31.
61. See e.g. *RMCA Reinsurance Limited* [1994] BCC 378.
62. *Supra* especially at paragraphs 23 and following.
63. Supra.
64. See also *Re Osiris Insurance Limited* [1999] 1 BCLC 112 where the same approach is applied even though the creditors held different types of insurance policies.
65. e.g. *Re Equitable Life Assurance Society* [2002] 2 BCLC 510; *Re: UDL Argos Engineering* [2002] 1 HKC 172; *Re Telewest (No. 2)* [2005] 1 BCLC 772 and in the matter of *MyTravel Group Plc* [2005] 2 BCLC 123.

company it is likely that holders of matured policies may constitute different classes to those who hold current policies but much will turn upon the scheme's terms. In the leading case of *Sovereign Life Assurance Co v. Dodd*[66] those two types of creditors were treated differently principally because the rights enjoyed by both classes within the Scheme were markedly different. In general debenture holders who hold debentures of a similar type, i.e. in the same series will form the same class. Whether debenture holders do belong to the same class will therefore depend on an analysis of the nature of the transactions between the company and the particular debenture holders. An example which is often given is that of a property development company which buys land in order to build properties but will then raise money on a series of successive mortgages: in such a case the various mortgagees will probably be regarded as sufficiently distinct so as to constitute a series of separate classes. It is rights, and not interests, which constitute the governing factor in the composition of classes, and it is the extent to which the relevant rights are dissimilar that determines the composition of classes in any particular case.[67]

In the wake of the *Re Hawk* decision the Companies Court issued a Practice Statement of 15 April 2002 (2002 Practice Statement) to replace an earlier direction in 1934; in order, as it was put, to enable the issues concerning the composition of classes of creditors and the summoning of meetings to be identified and if appropriate resolved early in the proceedings. It is now the express responsibility of the applicant, invariably the company, to determine whether more than one meeting of creditors is required by a scheme and if so to ensure that those meetings are properly constituted by a class of creditors so that each meeting consists of creditors whose rights are not so dissimilar as to make it impossible for them to consult together with a view to their common interest.[68]

In *Re British Aviation Insurance Co Limited*,[69] an insurance company insolvent run-off proposed a Scheme with some of its creditors who had insurance and reinsurance claims in the aviation sector. The claims were made under so-called currency policies which provided unlimited prospective coverage falling within three principal categories, namely unsettled paid claims, outstanding loss and incurred, but not reported claims. Proposing creditors in this last category objected that the Scheme was unfair. The court held that in deciding whether all the policyholders formed a single class, it was important to identify the appropriate comparator which in the case of a solvent company which had ceased to write insurance business was a continuing solvent run-off. In the latter case, policyholders with incurred but not reported claims would enjoy a full indemnity from the company, whilst under the Scheme they were at risk of having inadequate resources to meet their claims. In the case such as the Scheme before the court where a solvent liquidation was not a realistic alternative, those creditors within the first and third categories did not have interests that were insufficiently different as to make it impossible to say that they could not consult together 'in their common interests'.

---

66. [1892] 2 QB 573.
67. *Re Telewest Communications Plc* [2005] 1 BCLC 752.
68. *See* generally [2002] 1 WLR 1345.
69. (2006) BCC 14.

The *British Aviation* decision should be compared with the subsequent decision of *Re Sovereign Marine & General Insurance Co Limited*[70] where all the Scheme companies in that case were solvent, but as in the earlier case, all save one of those companies were in run-off having written a currency policy. The opposing creditors consisted principally of those with incurred but not reported claims who argued that a single class meeting was inappropriate as they constituted a separate class which, for voting purposes represented a distinct interest from the class which comprised notified claims. The court applied the same comparator as in the *British Aviation* decision, pointing out the policyholders with incurred but not reported claims under the Scheme would be paid cash up front which could be less or more than the claims they would have been entitled to make under a solvent run-off. In the particular circumstances of the case therefore, since there was greater uncertainty in estimating such claims, the court held that they should be constituted as two separate classes in relation to the solvent companies to enable Scheme creditors to vote, first in relation to their unpaid reclaims and secondly in relation to claims which were incurred, but not yet reported.

Such an application can be brought before a registrar or a judge of the Companies Court but the Practice Statement suggests that 'substantial schemes' should go before a judge, and where possible the same judge should retain the matter. It is the responsibility of the applicant to bring to the attention of the court any so called creditor issues, i.e. issues which go to the constitution of meetings or which affect the conduct of the meeting or meetings in question. Therefore, unless there are good reasons for not doing so, the applicant should take all reasonable steps to notify any potentially affected person of the Scheme, the purpose of the Scheme, the fact of the holding of the appropriate meeting or meetings and their composition when the court then comes to consider whether to make what is known as a 'meetings order' on which occasion the court will consider whether more than one meeting is required and if so the composition of such meeting or meetings.[71] If a particular issue needs to be determined, the meetings will generally be adjourned and anyone served with notice of this issue can apply, if necessary, to vary or discharge any order that has been made. Any creditor who feels that he has been unfairly treated at the meetings stage can apply later, i.e. when the Scheme comes to be sanctioned but he or it will have to state good reason why they did not raise a class issue at an earlier stage.

It has recently been confirmed that the hearing of an application for leave to convene meetings of creditors to consider a Scheme is not the time to determine the merits of the Scheme.[72]

The importance of the 2002 Practice Statement is that prior to the applicant issuing the initial application for the leave to convene meetings, it should circulate creditors in order to ascertain whether any creditors are of the view that there is more

---

70. (2006) BCC 774.
71. In *Re Altitude Scaffolding Limited* (2006) BCC 904, it was held that in the absence of evidence there existed only one creditor in any particular class, the attendance of one person would not constitute a proper meeting for the purposes of section 425 of the Companies Act 1985.
72. *See* generally *Re Telewest Communications Plc* [2005] 1 BCLC 752.

than one class involved. Part of the object of the 2002 Practice Statement is to ensure that if any creditor wishes to argue issues regarding the constitution of classes, it must do so at the initial stage and not at the time when the court considers whether it should sanction the Scheme. However, there are occasions where an application can be made to the court to dispense with any initial approach to creditors on the premise that time is of the essence where there is evidence of delay in proceeding with the Scheme. Alternative, such an application can be made if the preliminary views of creditors were sought, but the resultant delay could prejudice the Scheme as a whole.[73]

I. ESTIMATE OF DEBTS

As indicated *above*, for an arrangement to be approved there must be a majority by way of number (often colloquially referred to as 'the numerosity test') representing at least ¾ majority in value of creditors present and voting. Section 425 of the Companies Act 1985 cannot apply if it is not possible to estimate the amount of the claims of individual creditors. If, in the case of a life assurance company, there are different values of policies otherwise securing the same amount, albeit on different lives and if in particular it is uncertain in what cases there may have been a novation by policy holders of their policies, it may be impossible to estimate the amount of the claims of individual creditors. In this case, the court would be unable to act under the section.[74]

J. THE CONDUCT OF CLASS MEETINGS

As indicated *above*, the court's function at the first stage is to consider whether more than one meeting of creditors is required and the appropriate constitution of such meeting or meetings. In addition, if a creditor issue is drawn to the attention of the court, the court should consider what directions are appropriate including any order as to postponement. If any person is affected by any such order, the court can give that person permission to vary or discharge any order which otherwise convenes a meeting. However, although section 425 of the Companies Act 1985 speaks of the meeting or meetings being 'summoned in such manner as the court shall direct' the court in fact does not control the meeting or meetings. It merely has the right to issue directions as to the manner in which the meeting or meetings should be held and may even waive non-compliance with any direction that it might otherwise have given.[75] Failure to serve certain shareholders with notice might be accidental and in such a case, any meeting will not necessarily be invalidated.[76]

If there is no prospect that the Scheme will be approved by any of the meetings or equally if there is no prospect that the company itself will consent to the Scheme,

---

73. See e.g. *Re Marconi Plc* (unreported: 24 March 2003).
74. See e.g. *Re Albert Life Assurance Co* (1871) 6 Ch App 381.
75. *Re Anglo-Spanish Tartar Refineries* [1924] WN 222. As to the :court's inherent jurisdiction see *Re English, Scottish and Australian Chartered Bank* [1893] 3 Ch 385 particularly at 395.
76. *Re Peninsular & Oriental Steam Navigation Co* (2 March 2006).

in general the court will not sanction the calling of meetings at all.[77] Clearly if a class is not concerned in or affected by a scheme, no meeting of that class should be held.[78] A common situation involves ordinary shareholders who although forming a class will have no interest because all the available assets will be used up in favour of those who have rights ranking in priority to such shareholders.[79] The critical test is whether a class of creditors who might otherwise be affected in fact have a genuine and tangible economic interest in the outcome and not one which is merely theoretical or fanciful.[80]

When the court is considering whether it is appropriate to summon a meeting, it is not at that stage concerned with the merits or demerits of the Scheme.[81] In general if a class is small in number and there is evidence that its members agree to the Scheme a meeting may well be dispensed with.[82]

The use of proxies is in practice universal. Proxy forms can be sent out with notices of the meetings in such form as is 'considered appropriate'.[83] However, it has been confirmed that even a proxy in some other form may be acceptable provided the same is lodged within any time period that may have been specified.[84] Generally however, proxies which are lodged after the appropriate time limit will be rejected,[85] subject to any direction that may for example specify that later proxies can be delivered to the chairman of the meeting. In such a case, this would normally result in the chairman being able to disclose to the meeting how many late proxies had been lodged in order to ascertain whether objection was taken.

Many irregularities on a proxy form will be disregarded, e.g. where the agent's name (as distinct from that of the principal) appears on the form.[86] A form of proxy may even entitle a chairman to vote on a motion for adjournment.[87] In such a case the practice is for the chairman to vote for an adjournment employing proxies which vote in favour of the Scheme.[88]

---

77. *Re Savoy Hotel Limited* [1981] Ch 351.
78. *Re Tea Corporation* [1904] 1 Ch 12. See also *Re MyTravel Group Plc* [2004] EWHC 2741: there is no need even to recite in any order the existence of a class whose economic interests are not otherwise affected by the proposed Scheme.
79. *Re Tea Corporation supra*. There can be no complaint on the part of ordinary shareholders should they receive an unexpected dividend, i.e. one to which they were not otherwise entitled under the proposed Scheme.
80. See *Re MyTravel Group Plc* supra.
81. *Re Telewest Communications Plc* [2004] BCC 342 and 348; *Re British Aviation Insurance Co Limited* (2006) 1 BCC 14.
82. *Re RMCA Reinsurance Limited* [1994] BCC 378. *See also Altitude Scaffolding* (2006) BCC 904 which stated that in general, the attendance of one person will not constitute a class meeting.
83. See e.g. *Re English, Scottish and Australian Chartered Bank* [1893] 3 Ch 385 especially at 395.
84. *Re Dorman Long & Co Limited* [1934] Ch 633 at 662–4.
85. *Re Equitable Life Assurance Society* [2002] 2 BCLC 510.
86. *Re English, Scottish and Australian Chartered Bank supra*.
87. *Re Waxed Papers Limited* [1937] 2 All ER 481.
88. *Re Waxed Papers Limited* supra and *Re BTR Plc* [1999] 2 BCLC 679 especially at 684.

The proxy-holder need not be a class member: even a liquidator can appoint the chairman of the meeting as proxy.[89]

There are occasionally cases in which it will be alleged that a creditor or member of a company has some form of collateral interest in voting in favour of a proposed scheme: in such a case, there must be proper evidence of such an ulterior motive before a court will consider disenfranchising a class member who would otherwise be entitled to vote.[90]

K.   NOTICE OF MEETINGS

Invariably notice of any meeting or meetings should be advertised. This will be the case where the instrument which grants its holder rights against the company is held not in the name of a named party but only as a bearer or registered shareholder.[91] Any creditor who has no rights against the company need not be given notice.[92] Otherwise the company must have taken all sufficient steps to notify all those who are eligible to attend the meeting.[93] However, if there is an accidental or inadvertent failure to notify the relevant creditors, the process will not necessarily be invalidated.[94] If, for example, excessive time and expenditure would be incurred, then an advertisement may well be regarded as unnecessary and dispensed with. Any deficiency in the notice procedure will be taken into account at the time the scheme as a whole comes to be approved by the court.[95]

If the court orders a meeting to be convened, 'at least' a stated number of days that expression denotes a required number of clear days as to the required number.[96]

The court has a discretion to decide whether or not a meeting can be convened without the consent of the company.[97] As explained *above*, it is a responsibility of the applicant, invariably the company itself, to select the correct class. Consequently, wherever practicable, therefore, the application must take all reasonable steps necessary to notify those interested of the proposed order.[98]

In most cases the court which makes a meetings order will give directions as to the manner in which the meeting or meetings is or are to be convened, the appointment of a chairman, the form of the appropriate notice (generally directed to be

---

89. *Re General Mortgage Society (Great Britain) Limited* [1942] Ch 274.
90. *Re Linton Park Plc* (unreported: 14 March 2005).
91. *Mercantile Investments and General Trust Co v. International Co of Mexico* [1893] 1 Ch 484n.
92. *The Oceanic Steam Navigation Co Limited* [1939] Ch 421.
93. *Re Osiris Insurance Limited* [1999] 1 BCLC 182 at 186.
94. *Re Equitable Life Assurance Society* [2002] 2 BCLC 510.
95. *Re British Aviation Insurance Co Ltd* (2006) 1 BCC 14.
96. *Mercantile Investment and General Trust Co v. International Co of Mexico* [1893] 1 Ch 488n at 489n.
97. *Re Savoy Hotels Limited* [1981] Ch 351.
98. *See* e.g. *Re Marconi Plc* [2003] All ER (D) 362.

given by post)[99] and the form of proxy or proxies to be used. Almost invariably the meetings order will direct the chairman to report to the court on the results of the meeting.

Section 425(2) of the Companies Act 1985 requires the sanction of a majority in number or representing three-quarters in value of the members of the class 'present and voting' in person or by proxy. This is so, even if, the requisite majority may not actually represent three-quarters in value nor even a majority of the total class. Voting agreements in the sense of a binding agreement between the company and some members of a class under which those members agree to vote in favour of the Scheme are not uncommon and are permissible. There is some discussion about the time and costs saving virtues of such agreements in *Re Telewest Communications Plc (No. 1)*.[100] However, the court will need to consider whether a member otherwise bound by such an agreement would not reasonably have voted differently had there been no such agreement. Any member who does sign up to such an agreement, however does not thereby constitute a separate class, unless the agreement confers upon him benefits otherwise not available to other members of the same class. Existence and disclosure of such an agreement however will be relevant to whether the court sanctions the Scheme.

L.   SANCTION

It is well established that when a court sanctions a Scheme, it does not do so merely as a formality.[101] Importantly, the court will not sanction a Scheme if it appears that the majority has not voted *bona fide* in the interests of the class in respect of which it is the majority[102] or if in all the circumstances the court does not approve of the Scheme.[103] The court must, in other words, ensure that the power otherwise vested in the majority is used for the benefit of the class as a whole and not for individual interests. The above principles are particularly engaged where a specific creditor or group of creditors who is or are members of the class also enjoy interests stemming from the fact that he or they are also members of another class where different interests are in play, e.g. debenture holders, who also hold shares.[104] In such a case, the court will scrutinize with even greater care the conduct and outcome of the relevant meetings.

The court's discretion to sanction a Scheme is therefore unfettered, but in general terms the discretion will be motivated by three principal considerations,

---

99. In the case of Schemes involving large and multiple bond issues, a variety of techniques will in practice be employed to discover the identity of all beneficial holders, e.g. company searches and web sites searches, etc.
100. [2004] BCC 342.
101. *Kempe v. The Ambassador Insurance Co* [1998] 1WLR 271, 276.
102. *Re Wedgwood Cole & Iron Co* (1877) 6 Ch D 627.
103. *Re Hickman XP Strawbridge* (1883) 25 Ch D 266.
104. See e.g. *Re Madras Irrigation and Canal Co* [1881] WN 172 and *Re Alabama, New Orleans, Texas & Pacific Junction Railway Co* [1891] 1 Ch 213 at 239.

namely: (1) whether there has been compliance with the statutory provisions; (2) whether the class or classes was or were fairly represented by those who attended the meetings and moreover that the statutory majority was acting in a *bona fide* manner, and in particular, was not coercing the minority in order to promote the former group's interest or interests adverse to those of the class they purported to represent; and, (3) that the arrangements were such as an intelligent and honest man being a member of the class concerned and acting in respect of his interests might reasonably approve.[105] The court will have regard to the amount and quality of the information that has been supplied to the creditors and which by virtue of the Report on the meeting will equally be available to the court at the sanction hearing. There might well be a case in which, at first, the petition is dismissed on account of the necessary majority or majorities not being obtained, but where such approval is later obtained; in such a case the court may sanction the Scheme on a fresh petition without requiring fresh meetings of the other classes.[106] Often a Scheme may be disadvantageous to some creditors, but the court may well take the view that overall the Scheme's advantages outweigh any disadvantages. In *Re T&N Limited*[107] it was held that a court would be unlikely to sanction a Scheme which resulted in creditors receiving less than in a winding-up assuming the return in a winding-up would be achieved within a reasonable timescale. However, it was important in such a case to take into account the interests of all dissenting creditors to ensure that they received at least as much under the proposed Scheme as in the formal liquidation. Generally, in such a case, the court should give all dissenting parties an opportunity to put forward their case with as much details as possible. This is especially so if a significant number of creditors has voted in support of the Scheme and all creditors were fully informed about it.[108] A Scheme will come into effect by the court's approval and by court order.[109] It was confirmed in *Re Equitable Life Assurance Society*[110] that approval of a Scheme which will bind dissentients does not breach the rights afforded by Article 1 of the First Protocol to the European Convention on Human Rights (ECHR) since the Scheme necessarily involves an exchange of rights and not any form of confiscation. However, it is thought that an order under section 425 of the Companies Act 1985 might still constitute an interference with the peaceful enjoyment of a persons' possessions under Article 1 of the First Protocol of the ECHR. It could be said that the State by its agencies, i.e. the courts are engaging in this activity by virtue of rendering a

---

105. See *Re Alabama, New Orleans, Texas & Pacific Junction Railway Co* [1891] 1 Ch 213, 219; *Re English Scottish & Australian Chartered Bank* [1893] 3 Ch 385, 408; *Re National Bank Limited* [1966] 1 WLR 819, 828. See also *Re BTR Plc* [1999] 2 BCLC 675, 680, [2000] 1 BCLC 740, 747.
106. *Re United Provident Assurance Co* [1911] WN40.
107. (2005) 2 BCLC 488.
108. See e.g. *Re Osiris Insurance Limited* [1999] 1 BCLC 182; *Re Equitable Life Assurance Society* [2002] 2 BCLC 510. In *Re British Aviation Insurance Co Limited* (2006) 1 BCC 14, the courts observed that there is no English case involving a court with jurisdiction to sanction a Scheme where refusal took place in the exercise of the court's discretion.
109. *Kempe v. Ambassador Insurance Co* [1998] 1 WLR 271.
110. [2002] BCC 319.

Scheme effective.[111] It follows from the *above* principles that although the court does not, and indeed should not, rubber-stamp the results of the creditors' meetings, it will not usually dissent from the results of those meetings unless it is shown that the class or classes have been improperly constituted, or the meetings or any of them have or has failed properly to consider the interests of the creditors' concerns, or if there is some blot on the Scheme.[112] A court is fully entitled to impose conditions prior to sanction. In *Re Canning Jarrah Timber Co*,[113] the court required the liquidator of a company to abandon certain underwriting agreements and to pay out unsecured creditors in full prior to the company's assets being passed over to a new company. In general, the court will not sanction a Scheme if a class whose interests are affected by the Scheme does not vote in its favour at the class meeting unless that class could not receive any assets in the event of an immediate distribution.[114] Although a court clearly cannot amend or alter the substance of any Scheme, in the sense of improving on the position in any arrangement which they have not properly considered, obvious mistakes or errors on the face of the Scheme can be corrected.[115] The Scheme hearing is clearly the opportunity for any creditor who feels he or it has been unfairly treated to raise any objections regarding sanction. The 2002 Practice Statement already referred to makes it clear[116] that if a creditor raises a creditor issue at the sanction hearing, good reason will need to be shown why that issue was not raised at an earlier stage. Examples of cases where objections to Schemes have been upheld are numerous, but they include cases in which a Scheme provided for the payment of costs and remuneration without making proper provision for making such costs or remuneration subject to court taxation or control.[117] Similarly, a court will not generally sanction a Scheme, if it empowers a majority of debenture holders to bind a majority in a way which could otherwise be regarded as a delegation to that majority of the court's own powers.[118] A Scheme which sought to include provisions which submitted all disputes including disputes as to the legal rights of creditors to an arbitrator or an adjudicator would probably also be objectionable.[119]

---

111. See *Re Hawk Insurance Co Limited* [2001] 2 BCLC 480; reversed on other grounds [2001] BCLC 508.
112. *Re English Scottish & Australian Chartered Bank* [1893] 3 Ch 385 especially at 409; *Re BTR Plc* [1999] 2 BCLC 675 at 680. A blot on the Scheme is in effect a defect in the Scheme which comes to light after the meetings: see *Re English Scottish & Australian Chartered Bank* supra at 409 quoted in *Re Equitable Life Assurance Society* [2002] 2 BCLC 510 at paragraph 95.
113. [1900] 1 Ch 708.
114. *Re Hellenic & General Trust Limited* [1976] 1 WLR 123; *Re Tea Corporation Limited* [1904] 1 Ch 12. See also *Re Telewest Communications Plc* [2005] 1 BCLC 772 approved in (2005) BCC 29, where the court upheld the adoption of a currency conversion rate which though on the facts produced a less favourable result for certain bondholder creditors, represented a formula which was not inherently unfair. See generally *below* at II.M.
115. *Kempe v. Ambassador Insurance Co* [1998] 1 WLR 270 especially at 276.
116. See *above* at II.H.
117. See *Re Mortgage Insurance Corporation* [1886] WN 4.
118. *Re Land Mortgage Bank of Florida* [1896] WN 48.
119. *Re Hawk Insurance Co Limited* [2001] 2 BCLC 480. At first instance the court held that it had no jurisdiction to sanction the Scheme as the appropriate class meetings had not been held. On appeal it was held that it was not necessary to have separate meetings: *see* [2001] 2 BCLC 48.

The position might be different if certain types of claim against the company, e.g. insurance claims, were determined by an expert.[120] Once an order is made sanctioning the Scheme, it is immediately binding on the creditors as well as the company and all those representing the company, e.g. a liquidator, subject to any appeal arising out of the sanction hearing. Once an order is made, the Scheme cannot thereafter be questioned;[121] so for example, following the making of an order, a company cannot subsequently challenge the Scheme on the ground that it is, in substance, no more than an unlawful return of capital.[122] It has been held that if claims are likely to arise over a long period against a company in circumstances in which there was inadequate insurance cover, it will in general be appropriate to sanction what would otherwise be regarded as an unusual scheme in order to provide long term finance for claims and to protect the Scheme company or companies from the risk of insolvency. Such an approval will generally fulfil the test as to whether the proposed scheme would be one which in principle an intelligent and honest member of the class or classes of all relevant creditors could reasonably approve.[123] The position is different, however, if there has been a defect or irregularity in the procedure whereby sanction of the Scheme was obtained.[124] Proof of fraud may well however justify setting aside the Scheme unless it can be shown that the Scheme would have been sanctioned if the fraud had not been perpetrated.[125] The Scheme in fact takes effect once the order expressing the court's sanction has been delivered to the Registrar of Companies.[126]

The court will sometimes sanction a Scheme that contains a power of amendment which might operate after sanction: alternatively, it can sanction a Scheme that authorized ancillary documents which contained a power to amend subsequent provisions within the Scheme. However, in general a court will be predisposed not to sanction such a Scheme.[127]

M.   Meetings and Sanction: A Recent Example

In *Re Telewest Communications Plc*,[128] the company and its wholly owned Jersey subsidiary made applications for leave to convene creditors' meetings to consider proposals for a Scheme of arrangement regarding both companies. The main creditors were USD and GBP bondholders respectively. The Schemes proposed a debt for equity swap involving the cancellation of the bonds in exchange for shares in a new Delaware holding company pro rata to the total claims of each

---

120. See e.g. *Re Pan Atlantic Insurance Co Limited* [2003] 2 BCLC 678.
121. *Nicholl v. Eberhardt Co* (1888) 59 LT 860.
122. See e.g. *British & Commonwealth Holdings Plc v. Barclays Bank Plc* [1996] 1 BCLC 1.
123. See *Re Cape Plc* [2006] EWHC 1446 (Ch): 10 June 2006.
124. *Sovereign Life Assurance Co v. Dodd* [1892] 2 QB 573. *cf.* the Australian position where Schemes have been held binding irrespective of any defects, See e.g. *Chief Commissioner of Pay-Roll Tax v. Group Four Industries* (1983) 8 ACLR 973.
125. *Fletcher v. Royal Automobile Club Limited* [2000] 1 BCLC 331.
126. Section 425(3) of the Companies Act 1985.
127. See *Re Cape Plc supra* applying *Horrocks v. Broome* (2000) BCC 251.
128. [2005] 1 BCLC 752 confirmed at (2005) BCC 29.

bondholder. To determine the number of new shares to be granted to each bondholder, all claims covered by the Scheme had to be expressed in a single currency. It was provided in the Schemes that GBP claims should be converted into USD amounts using a particular spot-rate formula, dependent in large part on the fluctuations and rates in the period between the date on which the bonds first defaulted and the last date prior to the posting of the explanatory statement to the Scheme. A group of bondholders argued that the conversion rate should depend on a specified spot-rate and not on the proposed average rate, since the latter was bound to be less favourable.

The bondholders contended that the meeting should not be held unless the Scheme was amended to correct the unfairness complained of. In the alternative, they claimed that if the Scheme was to continue, there should be separate meetings of the USD and the GBP bondholders. The court held that it should give leave for the meetings to be convened. It stressed first that at the stage at which application for leave was sought, the court should not consider questions which went to the fairness of the Scheme: they were questions to be determined at the sanction stage. Secondly, any issues as to whether creditors formed one or more classes was a question of judgment to be decided according the facts of each case. In the present case, all bondholders had substantially the same rights and interests: in particular, they all represented unsecured claims and would therefore rank *pari passu* in the liquidation.

The court also pointed out that the proper comparator in such a case as the present case before it where a Scheme was put forward as an alternative to winding-up, was an insolvent liquidation. A spot-rate was an intrinsic part of the *pari passu* distribution machinery in a liquidation, and therefore it was conceivable that a Scheme which provided for conversion on a different basis might give rise to class issues if the difference in creditor claims' treatment was material. However, in the present case, the court found that there was insufficient dissimilarity to constitute separate classes and enough similarity to place both sets of bondholders in the same class. The case therefore confirms as in the case of another unreported Scheme[129] that where a Scheme was proposed as an alternative to liquidation or administration, it is relevant to ask what treatment creditors would receive in a formal liquidation.

By the time of the subsequent sanction hearing[130] and at the creditor's meetings, the Scheme had been approved by the statutory majorities. However, as the sanction hearing, a significant minority of the GBP bondholders (all but one of whom had voted against the Scheme) raised the exchange rate issue as going to the question of fairness. This was on the basis that the average rate unfairly discriminated against the GBP bondholders. The court recognized there existed a difference in the positions of the GBP and USD bondholders. The question was whether the difference was not so large as to prevent them from consulting together in a single meeting with a view to their common interests.[131] On the

---

129. *See* e.g. the Schemes involving *Marconi Corporation Plc* and *Marconi Plc* (*below* at IV).
130. [2005] 1 BCLC 772.
131. *See* the case of *Re National Bank Limited* [1966] 1 WLR 879.

England & Wales

facts, it was found that the average rate was not unfair principally on the basis first that the Scheme would lead to a better result for the bondholders than they would otherwise obtain in a liquidation, and secondly that the majority of the relevant creditors had approved the Scheme. It followed from this decision that a Scheme can depart from the normal liquidation rules, e.g. as to the rates of exchange, if the departure is overall fair in all the circumstances.

N. COSTS

In general, the costs of an unsuccessful opposing party to a Scheme at the sanction stage will be borne by the applicant unless the position was clearly frivolous or vexatious.[132] However, if the Scheme is supported by some creditors or members, but not others, and the Scheme fails, the court will be inclined to order those supporting the Scheme to bear the costs of those who opposed it.[133] If a party objects to a Scheme, but withdraws the objections prior to the sanction hearing, it will in general not recover its costs.[134]

In cases where the grounds of those objecting to the Scheme are known prior to the sanction hearing, the company can even obtain a pre-emptive costs order in favour of the objector which will enable the objector or objectors to be paid those costs up to and including the sanction hearing.[135]

O. THE EFFECT OF LIQUIDATION

When a company is in liquidation, either by way of voluntary winding up or in compulsory liquidation, the Insolvency Act 1986 grants an extensive range of powers to liquidators to effect compromises or arrangements with creditors or those alleging themselves to be creditors.[136] Section 425 of the Companies Act 1985 can justifiably be regarded as an enlargement of those provisions so that if the compromise or arrangement in question constitutes a distribution otherwise than strictly in accordance with rights, a section 425 of the Companies Act 1985 Scheme should be employed.[137] A section 425 of the Companies Act 1985 Scheme may even involve the imposition of terms which differ from those which obtain in the normal liquidation: a Scheme would inevitably bind the liquidator, but the court would generally be careful before sanction is granted in such a case.[138] In most

---

132. See e.g. *Re National Bank Limited* [1966] 1 WLR 819.
133. See e.g. *Re Esal (Commodities) Limited* [1985] BCLC 450.
134. *Re Alliance Assurance Co Limited* ([2006] EWHC 2947 17 October 2006).
135. See e.g. *Re AXA Equity & Law Life Assurance Society Plc* [2001] 1 BCLC 447. The court may well impose a cap on the amount.
136. See generally sections 165–167 and Schedule 4 of the Insolvency Act as well as Schedule 4, Part I, paragraph 2 to the said Act.
137. *Re Trix Limited* [1970] 1 WLR 1721.
138. See e.g. *Re Anglo-American Insurance Limited* [2001] 1 BCLC 755.

cases in which the company is in liquidation, the applicant proposing the Scheme will be the liquidator. The court will not have jurisdiction to order a sanction between a company in liquidation and its creditors unless the Scheme is approved by the liquidator.[139] If on the other hand the company is not in liquidation, the company's board or alternatively, a simple majority of members in general meeting, will need formally to approve the proposal.

P. APPEAL

Any party who appears at the sanction hearing can appeal. However, a creditor or contributory who did not appear at that hearing will not be able to appeal except with permission. In any event, permission is required for any appeal under section 425 of the Companies Act 1985.[140]

Q. PARTICULAR ISSUES: DEBENTURE DEEDS

It is not uncommon for a debenture deed to contain a provision that a stated majority of the debenture holders can sanction 'any modification or compromise of the rights of the debenture holders against the company or against its property'. By doing so, the majority would bind the minority. It has been held that a power to effect a modification will not entitle the majority to relinquish or extinguish rights. As indicated at the outset of this chapter, in relation to the general notion of 'compromise', there must be an element of give and take, and no element of outright gift or total extinction of rights.[141] However, a modification of rights would include a resolution to raise money by way of priority over the debentures (as well as any form of debt for equity swap);[142] equally, a resolution to increase the amount of debenture stock and to extend the time or date for redemption, where a company was not otherwise able to effect redemption, would probably be a 'compromise' of claims.[143] A power on the part of a majority to sanction modifications of rights will not entitle the majority to delegate that power to others, e.g. to a committee.[144] As also indicated *above* at II. M, at the sanction hearing the court will be particularly concerned that the statutory majority have acted *bona fide* and have not coerced the minority. However, it may well be that certain debenture holders will hold or enjoy particular interests which will be reflected in the

---

139. *Re International Contract Co (Hankey's Case)* (1872) 26 LT358.
140. Section 54 of the UK Access to Justice Act 1999.
141. *See above* at II.C and *Mercantile Investment & General Trust Co v. International Co of Mexico (1891)* [1893] 1 Ch 484n.
142. *See e.g. Follitt v. Eddystone Granite Quarries* [1892] 3 Ch 75.
143. *Walker v. Elmore's German and A-H Metal Co* (1901) 85 LT 767.
144. *British America Nickel Corporation v. O'Brien* [1927] AC 369 especially at 379. A committee might however be set up under the Scheme to deal e.g. with scheme administration decisions and fees, etc.

appropriate resolutions: if the latter is the case, such debenture holders can vote on the resolution or resolutions, but the court will need carefully to consider the overall fairness of the scheme.[145]

R. SECTION 426 OF THE COMPANIES ACT 1985: GENERAL

Section 426 of the Companies Act 1985 deals more specifically with the information which has to be circulated about the proposed Scheme to a company's creditors and members. According to section 426(2) of the Companies Act 1985, the statement must explain the effect of the compromise or arrangement and in particular it should state 'any material interests' of the company's directors (whether as directors or as members or as creditors or otherwise) and the effect of such interests on the proposed Scheme. Section 426(4) of the Companies Act 1985 provides that where the proposed scheme affects the rights of the company's debenture holders, the same information as that which relates to the company's directors must be given. In practice this means that apart from the *above* specific requirements under section 426(2) and (4) of the Companies Act 1985, the circular must set out all the principal facts which will enable those parties who are in receipt of the circular to exercise their independent judgment as to the proposed scheme. It should be assumed that the creditors and members will have read the circular itself.[146] There may be cases in which it could be said that the information provided falls short of what is essentially required by section 426 of the Companies Act 1985, but where the court will nevertheless sanction the Scheme because even in the light of the admitted information, no creditor or member would have altered his or its view as to the perceived benefits offered by the Scheme.[147] It follows that if material facts come to light between the provision of the circular and the creditors' meetings, such facts should be disclosed at the meetings.[148] It is to be noted that section 426(2) of the Companies Act 1985 states merely that the directors' 'material interest' must be disclosed as distinct from the effect of the proposed Scheme on such interest. The concept of a 'material interest' is a broad one, and apart from including such relatively obvious matters as interests in other companies, particularly associated ones and related benefits, the circular should address any matter which is likely to or could be said to be likely to effect the interests of the director, and in particular, his willingness or otherwise to accept or reject the scheme.[149] Failure to comply with any provision of section 426 of the Companies Act 1985 will generally invalidate any resolution to approve the Scheme.[150]

---

145. *See* e.g. *Goodfellow v. Nelson Line (Liverpool)* [1912] Ch 324.
146. *See* e.g. certain comments in *Re British Aviation Insurance Co* (2006) 1 BCC 74.
147. As in *Re Heron International BV* [1994] 1 BCLC 667.
148. *See Re MB Group Plc* [1989] BCLC 672.
149. *See* e.g. *Rankin & BlackmoreLimited* (1950) SC 218.
150. e.g. if the advertisements covering the meeting do not state where a copy of the statement can be obtained contrary to section 426(3).

S. SECTION 427 OF THE COMPANIES ACT 1985: THE FACILITATION OF A COMPANY RECONSTRUCTION OR AMALGAMATION

If a Scheme under section 425 of the Companies Act 1985 involves a transfer of company's assets to a new company, it will not be appropriate to sanction the proposed transfer as a Scheme under section 425, since it will involve an attempt to bind the company that has yet to come into existence. The court will, however, make an order binding only the existing company and its members and creditors. Section 427 of the Companies Act 1985 provides by subsection (2) that if it is shown:

(a) *that the compromise or arrangements has been proposed for the purposes of, or in connection with, a scheme for the reconstruction of any company or companies or the amalgamation of any two or more companies, and*

(b) *that under the scheme the whole or any part of the undertaking or the property of any company concerned in the scheme ('a transferor company') is to be transferred to another company ('the transferee company'), the court may, either by the order of sanction in the compromise or arrangement or by any subsequent order, make provision for all or any of the following matters.*

(c) *The matters for which the court's order may make provision are:*
   (a) *the transfer to the transferee company of the whole or any part of the undertaking and of the property or liabilities of any transferor company,*
   (b) *the allotting or appropriation by the transferee company of any shares, debentures, policies or other like interests in that company which under the compromise or arrangement are to be allotted or appropriated by that company to or for any person,*
   (c) *the continuation by or against the transferee company of any legal proceedings pending by or against any transferor company,*
   (d) *the dissolution, without winding up, of any transferor company,*
   (e) *the provision to be made for any persons who, within such time and in such manner as the court directs, dissent from the compromise or arrangement,*
   (f) *such incidental, consequential and supplemental matters as are necessary to secure the reconstruction or amalgamation is fully and effectively carried out.*

The court only has the power to make an order under section 427 of the Companies Act 1985 where the Scheme or arrangement is related to a reconstruction or an amalgamation. In *Re MyTravel Group*,[151] it was held that a reconstruction requires that there be a substantial identity between the body of the shareholders in both the old, i.e. the transferor company and the new, i.e. the transferee company. The

---

151. [2005] 1 WLR 2365.

various matters listed in section 427 subsection (3) of the Companies Act 1985 are self explanatory. Insofar as provision is made in section 427 subsection (3)(e) of the Companies Act 1985 as to the position of persons who dissent from the compromise or arrangement is concerned, such provision can, and usually will, take the form of a provision authorizing or sanctioning the purchase of a dissenting party's interests.

III. COMPANY VOLUNTARY ARRANGEMENTS

A. GENERAL

Company Voluntary Arrangements (CVAs) were introduced by Part 1 of the Insolvency Act 1986. The original provisions in the 1986 Act have been the subject of major statutory reform principally in the form of sections 1 and 2 of the Insolvency Act 2000. The main effect of such reforms has been to introduce a new optional form of CVA embodying a moratorium for small eligible companies. In addition, amendments were introduced as regards the general CVA model.

The Cork Committee in its 1982 Report,[152] particularly at paragraphs 400–403, felt it was desirable to introduce a system whereby a company could enter into a binding arrangement with its creditors in order for there to be a composition of its overall liabilities undertaken by means of a relatively simple process. Prior to the introduction of CVAs the only options were, for present purposes, principally represented by formal Schemes under section 425 of the Companies Act 1985 previously dealt with in this chapter. However, section 425 of the Companies Law 1985 is by any standards a time consuming and costly procedure.

Although CVAs have now been utilized for a number of years, it could be said that despite their simplicity and relative informality, two factors have perhaps hampered their overall effectiveness and somewhat restricted their use to an extent smaller than might otherwise have been originally envisaged. First, no secured or preferential creditors will be bound by a CVA without their express consent, and secondly, until the introduction of section 1A of the Insolvency Act 1986 by the Insolvency Act 2000 with regard to small eligible companies, there was no provision in the legislation which enabled a moratorium to be obtained or applied for while the proposal for an arrangement was being drawn up (unlike the case of individuals who in the case of Individual Voluntary Arrangements (IVAs) have always been able to apply for an interim order.

The only exception to the second restriction is that a moratorium can be sought if a proposal for a voluntary arrangement is combined with an application to seek the appointment of an administrator under what is now Schedule B1 to the Insolvency Act 1986. It is to be noted, however, that the moratorium arises solely out of and by virtue of the administration proceedings. Since 1 December 1994, a voluntary arrangement procedure based on CVAs has been available for insolvent

---

152. Insolvency Law and Practice, Report of the Review Committee, HMSO, Cmnd. 8558, 1982.

partnerships[153] and the CVA model has been extended to building societies by virtue of the Building Societies Act 1986.[154] Section 426 of the Insolvency Act 1986 affords judicial cooperation between various countries including the Channel Islands and the Isle of Man, and the UK allows even a foreign company to use a CVA procedure.[155]

The basic procedure regarding a CVA is based on a proposal to enter into a suitable arrangement made either by the directors, or if the company is in liquidation or in administration, by the liquidator or administrator. The proposal which is put forward is then put before and considered by meetings of the company's creditors and members. If the proposal is accepted following such meetings and as a result of them, the arrangement becomes operative and binding on both the company and all its creditors. The proposal is even binding upon those creditors who did not support it. A CVA cannot be imposed on creditors without, in general terms, the agreement in value of 75 per cent by value of the creditors. Once in place, the company and indeed all parties are bound by the arrangement, and must keep to its terms unless there is agreement amongst the creditors to vary those terms.

B. COMPOSITION OR SCHEME OF ARRANGEMENT?

Section 1 of the Insolvency Act 1986 refers to the principle that the directors of a company may make a proposal under this part to the company and to its creditors for a composition in satisfaction of its debts or a scheme of arrangements of its affairs. The terms 'composition' and 'scheme of arrangement' are not synonymous; a scheme concerns an arrangement stopping short of a full release or discharge of a creditor's debts such as a moratorium.[156] Consequently, if creditors are being asked to accept a sum which is less than payment in full, it is advisable for the proposal to state at the outset that what is being sought is a composition.

C. NATURE OF A CVA

The CVA is essentially a contractual arrangement, but there remain significant distinctions from a classic form of contract. With a CVA, there is no strict need for an offer and acceptance, so a creditor can be bound even if he has not accepted the CVAs terms, e.g. when he has been out-voted. It is however useful in general terms to regard a CVA as a binding form of contract.[157]

---

153. *See* Insolvency Partnerships Order 1994 (SI 1994 No 2421).
154. Section 90A.
155. *Re Television Trade Rentals Limited* [2002] BCC 807.
156. Generally a 'composition' is an agreement to pay a sum instead of a larger debt or other obligation: See e.g. *Inland Revenue v. Adam* [2002] BCC 247.
157. *See* generally *Johnson v. Davies* [1999] BCC 275, especially at 289; *Alman v. Approach Housing Limited* (2002) BCC 723.

D. Procedure: The Basic Steps

With regard to CVAs there are three basic stages. The first concerns the making of the proposal. This step will entail the preparation of the proposal commonly undertaken in practical terms by a qualified insolvency practitioner who in due course prepares his own report. In addition, there will be a statement of affairs. The second principal stage involves a moratorium if the company is suitably eligible. There are a number of detailed provisions involving the need to submit additional documents in connection with the moratorium including requirements as to advertisement and as to the convening of meetings. Thirdly and finally, there are separate provisions regarding the convening of the requisite meetings with regard to CVAs whether or not they were previously eligible for a moratorium.

E. Practical Factors

It is a fundamental feature of a CVA that the company's directors remain in day-to-day charge of the company. Once the CVA has been approved, the proposed nominee, i.e. the licensed insolvency practitioner who will have reported prior to approval on the prospective benefits of the CVA, will normally become the supervisor of the CVA itself. Although the terms of a proposal for the CVA may include a provision that a supervisor is empowered to remove or appoint a director, whether he can in law and in fact do so, will depend upon the company's own constitutional documents. It is therefore suggested that it is extremely doubtful that even where the CVA contains such a term, this power can validly be exercised by the supervisor without further ado.

An equally fundamental feature, at least in practice, of a CVA is the need to reflect the availability of suitable funding in order to underwrite the operation of the CVA. A well drafted CVA should at least refer to the means whereby additional working capital is to be raised as well allude to the relevant amounts and to the timing considerations which might affect the raising of funds. The means whereby new cash is raised are many and varied. For example, a bank may require fresh advances to be matched by funds raised by directors or shareholders. The latter may do so by means of new share subscriptions. However, as the law now stands, any such new funding would not attract what is sometimes called any 'super priority' thereby ranking ahead of any existing security claims.

F. The Role of the Court

Although in the large majority of CVAs, the role of the court is, to say the least, minimal (at least where no moratorium is involved), the CVA proposal and the nominee's report must be lodged with the court.[158] The court however makes no order in

---

158. *See* Insolvency Act 1986 section 2; Insolvency Rule 1986, Rule 1.7.

contradistinction to the case of an IVA where it will be asked to grant an interim order provided the proposal is 'serious and viable'.[159] Indeed, it does not appear as if the court can in some way disallow the proposal, let alone make any observations about any relevant aspect of it. As will be explained in *further* detail *below*,[160] effectively the only involvement in the CVA process by a court will be triggered by a challenge to the CVA under sections 6 and 7 of the Insolvency Act 1986 or where there has been a default or where there is an application that there has been a transaction defrauding creditors under section 423 of the Insolvency Act 1986.

G.   MEMBERS' INVOLVEMENT

Although creditors must sanction a CVA in accordance with the requirement that a majority of 75 per cent in value must approve the proposal, it is also provided that the shareholders by a simple majority may approve the proposal. Moreover, the term 'member' would seem to include persons to whom shares have been transferred by operation of law. It is however, not immediately clear why members must express their approval: a CVA is an agreement between the company and its creditors. Indeed, there may well be cases where the seeking of members' approval may hinder the implementation of the proposal, e.g. where there is a dispute as to who the members are or whether as a dispute between various factions of the company's membership.

Admittedly under section 4A of the Insolvency Act 1986,[161] a CVA will take effect notwithstanding that the members of the company do not vote in its favour. It is also provided that if the decision taken by the creditors' meeting differs from that taken by the members' meeting, a member may within 28 days apply to the court for an order that the decision of the company meeting, i.e. that of the members is to have effect instead of that of the creditors' meeting. At present, there is no judicial indication of the circumstances in which that provision might be applied.

H.   PROCEDURE

1.   The Proposal

As part of the preparation of any set of proposals, a company acting by its directors, must satisfy itself that a CVA is viable. The company may already be in a formal insolvency, in which case the proposal will be the responsibility of the liquidator or administrator. In general terms, should an administrator prepare a proposal, the same will represent a formal means of distribution of the available funds to the company's creditors. Almost invariably the drafting of the proposal will be in

---

159.   See e.g. *Hook v. Jewson Limited* [1997] 1 BCLC 664.
160.   See III.K *below*
161.   Introduced by paragraph 5 of Schedule 2 to the 2000 Act: *see* especially section 4A(2).

the hands of an insolvency practitioner and/or legal advisers instructed by the directors. A well prepared proposal should incorporate provisions as to trading and cash flow forecasts. Both the Insolvency Act 1986 and the UK Insolvency Rules (Insolvency Rules) specify[162] that the directors must prepare a statement of affairs for the information of creditors. This should show the likely return for creditors after deduction of costs and it should also show comparative figures in respect of any possible alternative form of insolvency procedure, e.g. a creditors' voluntary liquidation. It is highly desirable that a formal meeting of the full board of the company should be convened in order to approve the proposal. This is partly because section 1(1) of the Insolvency Act 1986 states that 'the directors of a company' may make a proposal which suggests that the directors as a whole should make the appropriate decision. It is, however, equally important that the company's Articles of Association be respected so that if, for example, the constitution of the company is not adhered to, there may then be a challenge to the validity of the proposal, despite any subsequent purported ratification.

2. The Moratorium

In practice it is highly likely[163] that a so-called free-standing CVA, i.e. one which is not linked with a pre-existing administration or liquidation, will entail consideration of a moratorium. If the directors wish to apply for a moratorium, they must supply the nominee with a copy of each of the following, namely: (1) the proposed arrangement; (2) a statement of affairs; (3) such other information as is described in the appropriate Insolvency Rules; and, (4) such other information as the nominee requires to enable him to form an opinion as to whether the proposal is viable. Such information is likely to include an explanation as to how the arrangement is to be financed.[164]

Following the receipt of the above documents, the nominee must then issue a statement indicating whether or not, in his opinion, the proposal is viable and whether creditors' and members' meetings should be convened.[165] In particular, the nominee is required by Schedule A1, paragraph 6(2) of the Insolvency Act 1986 to indicate whether or not, in his opinion, the proposed arrangement has a reasonable prospect of being approved and implemented and whether the company is likely to have sufficient funds.

There is as yet no clear guidance as to how these provisions are to be addressed. A nominee will now have to make some enquiries of the directors and probably of the major creditors prior to completion of his report as nominee. It should be noted that by Insolvency Rule 1.35,[166] the directors can amend the proposal

---

162. Insolvency Act 1986, section 2(3)(b) Insolvency Rules, Rule 1.5.
163. In practice only in the case of a small non public company which is not part of a group.
164. *See generally* Insolvency Act 1986, Schedule A1, paragraph 6(1) inserted by Insolvency Act 2000 in Schedule 1, paragraph 4.
165. *See* previous footnote; paragraph 6(2).
166. Introduced by the Insolvency Act 2000, Schedule 1, paragraph 4.

prior to the nominee issuing his statement under Schedule A1 paragraph 6(2) of the Insolvency Act 1986 which would allow the directors to change the proposal if the nominee is not satisfied with the proposal as initially presented to him.

Insolvency Rule 1.38[167] now provides that the nominee must submit his Schedule A1 paragraph 6(2) statement to the directors within 28 days of his receipt of the proposal. The statement must have annexed to it Form 1.8 which consists of the nominee's comments on the proposal and the statement of his consent to act. After the nominee has prepared a statement, the directors must file the following documents in court, namely: (1) the proposed arrangement; (2) the statement of affairs; and, (3) a statement that the company is eligible for a moratorium. In addition, they must file a statement that the nominee has consented to act and the nominee statement as to the viability of the proposal and as to funding.[168]

Insolvency Rule 1.39 now provides that the documents are to be delivered with four copies of a schedule listing them within 3 working days of the submission by the nominee of a statement under Schedule A1 paragraph 6(2) of the Insolvency Act 1986.[169] The directors are also required to file a copy of any reasons why the nominee agreed to the statement of affairs being drawn up to a date more than 2 weeks prior to his receipt of the proposal: they are also required to file in court a copy of the nominee's comments on the proposal.

The moratorium comes into effect at the time when the documents are filed in court. The court endorses the schedule of filed documents under Insolvency Rule 1.39(3). The moratorium normally lasts 28 days, but that period can be extended with the agreement of the meetings of the creditors and members, although not beyond two months in total beyond the date on which the notices of the meetings were sent out.[170]

Any meeting convened to extend the moratorium may appoint a new nominee in place of the original nominee.[171] Notice of any extension must be filed with the Registrar of Companies and with the court. Although in practice, in most cases, the nominee would no doubt be aware of the coming into force of the moratorium, the directors must inform him once it is in force[172] and he must then advertise the moratorium notifying the Registrar of Companies as well as the company, and importantly, notify any creditor of whom he is aware who has presented a winding up petition which has not been dismissed or withdrawn. There are similar advertisements and notifications required in the case of the moratorium coming to an end or being extended.[173]

---

167. Also as inserted by the Insolvency Act 2000, Schedule 1, paragraph 4.
168. Insolvency Act 1986, Schedule A1, paragraph 7 is inserted by the Insolvency Act 2000, Schedule 1, paragraph 4.
169. The forms are prescribed: *See* in particular Forms 1.2 and 1.9.
170. Insolvency Act 1986, Schedule A1, paragraphs 8 and 32.
171. Insolvency Act 1986, Schedule A1, paragraph 33.
172. Insolvency Act 1986, Schedule A1, paragraph 9.
173. *See* e.g. Insolvency Rules 1.40, 1.41 and 1.42.

3. Effect of the Moratorium

During the period of the moratorium, no legal proceedings, execution or other legal process can be commenced or continued without the leave of the court. Moreover, no creditor can exercise his or its security rights except with leave. In practical terms, this will mean that a bank cannot appoint a receiver whilst a moratorium is in force. Equally, no meeting of the company can be held without the consent of the nominee or with the leave of the court.[174] Although in the case of a pending administration, prior notice must be given to a debenture holder, no such prior notice is required in the case of an imminent initiation of a pre-CVA moratorium. The existence of a moratorium must be stated on the company's letterhead and other company-generated documents. There are limits as to the security that can be granted by the company during the moratorium, and the company cannot get credit of more than GBP 250 without disclosure of the moratorium to its creditors.

During the moratorium period in certain circumstances, and particularly if it can be shown that it would be in the best interests of the company to do so, the company may dispose of its assets even if a winding up petition has been issued.[175] This principle when read together with Insolvency Act 1986, Schedule A1, paragraph 12(2) appears to override the restrictions which are normally imposed by section 127 of same, which renders void any transactions made in the twilight period between the presentation of a winding up petition and the date of any winding up order. Indeed, there even seems no reason why a company should not be able to dispose of or charge its property during the moratorium period. The Insolvency Act 1986, Schedule A1, paragraph 24 provides that during the moratorium period, the nominee must monitor the company's affairs and satisfy himself that the proposed CVA continues to be likely to be viable, particularly as regards funding.

If, however, having accepted his nomination, the nominee then forms an adverse view, he must withdraw his consent to act; at which point the moratorium will come to an end and appropriate notices must be given to the court, the Registrar of Companies, the company and the company's creditors. The question of withdrawal of consent is extremely important. Should a nominee withdraw without due consent, he may be accused of damaging the ability of the company to survive. If he withdraws consent too late or not at all, he may well be attacked or even proceeded against by creditors who have provided credit in the moratorium period. It follows that he will be well advised to chronicle the reasons for his withdrawal with as much detail as possible and as frequently as possible.

A creditor, member or director affected by the moratorium can apply to the court[176] if he or it is dissatisfied, in which case the court can make an interim appointment to replace the original nominee. Such a situation may arise if a creditor alleges that the nominee's activities are damaging the company, or if such

---

174. Insolvency Act 1986, Schedule A1, paragraph 12.
175. *See* Insolvency Act 1986, Schedule A1, paragraph 17.
176. *See* Insolvency Act 1986, Schedule A1, paragraph 26(i).

actions are unfairly prejudicial to the company or its creditors. If an application for replacement is made, a seven day notice must be provided to the existing nominee.

Any provision in a floating charge which provides for it to crystallize on the obtaining of a moratorium is void.[177] Although a company is bound to seek a moratorium, if it in fact does so, the company must abide by the 1986 and therefore pre-Insolvency Act 2000 legislation if it should then seek to obtain a binding arrangement. If at the end of the moratorium, no voluntary arrangement has been approved, there is provision for the making of a compulsory winding up order.[178]

4.   Post-Moratorium Procedure

The institution of the moratorium is followed by meetings of both creditors and members which will invariably be held on the same day with the latter following upon the former. As an additional practical matter, in the event of there being one dominant creditor, i.e. one whose vote might radically affect the prospect of a 75 per cent majority approval, a nominee must take care not to be seen to, or in fact, be taking any step which might suggest that he is soliciting for proxies; nor should he be in receipt of any payment in relation to being approached to assume the role of prospective nominee,[179] as distinct from fees received in respect of any appointment as a nominee.

The relevant meetings must be summoned for a date not more than 28 days later than that on which the moratorium comes into force and at least 14 days written notice must be given. Insofar as the meeting of the company's members is concerned, the said meeting must be convened and held in accordance with the company's Articles of Incorporation as well as the relevant provisions of the company's legislation,[180] including terms of any applicable shareholders' agreement.

Although reference should be made to specialist works on company law and procedures for further discussion of all topics relating to when and how company meetings should be held, it is important to note that due consideration should be given to empowering the nominee, by virtue of appropriate terms to the proposal, to convene creditors' meetings during the conduct of the CVA, mindful of the fact that the power to convene an Annual General Meeting will remain vested in the directors. In addition, even if the CVA proposal provides for an increase in authorized and issued share capital, it will be for the directors and not the supervisor to implement the procedure and convene the relevant meetings.

5.   Role of the Nominee. The Nominee's Report

As should be apparent from the preceding discussion, a nominee whether prior to as well as upon his appointment, should not in fact seek or be seen to act on behalf of the directors. The precise confines of his role have yet to be fully established

---

177. Insolvency Act 1986, Schedule A1, paragraph 43.
178. Insolvency Act 1986, section 122(1)(fa) as inserted by the 2000 Act, Schedule 1, paragraph 6.
179. *See* e.g. Institute of Chartered Accountants of England and Wales Statement 1.202.
180. *See* e.g. sections 366–383 Companies Act 1985.

in the relevant case law but a fundamental aspect of his function involves the facilitation of the proposal with the nominee in effect occupying a position akin to that of a mediator. This appears to remain the position even though at some stage and at least initially, the nominee may well have provided advice to the directors. The neutrality of his position is demonstrated by the fact that should there be a default in the subsequent implementation of the CVA, it will be for the supervisor to petition for the company's winding up.

Overall the nominee should satisfy himself that the information in the proposal is accurate and fair. A Statement of Insolvency Practice[181] or SIP (No.3)[182] provides that a nominee 'should bear in mind his overriding duty to ensure a fair balance between the interests of the company, the creditors and any other parties involved'. This SIP further comments on the nominee's initial contact with the directors and the need to explain and demonstrate professional independence.

A nominee in general has an obligation to creditors but equally he is entitled to rely on what a debtor, i.e. normally the directors will have told him, albeit subject to a reasonable degree of verification on the part of the nominee.[183] It follows that in assuming the role of nominee, an insolvency practitioner has a clear duty to ensure that the directors have read and understood the proposal which they are making and which he will quite possibly have drafted. In practical terms he should therefore explain the company's obligations and perhaps more importantly he should verify and if he thinks it appropriate, investigate any information given to him by the directors if he believes any such information to be inaccurate or misleading.

Section 2 of the Insolvency Act 1986 provides that the nominee must report to the court within 28 days of his being given notice of the company's proposal. It has been judicially observed that at this juncture the nominee must bring a 'considered opinion of the sort which would expect of a professional accountant and a licensed insolvency practitioner to bear upon the nature of the proposal'.[184] The nominee should therefore attempt to assess not only whether the proposal is in accordance with the rules but whether as the court remarked, it is 'fit for consideration'. The Insolvency Service[185] has, in the wake of these observations, suggested that

---

181. As stated in the explanatory foreword of the Statements of Insolvency Practice (available at <http://www.r3.org.uk/publications/?p=80&s=0&id=293>), the Statements of Insolvency Practice are issued to members of the UK Society of Practitioners of Insolvency and give guidance as to the best practice to be adopted by authorized insolvency practitioners having regard to the relevant legislation. They are adopted by each of the Recognized Professional Bodies for promulgation as part of each Recognized Professional Bodies' regulatory regime and are issued to insolvency practitioners authorized by the Secretary of State for Trade and Industry.
182. Published by the Association of Business Recovery Professionals.
183. See *Pitt v. Mond* [2001] BPIR 624 cf *Prosser v. Castle Sanderson* (2003) BCC 440.
184. *Re A Debtor (No 222 of 1990)* [1993] BCLC 237.
185. The Insolvency Service is an executive agency of the UK's Department of Trade and Industry (DTI) which: (1) administers and investigates the affairs of bankrupts, of companies and partnerships wound up by the court, and establish why they became insolvent; (2) acts as trustee/liquidator where no private sector insolvency practitioner is appointed; (3) acts as nominee and supervisor in fast-track individual voluntary arrangements; (4) takes forward reports of bankrupts' and directors' misconduct; (5) deals with the disqualification of unfit

practitioners now consider the following issues in relation to a proposed arrangement, namely: (1) whether the proposal is feasible; (2) whether it is fair to creditors; (3) whether it represents an acceptable alternative to a formal insolvency, e.g. administration or liquidation; (4) whether the proposal is fit to be considered by the creditors; and, (5) whether in all the circumstances the proposal is fair to the debtor.

In the leading case of *Re Greystoke*,[186] the court in effect confirmed these principles by holding that a nominee must satisfy himself first that a debtor's true position as to his or its assets or liabilities should not appear to be materially different from the information which is imparted to the creditors, secondly that the proposal has a real prospect of being implemented and that there is no avoidable manifest unfairness.[187] It is therefore vital that the nominee engages himself in an independent assessment of the matters reflected in the above requirements. Clearly the extent to which any proposal is viable will depend upon such matters as management and will thereby involve matters which are clearly beyond the remit of the nominee, but overall the nominee must also satisfy himself that the proposal is 'serious and viable'. It has been noted above, however, that in relation to a moratorium,[188] the legislation now requires the nominee to report whether in his opinion first whether the proposed arrangement has a reasonable prospect of being approved and implemented[189] and secondly that the company is likely to have sufficient funds to enable it to carry on its business. In such a case, it now appears that a practitioner will need to address any concerns he may reasonably have or reasonably entertain as regards matters which could impact upon the funding underlying the proposal and questions of management. A practitioner must, in other words, ask himself whether the company will be able to comply with the terms of its proposal. Again though, this overriding requirement is subject to an entitlement on the part of the nominee to be able to rely on information submitted to him by the directors unless he has reason to doubt its accuracy.[190] It remains to be seen whether in practice this will hinder the growth of the moratorium procedure.[191]

---

directors in all corporate failures; (6) deals with bankruptcy restrictions orders and undertakings; (7) authorizes and regulate the insolvency profession; (8) assesses and pays statutory entitlement to redundancy payments when an employer cannot or will not pay its employees; (9) provide banking and investment services for bankruptcy and liquidation estate funds; (10) advises DTI ministers and other government departments and agencies on insolvency, redundancy and related issues; (11) provides information to the public on insolvency and redundancy matters via its website and other means; and, (12) conducts confidential fact-finding investigations into companies where it is in the public interest to do so. These enquiries are carried out by Companies Investigation Branch. *See* <http://www.insolvency.gov.uk/index.htm>.

186. [1996] BCLC 429.
187. *See also Hook v. Jewson Limited* [1997] 1 BCLC 664.
188. *See above* at III.H.2.
189. *See* generally Insolvency Act 1986 schedule A1 para 6(2) asserted by the Insolvency Act 2000, *See also* Insolvency (Amendment No 2) 2002 schedule 1 para 3 amending rule 1.7.
190. *See* Insolvency Act 1986 schedule A1 para 6(3).
191. *See Hurst v. BDO Stoy Haywood* (unreported 20 September 2002) in which a claim in negligence against accountants for summary judgment was dismissed in relation to their

6. The Nominee's Costs

It is clearly incumbent on the nominee to explain in advance what his likely costs and charges will be. A voluntary arrangement should not continue if virtually all the funds in the arrangement are to be used up in fees and costs.[192] Consequently, the proposal should set out what fees are likely to be charged both by the nominee as well as by his advisors. It is also good practice for a proposal to identify the party or parties if applicable who are responsible for having introduced the directors to the nominee and the amount paid or to be paid in respect of such introduction. The *above* are no more than illustrations of the need for overall transparency with regard to the proposal.

Insolvency Rule 1986 4.128(3) provides that if a liquidator is a solicitor and he uses his own firm to act on behalf of the company, any profit costs will not be paid unless they have been authorized by the liquidation committee, the creditors or the court. Consequently, in the case of a CVA if the supervisor is a solicitor, no profit costs should be taken unless they are permitted by the proposal.

Outside the particular context of CVAs, a supervisor should regularly review his costs. Just as in the case of a liquidation where a practitioner should not spend undue time investigating or agreeing the claims of unsecured creditors when there is no prospect of a dividend to such creditors, so a supervisor should not expend too much time and cost in attending upon the management at the company's premises if there is no resultant benefit to creditors. Equally, the practitioner should not employ solicitors to carry out work which he or his staff can just as easily perform.

I.   THE PROPOSAL: CONTENTS

Insolvency Rule 1986 1.3 sets out the contents of a proposal document. However, the contents of the Rule are not exhaustive and it is wise to consult the practitioner guidelines set out in SIP 3,[193] though it may well be that even compliance with such guidelines may be insufficient in a given particular case. Since the introduction of the voluntary arrangement procedure, two desirable practical requirements have emerged. First, the language of the proposal must be clear, intelligible and not open to doubt or ambiguity. It is unlikely that a court would readily infer any implied term. Secondly, the proposal should make express and due allowance for further amendments and modifications.[194] This is not to say that there exists any standard or universally acceptable form of proposal. The requirements for a well drafted proposal are constantly evolving, quite apart from the distinct commercial and legal

---

preparation of a proposal, partly on the grounds that presentation of a non-negligent proposal would have made no different to the court's refusal to approve the arrangement in any event.
192. *Vadher v. Weisgard* [1997] BCC 219.
193. Published by the Association of Business Recovery Professionals. *See* note 181
194. *See above* at III.H.2.

needs of the debtor company.[195] As noted *above* with regard to the role of the nominee,[196] if a moratorium is being sought, the proposal must state the address to which the notice of the consent of the nominee to act is to be sent.[197] The rules, especially Insolvency Rule 1.35, also enable the directors to amend the proposal prior to submission to them by the nominee. If the statement by the nominee is required in connection with the obtaining of a moratorium as required by paragraph 6(2) of schedule A1 of the Insolvency Act 1986, that statement should indicate whether in the nominee's opinion first, the proposed voluntary arrangement has a reasonable prospect of being approved and implemented, secondly, that the company is likely to have sufficient funds available to endure the proposed moratorium to enable it to carry on business and finally, that meetings of the company and its creditors should be summoned to consider the proposed voluntary arrangement.

A well drafted proposal should begin with some general description regarding the company which is advancing the proposal including all relevant background and history. Given the need to ensure that the proposal should be clear and unambiguous, this section of the proposal should be drafted in such a way that creditors can understand what has happened in the past and what steps are envisaged regarding the possible return to profitability. There should also be a section describing whether and, if so, what other forms of insolvency process have been considered. More importantly, a statement of affairs should be attached and commented upon, not only with a view to indicating to creditors what dividend might be anticipated but also to provide a comparative analysis with whatever alternative forms of insolvency might be applicable.

A subsequent section of the proposal should then provide details about the company's assets. If, as often happens, it is intended that a director or directors is or are to acquire particular assets, full details of the contemplated transaction should be provided since it is important that the proposal in no way suggests that the company is likely to enter into a preference or transfer at an under value. Any action involving directors' approval should be set out with suitable reference to the company's articles. Particular care should be taken to have regard to section 320 of the Companies Act 1985 which entails members' prior approval if a director is to acquire a non-cash asset from the company worth GBP 100,000 or more. Engagement of sections 317 to 320 of the Companies Act 1985 means that specific resolutions will have to be minuted at the appropriate directors' and members' meetings convened to approve the proposal.[198]

Unlike a liquidator, a supervisor cannot disclaim onerous property. Moreover a voluntary arrangement will not normally protect a company against forfeiture or distress, since the latter do not constitute processes of a judicial nature. Unless a moratorium is in place, there is no bar to a landlord exercising his rights to forfeiture.

---

195. There are standard forms published by the Association of Business Recovery Professionals but it is questionable whether the suggested terms which are lengthy remain fit for most cases.
196. *See above* at paragraph 5.
197. Insolvency Rule 1986 1.35 introduced by the Insolvency (Amendment) (No. 2) Rules 2002.
198. *See* generally *Demite v. Protec Health Limited* [1998] BCC 638.

If, however, a moratorium is in force, a landlord must obtain the court's leave which can be granted subject to such conditions as the court thinks fit.[199] Consequently, it is advisable that all matters relating to any landlords who might be affected by the proposal be set out in as much detail as possible. Equally, the position regarding the company's secured creditors should be set out with as much explanation as possible, especially all facts relating to the degree of support such creditors are prepared to demonstrate. It is now customary for a proposal expressly to confirm that the assets will be held on trust for the benefit of creditors of the voluntary arrangement together with an undertaking that the company will not dispose of any of its assets other than in the ordinary course of business.[200] There are cases in which it will be appropriate that a supervisor should be given authority to take all steps reasonably necessary to prevent the improper disposal of assets otherwise subject to the arrangement. In such cases the supervisor may well be granted a charge over the land and buildings as well as a chattel mortgage or similar security over such assets as plant and machinery, details of which should again be set out in the proposal.

A further section in the proposal should deal with the company's liabilities. The manner in which preferential and unsecured creditors will be addressed will be dealt with later.[201] The rules also require that the details of any and all legal proceedings which have been commenced against the company should be referred to in the proposal. In practice it is advisable that a draft proposal be circulated to the HM Revenue and Customs.[202] A company will need to continue to submit returns in the wake of approval of a proposal: it is even desirable expressly to provide that should a company fail to make returns or payments in the period following approval, the arrangement should be terminated.

Yet another section should set out the normal provisions regarding the submission of proofs of debt and the agreement of claims. In addition a proposal should contain details of any procedures which are decided upon to resolve disputes as to the admission and quantification of claims. It may well be that the directors and the nominee decide that certain suppliers and their claims be excluded from the CVA on the ground that such parties are essential for the continuing trading activities of the company.

Even though, as will be set out below,[203] the Insolvency Act addresses the position of creditors who have not been given due notice of the proposal, a well-drafted proposal will specifically cater for how and if so, to what extent, additional liabilities can be admitted. A particularly significant set of provisions should concern the company's obligations to make payments under the arrangement. It is important for creditors to see how the company has arrived at the amount which it is offering to pay. This will mean that the proposal should incorporate suitable cash flows and related forecasts showing the amounts which it is envisaged the

---

199. Insolvency Act 1986 schedule A1 para. 12(1)(f).
200. *See* generally *Re N T Gallagher & Son Limited* [2001] 2 BCLC 133.
201. *See below* at III.J.1 and III.J.3.
202. HM Revenue & Customs is the result of the merger between the Inland Revenue and HM Customs and Excise Departments and is the UK's tax authority.
203. *See below* at III.J.10.

company can pay and the relevant time period during which such payments will continue. The supervisor should also be given the power to conduct periodic reviews of the company's profitability and the proposal should also cater for the possibility of increased contributions should profitability outstrip the forecast level of profits. Key terms include not only a provision that failure to maintain monthly payments will constitute a default but also a clear description of those events which constitute default under the arrangement.[204] It is possible that some dividends will remain unclaimed, in which case provision should also be made for such sums to be paid into the Insolvency Services account or alternatively repaid into the arrangement.

The need for co-operation between the company and the supervisor should also find expression in a well drafted arrangement. Indeed lack of co-operation can constitute a ground on which a supervisor can seek a winding up order. Separate sections should deal with funding arrangements, guarantees, third party funds and details of all applicable bank accounts. It is particularly important to make a clear differentiation between pre and post CVA liabilities since a supervisor should not allow a CVA to continue if contributions are maintained solely at the expense of post CVA creditors.

All the powers, duties and even potential liabilities of the supervisor should be carefully specified. The supervisor will be anxious to avoid being treated as a shadow or de facto director and a suitable provision should be inserted in an attempt to address this possibility. Express allowance should also be made for the death, resignation or removal of a supervisor. The rules specify the need to set out all the relevant legal provisions regarding the possibility of voidable transactions and as indicated *above* detailed provisions should be included to deal with all questions of amendment and modification.

J.   CREDITORS

The general rule with regard to CVAs is the so called *pari passu* principle that all creditors should be treated alike. The position in practice is far from being as straightforward as that principle might otherwise suggest however.

Secured creditors are invariably entitled to be paid in full out of any proceeds which represent fixed charged realizations. There are, however, occasions where a CVA supervisor will be empowered by the terms of the CVA to sell assets which are subject to a fixed charge: in such a case he would be well advised to come to an agreement with the fixed charge holder as to the basis of his remuneration attributable to his efforts.

In cases in which the supervisor is in receipt or in control of funds which are not the subject of fixed charges, then in most cases the fund will be applied in the following order subject to the creditors' agreement. First, the fund will be appropriated towards the nominee's fee and thereafter in favour of the outstanding fees and disbursements of any previous officeholder including the Official Receiver.

---

204. *See below* at III.M.

Next, the funds should be applied in favour of the costs of any petitioning creditor who sought the compulsory winding up of the company and, subject to those costs, any costs which the supervisor will incur in petitioning for the winding up of the company in the event of the company's default under the terms of the CVA. Thereafter, subject to provision for the supervisor's own fees, the fund will be applied in the order normally prescribed for in a formal insolvency, namely the claims of preferential creditors, any prescribed part (as to which see the next section), floating charge holders, unconnected unsecured creditors and finally connected unsecured creditors.

Note should also be made of the two fundamental means by which creditors' claims are to be quantified, namely first in relation to voting purposes and thereafter in relation to dividend purposes. In the case of the former, votes will be calculated according to the amount of the debt as at the date of the creditors' meeting or, in certain circumstances, as at the date of a prior liquidation or administration. However, a separate calculation will need to be made as at the date of the computation of the dividend to cater for such subsequent eventualities such as mitigation of loss.

1. Preferential Debts

Preferential debts are listed in Schedule 6 to the Insolvency Act 1986.[205] The Enterprise Act 2002 abolished Crown preferential debts.[206] The principal heads of preferential debts are represented by contributions to occupational pension schemes and employee remuneration. A CVA supervisor will therefore need to consider such matters as holiday pay and arrears of pay if redundancies need to be made to ensure the continued viability of the business. Provision will sometimes also have to be made for the so called prescribed part which represents a fund otherwise payable to a floating chargeholder but made available to unsecured creditors.

Although Crown debts no longer constitute preferential debts, it is advisable that if possible the amount of any Revenue and Customs claims be embodied in the CVA e.g. the amounts of all sums due as at the date of the creditors' meeting, although there is no longer any obligation for a particular date to be selected. Whether provision should be made for any further such sums due in the period leading up to approval will depend on the proposal and the views of the creditors and members generally.

Section 4(4) of the Insolvency Act 1986 prevents a CVA from proposing that certain preferential debts are to be paid in full whilst others are not. However, it does not preclude the payment by a third party of non preferential creditors out of the third party's own assets.[207]

---

205. See Section 386 of the 1986 Act
206. Section 251 of the 2002 Act, with effect from 15 September 2003. A number of items were therefore removed from the list contained in Schedule 6. The underlying motive was that floating charge holders would be compensated in respect of a reserved fund set up at their expense in favour of unsecured creditors.
207. See e.g. *Inland Revenue v. Wimbledon Football Club Limited* [2005] 1 BCLC 66.

2. Secured Creditors

A secured creditor is not limited by the terms of the CVA, since his or its debt is covered by the value of security. In other words the secured creditor remains free to enforce his or its security even if a CVA has been approved; the only exception to this principle is where a moratorium is in force, in which case the court's consent is required.[208]

Section 4(2) of the Insolvency Act 1986 provides that the terms of a voluntary arrangement cannot affect the right of a secured creditor to enforce the security except with the consent of the creditor in question.[209] Any clause in a voluntary arrangement which attempts to preclude all creditors from commencing or continuing legal proceedings in respect of any personal liability of the debtor company cannot preclude a secured creditor from enforcing his security.[210]

Section 248 of the Insolvency Act 1986 defines a secured creditor of the company as a creditor who holds in respect of his debt a security over the property of the company and for this purpose security is defined as meaning any mortgage, charge, lien or other security.

Section 248 of the Insolvency Act 1986 makes it clear that the term secured creditor excludes execution creditors. Section 183 of the of the Insolvency Act 1986 provides that an execution creditor is not entitled to retain the benefit of execution unless the execution has been completed prior to the commencement of the winding up. Consequently, in the context of a moratorium, an execution creditor will be deprived of the benefit of execution if the execution has not been completed at the time of the institution of the moratorium. Execution is completed for these purposes when there has been seizure and sale in the case of personal chattels, the making of a final third party debt order and a charging order absolute.

A creditor can neither levy nor complete distress whilst a moratorium is in force.[211] A landlord, however, is not a secured creditor even though he enjoys rights of forfeiture and distraint.[212] The landlord cannot exercise his rights to forfeiture in a moratorium except with the court's permission.[213] A voluntary arrangement cannot affect the right of a landlord to forfeiture or peaceable re-entry where there has been a failure to pay future instalments of rent reserved under the lease.

Apart from landlords, the Crown enjoys a right of distress where there are unpaid taxes. The advisable course in cases in which either the landlord or the Crown is likely to threaten distress is to incorporate specific terms in the proposal to prevent the possible loss of assets which are or might be important for the continued viability of the company's business.

---

208. *See* Insolvency Act 1986 Schedule A1, para. 12.
209. *See* e.g *Frost v. Unity Trust Bank Plc* [1998] BPIR 459 cf *Khan v. Permayer* [2001] BPIR 95.
210. *Rey and Rey v. FNCB Limited* (2006) NPC 71.
211. Insolvency Act 1986 Schedule A1 para. 12(1)(h).
212. *See* generally *Re Lomax Leisure Limited* [200] Ch 502.
213. Insolvency Act 1986 Schedule A1 para. 12(1)(f).

England & Wales

A creditor might be only partially secured. In such a case, the creditor can vote at the creditors' meeting in respect of the unsecured component of his claim.[214] It will be open to such a creditor to attach a relatively low value to his security for voting purposes but to reserve a much higher value at such time as the security is eventually realized. There is power to alter the value attached to a security[215] but only with the agreement of the supervisor or leave of the court.

However, if the CVA is silent as to whether or not the secured creditor has any right to alter the value of the security, there seems no reason why the creditor should not be able to do so.[216] In practice, however, a secured creditor would be well advised to insist that such a right be expressly reflected in the CVA in order to represent the real possibility that the value of the assets secured may well rise during the duration of the CVA. It should be noted, however, that Insolvency Rule 1.52(3) provides that a secured or partially secured creditor can vote in respect of the gross value of the claim without making any allowance for the value of the security, whenever there is a vote on whether to extend the moratorium or to terminate a moratorium prior to the end of an existing extension. This Rule does no more than reflect the new provisions in Schedule A1 of the Insolvency Act 1986[217] which relate to the institution of a moratorium and which provide that during a moratorium no steps can be taken to enforce any security without the court's leave.

In practical terms the main, if not only, secured creditor is likely to be a bank. If a bank is to be expected to support a CVA, it should be approached prior to the proposal since a CVA cannot in reality expect to succeed without proper funding.

3. Unsecured Creditors

The terms of a CVA can naturally provide in any particular manner which may be appropriate as to how creditors may be ranked but it is normal to deal with all unsecured creditors in the same fashion. One possible exception is in the case of a creditor who may have petitioned for a winding up order: in such a case he is likely to be paid in priority to all other creditors.

The *pari passu* principle referred to *above*[218] can be displaced by agreement. The question, therefore, arises as to which, if any adjustment to the *pari passu* principle could give rise to any impeachment of the proposal e.g. by virtue of any such adjustment being alleged to constitute a matter which is unfairly prejudicial to an aggrieved party. Indeed it has been confirmed that it is fair that a creditor, whose claim had been improperly rejected at a creditors' meeting convened to consider a proposed CVA and who had gone on to obtain judgment against the

---

214. *See Re Calor Gas Limited v. Piercy* [1994] BCC 69.
215. *See* Insolvency Rule 1986 Rule 4.95.
216. *See Khan and Khan v. Mortgage Express* [2000] BPIR 473.
217. *See* in particular para. 12(1)(g).
218. *See above* at III.J.

company, should only be permitted to enforce his judgment *pari passu* against the company.[219]

In *Re A Debtor (No. 100 of 1999)*[220] the court held that the fact that some creditors might be treated differently from others in an IVA did not necessarily establish the existence of unfair prejudice: all relevant matters have to be taken into account.[221]

There can be little doubt but that there is ample commercial justification for drawing a viable distinction between customers of a trading company who would normally no doubt be made up of members of the public on the one hand and on the other the major trade creditors of such a company. Many major suppliers will enjoy the benefit of retention of title clauses which may of themselves justify some form of preferential treatment in favour of those creditors. There therefore seems no reason in principle why a CVA cannot be drafted so as to confer some particular advantage in favour of a specified group of unsecured creditors.

4. Future and Uncertain Claims

Many claims may be the subject of genuine disputes or be subject to the outcome of a future event. The current practice is no longer to attribute a nominal sum of GBP1 to such creditors: those drafting the proposal, invariably the nominee and his staff, must make a best estimate of the amount which is outstanding. Votes at the creditors' meeting must be calculated according to the amount of the debt due as at the date of the meeting, even though the debt may be valued differently when the time comes to distribute a dividend.

Formerly, a creditor could not vote if his claim was for an unliquidated amount or its value was not ascertained, except where the chairman agreed to put an estimated minimum valuation on it.[222] The replacement Insolvency Rule 1.17(3) now provides that a creditor for unliquidated or unascertained debt is to have his debt valued at GBP 1 unless the chairman agrees to put a higher value on it.[223]

In *Doorbar v. Alltime Securities Limited*,[224] it was confirmed that the valuation of a landlord's claim under a lease which had several more years to run, which value represented a year's rent, was reasonable, even though the landlord had

---

219. See *Oakley-Smith v. Greenberg* sub nom *Re TBL Realizations* (2004) BCC 81. This was because the creditor's only other remedy, namely the presentation of a winding-up petition would not yield him a more favourable result.
220. [2000] BPIR 998.
221. At a further hearing reported at *Re A Debtor (100 of 1999) (No 2)* [2001] BPIR 996, it was held that where the voluntary arrangement had been set aside on account of unfair prejudice, the court had to satisfy itself the proposal was viable before ordering a further meeting of creditors.
222. See the former Insolvency Rule at Rule 1.17(3) which was considered in detail in *Re Cranley Mansions Limited* [1994] BCC 576.
223. See also *Re Newlands (Seaford) Educational Trust* (2006) 33 EG 10 where it was confirmed that a chairman had no option but to value an unascertained and unliquidated debt at GBP1.
224. [1995] BCC 1149.

objected and sought to vote for the whole of the rent payable for the remaining term. It was held that reference to an agreement in the amended rule did not necessitate an agreement between the chairman and any other party including, but not limited, to the creditor. In other words it was held that the chairman alone could decide what the claim was probably worth: no form of belated agreement was required.[225]

In *Re TBL Realizations Plc*[226] administrators proposed a CVA of which they were to be the supervisors. The chairman refused to put any value on the respondents' claim, as a result of which the respondents could not vote. It was held that the respondents were not bound by the CVA and that they should be paid out of the funds which were not paid into the arrangement. Under the present Rule 1.17(3) referred to *above,* the chairman would now have to allow the creditor to vote for at least GBP 1.

In the event of a genuine dispute as to the amount of a claim, the claim should be admitted at the amount indicated by the creditor but the claim should be marked disputed.[227]

If a creditor's claim is wrongfully rejected at a meeting convened to consider a CVA proposal, the creditor in question should only be permitted to enforce his claim *pari passu* with the other CVA creditors in a case where a creditor's claim is unliquidated but the chairman does not give it any value for voting purposes, as a result of which the creditor will not be bound by the CVA.[228] If there is any doubt regarding whether a creditor has a legitimate claim, the prudent course is for the chairman to mark the claim as objected to but to allow the creditor to vote subject to the vote later being declared to be invalid in accordance with Insolvency Rule 1.17A(4). This is because it is for the court (or indeed an arbitrator) to determine the amount of the claim.[229]

There is no statutory definition of a contingent debt or contingent liability: in general terms a contingent creditor is a person with an existing claim in respect of which the company may or will become liability on the happening of a future event or in the future.[230]

It has been held that the term 'creditor' includes persons who are owed a future debt which has not yet fallen due.[231] In such a case the chairman may have to

---

225. See also Re Streatfield Limited [1997] BCC 744.
226. [2001] All ER (D) 229.
227. See now Insolvency Rule 1.17A.
228. See Re TBL Realizations (2004) BCC 81.
229. See Re A Debtor (No. 222 of 1990) (Nos. 1 and 2) ex p Bank of Ireland [1993] BCLC 233; Re A Debtor (Nos. 400 10 and 410 10 1996) [1997] BCC 867.
230. See generally *Re William Hockley Limited* [1962] 1 WLR 555. In *Re T & N Limited* [2006] 1 WLR 1728 it was determined that a company which was formerly engaged in asbestos mining was the subject of contingent liabilities in respect of future asbestos claims and the future victims of asbestos related diseases who were creditors for the purposes of Part I of the Insolvency Act 1986, i.e. for the purposes of a CVA. See also *Country Bookshops Limited v. Grove* (2002) BPIR 772 in which it was held that a liability to pay on the presentation of an invoice was not a contingent liability for the purposes of a CVA although the question was ultimately one of construction of the terms of the actual CVA in question.
231. Re Cancol Limited [1995] BCC 1133.

discount the claim to a net present value to take into account the fact that money paid immediately will be worth more than money payable at some indeterminate future date. The new Insolvency Rule 1.17A referred to *above* sets out the procedures by which a chairman can reject the claim for voting purposes following which the creditor can challenge the rejection. Although at face value the new rule largely repeats the pre-existing regime, it now appears that the effect of the new rule means that creditors with liquidated or unliquidated claims will be bound by the arrangement if for some reason they do not receive notice of the meeting.

A similar form of discount as might apply in the case of a debt payable at a future time operates in the context of the payment of dividends in a winding up and bankruptcy. In such cases Insolvency Rule 11.13 provides for the discounting of payments made by way of dividend where a creditor has proved for a debt of which payment was not due at the date of the dividend declaration. Although the legislation does not refer to the discounting of value to be attributed to a claim for voting purposes, there seems to be no reason why discounting is inappropriate for voting purposes as well as for dividend purposes.

5. Creditors with Rights of Set-Off

A well drafted proposal should specifically refer to the fact that a creditor is also a debtor, if such be the case, and should make additional reference to the applicability of the set off provisions in Insolvency Rule 4.90. The latter rule does not apply to CVAs unless specifically embodied in the proposal. The Rule provides that set-off 'shall' apply where there has been mutual trading. If a company has assigned its debts (e.g. to a factoring company) set off will not be permissible even if Insolvency Rule 4.90 (which deals with mutual set of in a formal insolvency) has been imported into the proposal. To justify set-off, both debts must have arisen prior to the commencement of the arrangement and must both be 'mutual' in the sense of being of the same type.[232]

The Crown, however, is entitled to set off a debt owed by one Crown department against a debt due to another but again the respective liabilities must relate to periods arising prior to the CVA's approval.

6. Connected Creditors

According to Insolvency Rule 1.19(4), a proposal cannot be approved unless it is approved first by more than 50 per cent by value of all unconnected unsecured creditors who have given notice to the chairman (whether or not they have voted) and secondly by 75 per cent in value of all voting unsecured creditors. In other words the relevant creditors for the purposes of these rules are not only those who are unsecured and who have been given notice of the meeting but also those who

---

232. *See* generally *Stein v. Blake* [1995] BCC 543. There would be no mutuality for example as between a liability for unpaid share capital and a loan account liability.

have given written notice of their claims to the chairman and who are not connected.

According to Insolvency Rules 1.19(5) and 1.52(6) (which applies to a moratorium), it is for the chairman of the meeting to decide whether a person is a connected person. In this respect the chairman is entitled to rely on the information provided by the statement of the company's affairs 'or otherwise in accordance with this Part of the Rules'.

Any decision as to connected creditors made by the chairman is subject to appeal in accordance with Insolvency Rule 1.19(7). A situation may arise where a 50 per cent majority is achieved without taking into account connected creditors but where a 75 per cent majority is achieved only taking into account connected creditors' votes. Insolvency Rule 1.17A(4) states that if the chairman is in doubt whether a claim should be admitted or rejected, he should mark it as objected to but nevertheless allow the creditor to vote subject to the vote being subsequently declared invalid. If, therefore, a chairman has doubts as to the validity of the amount claimed by a connected person, he should first adjourn the meeting in order for the creditor to supply further evidence. If there is no such evidence over and above a confirmatory letter or even an affidavit, the benefit of the doubt should be afforded to the creditor and the claim should be admitted.[233]

Overall, however, a balance should be struck between the rights of connected persons and the rights of the general body of creditors. The position is not entirely clear and ideally a chairman should consider carefully whether he should disallow the votes of connected persons, unless there is clear evidence substantiating the vote.

7. Guarantors

Insolvency Rule 1.3(2)(d) provides that a proposal for a CVA must state whether any and, if so what, guarantees have been given of the company's debts by others.

As a general rule, a creditor will reserve all his rights against a guarantor and such reservation will be reflected within the terms of the CVA. Consequently, it is the practice for notice of a creditors' meeting (whether it be the first or not) to be given to the guarantors as well as to the principal creditor. Much will depend on whether the creditor has made a formal demand on the guarantor. Should a demand have been made, the guarantor's liability will be an actual one: otherwise it will merely be contingent. In either event, however, approval of the arrangement will not of itself discharge the liability of the guarantor.

Voting rights usually reflect the anticipated dividend. It is not uncommon for the principal creditor to be allowed to vote at the first meeting for an amount representing that proportion of the debt which is likely to be expected to be paid with the guarantor voting for the balance. However, if the guarantor has paid the debt in full, he should of course, be allowed to vote for the entirety of the debt.

---

233. *See* generally *Re A Debtor (No. 222 of 1990)* [1993] BCLC 233.

Payment in full by a guarantor entitles him as a matter of law to be subrogated to the creditor's rights. If the guarantor has paid off the debt by the time a dividend is to be declared in the CVA, he and not the creditor should be paid, subject to any provision in the guarantee, e.g. as to waiver. Although a voluntary arrangement will not operate directly to release a third party guarantor from its liability to a creditor under the arrangement, the arrangement could contain a valid provision which compelled the creditor not to claim against the guarantor.[234]

8. Creditors' Committees

There is no provision in the relevant legislation which addresses the possibility of having a creditors' committee in connection with any form of voluntary arrangement. It is, however, suggested that the supervisor and the creditors consider the constitution of such a committee in an appropriate case particularly where there is a dominant group of creditors. Such a committee may also be useful where it is anticipated that a variation in the CVA may be anticipated.

9. Creditors' Meetings

In general terms a CVA proposal is binding, provided it is approved by creditors who have been given proper notice of the meeting and represent at least 75 per cent by value of creditors who vote at the meeting. Once a creditor has been admitted for voting purposes, he is effectively stopped from denying that he has such a status.[235] A SIP specifically deals with the summoning and holding of creditors' meetings in liquidation proceedings. It is suggested that parts of the same SIP should be borne in mind in the context of CVAs. In practical terms the proposal should deal with any issue that creditors might be expected to raise at the creditors' meetings. It is also good practice to circulate additional relevant information that has arisen since the proposal to all affected parties prior to the meeting, if at all possible.

Insolvency Rule 1.9 provides that the creditors' meeting must be held not less than 14 days but not more than 28 days from the date on which the nominee's report is filed in court. It is the nominee and not the directors who carries the responsibility for convening the meeting. Reference to 14 days means 14 clear days, i.e. excluding the date of the meeting as well as the day on which notice is served.[236] Insolvency Rule 12.10(2)[237] provides that where first class post is used, the document is treated as served on the second business day after the date of posting unless the contrary is shown. This suggests that if notice is posted by first class post on Day 1, e.g. Friday, it will not be treated as served until Day 3, i.e. in the example

---

234. Prudential Assurance Co. Ltd v. PRG Powerhaise Ltd [2007] EWHC 1002 (Ch).
235. *Re Millwall Football Club Limited* [1998] 2 BCLC 272.
236. *See Mytre Investments Limited v. Reynolds* [1996] BPIR 464.
237. In *Re T&N Limited* [2006] 1 WLR 283, it was confirmed that although Rule 12.10 applied to CVAs, Rule 12.12 did not so there is no requirement for an application to court or for the court's permission in order for notice of such meetings to be given to creditors outside the jurisdiction.

suggested, the following Tuesday and therefore the clear days' notice will start from Day 4 being, in the example given, Wednesday.

If notice is sent to a creditor's solicitor then either the solicitor must be authorized to accept service or the solicitor must have a reasonable opportunity to pass the notice on to his client in such a way that the client has 14 clear days' notice. Since it is generally advantageous to the implementation of the proposal that the creditors be given every opportunity to take advice, it is good practice to give the creditor more than 14 clear days' notice. Indeed the practice has developed of giving creditors up to 28 days notice of meetings called during the course of an arrangement with a view to varying the terms of the arrangement.

All creditors whose names appear in the statement of affairs must be circulated as well as any other creditor of which the nominee is aware. Although there is no specific obligation to do so, it is advisable that secured as well as unsecured creditors be notified as well as contingent creditors and creditors whose claims may be disputed in whole or in part. It is also good practice to send a notice of the meeting to HM Revenue & Customs[238] even if there appears to be no tax or arrears and where it is intended that any outstanding amount will be paid on the due dates.

The nominee would be ill advised not to notify any specific creditor or group of creditors, e.g. at the behest of the company. Such an action would be contrary to the provisions of Insolvency Rule 1.9(2) if nothing else and it is difficult, if not impossible, to see how such a breach could be justified. Even if a proposal contemplated the express exclusion from the arrangement of a certain number of unsecured creditors, it would still be necessary to send notice to such creditors of the meeting in the light of the clear words of Insolvency Rule 1.9.

Somewhat surprisingly, there is no provision for notice of either the creditors' or the members' meetings needing to be advertised in the London Gazette. This reflects the essentially private nature of a voluntary arrangement: it is only necessary that certain forms be lodged at the Companies Registry. However, in the light of the changes introduced by the Insolvency Act 2000 to the general effect that the creditors will be bound by a voluntary arrangement even if they have not been given notice, there is a strong practical argument justifying the insertion of a suitable advertisement of a creditors' meeting both in the London Gazette and in one or more local or even national newspapers.

No particular form of notice as to the meeting is prescribed. However, such form as is used should be accompanied by the following documents, namely: (1) a proposal; (2) the statement of affairs; (3) comments on the proposal by the nominee and if applicable, the moratorium, including the statement required under paragraph 6(2) of Schedule A1 to the Insolvency Act 1986; (4) a statement regarding Insolvency Rule 1.19 as to the requisite majorities; (5) a form of proxy; and, (6) a statement concerning the authorization of the nominees and supervisor's fees. It is generally practical to issue a similar form of notice as exists in other insolvency processes.

---

238. The Revenue has a section which deals with voluntary arrangements: ideally the local office should also be notified.

Insolvency Rule 1.13 provides that in fixing the venue of the creditors' meeting the person summoning the meeting is to have regard primarily to the convenience of the creditor. SIP No. 8 which applies to creditors' meetings in relation to a liquidation states that the insolvency practitioner must ensure that the accommodation is adequate and convenient, that the meeting can be held at the practitioner's offices and that a reasonable charge can be made for the use of the room. The meeting must be held between 10:00 am and 4:00 pm on a business day. In the case of a liquidation the court can vary such requirements but this does not seem possible in relation to meetings held regarding a CVA.

Insolvency Rule 1.13 provides that the form of proxy should comply with Form 8.1. The presence of only one creditor in person or by proxy is sufficient to constitute a quorum.[239] As a practical matter, if, as is often the case, it has been indicated that the creditor can attend by representative and if, as at the commencement of the meeting, the representative is not present, the meeting should be adjourned by 15 minutes. This reflects the requirement of Insolvency Rule 12.4A(4).

10. Creditors Not In Receipt of Notice

As a general rule, a creditor will not be bound by the decision of the creditors' meeting if he was not given proper notice. This follows from the clear provisions of section 5(2) of the Insolvency Act 1986.

In *Re A Debtor (No 64 of 1982)*,[240] notice of a creditors' meeting sent to the offices of a building society which were not yet fully operative and out of which the society's mortgage business did not operate, was held to be ineffective. However, the rigour of this principle is to some extent tempered to the extent that a creditor will be bound by a creditors' meeting even though he may not have been given notice of it but where he nonetheless become aware of the proposal and of the meeting, e.g. by virtue of having been acquainted of these matters by a third party.[241]

It has also been held that a creditor was entitled to vote even though he had not received notice but where the solicitors acting for the creditor had discovered that a meeting was to be held after examination of the court file.[242]

In the early days of CVAs, many problems arose in relation to the consequences of the inadequacy of a company's accounting records and oversight or human error, leading to a failure to give adequate notice of a creditors' meeting to all affected creditors. The effect of the primary legislation in its 1986 unamended form was that such creditors were not bound by the decision of the creditors' meeting which thereby enabled them to pursue their normal legal remedies against the company albeit in voluntary arrangement.

---

239. Insolvency Rule 12.4A(2)(a).
240. [1994] BCC 55.
241. Confirmed in *Beverley Group Plc v. McClure* [19995] BCC 751.
242. *Re A Debtor (No 400 10 and 101 10 of 1996)* [1997] BCC 867.

The Insolvency Act 1986 was subsequently reformed to provide that the creditors not given notice will in general be bound by the decision of the creditors' meeting, subject to a right of challenge.

Such a challenge would invariably be made by virtue of the provisions of Section 6 of the Insolvency Act 1986. This section provides in relevant part that a 'person entitled in accordance with the rules, to vote at either of the meetings' (ie a creditor or a member) or a 'person who would have been entitled, in accordance with the rules, to vote at the creditors' meeting if he had notice of it' can apply to court on the ground that there has been 'some material irregularity or some material irregularity at or in relation to either of the meetings'. In *Re A Debtor (No 259 of 1990)*,[243] it was held that failure to give notice of the creditors' meeting to a creditor was and is not a material irregularity unless the vote of that creditor could have altered the decision of the meeting.

Paragraph 37 of Schedule A1 to the 1986 Act, now imported into the Insolvency Act 1986 by virtue of the Insolvency Act 2000, provides by Insolvency Rule (2) that:

The approved voluntary arrangement . . .

(b) *binds every person who in accordance with the rules -*
  (i) *was entitled to vote [at the creditors'] meeting (whether or not he was present or represented at it) or*
  (ii) *would have been so entitled if he had had notice of it.*

Although the *above* cited provisions relate to a CVA which follows upon the imposition of a moratorium, the same wording has been introduced into Schedule 2 to the Insolvency Act 1986 and which relates to CVAs generally. Schedule 2, paragraph 6 revises Section 5 of the Insolvency Act 1986 so as to include creditors who have not been given notice but who would have been entitled to vote if they had been given notice.

Similarly, Schedule 2, paragraph 7 of the Insolvency Act 2000 revises section 6 of the Insolvency Act 1986 referred to *above* so as to extend rights of challenge to creditors not given notice. It might be thought that the inclusion of creditors who would have been entitled to vote had they received notice of the meeting would enable the company and its nominee to avoid giving notice to those creditors who might otherwise have been expected to vote against the proposal. There is as yet no reported decision dealing with this possible eventuality but the risk remains that an unscrupulous director or board of directors might seek to conceal the existence of or identity of such creditors from a nominee.

There are, however, three weighty countervailing factors which would tend to suggest that such a risk is perhaps more apparent than real. First, any concealment regarding a creditor (which would normally constitute a material irregularity) would also constitute an offence under Section 6A of the Insolvency Act 1986. Secondly, a well drafted proposal should contain a provision specifying that a

---

243. [1992] 1 WLR 226.

material underestimate of the company's liabilities will constitute a ground or grounds on which the supervisor will be obliged to convene a meeting of creditors, and if so instructed by the meeting, petition for the company's winding up. The third factor is reflected in paragraph 37(3) of Schedule A1 of the Insolvency Act 1986 which provides in general terms that if, when the arrangement ceases to have effect, any amount payable under the arrangement to a person bound by virtue of sub-paragraph (2)(b)(ii), i.e. one who has not been given notice, has not been paid and the arrangement does not come to an end prematurely, then the company shall at that time become liable to pay for that person the amount payable under the arrangement. It will be noted that this last provision will protect the non-notified creditors' rights to a dividend, however, it will not restore his voting rights.

11.   The Chair of the Creditors' Meeting

There is no requirement that the creditors' meeting need be chaired by the nominee. The meeting can indeed be chaired by another person who is an insolvency practitioner or by an employee experienced in insolvency matters. In a liquidation, the first meeting of creditors must be chaired by a director appointed for that purpose,[244] albeit with the prospective liquidator present.[245] It is therefore suggested that a similar procedure should be followed in a CVA: the position may, however, be different if the nominee has previously been or is the liquidator or administrator of the company in question; he will therefore be expected to have considerable knowledge of the affairs of the company.

12.   Adjournments of Creditors' Meetings

Insolvency Rule 1.21 enables a creditors' meeting to be adjourned for a period not exceeding 14 days. This period will normally be sufficient to enable there to be further negotiations between the company and its creditors and to enable further information to be made available to the adjourned meeting. Amendments in 2002 to Insolvency Rule 1.21 now enable the creditors' and members' meetings to be held on different days, whereas previously they had to be held on the same day.[246] Formal notice of any adjourned meeting should be given to all creditors who were or ought to have been given notice of the original meeting, and any such notice should be accompanied by a report on the original meeting setting out reasons for the adjournment.

Such an exercise is likely to be both time consuming and expensive and it may be that the proposal should specifically cater for an uplift in the nominee's fee should there be a need to adjourn a meeting through no fault of the nominee. In the realm of personal insolvency, section 376 of the Insolvency Act 1986 enables

---

244. *See* section 99(1) of the Insolvency Act 1986.
245. *See* section 166(4) of the Insolvency Act 1986.
246. *See* Insolvency Rule 1.21 and 1.13(3) as amended by paragraph 6 of the Schedule to Insolvency (Amendment)(No. 2) Rules 2002.

the court in the context of any provision, whether in the Insolvency Act 1986 or in the Insolvency Rules, prescribing a relevant time limit, to extend the time, whether or not the period has expired on any terms it thinks fit.[247] There is no corresponding provision regarding corporate insolvency.[248]

There is some doubt, even in the case of personal insolvency, however, whether a court can validly extend a time period after the relevant period has elapsed, despite the apparently contrary wording of section 376 of the Insolvency Act 1986.[249] It is suggested that in any event, it is prudent for an insolvency practitioner to recommence the voluntary arrangement should he face a situation in which the original meeting has resulted in a rejection of the proposal, but where subsequently the rejecting creditors have indicated that they might support a modified proposal.

13. Attendance by Directors of the Creditors' Meetings

Insolvency Rule 1.16 requires that the person convening a creditors' meeting must give 'notice to attend' the meeting to all directors, even though there is no specific statutory requirement for a director to attend. A principal reason why it is generally desirable for a director to attend is to explain to the meeting any matters which are, or may be, of assistance or relevance to the creditors. Although this topic is not within the scope of the chapter, there may be an issue of self-incrimination which emerges in the course of any questions put to the director. SIP 8[250] which relates only to liquidations states that a director may refuse to answer a question if principally the question is put by neither a creditor nor a creditor's representative, or indeed anyone who admits to being such a party and the answer could be seen to prejudice the directors' interest.

14. Proxies

Any proxy to be used at a meeting of members or creditors must be in the prescribed form.[251] A proxy will be valid even if it is lodged after the commencement of the creditors' meeting as long as it is lodged prior to the time when the formal vote is taken.[252] Such relative flexibility should be compared with the principles which apply in relation to a creditors' voluntary liquidation. In the latter case, Insolvency Rule 4.67(1)(b) provides that in order to be valid, a proxy must be lodged by the time and date stated on the face of the notice of the meeting: normally the close of business on the day prior to the meeting, or at the latest, noon on the day

---

247. See *Tager v. Westpac Incorporation* [1998] BCC 73.
248. *Re Bournemouth and Boscombe Athletic Football Club* [1991] BPIR 183.
249. See *Re Symes (a debtor)* [1996] BCC 137.
250. Paragraph 41.
251. i.e. Form 8.1
252. See *Re Cardona* [1997] BCC 697 and see in the context of administrations *Re Philip Alexander Securities and Futures Limited* [1998] BCC 819.

prior to the meeting. Proxies can also be sent by fax. It is therefore entirely possible for a proxy to be validly lodged in this fashion within a matter of hours, or perhaps less, prior to the meeting.[253] At the moment there is no bar to this practice which can cause serious practical difficulties if the proxy proposes substantial modifications to the proposal. It is therefore clearly desirable for the nominee or the company to circulate all known creditors with a formal request that proxies be lodged no later than noon on the business day prior to the creditors' meeting.

Insolvency Rule 8.2 emphasizes that any proxy form sent to creditors should not have inserted or placed on it the name or description of any person who might be appointed as an insolvency office-holder or as a member of the committee or as a proxy-holder. Rule 8.7 provides that a proxy should be accompanied by a suitable corporate resolution which confirms the proxy-holder's authority. It is not, it is suggested, conducive to the efficient and proper pursuit of a CVA if the chairman chooses to reject the proxy on the grounds of minor technical irregularity, e.g. failure by the person signing the form formally to declare or state his position with his relationship to the creditor or because no copy resolution was attached. If nothing else, any rejection on such grounds may well lead to a challenge under section 6 of the Insolvency Act 1986.[254]

15. Modifications and Adjournments

A last minute proxy which requires a modification may prompt the chairman to adjourn the meeting particularly where the proposed modification is ambiguous or inconsistent with another proposed modification. Each case will differ and there may be instances in which some creditors will vote for the proposal without modification, whilst other creditors will require some form of modification: in such a case as the latter case, it may not be necessary for the meeting to be adjourned at all. The position may well be different if the modifications which are proposed risk effecting a reduction of the level of dividend. Ideally, and if necessary by means of a suitable adjournment, all modifications should be reviewed to ensure that no inconsistencies are likely to arise. It is not customary for the HM Revenue and Customs to insist upon a clause or section in the arrangement to the effect that in the event that there do arise any modifications, the modifications take priority. One common modification concerns the proposed limitation or capping of the nominee's fees. Such a matter may well need to be properly ventilated before the creditors. It is however doubtful whether creditors can in effect validly intervene in an arrangement which is effectively a bargain struck only as between the company and the nominee.[255]

---

253. *See* e.g. *Inland Revenue Commissioners v. Conbeer* [1996] BCC 189.
254. SIP 8 already referred to which applies only in the context of voluntary liquidations, deters a chairman from rejecting a proxy on account of minor errors provided the proper form sent with notice of the meeting has been used and it is clear who the creditor proxy-holder are, together with the nature of the authority and the relevant instructions.
255. *See* generally Insolvency Rule 1.28 as to disbursements, fees, costs, charges and expenses of the nominee. cf supervisor's fees which have to be 'sanctioned by the terms of the arrangement'.

16. Creditors' and Members' Meetings: The Chairman's Report

Following the convening and holding of the relevant meetings, the chairman must prepare and submit a report.[256] The report must state and set out first whether the proposal was approved or rejected, secondly which if any modifications were agreed, thirdly details of how votes were cast, and finally whether, in the opinion of the supervisor, the EC Insolvency Regulation applies to the voluntary arrangement, (and if so whether the proceedings are main, secondary or territorial within the meaning and scope of the EC Insolvency Regulation). In addition, a copy of the report must be sent to the creditors, the members, as well as to the court. A return must also be submitted to the Registrar of Companies. A SIP[257] entitled 'Records of meetings and formal insolvency proceedings' provides that even though the legislation does not formally require that a full record be maintained of all meetings held as part of the CVA procedure, it is desirable that the chairman compile a record and sign it. Apart from constituting a note of purely formal matters, e.g. date, time and venue, as well as a list of those attending and details of all resolutions put and voted upon, the SIP suggests that a record be kept of any other information required arising out of the voluntary arrangement proposal as modified, as well as any other information provided regarding the office-holder's remuneration.

K. Members' Meetings: General

In general terms, a nominee will not have to bear the cost of a challenge. In *Re Naeem*,[258] an application was made under the IVA equivalent of section 6 of the Insolvency Act 1986, namely, section 262 of same Act by a landlord claiming that his rights had been prejudiced: it was held that in a case where prejudice was demonstrated, the nominee should not be ordered to pay, but to contribute towards the costs of a challenge unless he had committed some act which justified an order for costs against him. Such conduct may in certain cases take the form of acting unreasonably.[259]

There are various classes of persons who can apply to court to overturn the result and decision of a creditors' meeting or a decision of the chairman made at or during such meetings. Those who may apply include any person entitled to vote at the respective meeting or meetings, or should the company be in the course of being wound up or in administration, the appropriate liquidator or administrator. Neither the company nor the directors can apply if the company is either in liquidation nor in administration.

---

256. As for the procedures, see section 4(6) of the Insolvency Act 1986 and Insolvency Rule 1.24.
257. SIP12.
258. [1990] 1 WLR 48
259. *See* e.g. *Re A Debtor (No. 222 of 1990) (No. 2)* [1993] BCLC 233.

As also indicated *above*,[260] section 6 of the Insolvency Act 1986 enables an applicant to apply on one or both of the following grounds, namely first that a voluntary arrangement approved at meetings summoned under section 3 of the Insolvency Act 1986 unfairly prejudices the interests of the creditor, member or contributory of the company, and/or there has been some material irregularity at/or in relation to either of the meetings. Examples of the latter category might include changing the venue of the creditors' meeting without proper notice, failure to supply the requisite information, in certain circumstances failure on the part of the debtor to be present at the creditors' meeting, infringement of the rules regarding the admissibility of claims, the inappropriate application of the voting rules, in an appropriate case failure by the chairman to adjourn, and again, in appropriate cases failure to deal properly, or at all, with proposed modifications.[261] Any application under section 6 of the Insolvency Act 1986 must be made within 28 days. On the hearing of an application under section 6 of the Insolvency Act 1986, the court will have close regard to whether an applicant enjoyed or might enjoy sufficient voting power to effect the outcome of a meeting even if the complaint were upheld.[262] Moreover in considering whether a voluntary arrangement was unfairly prejudicial to the interests of a particular creditor, the court must consider the whole range of options available to a creditor in the event of an arrangement not being approved and not simply whether the creditor would receive, more or less, the same amount or return under the arrangement as in a formal insolvency.

There is clearly no exhaustive list of the circumstances in which it can be said that an applicant's interests have been prejudiced. A critical, though by no means determinative, test is whether the applicant's interests will be, or would be likely to be, prejudiced as against the interests of other creditors. The notion of unfair prejudice is well known at least in other statutory contexts e.g. petitions under section 459 and following of the Companies Act 1985.[263] In *Inland Revenue v. Wimbledon Football Club*,[264] it was confirmed that to constitute unfair prejudice, the prejudice had to be caused by the CVAs terms themselves so that the existence of unequal or differential treatment of creditors of the same class will not of itself constitute unfairness although it may give rise to complaints and may even require explanation. It is important to consider whether in all the circumstances a fairer scheme is possible and whether differential treatment may be necessary, not only to ensure some fairness, but also to serve the continuation of the company's business

---

260. *See* paragraph 3.40
261. Sub-paragraph 3b. *See* e.g. in the context of an IVA *Pender v. Inland Revenue* (unreported: 18 July 2003) (serious shortcomings in relation to the manner in which a supervisor conducted himself in depriving the creditors of the independent scrutiny they deserved); *Roberts v. Pinnacle Entertainment* (2004) BPIR 208 (improper disallowance of a main creditor's vote). cf *Re Trident Fashions Plc* [2004] 2 BCLC 35 (failure to disclose existence of offer to buyer company, even though irregularity not held to be material).
262. *See* e.g. *Re A Debtor (No. 259 of 1990)* [1992] 1 WLR 226.
263. *See* generally *O'Neill v. Phillips* [1999] 1 WLR 1092.
264. [2005] 1 BCLC 66: *See* in particular Lightman J's judgment upheld on different grounds. *See* also *Inland Revenue v. Exeter City AFC Limited* [2005] BCC 519.

which underlies the arrangement. In *Sisu Capital Fund Ltd v. Tucker & Others*[265] a series of complex interlocking CVAs were proposed. In rejecting a claim for unfair prejudice made by a group of aggrieved creditors, the court confirmed that the package of compromises put forward in the CVAs was the only way in which the respondent administrators believed it was reasonably possible to command the approval of the necessary majority of creditors in order for the CVAs as a whole properly to implement the negotiating strengths of the interested creditor groups: in all the circumstances, the series of interlocking CVAs represented a better alternative to liquidation. The court added that if there was any conflict of interest in such cases involving an office-holder and a breach or breaches by him of his professional rules or obligations, such a conflict would not of itself be sufficient to establish unfair prejudice for the purposes of revoking the arrangements.

It has been observed that in general terms, it is difficult to envisage a case where the court would not interfere with a CVA that was an alternative to a winding-up and that was likely to result in creditors, or some of them, receiving less than they would in a winding-up, assuming that the return in the winding-up would in reality be achieved within a reasonable timescale.[266]

Should the court determine that there has occurred unfair prejudice as against the applicant's interests, or should it find that there has been a material irregularity, the court may revoke or suspend the approval which has already been granted or it may give directions for the summoning of further meetings as well as any other directions it thinks fit. A successful applicant has to serve a copy of any order made on the supervisor, directors, if appropriate the liquidator or administrator, and the company itself.[267] A copy must also be sent to the Registrar of Companies.

The provisions of section 6 of the Insolvency Act 1986 have been extended to apply to meetings which have agreed a company moratorium.[268] Under the extended rules, not only can a person entitled to vote bring a challenge, but such a challenge can be brought by a person who would have been entitled to vote if he or it had had notice of the meeting in question. Yet again, as with the original principles governing section 6 of the Insolvency Act 1986, a challenge cannot be made by the company or its directors.

Should a supervisor successfully resist an application made under section 6 of the Insolvency Act 1986, he will not necessarily be entitled to recover his costs in respect of the time spent other than matters within his own professional expertise.[269]

---

265. (2006) BCC 463 where the court cited with approval the principles in the *Wimbledon Football Club* decision. *See* also *Prudential Assurance Co. Ltd v. PRG Powerhouse Ltd* [2007] EWCH 1002 (Ch).
266. *See* generally *Re T&N Limited* [2005] 2 BCLC 488: on the facts of that case which were complicated involving the possibility of formal Schemes or CVAs being entered into with a variety of related companies, the court determined that it was premature to decide at the stage at which matters had reached whether certain issues which had been raised rendered any Scheme or CVA unfair.
267. *See* generally Insolvency Rules, Rule 1.25.
268. *See* Insolvency Act 1986, Schedule A1, paragraph 38 inserted by the Insolvency Act 2000.
269. *See Sisu Capital Fund Limited v. Tucker Wallace & Others* (2006) BCC 463

L. CVAs: Implementation

1. Publicity

Schedule 1A, paragraph 9 of the of the Insolvency Act 1986 introduced by the Insolvency Act 2000 provides that when a moratorium comes into force, the nominee must advertise the fact forthwith as well as notifying the Registrar of Companies. Equally, the end of a moratorium must be advertised under Schedule 1A, paragraph 11 of the Insolvency Act 1986. Under Schedule 1A, paragraph 16 of the Insolvency Act 1986, during a period of a moratorium, every invoice, order for goods or business letter issued on behalf of the company and on which the company's name appears must also contain the nominee's name and a statement that the moratorium is in force. Under Schedule 1A, paragraph 17 of the Insolvency Act 1986, a company in moratorium cannot obtain credit of GBP250 or more from someone who has not been informed that the moratorium is in place. Curiously, no such rules apply to a company which is in a CVA and which is no longer in a moratorium.

Under Insolvency Rule 1.24(5), a supervisor must send a report to the Registrar of Companies and to the court on the outcome of the members' and creditors' meetings which would have approved the proposal. In addition, abstracts of receipts and payments must be filed, together with 'comments on the progress and efficiency of the arrangements' which a supervisor may have.[270] It follows from this rule that the Registrar of Companies and the courts should in addition be sent copies of reports on any meetings which are held during the course of the arrangement, particularly those which sanction any variations in the terms of the arrangement.

2. Formal Considerations: Complaints, Replacements, More Than One Supervisor and Notifications

Section 7(3) of the Insolvency Act 1986 provides that if any creditor or any other person is dissatisfied by any act, omission or decision of the supervisor, he may apply to the court for an order. This right co-exists with the right of an aggrieved creditor to apply to court under section 6 of the Insolvency Act 1986.[271] However, unlike the time limits applicable to section 6 of the Insolvency Act 1986, an application under section 7 of the Insolvency Act 1986 need not be made within 28 days of the creditors' meeting. The language and intention of section 7(3) reflect the provisions of section 168(5) of the Insolvency Act 1986, which enable an application to be made to court regarding the acts or omissions of a liquidator at the instance of a creditor or contributory. In general terms, a court is reluctant to interfere with the day-to-day administration of a liquidation, unless the liquidator

---

270. *See* Insolvency Rule 1.26.
271. *See above* III.K.

or is engaging in activities fraudulently, or in a way in which no reasonable liquidator would have acted or act: negligence in other words is not sufficient.

There are very few reported instances of a court considering section 7 of the Insolvency Act 1986. Refusal to admit a debt by CVA supervisors who are also administrators has held susceptible to challenge under section 7 of the Insolvency Act 1986,[272] despite their argument that challenge under the section represented an attempt to circumvent section 11 of the Insolvency Act 1986 which then established a moratorium on account of the administration. It is difficult to conceive of cases in which a viable challenge can be made under section 7 of the Insolvency Act 1986 if the 28 day time limit has expired under section 6 the same Act. In any case, when there is a dispute between a supervisor and a creditor regarding the amount, if any, at which a claim should be admitted for dividend in the liquidation, it is conceivable that such a dispute could be adjudicated upon under section 7 of the Insolvency Act 1986. However, the CVA should specifically provide a machinery for resolution of such disputes if necessary by express incorporation of the appropriate rules regarding dividends in the Insolvency Rules.[273] This technique will enable a supervisor to reject a creditor's claim in whole or in part, and entitle the creditor to apply to court for the decision to be reversed or varied.

Other alleged failures by a supervisor, e.g. delay or total failure to deal with claims may justify an application under section 7 of the Insolvency Act 1986. It is to be noted, however, that section 7(4) of the Insolvency Act 1986 enables a supervisor to apply to court either for directions, a winding up order or an administration order. Invariably, the terms of a CVA will provide that on default a supervisor will be obliged to petition for the compulsory winding up of the company.

If a vacancy arises in relation to the position of supervisor, e.g. through death or resignation, section 7(5) of the Insolvency Act 1986 enables the court to appoint a new supervisor. However, as in the case of the other matters listed *above*, the CVA should itself provide the machinery for such an eventuality.

Insolvency Rule 1.22 provides for the possible resolutions by both the creditors' and members' meetings that two or more insolvency practitioners be appointed to act as supervisors. In particular, the Rule entitles the meetings to pass a resolution to determine which work is to be done by each of the appointees, and both of them respectively. If a person who is not the nominee is proposed as a supervisor, then he must provide his written consent to act.

3. Report of the Meetings and other Reports

Under Insolvency Rule 1.24, the chairman of the meetings must report on the meetings. This will usually be done by the nominee or his representative. The contents of the report are fairly straightforward and consist of setting out the fact of approval, the content of all resolutions passed, a list of creditors and members

---

272. *Holdenhurst Securities Plc v. Cohen* [2001] 1 BCLC 460.
273. i.e. Rules 4.73–4.9 inclusive.

who were present in person or by proxy, the extent to which the EC Insolvency Regulation applies and any other matters regarded as material, e.g. details of any anticipated dividend.

The reports will be sent to the creditors, the court and to the Registrar of Companies.[274] If the court makes an order following the challenge of a decision made in a meeting under section 6 of the Insolvency Act 1986, then in accordance with Insolvency Rule 1.25, copies of the court order should be served on the applicant, the supervisor, the directors and any administrator or liquidator. The directors, administrator or liquidator must in turn give notice to the creditors of the effect of the court decision: they must also advise the court whether it is intended to make a revised proposal.

4. Accounts and Records

Insolvency Rule 1.26 requires a supervisor to keep proper accounts and records as well as summaries of receipts and payments.[275] Such summaries must be prepared at least every 12 months and sent with annual reports to the court, the Registrar of Companies, the company, the creditors, members and auditors. A supervisor should also submit returns to the Registrar of Companies every 12 months.[276] Persistent failure to submit returns to the Registrar may well entail disciplinary problems for the practitioner with his professional body: he may also risk facing disqualification proceedings.

5. Fees and Remuneration

Insolvency Rule 1.28 defines the fees, costs, charges and expenses that may be incurred for the purposes of the CVA. These are defined as any disbursements made by the nominee prior to the approval of the arrangement as well as any remuneration for his services as such agreed between himself and the company, together with any fees, costs, charges or expenses sanctioned by the CVA.

6. Completion of the Arrangement

Insolvency Rule 1.29 provides that a supervisor is required to submit a final report and return to the court, the creditors, members and the Registrar of Companies within 28 days of the final completion of the voluntary arrangement. The report must include a summarized receipts and payments statement and will invariably include a certificate of compliance and should be compared with a certificate of non-compliance which is usually issued in the event of a default. Under Insolvency Rule 1.29, there is no power to extend the 28 day limit. In addition, a supervisor is

---

274. Using Form 1.1.
275. *See* Statement of Insolvency Practice SIP7: Preparation of Insolvency Holder's Receipts and Payments Accounts.
276. *Ibid.*

not to vacate office until after copies of his final notice and report have been sent. The report to the Registrar of Companies must be accompanied by a form known as Form 1.4.

7. Payments of Dividend

A well drafted CVA should clearly set out how and when dividend payments are to be made to creditors. Part 11 of the Insolvency Rules provides that prior to his declaring of dividends, a supervisor should give notice of his intention to do so to all creditors who have not proved their debts. In particular, Insolvency Rule 11.2 also provides for a last date for proving. The same rule also provides that a responsible insolvency practitioner should publicly advertise the notice regarding the intended dividend. It is perhaps curious that a public advertisement is thought necessary in the case of advertising the intended dividend in a voluntary arrangement, particularly since Insolvency Rule 4.180 which also relates to the distribution to dividends does not refer to any such public advertisement.

If a creditor submits a claim in a foreign currency, it appears that the claim should be converted at the rate of exchange applicable as at the date of the voluntary arrangement, rather than as at the date of the dividend. A supervisor should also ensure that he does not pay a greater amount by way of dividend than the amount to which the creditor is properly entitled.[277] In practice, the supervisor should obtain an up-to-date receipts and payments summary and he should also ensure that all the costs of the arrangement have been provided for. Such costs will invariably include any taxes, e.g. VAT for which the supervisor is liable as well as the costs, charges and expenses of any agents of professional advisors, apart from the supervisor's own firm's costs. If, as often is the case, the CVA has been preceded by liquidation or administration, then the supervisor will need in addition to ensure that all costs relating to any prior insolvency have been settled or paid. Insolvency Rule 1.3(2)(l) states that a CVA proposal must provide how it is intended to deal with unclaimed dividends.[278]

8. Challenge of Directors' Actions

Ideally, a proposal should set out fully and clearly the powers which are to be conferred on the supervisor. It may be that such powers can appropriately be exercised by the supervisor alone, whilst others should be exercised only with the consent of the creditors given that a voluntary arrangement is predominantly, if not exclusively, for these purposes at least an arrangement between the company

---

277. *cf AMF International Limited v.* Ellis [1996] BCC 335 where it was held appropriate to replace an insolvency practitioner who had over-distributed funds in a members' voluntary liquidation having refused to admit a landlord's claim in full. The winding up was converted into a creditors' voluntary liquidation and the liquidator was ordered to pay the costs.
278. *See also* Insolvency Technical Reminder No.2 issued by the Association of Business Recovery Professionals.

and its creditors. The original legislation as set out in the unamended Insolvency Act 1986 gave a supervisor very limited powers. These included primarily the power to apply for directions under section 7(4) of the Insolvency Act 1986, the power to apply to petition for the compulsory winding up of the company and the power to apply under section 423 of the Insolvency Act 1986 with regard to transactions which allegedly involved the defrauding of creditors on account of transactions having been entered into at an undervalue.

It might be thought the occasions on which a supervisor might impeach a transaction on the basis of an undervalue are relatively rare. However, various recently introduced techniques, such as conditional fee arrangements and more specifically insurance related products, may have increased the opportunity for this to happen, coupled with the ability of a creditor to make claims on his or its own account under section 423 of the Insolvency Act 1986.[279]

However, even though there are restrictions to a supervisor being able to set aside prior transactions other than those under section 423 of the Insolvency Act 1986, the Insolvency Rules clearly provide that a proposal for a CVA must state whether, should a company go into liquidation, there might be a claim regarding transactions at an undervalue, preferences, extortionate credit transactions or invalid floating charges.

9. Variation

The legislation does not provide for the terms of a CVA to be varied during the CVA period. Neither does the court have any power to vary the terms of a CVA.[280] It is therefore extremely important that the proposal itself should empower the supervisor to call creditors' meetings during the course of the arrangement in order to approve any suitable variation, e.g. as to a possible extension of the duration of the arrangement preceded by some form of 'variation meeting' at which creditors' views can be canvassed and voted upon.

Another common reason for an extension is to address the level of a supervisor's fees which normally should not exceed a specified level except with specific authority. It is important to note that should such a variation meeting be called, a report on the outcome must be sent to the creditors, the members, the company, the court and the Registrar of Companies.[281] In *Raja v. Rubin*,[282] it was held that where the proposal does not contain an express power to vary the arrangement, it can still be varied provided all creditors entitled to share in the proceeds of the assets which are subject to the arrangement unanimously agree. Unanimity may in practice be very difficult to achieve during the course of an

---

279. *See* e.g. *National Westminster Bank v. Jones* [2000] BPIR 1092 [2002] BPIR 361.
280. *See Re Alpa Lighting Limited* [1997] BPIR 341; *See also Re Broome (A Debtor)* [1999] BCLC 336. cf *Tanner v. Everitt* (unreported: 28 May 2004), where the variation involved the appointment of a new supervisor even though there was no express power to vary.
281. *See* Insolvency Rule 1.24.
282. [1999] 1 BCLC 621.

arrangement and reliance may have to be placed upon any power vested in the supervisor, not only to convene meetings during the arrangement, but also to ensure that decisions can be carried by a 75 per cent by value of majority of those creditors who vote.

It should be noted that voting rights at the time of any variation meeting may have to be reduced in order to take into account the effect, for example, of any dividends that may have already been paid and distributed, or any amounts received by third parties, e.g. guarantors. There seems no reason why the challenge procedures contained in section 6 of the Insolvency Act 1986 should not apply to any subsequent 'variation meeting'. However, there may be doubt as to whether section 6A of the Insolvency Act 1986 (which makes it an offence to make false representations in relation to any original proposal) extends to representations made to induce creditors to agree to any variation of a CVA.

10. CVA Following a Liquidation

There is no bar to entering into a CVA following a formal liquidation either in the form of a compulsory winding up or a voluntary winding up. However, unlike the case of a bankruptcy, where a bankruptcy order will be annulled in the event of a subsequent voluntary arrangements, no such effect is achieved in the case of a company entering into a CVA following liquidation. Section 5(3) of the Insolvency Act 1986 presently provides that if a company is being wound up the court may (1) by order stay all proceedings of the winding up; or, (2) give such directions with respect to the conduct of the winding up as it thinks appropriate for facilitating the implementation of the approved voluntary arrangement. Although those provisions contemplate a stay, it is unclear to what extent, if any, the company emerges from liquidation. At the moment it seems that the best course is that in the event of a surplus following upon the implementation of the CVA, the company shall be placed into members' voluntary liquidation following whatever form of liquidation it had previously been subject to. If the CVA follows upon a liquidation, the supervisor must discharge the remuneration and costs of the outgoing practitioner.[283]

Although there is clear power in the Insolvency Rules[284] to enable every court having jurisdiction to wind up companies to review, rescind or vary any order made by the court, it may well be far easier to obtain a stay of a winding up order than to obtain its rescission.[285] It may however be possible for the court to rescind a winding up order where a CVA proposal had been approved by both creditors and members.[286]

---

283. *See* Insolvency Rule 1.23(2).
284. *See* e.g. Insolvency Rule 7.47.
285. *See* generally *Re Calgary & Edmonton Land Co Limited* [1975] 1 All E.R. 1046.
286. *See* e.g. *Re Dollar Land (Feltham) Limited* [1995] BCC 740.

11. Change of Supervisor

The appointment of a supervisor attaches personally to the supervisor and not to his firm. Section 7(5) of the Insolvency Act 1986 gives a court power to remove a supervisor or to appoint a new one should a vacancy occur, as well as power to replace a supervisor. In addition, the court has the power to appoint an additional supervisor on a temporary basis.[287]

Overall, it is necessary to show a good reason why there should be a change, e.g. a change of firms by the supervisor and the supervisor's inability to fulfil his role at the new firm.[288] Whether it is necessary in any particular case to circulate the creditors will depend on the facts.[289] In practice it is desirable that creditors be circulated with the suggested change. There is no entitlement on the part of creditors to remove or change a supervisor without a court order. Equally, it is not possible for a supervisor to resign, e.g. on grounds of alleged complexity or inadequate remuneration except in cases of loss of licence, illness, death, change of firm or any other reason which forms the subject matter of a court application and subsequent order, a supervisor must remain an office-holder until the terms of the arrangement have been completed.

12. Implementation and Termination

In practice, even though the CVA has reached its allotted termination date, the nominee should carefully ensure that all the obligations of the company under the CVA have been completed and complied with, that all fees have been drawn in accordance with its terms, that all creditors' claims have been properly submitted and agreed and that all necessary receipts and payment summaries have been prepared and finalized.

Insolvency Rule 1.29 provides that a final report is to be sent to creditors and members not more than 28 days after completion of the CVA. A copy should also go to the court and to the Registrar of Companies. The report should include a paragraph stating the purpose of the report and describing the nature of asset realizations and periodic contributions achieved and made during the course of the arrangement. The report should also itemize all dividends paid and compare them with those anticipated at the time of the original creditors' meetings. A summary of the supervisor's receipts and payments account should also be attached. Although questions regarding a supervisor's fees have already been dealt with,[290] the final report should explain as fully and as clearly as possible the manner in which fees have been charged, setting out if necessary how, if at all, the fees taken differ from those envisaged at the outset of the arrangement.

---

287. *See Clement v. Udall* [2001] 1 BPIR 454.
288. *See* e.g. *Re Parkdown* (1993) 15 June: unreported.
289. It is generally desirable that creditors be circulated with the suggested change: *see Re Equity Nominees Limited* [2000] BCC 84.
290. *See above* at III.H.6 and III.L.5.

M. DEFAULT AND FAILURE

A supervisor must bring a CVA to an end if a company defaults in its obligations and there is no scope for agreement as to any variation. Indeed, a supervisor should do so even where there is a lack of funds to do so in a manner otherwise envisaged by the CVA. Invariably any default will be formally indicated by the supervisor issuing a certificate of non-compliance.[291] Such a certificate will constitute a report to creditors as well as to the court in which the nature of the default will be set out. There is no statutory definition of the term 'default'. The exact ambit and meaning of the default or defaults in question can only be drawn from a close consideration of the company's obligations under the arrangement. It is unlikely that relatively minor obligations borne by the company under the arrangement will trigger a default such as to justify the termination of the arrangement. An analogy can be drawn with a position which applies in the case of individual voluntary arrangements. Section 276(1) of the Insolvency Act 1986 provides that a court shall not make a bankruptcy order on a supervisor's petition or on a petition presented by a person bound by the arrangement unless it is satisfied that first the debtor has failed to comply with his obligations under the arrangement, secondly that information that was false or misleading or which contained material omissions was contained in any statement of affairs or other documents supplied by the debtor to any person who was otherwise made available by the debtor to his creditors or thirdly and finally, the debtor has failed to do all such things as may have been reasonably required of him by the supervisor.

An obvious example of default would be significant failure by the company to meet its monthly payments under the arrangement. It has been held that a default petition presented by a supervisor can be maintained even if the alleged breach or breaches relied on were not continuing as at the date of the hearing of the petition.[292] It is, however, arguable that it may not be in the best interests of the creditors for the supervisor to persist with the presentation of such a petition and that the creditors' views should be canvassed as to whether the petition should continue.[293] Subject to its being reflected in the considered views of the creditors, the culpability of the directors is not a relevant issue.[294] In *Cadbury Schweppes Plc v. Somji*[295] it was held that the test of determining whether there had been a material omission was whether, had the truth been told, it would have made a material difference to the reaction of the creditors as a whole. In that case it was held that failure to disclose the fact, that if the arrangement were approved, two creditors would receive substantial benefits in addition to those which they would have got from a proportionate distribution of the debtor's estate, constituted

---

291. *See* Insolvency Rule 1.29(2) introduced by the Insolvency (Amendment) (No.2) Rules 2002.
292. *See Carter-Knight v. Peat* [2000] BPIR 968.
293. Compare *Vickers v. Mansell* (2002) 10 May: unreported.
294. *See* in the case of an IVA *Re Keenan* [1998] BPIR 205.
295. [2001] 1 WLR 615 and [2001] BPIR 172.

a material omission.[296] Now section 64 of the Insolvency Act 1986 (which replaced a former rule, namely Rule 1.30) provides that the making of false representations will constitute a criminal offence. A common illustration of default will be the company's failure to pay post-arrangement creditors.[297]

1. Supervisor's Liability

The role and function of the supervisor are prescribed by statute. Consequently the only right of action available is that set out in statute. A supervisor is an officer of the court: consequently he is general protected whether or a moratorium has been obtained,[298] so that in *Heritage Joinery v. Crasner*,[299] it was held that a supervisor had no general duty of care to post-arrangement creditors unless he had made or was responsible for a negligent misrepresentation on which reliance had been placed.[300]

In practical terms, however, it may be difficult for a supervisor to know precisely when to bring an arrangement to an end, mindful of the fact that creditors have no power to extend an arrangement that has already expired.[301] The best course may be in cases in which default has occurred shortly prior to the arrangement's termination date, to send a letter to the directors notifying them that a default has occurred, followed shortly afterwards by a letter in similar terms to creditors. The supervisor should also convene a creditors' meeting to authorize the ending of the arrangement, and if no variations are agreed upon, he should then formally terminate the arrangement. The benefit of convening a meeting is to ensure that the creditors are presented with a clear option either to extend the arrangement or to terminate it.

A winding up order can be made following the presentation of a petition even after the date of the termination of the arrangement.[302] There seems no reason why an arrangement cannot be revived even after the presentation of a winding up petition by the supervisor and prior to the making of a winding up order at least with the creditors' consent. Such a situation should perhaps be specifically provided for within the terms of the arrangement.

In practice, the main, if not only, risk as to a potential liability which might attach itself to a supervisor will be in cases in which he acts as a *de facto* or shadow director. It is therefore vital that the supervisor be neither seen, nor in fact take part in any company management function. He must however take all reasonable steps to ensure that he monitors the financial results of the company's business, mindful

---

296. See also *Re Tack* [2000] BPIR 164 and *Re Bradburn Subnom Bradburn v. Kaye* (unreported: 19 April 2006).
297. See *Re McKeen* [1995] BCC 412.
298. See, in the context of an IVA *King v. Anthony* [1999] BPIR 73.
299. [1999] BPIR 683.
300. See also *Re Central Crest Engineering Limited* [2000] BCC 627 (misfeasance by a liquidator who had allowed loss making trading to continue without court of liquidation committee sanction).
301. *Strongmaster Limited v. Kaye* [2002] BPIR 1259.
302. See in the context of an IVA *Harris v. Cross* [2001] BPIR 586.

of the terms of the arrangement. If the operation of the arrangement depends on its continued ability to discharge post-arrangement liabilities, it will not be for the supervisor to decide on whether the arrangement has failed.[303] The position may be different however if despite such failure, the default is triggered by the issuance on the part of the supervisor of a certificate of non-compliance.[304]

2. Liability of Directors

A proposal should allow for the views of creditors to contribute to the determination of whether a company otherwise in default under an arrangement should then be placed into liquidation. It may be appropriate in many cases for a company, albeit in default, to continue trading. Should the creditors resolve upon the need to put the company into liquidation, then in the face of resistance in that respect on the part of the directors, the supervisor should present a winding up petition.[305] Once in liquidation, the company by its liquidator can then investigate the actions of the directors during the currency of the arrangement.

3. Certificate of Non-compliance

Insolvency Rule 1.29 requires a supervisor to send to all creditors and members a notice that the arrangement has been fully implemented. Although the Insolvency Act 1986 is silent on the question, the practice has now developed for the supervisor to issue a certificate of non-compliance whenever a company has defaulted in relation to the obligations set out in the arrangement.

The certificate should inform both the creditors and the members not only as to the nature of the default but also as to the remedies and other steps, if any, which the supervisors might need to take. The latter, if thought appropriate by the supervisor, should reflect the terms of the proposal. A certificate of non-compliance is also the proper means by which to inform the creditors that they are no longer bound by the arrangement and are thus free to petition for the winding up of the company.

A voluntary arrangement cannot be revived after the issuance of a certificate of non-compliance, especially one which follows upon a default. In such a case, the voluntary arrangement will have to come to an end, though it is arguable that should the creditors and members indicate even after the issuance of the certificate that they wish the arrangement to continue or, put more strongly perhaps, be revived, then the supervisor can apply to court under section 7 of the Insolvency Act 1986 for authority to continue the conduct of the arrangement. However, this is subject to the abiding difficulty that it is difficult to see what *locus standi* in such cases the supervisor would generally have. It is however possible that the terms of the proposal do provide for such a revival, not only after the

---

303. *Re Maple Environmental Services Limited* [2000] BCC 93.
304. *Re Brelec Installations Limited* [2001] BCC 421.
305. Which reads section 7(4) Insolvency Act 1986, giving the supervisor specific power to do so.

issuance of a certificate for non-compliance, but also following upon the presentation of a winding up petition. In this respect, the position is perhaps analogous with one in which in the context of winding up and bankruptcy petitions, payment is proferred by means, e.g. of a banker's draft in consequence of which the court will then invariably dismiss the petition.

N. THE EFFECT ON THE UNDERLYING TRUST

It is well established that subject to any contrary wording in the proposal, all funds and assets included in the voluntary arrangement constitute trust assets for the benefit of the creditors bound by the arrangement. In the early days of the voluntary arrangement regime, there were conflicting decisions as to whether the trust created by the arrangement came to the end on the making of the winding up order or on the passage of the resolution to wind up the company voluntarily.[306]

Proposals are sometimes drafted in such a way as to provide that on default initially the supervisor serves a notice to the directors requiring them to institute a voluntary winding up of the company failing which the supervisor himself will then be at liberty to petition for the compulsory winding up of the company. In the light of the distinctions drawn in the early case law, it appeared to follow in practice that if the directors complied with the request, the trust was not treated as broken, whilst if they did not comply, forcing the supervisor to petition, the trust was treated as at an end.

In the event of the latter event occurring, it was and remains prudent for the supervisor to effect any distributions to the arrangement creditors prior to the presentation of any petition. This is on the ground that the provisions of section 127 of the Insolvency Act 1986 would otherwise invalidate any such distributions as being dispositions void as against the company after the commencement of a winding up.

As referred to *above*, the Court of Appeal in *Re N.T. Gallagher & Son Limited*[307] has now confirmed that funds held by the supervisor are held in trust for the benefit of CVA creditors even though the company might have subsequently gone into voluntary liquidation, secondly that the trust created by the proposal continues to be binding even after liquidation, and finally that if CVA creditors surrender their security, they can claim a dividend in the CVA whilst remaining able to prove in the winding up for the balance. The Court of Appeal, however, emphasized that assets specifically excluded from the CVA would not fall into the trust created for CVA creditors but would instead be available to the liquidator should the company later go into voluntary liquidation. It also stated that the trust continued, whether or not any petition for the winding up for the company was presented by the supervisor. It is therefore now desirable for the proposal to specify

---

306. As to the former approach, *see* e.g. *Re Arthur Rathbone Kitchens* [1997] BCC 450 to be compared with e.g. *Re Brelec* [2001] BPIR 210.
307. Recently applied in *Re Zebra Industrial Products Limited* (2005) BPIR 1022.

that assets in the CVA are held in trust for the arrangement of creditors irrespective of whether the supervisor presents a winding up petition, even though it follows from this that there may be few, if any, assets left available to finance a liquidation in the wake of a default. There is no reason why the proposal should not also provide that the CVA must cease, save in respect of assets already realized which can be distributed to creditors in the arrangement.

O.	DEFAULT AND SUBSEQUENT LIQUIDATION

Section 7(4) of the Insolvency Act 1986 grants the supervisor of an arrangement power to present a winding up petition. The Insolvency Act 1986, however, is silent on the form and content of the petition, so that it is important that the default, as well as the reasons for the making of a winding up order, are clearly set out. Although it is the normal practice for the Official Receiver[308] to be appointed liquidator at least initially on the making of a winding up order (Official Receiver), the court has power under section 140 of the Insolvency Act 1986 to appoint the supervisor to the position of liquidator.

P.	THE SUPERVISOR AS LIQUIDATOR

Although most professional bodies such as the Institute of Chartered Accountants stress the need for independence whenever an insolvency practitioner assumes a new appointment, not only can the practitioner act first as administrator and thereafter as supervisor or liquidator of the same company, but a supervisor of an individual voluntary arrangement can act as a Trustee in bankruptcy even after there has been default under the arrangement.[309]

Consequently, there seems no reason why a supervisor in a CVA cannot subsequently act as liquidator of the same company. Indeed, section 137 of the Insolvency Act 1986 would enable him to be so appointed by the Secretary of State albeit at the suggestion of the Official Receiver.

Rule 4.102 in the Insolvency Rules 1986 specifically provides for the court to be able to appoint the supervisor to the position of liquidator. The requirements are first that the supervisor must confirm that he is qualified to act and that he consents so to do, secondly that a copy of the order is sent to the Official Receiver, thirdly that the appointment as liquidator takes effect from the date of the order and finally the notice of the appointment be given to the company's members and creditors setting out certain stipulated information.

In practice, however, a supervisor should be reluctant to put himself forward in the wake of a failed arrangement where his relationship with the directors was

---

308. The Official Receiver is a civil servant in The Insolvency Service and an officer of the court.
309. This is expressly reflected in the terms of section 297(5) of the Insolvency Act 1986.

problematic, although clearly the views of creditors would be important in this respect.

IV. SCHEMES AND CVAS CASE STUDIES

This section of the chapter will provide actual case studies to demonstrate how Schemes and CVAs work in practice. The two case studies to be analyzed are the Marconi plc and Marconi Corporation plc Schemes and the TXU Europe group CVA. Although the CVA case study provided was used in an administration it is very useful to illustrate how a CVA actually works.

A. SCHEMES CASE STUDY: THE MARCONI PLC AND MARCONI CORPORATION PLC

1. Introduction

The restructuring of the Marconi group in 2002–2003 was one of the largest and most complex ever carried out. A consensual restructuring of circa GBP5 billion of debt was implemented without the need for an insolvency process, using Schemes of arrangement under section 425 of the Companies Act 1985 (Schemes), combined with section 304 of the US Bankruptcy Code orders for the top two companies of this multinational group (i.e. Marconi plc and Marconi Corporation plc). The remainder of the group was left free to operate normally.

2. Background

The Marconi group arose from a stalwart of UK industry, General Electric Company, and had decades of corporate history in a variety of engineering related industries. At the end of the nineties its traditional businesses were sold and it focused heavily on the telecommunications market. At that time it had operations in around 40 jurisdictions across the world. When the telecoms market turned down at the beginning of the twenty-first century, the group's performance suffered and it became clear that it was excessively indebted.

The group structure, in summary, consisted of an ultimate parent company, Marconi plc (plc), which was a London Stock Exchange and NASDAQ listed entity with some 200,000 shareholders. Its key subsidiary was Marconi Corporation plc (Corp). Corp was the holding company of some 300 operating subsidiaries across the world. Plc had one other subsidiary that would be crucial to the restructuring, which had been established to buy back some of the outstanding bond debt.

The group's debt mainly resulted from unsecured bank and bond lending in approximately equal proportions. The financial debt was denominated in GBP, USD and EUR. Corp was the principal obligor of the bank lending and the issuer of the bonds. Both these exposures were guaranteed by plc.

3. The terms of the restructuring

Two Schemes were proposed, one at plc and one at Corp, to compromise the circa GBP5 billion debt in exchange for cash, new debt instruments and new equity (which would be publicly tradable). The plc Scheme was dependent on the Corp Scheme being passed, although the Corp Scheme was not conditional on the successful implementation of the plc Scheme. No other companies were to be made subject to a Scheme, and the rest of the group was to continue trading as normal. The Schemes were 'all creditor' and the majority of the consideration was to be distributed immediately upon the Schemes becoming effective: the so-called 'first day distribution'.

The restructuring fell into the following areas: (1) creditor identification, quantification and notification; (2) key factors of the schemes; and, (3) the nature and distribution of the consideration.

4. Scheme creditors

The creditor profile of Marconi (plc and Corp) was as follows:

(1) Bank debt – the bank debt was syndicated, and so control and communication could be established through the agent bank for the syndicate. This bank was also a member of the bank co-ordinating committee.
(2) USD and EUR denominated bond issues – there was an ad-hoc committee of the bondholders but the beneficial ownership was widely spread.
(3) Other creditors.

There were four aspects of convening that needed to be addressed: (1) classes; (2) identification; (3) notification; and, (4) voting.

a. Identification of Creditors

Identification of creditors was an issue of concern to all parties, to ensure that there was a clear understanding of the level of liabilities (and therefore prospective dividends and provisions for unascertained and/or unknown creditors) prior to the Schemes being promulgated.

For the bank syndicate, identification was complicated by the active trading market in the Marconi bank debt. This was addressed by taking a record date at which point the syndicate participants then extant would be those which would be notified of the Schemes. If the bank debt were subsequently traded, then the seller would need to pass on the information to the buyer and notify the syndicate agent bank, Marconi and its advisers.

Identification of the bondholders was difficult. The initial concern that arose was which party constituted the creditor for the purposes of voting and/or proof of debt. Was it the bond trustee, the depository at which the bond was held, or the beneficial holder of the economic interest in the bond? The bond issues were originally held as one global note per issue, with holders of parts of that bond issue being recorded only as memo entries against the global note. The existence of the global note would have meant that technically there was only one creditor, for the whole amount of the issue, for each one of the bond issues – i.e. four creditors. Depending on the terms of the bond documentation, there existed the possibility that the bond trustee would give a split vote by way of omnibus proxy (GBP x in value for the Scheme; GBP y in value against) which could result in one vote for and one against; or one vote in favour; or one vote against (in the latter two cases where a majority of the bondholders voting at a bondholder meeting to instruct the bond trustee would vote either for or against. This would then result in the whole value of the bond issue being voted either for or against the Schemes).

In terms of achieving the required majority in number (one half of those present and voting) none of these possibilities were attractive. There was concern that although it was very likely that the Schemes would be passed by a three-quarters majority in value, the majority in number (colloquially known as 'numerosity') test was less certain. In addition, for the bond trustee to be authorized to cast a vote they would need to call a meeting of bondholders which would take valuable time. The solution, for the Marconi bond issues, was for the global notes to be 'definitised', i.e. for the global note to be split into definitive notes issued (in either individual global note or definitive registered form) to each individual holder. Although this was a complex legal drafting exercise, it took less time than convening bondholder meetings, with the risk that these would need to be adjourned to achieve a quorum, would have done.

The practical result of the definitivisation process was that the actual creditor who was entitled to vote was the ultimate beneficial owner. It is worth noting that if the process had been a CVA then there would not have been a numerosity test to satisfy and this reason for definitising would not have been necessary (a discussion of other reasons for doing so in a CVA is contained in the TXU Europe group example given *below* where a practical example of the use of CVAs is provided).

Whilst the definitisation process was proceeding through its legal requirements, an agency which specialized in identifying and notifying bondholders was instructed to begin the process of identifying the holders of the Marconi bonds issues. The details of holders are kept confidential by the depositories and therefore it was not possible simply to request a list of holders. In any event the Marconi bonds were publicly traded and the holders were constantly changing.

Because the Marconi Schemes were 'all creditor' Schemes it was also necessary to identify the other creditors of plc and Corp. This was done by reviewing the books and ledgers of the companies, hedging contracts, sale and purchase contracts, leases, pension schemes, employee contracts, extant or threatened legal proceedings, tax affairs, and intercompany transaction matrices; and considering and reviewing any areas of activity which might give rise to contingent or unascertained creditors. This was done jointly by the companies, their legal and financial advisers and the prospective Scheme supervisors. However, it should be noted that the final responsibility for identifying creditors who were to be notified and given an opportunity to vote rested with the companies proposing the Schemes.

In addition to these actions, Marconi placed advertisements in various international newspapers to attempt to identify any previously unknown creditors.

Notices were also placed into the Clearstream, Euroclear and DTC notification systems, to alert bondholders. If previously unknown creditors arose as a result of these processes, their claims were considered to assess whether they were correctly made against the Scheme companies and were not spurious. In most cases the claims made turned out to be against other group companies and therefore did not relate to, or affect, the Schemes.

The final step relating to creditor identification was to try to quantify the amount of their claim. This was done on a prudent basis following the liquidation rules relating to creditor claim agreement contained in the Insolvency Act 1986.

Certain types of creditor claim were excluded from the Schemes, in particular creditors which would have been preferential in a liquidation, pensions-related liabilities which could not be compromised by way of a Scheme, unsecured creditor claims of less than GBP 5,000 and trade and other obligations relating to the operating subsidiaries which would have impaired the group's ability to trade normally and carry on its business following the restructuring.

These exclusions were approved by the court at the sanction hearings. The ability to exclude certain categories of creditor was one of the reasons why, for Marconi, a Scheme was considered to be a more advantageous process than, say, a CVA, in which all creditors would have to be included for notification and voting purposes.

b.   *Notification*

Following the identification of creditors, it was necessary to devise a way of notifying them of the Scheme proposals and meeting date and venue; to provide them with voting forms and to receive and collate the proxies and proofs of debt. Again, advertisement in international newspapers and notification through Clearstream, Euroclear and DTC was used.

Where names and addresses of creditors were known, the proposals and all relevant documentation could be posted. Given that the Scheme proposals and appendices ran to over 1,000 pages, and that many creditors were based outside the UK, this had considerable cost and delivery time implications. Partially to alleviate this, the document could be printed in both the UK and the US. In addition, a secure website from which the proposals could be downloaded was established, together with telephone and e-mail help lines.

Creditors were asked to supply proxies in respect of their voting preference and proofs of debt. Other than for bondholders (discussed *below*) the proxy and accompanying proof of debt form were to be completed by the Scheme creditor. These forms were specifically designed and gave/requested more detail than the corresponding forms which would have been used under the Insolvency Act 1986, as this would not have given sufficient information to deal with all the issues which needed to be resolved for each creditor (this is discussed in more detail *below*).[310] Proxy forms and proofs of debt were colour coded to make it easier for creditors to

---

310. See IV.A. 6 *below*.

determine which should be submitted in respect of each claim and/or Scheme company.

For bondholders, no proof of debt form was required to be submitted. One proof for the whole of the bond issue was submitted by the bond trustee for each issue. Beneficial owners who wished to attend and/or vote at the Scheme meetings were required to instruct their 'Account Holder' (being the financial institution which held an account with the depositories, being DTC, Clearstream and Euroclear) to deliver an Account Holder letter to the bond identification agent and to 'block' the relevant holding of bonds. This was to ensure that, once voting instructions had been given, there could be no transfer of the bonds. This letter could be completed, checked and submitted in person, by post, or via a website. The result of the bondholder voting process was to produce an omnibus proxy which was then used to vote at each of the Scheme meetings.

c.   *Classes*

There were two matters which complicated the consideration of the classes to be included in the Schemes. The first was a 'lock-box' arrangement: an interim security granted to certain financial creditors over the group's cash of circa GBP 800 million. It was agreed that this security would be released, under certain conditions, prior to the Scheme meetings. These conditions became one of the most interesting aspects of the period leading up to the effective date.

Essentially, the financial creditors were concerned that, should they release their security prior to the effective date of the Scheme, if either Corp or plc were forced to file for insolvency, they would be unsecured creditors. The issue that arose centred around providing comfort to the financial creditors that no previously unknown claims were arising which would put the financial basis of the Schemes in doubt. The process adopted became known as the 'stop-go' letters, in which Corp and plc were required to confirm at key dates in the process that the provisions and reserves remained adequate to make distributions to all creditors under the Schemes. The prospective supervisors had to confirm, in turn, that they had no reason to disagree with these views. If these confirmations could not be given then the financial creditors would not release their security and the Schemes would not proceed. The second complication was the existence of an employee share option plan, for which a settlement of the claim was agreed prior to the Schemes (but payable only if the Schemes became effective).

As has now become usual, there were also agreements in place from certain Scheme creditors committing those creditors to vote in favour of the Scheme. These were not considered to give rise to a class issue.

The groups of excluded creditors (who would be dealt with in the ordinary course of business) included those which might have formed separate classes, e.g. those creditors which would have been preferential in the event of a winding up.

The resolution of these issues meant that all creditors were unsecured and all would have had equal rights against the company had an insolvency occurred.

If these conditions had not been met, neither Corp nor plc would have proceeded with their respective Schemes. The court was satisfied that this was acceptable. The result of this was that only one class, of ordinary unsecured creditors, existed for each Scheme.

5. Key Features of the Schemes

a.   *Shareholder Issues*

Although the Marconi group was in financial difficulty, and the Scheme was designed to compromise the claims of creditors of plc and Corp, shareholder issues could not be ignored. Because the new shares to be issued by Corp as part of the Scheme were to be listed, certain aspects of the Stock Exchange Listing Rules relating to prospectuses had to be complied with in the proposal documents. In addition, announcements had to be made to the market at appropriate points during the restructuring process. Practically, these had to be carefully considered in order to ensure that the market was not misled but that the restructuring process was not compromised. Both of these aspects added complexity, and thus cost, to the process.

The conversion of debt into equity resulted in the creditors becoming owners of 99.5 per cent of the re-issued equity, pro-rata to their debts. Existing shareholders were given 0.5 per cent of the reissued equity, in proportion to their existing shareholdings. Normally, a material dilution of existing shareholdings requires shareholder approval. However, permission was obtained from the UK Listing Authority for plc not to call such a meeting, under a dispensation available to companies in financial distress.

b.   *Proposals*

The proposal document enclosed all the information considered necessary for creditors to make an informed decision on the Schemes, to prove their debts and to vote at the meetings. It was divided into several parts: (1) important information, notices and instructions to creditors; (2) a letter from the Chairman of plc and Corp briefly explaining the reasons for proposing Schemes, the purpose of the rest of the documents, and recommending that the creditors vote in favour (this was different from a Scheme proposed by a liquidator or administrator, where such a recommendation would be less usual); (3) the explanatory statement; (4) the terms of the Corp and plc Schemes; and, (5) detailed information supporting the proposal in the appendices. The proposals and ancillary documents ran to over 1,000 pages. This was much longer than proposals would normally be expected to be in a CVA (by comparison the TXU Europe group proposals discussed *below* ran to some 200 pages), but the length was greatly increased due to the complexity of the consideration and the requirement to include the majority, if not all, of the information needed for the listing of the new equity in Corp.

c.   *Information*

From the point of view of providing creditors with sufficient information to make an informed decision, Marconi provided a description of all the key matters which might affect the creditors' view of the Scheme, how the group had got to its current position, historical financial information for both Corp and plc; a discussion of the current financial position; and the most recent (unaudited) quarterly report. In addition, and similarly to that information which would be expected to be provided to creditors in a CVA, an insolvency analysis was prepared and presented. This was given in order that creditors could form a view of the relative returns which the scheme would give them compared to an illustration of what might be expected on an administration. An administration was chosen as the comparative process as Corp and plc believed that there were only two possible outcomes from the position: the restructuring as comprised in the Schemes, or an administration[311] or liquidation of the companies under the Insolvency Act 1986. As it was believed that an administration would give rise to a better realization of the assets than could be obtained in a liquidation, administration was chosen as the comparative in order that an unduly pessimistic, and potentially misleading, comparative was not shown.

Listing particulars relating to the new shares were included in the proposal so that the requirements of the London Stock Exchange when issuing shares would be complied with.

d.   *Operative Provisions*

The operative provisions of the Schemes: i.e. the technical and mechanical provisions necessary to determine claims, make distributions, resolve disagreements and terminate the Schemes; together with the powers of the Scheme supervisors, were included in the Scheme documentation so that creditors would be informed as to how the Schemes would operate in practice. The terms relating to claim agreement and dispute resolution largely followed the provisions of the Insolvency Act 1986. The way in which distributions would be calculated was explained in detail, as this was a matter of considerable interest to the creditors. Terms were included to allow the constitution of a creditors' committee; to hold meetings of creditors; and to deal with the remuneration of the supervisors.

e.   *Other Key Items*

Because Marconi was a geographically diverse group with publicly traded debt, creditors were located in many jurisdictions. Each jurisdiction had different rules relating to the ability of creditors to accept new debt or equity instruments

---

311. A company can apply for an administration order – a court based procedure – to receive protection from its creditors to rescue a troubled company as a going concern avoiding liquidation.

in exchange for its existing debt, and brief details of this had to be given in order for creditors to take their own advice on their positions. The same was true for tax. The jurisdictional issues would not necessarily have been any different had a CVA been proposed instead of a Scheme: certain jurisdictions would still have had restrictions on the ability of creditors to receive new debt and/or new equity.

The proposal described in detail the actions to be taken by creditors in respect of their claims, whether they were bondholders or other types of creditor.

f.   *Other Key Documents*

The key terms of other documents which were required to implement the Schemes successfully were also included in the proposals sent to Scheme creditors. These included the terms of the new debt instruments, the proposed section 304 US Bankruptcy Code orders; details relating to the Scheme supervisors; and provisions of the company constitution of Corp following the restructuring.

There were two other critical documents: the Scheme Implementation Deed, which was to put in place legally binding arrangements which governed the interactions between Corp and plc relating to the Schemes and which would (inter alia) protect the ongoing group (i.e. Corp and its subsidiaries) should plc's Scheme fail and plc be placed into an insolvency process before the Corp Scheme was formally implemented; and the Escrow and Distribution Agreement, which appointed an escrow trustee and distribution agent who would hold the Scheme consideration and distribute it as instructed by the Scheme supervisors.

g.   *Separate Documents*

Creditors were sent the proposal document, account holder letters, forms of proxy and proof of debt forms as separate letters so that they could complete and return the proxies, proofs and/or account holder letters without difficulty. This conforms with normal insolvency practice in the UK where forms of proxy and proof of debt forms are sent as separate documents with the notices convening meetings of creditors and members.

h.   *Effective Date*

For a Scheme to become effective, firstly, there must be a majority in number representing three-quarter in value of those creditors present and voting in favour, secondly the court must sanction the Scheme and finally a notice confirming this must be delivered to the Registrar of Companies. On Marconi, the time pressures following the meetings were acute. This was the result of the necessity for the bonds to be blocked from trading once an account holder letter had been issued, and the desire of the major creditors to receive the consideration due to them immediately. As a result, the sanction hearings were planned to occur as quickly as possible after the meetings (in practice, about two weeks later) and the effective date was one week after that. It should be noted that, absent a challenge to a CVA, it would be effective immediately following approval by the creditors' and members' meetings

6. Consideration and Distributions

a.   Consideration

Creditors were offered a mixture of cash, new debt instruments and equity, pro rata to their existing claims against each company. There was a cash-out option for creditors in jurisdictions which did not allow certain creditors to receive equity and/or debt instruments. Creditors were required to confirm on their proof of debt forms that they were not subject to any such restrictions. The proof of debt forms therefore had to be specially designed to allow this confirmation to be given. This was a clear advantage to the Scheme process over a CVA, as in a CVA both proof and proxy forms would have had to conform to the format given in the Insolvency Act 1986 in every detail, necessitating an extra form to allow the confirmations to be provided.

b.   Funds Flows

Plc's main source of funds was distributions from Corp, in some cases via plc's bondholding vehicle. Plc was the sole shareholder of this vehicle and therefore received the distribution in its capacity as shareholder. However, plc was also a debtor of the vehicle (as guarantor of the bonds), and so it also received distributions from plc. The circular nature of the intercompany matrix between Corp, plc and the bondholding vehicle required a complex model to establish the funds flows, model the circularity and thus calculate the final distributions to be received after all the funds flows had been iterated to infinity. This allowed the first day distributions to be maximized, saving the time and cost of making ever smaller distributions separately.

c.   First Day Distributions

The creditors had required that the majority of the considerations should be distributed immediately upon the Schemes becoming effective. That had in turn meant that creditor claims had to be quantified and, as far as possible, agreed, prior to the effective date. Formal agreement of the claims in the Schemes could only be given once court sanction had been given. The proposals included strict time limits for claims to be made if the creditor wished to receive a first day distribution. If these were missed, the first distribution to that creditor would be made as soon as possible but they would not be part of the initial payment.

As well as agreeing known creditors, reserves had to be made for unascertained and unknown creditors. Known creditors, who would receive the first day distribution, wished the reserves to be lower to maximize their payment; the Scheme supervisors wished to minimize the risk that late-appearing creditors would be disadvantaged. The differing views were accommodated partly because of the extensive identification and quantification exercises already undertaken and partly by requiring Corp and plc to confirm at key dates in the process that the provisions and reserves remained adequate to make distributions to all creditors under the Schemes. The prospective supervisors had to confirm, in turn, that they had no reason to disagree with these views. A key agreement which assisted in resolving the level of provision to be maintained related to a class action claim of hundreds of millions of GBP, which was known and thus had to be provided for in full. It was agreed that, should this be settled at a materially lower figure, then the balance would be distributed immediately. The court accepted that all of these matters constituted reasonable ways in which to deal with the risks of a first day distribution.

7. Conclusion

The Marconi Schemes remain among the most complex ever implemented, and developed the process to become a key restructuring tool which minimizes the reputational issues which a formal insolvency process such as a CVA can bring to an ongoing trading business. With a Scheme, it is possible to be very flexible as to the creditors that are included and the design of forms of proof and proxy. However, Schemes of this nature remain the province of larger companies and groups due to the formalities to which they are subject and the costs of the exercise.

B. CVA CASE STUDY: TXU EUROPE GROUP

1. Introduction

In the insolvency of the TXU Europe power group (TXU Europe group), the distribution and exit procedure chosen to conclude the administrations and certain liquidations of the Holding Companies was the Company Voluntary Arrangement ('CVA'). Why were CVAs chosen, and what were their advantages over section 425 of the Companies Act 1985 Schemes in this case?

2. Background to the CVAs

The insolvency of the TXU Europe group was the largest ever in the UK. The group fell into two parts, the operating companies, with assets of some GBP 2.1 billion and liabilities of some GBP 2.3 billion (Operating Companies); and the holding companies, with assets of GBP 0.6 billion and liabilities of GBP 2.5 billion (Holding Companies). Complex, interlocking CVAs for sixteen of the Holding Companies were proposed, in order to resolve the outstanding intercompany and intercreditor disputes and to distribute the available funds.

Under the Insolvency Act 1986, an administrator was not permitted to make distributions to creditors (this has been partially altered by the Enterprise Act 2002). Therefore an exit procedure to distribute funds to creditors had to be put in place. There are three main exit procedures:

1. CVAs;
2. Schemes; or,
3. Liquidation.

Liquidation was not an option in these cases due to the adverse tax consequences on the whole of the group, which would have significantly reduced the funds available to creditors. The choice was therefore between CVAs and Schemes.

Although the paramount purpose of the CVAs was to distribute funds to creditors, in many ways the TXU Europe group CVAs were akin to a debt restructuring process. In particular, the CVAs:

(1) resolved the allocation of disputed funds between estates;
(2) agreed creditors' claims against each estate;
(3) provided certainty of position;
(4) were working to a deadline after which a key asset would no longer be 'on the table'
(5) had groups of creditors with disparate holdings in different debt instruments, where the principal debtors for the instruments were different estates.

There were seven issues which had to be compromised between the Holding Company estates, of which the key issue was the allocation of a settlement of potential litigation against the directors and the ultimate holding company, TXU Corporation, valued at some USD220 million ('the Corp settlement'). The Corp settlement was the driving factor behind many of the critical issues in the case, as:

(1) it mandated a long-stop date for the holding of meetings to approve the compromises;
(2) it required any challenge to the compromises to be disposed of by 30 November 2005, or else the settlement would fall away;
(3) it required releases to be given by all of the key Holding Companies; and
(4) it required section 304 relief to be given under the US Bankruptcy Code by the key Holding Companies and certain Operating Companies.

The other issues comprised:

(1) the allocation of GBP 67 million arising from swaps encashed pre-insolvency;
(2) the allocation of GBP 11.5 million receipts from certain power companies;
(3) whether the on-lending of proceeds from several bond issues (totalling approximately GBP 1.4 billion) from a special purpose vehicle to TXU Europe Ltd. was subordinated;
(4) whether another special purpose vehicle, known as EGO BV, had a guarantee claim of approximately GBP 400 million against Energy Holdings No 3 Limited (EH3);

England & Wales

(5) which would be the most appropriate date for valuing claims (significant amounts of debt were in EUR, USD and GBP); and,
(6) the agreement of inter-company balances.

In order to be as efficient and cost-effective as possible in satisfying the requirements of the Corp settlement, all key companies had to enter the same procedure, on the same terms. This was especially important for two reasons:

(1) the Corp settlement required releases from all the key companies in order to become effective; and,
(2) the complex inter-company balances, which gave rise to a circular flow of funds within the group. This forced the creation of an extremely complex computer program to model outcomes and distributions on an entity priority basis ('the Model'). The key to the Model was the iterative funds flow through all the inter-company balances, resulting in the eventual distributions to third parties. The Model had to assume that all the funds flows took place, otherwise external creditors would not receive as high a distribution as they were expecting. But for this to function in reality, as opposed to in the Model, all the companies through which significant funds were to flow had to be part of the process.

If any key company did not enter a distribution process, then none could, as a result of the two points above. There were six of these key companies, which were termed the Core Companies. It was not necessary for all of the other companies to enter the process, although the more that did, the simpler the process would be. The Core Companies comprised all the companies through which there were material flows of funds, those companies who had significant external creditors, and those from which TXU Corp required releases.

Sixteen interlocking CVAs were proposed, each on exactly the same terms, to settle each of the *above* items.

The creditors comprised a bank syndicate owed approximately GBP0.7 billion and two groups of bondholders, owed GBP 1.4 billion and GBP 0.3 billion. The bond issues were traded on both the US and European markets.

3. Ability to Bind Third Parties

A key factor in the process was the ability for creditors to give releases to third parties by contracting so to do as part of the CVA.

4. Creditor Issues

a. *Notification of Creditors*

Under section 5(2)(a) of the Insolvency Act 1986, since amended, creditors would only be bound by the compromise made in a CVA if they had been notified of the creditors' meeting. This gave rise to considerable problems in large cases: identifying every creditor would be difficult even in the best run companies, and insolvent companies are not generally noted for the excellence of their record-keeping. The difficulty that arose was that a creditor which was not bound by the CVA would retain all its rights against the company, including the right to petition for its winding-up. The consequence of this was that the administration or liquidation would have to be maintained in order to protect the company from an unknown creditor, regardless of whether this was necessary for any other reason.

The provision was amended by the Insolvency Act 2000, inserting section 5(2)(b). This provides that the CVA would bind every creditor which was entitled to vote at the creditors' meeting. Of course, fully secured creditors are not entitled to vote, but the effect of the amendment is to make the CVA procedure far more certain.

For a CVA, the Insolvency Act 1986 requires that notice of the CVA meetings must be in writing and sent, which is interpreted to mean by physical post. Clearly for traded bond issues this is not practical – even the best identification systems will never pick up 100 per cent of holders, still less their postal addresses. Were this to be rigidly adhered to, then a CVA would remain generally unachievable in large and complex cases.

For TXU Europe group, a directions application was made in relation to these matters. The Court agreed that, in addition to posting the papers to all creditors whose addresses were known and to advertising in internationally read newspapers, creditors could also be notified by sending electronic copies of the documents, and/or by notice through the clearing systems. In both cases the Court permitted a link in the notification which would direct creditors to the TXU website where the proposal documents could be downloaded, rather than sending documents physically. Again, this allowed CVAs to continue to be considered.

Proxy forms had to be provided in hard copy and in the specific format required by the Insolvency Act 1986. It is not permitted to alter the format or to allow them to be filled in and submitted electronically (e.g. via a website) In a Scheme, it would have been possible to provide an electronic proxy form, tailored to specific creditor groups, which could be filled in, checked, and transmitted on-line. This would have simplified the voting process for bondholders, and also reduced the cost. Recent commentary suggests, however, that submitting a proxy form by scanning and e-mailing a form which has been filled in physically may be acceptable. If confirmed, this may simplify and speed up the process of voting, especially where overseas creditors are involved.

In a CVA it is possible to impose a bar date, beyond which creditors will not be permitted to claim. Recent case law has established that this must be of a reasonable length, however it provides certainty to creditors and the company on the duration of the procedure.

b.   *Identification of Creditors*

As noted *above*, within the Holding Companies' creditors there were significant numbers of bondholders. As the bonds were traded, and in fact there was a relatively liquid market, although identification of a large number of holders was possible it would never have been possible to identify all holders. Had it not been for the provisions of section 5(2)(b) of the Insolvency Act 1986, a CVA would have been impossible to implement in any case where bondholders formed one of the creditor groups: there would always have been unknown, and hence unnotified, creditors who could have derailed the CVA after its implementation. Thus these provisions were critical even to be able to consider, let alone propose, CVAs for the Holding Companies.

In the case of bondholders, there is a question of the identity of the creditor. Is it the Trustee of the bond issue, is it the Account Holder (generally a major bank who has a clearing system account and holds on behalf of a number of ultimate beneficial owners) or is it the beneficial owner itself?

Where there is a bond issue represented by a global note, if the Trustee were to be treated as the creditor then there would only be one creditor. If the Account Holders or the beneficial owners are the creditors, then there are many. The Trustee may be directed at a bondholder meeting to vote in a specific way – all for or all against—or its vote may be exercised as a value for and a value against representing the sums of individual wishes of the holders. Which it is depends on the terms of the indenture or trust deed. In previous cases, which have used Schemes, most notably Marconi, this has been resolved by issuing definitive notes to all bondholders. This is expensive and time-consuming, and gives rise to the need to identify bondholders by clearing system notice and advertisement. However, it was very carefully considered as a potential course of action to permit voting by the individual bondholders of the TXU bond issues.

In the CVAs, the first concern was the creditors which should be notified. If the Trustee were the creditor, only one letter would be needed and the process would be very simple. If it were the bondholder, then an identification exercise would have to be carried out. The second concern was the timing. For the Trustee to vote, it would need to be instructed by a meeting of bondholders. Typically, bondholder notice periods are between 30 and 90 days, and if a quorum is not achieved a second meeting must be held with a further notice period. Between 14 and 28 days' notice must be given for holding the creditors' meeting for a CVA (Insolvency Rule 1.9). The issue is that the bondholders cannot instruct the Trustee to vote if they have not been provided with a copy of the proposals, but the notice period for the bondholder meeting is much longer than the maximum notice period permitted by law for the CVA meetings. The solution used in a similar situation for the Operating Companies CVAs was to provide bondholders with an Information Memorandum, which then became the Explanatory Statement sent as part of the CVA proposals. Unfortunately, this solution would not be possible in the TXU Holding Company CVAs, as there was a long-stop deadline for holding the CVA meetings imposed by the requirements of a settlement with TXU Corp, worth circa USD 220 million. This long-stop date would not have allowed time to hold second meetings had any bondholder meetings been inquorate.

On TXU Europe group, a chain of reasoning was developed which allowed the office-holders to treat the individual bondholders (Account Holders for the Eurobonds and beneficial owners for the Yankee bonds: the difference was a result of the different terms of the indentures) as the creditor and therefore as the person with the entitlement to vote. This relied on an analysis of the bondholder's contingent creditor claim. Each of the Trustees confirmed that they would not seek to vote, leaving the contingent creditors to vote individually. There was then no need to convert the global notes into definitive bonds. This treatment cured the problem of differing notice periods for the CVA and bondholder meetings, but used identification procedures similar to those which have previously been developed for Schemes. Such procedures are becoming familiar to bondholders, who have responded to them in large restructurings previously.

5. Class Issues

In a CVA there is only one class of unsecured creditor. A CVA is thus simpler to implement than a Scheme, as no unsecured class issues need to be considered. However, it is not possible to exclude any unsecured creditors from a CVA. Instead, it is necessary to propose different treatments (for example paying key trade creditors in full) for different commercial types of creditor, and to have this agreed by the statutory majorities. This leaves the commercial settlement in a debt restructuring open to ransom.

In TXU Europe group, it did not appear to the office-holders that there would be separate classes whether a Scheme or a CVA was proposed, as each company was already in an insolvency process in which all creditors were unsecured. Had Schemes been proposed, only one class would have been put forward. However, in a subsequent unfair prejudice application, the challenging creditors argued that they had been prejudiced by the use of a CVA procedure, as, they alleged, they would have formed a separate class in a Scheme. Their argument rested on the contention that as they had interests in only one bond issue, whereas other creditors had interests in other bond issues and/or in the bank syndicate, the votes of these other creditors were cast on the basis of collateral interests and not on whether the CVA represented the best outcome for the creditors of the individual company. The CVA officeholders disputed that they would have formed a separate class.

There has previously been little guidance on whether, or when, administrators should choose a CVA or a Scheme. The TXU Europe group judgment makes it clear that there is no reason in law that one or other should be preferred. There is no obligation to propose a Scheme – which can be more expensive and protracted than a CVA – in preference to a CVA, where different unsecured creditors have differing balances of interests overall. The mere fact that there might be separate classes in a Scheme will not render a CVA unfair. This is so even if the creditors who complain would form a separate class in a Scheme, and therefore have the power to block the Scheme, but do not have the power to block the CVA. This opens the way to use the CVA procedure more widely, making an exit from administration or liquidation potentially faster and cheaper. As long as the CVA is not itself unfair, then the use of that procedure reduces the chance of a 'ransom' creditor, who might argue that it is a constituent of a separate class, trying to improve its position by threatening to block a Scheme, although they may still bring an unfair prejudice challenge under section 6 of the Insolvency Act 1986.

There is an argument that in a Scheme the sanction hearing would discount the votes of creditors having collateral interests. This would be a matter for the Court's discretion. There is no basis in the Insolvency Act 1986 for this contention in a CVA: it is clear that the basis of voting is the value of the claim against the estate. The protection available is that at least half of the unconnected creditors must vote in favour. Creditors having collateral interests in other estates are not connected, and the remedy here is an unfair prejudice challenge. The suggestion that creditors with other interests should have been 'disenfranchised' in a CVA was dismissed in the TXU Europe group case.

6. The US Angle and the Need for Section 304 Bankruptcy Code Relief

Obtaining relief under section 304 of the US Bankruptcy Code was a pre-condition to receipt of the TXU Corp settlement sum. Traditionally, relief under section 304 has not been considered available where a CVA is being considered, as it had been uncertain whether that a CVA would qualify as a collective, court supervised, procedure for the purposes of that section. Therefore where section 304 relief is sought a Scheme has been the process of choice. The availability, or otherwise, of section 304 relief was a critical factor. The officeholders were advised that, due to the administrations being a court supervised process, even if a CVA were put in place the US courts would look favourably on a request for relief. On balance, therefore, there seemed no reason why a CVA should not be given relief in the same way as a Scheme would.

A request for relief was duly made, and granted, in order to perfect the TXU Corp settlement. The decision rested on the Judge's finding that the administration proceedings, and their resolution through the statutory provisions of the Insolvency Act 1986 (i.e. the CVAs), satisfied the standards required by section 304(c) of the US Bankruptcy Code. It seems that the existence of the administration order gave the Court comfort, although the Court saw no problem in enforcing the CVAs and indeed appears to have agreed that the CVAs were foreign proceedings. This decision means that there is now no reason not to propose a CVA to exit administration where US interests are involved.

It seems likely that this reasoning would be followed in a new Chapter 15 proceeding.

7. Is There a Requirement for Sanction by the Liquidation Committee?

The TXU Europe group case has made it clear that by making proposals for a CVA, the officeholder does not enter into a compromise requiring sanction. This is a welcome clarification which will make proposing CVAs in liquidations with conflicting creditor views much simpler. Of course, the CVA must still have a substantial chance of being passed by the statutory majorities. But a creditor who does not have a blocking vote (over 25 per cent) cannot create a hold-up simply by being on a committee and refusing to sanction the proposal. Of course, in an administration there is no requirement for sanction.

It is, however, still a moot point whether voting in a CVA following a liquidation would require liquidation committee sanction. This, it seems, will depend on the terms of the CVA. In the TXU Holding Company CVAs, the proposals were all interconditional. This was held not to require sanction in order to vote.

8. Challenges to the Compromise

In a Scheme, following the creditors' meetings there is a Court hearing (the sanction hearing) at which the overall fairness of the Scheme is considered. This gives dissenting creditors the right to be heard, despite the creditors' meetings having approved the Scheme by the requisite majorities. Once this hearing process (including any appeals) is exhausted there can be no further challenge to the Scheme.

In a CVA, any challenge to the compromises agreed by the creditors' meeting can only be made by applying to the Court under section 6 of the Insolvency Act 1986 to suspend or revoke the CVAs, or require a revised compromise proposal, on the grounds that the original proposal causes unfair prejudice or that there was a material irregularity at the meetings. A dissenting creditor has 28 days to bring such an application following the date on which the report of the creditors' meetings is filed at Court. In addition to this immediate 28 day period, there is a further risk, in that creditors who are not aware of the CVA have 28 days from the date on which they become aware of it to bring a section 6 of the Insolvency Act 1986 challenge. It is extremely unclear what practical redress such creditors might have, since in the elapsed period the CVA will have been implemented and some, if not all, of the assets are likely to have been distributed. In any event, appropriate advertising will provide protection against this type of challenge.

The difference in the ability to challenge is a double-edged sword. The necessity for a sanction hearing in a Scheme adds time and cost to the procedure. The ability to argue at that hearing, for which the costs of all parties are usually met by the estates, may encourage creditors to argue points for which they would not initiate (or fund) proceedings themselves. However, once the sanction hearing (including any appeal process) has approved the Scheme then the Scheme cannot be further challenged. In a CVA, by contrast, the need to bring proceedings under section 6 of the Insolvency Act 1986, the costs of which may not be met by the estates if the application is lost, may discourage creditors from challenging it without good grounds. Necessarily, though, it also means that after approval there is a risk that the implementation of the CVA will be delayed for an indefinite period until any challenge is finally disposed of. If, as in the TXU Europe group case, the challenge to the CVAs is coupled with a removal application, then there is also a continuing personal risk to the office-holders.

In the TXU Europe group CVAs, challenges were brought on the grounds both of unfair prejudice and of material irregularity (that (1) Schemes had not been proposed which would have treated the challenging creditors as a separate class; and, (2) that creditors having collateral interests were allowed to vote their creditor claims in full). The challenges were made on the last day permitted.

The challenges required a full court hearing to dispose of. The evidence comprised eight witness statements from the challengers; nine witness statements in reply; written submissions and case summaries, letters of support for the CVAs from certain major creditors; a full disclosure process requiring the review of more than 1200 physical files and more than 70,000 e-mails; and a ten day trial at which the challenging creditors and the office-holders were cross-examined. All of this was completed within four months of the challenge being served. Judgment was given less than a month later and the challenges were dismissed on all counts.

It was necessary to expedite the proceedings in order to be able to deal with an appeal within the long-stop date for perfecting the TXU Corp settlement. In the event, no appeal was brought and the settlement was completed.

9. Conclusions

In view of all the considerations *above*, it is only a matter of commercial judgment whether a CVA or a Scheme should be used. There is no technical reason to prefer one over the other. Practically, a CVA is as flexible as a Scheme, faster to implement in that it does not require the same degree of Court involvement, and has only one class of unsecured creditor. It should therefore be given serious consideration in any size of case.

Chapter 7
France

The Idiosyncrasy of the French Judicial System and its Preventive Procedures for Expedited Debt Restructurings

Isabelle Didier

ACRONYMS, ABBREVIATIONS & DEFINED TERMS

ADR	Alternative Dispute Resolution Mechanisms
AGS	Association pour la Gestion du Régime de garantie des créances des Salariés (French Salary Insurance System)
BNP	Banque Nationale de Paris, merged to form BNP Paribas
COB	Commission des Opérations de Bourse
COMI	Center of Main Interest
Company Rescue Act	'Loi de Sauvegarde', Act n° 2005–845 dated 26 July 2005
Council	National Council of Commercial Courts
Decree	Decree n° 2005–1677 dated 28 December 2005, which came into force on 1 January 2006 and is the implementing decree of the Company Rescue Act
EU	European Union
EUR	Euro
Eurotunnel	Eurotunnel S.A.
IP	Insolvency Practitioners
PMEs	Small and Medium-sized Companies
Rescue proceedings	a preventive procedure, under the supervision of French courts, intended to facilitate the reorganization of a company while still solvent.

I. INTRODUCTION

A. Overview

In July 2005, France equipped itself with a new statute for the treatment of insolvency, namely the 'Loi de Sauvegarde', Act n° 2005–845 dated 26 July 2005 (*'Company Rescue Act'*) which amended the French bankruptcy law included in the Commercial Code. The Company Rescue Act is supported by its implementing decree No. 2005–1677 dated 28 December 2005, which came into force on 1 January 2006 ('Decree').

The Company Rescue Act is the successful culmination of lengthy consultations with its stakeholders, professional organizations and concerned lobbies. The French Justice Department, the French National Assembly and the Senate all led the push for reform; foreign systems were also taken into consideration.

Observers will note that every twenty years or so, French laws on insolvency undergo changes in an effort at modernization: 1967, 1985 and most recently 2005.

The *Company Rescue Act* also attempts to throw off the all-too-frequent image of the French insolvency system as being inefficient, operating with a minimum of transparency and lacking in predictability.

Legislative reform sends a loud message. This new law is a national step forward directed at the country's businessmen and equally to their representative bodies (official representatives/trade associations, respective unions, etc), and to professional practitioners directly involved in the management of companies in distress. It is a call for co-operation among financial and judicial authorities at an international level.

The generally-held conviction by most parties to the process is that previous laws had not succeeded in protecting the French economy or in saving jobs, although these were precisely the objectives that had been sought in the 1985 amendments.

The strong words 'instilling fear', 'the obsolescence of the system' and 'destructive law' are used to describe the past. The hopes for the future are repeated over and over through the slogan: we must create a climate of 'trust'.

Companies will be provided with the necessary tools and support through the new laws to find appropriate solutions to their problems.

Problems can be multiple, solutions can therefore be numerous. The government hopes to convince business leaders to react before the fatal outcome of compulsory liquidation becomes their only option.

Having said all this, the reform, which was widely publicized has not succeeded in changing the very essence of French insolvency procedures. Judicially controlled they were, judicially controlled they remain. Should prevention be desirable, it continues to be organized by the court having local jurisdiction.

Furthermore, as before, the new and expanded preventive measures are reserved exclusively for those businesses not having suspended payments as defined by law. Insolvency, under French rules, occurs when accounts payable and due exceed current and available assets. The rigid application of the letter of the law severely limits a company's eligibility to apply for preventive measures.

No 'forum shopping'. In France, jurisdiction is tied to the company headquarters. The first article of the Decree stipulates that a change in address of the headquarters can only be recognized six months after the date of official publication.

By putting the focus on reforming the law rather than on the badly-needed reorganization of the Commercial Courts, the government deliberately, and again for political reasons, brushed aside changes to the archaic French judicial system which has existed since 1563. Perhaps the political and financial costs of this type of reform are too high.

The background in a few figures:

In 2004, France had:

- a population of ca. 61,000,000;
- approximately 2,568,000 businesses including some 230,000 businesses created in 2004;
- Some 42,000 insolvency proceedings opened. France requires insolvency proceedings for the legal and accounting discontinuation of any business, even devoid of assets;
- 184 Commercial Courts;
- 3,100 Commercial Court judges;
- 307 liquidators; and
- 121 administrators.

B. LEGAL FRAMEWORK

1. The Commercial Courts

There are 184 Commercial Courts and 3,100 elected judges handling insolvency proceedings in France. Of these courts, 25 are made up of more than 25 judges, the largest court being the Tribunal de Commerce de Paris (Paris Commercial Court) with 180 judges. According to data provided by the supervisory body of the Commercial Courts (*Observatoire du Tribunal de Commerce*), in 2004 these 25 Courts handled approximately 40 per cent of the insolvency proceedings, i.e. 21,000 cases of a total annual average of 45,000. Out of this figure, 900 are voluntary arrangements and mediations.

The judges are elected by their peers for a maximum term of 14 years. They are volunteers and hold a business occupation when designated. While in office, it is understood that they will lobby actively for their company's interests when required. As a matter of note, banking circles and industry are most represented among the judges in the Commercial Court of Paris.

Certain judges are lawyers; others have little or no legal training at all. Due to limited resources for training, elected judges are prone to wide variances in performance delivery.

The idea of volunteers financed by the businesses they work in, while fulfilling this public service role is naturally based on an expectation.

France

There is a price to pay for a legal system's independence. Even the best of women and men cannot guarantee the independence of their decisions if they are both judge and party to the matter.

For the time being, the elective system endures because of the costs issue. Perhaps this system is the best under the circumstances?

The need for impartiality would have been assured by the presence of professional judges sitting alongside the elected judges, a recommendation which had been made during the 2005 reform but which was unfortunately rejected due to political pressures.

In the meantime, changes are being sought making the elected judges accountable for their decisions.

The National Council of Commercial Courts was created by Decree n° 2005–1201 on 23 September 2005. The National Council of Commercial Courts is an advisory body reporting to the French Minister of Justice competent in advising the Minister in three areas:

1. The code of ethics and the training of elected judges;
2. The functioning and organization of the Commercial Courts; and
3. The establishment and subject-matter jurisdiction of the Commercial Courts.

The creation of this Council is part of the reform package aimed at reorganizing the Commercial Court system. It will allow discussions to go forward on a number of important questions affecting the future of the commercial courts' system such as amendments to the territorial map, the specialization of courts, or the implementation of the *Company Rescue Act* voted in on 26 July 2005.

Justice, in order to be well-administered and accepted, must be fair.

2. The Public Prosecutor's Office

Insolvency proceedings in France are under judicial authority and fall under the auspices of the Public Prosecutor's Office. The Public Prosecutor represents in court the side of public law and order, for both social and economic interests.

The Company Rescue Act confirmed the legislative intent to see the Public Prosecutor become more involved in the day-to-day management of the prevention and handling of distressed companies.

The Public Prosecutor's Office is involved during the rescue proceedings. The proposed plan resulting from the negotiations must be submitted to his office for review, before the court can move forward and rule on it. Once a company exceeds a certain size, the Public Prosecutor's Office must be present at a mandatory hearing. The court does not have the power to replace company directors; this type of initiative remains within the purview of the Public Prosecutor's Office.

3. The Judicial Auxiliary Officers

Under the Company Rescue Act, the judicial auxiliary officers are now referred to as Judicial Administrators and Liquidators. These professionals, who were known as '*syndic judiciaires*' as early as 1838, were split into two professions in 1985:

1. The Judicial Administrators, who oversee the restructuring of distressed companies; and

2. The Liquidators, who realize the remaining assets and who represent the interests of creditors in receiverships. They also handle payment to the employees through the *Association pour la Gestion du Régime de garantie des créances des Salariés* or AGS (National Insurance System).

These two professions are another peculiarity of the French system inasmuch as they enjoy quasi-judicial powers. Appointed by the courts, legally competent over the entire French territory but operating locally by custom, they are organized into two parallel professions under the same governing body, the National Council. They also benefit from the same insurance underwritten by the Caisse de Garantie (Professional Mutual Insurance).

This small profession numbering 428 members, of whom 121 are Judicial Administrators, oversees the entire French territory. Moreover, the profession's members are subject to a rule of joint liability secured by their own personal property.

Furthermore, the mandates of each office (administrator and liquidator) are incompatible with all other professions, and are as well intrinsically different from each other by their very nature. Only the professions of lawyer and administrator are compatible, but examples of such combinations are rare.

C. THE ALERT PROCESS

It is normally given that late awareness of company difficulties is one of the main reasons why restructurings fail. It was therefore considered essential to provide the economic and judicial world with legal tools allowing intervention well upstream, as soon as the very first distress signal appears.

Prevention is better than cure.

1. Sounding the Alarm

An auditor must sound the alarm in a company when it is revealed that there are 'events likely to compromise the continuity of business' (L611–2 *of the* Commercial Code). He does this by informing the managers.

The concern raised by the auditor is neither transmitted to the shareholders, nor to the Employee Works Council (*Comité d'Entreprise*) in order to avoid complicating the situation if it can be resolved at an early stage. This first phase remains confidential if the explanations given by the management, which should be provided within 15 days, are satisfactory to the auditor.

In the event that the response is not considered satisfactory, the auditor must establish a special report that is submitted to the management of the company and, depending on the type of company, to the shareholders, the Board of Directors, the Supervisory Board and the Employee Works Council.

If there are doubts about the company's ability to continue operating, the auditor must inform the President of the Commercial Court and this information must be accompanied by all the documentation supporting the justification of the

France

steps taken, together with the auditor's reasoned opinion. The absence of the filing of annual statements is regarded as an additional indication of economic difficulty.

The result will be either: (1) the commencement of proceedings if the President of the Commercial Court believes that the company is no longer able to pay its debts; or, (2) a meeting with the management in order to address the problems of the company together, making the management aware that the situation could become serious if nothing is done, and to consider suitable measures to remedy the situation.

Despite the importance of the auditor's role, there is always a time lag. The auditor intervenes in the producing of the financial statements – in essence several months after the first difficulties really occurred.

As a result of this delayed intervention, it is up to the company's entire environment and advisers, to help the management to become aware of the seriousness of events and the consequences they could have on the company. The goal is to enable the management to react to the situation.

However, if this does not have any effect, the law provides for a judicial authority, the President of the Commercial Court (or Civil Court), to be empowered with the means to make the management face up to the reality of the impending crisis.

2. The Role of the President of the Commercial Court and/or Civil Court

Company audits are published in the National Registry of Commerce *(Régistre National du Commerce)*, which is maintained by the Clerk's Office. Reports revealing businesses in difficulty may lead to the summoning of company officials to appear before the President of the Commercial Court to discuss potential remedies to the situation.

The President of the court, who has exorbitant powers under the Company Rescue Act, may also obtain from the auditor, employees, tax authorities, social security authorities and financial authorities any useful information that may help him assess the debtor's economic and financial situation.

To prevent abuse and arbitrary measures, the Decree wisely requires the President of the Commercial Court to include an appendix containing a memorandum explaining the facts motivating his summons. In the same manner as the public authorities, parties contacted by the President of the Commercial Court in order to provide information will be able to exonerate themselves from this duty if the format required by law is not respected

Should the debtor not comply with the annual filing of accounting statements, the Commercial Court may order a penalty to be paid without recourse to appeal (if the fine does not exceed EUR 4,000). The President of the Commercial Court decides on the amount of the penalty on amounts greater than EUR 4,000 and the defendant may appeal. To no one's surprise, certain companies prefer not filing for reasons of confidentiality and are willing to absorb the fines as part of the cost of doing business.

The Paris Commercial Court is promoting the preventive measures available of under the new Company Rescue Act as an alternative to insolvency proceedings. However, convincing managers and their advisers to take advantage of the new measures requires more than the opportunity created by the law. It remains difficult for French managers to overcome their fear of entering into discussions with judicial authorities. This is because the latter, in the role of 'prevention' expert, also represents the institution that will judge the executive's actions and responsibility if the rescue process fails.

At the very least, the new prevention-focused judicial environment may act as catalyst in alerting the management of the state of affairs, which may lead to seek out appropriate business and professional assistance.

In terms of protocol, the President of the Commercial Court normally convenes company officials with a view to discussing problems and seeking solutions. They are not obligated to appear before the President of the Commercial Court but if insolvency proceedings begin later; their unwillingness to cooperate could weigh against them if sanctions are adopted.

It is important to stress that the success of the encounter between the President and the manager will depend above all on the 'charisma' and recognized humanity of the President of the Commercial Court.

3. Roles of Advisors. Other Parties to the Process

The shareholders of a company as well as the Employee Works Council also have the right to sound the alarm should the company be experiencing difficulties. They may also question the management and, if there is no response, they can either inform the auditor to begin proceedings or they can alert the President of the Commercial Court directly.

Approved parties such as professional bodies (*Centre de Gestion Agrée, etc.*) experienced in preventive procedures may also sound the alarm.

The usual advisers, lawyers and experts – for their part – have a duty to inform the management to help it make a decision that each party recognizes is extremely difficult to adopt.

After having provided a brief overview of the French legal idiosyncrasy, the judicial system and the internal process to alerting a company in distress, it is now time to analyze the expedited debt restructuring procedures available under French law. There are three expedited debt restructuring procedures, these are: (1) Mandat ad hoc; (2) the conciliation procedure; and, (3) the rescue procedure. These three expedited mechanisms will be analyzed *below*.

II. PREVENTIVE PROCEDURES

A. MANDAT AD HOC

1. Definition

The law does not provide a definition for this procedure. It simply states, in article L.611-3 of the Commercial Code that the President of the Court (Commercial or

Civil) may, at the request of a company's representative, designate an ad hoc receiver whose mission he will determine.

The Mandat ad hoc was used primarily by the Paris Commercial Court during the real estate crash of 1993–1996. The strength of the Mandat ad hoc lies in its lack of legal rules and in its confidentiality. It relies on the tools of informal mediation. Due to its great flexibility, the procedure has enjoyed laudable success, recording a 70 per cent satisfaction rate among its users, as stressed by the Judicial Administrators Society (*Compagnie des Administrateurs Judiciaires*).

2. Main Characteristics

The main characteristics of the Mandat ad hoc are:

(1) *Flexible:* The procedure is not bound by a set period of time except as determined by the President's order. This period may be extended without any statutory limitation. The Mandat ad hoc option has been employed for over ten years now. During this time it has continually proved itself to be a flexible contractual tool appreciated by all concerned parties.

(2) *Confidential:* It remains confidential, an obligation prescribed by Article L.611–15 of the Commercial Code. This obligation is applicable to any person informed of its existence. The only restriction on confidentiality is contained in the new Article L.621–1 of the Commercial Code which provides that, if a rescue proceeding is opened within 18 months after appointment of the ad hoc receiver, the Public Prosecutor's office shall be in attendance and may obtain disclosure of the documents and instruments relating to an earlier procedure. This raises the possibility of having the date of suspension of payments backdated to the period of the Mandat ad hoc.

(3) *Debtor chooses mediator:* The Mandat ad hoc's chance of success lies in the choice of the ad hoc receiver, who can be selected by the debtor.

The President of the Commercial Court is not bound to agree with the selection however it is not likely that he would go against the debtor's choice.

3. Some Notes on the Rescue Proceeding

a. *Scope of Application*

The new Company Rescue Act did not seek to regulate counselling, but has now endorsed it in Article L.611–3 of the Commercial Code. It provides that the Presidents of Courts (Civil or Commercial) located in the geographical jurisdiction of the company's head office may, upon application of the business' legal representative, appoint an ad hoc receiver, whose assignment the Court shall determine. This application must be made in writing and should contain a statement of the reasons of the appointment (see Article 11 of the Decree).

b.　　　　　*Who May Initiate Mandat ad hoc Proceedings?*

As previously mentioned French law states that the Mandat ad hoc is reserved for businesses not having suspended payments, i.e. when debts immediately payable exceed available assets.

It is now clearly provided that only the Managing Director may take the initiative of applying for the Mandat ad hoc by a motion supported by any appropriate documents. The Court may accordingly no longer act *sua sponte*.

c.　　　　　*Eligibility Criteria for Opening of the Mandat ad hoc Proceeding*

A personal statement from the company's director attesting to the solvent nature of the business suffices for Mandat ad hoc application purposes. The courts do not require proof from the debtor to support this procedure as they do for Conciliation and Rescue proceedings (see B and C *below*).

In fact, the documentation normally provided voluntarily by the Mandat ad hoc applicant is the same as the one required by law for the conciliation procedure (see 4 *below*). The only difference is that in the Mandat ad hoc application, there is no formal legal requirement to provide such documentation.

d.　　　　　*Participants to the Process*

Based on prior personal experience, it is highly probable that the debtor will not enjoy full autonomy, even though there will be a favourable background for harmonious cooperation, in all parties' interest, when the debtor trusts the ad hoc receiver appointed.

e.　　　　　*Mission and Remuneration of the Ad Hoc Receiver*

As per articles 12 to 14 of the Decree, the ad hoc receiver must be a specialist in the management of distressed businesses. This normally means – although not exclusively – that judicial administrators listed on the national registry are selected because of the security they provide, i.e., their professional ethic according to the code of conduct, their supervisory role and their professional insurance. The only requirement to be observed is the absence of a conflict of interest and more specifically, not having received compensation from the business counselled or one of its creditors within the past 24 months.

An ad hoc receiver may also be a former Commercial Court judge, but it is essential that he/she has not held office during the previous five years. This restriction is intended to put an end to contested practices and is tied to the legislator's intent to create a trust-building environment.

The ad hoc receiver's assignment may vary. It may be to assist in resolving a dispute/s relating to funding or employment matters, be it between shareholders, with suppliers or with financial institutions.

The receiver's remuneration is negotiated freely between the different parties of which the terms must be officialised by the President of the Court before the

France

assignment starts. The remuneration may be increased upon mutual agreement of both parties with the consent of the President of the Court.

4. The Procedure Illustrated in Steps

The *following* box illustrates the steps that should be followed in the process of appointing an ad hoc receiver:

> 1. The President receives the application* for appointment of an ad hoc receiver.
> 2. Upon receipt of the application, the President immediately instructs the clerk to call the debtor to a meeting.
> 3. After the meeting, the President may take up to one month to issue the order appointing the ad hoc receiver.
> 4. If no ad hoc receiver is appointed, the application is deemed to have been denied.
> 5. If the President agrees on the opening of a Mandat ad hoc procedure, he then issues an order defining the purpose of the assignment and setting the terms of remuneration.
>
> * The Application includes the following:
>   – Official company registration documents.
>   – Company organization charts.
>   – All financial statements.
>   – Update on liabilities and payment schedules, etc.
>   – Update on securities and commitments/publicly listed or not.
>   – Cash flow statements.
>   – Letter of acceptance of ad hoc receiver including details on mission.
>   – Declaration of solvency.

5. Potential Outcomes of the Proceedings

The potential outcomes of the Mandat ad hoc are the following:

1. No agreement;
2. Agreement/s, i.e. binding contracts which remain confidential and affects the parties to the process only; OR
3. Agreement/s, where the parties have agreed to move on to conciliation to have the agreement/s court-registered and therefore publicized.

6. Advantages and Inconveniences of the Mandat ad hoc

The advantages of the Mandat ad hoc can be summarized as follows:

1. Ability to use the ad hoc receiver as an informal mediator to restore the communication between the opposing parties;
2. Mandat ad hoc remains confidential;
3. It is of no specific duration and is not subject to time limitations; and

4. Can be used as a preparatory phase for conciliation or rescue. Does not bind third parties through approval of the agreement or adoption of the plan.

a. *Disadvantages*

On the other hand, the disadvantages of the Mandat ad hoc are:

  1. Contracts emanating from negotiations only bind parties to the process, third parties are exempt. The advantage of the Mandat ad hoc is also its drawback. Flexible and contractual, it has no effect on parties excluded from the negotiations. So that in the event of a future insolvency, contracts may potentially be voided through legal actions.
  2. No facility is granted in amicable negotiations with public agencies such as Union de Recouvrement des Cotisations de Sécurité Sociale et d'Allocations Familiales or URSSAF (the French Social Security Agency).
  3. No relief granted on payments schedule and no automatic stay on proceedings.
  4. No help from government authorities (AGS insurance) for downsizing workforce or restructuring plans.

b. *General comments*

The appointment of an ad hoc receiver allows the debtor-management to have access to an independent specialist who will provide an independent and objective view of the company. Besides the debtor's regular channel of contacts, i.e., accountants, solicitors, the management will find itself benefiting from the ad hoc receiver's expertise on business matters, which can only help to rebuild confidence. Further, the receiver is also there to provide assistance on next steps to be adopted, i.e., transactions, contracts, etc.

B. CONCILIATION PROCEDURE

1.   Definition

As per Article L. 611-4 of the Commercial Code, Conciliation is a preventive procedure initiated by the debtor, who is still solvent (or who has been insolvent for less than 45 days) and who is experiencing difficulties or anticipates them in the foreseeable future. It is worth stressing that conciliation presents two alternatives: (1) a conciliation procedure approved by the President of the Commercial Court; or, (2) a conciliation procedure registered with a court. The main difference between the two is that while the former remains confidential, the latter no. In most cases, the debtor opts for the Commercial Court President's approval to maintain confidentiality.

2.   Main Characteristics

The main characteristics of the conciliation procedure are as follows:

  1. *Debtor-initiated*: The debtor has the initiative of beginning proceedings, by motion to the President of the Court.

2. *Confidential*: The conciliation process remains confidential on the condition that the participants opt for President-approval (fewer financial advantages) rather than for Court-registration (better financial conditions but agreements publicized hence loss of privacy) when finalizing their agreement/s.
3. *Briefness:* It lasts four months with an additional one-month possible extension. The common practice is to have a conciliation preceded by a Mandat ad hoc or mediation phase to prepare the case, establish the guiding principles, study possible solutions, and finally submit agreements.
4. *Flexibility*: The parties are not bound by any specific rules, provided that they consider in mind third-party interests when drafting up their agreement/s.

3. Conditions for Opening the Proceeding (L.611–4 and 5 of the Commercial Code)

a.   Scope of Application

The conciliation procedure is available to individuals or legal entities engaging in commercial or professional activities and undergoing or foreseeing legal, economic or financial difficulties.

This prospective element is particularly innovative in the new Company Rescue Act as it now allows the procedure to be used in finding solutions to avoid future difficulties.

The Company Rescue Act has also accepted that suspension of payments is no longer an essential criterion. A debtor *in bonis* or having suspended payments within the last 45 days is eligible for conciliation.

b.   Who May Initiate the Conciliation Proceedings?

The debtor may initiate proceedings, i.e. businesses (both, privately-owned or incorporated) independent workers, licensed professionals, etc. Farmers are excluded as well as personal bankruptcies. These are handled under separate legislation.

c.   Eligibility Criteria for Opening the Procedure

The debtor, still solvent or having been insolvent for less than 45 days, must provide written documentation to the court's satisfaction justifying the request for conciliation.

d.   Participants to the Process

i.   The Debtor
The debtor initiates the request for conciliation and retains full decision-making authority over the company during the proceedings.

ii.   The Conciliator

The conciliator, who is normally a judicial administrator, is responsible for fostering agreements with the main creditors and/or contracting parties (Article L.611–7 of the Commercial Code). The conciliator is also responsible for the submission of proposals to rescue the business, to continue operations and maintain employment.

iii.   The Expert Appraiser

A new player has appeared as result of the new Company Rescue Act: an appraiser. His intervention has to be decided by the President of the Commercial Court. In the event of his appointment, the expert has to draft a report on the company's position.

The role of the appraiser can be understood as a formalization by the Company Rescue Act of the practice of appointing a certified accountants or auditors to review the accounts to the court's satisfaction. Furthermore, this second opinion supports the conciliator in establishing proposals for review and acceptance by third parties.

iv.   The President of the Commercial Court

He makes appointments and sets limits to assignments and their remuneration. He is the authority approving the agreement/s; should both parties require this formality. In this case, he does not validate the legitimacy of the agreement; he simply requests that the conciliator provide him with the evidence that third parties are not prejudiced by the agreement/s.

v.   The Public Prosecutor's Office

The Public Prosecutor's Office is informed of initiated proceedings. The opening of proceedings ruling is not subject to appeal. Should conciliation succeed and the agreement/s is to be court-registered, the Public Prosecutor's Office is required to attend the proceedings. The Public Prosecutor Office may provide its opinion at this time. The Public Prosecutor's Office may only appeal conciliation proceedings when the agreement/s are court-registered and not simply President-approved.

e.   *Mission and Remuneration of the Conciliator*

The debtor may suggest a conciliator. The President of the Court reviews the proposal and has final say on the appointment of the conciliator. As in all preventive procedures, it is propitious for the Court to accept the debtor-selected professional in order to improve the conciliation's chances of success.

The conciliator's role is to foster agreements and submit proposals. This implies that a successful conciliation requires genuine cooperation between the debtor who develops the proposals and the conciliator who prepares the stage to reach a successful agreement and have its terms accepted.

The Company Rescue Act is intended to provide the conciliator with resources to obtain a full view of the company's real situation, even though he has no powers of investigation. The Conciliator may obtain from the debtor any

France 271

appropriate information. In addition, the President of the Court will provide the conciliator with the information obtained from public agencies, banks, lending institutions, etc.

Naturally, the conciliator is subject to the rules of incompatibility of offices arising out of conflicts of interest.

A challenge procedure has been provided enabling the President of the Commercial Court to issue a ruling when necessary or when anomalies require it.

The conciliator is also subject to a confidentiality duty, and reports directly to the President of the Commercial Court.

The conciliator's assignment and remuneration is negotiated beforehand and formalized in writing. A copy of the terms of appointment must be attached to the application allowing the President to deliver his order.

Due to reasons of confidentiality, the conciliator is usually a judicial administrator. Nevertheless, other professionals may also be appointed, such as a certified accountants, lawyers, and professionals performing executive duties in the company or former Commercial Court judges (five years after ceasing to hold office).

Conciliators are appointed on the basis of their skills or reputation and they then become auxiliary judicial officers on a temporary basis.

4. The procedure Illustrated in Steps

The *following* box illustrates the steps that should be followed in the process of appointing a conciliator:

1. The debtor provides written documents to the President of the Court detailing the economic, social and financial situation of his company including financing requirements and potential solutions.
2. The debtor is summoned to appear before the President of the Court.
3. If the decision is favourable, the President then appoints a conciliator who assists the debtor in negotiating a plan with a view to overcoming the difficulties.
4. The proposed conciliator must confirm acceptance of the mission and negotiate his fees.
5. Conciliation is bound by strict time limits (four months, with a possible one-month extension).

5. During Conciliation

The company goes on trading; the management remains in control and does not need to obtain agreement from the court in running its business. It is expected however, by both the court and the main creditors, that during this period of 'borderline' insolvency, the debtor should avoid entering into uncertain transactions and remain transparent with the court and the conciliator.

Since no approval is necessary to carry on trading, the conciliator will analyze the business' transactions to ensure that third parties' rights are not infringed upon. Fairness and transparency are obviously required. If the conciliator is unsatisfied with the plan or disagrees with the management's performance during conciliation, he resigns from the proceedings and provides his reasons for doing so to the President of the Court.

As result of the short timeframes of this proceeding, there is a pressure to compromise and move forward. The conciliator has only four months to negotiate and one month to get both or more parties to validate the negotiations. Should conciliation fail, the likely outcome will be receivership or liquidation.

6. Potential Outcomes of the Conciliation Procedure (Art. L611–7, 8, 9 and 10 of the Commercial Code)

The Company Rescue Act provides for several possible outcomes. These are listed *below*.

a. *Conciliator-terminated*

The conciliator may terminate his duties if the debtor does not accede to the conciliator's recommendations (Article 29 of the Decree)

b. *No Agreement Failure*

Upon receipt of the conciliator's report, the President of the Commercial Court terminates the proceedings and the conciliator's assignment. There is no possible recourse against this ruling. The debtor himself may apply to end conciliation.

Article 631–4 of the Commercial Code provides that if the conciliation fails and the conciliator's report shows that payments have been suspended, the court shall act *sua sponte* by opening a judicial reorganization.

c. *Successful Conciliation and Conclusion of Agreement/s. Two options: President-approved or Court-registered*

The debtor may successfully conciliate with its creditors and conclude an agreement. These agreements may be made official in two ways:

1. the President of the Commercial Court approves the agreement; or,
2. the Court officially approves and registers the agreement.

i. President-approved (no publicity)

Upon joint motion by the parties, the President's order acknowledging the agreement makes it enforceable. In that case, the President is not required to review the scope of the agreement.

The debtor attests that it has not suspended payments, as the negotiations conducted are supposed to have put an end to an earlier suspension of payments.

The order is not published and there is no means of recourse. It puts an end to the conciliation procedure and the process allows for the maintenance of confidentiality.

ii. Court-registered (officially advertised)

Sometimes the parties prefer to make their agreements public. In these cases, the debtor (exclusively) will apply for an approval of the agreement by the court. In that case, the court will call for evidence (for example an acknowledgement) of the absence of suspension of payments, but also that the agreement:

1. secures durable operation of the business; and,
2. is not detrimental to the interests of third parties.

The latter criterion is interesting, in that it has drawn a lesson from recent past experiences: the end (sometimes) justifies the means. Many agreements made between 1995 and 1998 were criticized for taking into account only the interests of parties to the agreement, in detriment of unsecured creditors. This new requirement is a necessary precaution and plays a part in balancing the rights of the parties involved, and therefore in improving the practice and image of French proceedings.

Once the approval procedure has started, the court summons and hears the parties to the agreement and: (1) the employee representatives; (2) the Public Prosecutor's Office; and, (3) the conciliator (if applicable in the case of regulated professions, the professional governing body is invited to attend as well). The summoned parties are informed of the agreement on a confidential basis.

The Act has ingeniously provided for protection of confidentiality while securing the judgment's publication. The judgment does not mention the contents of the agreement, it only refers to the existence of that agreement and the amount of beneficiaries of priority relating to 'new money' and the security provided. Any third party may object to the approval ruling within 10 days as of publication.

Parties involved in the agreement may appeal against a judgment denying its approval.

The agreement remains confidential and in the event of approval, a copy of it is provided to the statutory auditor whose role is to ensure that company accounts comply with reporting requirements as determined by French legislation. The statutory auditor must also signal the alert when a company begins to show signs of financial distress.

d. *Termination of the Agreement*

The opening of a rescue proceeding, a judicial reorganization or a judicial liquidation automatically terminates the agreement achieved and the creditors recover the full remaining amount of their debt.

In the event of failure to perform one of the commitments under the agreement, the court is required by law (L611–10 of the Commercial Code) to rescind the agreement, regardless of the seriousness of the breach.

7. Advantages/Disadvantages of Conciliation

a. *For all Conciliation Agreements Whether President-approved or Court-registered*

i. Advantages

In the event that a conciliation agreement is reached, it will produce various advantages. These are:

1. *Manager retains control.*

    The debtor remains in control of the company but must commit to good corporate governance during the conciliation phase, especially with regard to third parties
2. *Company may sell sectors of business in order to support reorganization efforts*
3. *Financial liability and/or/professional misconduct charges do not apply in the event of insolvency proceedings (criminal or fraudulent intent)*
4. *Predictability on grace periods of up to two years (consolidating debt deferrals)*

    While it does not allow for a stay of proceedings, it allows for the application for deferrals not to the court having jurisdiction over the disputed contractual relationship, but to the judge to whom the conciliation is submitted. The defendant debtor may refer to the President of the Commercial Court, acting in summary proceedings, thereby freezing the proceedings brought by creditors. The President may allow up to a two-year grace (Article L.1244–1 of the Civil Code). These periods are not cumulative.

    This referral request made before the President of the Court is naturally revealing of the company's position, resulting in a termination of the confidential status.
5. *Deferrals and/or waiver of taxes (Income tax, social security contributions, etc.)*

    This procedure provides an opportunity to obtain forgiveness of debts from the tax and welfare agencies. With a concern for fostering negotiations between the debtor and its creditors and allowing a restoration of the distressed business, the Company Rescue Act contains an extremely important provision which further restricts the State's priority. The tax and welfare (and unemployment-insurance) agencies may waive debts (Articles L.611–7 Par. 3 and L.626–6 of the Commercial Code) provided that their effort is concurrent with those of other creditors.

    The Company Rescue Act refers mainly to a concept of similarity in efforts. The public agencies' efforts will be contingent on those of other creditors in order to avoid any EU accusations of receiving state aid, the Company Rescue Act provides that 'the waivers shall comply with ordinary market conditions and shall be those which a private party/entity in the same situation would grant'. (L626–6 of the Commercial Code).

However, the scheduling and percentage of abatement that the public agencies may grant and the nature of security requested are unknown to date. Unless these actions are substantial, the existence of priority liabilities will require companies to opt for insolvency or rescue proceedings (if there is no suspension of payments).

6. *Creditor-driven motions for reorganization or liquidation inadmissible during conciliation*

Likewise, Article L.631–5 of the Commercial Code, which provides that during a conciliation procedure, actions for judicial reorganization may not be brought against the debtor, creates a reassuring background for the course of negotiations. However, on the other hand it also results in the disclosure of information regarding the conciliation's existence.

7. *Conciliation allows prior creditors to be satisfied.*
8. *Individuals standing surety, having granted independent security or acting as co-obligors may assert the terms of the agreement (Art. L.611–10 of the Commercial Code). These individuals benefit from the advantages that were negotiated during conciliation.*

ii. Disadvantages

The following are the disadvantages of reaching a conciliation agreement:

1. No automatic suspension of payments;
2. No automatic stay on proceedings; and
3. No government insurance scheme to assist with downsizing of workforce (non-intervention of AGS).

b. *Exclusive to Conciliation Agreements which are President-approved:*

i. Advantages

These are the advantages which are exclusive to a conciliation agreement approved by the President of the Commercial Court:

1. *Agreement remains confidential*

It will be noted that an agreement that has been acknowledged by the President of the Commercial Court is not binding on third parties, so that the advantages of conciliation lie rather on the side of approval.

2. *Full autonomy as to agreement's contents and implementation*

The content of the agreement/s is not challenged by the President of the Commercial Court as long as the company remains solvent, operations are sustainable and third parties' rights are not infringed.

c. *Exclusive to Conciliation Agreements which are Court-registered:*

i. Advantages

These are the advantages which are exclusive to a conciliation agreement registered with the court:

1. *Obtaining Financing and advantage of New Money*
   Only the court-approval provides creditors with sufficient confidence to contribute further cash or further goods/services to secure maintenance of the company together with the 'new money' which will enjoy priority ranking immediately after salaries and judicial costs (Article L.622–17 for rescue and judicial reorganization, L.641–13 for judicial liquidation, both of the Commercial Code) and ahead of earlier creditors secured by collateral. But in the event of failure and opening of collective proceedings, these debts are to be notified to the administrators within one year of the finalization of the observation period. Upon default, such a creditor's 'new money' powers would be forfeited.

   What will be the practical scope of this 'new money' priority which has provided so much debate? With the setting of ratios of equity in relation to the rating of risk provided for under the Basel II Accord, one may wonder whether banks, cautious by nature, will grant further credit. In addition, shareholders will obtain its benefit only by making contributions in shareholders' accounts or securities, and not through a recapitalization. If that contribution is capitalized after the approval, they may be expected to lose their priority since it would be tantamount to disregarding two principles: the corporate capital is security for the creditors collectively and the shareholders are paid after the other creditors.

   It shall be noted, however, that in France suppliers are one of the means of obtaining funding (extensions on payments deadlines) for small and medium sized companies (*PMEs*) and that the Company Rescue Act provides that suppliers as well as banks will be eligible for this new priority.

2. *Transactions occurring during conciliation are not subject to review or cancellation in the event that the company goes into receivership*
   Only approval interrupts the risk of postponement of the date of suspension of payments (see Article L.631–8 of the Commercial Code) since the date of suspension of payments may not be earlier than the date of the judgment approving the agreement reached by the parties. So, actions taken prior to the approval will remain valid.

3. *Suspension of proceedings against all guarantors whether party or not to the conciliation procedure*
   The Company Rescue Act provides for a stay of proceedings only if the conciliation agreement is approved, which corroborates the procedure's purpose, to wit, fostering one or more agreements reached by the parties on an out-of-court basis putting an end to difficulties between the debtor and the main creditors and/or contracting parties.

France 277

ii. Disadvantages
1. The Court registration of the conciliation agreement renders the decision executory but the decision will not become final until all possibilities of appeal have been exhausted. Therefore there is an element of risk, uncertainty, which may impact on the date of suspension of payments and other matters until the appeal period is over or all appeals have been heard.
2. The risk of third-party objections is increased by disclosure to third parties. Any third party considering that the agreement is detrimental may enter an objection but the risk is restricted as the agreement is publicized on a limited basis.
3. Loss of confidentiality with associated risks.

iii. General comments

One disadvantage or rather complication for businesses pursuing conciliation is the imperative of ensuring that equal classes of creditors receive equal treatment. However, the advantage to creditors is obvious – it guarantees fair treatment.

C. RESCUE

1. Definition

The Rescue proceedings consist of a new preventive procedure, under the supervision of French courts, intended to facilitate the reorganization of a company while still solvent. It allows for restructuring and streamlining activities, as well as for the downsizing of its workforce. This procedure provides the management with the facilities to reorganize the company debt, as well as with dispositions regarding the discharge of certain liabilities.

2. Main Characteristics

a. *Debtor initiates Rescue*

As per Article L.620–1 of the Commercial Code, the debtor may request the opening of Rescue proceedings based on his appreciation that the company **will soon experience** financial difficulties, which it is not able to overcome on its own, and which will lead to insolvency.

Rescue proceedings are available to all trades, businesses, farmers and professions in France, whether incorporated or not. It is also open to independent workers, whether or not subject to government regulations or licensed by a professional body.

b. *Automatic suspension of payments upon opening of Rescue proceedings*

As per Article L. 622–7 of the Commercial Code, automatic relief is granted to the applicant in that all claims are automatically frozen upon opening of the proceedings, despite the solvency of the debtor. Further there is a stay of proceedings against the debtor.

c. *New payment schedules possible with banks and main suppliers*

The Rescue proceedings allow negotiations to begin with creditors before the suspension of payments. Payment schedules and terms can be renegotiated with banks and suppliers.

d. *Debtor remains in control, but under supervision of court*

Rescue proceedings are of a contractual nature, the negotiation of a rescue plan between the debtor and its main creditors is the first priority. However, it is also a genuine judicial procedure, unlike conciliation.

This procedure is publicized at the Business and Commerce Registry.

Judicial auxiliary officers are appointed by the court. An Administrator is mandated with the elaboration of a rescue plan. The bankruptcy judge oversees the proceedings to ensure coherence with the law. The creditors are represented by two main committees and up to five controllers. The admissibility of claims is reviewed by the judicial liquidator.

3. SOME NOTES ON THE RESCUE PROCEEDING

a. *Scope of Application*

The proceedings apply to any legal entity or individual, engaging in commerce, crafts, farming or a profession. The Civil Court has jurisdiction over the professionals, farmers and unregistered craftsmen; while the Commercial Court over all others.

If there is a fictional entity or a commingling of patrimonies, the new Company Rescue Act uses earlier case law and provides an opportunity to extend the initial judgments to related entities/companies.

b. *Who May Initiate Rescue Proceedings?*

The proceedings can only be initiated by the debtor as it is a preventative procedure. There is no suspension of payments, and therefore creditors do not have a right to oppose.

c. *Eligibility Criteria for Opening*

The debtor must prove, with supporting documentation that he is not in a position of insolvency as defined by French law (L631–1 of the Commercial Code), which

France

is when amounts payable and due exceed available assets. He also must provide sufficient evidence to demonstrate that his company is in difficulty or that distress is imminent.

d. *Participants to the Process*

i. The Debtor

Apart from being the initiator of the Rescue proceedings, the debtor retains control of the company during the procedure and runs business operations as usual.

ii. The Bankruptcy Judge/s

Upon opening of the proceeding, one or more bankruptcy judges are appointed to ensure that proceedings take place expeditiously and that interests of all parties concerned are protected.

iii. The Judicial Administrator

The administrator does not replace the debtor in the day-to-day management of the company; however he does have extensive powers. He institutes protective and temporary measures, he decides upon the maintenance or termination of contracts, he may make proposals to discontinue sectors/units of the business, and most importantly he can apply for termination of the rescue proceedings with a view to converting the procedure into a judicial reorganization (receivership) or liquidation.

The appointment of an administrator is optional for companies with gross sales not exceeding EUR 3,000,000 or with less than 20 employees.

iv. The Judicial Liquidator

This judicial auxiliary officer is appointed by the court and has exclusive authority to act in the name of the creditors (see f *below*).

v. The Creditor Committees

The incorporation of two creditors' committees is a new feature of the Company Rescue Act. One committee reunites financial institutions and the other the main suppliers of goods and services. The debtor must negotiate with both committees with a view to make a common proposal, which must receive a majority vote representing at least 2/3 of the debt of each committee in order to be adopted.

Committee members do not receive any renumeration for sitting.

vi. Staff-representative Bodies

A staff representative is appointed or elected by the employees of the business to represent their interests in the negotiation.

vii.   Bailiff or Auctioneer

In the proceeding, a bailiff or auctioneer is appointed being its mission is to inventory property and to prepare a list of assets and liabilities.

viii.   Controllers

As per Article L.621–10 of the Commercial Code, the bankruptcy judge appoints from one to five controllers among the creditors who had applied to perform this duty. When several controllers are appointed, the judge ensures that at least one controller oversees secured creditors and another one the interests of unsecured creditors. Obviously, there are strict measures to avoid collusion or conflict of interest.

f.   *Mission and Remuneration of Insolvency Professionals*

i.   The Liquidator

The liquidator has exclusive authority to act on behalf of creditors.

Nevertheless, in the event that the liquidator does not bear up to his responsibilities, the controllers may intervene under certain conditions as defined by the Decree (formal notice is sent to the liquidator by way of Registered Mail with acknowledgment of receipt; and, 2-months' notice given from the date of receipt of the letter).

The liquidator gathers creditors' claims and communicates the information and/or observations made by the controllers to the judge and to the Public Prosecutor's Office.

ii.   The Judicial Administrator

The judicial administrator oversees the debtor in the management of the company and assists him in certain or all management functions (if necessary). The judicial administrator sets up the creditor committees and presents the Rescue plan.

iii.   Their Remuneration

Regulations on insolvency practitioners ('IP') remuneration can be found in decree No. 85–1390 dated 27 December 1985, modified on 27 July 2005.[1]

The Administrator is paid based on the size of the workforce of the affected company, and also according to a sliding scale on the percentage of financial turnover during the overseeing period. Usually, the percentage is more or less high depending on the nature of the intervention, whether it is of an advisory/supervisory nature or more involved as in the case of debtor-replacement.

As regards, the liquidator, remuneration depends on the number of employees but also on the number and value amount of the claims.

iv.   Pay Scales for Administrators and Liquidators

For rescue proceedings, an administrator receives a fixed fee of EUR 2,287 at the opening of the procedure. He then receives a fee based on the company's

---

1. *See* <http://www.legifrance.gouv.fr>.

workforce, i.e., an amount of EUR 69 per employee multiplied by a sliding scale based on the number of employees concerned. He furthers receives a percentage based on the company's turnover during the observation period, anywhere from 2 per cent to 0.35 per cent based on company earnings from EUR 0 to above EUR 4,500,000.

Should there be a sale of a branch/division of the company, he receives a percentage based on the sale price, anywhere between 4 per cent (up to EUR 45, 735) to a 0.10 per cent (if the amount of the sale exceeds EUR 7, 622, 450).

The liquidator, for his duties, receives a fixed fee of EUR 2,287. In addition, he receives EUR 30 to EUR 50 per claim reviewed. To establish the workforce claims, he receives EUR 120 per employee.

4. The Procedure Illustrated in Steps

a. Major Steps

The main steps of the procedure are as follows:

1. Debtor applies to the competent court, within the territorial jurisdiction.
2. The Court examines the request, ensures that suspension of payments does not exist at the time of the filing. Burden of proof is on the debtor to prove solvency and existence of foreseeable difficulty, whether it is of an environmental, labour, legal or economic nature.
3. A court hearing takes place where the judge receives testimony from the most senior business manager, the staff representatives, in the case of a licensed profession he hears the competent professional association, and from other experts as required, i.e., auditor, expert appraiser, etc. The court may also retain the services of an IP to conduct an investigation to ascertain the company's financial position or other. This is a second hearing after the initial 'exploratory' hearing is held in order to asses whether the proceeding should be opened.
4. If the President decides in favour of initiating the proceeding, an opening hearing is held (the second hearing). The Public Prosecutor's Office is present at the opening hearing, and should there have been an earlier proceeding (Mandat ad hoc or conciliation) this fact must be reported. If so, the ad hoc receiver and/or conciliator must attend.
5. The observation period begins when the opening judgment is pronounced and lasts six months. Two possible six-month extensions can be granted, up to a maximum of 18 months.
6. The court designates a bankruptcy judge, a judicial liquidator (representing the creditors), a judicial administrator (representing the debtor), and experts.

7. The debtor remains in possession, continues to manage the company but all his decisions must be submitted by the Administrator to the court for approval.
8. An inventory of the debtor's patrimony is made.
9. The creditors submit their claims to the liquidator, which he in turn examines as to their legitimacy.
10. The Administrator establishes the creditors' committees.
11. A rescue plan is proposed and submitted to the committees.
12. If the plan is approved, then it is submitted to the court for approval.
13. The acceptance of the plan by the court, puts an end to the observation period.
14. The plan details prospects for recovery, sales of divisions, debt payment, etc.
15. The court makes a ruling. This ruling is opposable by the parties.
16. The plan may not exceed 10 years.
17. An insolvency practitioner is mandated with overseeing the plan's enforcement.
18. If insolvency occurs, then the plan is cancelled and the proceeding is converted to liquidation.
19. Upon completion and full execution of the plan, an official record is made evidencing said and that the debtor has no pending obligations to the parties to the plan.

b. *Certain Steps of the Procedure. Further Discussion*

Should it be discovered subsequent to the opening of a Rescue proceeding, that a suspension of payments existed at the date of opening of said proceeding, it is entirely possible (not automatic though, e.g. see the current Eurotunnel S.A. (Eurotunnel)[2] proceedings at the Paris Commercial Court) that the Rescue proceedings be reclassified to a judicial reorganization (official receivership where debtor loses control of management decisions).

Another peculiarity of the Rescue proceeding is that, should suspension of payments occurs during the proceeding, it will automatically be converted to a

---

2. Eurotunnel is the company who built the tunnel under the Channel linking France to Britain, and who sell transportation rights for its use.

France 283

judicial liquidation. Not likely though, as the opening of Rescue proceedings provide an automatic relief, stay of proceedings against the debtor, and payments are frozen.

While the debtor may apply for opening of the proceedings, he is not free to appoint liquidators and judicial administrators. The court controls the procedures, and appoints the agents.

c. *During the Observation Period*

During the observation period phase the liquidator gathers claims, the administrator reviews contracts to decide which should be terminated or maintained, the business continues to operate normally. This time allows the judicial auxiliaries along with the debtor-in-possession to develop a rescue plan suitable to the economic conditions and business prospects of the company.

d. *End of the Difficulties*

Should difficulties cease during the Rescue proceedings, the legal process is discontinued upon the debtor's application.

5. Potential Outcomes of the Rescue Proceeding

The possible outcomes of the rescue proceeding are as follows:

1. Successful conclusion of the Rescue proceedings, adoption of plan by the committees, and approval by the court. Enforcement begins. There is a statutory maximum period of 10 years to complete the plan. The liquidator oversees the enforcement of the plan.
2. Discontinuation of the company's operations. The rescue proceeding is converted into a judicial reorganization or judicial liquidation.
3. Close for discharge of the liabilities (Article L.631–16 of the Commercial Code). If the debtor has sufficient funds to satisfy his creditors and bear the costs of proceedings, the court may put an end to the proceedings.
4. End of the monitoring period with a conversion into judicial reorganization or judicial liquidation.

6. Advantages and Disadvantages of the Rescue proceedings

a. *Advantages*

The main advantages of the rescue proceedings are:

1. *Automatic debt relief.* The Company Rescue Act provides for one substantial innovation, i.e. the business is entitled to cease paying its debts, even though it is not in distress (see Article L.622–7 of the Commercial Code).

2. *Debtor remains above reproach.* According to the amendments introduced by the Company Rescue Act, a proper and correct business status is accorded to the debtor: 'Hold-your-head-high as it is not your fault, it is the economy'. Debtor retains dignity, a very important feature of the Rescue proceedings in France. Accordingly, civil and criminal immunity is granted to the debtor upon application for a rescue proceeding. No fear of personal sanctions for the debtor who comes forward for help. A judicial administrator is appointed only to assist or to supervise the proceedings.

b. *Disadvantages*

The main disadvantages of the rescue proceedings are:

1. *Rescue proceedings are judicial.* Not pre-packaged plans as in the US Chapter 11 are contemplated under the Rescue proceedings. The entire Rescue procedure is under court control and supervision. The debtor must get the administrator to agree and the court must – at a later stage – approve the plan.
2. *The Company property is not exempt from title claims.* Claims from suppliers for restitution of personal property are allowed during the Rescue proceedings (Article L.624–9 of the Commercial Code), which is odd since the business is *in bonis*.
3. *Limited intervention of government insurance assistance for the restructuring.* According to Article L.625–9 of the Commercial Code, the AGS will not provide unconditional assistance for the labour restructuring. Article 143–11 Para. 1 of the Labour Code provides that all employers are required to insure their employees, including against the risk of failure to pay the amounts due in respect of their contracts of employment, in connection with rescue proceedings. Termination of the contract pursuant to the rescue proceedings is to be carried out within one month after the judgment adopting the plan. The Company Rescue Act provides that if the company undergoing rescue (*in bonis*) does not have sufficient funds to meet the employment liabilities arising out of restructuring action, the Administrator shall require them to be advanced and shall provide evidence of the insufficiency in assets. The statement of the Administrator may be challenged by the bankruptcy judge, whose permission for the advance payment shall be required. The advance shall be repayable against the first revenues.

c. *General Comments*

Should the rescue plan not be submitted in due time, i.e. before the end of the monitoring period, as per Article 134 of the Decree, the court shall close the proceedings.

France

The plan shall provide for the persons appointed to enforce it, and for the honouring of commitments made with respect to the business' future, discharge of liabilities and employment prospects. The inalienability of certain assets may be decided during the duration of the plan and for a term not exceeding the plan's duration.

The court will observe the deferrals and abatements granted by creditors. As for other parties involved, it shall set standard time limits for discharge.

The plan may not exceed ten years. The first due date shall be within one year following implementation of the plan and instalments made may not be less than 10 per cent of the amount of liabilities.

The overlap of duties between the administrators and liquidators will inevitably be a source of friction within the implementation of the plan. Article L. 626-4 of the Commercial Code has provided that the administrator shall take all necessary action to see that the plan is implemented.

The administrator shall remain in office to finalize all issues related to claims. All sales will be carried out under liquidation regulations. The liquidator shall collect and pay out all proceeds.

Either the Administrator or the Liquidator may be appointed as Commissioner to carry out the plan's enforcement.

D. PROGRESS REPORT ON NEW LEGISLATION

Six months after the entry into force of the Company Rescue Act, the Rescue proceeding is meeting with moderate success.

Since 1 January 2006, of the 20,000 insolvency proceedings opened in France, only 203 were Company Rescue proceedings. Fourteen of them were opened in Lyon and 11 in Tarascon, in other words most French courts were reluctant to grant Rescue status to distressed companies. In all cases, a judicial administrator (receiver) was appointed. Further, until August, Rescue proceedings had only concerned small and medium-sized companies.

On 2 August 2006, the Paris Commercial Court opened the rescue proceedings for Eurotunnel – this procedure being the first Rescue proceeding opened by the Paris court under the new Company Rescue Act. Eurotunnel lists debts of EUR 9 billion and has been undergoing financial difficulty for over 10 years. At the very least this case will serve as a ground-breaker for the French Rescue procedure. Interestingly enough, the criteria of the French notion of solvency 'no suspension of payments' was completely overlooked in this case.

Again, only the future can tell, but it is possible that the French Rescue will become a very interesting proposition for the larger companies – meaning those 'benefiting' from public pressure for Rescue.

So far, the companies accepted under the Rescue programme, can be broken down into the following sectors:

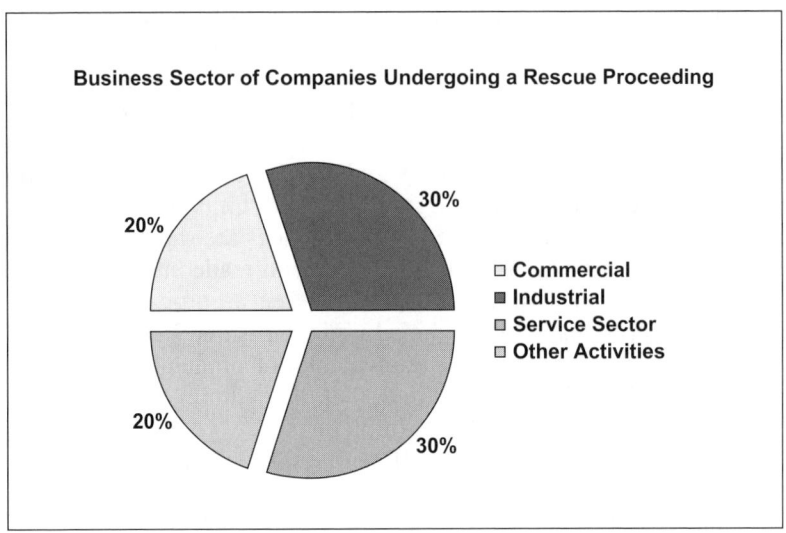

To note:

- 45 per cent of rescue proceedings concern companies with less than 10 employees;
- 85 per cent concern companies with less than 50 employees; and
- 65 per cent of the proceedings, an administrator is appointed (due to court's hesitation on debtor-manager's ability to overcome difficulty).

Of the 203 rescue proceedings, 11 were converted to receiverships, 6 to liquidation and in the first six months only two company rescue plans have been adopted.

So why aren't more companies taking advantage of the new Rescue? The answer might be that some courts are applying overly strict rules in the definition of insolvency, especially with regards to the criteria concerning payments due. They are not accepting company applications at face value.

Also, another interpretation is that because, the work required by a small to medium-sized company to prove that it is still solvent takes up too much valuable time and money and ends up provoking the insolvency before the Rescue proceeding can begin.

Courts in southern France however, who have been more favourable to opening rescue proceedings, argue that the provisions under the new Company Rescue Act allow the Public Prosecutor's Office to antedate the beginning of insolvency should it be proven that erroneous or deliberately false statements were made at the time of filing.

Another factor in Rescue proceedings that is not working as well as intended is that potential applicants are often discouraged when they find out that the process of Rescue remains a judicial procedure. Courts oversee the process, along with court-appointed judicial auxiliary officers, i.e., insolvency practitioners. This is too heavy and restrictive for a company – they do not want to relinquish control over policy or strategy. Foreign groups, especially, do not wish to communicate to third parties (courts, administrators, etc) while undergoing restructuring or pursuing negotiations with their suppliers. They want to prepare a pre-packaged plan, which all parties have agreed to, before presenting it to the court. As well, there is often the misconception that a Rescue proceeding is the French version of the American Chapter 11 – which is definitely not the case. Rescue operates strictly under court supervision, while under US law there is an option for pre-packaged plans with very little – almost inexistent – court supervision.

There is also the psychological factor – when a company must cooperate alongside court–appointed officials when restructuring their ailing company, there is the notion that they have failed in the fact that they needed external assistance to resolve their situation.

The banking industry also shares a mitigated view on the success of Rescue proceedings; even though their interests have been largely protected by the creation of the creditor committees.

Far from being an exchange forum, the committees are mainly used as an information vehicle and are not able to participate actively in seeking solutions to help the company get back on its feet.

Further, progress is needed in changing the attitude and behaviour of the personnel operating in the judicial environment. Administrators must adopt new modus operandi, and drape the apparel of negotiation – to convince and not to impose.

For those not used to conciliation and amicable negotiations, this shift in working methods is a challenge.

In fact, the principles of negotiation, mediation and conciliation influenced legislators in drawing up the new law; a 'new attitude' is the order of the day for judges, professionals, businessmen/women and their advisors.

E.   BEST PRACTICES

> **Alternative tools: Arbitration and Informal Mediation**
>
> Alternative dispute resolution methods, e.g. arbitration and informal mediation (ADR) are being used more and more frequently in every field of law and have proven over the past ten years their ability to resolve the most difficult situations painlessly.
>
> Company difficulties, long considered a ghetto area, have kept business managers away from the tools used in more favourable circumstances. This attitude has to change – fortunately the Mandat ad hoc, which relies heavily on mediation, is being used more extensively.
>
> The fact that a business is defaulting is not a reason for neglecting it from the economic and social community, even partially. And the fact that a manager stumbles is not a reason to exclude him, actually it is precisely at this moment that help should come forward.

> Experience shows that the area of company distress is particularly well suited to informal mediation or out-of-court settlement. Everyone is only too aware, that if legal proceedings go forward, all parties are sure to suffer large losses. Negotiated settlement opens the way to a possible improvement, however small, in their own situations.

This view, which I personally have been advocating for over 15 years, is no longer a mere statement of principle. It now has its defenders internationally, and has shown its merit domestically.

These cases, faced with a positive attitude and hard work, can benefit all parties since:

1. the legal system, can spare the management with complex and time-consuming litigation;
2. the creditors, can be better compensated with in-kind or in cash than what they would expect with insolvency;
3. the debtors, are able to contribute towards resolving problems with third parties and recover their dignity, or even in some cases experience a fresh start.

The decision to apply alternative dispute resolution methods is often found to be the only pragmatic and effective solution.

As per articles L.622–7 and L.642–24 of the Commercial Code, French law allows ADR in both rescue proceedings and in proceedings for reorganization or judicial liquidation, providing that the court-appointed agent has received permission to compromise and settle (sanctions excluded). Decisions of collective interest to the creditors are subject to approval by the bankruptcy judge and court approval of the agreement made.

It is the ambition of international organizations such as GRIP 21, INSOL Europe, the IBA and the ICC to recommend the use of ADR in insolvency proceedings. All parties should monitor with interest this positive development which, by restoring dialogue among the frustrated parties to the process, allows the creation of value.

Arbitration, for its part, is now recommended for the resolution of jurisdictional disputes: it seems appropriate to find in cross-border cases a means of resolving expeditiously, with increased legal certainly, the issue of courts' jurisdiction.

Analysis by one or more neutral arbitrators of the evidence allowing a determination of the COMI seems an attractive solution, more satisfactory than a costly and excessively time-consuming recourse to domestic or EU Courts. It is good to see that, in 2006, all the major international organizations have acknowledged the interest of combining insolvency law with arbitration law and the IBA and Chamber of Commerce and Industry mediation rules.

III.   CASE STUDIES

It is not possible to discuss ongoing Mandat ad hoc and Conciliation cases, due to their confidential nature.

France

However, for illustration purposes and to provide more information on these type of procedures, two successful files involving now-closed cases will be discussed.

The first case study involves a major real estate company/construction firm undergoing a financial crisis originated by management choices during the French real estate crisis of 1993–1996.

The second case study is useful to demonstrate that the Mandat ad hoc is comparable to mediation in that it can be employed both before and throughout the insolvency proceedings. It is also a tool, which can be deployed on a daily basis, to help seek out workable solutions in the difficult context of insolvency.

A.   CASE STUDY NO. 1 : THE JRH FILE: A SUCCESSFUL DEPLOYMENT OF THE MANDAT AD HOC PROCESS

1. Executive Summary of the JRH Group of Companies

The JRH group was created in 1976 by Messrs. JR and H. In 1985, Doctor P joined them, all three taking an active part in the management and day-to-day business of the JHR Group.

Since its incorporation, the JHR Group concentrated its activities in the development, sale and management of diversified up-market real estate products, which were made available to wealthy investors, both individual and corporate, who were looking for sizeable tax breaks while building up their property holdings.

Until 1991, the JRH group pursued its venture with success through its building restoration programme, falling within the scope of the *Loi Malraux*, (Law No. 62–903 dated 4 August 1962) in both Paris and in the provinces, mainly in Bordeaux.

Starting in 1991 and subsequent to the new law on urbanization '*Loi d'orientation pour la Ville du 13 juillet 1991*', which extensively modified existing tax breaks, the JRH group of companies diversified its activities and began offering new and more complex tax-deductible investment opportunities to its clients.

JRH began investing in furnished accommodation for professionals, hotel-apartments, and parking lots. As these new tax write-off products were more sophisticated, highly-qualified personnel became necessary to manage the programme. Tax experts, lawyers, notaries, chartered accountants, were hired to manage the intricacies of the new investment programme.

To support their new structures, the JRH group founded a property maintenance and real-estate agency known as E, which oversaw the day-to-day administration of the properties, i.e., tenant searches, rent collection, building maintenance, management of the co-ownerships, and sales of properties.

Further, a hotel management company was set up, the G, and a travel agency, T, were created to ensure occupancy of the hotel-apartments.

The JRH Group retained co-ownership of certain shared properties in the majority of the buildings.

The activities of the JRH Group relied on two main financiers: (1) the BNPI bank (a subsidiary of the Banque Nationale de Paris, since privatized and having merged with Paribas to form BNP Paribas); and, (2) SOFAL bank (now defunct). The banks were also involved in setting up the tax write-off contracts with the several hundred investors of the group.

2. 1992: the JRH Group Begins Experiencing Difficulties

The JHR Group began experiencing financial difficulty in 1992 due to a combination of factors, the majority of problems being linked to the two major business axes of the group, real estate and the ensuing tax exemption transactions.

The real estate crisis, coupled with the reform introduced in 1991 to the *Loi des Finances* which significantly modified the tax deduction opportunities of the *Loi Malraux*. All this, brutally halted the activity of the group. As a result, the two major banking partners of the group – BNPI and SOFAL – started developing a thorny attitude towards the JRH Group.

3. The 30 August 1993 Memorandum of Agreement

The ongoing difficulties of the group led the JRH management to sign a memorandum of agreement with its main creditor, the BNPI bank on 30 August 1993. This agreement on protocol took on significant importance as the case developed, eventually becoming the cornerstone of the negotiations which followed.

The agreement foresaw the out-of-court liquidation of the assets and liabilities of the JRH Group. And it paved the way for the conciliation process to begin.

4. Conciliation Begins (7 September 1993)

The memorandum of agreement took into account the intention of the parties, and particularly that of the BNPI, of entering into a phase of conciliation permitting the out-of-court liquidation of the company. Unfortunately, the parties were in for a surprise. They had all vastly underestimated the size of the debt, and the true state of affairs surrounding the condition of the assets.

The reaction was immediate and to avoid insolvency, both the company and the main banks, went before the court requesting conciliation. The application was granted, and the designated conciliators consisted of a trio composed of a former Commercial Court judge, a real estate expert and an auditor/chartered accountant.

For the next 18 months, the companies continued to operate and the conciliators were mandated with realizing the assets under the best possible conditions to both satisfy the demands of clients and to reduce the sizeable debt.

The banks agreed to continue to finance the ongoing business. Structures were cut but overall very little progress was made over the 18 months other than a reduction in commitments, i.e. no new purchases and a willingness to sell off assets on an expedited basis (clearance sale).

These 18 months were ultimately a failure as the conciliation focused almost entirely on the bank's needs – the company did not take into account the other participants to the process: real estate investors, sub-contractors, employees, building maintenance staff, tax authorities, etc.

As no mechanism or directive had been established prior to conciliation, which would have ensured the organized and fair treatment to all classes of creditors, chaos became the order of the day. Potential claims and impending law suits were waved in all directions. It was not a surprise when the conciliation process failed and the case ended up being converted into a liquidation proceeding.

It is not a coincidence that the bank's interest in conciliation coincided with the privatization of its parent company, the BNP bank and its impending listing on the French equivalent of the Securities and Exchange Commission, la Commission des Operations Bourses (COB).

5. The JRH Group Was Placed in Court-ordered Receivership (27 February 1995)

It was in the *above* circumstances and even before the debtor had a chance to file for insolvency that the Paris Commercial Court was seized and the company placed in receivership on 27 February 1995.

The compulsory liquidation involved 21 different parties, 3 natural persons and 18 legal entities. Two *mandataires judiciaires* (insolvency practitioners) were named, Patrice Frechou and myself, Isabelle Didier.

The illogical distribution of the files to the liquidators presented many problems, due to the many financial and economic links between the different companies of the JRH Group. Furthermore, the cancellation of the property management contracts by Mr. Frechou had a direct effect on the files as the real estate holding companies suddenly found themselves without property managers. No other choice was left but to take immediate and effective action to protect the interests of clients and maximize the value of the assets before liquidation.

6. Management of the JRH Liquidation Proceedings

The following provides a general overview of the numerous measures, which were undertaken to bring the liquidation file to satisfactory closure. It must be understood that the interest of this file lies in the approach. It was anything but conventional or linear. There were interwoven negotiations, and sharing of information at appropriate moments as well as reliance on experts' opinions. As many parties as possible were involved in the process, the stakes were high for both creditors and debtors. Transparent information was provided to all parties during the negotiations, written opinions, results of studies commissioned, etc. All participants, by category of creditors, enjoyed the same rights which generated trust. All were kept informed on potential consequences of pursuing legal battles in the courts, i.e., financial losses due to time delays, possible convictions, costs involved in litigation, etc.

It was in everyone's interest to reach an agreement. Mediation and concession-making were encouraged. Creative solutions were put forward to enhance the value of the assets before liquidation. At the time, the real estate slump was such that it was extremely unwise to sell off the assets immediately. It was a timely opportunity to deploy mediation at its finest.

One of the most important aspects of the management style adopted by the insolvency professionals in this file was their ability to move exceptionally fast, to manage the hundreds of ongoing negotiations simultaneously, without waiting for one to end before proceeding with the next. Making good use of experts, the vital information arrived in time to make decisions, to have them approved by the courts, hence saving the company from immediate liquidation, and operating it as a going concern eventually wiping out the entire debt, that is to say EUR 1.37 billion.

Former Justice Minister Robert Badinter once said '[f]*irst analyze and negotiate, think afterwards*', this is precisely the modus operandi used in the JRH file.

7. Author's Comments

In this file the Mandat Ad hoc had to be sold to the parties as innovative, providing solutions even when liquidation was in the process. This method, unique to France, enables many business establishments and private individuals to escape bankruptcy.

Negotiations began with the banks, using mediation. Uneven commercial negotiations would have likely precipitated litigation against the banks, which in turn would have led to further damage through lowered bank ratings.

The banks had an interest in negotiating since they did not want to go to court especially at a time when the flagship parent company of one of the banks, known as a first-rate institution, was entering the stock market.

Likewise, the physical persons (the three partners) could have anticipated extensions of law suits against both themselves and their families as at that time the law allowed for such extensions when recovering assets. They as well were willing to negotiate.

Negotiations often take time, but are usually worth the effort.

Another complication was that many contracts (construction, supply, etc.) in the building industry were at stake. Not honouring them would have resulted in more litigation, loss of jobs, unfinished buildings, semi-finished unsafe dwellings, etc.

When things go wrong people are only willing to make concessions in order to not loose all. To illustrate this situation, I will use the following analogy: when a drycleaner closes its business unexpectedly, what do you prefer? 20 per cent of the cost of your clothing or all your clothing back ... dirty, of course?

This is how we operated: always negotiating in the context of damage control, trying to make the best deal out of an impossible situation. And, not only did we manage to give all the clothes back. But we gave them back and clean.

Individual investors understood that they had to make concessions. There was too much at stake: their real-estate property, the loss of rental income, their tax deduction, the ongoing payment of their loan to finance their property acquisition, their unfinished property crumbling (hence their personal liability), etc. Everything tied in together.

They also quickly agreed to negotiate and paved the way for the plan to continue: get the banks to finance the remaining work on the buildings, obtain a moratorium on loan payments and wait out the real estate slump before selling off the important assets.

The individual investors agreed to the completion work necessary to finish the buildings. They were provided with a detailed list building by building of the work to be done to bring them up to standard. Things went very quickly after that and all creditors, contracting partners, banks, court and prosecutor reached an agreement. All 450 protocols were signed within the first 18 months. It took six years to finish the buildings. Then another six years to ensure that all obligations were respected, all litigations were resolved, and all matters of contention dealt with.

The JRH file continued for 12 years before all loose ends were tied up, but the major problems were resolved within the first 18 months. 99.8 per cent of creditors received satisfaction and 100 per cent of the debt EUR 1.37 billion was completely wiped-out through the propitious use of Mandat ad hoc.

B.   CASE STUDY NO. 2: PAX HOTEL

Despite the rigidity of the legal framework surrounding insolvency proceedings in France, it is possible to work out solutions through consensus-seeking and agreement-making in the interest of the creditors.

Indeed, the law stipulates, by way of two important provisions, that in the event of a judicial liquidation, the liquidator can compromise with the permission of the judge (Art. L.642–24 of the Commercial Code). The court will approve and officially register the transaction if it is in the collective interest. In the case of a judicial reorganization, although the law is silent in this matter, the administrator may also compromise to reach agreement.

These two articles anticipated the possibility of negotiations taking place between parties; on the one hand, the company undergoing proceedings, and on the other, a contracting partner or even a group of creditors. Many times, these legal provisions came in handy.

It was through the seasoned use of the *above* legal facilities that the insolvency procedure became a tool allowing damaged contractual relationships to be overcome. Many cases initiated before the Paris court, which benefited from this approach to compromise and negotiation, were brought to a successful finalization.

In two very pertinent cases, the extensive use of this type of transaction was source for dropping all outstanding litigation between parties on damaged contractual relationships.

Let us now discuss in detail the Pax Hotel case.

The manager was 80 years old at the time of the case, which rendered her physically incapable of properly managing a busy restaurant situated in the heart of Paris. She no longer had the ability to supervise staff as is required when running a busy restaurant with 20 employees.

The court estimated that the situation was irreversible. In addition, the court considered that since the company's legal duration (99 years) had expired it could not benefit from a judicial reorganization proceeding, and that liquidation was the only available option.

The liquidation was therefore pronounced despite the opposition of the manager. The business was to be put up for sale despite concerns raised by both the creditors and employees on – among other things – conflicting valuation and uncertainty of the assets and contested property.

Consulted by both the employee committee and company manager, I was able to develop a plan that was both feasible and interesting for all parties concerned. I decided to demonstrate to both the liquidator and court, that the creditors had an interest in considering a more proactive management option; that they were in fact favourable to other more creative solutions rather than simply liquidating the business through public auction.

In fact, since the beginning of the procedure, the manager, advanced in age and without children, had explained, and curiously was not listened to, that in order to preserve the restaurant, she was prepared to pledge her personal assets as guarantee, a realistic option, as her properties and estate were of significant worth.

By substituting the debtor's personal assets in order to pay off liabilities and creditor claims, the restaurant was able to completely wipe out the debt during the proceedings. This to the complete satisfaction of the creditors who as well reduced their claims in order to facilitate the process, and who saw the procedure come to a satisfactory close without their having to invest time in court proceedings, thereby saving considerable legal and other fees. Surprisingly, at the earlier stages the court and the liquidator involved did not want to endorse this plan. Despite their resistance, and due to the good business sense of the administrator and creditors the file came to a judicial closure much earlier than expected – the entire procedure was over in less than six months.

The negotiations resulted in discouraging the judicial liquidator from any interest in acting, it prepared the conditions to renew a relationship with the property owner and to negotiate a more suitable lease, to renegotiate the business relationships, and better yet, to restore a more professional atmosphere. One the causes of the earlier difficulties had been the too-friendly relations among the staff.

Certain employees, who were at the root of the restaurant's problems, were laid off under negotiated conditions; the entire social plan was approved without needing to resort to the courts.

France

One year after this showdown – which enabled the restaurant to be saved, the creditors to be satisfied and the majority of the staff to be maintained – it is nice to observe that the restaurant is doing very well with improved financial results.

Suffice it to say, the liquidator's solution if brought to fruition, would only have resulted in reduced employment, financial losses to creditors and perhaps a good deal for an informed buyer.

Today, the nice old lady and former owner comes to help out everyday at lunchtime, she encourages the young staff and looks after the customers.

So next time you are in Paris please come and visit Au Gamin de Paris in the Marais, 51 rue Vieille du Temple 75004 for an always delicious Parisian meal.

IV. CONCLUDING WORDS

Until now, expedited corporate debt restructuring in France has been best managed by the Mandat ad hoc. The 2005 Company Rescue Act has given official status to the Mandat ad hoc procedure; prior to this it was used on an informal basis by insolvency professionals.

The former voluntary arrangement procedure was also deployed to the general satisfaction of the insolvency community.

The new Conciliation procedure, which derives from the former voluntary arrangement process, offers flexibility to both the debtor and creditor through new features. The new money option (must be court registered though/loss of confidentiality) gives creditors the extra protection they need. Also, the debtor and creditor can decide on whether agreements are to remain confidential (President-approval only). The new and improved 'voluntary arrangement', has not been in place long enough for practitioners to decide its merits. However, law professors and many insolvency professionals working in the area of company rescue, feel that it should produce favourable results.

Likewise, it is too soon to form an opinion on the new Rescue procedure introduced earlier this year. Time will tell, perhaps the Eurotunnel case will shed more light on the procedure's strengths and weaknesses, and will seal its fate as a tool in safeguarding companies.

But one thing has become clear. Now, more than ever, insolvency practitioners the world over must take into account the international context in which companies operate. Judicial cooperation, best practices, ADR and the sharing of good ideas are not only progressive and effective tools at the service of business; but they have also become the lifebuoy for many a distressed company.

Chapter 8
Hong Kong

Corporate Rescue in Hong Kong[1]

Charles D. Booth, Stephen Briscoe and Philip Smart

---

1. The three co-authors of this chapter have written extensively about corporate rescue in Hong Kong and this article incorporates and/or adapts some of their earlier work, including the following: Charles D. Booth, *Corporate Reorganization in Hong Kong: Can Provisional Liquidation Come to the Rescue?*, 2 Journal of Restructuring Finance Law and Practice 183 (September 2005); Philip Smart, Charles D. Booth & Stephen Briscoe (eds.) *Hong Kong Corporate Insolvency Manual* (Hong Kong: Hong Kong Society of Accountants, 2002), Chapter 10; Philip Smart & Charles D. Booth, *Corporate Rescue: Hong Kong Developments*, 10 American Bankruptcy Law Review 41 (2002); Charles D. Booth, *Hong Kong corporate rescue proposals – making secured creditors more secure*, 14 Insolvency Law and Practice 248 (1998).

ACRONYMS, ABBREVIATIONS & DEFINED TERMS

2000 Bill	Companies (Amendment) Bill 2000, *Hong Kong Government Gazette,* Legal Supplement No. 3, C5 (7 January 2000)
2001 Bill	Companies (Corporate Rescue) Bill 2001, *Hong Kong Government Gazette,* Legal Supplement No. 3, C615 (18 May 2001)
2002 Consultation Paper	Consultation Paper on Proposals Relating to the Trust Account Arrangement under the Companies (Corporate Rescue) Bill
CMH	Construction Management Handbook
CO	Hong Kong Companies Ordinance, Cap. 32, L.H.K. (1999).
HKAB	Hong Kong Association of Banks
HKAB/HKMA Guidelines	HKAB and HKMA Guidelines on the Hong Kong Approach to Corporate Difficulties
HKCFA	Court of Final Appeal of Hong Kong (the highest appellate court)
HKD	Hong Kong Dollar
HKMA	Hong Kong Monetary Authority
ISO	International Organization for Standardization
Keview	Re Keview Technology (BVI) Ltd, [2002] 2 HKLRD 290
Legend	Re Legend International Resorts Ltd, [2006] 2 HKLRD 192
LRC	Law Reform Commission of Hong Kong
PRC	People's Republic of China
PWIF	Protection of Wages on Insolvency Fund
Scheme	Scheme of Arrangement under section 166 of the CO
USD	US dollar
Works Bureau	Environment, Transport and Works Bureau

I. INTRODUCTION

Parts II–V of this chapter discuss existing and proposed procedures to facilitate corporate debt restructuring in Hong Kong. Hong Kong remains one of the few jurisdictions in Asia without a modern, effective statutory rescue procedure on the statute books. Part II of this chapter discusses the only statutory workout procedure currently available in Hong Kong – for entering into schemes of arrangement – which is contained in section 166 of the Companies Ordinance ('CO')[2] and is a replica of the UK scheme of arrangement procedure.[3] Part III of this chapter discusses insolvency law reform in Hong Kong. Ironically, Hong Kong was the first jurisdiction in Asia to commence insolvency law reform. The process began back in 1990, a good seven years before the onslaught of the Asian financial crisis. However, to date, significant amendments have only been made to the Bankruptcy Ordinance and it appears probable that the government's proposed corporate rescue procedure, which is called Provisional Supervision, is dead. Part IV of this chapter notes that in the interim – since 2002 – the Hong Kong courts have proved flexible in adapting provisional liquidation for use as a corporate rescue procedure. However, the recent case of *Legend,* in narrowly re-interpreting this case law, may well complicate this development. Part V, in turn, discusses another post-financial crisis development in Hong Kong, the use of out-of-court rescue guidelines that have been promulgated by the HKAB and the HKMA. Part VI sets out an example of how a scheme of arrangement, when used with provisional liquidation, may be used to rescue an insolvent construction company in Hong Kong. The chapter concludes with Part VII, which suggests that although successful restructurings are achievable under the current variety of mechanisms in, Hong Kong still needs to enact a formal corporate rescue procedure.

II. SCHEMES OF ARRANGEMENT

A. Overview

CO section 166 establishes a procedure whereby a company can come to a binding compromise or arrangement with its shareholders and/or creditors. At the outset, it is important to keep in mind that although section 166 may be used to facilitate the reorganization of insolvent companies, it is not solely an insolvency provision and its use is not limited to insolvent companies. Rather, it is available to all companies and most schemes of arrangement have involved solvent companies that have wished to re-organize their capital structure.[4]

---

2. Cap. 32, L.H.K.
3. Section 425 of the Companies Act 1985.
4. In the 1990s, with the onset of Hong Kong's handover to Chinese rule looming, several Hong Kong companies used the scheme of arrangement procedure to re-locate their corporate domicile to overseas jurisdictions, such as Bermuda or the United Kingdom. Perhaps the best known pre-1997 re-domiciling was of HSBC from Hong Kong to the United Kingdom.

A scheme of arrangement can be used effectively to restructure an insolvent company and to bind dissenting creditors to a plan when certain criteria are met. In short, CO section 166 enables a scheme of arrangement to be made binding on *all* the company's creditors where: (1) it has been voted on and accepted by all the various classes of the company's creditors (each class must have a separate meeting and approval is by a majority in number of the creditors present and voting and by a three-quarter majority in terms of value at the relevant meeting/s); and, (2) the scheme is subsequently approved by the court.

B.   DIFFICULTIES

There are several weaknesses with the scheme of arrangement procedure. First of all, the initiation of the scheme of arrangement process does not trigger a moratorium on creditor actions. A moratorium only comes into operation when CO section 166 is utilized in the context of a winding up.[5] In other words, the fact that a company is pursuing a scheme of arrangement does not prevent an individual creditor from suing the company, seizing the company's property or presenting a winding-up petition. In fact, some (often smaller) creditors will deliberately take such actions once they know that major creditors are in favour of a scheme of arrangement – since a small creditor can in this way make such a nuisance of himself, there is always the chance that he will get a better deal or even be paid off in full. It is fair to say that the fact that a scheme of arrangement has no moratorium actually encourages strategic behaviour by individual creditors against the best interests of the general body of creditors.

Secondly, there is no mechanism to force unwilling or uncooperative secured creditors to come to the table to negotiate. Secured creditors may continue to act outside the scheme of arrangement procedure and thus in many cases retain an effective veto power over the restructuring process.

Thirdly, the CO section 166 procedure is an expensive and time-consuming process. From the *above* discussion it is apparent that a dissenting creditor will only be bound after: (1) relevant meetings of the separate classes of creditors have been convened; (2) each meeting approves the scheme by a majority in value of three-quarter (and a simple majority in terms of the number of creditors voting for or against); and, (3) the scheme is thereafter approved by the court. Since the company has also to go to court to get permission to convene the meetings in the first place, it often takes several months or even longer for a scheme of arrangement to be put into effect.

Further complicating and delaying the process is that section 166 requires separate meetings (and approvals) by each 'class' of creditors. Legal advice must always be taken on what constitutes a 'class' of creditors in any particular case. The question of what constitutes a 'class' has provoked considerable

---

5. The moratorium would come into operation upon the earlier of the making of a winding-up order or the appointment of a provisional liquidator. See section 186 of the CO.

litigation in the past, although a number of issues have been made clearer by the recent decision of the Court of Final Appeal in *UDL Argos Engineering & Heavy Industries Co Ltd v Li Oi Lin & Others ('UDL Argos Engineering & Heavy Industries Co').*[6]

In the light of these difficulties, it should not be surprising that there are relatively few successful restructurings of substantial companies in Hong Kong under section 166 of the CO.[7]

III. PROPOSED PROVISIONAL SUPERVISION PROCEDURE

A. LEGISLATIVE BACKGROUND

Insolvency law reform efforts began in 1990 when the LRC appointed the Sub-Committee on Insolvency. The Sub-Committee began work in November 1990 and issued three consultative documents: the first on personal bankruptcy and voluntary arrangement in 1993,[8] the second on corporate rescue and insolvent trading in 1995,[9] and the third on corporate liquidation in 1998.[10] After each of these documents was circulated among relevant professional bodies and others for consultation, the LRC issued its own report: on bankruptcy and voluntary arrangements in 1995;[11] on corporate rescue and insolvent trading in 1996,[12] and on corporate liquidation in 1999.[13]

If the LRC Sub-Committee on Insolvency had first turned to corporate rescue in 1990, it is quite likely that a law in some form would have been enacted and in place by the time the Asian financial crisis hit Hong Kong in 1997. However, since the Sub-Committee did not turn to corporate rescue until after first completing its review of personal insolvency, its corporate rescue proposals were in the process of being considered when the financial crisis struck. The magnitude of the crisis led the government to abandon a significant proposal of the LRC relating to workers'

---

6. [2001] 3 HKLRD 634. See further Part VI, Section F, infra.
7. For historical background, see LRC Sub-Committee on Insolvency, *Consultation Paper on Corporate Rescue and Insolvent Trading* (June 1995), para 1.5, at p 8; available at <http://www.info.gov.hk/hkreform/reports/index.htm>.
8. LRC Sub-Committee on Insolvency, *Consultative Document on Bankruptcy* (August 1993), available at <http://www.info.gov.hk/hkreform/reports/index.htm>.
9. See supra note 7.
10. LRC Sub-Committee on Insolvency, *Consultation Paper on the Winding-Up Provisions of the Companies Ordinance* (April 1998), available at <http://www.info.gov.hk/hkreform/reports/index.htm.
11. LRC, *Report on Bankruptcy* (May 1995), available at <http://www.info.gov.hk/hkreform/reports/index.htm>.
12. LRC, *Report on Corporate Rescue and Insolvent Trading* (October 1996), available at <http://www.info.gov.hk/hkreform/reports/index.htm>.
13. LRC, *Report on the Winding-Up Provisions of the Companies Ordinance* (July 1999), available at <http://www.info.gov.hk/hkreform/reports/index.htm>.

rights in corporate rescues in favour of a modified proposal that appears to have doomed the government's recommendations to failure.[14]

B.   OVERVIEW OF THE PROVISIONAL SUPERVISION PROCEDURE

There was general agreement in Hong Kong that the scheme of arrangement procedure should be replaced or supplemented (as in Singapore) with a more modern, detailed formal corporate rescue procedure. The disagreement that has arisen has been in relation to some of the substantive provisions that have been included in the draft bills.

'Provisional supervision' is the name of the statutory corporate rescue mechanism that was proposed in Hong Kong by the LRC as long ago as 1996.[15] Legislation, in turn, has been proposed in the form of the Companies (Amendment) Bill 2000 (the '2000 Bill')[16] and the Companies (Corporate Rescue) Bill 2001 (the '2001 Bill'),[17] but there remain very real doubts as to whether or not the regime will ever be enacted.

At the heart of provisional supervision is the idea that an independent insolvency specialist (the 'provisional supervisor', who would normally be an accountant with extensive insolvency experience) may be appointed to take over the management of a financially troubled company from the directors. Under the protection of a moratorium against creditor actions (including winding-up petitions, etc.), the provisional supervisor would ascertain whether a rescue plan was feasible. Appointment of the provisional supervisor would normally be made by the directors and would not require the approval of the court. A creditor holding fixed or floating charges over the whole or substantially the whole of the company's assets – a 'major secured creditor' – would have the power to veto the appointment of a provisional supervisor.[18] The appointment of a provisional supervisor would trigger an initial 30-day moratorium, which could thereafter be extended by the court (up to six months). The moratorium would extend to consenting major secured creditors.[19] To facilitate a provisional supervisor's attempts to rescue a company, super-priority funding was contemplated – the 2001 Bill provided that working capital provided by a lender after the commencement of provisional supervision could be given priority over all of the other company's debts, with the exception of fixed charges.[20]

If a rescue or restructuring was not feasible, provisional supervision would end and the company would go into liquidation. But if the provisional supervisor

---

14. These proposals are discussed in detail at Part III.B, infra.
15. In fact, the LRC Sub-Committee on Insolvency proposed 'provisional supervision' in its June 1995 *Consultation Paper on Corporate Rescue and Insolvent Trading*. See supra note 7.
16. *Hong Kong Government Gazette,* Legal Supplement No. 3, C5 (7 January 2000) (the 2000 Bill).
17. *Hong Kong Government Gazette,* Legal Supplement No. 3, C615 (18 May 2001), available at <http://legco.gov.hk/yr00-01/english/bills/c025-e.pdf> (the 2001 Bill).
18. 2001 Bill, s 19(5)(a) and s 19(5)(b) regarding a holder of two or more charges.
19. *Ibid.,* s 11.
20. *Ibid.,* s 18.

believed that a rescue was possible, he would formulate a proposal to be put in due course to the creditors for approval. Approval would be obtained by a vote of a majority in number and ⅔ in value of the creditors present and voting in one single class.[21] Once approved, the plan would, of course, bind the company and all creditors (including those who voted against it). At this point the provisional supervisor would hand control of the company back to the directors, whilst remaining responsible for ensuring that the company duly complied with all the terms of the rescue plan.

From this brief overview it can be seen that provisional supervision was intended as a streamlined procedure that did not suffer from the defects of schemes of arrangement – a moratorium would come into effect at the outset, there would be little court involvement and creditors vote in a single class.

C. THE PROBLEM – WORKERS' WAGES

The LRC had initially proposed that the Protection of Wages on Insolvency Fund (PWIF),[22] which is currently available to workers of companies that enter compulsory liquidation, should be extended for use in provisional supervision.[23] The government objected to using the PWIF for provisional supervision for fear that the fund would become a corporate bailout fund and might eventually go bust and decided against including this recommendation of the LRC in the provisional supervision legislative proposals. Ironically, the PWIF became insolvent anyway – in October 2002 the PWIF was rescued by the commitment of the Hong Kong government to extend the PWIF up to a HKD 695 million (approximately USD 90 million) bridging loan between 2002–2003 and 2005–2006.

The 2000 Bill proposed that before a company could initiate provisional supervision it would first have to pay, in full, all the wages and other entitlements owing to the company's workers, or set up a trust account with sufficient funds to make such payments. Of course, the obvious question raised by the business and banking sectors, as well as by academic commentators, was how a company in financial distress was supposed to find sufficient funds to pay all workers their full entitlements. Rather than addressing this concern, the government inserted the same proposal in the 2001 Bill.

Thus, the major sticking point in relation to provisional supervision remains the treatment of workers' wages: the 2001 Bill proposed that, in effect, a company could not go into provisional supervision unless it first pays off everything it owes to its workers – this included not only unpaid wages, but also any other entitlements

---

21. *Ibid.*, schedule 7, para 15.
22. The PWIF is a fund that will cover – upon employees' application – an ex gratia payment in respect of the wages, wages in lieu of notice and severance payment owed by an insolvent employer. Certain limitations apply.
23. LRC, *Report on Corporate Rescue and Insolvent Trading,* supra note 12, at paras 5.40 to 5.47, at pp 41–43.

(such as severance payments) due under the Employment Ordinance.[24] Section 8 and the Second Schedule to the 2001 Bill provided that no provisional supervision may commence until the company has paid off in full (or set up a trust account with a licensed bank containing sufficient funds to pay off in full): (1) all wage claims owing to its employees; and, (2) all entitlements arising under the Employment Ordinance (e.g. severance payments) owed to its 'former employees'. Moreover, 'former employees' is very widely defined. It includes not just workers who have already been laid off, but also workers whose employment *will* be terminated on or after the commencement of the provisional supervision. For example, if a company intends to go into provisional supervision and then lay off half its workers as part of a restructuring, the company will have to calculate and pay, in advance, not only the wages it owes to all its employees but also any severance payments that will become due once the lay-offs are put into effect.

There can be no doubt but that the treatment of workers' entitlements under the 2001 Bill would act as a major obstacle to many companies that might otherwise seek to go into provisional supervision. Quite simply, how is a company that is already in a bad financial position expected to find the cash to pay off its workers in full (or set up a trust account)?

Finally, a compromise was suggested towards the end of 2001. The Bills Committee of the Legislative Council has (as of December 2001) suspended its deliberations on the Bill pending further consultations. In September 2002, the Secretary for Financial Services and the Treasury circulated the *Consultation Paper on Proposals Relating to the Trust Account Arrangement under the Companies (Corporate Rescue) Bill (the '2002 Consultation Paper')*, which proposed that instead of a company having to pay off its workers in full in advance (or set up a trust account in such amount), a limit or cap would be put on the amount to be set aside by the company before it could go into provisional supervision. This limit would be calculated by reference to the amounts payable by the PWIF where a company went into insolvent liquidation. However, these amounts could still be significant – the overall cap for workers whose employment is terminated before a provisional supervision starts would be HKD 278,500 (roughly USD 36,000).[25] Although this compromise proposal is an improvement on the original 'payment in full' approach, it still means that a company might have to pay out considerable sums before even going into provisional supervision. This would remain a major hurdle for many companies considering the use of provisional supervision.[26]

---

24. Cap. 57, H.K.L.
25. Up to HKD 36,000 for wages for services rendered within four months prior to the last day of service; up to HKD 22,500 or one month's wages, whichever is the lesser, for wages in lieu of notice; and up to HKD 220,000 for severance payment, for a total of HKD 278,500.
26. For further discussion of workers' rights and provisional supervision, see Philip Smart & Charles D. Booth, *Reforming Corporate Rescue Procedures in Hong Kong,* 1(2) Journal of Corporate Legal Studies 485, 497 (December 2001); Philip Smart & Charles D. Booth, *Provisional Supervision and Workers' Wages: An Alternative Proposal,* 31 Hong Kong Law Journal 188 (2001).

At the time of writing (November 2006) there appears to have been no progress made in relation to the compromise proposal. Doubts are increasing as to whether provisional supervision will be enacted in the near future, and it is becoming increasingly clear that the whole idea is now moribund.

IV. PROVISIONAL LIQUIDATION

As has already been noted, the scheme of arrangement procedure lacks a moratorium against creditor actions. Of course, pursuant to section 186 of the CO all actions against the company are automatically stayed where a winding-up order has been made by the court, or earlier upon the appointment of a provisional liquidator (at any time after the presentation of the winding-up petition). Historically, parties sought the appointment of a provisional liquidator before the making of a winding-up order where they feared that the company's assets were in jeopardy; thus, provisional liquidation was normally an interim period during which the assets of a company were protected while the court considered the merits of making a winding-up order. However, given the absence of an effective formal corporate rescue law, over the last several years insolvency practitioners in Hong Kong have been trying to adapt provisional liquidation for use as a corporate rescue procedure.

In 2002, in *Re Keview Technology (BVI) Ltd ('Keview')*,[27] the Hong Kong court addressed the relationship between provisional liquidation and a proposed restructuring. In *Keview,* the debtor company was part of a group of 27 companies, the ultimate holding company of which was listed on the Hong Kong stock exchange. Keview was the holding company of a wholly-foreign owned enterprise established in the People's Republic of China ('PRC') and had given various group-related guarantees that had been called in by HSBC. It was accepted that the company could not pay the debts under the guarantees. HSBC presented a winding-up petition and subsequently provisional liquidators were appointed. The company's major assets were situated in the PRC and it appeared that, if the company were to be wound up, there would be little chance of obtaining anything for the creditors. On the other hand, certain potential investors were proposing a restructuring of certain key elements in the group that could result in substantial sums becoming available to the company's creditors. The provisional liquidators had consulted all the company's creditors who were fully behind the restructuring proposal. The restructuring was intended only to become binding on a creditor if the creditor compromised its claim (i.e. expressly consented). The provisional liquidators applied to the court for an extension of their normal powers and permission to participate in the restructuring. Yuen J noted that the traditional role of the provisional liquidator was to maintain the status quo pending the hearing of the winding-up petition and that participating in a restructuring plan was quite outside the normal powers of a provisional liquidator. Nevertheless, the court held that it had jurisdiction to extend the provisional liquidators' powers and so ordered, Yuen J commenting:

---

27. [2002] 2 HKLRD 290.

If the proposed restructuring would be in the best interests of the creditors, given the level of their support for the provisional liquidators' participation, and in the absence of any evidence of mismanagement by directors such as would require the company to be wound up without delay for investigations to be done, I see no reason why the court should restrict the powers of provisional liquidators seeking to work out a rescue operation before the court has to determine whether the company should be wound-up. Having said that, each case should be considered on its own facts and I do not consider it appropriate to set out any hard and fast rules which may not be applicable in all circumstances ... However the *above* considerations would be consistent with what has been called the 'rescue culture', what is in effect an attempt to maximize recovery for creditors by saving the company if it is a viable alternative to a minimized recovery on a winding-up.

Keview was an innovative use of provisional liquidation, although the court did note that judges in both England and Hong Kong had taken similar action in the past in circumstances where schemes of arrangement were 'backed up' by the appointment of provisional liquidators.[28] *Keview* was a case in which the provisional liquidators had first secured the agreement of all of the company's creditors to a restructuring proposal before applying to the court for an extension of their normal powers and for permission to participate in the restructuring.

Whilst there was some uncertainty at the time *Keview* was decided as to what the effect and magnitude of the decision would be,[29] several subsequent decisions extended the holding of *Keview* and sanctioned the appointment of a provisional liquidator with powers to explore the feasibility of putting together a rescue plan. *Re Luen Cheong Tai International Holdings Ltd*,[30] *Re I-China Holdings Ltd*,[31] and *Re Fujian Group Ltd*.[32] all recognized 'the facilitation of corporate rescue as a rationale for appointing provisional liquidators in the first place'. Provisional liquidation was also used to assist in a corporate rescue in *Re Jinro (HK) International Ltd*[33] and in an application by SK Global Hong Kong Ltd to prevent a creditor from levying execution against the company's assets.[34] However, in its most recent pronouncement, the Court of Appeal in Hong Kong has taken a restricted view of when provisional liquidators may properly be appointed to carry forward a rescue plan.

---

28. See *Re English and American Insurance Co Ltd* (1994) and *Re HIH Insurance (Asia) Ltd*, 21 December 2001.
29. See *Hong Kong Corporate Rescue Manual,* supra note 1, at p 144.
30. [2002] 3 HKLRD 610, appeal dismissed, [2003] 2 HKLRD 719.
31. [2003] 1 HKLRD 629.
32. [2003] 1 HKC 659.
33. [2003] 3 HKLRD 459 (participation in a group-wide restructuring), which led to the sanctioning of a scheme of arrangement in [2004] HKCFI 673.
34. The application was made in response to the decision in *Credit Lyonnais v. SK Global Hong Kong Ltd* [2004] HKCA 250, discussed in Part V, infra.

In *Re Legend International Resorts Ltd* (*'Legend'*),[35] the company, incorporated in Hong Kong, carried on its business (running a casino at Subic Bay) entirely in the Philippines. The company had been making heavy losses for several years. A rehabilitation receiver had been appointed in the Philippines and the receiver was required regularly to report to the court in the Philippines. There appeared to be no property or assets in Hong Kong other than the statutory books of account and records.[36] Upon an application by a creditor for the appointment of a provisional liquidator, Kwan J at first instance[37] ruled, *inter alia*: (1) that the court could appoint provisional liquidators specifically for the purpose of exploring a corporate rescue, even though the company's assets were not shown to be in jeopardy;[38] but (2) on the facts, the court in the exercise of its discretion would not appoint provisional liquidators, since at that time[39] the rehabilitation receiver appeared to be functioning effectively and appointing provisional liquidators in Hong Kong would not lead to any practical benefit. The Court of Appeal[40] took a markedly different approach. Although not disagreeing with the judge as to the apparent exercise of her discretion,[41] the appellate court held that on principle provisional liquidators could not be appointed simply to explore the possibility of a corporate rescue. Their Lordships re-asserted the traditional doctrine that the appointment of provisional liquidators required that the company's assets be in jeopardy, Rogers VP observing that there was:[42]

> a significant difference between the appointment of provisional liquidators on the basis that the company is insolvent and that the assets are in jeopardy and the appointment of the provisional liquidators solely for the purpose of enabling a corporate rescue to take place. The difference, may, in most cases, be merely a matter of emphasis, but in the final analysis the difference exists.

In the sense, and to the extent, that a scheme of arrangement was being formulated as an *alternative* to a winding up, i.e. with the primary intention of avoiding there being any winding-up order made by the court, the court was of the view that it lacked jurisdiction to appoint provisional liquidators. The statutory power to appoint provisional liquidators was, *per* Rogers VP, for the purposes of winding up

---

35. [2006] 2 HKLRD 192.
36. *Ibid.,* at para 49.
37. [2005] 3 HKLRD 16.
38. 'I hold that it is within the jurisdiction of the court to appoint provisional liquidators to explore, formulate and pursue a corporate rescue'. *Ibid.,* para 92.
39. Subsequently the proposed rehabilitation in the Philippines failed and the rehabilitation receiver was removed by the Philippines court on account of a conflict of interest; see *per* Kwan J in *Re Legend International Resorts Ltd* [2006] 3 HKLRD 270, para 31 (the hearing of the winding-up petition).
40. The judges in the Court of Appeal were Rogers VP and Le Pichon JA; the latter merely agreed with Rogers VP.
41. *Legend,* supra note 35, at para. 43.
42. *Ibid.,* at para. 35.

the company, rather than to avoid the winding up of the company.[43] The Court of Appeal emphasized that, however convenient it might be, the statutory power to appoint provisional liquidators should not be extended beyond the situation where assets were in jeopardy and a winding-up order was likely. The introduction of a specific corporate rescue law in Hong Kong had been much debated pursuant to the recommendations of the LRC and had given rise to many difficult questions (as discussed in Part III, supra), but whether such a law ought to be introduced remained in the opinion of the court 'a matter of policy for the administration and the legislature'.[44]

At first sight it might appear that the Court of Appeal has placed a major, if not insurmountable, obstacle to using provisional liquidators to promote a rescue plan.[45] However, other passages in the judgment of Rogers VP make it plain that the court was only concerned with the 'threshold' question of whether or not there were appropriate grounds (such as jeopardy) for making an appointment. If such grounds were made out, there would be no objection to giving the provisional liquidators wide enough powers to explore the possibility of a rescue plan via, for example, a scheme of arrangement:[46]

> The law on the appointment of provisional liquidators at present is contained in s.192 and the following sections and it is clear on the wording of those sections that the appointment of a provisional liquidator must be for the purposes of the winding-up. *Provided that those purposes exist there is no objection to extra powers being given to the provisional liquidator(s)*, for example those that would enable the presentation of an application under s.166 [i.e. a scheme of arrangement].

The significance of this comment will not be lost on practitioners. Instead of approaching the court and blandly stating that a rescue plan is to be pursued by the provisional liquidators, the application may emphasize the risks to the company's assets and that the provisional liquidators will consider a scheme if it appears subsequently that a winding up can be avoided. It may also be noted that there is no objection to the continuation of provisional liquidation where, after the passage of some time, the making of a winding-up order is no longer the primary relief being sought and the petitioning creditor 'intends not to press with the winding-up order

---

43. 'The power of the court under s.192 is to appoint ... liquidators for the purposes of the winding-up not for the purposes of avoiding the winding-up. Whatever benefits may be said to arise and however convenient it may ... be for the court to be able to appoint provisional liquidators for other purposes it seems to me that [the] primary purpose of appointing provisional liquidators must always be the purposes of the winding-up. Restructuring a company is an alternative to a winding-up'. *Ibid.*, para 36.
44. *Ibid.*, para 34.
45. John Wacker notes that the decision of the appellate court in *Legend* 'seems to have curtailed the use of provisional liquidation as a means of corporate rescue'. Hong Kong Lawyer (August 2006), p 65.
46. *Legend, supra* note 35, at para 35, emphasis added.

because he believes that an alternative remedy, such as a scheme, will be eventually available and more likely to be in the interests of the creditors as a class'.[47]

Whilst the use of provisional liquidation as a rescue device leaves many unanswered questions,[48] and Hong Kong obviously needs specific legislation on the matter, the restricted approach of the Court of Appeal in *Legend* cannot escape criticism. Firstly, the court's reasoning reflects to a considerable degree a triumph of form over substance; in that, rather than being reasonably optimistic and stressing the likelihood of a rescue, the application for the appointment of provisional liquidators stands a greater chance of success if a pessimistic stance is taken, with the threats to the company and the chances of a winding up being played up. Second, an application of the approach in *Legend* may seem to lead to absurd consequences. To take a hypothetical illustration: a company may be in severe financial difficulties with the situation deteriorating every month; in January the chance of negotiating a scheme (and avoiding any winding up) may be quite high, let us say 75 per cent; by March that may have declined to 55 per cent and by April to less than 50 per cent, with creditors becoming more and more exasperated as the months progress. *Legend* suggests that there will be little difficulty in having provisional liquidators appointed in April, but they may not be appointed in January (when and because there is every chance of avoiding a winding up). But once appointed, i.e. in April, the provisional liquidators can try to put a scheme in place. The effect of *Legend* might well be to delay the appointment of provisional liquidators until the chance of achieving the solution that all the parties would prefer is seriously diminished. It is as if the Fire Brigade said that they would use hoses to put out the fire in your house, but only once the fire had spread to the upper floors! Third, it is unfortunate that the court was not referred to Australian authority,[49] where it has been expressly recognized that a provisional liquidator may be appointed in order to avoid an unnecessary winding up.

V.   OUT-OF-COURT WORKOUTS AND
         THE *HKAB/HKMA GUIDELINES*

Formal rescue laws are, of course, not the only – or necessarily the best – way to rescue companies. Where a company is in financial difficulty it is only natural that

---

47. *Re Esal (Commodities) Ltd* [1985] BCLC 450, *per* the headnote.
48. Rogers VP in his judgment in *Legend* correctly, it is respectfully submitted, pointed out (supra note 35, at paras 33–34) the various difficult policy issues that must be dealt with in any attempt to formulate a comprehensive corporate rescue law. One of those issues is how workers' wages and other entitlements should be treated; as noted in Part III, supra, this issue has caused considerable controversy in Hong Kong in recent years and was a major reason behind the failure of the proposed provisional supervision regime: see Smart & Booth, *Reforming Corporate Rescue Procedures in Hong Kong,* supra note 26.
49. Note *Re Denilikoon Nominees (No 2) Pty Ltd* (1981) 6 ACLR 262 (for later proceedings, see (1982) 6 ACLR 509). See also *Tickle v. Crest Insurance Co of Australia Ltd* (1984) 2 ACLC 493 and *Zempilas v. JN Taylor Holdings Pty Ltd (In Prov Liq) (No 3)* (1990) 9 ACLC 1 (court rejecting that jeopardy to assets and likelihood that a winding-up order would be made, although usually required before appointing a provisional liquidator, were always required as a rule of law).

it will wish to resolve those difficulties as rapidly as possible and without adverse publicity. If news that the company is in trouble is plastered all over the pages of the newspapers (or on the internet), creditor confidence may well collapse overnight. The best solution will often be for the company to come to an out-of-court agreement or workout with its major creditors for the re-scheduling of the company's debts and overall re-financing. The most significant of a company's major creditors will, of course, normally be its bankers. It is important to note that in Hong Kong it is almost universally the case that a company will not have just one or two bankers but several (or more).[50] Reaching an agreement with several banks might seem, at first sight, to present enormous difficulties; for different banks will have different policies and different attitudes. However, many potential problems in this area have been ameliorated by the joint *Hong Kong Association of Banks ('HKAB') and Hong Kong Monetary Authority ('HKMA') Guidelines on the Hong Kong Approach to Corporate Difficulties* (the '*HKAB/HKMA Guidelines*').

The background to the *HKAB/HKMA Guidelines* was explained by Mr. David Carse, Deputy Chief Executive of the HKMA, in November 1999, as follows:

> Usually the best way of achieving ... [the] best return [for lenders] is not to rush to put a company into liquidation at the first sign of financial difficulty, but instead to co-operate with the company and with the other lenders to try to salvage the company and keep it going. Keeping commercially viable companies going is in itself desirable as it preserves employment and productive capacity. But the more immediate advantage from the lenders' point of view is that giving such companies the time to restructure their operations and financial position can ultimately improve their ability to service and repay their debt. Bearing in mind the generally low recovery rate that unsecured creditors obtain from liquidations, workouts will usually be the better option as far as maximizing the lenders' return is concerned. But it is important to note that workouts should not be seen as a soft option for the debtor or an act of charity on the part of the creditors. Banks will generally only be prepared to embark on a workout if the prospect of eventual recovery is greater than it would be in a liquidation. And the threat of liquidation must always be there to provide an incentive for the debtor to face up to its problems and to agree to co-operate with the banks. Co-operation, and a recognition of shared interests, is integral to the workout process.[51]

The following are the main features of the *HKAB/HKMA Guidelines*:

1. Firstly, when it becomes apparent that a company is in financial difficulty, no bank should individually take steps to put the company into receivership or liquidation or withdraw banking facilities. Instead, there should be a 'standstill', so that a breathing space is given to the company, during

---

50. There are anecdotal reports of some companies having more than 20 bankers.
51. HKMA, *Quarterly Bulletin*, February 2000, p. 70.

which time an informed decision can be made as to whether the company is salvageable.
2. Second, during this process, a single bank should not act selfishly or try to gain some separate advantage for itself: the objective should be the best deal for all lenders. It will be noted that a bank that acted selfishly to maximize its own recovery at the expense of other lenders might find the position reversed in later cases.
3. Third, a lead bank should be nominated to head up negotiations with the company. But any agreement ultimately reached cannot be forced upon an individual bank without its agreement. Although it is obvious that if all the other banks have agreed, it may be difficult for one individual bank to hold out.
4. Fourth, during this collective process the banks should share relevant information, whilst ensuring that confidential information about the company's affairs does not leak out to third parties.

Although the *HKAB/HKMA Guidelines* have been in operation for several years and appear to have been generally well-received, it must be noted that the *HKAB/HKMA Guidelines* have a restricted role to play. Firstly, the *HKAB/HKMA Guidelines* have no statutory force and are not legally binding on any bank. For example, the Hong Kong Court of Appeal decision in *Credit Lyonnais v SK Global Hong Kong Ltd*[52] discusses the nonbinding nature of the HKAB/HKMA Guidelines. Second, and more importantly, the *HKAB/HKMA Guidelines* apply only to banks – in many cases, particularly where a company's financial position has deteriorated radically, there will be a considerable number of other, non-bank creditors who must be accommodated. Similarly, in certain types of insolvencies, such as in the construction sector, there are often a high percentage of non-bank creditors. The *HKAB/HKMA Guidelines* obviously do not seek to apply to such other creditors.

Where there are many creditors, drawn from different sectors and with differing interests, it will often be necessary to seek to arrive at an agreement which can be made legally binding all creditors, particularly the dissenting creditors. At present, under Hong Kong law, a scheme of arrangement may be the only option.

VI. AN EXAMPLE OF THE USE OF A SCHEME OF ARRANGEMENT AND PROVISIONAL LIQUIDATION TO RESCUE AN INSOLVENT CONSTRUCTION COMPANY IN HONG KONG

A. INTRODUCTION

Many companies experience financial difficulties at some time during their lifetime. Sometimes a company is able to trade out of its difficulties without its

---

52. See *supra* note 34. See also, Philip Smart, 'Cross Border Restructuring: Hong Kong Developments', 1(1) International Corporate Rescue 19, pp. 22-25.

predicament becoming public knowledge. For some companies, those financial difficulties can be terminal leading to its eventual demise by way of liquidation. For an increasing number of distressed companies the solution is to implement a scheme of arrangement (a 'Scheme') with its creditors. In Hong Kong, despite the many problems noted in Part II, supra – and because of the lack of an effective alternative – a Scheme remains in many cases, in effect the best alternative available to a company to formulate a rescue. The construction industry in general is one that is prone to the failure of some of its participants. Hong Kong is no different in this respect, but occasions arise where a Scheme can be instrumental in restructuring and rescuing a distressed company.

The construction industry in Hong Kong is notable for its system of licensing whereby a company can only apply for and undertake work for the government, incidentally the largest provider of construction work in the territory, if it has a licence to do so. The system of licensing allows companies in the construction industry to demonstrate to government that they can undertake work to the required standard, that they have sufficient financial resources to undertake the work and that they possess the appropriate technical resources and skills. Once they can demonstrate the *above* they are allowed to undertake contracts up to HKD 20 million.

Subsequently, and subject to successful completion of a required number of contracts, they can progress to larger contracts until eventually they can tender for the largest contracts valued at over HKD 250 million. In addition to classification of licences by value there are also numerous classes of licences by trade i.e. roads and drainage, electrical engineering, landscaping, etc. There are many different categories of licences, with some companies holding only one whilst others hold multiple licences.

However, the licence is not an asset of the company. It is not shown on its balance sheet and it cannot be sold. Nonetheless, that is not to say that value cannot be created from the licence for creditors in the event of the company being in financial difficulties.

A number of Schemes for insolvent construction companies in Hong Kong have been put in place with a view to creating value from their government licences. Although it is not a tradable commodity, the licence itself carries an intrinsic value, which is attractive in the eyes of investors. The value lies in the fact that to obtain a licence from scratch can take several years and a very substantial investment of time and money.

Unfortunately, when a company is in difficulties it is easy for it to fall foul of the regulations that govern the issue and retention of licences. It is in these circumstances that a Scheme can often be used to create value from the licence. At this point, it is crucial to be aware that if a company that has a licence is wound up, the licence will effectively be terminated and with it will be lost any chance of creating value for the construction company's creditors.

In this sample case, the construction-related issues are not addressed except where necessary. The aim is to highlight the way in which a Scheme can be used, often in conjunction the appointment of a provisional liquidator to rescue a failing company, but one which has a future when its business, as well as its balance sheet, has been restructured.

The fundamentals of using a Scheme to rescue a distressed company in any industry are similar, but in a construction-related company it better illustrates the benefits that can accrue from rescuing a company as opposed to selling its assets on a break up basis.

The sequence of events set out *below* is not based on a single company, but draws on the experience of dealing with many Schemes, usually undertaken in conjunction with the appointment of a provisional liquidator.

B.   Recognition of the Problem

The first stage of dealing with the affairs of a distressed company is, paradoxically, often the most challenging in that it relies not only on management recognizing its difficulties, but also in being prepared to take sometimes radical steps to address them. Once that hurdle has been surmounted and the company, its management and advisers are all pulling in the same direction, one of the major impediments to a successful rescue has been resolved.

A common problem seen in many Hong Kong restructurings in recent years has been that they have been balance sheet based – that is, the balance sheet has been restructured to restore it to solvency, but little or nothing has been done to look at the underlying causes of the company's financial difficulties. Increasingly, there is a recognition that for a restructuring to be completely successful, it requires the underlying business operations to be restructured, thus creating a profitable entity that is capable of servicing the debt which is part of the restructured balance sheet. The issue of operational restructuring is beyond the scope of this article, but must not be lost sight of in the context of the overall restructuring process.

Assuming that a company is capable of being rescued, thoughts immediately turn to the tools available to effect the restructuring. Hong Kong, although a world-class financial centre, suffers from having a legislative framework which, as noted above, at least in terms of rescuing distressed companies, has fallen far behind the times. There is no US Chapter 11,[53] no UK Administration,[54] no Australian Voluntary Arrangement.[55]

As a result, restructuring professionals have started to make greater use of the Scheme procedure, supplemented where necessary by the appointment of a provisional liquidator. The appointment of the provisional liquidator is often necessary as it triggers the protection from creditors offered by the CO, creating the moratorium, which otherwise is not available to protect the company's assets from action by aggressive creditors. This is especially important with a construction company with licences, because the appointment of a provisional liquidator does not trigger the termination of the licence.

---

53. Reorganization procedure under 11 U.S.C.
54. Schedule B1 of the Insolvency Act 1986.
55. Part5.3A of Australia's Corporations Act 2001.

Assuming there is pressure from creditors, and this is usually the case, the first stage of the process is to appoint a provisional liquidator. Unfortunately, as a result of recent court rulings, that is not necessarily as simple as might be supposed. As discussed in Part IV, supra, the Court of Appeal in Hong Kong recently ruled in *Legend* that it is not acceptable to appoint a provisional liquidator for the stated purpose of conducting a rescue, arguing that the reason for filing a winding up petition should be to wind up the company. The Court of Appeal went on to say that the purpose behind appointing a provisional liquidator should be to safeguard the assets of the company. However, it did leave the door open to a provisional liquidator, who had been appointed for that purpose, going back to court at a later date and seeking an extension of his powers to allow him to explore the possibility of restructuring the company. This is the route that the provisional liquidator must consider taking to rescue the company.

Once the provisional liquidator has been appointed, his role is to safeguard the assets of the company, and at the same time assess how best those assets can be realized for the benefit of its creditors. If the best result can be obtained by selling the assets on a break-up basis then he should proceed along those lines. However, in the context of a construction company with licences to do government work, it is almost certain that if an investor can be found who wants to acquire the company together with its licences, a better result can be obtained by restructuring the company through a Scheme.

At this point, a cautionary word must be raised in respect of the issue of costs. It is an unfortunate fact that Hong Kong is a jurisdiction with a high cost of doing business. Putting together a Scheme document and shepherding a company through the process from start to finish can be a time consuming and expensive exercise. Before embarking on this course of action, the company and its professional advisors must satisfy themselves that after taking into account the likely costs of the process, from the appointment of a provisional liquidator through to the implementation and completion of the Scheme, there will still be a better return for creditors than they would receive in the event of liquidation.

C. BACKGROUND TO THE PROBLEM

Let us assume we are approached by the directors of the company experiencing significant financial problems and struggling to complete its ongoing contracts. The company is on two of the government's Lists of Approved Contractors and Specialist Contractors. However, it has been suspended from tendering for government contracts under both licences due to its failure to meet the financial requirements regulated by the Environment, Transport and Works Bureau ('Works Bureau').

The company has three ongoing government contracts involving landslip preventive works for slopes throughout Hong Kong and general road works. At the time, a substantial part of the work on the landslip preventive works contract has yet to be completed with a remaining contract period of around eight months. The whole contract was sublet to a subcontractor who had to pay a fee to the company for 'borrowing' its licence. In respect of the two road works contracts, the rectification of defects will have to be completed before the government will agree to release retentions.

The company has no material fixed assets as most of its plant, equipment and motor vehicles were sold when the company first faced financial trouble. The company is facing considerable pressure from its financial creditors, suppliers, subcontractors and employees, and a number of them have taken proceedings and instructed the bailiff. The directors have given personal guarantees to banks and finance companies in respect of company debts. Moreover, all of the employees, except for one, have left the company due to unpaid salaries and have filed claims with the Labour Department to recover outstanding wages and entitlements.

The directors are aware that the company is insolvent in that its liabilities exceed its assets, and the company is incapable of paying its debts as and when they become due. After reviewing the affairs of the company, the directors are of the view that its financial position is unlikely to improve and that there is little or no prospect that the company will be able to trade out of its difficulties.

D. OPTIONS AVAILABLE

Following an initial review, it appears that the company has three options. The first is to maintain the status quo. However, the company is clearly insolvent, and the directors are advised that they have a duty to minimize the potential loss to creditors. The second option that must be considered is whether the company should be placed into liquidation. However, if that step is chosen, the contracts with government would be terminated, there would almost certainly be substantial contra-charges raised as a result of the breach of contract and in the circumstances, the prospects of there being anything other than a nominal recovery for creditors would be remote.

The company, as an approved government contractor and having a proven track record of completing contracts, is likely to be an attractive investment proposition. A third option would be to seek the use of a scheme of arrangement in the context of a provisional liquidation and to file a winding-up petition, being cognizant of the recent *Legend* guidelines. The role of the provisional liquidator would be to implement a Scheme and to continue the contracts to ensure that realizations were maximized for the benefit of creditors generally, and to find an investor who is prepared to put forward a rescue proposal under which the investor would inject funds into the company, allow the contracts to be completed satisfactorily and to preserve the company's licences. The return to creditors would be generated through a payment made for the 'value' of the licence and from receipts from the completion of the contracts.

E.   ONGOING CONTRACTS

In the event of a contractor on its approved list failing to complete a contract, or claims arising from work done on a contract, the government has the power to apply set-off amongst contracts whether the contracts are with a particular government department or across different departments. Therefore, a company's failure to complete one particular contract will almost certainly have an adverse effect on the financial position of other contracts with respect to the potential contract income, and is also likely to lead to disciplinary action being taken by the government on the company's licence/s. The disciplinary action is usually in the form of issuing adverse reports on the performance of a contractor on government contracts. The accumulation of these reports will ultimately lead to the suspension and downgrading of its licence/s. In a restructuring context, this means that any value associated with the company's licence/s will be reduced, and the amount that any investor will be prepared to pay will be consequently reduced.

It is therefore essential that steps are taken to ensure the contracts are completed to the satisfaction of the government and that the company continues to comply with its obligations so that it can remain on the government's lists.

The provisional liquidator is likely to have a number of options to ensure completion of the contract. These could vary from arranging for completion by sub-contractors supervised by the provisional liquidator, to finding a new contractor to complete or possibly negotiating an agreement with the investor to fund and/or supervise completion. The third option is attractive because the investor, who is likely to be an existing participant in the construction industry, will have a vested interest in ensuring the work is undertaken to a satisfactory standard thus ensuring that the company retains its licences. It is also probable that this option that will maximize recoveries from the remaining work on the contract.

The benefit to the company would accrue from taking a proportion of the income generated on the contract as a fee for allowing the replacement contractor to profit from the work involved in completing the contract. This will swell the pot of assets available to the general body of creditors.

Meanwhile, the role of the provisional liquidator is to prepare the Scheme documentation and proceed with the applications to court to bring the Scheme to fruition. The Scheme documentation comes in two parts. The first is the Scheme itself, which sets out (1) the assets that are available and how they are to be realized; and, (2) the extent of the liabilities covered by the Scheme and how they are to be dealt with. The second document is the explanatory statement that deals with the terms and conditions of the Scheme in such a way that creditors should be able to fully understand what the Scheme is all about and how it will work in practice.

Both of these documents will be closely scrutinized by the court at the initial application for sanction to convene the meetings of creditors and shareholders. The wording of the explanatory documents will to an extent vary depending upon the audience. For example, if the general body of creditors is composed of global financial creditors, the wording would be different compared to a Scheme where the majority of creditors are sub-contractors in the construction industry.

Above all, at the initial sanction hearing, the court will need to be completely satisfied that the Scheme is clearly and accurately explained to all the creditors and shareholders to whom it applies.

The court's scrutiny will extend to the agreement of the precise wording and form of the notices and proxy forms to be sent to creditors.

F.   CLASSES

For a Scheme to be effective, it will require the agreement by 75 per cent in value and a majority in number of the creditors and/or shareholders present and voting in each class at the relevant meeting/s. The constitution of classes of creditors in particular is one of the thorniest issues in the whole scheme of arrangement procedure and it has spawned numerous legal battles in every jurisdiction in which Schemes are used.[56] The issue of the constitution of classes is outside the scope of this article, but was set out by Bowen LJ in *Sovereign Life Assurance Co v Dodd*:[57]

> It seems plain that we must give such a meaning to the term 'class' as will prevent the section being so worked as to result in confiscation and injustice, and that it must be confined to those persons whose rights are not so dissimilar as to make it impossible for them to consult together with a view to their common interest.

Traditionally, if creditors were unhappy with the constitution of classes, it would be left until the final sanction hearing for their objections to be considered. This practice has been explained by Lord Millett NPJ in *UDL Argos Engineering & Heavy Industries Co*[58] as follows:

> The present practice ensures that those advising the company take their responsibility seriously, since an error on their part will be fatal to the Scheme. At the same time it leaves the question, which goes to the jurisdiction of the Court to sanction the Scheme, to be decided at the appropriate time, that is to say when the Court is asked to sanction it. By then the outcome of the meeting or meetings will be known and the question, which will no longer be hypothetical, can be argued between the appropriate parties, that is to say the company on the one hand and those who object to the Scheme on the other.

---

56. For a recent example where it was held that the classes had not been properly constituted, see *Re HIH Casualty and General Insurance Ltd*, [2006] NSWSC 485.
57. [1892] 2 QB 573 at 582–3, quoted with approval by Lord Millett NPJ in *UDL Argos Engineering & Heavy Industries Co*, supra note 6, at para 18. Lord Millett observed (para 27): 'The test is based on similarity or dissimilarity of legal rights against the company, not on similarity or dissimilarity of interests not derived from such legal rights. The fact that individuals may hold divergent views based on their private interests not derived from their legal rights against the company is not a ground for calling separate meetings'. (Lord Millett is a non-permanent judge of the Hong Kong Court of Final Appeal.)
58. *UDL Argos Engineering & Heavy Industries Co*, ibid., at para 14.

In England, the traditional practice has been altered as a result of a Practice Statement[59] and now, as far as possible, questions concerning the composition of classes should be decided at the initial hearing (to order the convening of meetings) rather than at the subsequent hearing to sanction the scheme (after it has been approved by the meeting/s of creditors). No such Practice Statement has been issued in Hong Kong. Nevertheless, it appears that on at least one occasion the court has determined issues as to the constitution of classes at an *inter partes* hearing of the application to summon meetings.[60] Because there is no Practice Statement in Hong Kong, it remains more than a little uncertain as to the basis of this change in a practice that was endorsed by Hong Kong's highest appellate court in *UDL Argos Engineering & Heavy Industries Co.*[61]

In recent years, in an effort to move with the times, Scheme Administrators have sought to obtain the sanction of the court to use electronic methods of communication. In *Re Sporting Options plc*,[62] which concerned a UK-based internet gaming company, the Administrators (in a case not involving a Scheme) asked the court to sanction the sending of notices to creditors by email rather than by post. The court rejected the application, noting that:

1. e-mail communication can be rejected by technology such as firewalls;
2. individual members of the particular class of creditors may not have retained their same e-mail addresses; and,
3. individuals may not access their e-mails with the same regularity as their Post Office deliveries.

The judge did, however, allow the Administrators to make available to creditors a full set of the documents concerning their proposals through a web-site. In Hong Kong, in the case involving HIH Insurance, due to the volume of documents the Court also allowed the Scheme Administrators to send a summarized version of the Scheme documentation to creditors, referring them to a web-site from where a full copy of the Scheme information could be obtained.

Once the court has sanctioned the convening of the meeting, notices will be sent to all the creditors and sharcholders in accordance with the terms of the explanatory statement.

G. MEETING OF CREDITORS

The Scheme Administrator is the chairman of the meeting. After the formalities, the votes are taken for each of the classes of creditors and shareholders. Crucially,

---

59. The Practice Statement is set out as *Practice Statement (Companies: Schemes of Arrangement)* [2002] 1 WLR 1345.
60. This appears from *Re Oxford Properties & Finance Ltd* [2004] 3 HKLRD 142, paras 32–34, where the court refers to an earlier unreported decision of Barma J in the litigation.
61. See supra note 6.
62. [2004] EWHC 3128 (Ch), [2005] BPIR 435.

Hong Kong 319

the Scheme Administrator must ensure that a proper record of the proceedings is maintained, particularly in the area of recording the votes cast, by whom and in favour of which resolution. The outcome of the meeting is then reported to the court setting out the resolutions considered and the voting on them. Most meetings are however, relatively uneventful, it is the sanction hearing which takes place a few days thereafter at which there tends to be much more discussion.

H.   Sanction Hearing

The sanction hearing will be before the same judge who ordered the meeting to be held. The court will consider the report of the Scheme Administrator and submissions by any interested parties. This usually means creditors who are, for some reason, opposed to the Scheme going ahead. Traditionally, it is at the sanction hearing that the issue of classes of creditors is brought to the fore. The problem is that historically, if the court finds at this late stage that the classes of creditors were not correctly drawn, it will refuse to sanction the Scheme. The rationale is that if the classes of creditors were not correctly drawn the court does not have the power to sanction the Scheme.[63] But, even if the scheme is approved by the requisite majority of creditors at properly constituted meetings, the court may yet refuse to sanction unless it is satisfied that 'the result of each meeting fairly reflect the views of the creditors concerned'.[64] In this regard it has been confirmed that the court may:[65]

> discount or disregard altogether the votes of those who, though entitled to vote at a meeting as a member of the class concerned, have such personal or special interests in supporting the proposals that their views cannot be regarded as fairly representative of the class in question.

Once the court has sanctioned the Scheme, an office copy of the order of the court sanctioning the Scheme is delivered to the Registrar of Companies for registration. As soon as this step has been taken the Scheme comes into operation. Occasionally, the court will make an order sanctioning the Scheme, but subject to conditions precedent. In that case, the Scheme Administrator should not file the court order until such conditions precedent have been met.

I.   Role of the Provisional Liquidator

Meanwhile, the provisional liquidator must continue to protect the value of the company, which to a large extent is tied to retaining its place on the government's list.

---

63. See *UDL Argos Engineering & Heavy Industries Co,* supra note 6, at para 27.
64. See *ibid., per* Lord Millett.
65. *Ibid., per* Lord Millett.

It is likely that prior to the provisional liquidator's appointment, the company would have progressively failed to comply with the technical and financial requirements set out in the Construction Management Handbook ('CMH'). A major task of the provisional liquidator will therefore be to restore the quality control system and the adequate level of staffing, plant and machinery to meet the technical criteria and to produce up to date audited accounts for assessment by the financial section of the Works Bureau.

The provisional liquidator is also likely to be operating under considerable time constraints in terms of reporting both to the court and to the Works Bureau with respect to the progress of the restructuring. A provisional liquidator may make an application to the court to adjourn the hearing of the winding-up petition to allow the restructuring to take place, but the court will want to be satisfied that progress is being made with the restructuring in order to assist in this respect.

As part of the requirements set out in the CMH, the company must maintain a quality control system sufficient to meet ISO (International Organization for Standardization) standards. The provisional liquidator will need to work with existing management and probably the investor to improve the system by employing a quality assurance consultant to produce the necessary documents and manuals for ISO inspection and audit.

In terms of staffing, the CMH specifies the requirement of employing a certain level of management and technical staff for retention of its licences, particularly in specialist categories. The provisional liquidator will most likely enter into discussion with the investor on providing the necessary staffing from its own organization, as it will be considered beneficial to creditors to reduce the cost of recruiting new staff. There will be an added advantage if the investor is also from the construction industry and is able to utilize its existing staff in the company.

The company is also required to own a particular level of plant and equipment. To meet these requirements, the provisional liquidator may need to acquire additional plant and equipment to meet the technical criteria in the CMH. Decisions of this nature will need to be taken in light of the ultimate commercial benefit to the creditors.

The company will also be required to maintain updated audited accounts for the Works Bureau to assess the financial status in order to retain the licences. If licences have been suspended prior to the appointment of the provisional liquidator who was advised by the Works Bureau, the provisional liquidator will need to communicate with the Works Bureau to show that the financial position of the restructured company will be sufficient to comply with the working capital and other requirements of the CMH.

J.   Success Achieved?

As a result of the nature of the construction industry and how construction companies operate, there are many practical issues arising from both the contract and management levels that need to be addressed in order to successfully restructure a construction company. In this example, the financial sourcing of the Scheme (i.e.

the funds available for the creditors) would be a combination of both the injection of money from the investor and the income generated under the contracts. It is through the successful management of the contracts that the creditors will receive a greater return.

The technical aspects of running and managing the contracts and the issue of maintaining the licences are at the core of creating value out of an insolvent construction company, and it requires both expertise and experience to extract the maximum value for creditors.

VII.   CONCLUSION

As can be seen from the example in Part VI *above*, as well as from the earlier discussion, although corporate rescue in Hong Kong is difficult and expensive, it is possible. There are some successes. Hong Kong probably is unique in that it has one of the ablest bodies of insolvency professionals in the world with the least amount of law to apply in attempting to rescue companies.

Hong Kong still needs an effective formal corporate rescue system. The government should admit defeat with respect to provisional supervision and start over by rethinking the insolvency law reform process. Given the difficulties that have arisen in attempting to enact a whole new regime for corporate rescue, the government should draft a new law that incorporates provisional liquidation into a formal corporate rescue law. However, rather than harking back to early 20th century notions of appointing provisional liquidators when the assets of a company are in jeopardy, it should propose that a formal corporate rescue process commence when it is in the best of interests of creditors to do so. Moreover, in drafting this new law, the government should abandon its requirement on pre-paying the workers in full as a condition precedent for starting the corporate rescue process. Perhaps a codified provisional liquidation scheme could come to the rescue of provisional supervision and provide Hong Kong with a workable statutory framework.

ANNEX: KEY LEGISLATION

A.   COMPANIES ORDINANCE

Arrangements and Reconstructions

Section 166. Power to compromise with creditors and members

(1) Where a compromise or arrangement is proposed between a company and its creditors or any class of them, or between the company and its members or any class of them, the court may, on the application in a summary way of the company or of any creditor or member of the company, or, in the case of a company being wound up, of the liquidator, order a meeting of the creditors or class of creditors, or of the members of the company or class of members, as the case may be, to be summoned in such manner as the court directs.

(2) If a majority in number representing three-fourths in value of the creditors or class of creditors, or members or class of members, as the case may be, present and voting either in person or by proxy at the meeting, agree to any compromise or arrangement, the compromise or arrangement shall, if sanctioned by the court, be binding on all the creditors or the class of creditors, or on the members or class of members, as the case may be, and also on the company or, in the case of a company in the course of being wound up, on the liquidator and contributories of the company.

(3) An order made under subsection (2) shall have no effect until an office copy of the order has been delivered to the Registrar for registration, and a copy of every such order shall be annexed to every copy of the memorandum of the company issued after the order has been made, or, in the case of a company not having a memorandum, of every copy so issued of the instrument constituting or defining the constitution of the company.

(4) If a company makes default in complying with subsection (3), the company and every officer of the company who is in default shall be liable to a fine for each copy respect of which default is made.

(5) In this section and in section 166A, the expression 'company' (公司) means any company liable to be wound up under this Ordinance, and the expression 'arrangement' (債務償還安排) includes a re-organization of the share capital of the company by the consolidation of shares of different classes or by the division of shares into shares of different classes or by both those methods.

Chapter 9
India

The Corporate Debt Restructuring Mechanisms in India

Rajiv Luthra

ACRONYMS, ABBREVIATIONS & DEFINED TERMS

Companies Act	Indian Companies Act (1956)
CRPS	Cumulative Redeemable Preference Shares
DRT Act	Recovery of Debts due to Banks and Financial Institutions Act (1993)
IFCI	Industrial Finance Corporation of India
INR	India Rupees
JVSL	Jindal Vijaynagar Steel Ltd.
Prudential Norms	Reserve Bank of India Master Circular dated 1 July 2005 on Prudential norms on Income Recognition, Asset Classification and Provisioning pertaining to Advances
RBI	Reserve Bank of India
SARFESI	Securitization and Reconstruction of Financial Assets and Enforcement of Security Interest Act (2002)
Sick Industrial Companies Act	Sick Industrial Companies Act (1985)
USSR	Union of Soviet Socialist Republics

I. INTRODUCTION: SOUTH EAST ASIAN CRISIS AND ADOPTION OF THE CORPORATE DEBT RESTRUCTURING MECHANISM IN INDIA

The economic health of the real sector and the financial sector are in many ways interrelated. While the latter provides capital to the former for its growth, it also is dependent on the real sector for business opportunities and return on the capital. The weakness of the financial sector and failures in it not only result in the drying up of the capital flow but also may (due to the terms on which credit is usually given) result in a sudden demand for return of capital. Moreover, failures amongst financial intermediaries do result in the drying up of money supply.

While other regions of the world have, at some time or the other, come to terms with this, for the expanding Asian economies, the defining moment was the South East Asian currency melt-down which occurred in 1997.[1] One of the reasons for the economic meltdown was the weakness of the financial sector, most importantly the banking sector. But the health of the sector itself was dependent upon the repayment of debt by the borrowers, most of whom unfortunately were unable to pay due to various reasons. So, drastic measures were needed to revitalize the economy and to save it from succumbing to cascading bankruptcies in the businesses.

Financial rehabilitation of the corporates was not only economically desirable but also the only politically feasible solution which was available. So most of the crisis ridden countries like Thailand, Korea, Malaysia followed a corporate debt-restructuring programme with variations. The logic of the exercise was two fold. Firstly, loans are not written off or adjusted in a healthy economy as a moral hazard (i.e. if those who do not pay up are treated with kid gloves then it serves as an incentive for others not to re-pay or not to take sufficient care of their affairs so that they are capable of repaying their debt as per the agreed terms and schedule). But in contrast to recessionary conditions everyone understands that those who are unable to pay up were put into that condition generally by circumstances beyond their control. The second rationale behind corporate debt restructuring was the realization that a corporate which was healthy and running, was also a source of much direct and indirect revenues and that no purpose would be served by declaring it bankrupt and putting it up for sale unless there were buyers who would pay enough so as to satisfy at least a substantial part of the debt, which generally would not be the case in a recession hit economy. It was recognized that more could be recovered in future from a running unit than from sale where every alternate business was going insolvent. The financial institutions hope to weather the storm and come out from the recession relatively unscathed along with their debtors.

---

1. For an enlargement on the Asian Crisis see G. Corsetti, P. Pesenti and N. Roubini, 'What Caused the Asian Currency and Financial Crises? Part I: A Macroeconomic View', available at <http://www.stern.nyu.edu/globalmacro/AsianCrisis.pdf> and 'What Caused the Asian Currency and Financial Crises? Part II: The Policy Debate', available at <http://www.stern.nyu.edu/globalmacro/asiacri2.pdf>. For a comprehensive list of papers on the topic available electronically, see <http://www.stern.nyu.edu/globalmacro/asian_crisis/basic_readings.html>.

India was amongst the few in the region which escaped, virtually unscathed, from the South East Asian currency meltdown. However, this by itself was no cause for celebration amongst the Indian policymakers. It was evident that the main reason why India was unaffected was the lack of free convertibility of the Indian Rupee and the restrictions on currency movements. Taking a cue from India, Malaysia re-imposed currency control to get out of the crisis. Another reason was, government ownership of most of the financial institutions,[2] which led to many depositors and financial market players to assume sovereign guarantee by implication (it may be noted that such sovereign guarantee has been explicitly provided for in statutes creating financial institutions such as the Life Insurance Corporation of India).[3]

Moreover, the Indian policymakers did realize that many of the ills which afflicted the South East Asian countries were present in India as well. The Indian financial system, more specifically the banking system was perhaps, at that point of time, weaker than that of some of the affected South East Asian countries. Further, in an economy which was integrating with the world economy and whose policy makers had ambitions of capital account convertibility, there was a need that the issues relating to corporate inability to pay were tackled before things deteriorated to a point of no return.

II. BACKGROUND TO THE CRISIS IN THE INDIAN FINANCIAL SYSTEM

In the mid-fifties, the Indian policymakers had decided that the public sector should attain the commanding heights of the Indian economy.[4] They had also come to the conclusion that planning was inevitable for India to develop as it needed to best utilize its scarce resources, especially capital, and for this reason financing and lending had to be directed. Moreover, there was the perceived need to spread the reach of the financial institutions, especially banks, so that they become instruments of savings. But for this, it was felt, there was a need to instil confidence in the general public in the long-term solvency of these institutions. Due to these considerations, the government, at the time of liberalization of the

---

2. The Banking Companies (Acquisition & Transfer of Undertakings) Act, 1970 and 1980, created banks which were managed by board of directors appointed by the central government in consultation with the Reserve Bank of India and were bound to be guided by the directions of the Central Government.
3. For example, Section 37 of the Life Insurance Corporation Act, 1956 explicitly provides for sovereign guarantee to the policyholders in relation to the sums assured by the policies issued by Life Insurance Corporation, including any bonuses thereof. It states as follows: 'The sums assured by all policies issued by the (Life Insurance) Corporation including any bonuses declared in respect thereof and, subject to the provisions contained in section 14 (of the Life Insurance Corporation Act, 1956) the amounts assured by all policies issued by any insurer the liabilities under which have vested in the (Life Insurance) Corporation under this Act, and all bonuses declared in respect thereof, whether before or after the appointed, day shall be guaranteed as to payment in cash by the Central Government'.
4. Industrial Policy Resolution dated April 30, 1956.

economy in the early nineties, owned and controlled most of the important financial institutions. The situation came about either by the government bringing in or creating new institutions e.g. Industrial Development Bank of India, Industrial Finance Corporation of India, etc.[5] or by nationalization of existing institutions.[6] In some cases it inherited the pre-independence institutions e.g. State Bank of India (formerly Imperial Bank of India). The public ownership of the financial institutions, though beneficial in some respect brought about its own set of pitfalls. The first set of problems was with regard to the objectivity of lending decisions. Secondly, the need to create productive assets and industrialization goals did result in the banks lending to companies which were overleveraged.

Both, the debt equity ratios of debtors and the cost of capital, were high. The latter was high due to high cost of servicing customers/depositors due to their geographical spread and the need to cater to small value accounts as well as the requirement to provide a certain portion of the loans at low cost to achieve socially desirable goals. Moreover, political control meant that lending decisions in quite a few cases were at least based upon over optimistic projections. The other set of problems were legal in nature. The public sector character of the financial institutions meant that quite a few times these institutions were answerable in a court of law for their refusal or unwillingness to provide loans. Though notionally the courts were not supposed to sit in judgment over commercial decisions of the institution, but the decision on whether to lend or not to lend by public financial institutions, unlike those by a private body, could not be arbitrary and needed to have some rationale. This was because, such financial institutions are considered to be 'State' under Article 12 of the Constitution of India.[7] So, the court has in quite a few instances enforced a specific performance of contract to lend (which is

---

5. IFCI was set up under the Industrial Finance Corporation Act, 1948 (Act 15 of 1948) with the object of making medium and long-term credit more readily available to eligible industrial concerns in India.
6. Fourteen major banks were nationalized by the Banking Companies (Acquisition & Transfer of Undertakings) Act, 1970. Later six more banks were nationalized by the Banking Companies (Acquisition & Transfer of Undertakings) Act, 1980. These were the largest banks in the private sector at that time. Further, the insurance business was nationalized by establishment of the Life Insurance Corporation of India under the Life Insurance Corporation of India Act, 1956 and by the General Insurance Business (Nationalization) Act, 1972.
7. Article 12 of the Constitution of India states 'In this Part, unless the context otherwise requires, 'the State' includes the Government and Parliament of India and the Government and the Legislature of each of the States and all local or other authorities within the territory of India or under the control of the Government of India'. In the case of *Sukhdev Singh v. Bhagatram*, Supreme Court of India 1975, it was held that statutory corporations like the Life Insurance Corporation of India and Industrial Finance Corporation of India are 'State'. Further, in the case of *Ajay Hasia v. Khalid Mujib*, Supreme Court of India 1981 it was held that several tests can be used to determine whether a corporation is 'state' or not. These tests are: (1) if the government is a shareholder of the corporation; (2) whether the State provides financial assistance to the corporation; (3) whether the corporation enjoys monopoly status which is State conferred or State protected; (4) whether there is State control; (5) whether the functions performed by the corporation are of public importance and related to functions of the government; and, (6) whether a department of the Government has been transferred to the corporation.

normally supposed to be only amenable to damages under Indian law).[8] The public sector character was a big drawback at the time of recovery as well. The enforcement of securities or other coercive measures were amenable to the writ jurisdiction of the courts, in addition to any limitations faced by their private sector peers. But unlike them, they also could not enter into any compromise with their debtors as the Central Vigilance Commissioner or the Comptroller and Auditor General of India, who had jurisdiction over these institutions might question the commercial judgment of the financial institution on the ground that public money had been given away, which would not only reflect on the future promotional avenues of those who took the decision but could also thereafter become a reason for crime investigating agencies to step in.

III. LIMITATIONS OF THE INDIAN LEGAL SYSTEM FOR RECOVERING THE DEBT DUE FROM DEBTORS

The Indian legal system is based on the premise that, between the creditor and the debtor, it is the former who is in the driver's seat and can, and usually does, drive a hard bargain. So the focus of the legal system has been to provide checks in this ability of the creditor to enforce an unreasonable contractual term which maybe the result of unequal bargaining power.[9] In addition to this handicap, enforcement of creditor's rights were subject to normal delays present in the Indian legal system.

Insolvency and liquidation proceedings were quite drawn out, and in an industrial undertaking, by the time an asset was disposed, neither the economy nor the creditor gained anything.[10] Usually, due to deterioration or pilferage of the assets of the company during the time of the proceedings, a productive asset was forever lost. Due to this the Sick Industrial Companies Act, 1985 (**'Sick Industrial Companies Act'**) was enacted.

A. SICK INDUSTRIAL COMPANIES ACT

Under the terms of Sick Industrial Companies Act, the Board for Industrial and Financial Reconstruction was constituted. The Board for Industrial and Financial Reconstruction is a quasi-judicial body. If and when an industrial company became sick, its board of directors is required to make a reference to the Board for Industrial and Financial Reconstruction within 60 days for it to determine and decide the

---

8. In the case of *Gujarat State Financial Corporation v. M/S. Lotus Hotels Pvt. Ltd*, Supreme Court of India 1983, it was held that that the Gujarat State Financial Corporation is bound due to the principle of promissory estoppel to fulfill its obligation arising from the solemn promise to lend made by the Gujarat State Financial Corporation to Lotus Hotels, which had acted on it and thus changed its position.
9. An example can be that India adopts the principles of English law with regard to clog on redemption. But on the other hand the law has restricted the availability of the right to entry and sale by the creditor, which are recognized in English mortgage.
10. Time taken to rehabilitate or liquidate distressed companies was 10 to 15 years under the old bankruptcy system.

measures that may be taken to revive the company. A sick company has been defined in the Act as one which has accumulated losses equal to or more than its net worth.[11] Thus, in effect, the Board for Industrial and Financial Reconstruction was given jurisdiction over manufacturing companies that were insolvent. If a reference has been made by the directors of a company to the Board for Industrial and Financial Reconstruction, its creditors were disallowed from pursuing any recovery or any other proceedings against the debtors till the Board for Industrial and Financial Reconstruction is seized of the matter. Though, the Board for Industrial and Financial Reconstruction is supposed to recommend measures for the revival and rehabilitation of the company only with the consent of the parties, the requirement of Board for Industrial and Financial Reconstruction proceedings and the oversight which the High Courts could exercise with their writ jurisdiction in effect meant that it became a means by which the debtors many a times sought to delay the creditors. It became another clog in the liquidation process and unfortunately, the misuse of it by the debtors meant that success in revival and rehabilitation were few and far between.

Due to definition of the term 'sick',[12] the very jurisdiction of the Board for Industrial and Financial Reconstruction related to companies that were insolvent and not just financially challenged due to temporary losses or cash flow problems. This definition of 'sick' in the Sick Industrial Companies Act prevents any intervention by the Board for Industrial and Financial Reconstruction until the accumulated losses have made any meaningful rehabilitation an impossibility.[13] Moreover, for a company which is technically insolvent, for a viable revival solution to emerge, the creditors have to be in a position to dictate, otherwise it merely hands over to the debtor an additional bargaining chip. It is not just the creditor, but also the debtor who has to take cuts. One of the favourite means which were usually sought to be adopted by the Board for Industrial and Financial Reconstruction was seeking a White Knight i.e. an outside investor who would buy out the company or its majority owners. But this usually was resisted by the group in control as loss of control usually entailed a loss of privileges associated with the control. This continued control, over an entity which in any case was technically insolvent, meant that the role of the controlling group could in the intervening period be more of a scavenger and thus worsen an already bad situation.

B.　　　　INDIAN COMPANIES ACT, 1956 ('COMPANIES ACT')

The second method to deal with the problem of distressed companies was provided in the Companies Act modelled on the English Companies Act. The Companies

---

11. See Section 2(o) of the Sick Industrial Companies Act (1985).
12. Section 2(o) of the Sick Industrial Companies Act states that a 'sick industrial company' means an industrial company (being a company registered for not less than five years) which has at the end of any financial year accumulated losses equal to or exceeding its entire net worth.
13. Nimrit Kang and Nitin Nayar, The Evolution of Corporate bankruptcy Law in India, (October 2003 – March 2004) *ICRA Bulletin – Money & Finance* 44. The few cases of success usually relate to disposal of real estate at historical book value in Company's books, inspite of the appreciation in the value during the intervening decades, to raise the cash for revival.

Act governs the setting up and governance of the companies that are formed and registered under it. Chapter V of the Companies Act provides the framework under which compromise and arrangements can be proposed between a company and its creditors. Such compromise and arrangements between the company and the creditor are however required to be sanctioned by the High Court with jurisdiction. The Companies Act also provides for the procedure for winding up of companies, in case the company is unable to pay its debts, and this can be voluntarily or pursuant to a court order.

IV.   DEVELOPMENTS IN THE NINETIES

In the nineties, alternate mechanisms were being thought of so as to increase the repayment rates of big borrowers. First, the feeling was that the reason for low repayment rate was the slow court process. So, for banks and financial institutions special debt recovery tribunals were constituted, upon the recommendation of the committee headed by Mr. M. Narasimham, so that loans could be speedily recovered.[14] But the process was bogged down by its own shortcomings. The recovery process, though now comparatively speedy, was still too slow to help the creditors.

The second method was takeover of assets as in English mortgage.[15] This facility was allowed to the State Financial Corporations[16] and it was thought fit that all banks and financial institutions should have it. So the Securitization and Reconstruction of Financial Assets and Enforcement of Security Interest Act, 2002 ('SARFESI') was enacted.[17] But even before it was passed, there was a realization

---

14. These special tribunals were set up under the Recovery of Debts due to Banks and Financial Institutions Act, 1993 ('DRT Act'). The DRT Act entitled banks and financial institutions to recover debts by filing a petition before the debt recovery tribunal for recovery of loans. The application of the provisions of the civil procedural law to the DRTs has been specifically excluded by the DRT Act. The debt recovery tribunals and the debt recovery appellate tribunal, subject to the procedure provided for in the DRT Act and the Debts Recovery Tribunal (Procedure) Rules, 1993, are free to determine their own procedure for dealing with the claims of the banks and financial institutions.
15. In certain specified circumstances, the mortgagee has the power to sell the mortgaged property or any part thereof without court intervention. One such circumstance is that the mortgage is an English mortgage and neither the mortgagor nor the mortgagee should be Hindu, Muhammadan or Buddhist or any other race, sect, tribe or calls specified by the state government from time to time. Further, another such circumstance is wherein sale without court intervention has been specifically permitted by the mortgage deed and the mortgaged property is situated within the towns of Calcutta, Madras, Bombay or in any other town or area which the State Government by notification has specified.
16. These corporations are incorporated under the State Financial Corporations Act of 1951 which contains a special provision for enforcement by state financial corporations. As per Section 29 of the said act, the corporation has a right to take over the management or possession or both of the industrial concerns who have defaulted in repayment of loan or advance obtained from the corporation. Further, the corporation has the right to transfer by way of lease or sale and realize the property pledged, mortgaged, hypothecated or assigned to it.
17. SARFESI allows secured creditors to take possession of the securities in the event of default and sell such securities for the purpose of recovery of the loan. Section 13(1) of the SARFESI states

that at the most it would serve as a stick or a negotiating platform. Many financial institutions had with them the pledged shares of the promoter group, but there was a realization that such clauses in the loan contract were not by themselves useful in a running company unless one got the cooperation of the promoter who had the documents in his possession and also many a times the key personnel were his personal loyalists. Further, many a times, some key property like trademark, etc. were owned by the promoters. Moreover, the raw material suppliers to the company and distributors of company products could be related to the promoter or controlled by him. Thus, it was difficult for the financial institution to break this web of control without the cooperation of the promoters. Also many of the securities were illiquid and made more so by the different laws.[18] If it was a big industrial company, the labour laws were unhelpful.[19] There was a realization that some of the failed projects were not just because of the failure of promoters. The concerned promoters were in many cases a victim of the business environment they had been used to and the change in circumstances bought about by the policy makers. After the liberalization of 1991, when industrial licensing had been done away with, there was a sudden rush to set up industries. This led to a sudden glut of the concerned produce in the market which worsened the situation when considered along with the fact that most of the time the concerned company was, as per the traditional way of doing business, overleveraged with debt. This situation was compounded by high interest rates which were charged because of policy of monetary contraction in the mid nineties. Steady lowering of import duties and also a global glut, especially in metals (due to break up of USSR), worsened the situation. It also meant that there were no takers for

---

as follows: 'Notwithstanding anything contained in section 69 or section 69A of the Transfer of Property Act, 1882 (4 of 1882), any security interest created in favour of any secured creditor may be enforced, without the intervention of the court or tribunal, by such creditor in accordance with the provisions of this Act'. Further, Section 13 (4) of the SARFESI states that in case the borrower fails to discharge his liability in full within the period specified, the secured creditor may take possession of the secured assets of the borrower including the right to transfer by way of lease, assignment or sale for realizing the secured asset.

18. Transfer of land is often restricted by restrictions in the nature of urban land ceilings laws, zoning plans, etc. For instance, several states like Maharashtra have urban land ceiling laws wherein a ceiling is imposed on the amount of urban land that can be held by an individual. Further, use of land in urban areas is also usually regulated by certain zoning regulations. For example, in terms of the Delhi Development Act, 1957, land is to be used in conformity with the master plans made there under. Also, often industrial land is not held on freehold basis but is leased out by a governmental authority. Certain restrictions on transfer of land might have been incorporated in the lease deed. In the event a lender wants to recover the amount lent by him by sale of the secured land, it would be difficult for him to do so taking into account the *above-mentioned* restrictions

19. For example the Industrial Disputes Act, 1947 imposes certain notice and compensation requirements that need to be fulfilled before the services of a workman are interrupted due to transfer of an undertaking. Hence, before the lender can sell an undertaking belonging to its borrower to make good his loss, such requirements would have to be complied with. Further, in terms of Section 25-O of the Industrial Disputes Act, 1947, an employer intending to close an undertaking employing more than 100 workers is required to obtain requisite permission from the relevant government authority and compensate every workman on the closure of the undertaking. But getting the permission is often very difficult because of negative political implications.

those assets, when secured, even if sold in market either on piece meal basis or as one running unit. So the need of the hour in many cases was to come up with a means to restructure the debt before the unit became sick.

Chapter V of the Companies Act does provide for a mechanism for the same. But it has serious practical limitations. First of all, the concerned company should be liable to be wound up under the Companies Act,[20] virtually implying that it should be insolvent. Secondly, the proposal for restructuring can be only within a class of creditors[21] and there will always be challenges in a court of law as to whether two creditors constitute a class unless they were members of a syndicate. Thirdly, since the process is court supervised the court has to be satisfied that the solution is fair and just and it is not bound to sanction it even if voted in by requisite majority.

On the other hand, individual settlements had their own limitations. Firstly, every creditor will be wary of the free rider problem i.e. the debtor is able to pay of the accounts of other creditors because of the concessions made by one, who does not derive any benefit of his own actions himself. Then one has to take into account

---

20. Section 433 of the Companies Act provides the circumstances under which a company may be wound up. It states as follows:
    'A company may be wound up by the Tribunal,

    (a) if the company has, by special resolution, resolved that the company be wound up by the Tribunal;
    (b) if default is made in delivering the statutory report to the Registrar or in holding the statutory meeting;
    (c) if the company does not commence its business within a year from its incorporation, or suspends its business for a whole year;
    (d) if the number of members is reduced, in the case of a public company, below seven, and in the case of a private company, below two;
    (e) if the company is unable to pay its debts;
    (f) if the Tribunal is of the opinion that it is just and equitable that the company should be wound up;
    (g) if the company has made a default in filing with the Registrar its balance sheet and profit and loss account or annual return for any five consecutive financial years;
    (h) if the company has acted against the interests of the sovereignty and integrity of India, the security of the State, friendly relations with foreign States, public order, decency or morality;
    (i) if the Tribunal is of the opinion that the company should be wound up under the circumstances specified in section 424G:

    Provided that the Tribunal shall make an order for winding up of a company under clause (h) on application made by the Central Government or a State Government'.
    Please note that the Tribunal referred to *above* and in the other sections that have been quoted from the Companies Act has not been constituted yet. Its functions are still being performed by a forum known as the Companies Court.

21. Section 391 read with section 394 of the Companies Act, 1956. Section 391 of the Companies Act states that where a compromise or arrangement is proposed –

    (a) between a company and its creditors or any class of them; or
    (b) between a company and its members or any class of them; the Tribunal may, on the application of the company or of any creditor or member of the company, or, in the case of a company which is being wound up, of the liquidator, order a meeting of the creditors or class of creditors, or of the members or class of members, as the case may be, to be called, held and conducted in such manner as the Tribunal directs.

India 333

the fact that most financial institutions and banks are in the public sector and therefore individual compromises might be put through the scanner by the Central Vigilance Commission, Comptroller and Auditor General and crime investigation agencies.[22] There had to be a mechanism which would take care of this problem.

V. CORPORATE DEBT RESTRUCTURING

It was in light of this that the Reserve Bank of India came up with the Corporate Debt Restructuring model in August 2001[23] providing detailed guidelines for establishing the corporate debt restructuring system. The present framework is provided by a November 2005 circular of the RBI.[24]

The model for corporate debt restructuring essentially has two elements – factual and legal. RBI is the regulatory body for most of the financial institutions and all banks. Also, the central government is either the sole or majority shareholder in most of them. As the regulatory agency (with the backing of the majority/sole owner), the RBI can prod such financial institutions to become involved in the corporate debt restructuring exercise. Those financial institutions which are not regulated by the RBI, e.g. Life Insurance Corporation of India, General Insurance Corporation of India and its subsidiaries, Unit Trust of India but are important players, are allowed to join either on individual case to case basis or become general members.[25] Thereafter the members are bound together by the Inter-Corporate Contractual Agreement entered into by the members. So the legal foundation of the arrangement rests on the basis of Inter-Corporate Contractual Agreement, which has come about because RBI regulates the entities which are signatories to it. In fact up to 2005, RBI was a member of the Corporate Debt Restructuring Standing Forum and oversaw some of the most important corporate debt restructuring cases and enabled the establishment of precedents for guidance in future cases.

A. STRUCTURE OF THE CORPORATE DEBT RESTRUCTURING MECHANISM

The corporate debt restructuring mechanism system has a three-tier structure. At the top is the Corporate Debt Restructuring Standing Forum and its Core Group. At the second layer is the corporate debt restructuring Empowered Group and thereafter we have the Corporate Debt Restructuring Cell.

The *Corporate Debt Restructuring Standing Forum* has as its permanent members Chairmen and Managing Directors of all banks, financial institutions such as the Industrial Development Bank of India, Industrial Finance Corporation of India and Chairman of Indian Banks Association. The Life Insurance Corporation of India &

---

22. There also exists a possibility of court intervention through public interest litigation.
23. RBI Circular dated 23 August 2001.
24. RBI Circular dated 10 November 2005.
25. As these institutions are owned by the central government, they generally comply with the directions issued.

Unit Trust of India can also participate in it. As the very structure and representative character of the Standing Forum suggests, this body is there essentially to lay down the policies and guidelines as to how the system of corporate debt restructuring should operate and thereafter review and monitor the programme. As a policy making body it lays down the important parameters to be taken into account in restructuring e.g. minimum level of promoter sacrifice, maximum period to be taken into account for a unit to become viable, which complicated cases should get special treatment, etc. The guidelines are also supposed to address the modalities for enforcement of the corporate debt restructuring mechanism, the time frame within which it should be done and as to how to deal with the operational difficulties which might be experienced in the functioning of the Empowered Group. One important area of concern of the guidelines is ensuring that over optimistic projections (e.g. of capacity utilization of the plant, future demand of products, price expected from sale of products, margin of profit in operations, raw material availability, comparative national and international competitiveness) are not assumed while preparing or approving the restructuring proposals. While the Corporate Debt Restructuring Standing Forum has to ensure the smooth functioning of the Empowered Group and Corporate Debt Restructuring Cell, there is a Core Group to guide and assist it in taking decisions relating to policy. The Core Group consists of Chief Executives of the financial institutions that have the greatest bearing on decision making because they are the biggest lenders and are associated with most of the big loans (Industrial Development Bank of India, State Bank of India, ICICI Bank Ltd., Bank of Baroda, Bank of India, Punjab National Bank and Chairman and Vice Chairman of Indian Banks Association). It is hoped that their wide-spread exposure would help in formulation of standards which will have a common thread through them.

The next layer is the Corporate Debt Restructuring Empowered Group which finally decides on the specific cases of corporate debt restructuring as per the guidelines of the Corporate Debt Restructuring Standing Forum. Since its work consists of looking into specific individual cases, the composition of the Corporate Debt Restructuring Empowered Group will first of all have to necessarily reflect the lenders of the troubled debtor. It consists of executive director level representatives of financial institutions and banks which have an exposure to the debtor. The high level of representation is there so that they can take decisions on behalf of their financial institution/banks. The RBI Circular issued in November 2005 also requires that the concerned creditor should authorize its chief executive officer and/or executive director to decide on the restructuring packages. In addition, so as to maintain a continuity in the discussion/decision making process and also so as to speed it up, the same person is required to represent the creditor in the Corporate Debt Restructuring Empowered Group meetings. For guidance of the creditors the Corporate Debt Restructuring Empowered Group also consists of representatives (executive director level) of Industrial Development Bank of India, ICICI Bank and State Bank of India as they bring their experience in corporate debt restructuring proposals and because most of the proposals generally involve them. Further, this ensures that individual restructuring proposals would follow certain broad parameters. However, it may be noted that they are not allowed to participate in the voting on the proposals.

The *Corporate Debt Restructuring Empowered Group* first of all looks into the preliminary reports of request for restructuring submitted to it by the Corporate Debt Restructuring Cell. Only after it ascertains that the restructuring is prima facie feasible and the enterprise has the potential to become viable as per policies and guidelines of the Corporate Debt Restructuring Standing Forum, will a detailed restructuring package be worked out by the Corporate Debt Restructuring Cell with the help of the lead institution (usually the major creditor to the enterprise). When the restructuring package is submitted to the Corporate Debt Restructuring Empowered Group, it will after examining the viability and chances of rehabilitation of the enterprise decide on the package within a time span of ninety days of reference to Corporate Debt Restructuring Cell. In some cases, for sufficient reasons, the time span may be extended to 180 days. To decide on whether the time span should be increased or not, the Corporate Debt Restructuring Empowered Group will have to take into account certain parameters, applied individually taking into account each enterprises' circumstances and peculiarities. The Corporate Debt Restructuring Empowered Group while deciding on the viability of restructuring has to take into account parameters like the return on capital employed, debt service coverage ratio, gap between internal rate of return and cost of fund and the extent of sacrifice entailed and proposed. The decision of the Corporate Debt Restructuring Empowered Group will be final and shall be taken on the basis of exposure of the creditors to the company, irrespective of the nature of exposure. So those who are secured or unsecured creditors, or who have provided term loan or working capital finance are on the same footing. Seventy five percent of creditors by value and 60 per cent of them by number have to vote in favour of the restructuring for it to pass.

The *Corporate Debt Restructuring Cell* is the first step in the restructuring exercise. It has staff on deputation from participating banks and financial institutions, but there is no prohibition on taking outside professional help. The costs are met by contributions by members of the corporate debt restructuring system. The cell does an initial scrutiny of restructuring proposals and after collecting information puts the matter before the Corporate Debt Restructuring Empowered Group, which within one month decides as to the prima facie feasibility of the restructuring proposal. If found to be feasible, then the Corporate Debt Restructuring Cell, and the lead institution or major creditor to the enterprise will work out a plan within 30 days with the help of other creditors and experts. It is based on this proposal that the final decision is taken by Empowered Group.

B. OPERATION OF THE CORPORATE DEBT RESTRUCTURING MECHANISM

The benefit of this mechanism is not available to those cases where there is only one creditor bank or financial institution. This is because the concerned creditor can in any case enter into a compromise with the defaulter and there is no need to bind the other creditors to the arrangement. Thereafter, it is at present applicable only to those cases where the exposure of banks and financial institutions is more than INR 100,000,000. The reason being that it is these cases which present a threat to the financial system and also the costs involved in working out the package and its implementation be justified. Cases which are with the Board for Industrial and Financial Reconstruction are not eligible to be considered under the system, so as to prevent conflict with the Board for Industrial and Financial Reconstruction, which also deals with the case on the same basis by and large. But the Core Group can recommend exceptional large value corporate debt restructuring cases for consideration on a case to case basis though the package can be implemented only after getting the approval of the Board for Industrial and Financial Reconstruction. Those corporates, which had in the past been found to be indulging in fraud or malfeasance, even if only with one bank or financial institution, are not eligible to be considered. The operation of the system involves the creditor waiving off his rights so as to enable repayment for an entity which is finding it difficult to repay due to genuine reasons. The system should not operate in a manner so that it creates a moral hazard of deliberate default so as to get concessions from creditors. The Core Group, however, can relax in those cases where it is satisfied that the concerned debtor was classified as a wilful defaulter, in a non-transparent manner and he can repay the loan if he is given an opportunity under the corporate debt restructuring system. But it is worth noting that there is no necessity that the company be sick or be in default or an account be a non-performing asset for reference to the corporate debt restructuring system.

For reference to corporate debt restructuring system of a concerned company/enterprise all that is required is that either creditor or creditors, having a minimum 20 per cent by value exposure to the debtor enterprise's working capital loans or term loans, refer it to the system or they support the application by the debtor for consideration. At the time of reference the debtor enterprise has to enter into a debtor-creditor agreement. In addition to contractually binding them to the future restructuring proposal upon their approaching the system, with necessary enforcement and penal clauses, the debtor-creditor agreement also has a stand still clause which is binding for 90 days or 180 days, as the case may be, on both the parties. This stand still clause prevents the parties from taking recourse to any legal action (other than criminal action) during the said period so that restructuring exercise takes place without any outside intervention. The directors of the referred company are not supposed to resign from the board of directors during this period and the debtor also agrees that the period of limitation on all relevant matters and documents is extended by the duration of the period.

C. VARIOUS RESTRUCTURING OPTIONS/METHODS EMPLOYED IN CORPORATE DEBT RESTRUCTURING SYSTEM

The corporate debt restructuring system has three different aspects broadly i.e. promoter sacrifice, creditor sacrifice and creditor's assistance. The system requires the creditors to forsake some of their rights and money. But before this is done or is agreeable to them, the concerned promoter of the company (who are the final beneficiaries) and shareholders are required to sacrifice as well. The various sacrifices are in the form of reduction in share capital, changing the composition of the share capital from pure equity to equity and preference with the latter being redeemable at a long date (under 20 years) with only a notional dividend (.01 per cent) being paid on them,[26] conversion of debt due from company to the promoter as equity or preference share, bringing in of additional capital by the promoter or merging the company with an another healthy profit making company controlled by the promoter.[27] The methods of extricating sacrifice from the promoter enumerated here are not exhaustive. But from the sacrifice entailed from the promoters, what is analyzed is whether the promoters are as keen and interested in revival of the unit as the creditors or whether the promoters are more free riders. The sacrifice also ensures that the moral hazard of indifferent/bad managements being rewarded with better and more lenient deals due to the operation of the corporate debt restructuring system is taken care of.

The second aspect of the corporate debt restructuring system is the sacrifice by the creditors. It can entail extension of the repayment period of the existing debt and rescheduling it, reduction of the high interest charged on loan (either the interest rate might be lowered uniformly for the full amount or the loan might be divided in two parts),[28] deferring the interest charged on loan or taking up zero coupon bonds in lieu of part of it, converting part of debt or accrued interest into capital of the company either as equity shares or cumulative redeemable preference shares (sometimes the promoter or promoter group company is required to guarantee its representation of future returns, i.e. internal rate of return on capital employed, by providing that it will buy the converted equity shares at a particular rate in future whenever offered to it)[29] and waiver of penalty. The package usually will be an amalgamation of the *above* with the weightage given to different components/methods taking into account the peculiarities of the case.[30]

---

26. The tool of cancellation of equity share and issuance of preference share in lieu of them was adopted in the restructuring of Essar Steel Limited that went in for corporate debt restructuring in 2002.
27. The restructuring of Jindal Vijaynagar Steel Ltd ('**JVSL**') would be a good example to study the contribution of the promoters to restructuring. Herein, first, a group company was demerged and a part of its business was merged with JSVL to give a boost to JVSL. Secondly, the company's promoters were obligated to contribute INR 1,080,000,000 only towards equity by a certain fixed date. Third, four equity shares out of every ten held by its shareholders were converted into four low interest, 0.01 per cent cumulative redeemable preference shares ('CRPS') of INR 10 each.
28. One part of the loan might an early repayment schedule and so low interest is charged on it while the other part of the loan could have a longer repayment schedule and so a higher interest rate is charged on it.
29. For example a key feature of the JVSL debt restructuring scheme was the imposition of a requirement on promoters to purchase equity shares worth INR 1,080,000,000 of the company by a certain fixed date.
30. In the Essar Steel corporate debt restructuring, debt owed by Essar Steel to secured Indian lenders was restructured in the following manner:

    1. All amounts towards penal interest and liquidated damages that remained due and unpaid up to a cut off date were waived off.
    2. Overdue and unpaid compound interest overdue and unpaid as on a fixed cut off date was converted to Zero Coupon Debt repayable in 48 equal monthly installments and secured by first *pari-passu* charge on the fixed assets of Essar Steel.

The third aspect of corporate debt restructuring system is provision of additional finance that may be required by the concerned corporate that is to be revived. Here, the corporate debt restructuring system discriminates between the types of debtors referred to it. Category I corporate debt restructuring scheme is applicable where the concerned account is a standard[31] or sub-standard account[32] (it is of this category if it is so in the books of minimum 90 per cent of its creditors by value). Since, the account is standard or substandard and 75 per cent of creditors by value have agreed, it is perceived that further lending to the concerned company is not that risky. So all creditors, whether working capital or term finance lenders, if there is in the package any provision for additional finance, have to provide loan at a pro-rata basis. Of course, they can arrange for a new or existing lender to take up their commitments. In case the concerned creditor is not the one which has voted for the proposal, then it also has the option of not providing the additional finance. But to ensure that the concerned creditor does not have the free rider advantage, in lieu of it, it will have to forego the first year's interest payable as per the restructured package and it will be paid, without compounding along with the last instalment of the principal. It not only entails a small financial price but also means the unco-operative bank or institution will be prevented from cleaning up its book for a year more. Category II corporate debt restructuring system is for those accounts which are classified as doubtful. In such cases, there is no requirement that under the package, the existing creditors shall provide any additional finance. It will be for the creditor to arrange for it.

Lastly all corporate debt restructuring which are approved will give a right to the debtor to prepay the credit and to the creditors to accelerate the payment.

---

3. Simple interest charged in excess of 14 per cent per annum in respect of Rupee term loans and Non Convertible Debentures, between a fixed time-period was converted into 10 per cent Cumulative Redeemable Preference Shares (CRPS) redeemable in 12 equal monthly installments.
4. All amount of Rupee debt, including, simple interest due and accrued as on a fixed cut off date, devolved deferred payment guarantees and lease assistance and non-convertible debentures after waiver and conversion as discussed *above* was restructured as follows:

   (a) Pro rata conversion of rupee debt aggregating up to INR 1,750,000,000 to equity share capital at par;
   (b) 40 per cent of the Rupee debt was converted to fixed rate foreign currency loan or reduced rate Rupee term loan, carrying fixed interest rate of 8 per cent per annum.
   (c) The balance amount of the Rupee debt continued as Rupee term loan, carrying fixed interest of 14 per cent per annum and repayable in 156 monthly installments.

31. As per RBI's Master Circular dated 1 July 2005 on Prudential norms on Income Recognition, Asset Classification and Provisioning pertaining to Advances ('Prudential Norms'), if arrears of interest and principal are paid by the borrower in the case of loan accounts classified as non-performing, the account should no longer be treated as non-performing and may be classified as 'standard' accounts.
32. As per Prudential Norms, a sub-standard asset would be one, which has remained non-performing for a period less than or equal to 12 months.

D.   Legal Aspects of the Corporate Debt Restructuring Mechanism

The Legal basis of the corporate debt restructuring mechanism is not based on any statutory provision. The RBI has come out with guidelines on it and has provided suitable carrots for the acceding banks. First of all, all the major financial institutions and all banks are part of the Inter Creditor Agreement, which has necessary enforcement and penal clauses. This agreement oversees that banks adhere to what was agreed.

Thereafter, the debtors are governed by the Debtor Creditor Agreements entered into. Now the RBI envisages that the debtors be required to, at the time of original loan documentation itself to accede to the Debtor Creditor Agreements. Though the Inter Creditor Agreements are valid for three years, however, if the Reserve Bank of India wants, it can have the agreement renewed. The provision for corporate debt restructuring in future debtor creditor agreements means that even if Inter Creditor Agreement is not renewed, the system may continue on the basis of an enforceable Debtor Creditor Agreement.

In addition the Reserve Bank of India has sought to provide some carrots in the form of treatment of assets on the balance sheet. For this purpose, the RBI has also sought to ensure that it does not become a source of window dressing by banks or financial institutions. So corporate debt restructuring benefit with regard to asset classification and write offs and provisioning will be available only if certain conditions are fulfilled. So first of all restructuring of the company should have been done for the first time only. The second condition is that unit should become viable in seven years and repayment period for restructured debts should not exceed ten years.[33] The third requirement is that promoters' sacrifice in the form of writing off of loans from group companies, reduction of capital, etc. or additional funds bought by them should be at least 15 per cent of the sacrifice made by the creditors. Lastly, the corporate debt restructuring requires that promoters should give personal guarantee except where the unit is affected by external factors like economic downturn or something which affects the concerned industry. It should be noted here that the corporate debt restructuring is not barred in cases which do not come within the *above*. Only the palliatives to banks will be unavailable.

Different components and different accounts i.e. standard, sub-standard or doubtful are restructured differently. The restructuring may involve rescheduling of the payment of principal, moratorium on payment of interest or extension of moratorium, conversion of principal into equity and interest into equity, conversion of principal and interest (either or both) into other marketable securities like debentures and zero coupon bounds.

---

33. Here it is not clear as to whether the ten year period within which the debt should be repaid begins from the date of viability or restructuring. Further, it is unclear whether the benefit is denied to the entire tranche of restructured debt or only to that tranche which is to be paid after the expiry of ten years.

In case of rescheduling of instalments of principal, if the four conditions mentioned *above* are satisfied and if the loan/credit facility is fully secured, then the assets would be continued to be treated as they were before the rescheduling of the principal. Similar is the treatment of reduction in interest. So standard asset continues as standard and sub-standard and doubtful continues to be so as they were before rescheduling. But the advantage here is that if the bank has provided for the sacrifice in its balance sheet then one year after the date when the first payment or interest became due, subsequent to corporate debt restructuring, the bank can upgrade the asset to the standard category.

Where the outstanding asset is converted into equity, in those cases, if it is quoted equity,[34] then the quoted value will have to be taken into account. If it is not quoted then the value is break-up value[35] in case of standard assets and Rupee one in other cases until it is upgraded. If interest is converted into equity then it shall be the amount of interest or quoted value whichever is lower, but if it is not quoted then it shall not be recognized.

If the debt is converted into other debt instruments i.e. debentures, zero coupon bonds, etc. then the asset class does not change and therefore if it is sub-standard or doubtful then income will be recognized only on realization basis. Also, in those cases where by corporate debt restructuring, moratorium on interest payment is bought about or moratorium is extended the loan asset is downgraded.

So we observe that the RBI, though it has given some benefits to banks when corporate debt restructuring is implemented in an account, but it has still sought to ensure that the balance sheet of the banks should reflect the true state of the account. Also, one should remember that balance sheet treatment is bank specific and not of all banks involved in the concerned corporate debt restructuring.

VI. CONCLUSION

Corporate debt restructuring was introduced by the RBI in 2001. In the approximately five years of its functioning 175 accounts involving INR 817,160,000,000 have been referred to corporate debt restructuring system. Many of these units have turned around, so in a way it can be said that corporate debt restructuring system has been helpful in arresting and to some extent reversing the ballooning of non performing assets in the balance sheets of the banks. But it should be remembered that one of the reasons for the smooth running and relative success of the mechanism has been that almost all the big lenders (except ICICI Bank) were owned or controlled by the Government. In future, as the corporate bond market grows and different funds or financial intermediaries neither owned or controlled by the Government nor regulated by RBI, play an increasingly important role, the corporate debt restructuring mechanism might face problems. These new players,

---

34. That is, if it is quoted in a stock exchange.
35. Break up value is the value which the share would command if the company winds up. Practically, it is the book value in most of the cases.

together with individual investors might not be willing to agree to the reduction in their dues nor to lend further cash. There might even be cases where there is another regulator which prohibits further lending. So while the success of corporate debt restructuring has prompted the RBI to envisage its continuance in future, the evolution of Indian capital and financial markets might not make its operation as smooth in future and one may have to revert to the Companies Act to resolve the problem.

ANNEX: KEY LEGISLATION

1. BACKGROUND

1.1. In spite of their best efforts and intentions, sometimes corporates find themselves in financial difficulty because of factors beyond their control and also due to certain internal reasons. For the revival of the corporates as well as for the safety of the money lent by the banks and FIs, timely support through restructuring in genuine cases is called for. However, delay in agreement amongst different lending institutions often comes in the way of such endeavours.

1.2. Based on the experience in other countries like the U.K., Thailand, Korea, etc. of putting in place institutional mechanism for restructuring of corporate debt and need for a similar mechanism in India, a Corporate Debt Restructuring System was evolved, and detailed guidelines were issued vide circular DBOD No. BP.BC. 15/21.04.114/2000–01 dated August 23, 2001 for implementation by banks. Subsequently based on the recommendations made by the Working Group to make the operations of the CDR mechanism more efficient (Chairman: Shri Vepa Kamesam, Deputy Governor, RBI. The group was constituted pursuant to the announcement made by the Finance Minister in the Union Budget 2002–2003), and consultations with the Government, the guidelines on Corporate Debt Restructuring system were revised in terms of our circular DBOD No. BP.BC. 68/21.04.114/2002–03 dated February 5, 2003.

1.3. A Special Group was constituted in September 2004 with Smt. S. Gopinath, Deputy Governor, RBI, as the Chairperson to review and suggest changes/improvements, if any, in the CDR mechanism. Based on the suggestions of the Special Group, and the feedback received on the draft guidelines, the CDR Guidelines have been further revised. The revised guidelines are in supersession of the extant guidelines outlined in the aforesaid circular dated February 5, 2003.

1.4. One of the main features of the restructuring under CDR system is the provision of two categories of debt restructuring under the CDR system. Accounts, which are classified as 'standard' and 'sub-standard' in the books of the creditors, will be restructured under the first category (Category 1). Accounts which are classified as 'doubtful' in the books of the creditors would be restructured under the second category (Category 2).

The main features of the CDR mechanism are given *below*:

2. OBJECTIVE

The objective of the Corporate Debt Restructuring (CDR) framework is to ensure timely and transparent mechanism for restructuring the corporate debts of viable entities facing problems, outside the purview of BIFR, DRT and other legal proceedings, for the benefit of all concerned. In particular, the framework will aim at preserving viable corporates that are affected by certain internal and external

India 343

factors and minimize the losses to the creditors and other stakeholders through an orderly and coordinated restructuring programme.

3.   STRUCTURE

CDR system in the country will have a three tier structure:
- CDR Standing Forum and its Core Group
- CDR Empowered Group
- CDR Cell

3.1.   CDR Standing Forum

3.1.1. The CDR Standing Forum would be the representative general body of all financial institutions and banks participating in CDR system. All financial institutions and banks should participate in the system in their own interest. CDR Standing Forum will be a self-empowered body, which will lay down policies and guidelines, and monitor the progress of corporate debt restructuring.

3.1.2. The Forum will also provide an official platform for both the creditors and borrowers (by consultation) to amicably and collectively evolve policies and guidelines for working out debt restructuring plans in the interests of all concerned.

3.1.3. The CDR Standing Forum shall comprise of Chairman & Managing Director, Industrial Development Bank of India Ltd; Chairman, State Bank of India; Managing Director & CEO, ICICI Bank Limited; Chairman, Indian Banks' Association as well as Chairmen and Managing Directors of all banks and financial institutions participating as permanent members in the system. Since institutions like Unit Trust of India, General Insurance Corporation, Life Insurance Corporation may have assumed exposures on certain borrowers, these institutions may participate in the CDR system. The Forum will elect its Chairman for a period of one year and the principle of rotation will be followed in the subsequent years. However, the Forum may decide to have a Working Chairman as a whole-time officer to guide and carry out the decisions of the CDR Standing Forum. The RBI would not be a member of the CDR Standing Forum and Core Group. Its role will be confined to providing broad guidelines.

3.1.4 The CDR Standing Forum shall meet at least once every six months and would review and monitor the progress of corporate debt restructuring system. The Forum would also lay down the policies and guidelines including those relating to the critical parameters for restructuring (for example, maximum period for a unit to become viable under a restructuring package, minimum level of promoters' sacrifice etc.) to be followed by the CDR Empowered Group and CDR Cell for debt restructuring and would ensure their smooth functioning and adherence to the prescribed time schedules for debt restructuring. It can also review any individual decisions of the CDR Empowered Group and CDR Cell. The CDR Standing Forum may also formulate guidelines for dispensing special treatment to those cases, which are complicated and are likely to be delayed beyond the time frame prescribed for processing.

3.1.5. A CDR Core Group will be carved out of the CDR Standing Forum to assist the Standing Forum in convening the meetings and taking decisions relating to policy, on behalf of the Standing Forum. The Core Group will consist of Chief Executives of Industrial Development Bank of India Ltd., State Bank of India, ICICI Bank Ltd, Bank of Baroda, Bank of India, Punjab National Bank, Indian Banks' Association and Deputy Chairman of Indian Banks' Association representing foreign banks in India.

3.1.5. The CDR Core Group would lay down the policies and guidelines to be followed by the CDR Empowered Group and CDR Cell for debt restructuring. These guidelines shall also suitably address the operational difficulties experienced in the functioning of the CDR Empowered Group. The CDR Core Group shall also prescribe the PERT chart for processing of cases referred to the CDR system and decide on the modalities for enforcement of the time frame. The CDR Core Group shall also lay down guidelines to ensure that over-optimistic projections are not assumed while preparing/approving restructuring proposals especially with regard to capacity utilization, price of products, profit margin, demand, availability of raw materials, input-output ratio and likely impact of imports/international cost competitiveness.

3.2. CDR Empowered Group

3.2.1 The individual cases of corporate debt restructuring shall be decided by the CDR Empowered Group, consisting of ED level representatives of Industrial Development Bank of India Ltd., ICICI Bank Ltd. and State Bank of India as standing members, in addition to ED level representatives of financial institutions and banks who have an exposure to the concerned company. While the standing members will facilitate the conduct of the Group's meetings, voting will be in proportion to the exposure of the creditors only. In order to make the CDR Empowered Group effective and broad based and operate efficiently and smoothly, it would have to be ensured that participating institutions/banks approve a panel of senior officers to represent them in the CDR Empowered Group and ensure that they depute officials only from among the panel to attend the meetings of CDR Empowered Group. Further, nominees who attend the meeting pertaining to one account should invariably attend all the meetings pertaining to that account instead of deputing their representatives.

3.2.2 The level of representation of banks/financial institutions on the CDR Empowered Group should be at a sufficiently senior level to ensure that concerned bank/FI abides by the necessary commitments including sacrifices, made towards debt restructuring. There should be a general authorization by the respective Boards of the participating institutions/banks in favour of their representatives on the CDR Empowered Group, authorizing them to take decisions on behalf of their organization, regarding restructuring of debts of individual corporates.

3.2.3 The CDR Empowered Group will consider the preliminary report of all cases of requests of restructuring, submitted to it by the CDR Cell. After the Empowered Group decides that restructuring of the company is prima-facie feasible and the enterprise is potentially viable in terms of the policies and guidelines evolved by Standing Forum, the detailed restructuring package will be worked out by the CDR Cell in conjunction with the Lead Institution. However, if the lead institution faces difficulties in working out the detailed restructuring package, the participating banks/financial institutions should decide upon the alternate institution/bank which would work out the detailed restructuring package at the first meeting of the Empowered Group when the preliminary report of the CDR Cell comes up for consideration.

3.2.4 The CDR Empowered Group would be mandated to look into each case of debt restructuring, examine the viability and rehabilitation potential of the Company and approve the restructuring package within a specified time frame of 90 days, or at best within 180 days of reference to the Empowered Group. The CDR Empowered Group shall decide on the acceptable viability benchmark levels on the following illustrative parameters, which may be applied on a case-by-case basis, based on the merits of each case:

- Return on Capital Employed (ROCE),
- Debt Service Coverage Ratio (DSCR),
- Gap between the Internal Rate of Return (IRR) and the Cost of Fund (CoF),
- Extent of sacrifice.

3.2.5 The Board of each bank/FI should authorize its Chief Executive Officer (CEO) and/or Executive Director (ED) to decide on the restructuring package in respect of cases referred to the CDR system, with the requisite requirements to meet the control needs. CDR Empowered Group will meet on two or three occasions in respect of each borrowal account. This will provide an opportunity to the participating members to seek proper authorizations from their CEO/ED, in case of need, in respect of those cases where the critical parameters of restructuring are beyond the authority delegated to him/her.

3.2.6 The decisions of the CDR Empowered Group shall be final. If restructuring of debt is found to be viable and feasible and approved by the Empowered Group, the company would be put on the restructuring mode. If restructuring is not found viable, the creditors would then be free to take necessary steps for immediate recovery of dues and/or liquidation or winding up of the company, collectively or individually.

3.3.   CDR Cell

3.3.1 The CDR Standing Forum and the CDR Empowered Group will be assisted by a CDR Cell in all their functions. The CDR Cell will make the initial scrutiny of the proposals received from borrowers/creditors, by calling for proposed rehabilitation plan and other information and put up the matter before the CDR

Empowered Group, within one month to decide whether rehabilitation is prima facie feasible. If found feasible, the CDR Cell will proceed to prepare detailed Rehabilitation Plan with the help of creditors and, if necessary, experts to be engaged from outside. If not found prima facie feasible, the creditors may start action for recovery of their dues.

3.3.2 All references for corporate debt restructuring by creditors or borrowers will be made to the CDR Cell. It shall be the responsibility of the lead institution/ major stakeholder to the corporate, to work out a preliminary restructuring plan in consultation with other stakeholders and submit to the CDR Cell within one month. The CDR Cell will prepare the restructuring plan in terms of the general policies and guidelines approved by the CDR Standing Forum and place for consideration of the Empowered Group within 30 days for decision. The Empowered Group can approve or suggest modifications but ensure that a final decision is taken within a total period of 90 days. However, for sufficient reasons the period can be extended up to a maximum of 180 days from the date of reference to the CDR Cell.

3.4 The CDR Standing Forum, the CDR Empowered Group and CDR Cell is at present housed in Industrial Development Bank of India Ltd. However, it may be shifted to another place if considered necessary, as may be decided by the Standing Forum. The administrative and other costs shall be shared by all financial institutions and banks. The sharing pattern shall be as determined by the Standing Forum.

3.5 CDR Cell will have adequate members of staff deputed from banks and financial institutions. The CDR Cell may also take outside professional help. The cost in operating the CDR mechanism including CDR Cell will be met from contribution of the financial institutions and banks in the Core Group at the rate of Rs.50 lakh each and contribution from other institutions and banks at the rate of Rs.5 lakh each.

4. OTHER FEATURES

4.1. Eligibility Criteria

4.1.1 The scheme will not apply to accounts involving only one financial institution or one bank. The CDR mechanism will cover only multiple banking accounts/ syndication/consortium accounts of corporate borrowers with outstanding fund-based and non-fund based exposure of Rs.10 crore and above by banks and institutions.

4.1.2 The Category 1 CDR system will be applicable only to accounts classified as 'standard' and 'sub-standard'. There may be a situation where a small portion of debt by a bank might be classified as doubtful. In that situation, if the account has been classified as 'standard'/'substandard' in the books of at least 90 per cent of creditors (by value), the same would be treated as standard/substandard, only for the purpose of judging the account as eligible for CDR, in the books of the remaining 10 per cent of creditors. There would be no requirement of the account/company being sick, NPA or being in default for a specified period before reference to the CDR

India 347

system. However, potentially viable cases of NPAs will get priority. This approach would provide the necessary flexibility and facilitate timely intervention for debt restructuring. Prescribing any milestone(s) may not be necessary, since the debt restructuring exercise is being triggered by banks and financial institutions or with their consent.

4.1.3. While corporates indulging in frauds and malfeasance even in a single bank will continue to remain ineligible for restructuring under CDR mechanism as hitherto, the Core group may review the reasons for classification of the borrower as wilful defaulter specially in old cases where the manner of classification of a borrower as a wilful defaulter was not transparent and satisfy itself that the borrower is in a position to rectify the wilful default provided he is granted an opportunity under the CDR mechanism. Such exceptional cases may be admitted for restructuring with the approval of the Core Group only. The Core Group may ensure that cases involving frauds or diversion of funds with malafide intent are not covered.

4.1.4. The accounts where recovery suits have been filed by the creditors against the company, may be eligible for consideration under the CDR system provided, the initiative to resolve the case under the CDR system is taken by at least 75 per cent of the creditors (by value) and 60 per cent of creditors (by number).

4.1.5. BIFR cases are not eligible for restructuring under the CDR system. However, large value BIFR cases, may be eligible for restructuring under the CDR system if specifically recommended by the CDR Core Group. The Core Group shall recommend exceptional BIFR cases on a case-to-case basis for consideration under the CDR system. It should be ensured that the lending institutions complete all the formalities in seeking the approval from BIFR before implementing the package.

4.2. Reference to CDR System

4.2.1 Reference to Corporate Debt Restructuring System could be triggered by (i) any or more of the creditor who have minimum 20 per cent share in either working capital or term finance, or (ii) by the concerned corporate, if supported by a bank or financial institution having stake as in (i) *above*.

4.2.2 Though flexibility is available whereby the creditors could either consider restructuring outside the purview of the CDR system or even initiate legal proceedings where warranted, banks/FIs should review all eligible cases where the exposure of the financial system is more than Rs.100 crore and decide about referring the case to CDR system or to proceed under the new Securitization and Reconstruction of Financial Assets and Enforcement of Securities Interest Act, 2002 or to file a suit in DRT etc.

4.3. Legal Basis

4.3.1 CDR is a non-statutory mechanism which is a voluntary system based on Debtor-Creditor Agreement (DCA) and Inter-Creditor Agreement (ICA). The

Debtor-Creditor Agreement (DCA) and the Inter-Creditor Agreement (ICA) shall provide the legal basis to the CDR mechanism. The debtors shall have to accede to the DCA, either at the time of original loan documentation (for future cases) or at the time of reference to Corporate Debt Restructuring Cell. Similarly, all participants in the CDR mechanism through their membership of the Standing Forum shall have to enter into a legally binding agreement, with necessary enforcement and penal clauses, to operate the System through laid-down policies and guidelines. The ICA signed by the creditors will be initially valid for a period of 3 years and subject to renewal for further periods of 3 years thereafter. The lenders in foreign currency outside the country are not a part of CDR system. Such creditors and also creditors like GIC, LIC, UTI, etc., who have not joined the CDR system, could join CDR mechanism of a particular corporate by signing transaction to transaction ICA, wherever they have exposure to such corporate.

4.3.2 The Inter-Creditor Agreement would be a legally binding agreement amongst the creditors, with necessary enforcement and penal clauses, wherein the creditors would commit themselves to abide by the various elements of CDR system. Further, the creditors shall agree that if 75 per cent of creditors by value and 60 per cent of the creditors by number, agree to a restructuring package of an existing debt (i.e., debt outstanding), the same would be binding on the remaining creditors. Since Category 1 CDR Scheme covers only standard and sub-standard accounts, which in the opinion of 75 per cent of the creditors by value and 60 per cent of creditors by number, are likely to become performing after introduction of the CDR package, it is expected that all other creditors (i.e., those outside the minimum 75 per cent by value and 60 per cent by number) would be willing to participate in the entire CDR package, including the agreed additional financing.

Other Aspects

4.3.3 In order to improve effectiveness of the CDR mechanism a clause may be incorporated in the loan agreements involving consortium/syndicate accounts whereby all creditors, including those which are not members of the CDR mechanism, agree to be bound by the terms of the restructuring package that may be approved under the CDR mechanism, as and when restructuring may become necessary.

4.4. Stand-Still Clause

4.4.1 One of the most important elements of Debtor-Creditor Agreement would be 'stand still' agreement binding for 90 days, or 180 days by both sides. Under this clause, both the debtor and creditor(s) shall agree to a legally binding 'stand-still' whereby both the parties commit themselves not to take recourse to any other legal action during the 'stand-still' period, this would be necessary for enabling the CDR System to undertake the necessary debt restructuring exercise without any outside intervention, judicial or otherwise. However, the stand-still clause will be applicable only to any civil action either by the borrower or any lender against the other

India 349

party and will not cover any criminal action. Further, during the stand-still period, outstanding foreign exchange forward contracts, derivative products, etc., can be crystallized, provided the borrower is agreeable to such crystallization. The borrower will additionally undertake that during the stand-still period the documents will stand extended for the purpose of limitation and also that he will not approach any other authority for any relief and the directors of the borrowing company will not resign from the Board of Directors during the stand-still period.

4.4.2 During pendency of the case with the CDR system, the usual asset classification norms would continue to apply. The process of reclassification of an asset should not stop merely because the case is referred to the CDR Cell. However, if a restructuring package under the CDR system is approved by the Empowered Group, and the approved package is implemented within four months from the date of approval, the asset classification status may be restored to the position which existed when the reference to the Cell was made. Consequently, any additional provisions made by banks towards deterioration in the asset classification status during the pendency of the case with the CDR system may be reversed.

4.4.3 If an approved package is not implemented within four months after the date of approval by the Empowered Group, it would indicate that the success of the package is uncertain. In that case, the asset classification status of the account should not be restored to the position as on the date of reference to the CDR Cell.

4.5. Additional Finance

4.5.1 Additional finance, if any, is to be provided by all creditors of a 'standard' or 'substandard account' irrespective of whether they are working capital or term creditors, on a pro-rata basis. In case for any internal reason, any creditor (outside the minimum 75 per cent and 60 per cent) does not wish to commit additional financing, that creditor will have an option in accordance with the provisions of para 4.6.

4.5.2 The additional finance may be treated as 'standard asset', up to a period of one year after the first interest/principal payment, whichever is earlier, falls due under the approved restructuring package. However, in the case of accounts where the existing facilities are classified as 'sub-standard' and 'doubtful', interest income on the additional finance should be recognized only on cash basis. If the restructured asset does not qualify for upgradation at the end of the *above* specified one year period, the additional finance shall be placed in the same asset classification category as the restructured debt.

4.5.3 The providers of additional finance, whether existing creditors or new creditors, shall have a preferential claim, to be worked out under the restructuring package, over the providers of existing finance with respect to the cash flows out of recoveries, in respect of the additional exposure.

4.6. Exit Option

4.6.1. As stated in para 4.5.1 a creditor (outside the minimum 75 per cent and 60 per cent) who for any internal reason does not wish to commit additional finance will have an option. At the same time, in order to avoid the 'free rider' problem, it is necessary to provide some disincentive to the creditor who wishes to exercise this option. Such creditors can either (a) arrange for its share of additional finance to be provided by a new or existing creditor, or (b) agree to the deferment of the first year's interest due to it after the CDR package becomes effective. The first year's deferred interest as mentioned *above*, without compounding, will be payable along with the last instalment of the principal due to the creditor.

4.6.2. In addition, the exit option will also be available to all lenders within the minimum 75 per cent and 60 per cent provided the purchaser agrees to abide by restructuring package approved by the Empowered Group. The exiting lenders may be allowed to continue with their existing level of exposure to the borrower provided they tie up with either the existing lenders or fresh lenders taking up their share of additional finance.

4.6.3 The lenders who wish to exit from the package would have the option to sell their existing share to either the existing lenders or fresh lenders, at an appropriate price, which would be decided mutually between the exiting lender and the taking over lender. The new lenders shall rank on par with the existing lenders for repayment and servicing of the dues since they have taken over the existing dues to the exiting lender.

4.6.4. In order to bring more flexibility in the exit option, One Time Settlement can also be considered, wherever necessary, as a part of the restructuring package. If an account with any creditor is subjected to One Time Settlement (OTS) by a borrower before its reference to the CDR mechanism, any fulfilled commitments under such OTS may not be reversed under the restructured package. Further payment commitments of the borrower arising out of such OTS may be factored into the restructuring package.

4.7. Conversion Option

4.7.1 The CDR Empowered Group, while deciding the restructuring package, should decide on the issue regarding convertibility (into equity) option as a part of restructuring exercise whereby the banks/financial institutions shall have the right to convert a portion of the restructured amount into equity, keeping in view the statutory requirement under Section 19 of the Banking Regulation Act, 1949, (in the case of banks) and relevant SEBI regulations.

4.7.2 Equity acquired by way of conversion of debt/overdue interest under the CDR mechanism is allowed to be taken up without seeking prior approval from RBI, even if by such acquisition the prudential capital market exposure limit prescribed by the RBI is breached, subject to reporting such holdings to RBI, Department of Banking Supervision (DBS), every month along with the regular DSB Return on Asset Quality. However, banks will have to comply with the provisions of Section 19(2) of the Banking Regulation Act 1949.

4.7.3 Acquisition of non-SLR securities by way of conversion of debt is exempted from the mandatory rating requirement and the prudential limit on

India   351

investment in unlisted non-SLR securities prescribed by the RBI, subject to periodical reporting to RBI in the aforesaid DSB return.

4.7.4 The relaxations allowed under paras 4.7.2 and 4.7.3 would be reviewed after a year.

4.8.   Category 2 CDR System

4.8.1. There have been instances where the projects have been found to be viable by the creditors but the accounts could not be taken up for restructuring under the CDR system as they fell under 'doubtful' category. Hence, a second category of CDR is introduced for cases where the accounts have been classified as 'doubtful' in the books of creditors, and if a minimum of 75 per cent of creditors (by value) and 60 per cent creditors (by number) satisfy themselves of the viability of the account and consent for such restructuring, subject to the following conditions:

   i. It will not be binding on the creditors to take up additional financing worked out under the debt restructuring package and the decision to lend or not to lend will depend on each creditor bank/FI separately. In other words, under the proposed second category of the CDR mechanism, the existing loans will only be restructured and it would be up to the promoter to firm up additional financing arrangement with new or existing creditors individually.
   ii. All other norms under the CDR mechanism such as the standstill clause, asset classification status during the pendency of restructuring under CDR, etc., will continue to be applicable to this category also.

4.8.2 No individual case should be referred to RBI. CDR Core Group may take a final decision whether a particular case falls under the CDR guidelines or it does not.

4.8.3 All the other features of the CDR system as applicable to the First Category will also be applicable to cases restructured under the Second Category.

5.   CREDITORS' RIGHTS

All CDR approved packages must incorporate creditors' right to accelerate repayment and borrowers' right to pre-pay. The right of recompense should be based on certain performance criteria to be decided by the Standing Forum.

6.   PRUDENTIAL AND ACCOUNTING ISSUES

6.1.1 Restructuring of corporate debts under CDR system could take place in the following stages:
   a. before commencement of commercial production;
   b. after commencement of commercial production but before the asset has been classified as 'sub-standard';

c. after commencement of commercial production and the asset has been classified as 'sub-standard' or 'doubtful'.

6.1.2 Accounts restructured under CDR system, including accounts classified as 'doubtful' under Category 2 CDR, would be eligible for regulatory concession in asset classification and provisioning on writing off/providing for economic sacrifice stipulated in para 6.2.1(b) and 6.2.3(b) only if

i. Restructuring under CDR mechanism is done for the first time,
ii. The unit becomes viable in 7 years and the repayment period for the restructured debts does not exceed 10 years,
iii. Promoters' sacrifice and additional funds brought by them should be a minimum of 15 per cent of creditors' sacrifice, and
iv. Personal guarantee is offered by the promoter except when the unit is affected by external factors pertaining to the economy and industry.

6.2.1 Treatment of 'standard' accounts restructured under CDR

a. A rescheduling of the instalments of principal alone, at any of the aforesaid first two stages [paragraph 6.1.1 (a) and (b) *above*] would not cause a standard asset to be classified in the sub-standard category, provided conditions (i) to (iv) of Para 6.1.2 are complied with and the loan/credit facility is fully secured.
b. A rescheduling of interest element at any of the foregoing first two stages provided conditions (i) to (iv) of Para 6.1.2 are complied with would not cause an asset to be downgraded to sub-standard category on writing off/ providing for the amount of sacrifice, if any, in the element of interest measured in present value terms. For this purpose, the sacrifice should be computed as the difference between the present value of future interest income reckoned based on the current BPLR as on the date of restructuring plus the appropriate term premium and credit risk premium for the borrower category on the date of restructuring and the interest charged as per the restructuring package discounted by the current BPLR as on the date of restructuring plus appropriate term premium and credit risk premium as on the date of restructuring.

6.2.2 Moratorium under Restructuring

If a standard asset is taken up for restructuring before commencement of production and the restructuring package provides a longer period of moratorium on interest payments beyond the expected date of commercial production/date of commercial production vis-à-vis the original moratorium period, the asset can no more be treated as standard asset. It may, therefore, be classified as sub-standard. The same regulatory treatment will apply if a standard asset is taken up for restructuring after commencement of production and the restructuring package provides for a longer period of moratorium on interest payments than the original moratorium period.

6.2.3 Treatment of 'sub-standard'/'doubtful' accounts restructured under CDR

a. A rescheduling of the instalments of principal alone, would render a sub-standard/'doubtful' asset eligible to be continued in the sub-standard/'doubtful' category for the specified period, [defined in sub para (b) *below*] provided the conditions (i) to (iv) of Para 6.1.2 are complied with and the loan/credit facility is fully secured.
b. A rescheduling of interest element would render a sub-standard/'doubtful' asset eligible to be continued to be classified in sub-standard/'doubtful' category for the specified period, i.e., a period of one year after the date when first payment of interest or of principal, whichever is earlier, falls due under the rescheduled terms, provided the conditions (i) to (iv) of Para 6.1.2 are complied with and the amount of sacrifice, if any, in the element of interest, measured in present value terms computed as per the methodology described in Para 6.2.1(b) is either written off or provision is made to the extent of the sacrifice involved.

6.2.4 Treatment of Provision

a) Interest sacrifice involved in the amount of interest should be written off provided for necessarily by debit to Profit & Loss account and held in a distinct account.
b) Sacrifice may be re-computed on each balance sheet date till satisfactory completion of all repayment obligations and full repayment of the outstanding in the account, so as to capture the changes in the fair value on account of changes in BPLR, term premium and the credit category of the borrower. Consequently, banks may provide for the shortfall in provision or reverse the amount of excess provision held in the distinct account.
c) The amount of provision made for NPA, may be reversed when the account is re-classified as a 'standard asset'.
d) In the event any security is taken against interest sacrifice, it should be valued at Re.1/- till maturity of the security. This will ensure that the effect of charging off the economic sacrifice to the Profit & Loss account is not negated.

6.2.5 Upgradation of restructured accounts

The sub-standard/doubtful accounts at 6.2.3 (a) & (b) *above*, which have been subjected to restructuring, etc. whether in respect of principal instalment or interest amount, by whatever modality, would be eligible to be upgraded to the standard category only after the specified period, i.e. a period of one year after the date when first payment of 'interest or of principal, whichever is earlier, falls due under the rescheduled terms, subject to satisfactory performance during the period.

6.2.6 Asset classification status of restructured accounts

During the specified one-year period, the asset classification of sub-standard/doubtful status accounts will not deteriorate if satisfactory performance of the account is demonstrated during the specified period. In case, however, the satisfactory performance during the specified period is not evidenced, the asset classification of the restructured account would be governed as per the applicable prudential norms with reference to the pre-restructuring payment schedule. The asset classification would be bank-specific based on record of recovery of each bank/FI, as per the existing prudential norms applicable to banks/FIs.

6.2.7 Prudential norms on conversion

a) Where overdue interest is funded or outstanding principal and interest components are converted into equity, debentures, zero coupon bonds or other instruments and income is recognized in consequence, full provision should be made for the amount of income so recognized. Equity, debentures and other financial instruments acquired by way of conversion of outstanding principal and/or interest should be classified in the AFS category and valued in accordance with the extant instructions on valuation of banks' investment portfolio except to the extent that (a) equity may be valued as per market value, if quoted (b) in cases where equity is not quoted, valuation may be at break-up value in respect of standard assets and in respect of sub-standard/doubtful assets, equity may be initially valued at Re1 and at break-up value after restoration/up gradation to standard category.

b) If the conversion of interest into equity, which is quoted, interest income can be recognized after the account is upgraded to the standard category at market value of equity, on the date of such up gradation, not exceeding the amount of interest converted into equity. If the conversion of interest is into equity, which is not quoted, interest income should not be recognized.

c) In case of conversion of principal and/or interest into equity, debentures, bonds, etc., such instruments should be treated as NPA ab-initio in the same asset classification category as the loan if the loan's classification is sub-standard or doubtful on implementation of the restructuring package and provision should be made as per the norms. Consequently, income should be recognized on these instruments only on realization basis. The income in respect of unrealized interest which is converted into debentures or any fixed maturity instruments, would be recognized only on redemption of such instruments.

d) Banks may reverse the provisions made towards income recognized at the time of conversion of accrued interest into equity, bonds, debentures etc. when the instrument goes out of balance sheet on sale/realization of value/maturity.

7. ASSET CLASSIFICATION OF REPEATEDLY RESTRUCTURED ACCOUNTS

The regulatory concession in terms of paragraphs 6.2.1 and 6.2.3 would not be available if the account is restructured for the second or more times. In case a restructured asset, which is a standard asset on restructuring, is subjected to restructuring on a subsequent occasion, it should be classified as sub-standard. If the restructured asset is a sub-standard or a doubtful asset and is subjected to restructuring, on a subsequent occasion its asset classification would be reckoned from the date when it became NPA on the previous occasion. However, such assets

India

restructuring for the second or more time may be allowed to be upgraded to standard category after one year from the date of first payment of interest or repayment of principal whichever falls due earlier in terms of the current restructuring package subject to satisfactory performance.

8. DISCLOSURE

Banks/FIs should also disclose in their published annual Balance Sheets, under 'Notes on Accounts', the following information in respect of corporate debt restructuring undertaken during the year:

  a. Total number of accounts total amount of loan assets and the amount of sacrifice in the restructuring cases under CDR.
     [(a) = (b) + (c) + (d)]
  b. The number, amount and sacrifice in standard assets subjected to CDR.
  c. The number, amount and sacrifice in sub-standard assets subjected to CDR.
  d. The number, amount and sacrifice in doubtful assets subjected to CDR.

9. IMPLEMENTATION OF THE REVISED GUIDELINES

The *above* guidelines will be implemented with prospective effect. All accounts pending with CDR Cell, in respect of which restructuring packages are yet to be approved, will be covered under the revised guidelines. The ICA and DCA will have to be suitably amended for incorporating the changes introduced in the scheme.

Chapter 10

Italy

Article 182bis of Law 80/2005 and the Code of Conduct to Restructure Debt Issued by the Italian Bank Association

Antonio Auricchio[1]

---

1. The author wishes to thank Rita Gismondi, an associate in the Restructuring & Insolvency Department of the Rome office of Gianni, Origoni, Grippo & Partners, for her valuable contribution in writing this chapter.

ACRONYMS, ABBREVIATIONS & DEFINED TERMS

182bis DRA	debt restructuring agreements under article 182bis of the Italian bankruptcy Law
ABI	Italian Bank Association
Bankruptcy Reform Act or BRA	Legislative Decree No. 5 of 9 January 2006
Code	Code of Conduct for Debt Restructuring Agreements enacted in 2000 by the Italian Bank Association (*Codice di Comportamento tra Banche per Affrontare i Processi di Ristrutturazione atti a Superare le Crisi di Impresa*)
Committee	A small advising committee of creditors under the auspices of the Code
CP	Composition with Creditors Proceedings
DIP financing	Debtor-in-possession financing
DRA	Debt Restructuring Agreements
EUR	Euro
Fillattice S.p.A.	Company
HoldCo	A company incorporated in Luxembourg which acts as holding company of Fillattice S.p.A.
Italian Bankruptcy Law or IBL	Royal Decree No. 267 of 16 March 1942
Law 80/2005	Law decree No. 35 of 14 March 2005, as amended and restated by Law No. 80 of 14 May 2005
Marzano Law	Law decree No. 347 of 23 December 2003, as amended and restated by Law No. 39 of 18 February 2004.
Report	A report by an expert concerning the feasibility of article 182bis of the Italian Bankruptcy Law debt restructuring agreements
Subsidiary	A subsidiary company of Fillattice S.p.A.

I. BACKGROUND

Italian insolvency legislation was significantly amended and supplemented in the last three years. The new approach is mainly focused on corporate reorganization, rather than on liquidation of the company's assets, as well as on arrangements between financially troubled or insolvent companies and creditors. The new provisions of law are based on flexible legal tools aimed at the restructuring and reorganization of distressed companies and thus offer a new perspective in the Italian insolvency legislation, in line with the most advanced legal systems.

Reference shall be made, in particular, to the following legal framework:

1. Law decree No. 347 of 23 December 2003, as amended and restated by Law No. 39 of 18 February 2004 (the 'Marzano Law'), referring to the extraordinary administration procedure for large insolvent companies[2] and issued on the occasion of the Parmalat group companies collapse.
2. Law decree No. 35 of 14 March 2005, as amended and restated by Law No. 80 of 14 May 2005 ('Law 80/2005'), which (a) amended the outdated provisions of Royal Decree No. 267 of 16 March 1942 (the 'Italian Bankruptcy Law' or 'IBL') concerning claw-back actions and composition with creditors proceedings (the 'CP'); and, (b) set out new rules concerning debt restructuring agreements ('DRA') under article 182bis of the IBL (the '182bis DRA'),[3] which will be subject to an in-depth study in paragraph III *below*.
3. Legislative decree No. 5 of 9 January 2006 (the 'Bankruptcy Reform Act' or 'BRA') which amended the whole IBL (except for bankruptcy crimes) and provided for a comprehensive reform, applicable to bankruptcy proceedings opened after 16 July 2006.[4]

---

2. Both of the following requirements shall be met for the admission to the extraordinary administration procedure ruled by Marzano Law: (i) no fewer than 500 employees, since at least one year; and (ii) debts for an aggregated amount no fewer than EUR 300,000,000, including secured debts.
3. Article 182bis of the IBL reads as follows:

    Debt Restructuring Agreement. The debtor can file with the court – together with the statement and the documentation prescribed in article 161 – an agreement of reorganization reached with its creditors representing at least a 60 per cent of the debts along with a report by an expert on the feasibility of the agreement itself, with special reference to its suitability as to ensure the regular payment of the external creditors.

    The agreement is published in the Companies' Register and the creditors and every other interested can oppose within thirty days from the publication.

    The court decides the oppositions and proceeds to the approval in a council chamber with a decree.

    The decree of the court can be appealed with the court of appeals pursuant article 183, as applicable, within fifteen days from its publication in the Companies' Register.

    The agreement is effective as of the day of its publication in the Companies' Register.

4. Please note, however, that in case of further postponement the BRA would be effective as from 1 January 2007.

In the above legal framework, arrangements and/or settlements between distressed or insolvent companies and relevant stakeholders play no doubt a key role in order to achieve positive results in restructuring and reorganization.

Indeed, the success of a restructuring process may depend on many different factors, such as the company's debt structure, its cash generation capabilities or the legal environment within which said restructuring will be undertaken. Also important is the willingness of the stakeholders to negotiate constructively and in good faith with the debtor. In particular, banks play a decisive role in the restructuring process, since they are both major creditors of the company and lenders providing new money or DIP financing.

The 182bis DRA represent a further flexible legal instrument aimed at the restructuring of financially troubled and/or insolvent companies, provided that certain requirements and conditions are met (see below, paragraph III).

However, it is worth noting that debt restructuring agreements are not brand new in the Italian legal system. In fact, also before the issuance of law 80/2005, out-of-court restructurings had been attempted at the onset of financial difficulties to avoid the disadvantages arising from formal insolvency proceedings.

Said agreements spread as a reaction to the many problems arising from the existing Italian insolvency regime, which appeared to be rigid and not flexible. In fact, before the recent changes introduced by the BRA, several provisions of the IBL were outdated and ineffective, so as to imply some disadvantages (*e.g.* no priority for new money; no recover of unsecured creditors' claims; excessive length and high costs and expenses of insolvency proceedings; and, which used up a substantial proportion of the assets).

Therefore, the experience of out-of-court, informal agreements between the debtor and its creditors was already known in the Italian legal system, especially in relation to small and medium-sized companies. Banks often entered into private discussions with the debtor outside the insolvency proceedings framework, trying to get full (or better) repayment or improved security in exchange for helping a distressed company. In fact, creditor's claims were usually more protected than under insolvency proceedings, especially in terms of time and percentages of recovery.[5]

However, before the enactment in 2000 of the code of conduct for debt restructuring agreements (the 'Code') of the Italian Bank Association ('ABI'), the above out-of-court settlements were not an effective alternative device. Indeed, agreements between banks and the debtor were usually hard to achieve for the following reasons: (1) as a consequence of multiple lines of credit and multiple and self-interested initiatives taken by each bank, i.e. lacking a 'leading bank'; and, (2) financial unsuitability of restructuring programs, with specific reference to the small dimensions and familiar structure of most Italian companies.

---

5. According to a recent report of the Bank of Italy, time and percentages of recovery are, respectively: (i) 19 months and 60 per cent under out-of-court agreements; and (ii) 72 months and 30 per cent under formal insolvency proceedings.

Italy

The above background led to the issuance of the Code, based on the adoption of preventive consultations measures between the debtor and its creditors in order to pursue the advantages arising from a cooperative restructuring process.

II.   THE CODE

The Code is aimed to (1) give banks a valid tool for the compliance with out-of-court debt restructuring agreements, and (2) pursue transparency and fairness in the relationships between banks and financially troubled companies. The purpose of the Code falls within the area of cooperative payment solutions and the preservation of the company as a going concern, through the involvement and support of banks.

The reference pattern for the Code comes from England and, in particular, from the English practice (based on the London Approach) aimed at promoting the involvement of banks in the rescue of distressed companies, in order to maximize a return of profit for both shareholders and investors, by means of a due analysis of companies in financial difficulties.[6]

A.   MAIN PROVISIONS.

The Code highlights the general principles of transparency and fairness in reciprocal relations between the different banks participating in the restructuring process and the financially troubled company, so as to ensure uniform conducts based on cooperation and substantial equity. In other words, co-operation between the different banks and the debtor represents the first step in order to settle and solve problems of distressed companies. However, the provisions set forth by the Code are applicable only to companies whose indebtedness towards the banking or financial system is no lower than EUR 15,493,707.00.

As a general rule, banks shall:

1. Be diligent and prompt in understanding whether a company is facing financial difficulties.
2. Get long-term decisions on the basis of reliable and complete information. And,
3. Seek a uniform approach in order to support the financially troubled company.

Furthermore, article 1 of the Code provides that banks shall act in line with the principle of equal treatment of claims (the so called *pari passu* or *par condicio creditorum* principle) and foster the exchange of any relevant information among the participants in the restructuring process. In particular, banks shall ensure,

---

6. See Ghia, I controlli bancari: il 'London Approach' in *Temi romana*, II, 1995, 245.

among other things: (a) a fair behaviour, aimed at promoting a joint settlement and adhesion to the restructuring program; (b) full disclosure and circulation of relevant information; (c) cooperation with other classes of creditors; (d) an increasing value of the company; (e) equal and fair sharing of the participation to the new money or DIP financing; (f) the adoption of procedures aimed at reducing the expenses; (g) the respect of principles and provisions set forth by the Code; (h) the avoidance of private and one-to-one negotiations; (i) timely decisions; and, (j) settlement of any issue relating to the interpretation of the agreement and/or the dispute resolution.

A bank may propose a meeting to the other banks involved, provided that same had agreed to the Code, in order to open a procedure concerning the distressed company. The information provided for by the company shall be disclosed to all parties involved. However, said parties shall (1) keep confidential any relevant information; and, (2) declare the ranking of the respective claim.

After the first meeting, banks shall give an opinion about the feasibility of the restructuring process and decide with a qualified majority on the appointment of a small advising committee of creditors (the 'Committee').[7] After this stage, the non-compliance with the obligations provided for by the Code may determine the liability of banks.[8] In particular, an infringement of the provisions set forth by the Code by one of the participating banks might cause direct effects against same, only if the prosecution of the procedure is resolved by the majority and thus a Committee is appointed.

The Committee shall, among other things:[9]

1. settle a technical body with consulting functions on legal, financial and industrial issues;
2. gather from the company and its advisor any further information required for the evaluation of the restructuring process;
3. verify the correct and fair performance of the procedure;
4. suggest the adoption of amendments to the agreement in relation to any economic and patrimonial changes that might occur; and,
5. verify the amount of claims, the respective pre-emption rights and the past positions, so as to ensure transparency and fairness in the DIP financing allocation.

In case of disputes relating to the interpretation of the provisions set forth by the Code, remedies may be a court settlement with the intervention of the ABI, or arbitration devolved to a panel of three arbitrators.[10]

---

7. See article 5 of the Code.
8. See Maimeri, 'Sistemazioni stragiudiziali delle crisi d'impresa e codice di comportamento bancario', in *Banca, borsa e titoli di credito,* 2000, 422.
9. See article 6 of the Code.
10. See articles 8 and 9 of the Code.

B. THE IMPLEMENTATION OF THE CODE.

The Code is aimed at promoting a 'parallel system', which strengthens the role of the contractual freedom of the parties involved in financial crisis situations.

Unfortunately, the Code has not been implemented yet, since the adhesion of banks was not general. It is worth stressing that the Code provides for a non binding set of provisions for banks and operates on a 'moral suasion' level.[11] Although self-regulating codes of conducts are now part of the Italian legal system,[12] especially in the banking area,[13] the provisions set forth by the Code are not binding on banks unless same voluntarily agree to the Code.

Furthermore, some provisions of the Code are not clear and the principles of transparency and fairness are too general and lack of precision as to their scope. As a consequence, the application of said provisions might cause certain problems.

Moreover, the Code does not expressly deal either with issues relating to new money and claw-back action risks, which are the most relevant in the out-of-court settlements framework.

III. 182BIS DRA

182bis DRA seem to be an effective legal tool aimed at the restructuring of distressed companies. In particular, the new provisions of law set the 182bis DRA as an intermediate solution between the private out-of-court agreements (without the judicial confirmation) and the insolvency proceeding of CP. 182bis DRA lay outside the traditional judicial proceedings framework, but require also the approval by a Bankruptcy court. Therefore, 182bis DRA are different from informal, out-of-court debt restructuring agreements, which are mentioned and not directly ruled by IBL.[14]

A. MAIN STEPS OF 182BIS DRA

Article 182bis of the IBL provides for the following steps:

1. negotiations with creditors representing at least 60 per cent of the total amount of claims and drawing up of the 182bis DRA;

---

11. Desario, *Il ruolo delle banche nelle crisi d'impresa: il punto di vista della Banca d'Italia,* Italian Banking Association, 7 June 2000.
12. See the *Borsa Italiana s.p.a.* Code of Best Practice for listed companies, as amended on 14 March 2006, available at <http://www.borsaitalia.it/media/img/ico/pdf.gif>.
13. see, for instance, the recommendations against money-laundering, as well as the establishment of the banking *Ombudsman.*
14. Indeed, article 67, paragraph 3(d) of the IBL, as amended by Law 80/2005, provides for a claw-back exemption rule according to which are not clawed back acts, payments and securities carried out for the execution of the plan, which seems qualified (1) to ensure the reorganization of the indebtedness and ensure the rebalancing of the financial situation; and, (2) the reasonableness of the plan should be certified by an expert, pursuant to article 2501bis, paragraph 4, of the Italian Civil Code.

2. filing of the 182bis DRA with the Companies' Register;
3. possible challenge of the 182bis DRA before the court within a 30-day-term, starting from the date that the filing took place;
4. decision on any challenge and approval by the court.

B.   LEGAL REQUIREMENTS

The debtor is entitled to enter into a 182bis DRA, provided that same legal requirements for the admission to CP are met.[15] In other words, the debtor shall be:

1. an entrepreneur (either natural person or corporate entity) or a small businesses (according to the new provisions of law of the Bankruptcy Reform Act small businesses are those having (a) investments non exceeding EUR 300,000.00 and (b) yearly earnings not exceeding EUR 200,000.00);[16] and,
2. in a 'state of crisis'.

Even though Law 80/2005 does not provide for a clear and precise meaning for the expression 'state of crisis', according to the available case law and a recent amendment of the IBL, a 'state of crisis' is wider than a 'state of insolvency' and also includes an insolvency situation.[17] As a consequence, both companies in a temporary and reversible distress and insolvent companies are entitled to enter into a 182bis DRA (as well as apply for the admission to the CP).[18]

It is worth noting that Law 80/2005 also provides for the following requirements:

1. A 182bis DRA shall be entered into by the debtor and creditors (no matter if they are secured or unsecured creditors) representing at least 60 per cent of total claims. And,
2. A report by an expert concerning the feasibility of the 182bis DRA (the 'Report') which shall be filed with the competent court.

It is of particular note that according to an order dated 22 February 2006 of the Court of Brescia, the percentage of 60 per cent of creditors' claims shall be calculated on the basis of the total amount of claims.[19] Furthermore, the

---

15. Bonfatti – Censoni, La riforma della disciplina dell'azione revocatoria fallimentare, del concordato preventivo e degli accordi di ristrutturazione dei debiti, Padova, 2006, p. 275; Ambrosini-Demarchi, Il nuovo concordato preventivo e gli accordi di ristrutturazione dei debiti, Milano, 2005, p. 189.
16. See the decree of the Court of Bari, 21 November 2005.
17. See the decree of the Court of Bari, 21 November 2005. See also article 36 of the decree law No. 273, issued on 30 December 2005 that amended article 160 of the ABI and stated that '... *a state of crisis it also comprises insolvency*'.
18. See the decree of the Court of Bari, 21 November 2005.
19. However, according to an early scholars' opinion, secured claims should be not included in the total amount of claims, provided that they are fully satisfied by the debtor: Verna, Sugli accordi di ristrutturazione ex art. 182bis l. fall, unreported.

above percentage shall be met at the time of the filing of the 182bis DRA with the Companies' Register, although subsequent adhesion by creditors is permitted.

A 182bis DRA is binding only on those creditors which participated the negotiation. Therefore, a 182bis DRA shall ensure the 'regular payment' to the creditors which have not entered into the agreement: i.e. the so-called 'external creditors'. According to the prevailing scholars' opinion, the expression 'regular payment' should be interpreted as a timely (on the expiry/maturity date) full payment.[20]

However, in a recent decision of the Bankruptcy Court of Milan reductions of claims and amendments to the relevant expiry/maturity date have been provided also in relation to external creditors, which were not involved in the 182bis DRA.[21] Therefore, the above issue is debatable and early case law is not uniform.

C. THE CONTENT AND FILING OF 182BIS DRA

A 182bis DRA is a flexible legal tool, which may provide for different terms and conditions of payment for the outstanding claims, as well as provisions concerning the re-funding of the business, in order to allow restructuring and prosecution of the business activities. In this 'open' framework, the debtor and its creditors may agree, for instance, on: (a) set-off; (b) assignment of claims; (c) *pactum de non petendo* (agreement not to sue); (d) reduction of claims; (e) deferred claims; (f) debt-for-equity swaps.

Article 182bis of the IBL does not expressly provide for a typical and binding content of the 182bis DRA. As a consequence, some scholars suggested that a 182bis DRA would include, *inter alia*, (1) extension of payments; (2) partial or total waiver to the amount due and outstanding of the assets and the shares; (3) financing supply; (4) assumption of the bankruptcy liabilities by extraordinary transactions, such as issuance of bonds; (5) debt for equity swap; (6) prosecution of

---

20. Guglielmucci, *La riforma in via d'urgenza della legge fallimentare*, Torino, 2005, p. 125; Caramaschi, 'I nuovi accordi di ristrutturazione', in *Il nuovo diritto delle società*, 2006, 52; Grossi, *La riforma della legge fallimentare*, Milano, 2005, p. 333; Frascaroli Santi, 'Gli accordi di ristrutturazione dei debiti (art. 182 bis Legge Fallimentare) e gli effetti per coobbligati e fideiussori', in *Il diritto fallimentare*, 2005, 851; Bonfatti Censoni, *La riforma della disciplina dell'azione revocatoria fallimentare, del concordato preventivo e degli accordi di ristrutturazione*, Padova, 2006, p. 282; Ambrosini-De Marchi, *Il nuovo concordato preventivo egli accordi di ristrutturazione dei debiti*, Milano, 2005, p. 191; Frascaroli Santi, in Trattato di diritto commerciale e di diritto pubblico dell'economia, vol. 37, Padova, 2005, 205. The Court of Brescia (decree issued on 22 February 2006) and the Court of Bari (decree issued on 21 November 2005) stated that the 'regular' payment of so called external creditors (i.e. creditors who did not attend to the meeting or consent the agreement) means to pay the debts on the expiry date, rather than in line with the terms and conditions of the debt restructuring agreement.
21. For rough critics to this construction see Fabiani, 'In salvo chi ha votato contro', in *Il Sole 24 ore*, published on 16 April 2006, 17.

the business activities by the debtor or a third party (*e.g.* by means of a lease of business); and, (7) assignment of the debtor's assets to creditors.[22]

In light of the above, with respect to the contents of a 182bis DRA would be similar to the plan in the CP, as well as to the plan provided for extraordinary administration procedures ruled by the Marzano Law.

The filing of a 182bis DRA and the Report shall be supported by the following documentation:

1. An updated report on the financial and economic situation of the company.
2. A detailed list of assets and a list of creditors, with indication of the relevant claims and preferential rights, if any.
3. A list of creditors having a real or personal security on assets belonging to the debtor. And,
4. The value of the Company's assets.

D. THE EXPERT

It is worth stressing that the Report is of great importance, because the approval of a 182bis DRA by a Bankruptcy court is mainly based on the content of same. Indeed, the Report shall make specific reference to the suitability of the 182bis DRA, so as to ensure full payment to the external creditors (*i.e.* the creditors that did not participated in the DRA).

Furthermore, article 182bis of the IBL does not refer to a specific rule, providing for the eligibility requirements of the expert. In this respect, the 182bis DRA seems to be different from both CP and out-of-court debt restructuring agreements. Indeed, in the CP the expert shall hold same requirements provided for the appointment of the trustee in a bankruptcy proceeding. Moreover, as prescribed by article 28 of the IBL, in out-of-court debt restructuring agreements the expert shall be an auditor (or an auditing firm) enrolled in the Register kept by the Italian Ministry of Justice.

However, according to a scholars' opinion, article 28 of the IBL shall also apply analogically to 182bis DRAs. As a consequence, should the above opinion be confirmed by case law:

1. The expert shall be (a) a lawyer, an expert in commercial law or a professional accountant; or, (b) a person who directed, managed and controlled a company, provided that he was not declared bankrupt in the past. And,
2. The expert shall not be (a) a relative of the debtor, (b) a creditor of the debtor; (c) a person who contributed to the company's distress or crisis situation; and/or, (d) a person in conflict of interests.

---

22. Vitalone, *Il nuovo concordato preventivo*, Milano, 2005, p. 197; Caramaschi, 'I nuovi accordi di ristrutturazione', in *Il nuovo diritto delle società*, 2006, 53; Ambrosini, 'Gli accordi di ristrutturazione nella nuova legge fallimentare: prime riflessioni', in *Il fallimento*, 2005, 950.

Italy

Article 182bis of the IBL does not provide any rule concerning the expert's liability. However, it is reasonable that the expert shall perform his functions having a duty of professional diligence. Therefore, article 2236 of the Italian Civil Code[23] might apply, according to which the expert shall be liable only in case of intent or gross negligence, provided that the relevant activity involved the resolution of very difficult problems.[24]

E.   THE JUDICIAL PHASE

Unlike CP, in case of a 182bis DRA the debtor should not request to the competent court the opening of an insolvency proceeding. Furthermore, creditors are not entitled to vote upon the 182bis DRA, since the debtor shall have been previously gathered the consents of the creditors. In this respect, 182bis DRA would be considered as a private law contract.[25] However, a judicial phase is required for the approval of the 182bis DRA, in order to achieve stability of same.

The formalities requested in order to enter into the 182bis DRA are not provided for by the law. However, according to a recent decision by the Court of Bari, creditors' adhesions should be certified by a public officer, *i.e.* the authenticity of the creditor's signature and the date of the adhesion.

Creditors and each interested party are entitled to challenge objections to the 182bis DRA before the court within a 30-day-period, starting from the date of the filing of the 182bis DRA in the Companies Register. Some scholars stressed that the above deadline is extremely narrow, as well as not reasonable. Furthermore, it is not yet clear whether only creditors who did not enter into the agreement or also creditors who previously consented to the 182bis DRA (for instance, in case of subsequent discovery), are entitled to challenge same.[26]

According to a reliable opinion, external creditors could challenge a 182bis DRA in the following scenarios:

1. If the debtor breaches the 182bis DRA and, as a consequence, cannot ensure the regular payment of external creditors' claims (*i.e.* full and on the expiry/maturity date);
2. since the approval of the 182bis DRA by the court implies an exemption to claw-back actions with reference to any act, payment or guarantee performed for the execution of the 182bis DRA, the external creditors could be

---

23. Article 2236 of the Italian Civil Code reads as follows: '*Liability of the provider. If the performance implies the solution of technical problems with special difficulties, the provider will not respond for the damages unless he performed his acts with intention or severe negligence*'.
24. Fauceglia, 'Gli accordi di ristrutturazione dei debiti nella legge 80/2005', in *Il fallimento*, 2005, 1449.
25. See the decree of the Court of Bari, 21 November 2005.
26. Verna, Sugli accordi di ristrutturazione ex art. 182 bis legge fallimentare, in *Il diritto fallimentare*, 2005, 865; Vitalone, *Il nuovo concordato preventivo*, Milano, 2005, p. 198.

harmed, since the above acts (no more clawed back) could reduce the debtor's assets and, thus, the satisfaction of relevant claims.[27]

F. THE APPROVAL BY THE COURT

The court shall decide on any objections and then approve the 182bis DRA, provided that the relevant requirements are met. In particular, the court shall preliminarily ascertain (1) reliability of the expert report; (2) achievement of the above mentioned minimum percentage (60 per cent) of claims; and (3) fulfilment of other requirements for the admission to 182bis DRA (pursuant to article 160 of the IBL).[28]

Having all the requirements been met, the court shall approve the 182bis DRA by means of a confirmation decree. It is worth noting that the approval by the court is necessary, even if there were no challenges. In the light of a recent decision,[29] the court cannot modify terms and provisions of 182bis DRA. In other words, the court is only entitled to confirm or reject the 182bis DRA and thus cannot introduce any contractual amendments and/or suggest same to the parties.

After the 182bis DRA has been filed the court has a 30-day period to receive creditors' challenges to the DRA. After said period, the court will enact a confirmation decree. The confirmation decree may be challenged before the competent Court of Appeals within a 15-day-term, starting from the publication of same in the Companies' Register.

Should the 182bis DRA be not approved, however, the insolvency of the debtor would not be automatically declared by the court. Indeed, the state of insolvency (1) is not for granted upon the lack of approval of the 182bis DRA; and, (2) shall be carefully ascertained before declaring the admission of the company to bankruptcy.

---

27. Guglielmucci, *La riforma in via d'urgenza della legge fallimentare*, Torino, 2005, p. 133.
28. Article 160 of the IBL reads as follows: '*160. Conditions for the admission to the procedure. The entrepreneur who founds himself in a state of crisis can propose to the creditors a preventive reorganization agreement on the base of a plan that can include:*

    a) *the reorganization of the debts and the satisfaction of creditors through any means, also by means of assignment of assets, the assumption of debts by a third party or other extraordinary transactions, including the issuance of shares, participations, bonds, convertible bonds, other financial instruments and debt certificates to the creditors and their companies;*
    b) *the activities of the companies involved in the proposal of the reorganization agreement performed by a trustee – also the creditors or their companies can act as trustees – or companies which are to be established in the course of the procedure and whose shares are destined to be assigned to creditors as result of the reorganization agreement.*
    c) *the subdivision of the creditors in different classes related to their rights and homogeneous economic interests.*
    d) *differentiated treatment to creditors belonging different classes.*

    Every time the first paragraph refers to state of crisis it also comprises insolvency'.
29. See the decree of the Court of Brescia, 22 February 2006.

The IBL considers that revealing signs of insolvency are, among others, the following:

1. Significant economic and financial imbalance of the debtor.
2. Revocation of lines of credit and/or termination of overdraft facilities.
3. Payments made by the debtor not in cash or other usual means of payment. And,
4. Any enforcement proceedings brought by creditors, *vis-à-vis* the debtor.

Furthermore, it should be stressed that a debtor in a state of insolvency could avoid bankruptcy by filing a petition for the admission to CP.

G.   DISSOLUTION AND AVOIDANCE OF THE 182BIS DRA

Article 182bis of the IBL does not provide any express provision with reference to termination and/or breach of the DRA. Furthermore, the corresponding rules concerning dissolution or avoidance of the CP do not seem applicable to the 182bis DRA.

If the debtor does not carry out the obligations arising from the 182bis DRA, creditors who entered into the agreement could bring legal actions in order to ascertain (1) the termination for breach of the agreement (pursuant to articles 1453 and 1459 of the Italian Civil Code);[30] or, (2) the avoidance of same.

On the other hand, if the debtor does not pay in full and timely external creditors after the approval by the court said creditors could (1) file a petition for the declaration of insolvency; (2) start enforcement proceedings, provided that the relevant claim was outstanding and they had a valid writ of execution; or, (3) register a mortgage on the basis of a judgment or an injunction.[31]

H.   182BIS DRA MAIN AND DEBATABLE ISSUES

1.   Claw-back action exemption rule

Pursuant to article 67, paragraph 3(e) of the IBL, as amended by Law 80/2005, each act performed by the debtor in the execution of a 182bis DRA approved by the

---

30. Article 1453 of the Italian Code reads as follows: '*1453. Termination of contracts as result of breach of one of the parties. In the case of contracts with counter obligations, if one of the parties does not fulfil his obligations, the other party can either request the fulfilment or the termination of the contract irrespectively of its right to claim damages. The termination can be claimed even when a judicial claim has been filed to obtain the fulfilment of the accrued obligations but on the other hand the fulfilment cannot be claimed if the termination has already been requested. As of the date of the claim of termination the non-complying party cannot fulfil his obligation anymore*'. And, article 1459 states that '*1459. Termination of a multilateral contract. In the case of contracts included in article 1420* [contracts of more than two parties aiming for the same objective] *the non-fulfilment of one party does not imply the termination of the contract in respect to the others, unless the non-provided performance is essential*'.
31. Guglielmucci, *La riforma in via d'urgenza della legge fallimentare*, Torino, 2005, p. 134.

court is subject to a special claw-back action exemption rule, aimed at the rescuing of the business and the financial restructuring.[32] Indeed, should the debtor be subsequently declared bankrupt, any transactions, payments and guarantees performed in execution of the 182bis DRA cannot be declared null and void *vis-à-vis* the bankruptcy estate. This new provision of law would promote the use of the 182bis DRA, as a tool aimed at the restructuring of distressed companies. In fact, claw-back risks have always been perceived as one of the major obstacles in the relationships between financially troubled companies and creditors.

In this respect, it is worth stressing that the benefit of the above claw-back action exemption rule is provided not only in case of a 182bis DRA, but also, *inter alia*, for:

1. Informal, out-of-court restructuring agreements, based on a plan aimed at the reorganization of a distressed company and the economic and financial recovery of business activities, provided that an expert (*i.e.* an audit firm) confirmed the feasibility of the plan by means of a fairness opinion, pursuant to article 2501bis, paragraph 4 of Italian Civil Code[33] (article 67, paragraph 3(d) of the IBL).[34]
2. CP, with reference to any act, payment or guarantee performed in execution of same, provided the above acts were carried out after the filing of the petition for the opening of the CP (article 67, paragraph 3(e) of the IBL).

Said provisions are a clear advantage reserved to projects aimed at the restructuring and the recovery of financially troubled companies, even though laying outside the formal insolvency proceedings. Furthermore, the claw-back action exemption rule gives some (subsequent) protection to the informal debt restructuring agreements, since the so called 'stay of the enforcement proceedings' against the company (arising from the opening of a judicial insolvency proceeding) is lacking. Indeed, unlike CP, a 182bis DRA do not grant the debtor any protection from enforcement proceedings brought by external creditors. Furthermore, while the CP is binding on all creditors (also for dissenting or non voting creditors), the 182bis DRA is binding only on the creditors who entered into the agreement.

---

32. Article 67, par. 3(e) of the IBL states that '[t]*hese are not subject to claw-back actions:* ... (e) *the actions, the payments and the guarantees granted for the execution of the reorganization agreement, the controlled administration and the homologated agreement pursuant to article 182-bis*'.
33. Article 2501-bis par. 4 of the Italian Civil Code states reads as follows: '*2501bis. Merger as result of a leveraged acquisition.* ... *The report of the experts referred to in article 2501-sexies, attests the reasonableness of contents of the merger project according to the* [financial plan (2501-bis second paragraph)]'.
34. Article 67 par. 3(d) of the IBL reads as follows '[t]*hese are not subject to claw-back actions:* ... *(d) the actions, the payments and the guarantees granted on assets of the debtor provided that they are put in place in the execution of a plan which consent to the recovery of the debt exposure of the company; and, ensure the rebalancing of its financial situation and whose reasonableness is attested pursuant* [an expert's opinion (paragraph fourth of article 2501bis of the civil code)]'.

In this respect, it is advisable that the highest number of creditors agree on the 182bis DRA, in order to ensure the stability of the restructuring process and avoid the risk of individual enforcement proceedings *vis-à-vis* the distressed company.

Furthermore, it is worth stressing that, according to a reliable opinion, the claw black exemption rule would also exclude any criminal liability referring to acts performed by the debtor and/or the other party of the transaction.

2. DIP Financing

As far as additional cash resources to the debtor is concerned, lacking any express provision of law and case law in this sense, it is not clear whether or not any expenses and obligations arising after the filing of the 182bis DRA, shall be settled on a priority basis in the event of a possible subsequent bankruptcy proceedings of the debtor.

This issue may be a serious problem since no bank would grant a loan to the insolvent debtor, if such loans are not paid on a priority basis in case of subsequent declaration of bankruptcy of the debtor.

According to a reliable opinion,[35] DIP financing provided to the debtor in execution of the 182bis DRA, should not be considered as a preferred claim, since the 182bis DRA would not imply a judicial control over the debtor's activities. This is no doubt an issue which might reduce the spread of 182bis DRA.

IV. CASE STUDY

A recent decision of the Bankruptcy Court of Milan may be considered as an application test of the new provisions of law concerning 182bis DRA.

The petition was proposed by Fillattice S.p.A. (the 'Company'), operating in the area of marketing and sales of textile products. According to article 182bis of the IBL, the Company filed with the Companies' Register the following documents:

1. The agreement entered into with creditors representing 72 per cent of total amount of claims (*i.e.* banks and other financers).
2. The petition, which highlighted the main terms and conditions of the industrial and financial plan. And,

---

35. Ambrosini, 'Gli accordi di ristrutturazione nella nuova legge fallimentare: prime riflessioni', in *Il fallimento*, 2005, p. 951; Bonfatti, 'La promozione e la tutela delle procedure di composizione negoziale della crisi d'impresa nella riforma della legge fallimentare', in <www.judicium.it>, 11; Rovelli, Quale competitività per le imprese dopo le trasformazioni della legge fallimentare, in *Il fallimento*, 2006, 113; Bonfatti – Censoni, La riforma della disciplina dell'azione revocatoria fallimentare, del concordato preventivo e degli accordi di ristrutturazione dei debiti, Padova, 2006, p. 310; Ambrosini-Demarchi, Il nuovo concordato preventivo e gli accordi di ristrutturazione dei debiti, Milano, 2005, p. 195.

3. The report, drafted and executed by an expert concerning the feasibility of the 182bis DRA, which contained more details with reference to the whole operation.

The Company holds the shares of other subsidiary companies and is totally owned by a holding company incorporated in Luxembourg (the 'HoldCo'). The Company had already assigned its shares, held in two subsidiary companies, to the HoldCo, in order to ensure the success of the restructuring plan, which was composed by a business and financial reorganization.

The business restructuring plan, enclosed in the report drafted by the expert, provided for interventions in the short term, aimed at re-establishing profitability and earning power of the Company, and in the medium term, strengthening the market competitiveness of same. Referring to the medium term intervention, the report of the expert also addressed the development of joint venture contracts in other countries.

The financial plan involved the participation of the other companies of the group. In particular:

1. The HoldCo shall convert the Company's bonds into shares before the deadline, paying in advance the value of the shares to one of the subsidiary companies which will become a shareholder of the Company (the 'Subsidiary').
2. The HoldCo shall pay, directly or by guarantor banks, a fixed amount of money to the Company. And,
3. The Subsidiary shall pay to the Company an amount of money for the purchase of an immovable property of the Company, within a 15-day-term from the filing of the agreement with the Companies' Register.

The Company proposed a complex operation aimed at ensuring the payment of creditors who entered into the agreement upon certain conditions, as well as the regular payment (i.e. full and timely payment) of the external creditors that did not entered into the DRA (see III.B *above*).

The expert certified the feasibility of the plan, with specific reference to the regular payment of the external creditors, as well as the compatibility of the terms and conditions of the plan with the probable trend of the macroeconomic standing situation.

According to the report, the Company could recover/restore the financial balance, on the basis of (1) new deadline for secured loans; (2) new terms and conditions for redemption; and, (3) confirmation of lines of credit. The 182bis DRA shall be terminated in case of breach of any covenant or obligation which would make more difficult the fulfilment of the Company's obligations towards the banks.

On the basis of the first applications of the provisions of law concerning the 182bis DRA, it may be argued that the plans and the agreements need to be supported by the banks and other financers. The participation of the banks to the restructuring process of distressed companies is clearly essential in order to ensure the success of same.

V. CONCLUSIONS

Traditionally, the Italian insolvency legal framework has been hostile to investors, such as international private equity funds focusing on special situations, trying to extract value from turn-around investments in distressed companies. Claw-back risks were perceived as one of the major obstacles. This picture is very likely to change in the near future.

As mentioned above, Italian insolvency law appears to herald a new approach that focuses on corporate reorganization and restructuring rather than liquidation of the debtor's assets. In said legal framework, the possibility of providing for arrangements with creditors is to be welcomed. Said arrangements are an effective legal tool aimed at the restructuring of distressed companies, away from the traditional judicial proceedings.

Law 80/2005 provisions will facilitate the implementation of turn-around plans and hopefully permit the injection of cash into distressed companies aimed at preservation of a going concern and its goodwill, which is a pre-requisite for the entry of private equity or industrial investors.

The provisions contained in article 182bis of the IBL appear to be in line with the most advanced insolvency regimes and enables legal instruments based on negotiations between the debtor and its creditors, in order to solve in advance, if possible, financial crisis and problems of distressed companies, as well as to avoid insolvencies.

Likely, a 182bis DRA, together with the other legal tools implemented by the Italian legislator, will allow for the swift satisfaction of creditors' claims without any need for a lengthy insolvency procedure, which is always detrimental to the debtor's business, its value on the market and the creditors' interests.

The first applications of the new law provisions concerning a 182bis DRA may fuel speculation that Italian companies experiencing financial woes will increasingly seek to reorganize their debts through the above new legal tools.

A successful restructuring of a distressed company depends on many factors, such as the company's debt structure, its cash generation capabilities and the willingness of the company's stakeholders to negotiate constructively and in good faith. Also important is the legal environment within which the restructuring will be undertaken. Following Law 80/2005 the legal landscape in which distressed companies operate has been clearly altered.

Notwithstanding some criticism and questionable issues raised by the first commentators, the new provisions are no doubt an improvement of the Italian insolvency legislation. Being focused on corporate reorganization, rather than on liquidation of the company's assets, as well as on arrangements between the insolvent company and its creditors, said provisions offers a new perspective in the Italian insolvency framework, in line with the most advanced legal systems.

In other words, the above provisions of law represent the first substantive step towards rehabilitative insolvency solutions for distressed companies in Italy, as well as an application test for the latest amendments to the insolvency legislation. Reference shall be made, in particular, to the recent Bankruptcy Reform Act, effective as of July 2006, containing a more comprehensive reform of the IBL that would, among other things, make innovations to further insolvency procedures, such as bankruptcy procedures and the so called *concordato fallimentare* (*i.e.* a reorganization with creditors performed in the framework of bankruptcy).

In conclusion, the provisions concerning a 182bis DRA might restore efficiency in the Italian system, opening up a potential for significant investment opportunities and allow investors skilled in special situation to provide their contribution to the Italian market.

In Italy the debate on the rules aimed at governing crisis situations and ensuring uniform applicability of the insolvency law principles is, up to date, very lively. Today, on the basis of new provisions of law, players in the Italian market could be more willing to use the above mentioned flexible legal tools and devices in order to address and resolve the main issues facing distressed companies.

ANNEX: KEY LEGISLATION

Article 182bis of the Italian Bankruptcy Law

Debt Restructuring Agreement. The debtor can file with the court – together with the statement and the documentation prescribed in article 161 – an agreement of reorganization reached with its creditors representing at least a 60 per cent of the debts along with a report by an expert on the feasibility of the agreement itself, with special reference to its suitability as to ensure the regular payment of the external creditors.

The agreement is published in the Companies' Register and the creditors and every other interested can oppose within thirty days from the publication.

The court decides the oppositions and proceeds to the approval in a council chamber with a decree.

The decree of the court can be appealed with the court of appeals pursuant article 183, as applicable, within fifteen days from its publication in the Companies' Register.

The agreement is effective as of the day of its publication in the Companies' Register'.

Chapter 11
Japan

Expedited Corporate Debt Restructuring in Japan

Shinjiro Takagi

ACRONYMS, ABBREVIATIONS & DEFINED TERMS

CC	Commercial Code
Civil RL	Japanese Civil Rehabilitation Law
Co. RL	Corporation Reorganization Law
DIP	Debtor-in-possession
EDITDA	Earnings before interest, taxes, depreciation and amortization, excluding non-cash stock compensation expenses, loss on disposal of property and equipment, and impairment charges
Guideline	The *Guideline for Out-Of-Court Workout* established by the Japanese National Bankers' Association and other relevant organizations in 2001.
INSOL	INSOL International
IRCJ	Industrial Revitalization Corporation of Japan
JPY	Japanese Yen
M&A	Mergers and acquisitions
METI	Japanese Ministry of Economy, Trade and Industries
NPLs	Non-performing and sub-performing loans
RCC	Resolution and Collection Corporation of Japan
SME	Small and medium sized enterprises

I. OVERVIEW OF EXPEDITED CORPORATE DEBT RESTRUCTURING PROCEDURES IN JAPAN

There are three schemes available in Japan to address expedite corporate debt restructuring on an expedited basis: one out-of-court workout scheme; and, two statutory reorganization proceedings. These are:

(1) The *Guideline for Out-Of-Court Workout* established by the National Bankers' Association and other relevant organizations in 2001 (the 'Guideline').[1]
(2) A Civil Rehabilitation proceeding under the *Civil Rehabilitation Law* (*Minji Saizei-hô*) enacted in 1999 ('Civil RL'), which abolished the former Composition Law of 1927; and,
(3) A Corporate Reorganization proceeding under the *Corporation Reorganization Law* (*Kaisha kôsei-hô*) enacted in 1951, which was the subject of major reform in 2002 ('Co. RL').[2]

A. OUT-OF-COURT WORKOUT

The Guideline is a useful tool to facilitate the reorganization of the financial structure of a corporation with excessive debts owed to banks and other financial creditors at an early stage, without impairing trade creditors' claims. A number of large-size cases have been resolved by using the Guideline.[3] The most significant deficiency of the Guideline is that it requires unanimous consents from all creditors to obtain a debt forgiveness and/or a debt equity swap in the proposed restructuring plan, while no compulsory power exists to induce dissenting creditors to accept the plan. Contrary to the INSOL 8 Principles,[4] the Guideline specifies not only the procedural matters, but also the substantial requirements such as fair and equality rules.[5] Since the Guideline provides for rather rigid requirements, such as the replacement of managers and owners when creditors' rights are generally impaired, it is used to reorganize relatively large corporations. Informal, out-of-court workout proceedings for small and medium-sized corporations are to some extent less strict in applying the *above* procedures and requirements, while referencing the Guideline.

---

1. An English version of the Guideline for Out-Of-Court Workout is attached as Annex 1 to this chapter.
2. Law No. 172 of 1952 and No. 154 as amended and restated in 2002. Law No. 154 became effective in 2003.
3. Guideline cases include Seibu Department Stores, Nippon Yakin Kogyo and Hazama Construction.
4. These principles are statements of best practice for all multi-creditor workouts. They were drafted by INSOL and endorsed by the World Bank, Bank of England and the British Bankers Association. INSOL International, 'Statement of Principles for a Global Approach to Multi-Creditor Workouts', London 2000, available at <http://www.insol.org/pdf/Lenders.pdf>.
5. See section 2(1) of the Guidelines.

B.   STATUTORY REORGANIZATION PROCEEDINGS

Under the Japanese law, there are two statutory reorganization procedures: (1) Civil Rehabilitation; and, (2) Corporate Reorganization.

Recent reforms of relevant insolvency laws[6] have changed the practices involved in reorganization cases dramatically. This has led the Japanese courts to open their gates wider to reorganization cases, and cases are being handled more expeditiously. For example, the number of civil rehabilitation cases filed in the Tokyo district court in 2002 was almost ten times higher than the composition cases under the former Composition Law. Previously, judges were rather reluctant to begin composition and corporate reorganization cases where the prospects for successful rehabilitation were uncertain.

Today, reorganization cases are being handled expeditiously under the Civil RL. In general, a plan is confirmed by the court within approximately six months after the initial filing. In corporate reorganization cases which are generally larger than civil rehabilitation cases, a plan is confirmed within about one year after the adjudication to open the case.

A sale of a going-concern business operations is conducted at a very early stage of a special liquidation proceeding based on the Company Law and the Bankruptcy Law, may constitute a substantial reorganization of viable businesses.

C.   CIVIL REHABILITATION AND CORPORATE REORGANIZATION PROCEEDINGS

The major differences between the civil rehabilitation and corporate reorganization proceedings are the following:

(1) The *civil rehabilitation proceeding* is designed – in general – to rehabilitate small and medium sized enterprises ('SMEs') whereas the *corporate reorganization proceeding* is usually used to reorganize larger undertakings.
(2) In a *corporate reorganization* cases, the rights of secured creditors are stayed and secured claims can be altered under a corporate reorganization plan which is accepted by a majority of creditors; on the contrary, in a *civil rehabilitation* case, secured creditors' rights can neither be stayed nor altered without consent of individual secured creditors (with some exceptions as explained later).
(3) In a *civil rehabilitation* proceeding, in principle, a debtor is not deprived of its right to operate the business and dispose of its assets, whereas in a *corporate reorganization* case, incumbent managers are replaced by a trustee. The Co. RL, however, provides that a court is able to appoint an incumbent manager/s as a trustee or deputy trustees in some cases where a debtor in possession ('DIP') scheme is adopted.

---

6. Civil Rehabilitation Law of 1999, Law for Recognition and Assistance to Foreign Insolvency Proceedings of 2000, New Corporate Reorganization Law of 2002, New Bankruptcy Law of 2004 and New Company Law of 2006 were enacted and English translations of these statutes can be ordered by e-mail at 'order@ehs.or.jp'.

A problem common to both reorganization proceedings, i.e. civil and corporate reorganizations, is the rigid thinking about the application of equality principle regarding the rights of unsecured trade creditors and those of unsecured claims of financial creditors (including over-secured part of claims owed to creditors). Even in cases where almost all financial creditors have agreed to an out-of-court workout (that requested financial creditors to partly forgive their loans and/or accept debt/equity swaps before filing a petition to commence a statutory proceeding), the subsequent conversion of the case to a statutory reorganization proceedings with an intention to cram-down a minority of dissenting creditors (by taking advantage of a majority rule available in the court-supervised statutory proceedings) involves some risks, since trade creditors' rights cannot be left unimpaired. This then may cause a possible deterioration of business reputation and an erosion of enterprise value of the debtor corporation. The Japanese courts should take a more flexible attitude toward applying the principle of equality paying due respect to the economic rationality.

D. THE RESOLUTION & COLLECTION CORPORATION

The Resolution & Collection Corporation ('RCC') was established by the Japanese government in 1996 to take over loan assets owned by bankrupt housing loan companies. It was subsequently reformed in 1999, when another special purpose company which was established in 1995 to buy loan assets of bankrupt financial institutions was merged (by absorption) to the RCC, for the express purpose of buying non and sub-performing loans ('NPLs') from financial institutions including solvent banks and collecting these debts in order to accelerate the removal of significant amount of NPLs from the banks' balance sheet. The RCC has not only tried to enforce actions against bad and doubtful debts, but it also has actively advised distressed debtors in restructuring their debts and businesses by means of out-of-court workouts and statutory reorganization proceedings (i.e. civil rehabilitation and corporate reorganization proceedings). Although the statutory provisions that created the RCC established that the timeframe in which it can perform purchases of NPLs expires on March 2005, the RCC continues to help restructuring nonviable loan assets entrusted by financial institutions but without having the faculty to purchase NPLs anymore.

E. THE INDUSTRIAL REVITALIZATION CORPORATION

In addition to the RCC, in April 2003 the Japanese government established the Industrial Revitalization Corporation of Japan ('IRCJ'). Its purpose was to accelerate the disposal of NPLs and revitalize corporations with excessive debt by restoring their profitability. In contrast to the RCC, the IRCJ was expected to purchase only those loans owed by distressed debtor companies that are viable and therefore likely to be successfully rehabilitated. Before making a decision to help a troubled debtor corporation, the IRCJ and the 'main creditor bank/s'[7] will

---

7. Main bank/s is the bank/s with the largest credit exposure to the debtor, *cf.* Article 2(2) of the Guidelines regarding 'Major Creditor'.

carefully review the feasibility of the reorganization plan proposed by a heavily indebted and distressed corporation. The IRCJ has engaged suitably experienced and qualified professionals, including consultants, accountants, lawyers and restructuring advisors to operate its business. The decision to help distressed companies includes the declaration of the IRCJ's intention to buy the loans at the price designated by the IRCJ from financial institutions other than the 'main creditor bank/s' that hold the most substantial exposure. Financial creditors are neither legally obliged to sell their claims to the IRCJ nor to accept the proposed debt restructuring plan that provides for a partial debt waiver and/or debt equity swap. In addition to buying loan assets, the IRCJ has infused new money into the assisted companies in the form of capital or new loans. Significant dilutions were involved to wipe out the rights of former owners of the companies. The IRCJ was authorized to use up to JPY 10 trillion to purchase NPLs from banks and/or infuse new money into debtor companies. These funds were obtained in the short-term money market with the Japanese governmental guarantee.

By the end of March 2005, the IRCJ has helped 41 corporate groups (the total number of assisted companies amounts 197). The IRCJ must sell all the purchased assets, including restructured debts and equity, within three years from the date of purchase of the assets. Managers of the debtor companies were replaced by managers appointed by the new owners or the IRCJ. In some cases, the IRCJ has sent turnaround managers to debtor companies to revitalize their businesses operations. The IRCJ is a corporation with a limited life of five years at the maximum. It is now becoming likely that the IRCJ will successfully conclude its operations without incurring any losses before the end of the fiscal year 2006.

F. THE SMALL AND MEDIUM-SIZED ENTERPRISES TURNAROUND COMMITTEES

In 2003, under the initiative of the Ministry of Economy, Trade and Industries ('METI'), the SME Turnaround Committees were created in all 47 municipalities and prefectures in Japan for the purpose of assisting debt restructuring of small and medium-sized enterprises. Professional staff at the SME Turnaround Committees are advising ailing SMEs with excessive debts on how to turnaround their business operations and draft debt restructuring plans. The SME Turnaround Committees have also been taking a role of an intermediary between the debtor and financial creditors to make the drafted restructuring plan become feasible. By the end of 2005, the committees have advised and assisted more than 6,000 enterprises.

G. PRIVATE EQUITY FUNDS

Since 2000, inspired by activities of some foreign-originated funds, a lot of private equity funds have been created. They have been purchasing debt and equity of distressed corporations or acquiring debtors' businesses. They are restructuring the debt of acquired companies by means of out-of-court workouts or statutory reorganization proceedings, and revitalizing their business operations to restore their profitability. The number of M&As, including those not involving debt restructurings, has doubled between 1999 and 2004 and is still increasing year after year.

H. RESOLVED NON-PERFORMING LOANS PROBLEM

It has been reported by the Financial Services Agency of Japan that in March 2002 NPLs held by Japanese banks and financial institutions started to decline from the peak of over JPY 50 trillion to less than JPY 25 trillion by March 2005. The rate of NPLs owed to major Japanese banks and financial institutions (the ratio of non-performing loans over the total loans) was 8.7 per cent in March 2002 when the amount of NPLs was at its peak. It is worth noting that as of March 2005 this figure came down to 2.9 per cent, and as of March 2006 it came further down to 1.8 per cent. In the light of these developments, by the end of March 2005, the Japanese government declared that the NPLs problem was resolved.[8] However, small and medium-sized financial institutions including regional banks are still struggling, trying to reduce their NPLs. The Japanese economy has been sluggish as long as 13 years, but now it appears it is finally on the sustainable recovery path.

II. OUT-OF-COURT WORKOUT RESTRUCTURING

A. ESTABLISHMENT OF THE GUIDELINE FOR OUT-OF-COURT WORKOUT

The National Bankers Association, the Federation of Managers of Business Corporations, and other relevant organizations associated with the Financial Services Agency, Ministry of Finance, METI, Bank of Japan and the Deposit Insurance Corporation, created a committee that established the Guideline for Out-of-Court Workout in September 2001. The Guideline that references the INSOL 8 principles for international multi-creditors' workout was designed to clear out the immense amount of NPLs owed to multiple banks and financial institutions and restore the viability of debtor corporations.

B. PROCESS OF OUT-OF-COURT WORKOUT BASED ON THE GUIDELINE

The procedure established by the Guideline begins with the debtor corporation applying together with its 'main creditor bank'[9] for a multi-creditor out-of-court workout in cases where a number of financial creditors possess lending

---
8. <www.fsa.go.jp/en/regulated/npl/index.html>.
9. The Guidelines refer to 'Major Creditors'. This term is defined in Article 2(2) as '*usually multiple financial institutions, including the banks with the largest credit exposure to the debtor*'.

exposures.[10] The application must be accompanied by documents that describe the causes of the debtor becoming financially distressed and a proposed reorganization plan. The proposal should include not only a business reorganization plan but also a debt restructuring plan. The 'main creditor bank' then investigates the documents and the reorganization plan to determine whether the descriptions and statements are accurate and the proposed plan is both feasible and reasonable. If the 'main creditor bank' determines that the criteria has been met and agrees that the plan can be acceptable to all other non-main banks whose debts are to be forgiven under the reorganization plan, it will issue a notice of 'standstill' to all other 'relevant financial creditors' and convene the first meeting of creditors.[11]

The 'relevant creditors' are those creditors whose claims are requested to be waived in the proposed plan.[12] They usually consist of banks and other financial institutions, but trade creditors with significant exposures may be included in the category of 'relevant creditors' when the waiver of their trade claims are necessary to accomplish effective debt restructuring. The meeting must be held within two weeks after the notice of standstill was issued.[13]

At the first meeting of creditors, an unanimous consent among creditors must be obtained to extend the standstill period. If they all agree, then a creditors' committee may be elected. The committee can designate professionals (including lawyers, accountants and consultants) to examine the accuracy of the financial statements and the reasonableness and feasibility of the proposed reorganization plan. During the standstill period, the relevant creditors shall refrain from any collection efforts; enforcement or realization of secured rights; improvement of their exposures in relation to other relevant creditors; and, maintain the original balance of their claims.[14] Before the end of the third month after the first meeting was held, a second meeting must take place at which all relevant creditors are to indicate whether they accept the plan or not.[15] If all creditors whose rights will be impaired by reorganization plan grant their consent to the proposed plan, the reorganization plan becomes authorized and the debts owed to the relevant creditors will be changed according to the provisions contained in the plan.[16] If one or more creditors refuses to agree to the plan, the out-of-court workout process is terminated and the debtor should decide whether to file a petition with a court to begin statutory insolvency proceedings.[17]

C. REQUIREMENTS FOR A REORGANIZATION PLAN

The Guideline is designed to facilitate multiple financial creditor workouts to rehabilitate corporations burdened with enormous amounts of debt. In contrast to the INSOL 8 principles, the Guideline provides for substantial requirements

---

10. See Article 4(1) of the Guidelines.
11. See Article 4(5) of the Guidelines.
12. See Article 2(4) of the Guidelines.
13. See Article 5(1) of the Guidelines.
14. See Article 6(1)C of the Guidelines.
15. See Article 6(2) of the Guidelines.
16. See Article 8(4) of the Guidelines.
17. See Article 8(6) of the Guidelines.

Japan

for the reorganization. If the debtor is insolvent, which means that the total amount of debts exceeds the total value of assets, the proposed plan must provide feasible measures to resolve the problem within three years.[18] If the debtor has a negative operating loss, the plan must also show how that loss will be turned into a profit within the three-year period.[19] The plan should provide that the equity of the debtor's controlling shareholders should, in principle, be wiped out and divested, and the equity of existing shareholders should be diluted substantially or eliminated altogether through stock retirement and subsequent capital increases.[20] The plan should, in principle, also request that the debtor's incumbent managers resign upon the creditors' acceptance of the proposed plan.[21,22]

D. OUT-OF-COURT WORKOUTS FOR SMALL AND MEDIUM SIZED ENTERPRISES

In response to the criticisms by some practitioners regarding the severity of substantial requirements envisaged in the Guideline-based reorganization plans for the restructuring of SMEs, the practicing committee of the Guideline has discussed possible ways to promote a more popular use of the Guideline and a possible relaxation of the requirements (or allowance for some reasonable exceptions) only for SMEs. The Guideline is a valuable tool to reorganize the financial structure of a debtor with excessive debts at the early stage without impairing debts owed to trade creditors.

Although the Guideline has not been extensively used during the period in which the IRCJ has been active, its usage increased again after March 2005 and nearly 50 large corporations have been reorganized through an out-of-court workout resorting to the Guideline. Debts owed by SMEs have been restructured assisted by the RCC, the SME Turnaround Committees, private equity funds and other restructuring advisers who may not strictly adhere to the Guideline but refer to it. The RCC and the SME Turnaround Committees have their own guidelines that amend the Guideline making it more suitable to their needs.

E. NECESSITY OF A NEW STATUTE TO FACILITATE AN OUT-OF-COURT WORKOUT

It is a fact that it is not very easy to obtain unanimous consents of all relevant creditors in out-of-court workout processes. Even during the out-of-court workout stages, sizable amount of loans need to be provided by banks to finance operating overhead costs of the debtor corporations. When the unanimous consent is not reached, the debtor should convert the process to a statutory reorganization proceeding to avail themselves of the majority rule contained in the court-supervised reorganization procedures. However, there is no assurance that the loans provided

---

18. See Article 7(2) of the Guidelines.
19. See Article 7(3) of the Guidelines.
20. See Article 7(4) of the Guidelines.
21. See Article 7(5) of the Guidelines.
22. For a hypothetical case of out-of-court workout based on the Guideline, see section V *below*.

during the workout stages would be treated as priority claims, equivalent to the administrative expense status of DIP financing loans during the statutory proceedings that may succeed the workout. Therefore, banks may be reluctant to provide pre-DIP financing loans during workout stages without any assurance that the loans would be treated as priority claims in the subsequent statutory proceeding. Some kind of bridge would be needed in Japan similar to the new statutory schemes adopted by the English Enterprise Act of 2002. What the Enterprise Act is addressing is a means to facilitate out-of-court workouts, whereby a court approval to a proposed restructuring plan can be obtained when the majority of creditors agree to the proposed plan in out-of-court workout albeit reticent minority creditors refusing to consent to the plan, and the debts owed to dissenting creditors can be impaired according to the court-approved plan, cramming them down. The study group established by the METI and the Ministry of Justice is now discussing possible introduction of such a new legislation to facilitate debt restructuring at the early stage by out-of-court workout process.

F. NEW COMPANY LAW ENABLES 100 PER CENT WIPE-OUT OF EXISTING STOCKS IN AN OUT-OF-COURT WORKOUT PROCESS

The New Company Law of 2005[23] which become effective in May 2006 provides that a 100 per cent dilution of existing shareholders' rights can be accomplished by a resolution of a shareholders' meeting. Namely, by a special majority of voting shareholders who hold more than two-third of the 'designated class of stocks', it has become possible to wipe out all stocks of that designated class by the articles of incorporation of the company. The 'designated class of stocks' in this context is defined as the stocks that are purchased by the company and wiped out completely by a special resolution of the shareholders' meeting of the designated class. The capability of a company to create such a 'designated class of stocks' needs to be readily defined in the articles of incorporation; if not, the articles need to be amended to include that provision by a special resolution adopted by the shareholders. The resolution should state that the stock of the newly created class to be purchased and wiped out by the company. This resolution should be adopted by a special class meeting (shareholders of the newly created class of stock). It will also be resolved to issue new stock replacing the wiped-out stock. These three resolutions that should be adopted by the shareholders can be resolved at the same meeting. Before the enactment of the New Company Law, 100 per cent dilution of issued stock without consent of the shareholders was possible only in corporate reorganization proceedings under the Co. RL, but after May 2006 onwards, a complete wiping-out of existing shareholders rights becomes possible even in out-of-court workouts under the conditions described *above*.

---

23. Provisions regarding companies were previously included in the Commercial Code (CC), but the enacted New Company Law has entirely abolished former provisions with regard to business corporations included in the CC. The new law has made significant changes in terms of corporate governance, information disclosure, restructuring, founding, and so forth, for business corporations.

Japan

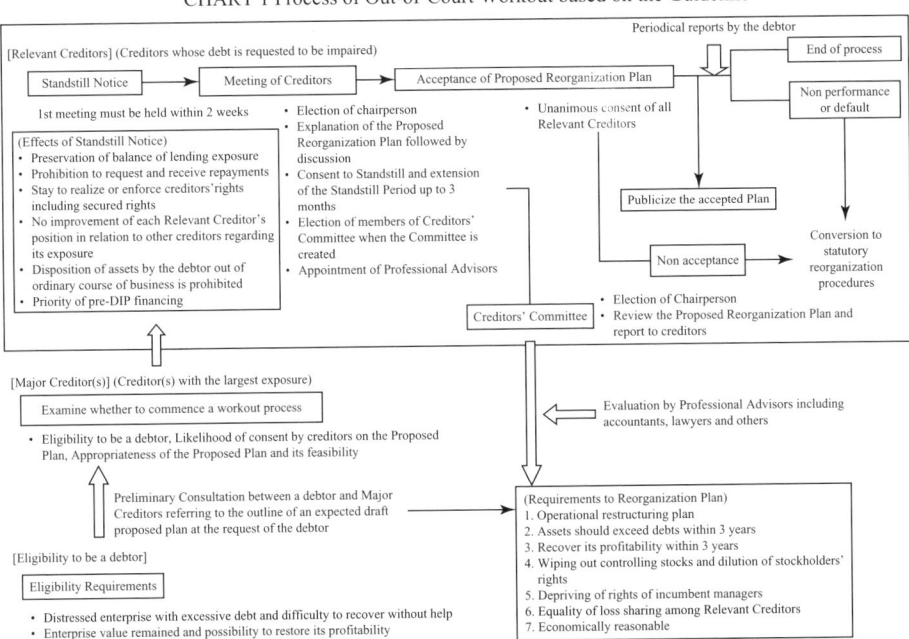

CHART 1 Process of Out-of-Court Workout based on the Guideline

III. CIVIL REHABILITATION PROCEEDING BASED ON CIVIL REHABILITATION LAW

The Civil RL was enacted to expedite proceedings, abolishing the former Composition Law, establishing the so-called 'rehabilitation proceeding'. In principle, only unsecured creditors are bound by the rehabilitation proceeding of the Civil RL and could be impaired by the rehabilitation plan. To change the rights of secured creditors and those of creditors with priority, e.g. employees' rights and tax and social security debts, the consent of each creditor is needed.

A. COURT SHOULD COMMENCE THE PROCEEDING UNLESS EXCEPTIONAL

A debtor is able to file a petition to commence a rehabilitation proceeding with a district court with competent jurisdiction, when: (1) there is a likelihood that the debtor is not generally able to pay debts becoming due or its debts exceed the value of its assets; or, (2) the debtor is not able to pay debts becoming due without seriously impeding the continuation of its business.[24] Upon filing a petition, the court may issue injunction orders which effectively stay creditors' general collection efforts.[25]

---

24. See Article 21 of the Civil RL.
25. See Articles 26–30 of the Civil RL.

Upon petition of the debtor, the court should issue an order to commence a rehabilitation case unless it is obvious that the debtor cannot be rehabilitated through the rehabilitation proceeding.[26] The Tokyo District Court usually issues the opening order within 15 days after the filing of the petition.

B. Debtor can Sell its Business with Court Permission During the Early Stage Without Shareholders' Consent

Outside a statutory reorganization proceeding, a special resolution with weighted majority of a shareholders' meeting is required to sell the company's business as a going concern.[27] However, after the commencement of the rehabilitation proceeding, the court may permit the sale of the debtor's business without the shareholders' resolution if the company is insolvent during the early stage of the proceeding and even before the filing of a proposed rehabilitation plan. M&As are an effective tool to revitalize a distressed business.[28] Speedy sale of the business before its deterioration is crucial to avoid the deterioration of the value of the going concern and the company's assets.

C. DIP in Normal Cases

Managers of a debtor company may be able to remain in their positions, and continue to operate the debtor's business and dispose of its assets in ordinary course of business. This may occur even after the commencement of a rehabilitation proceeding in a fashion similar to the US Chapter 11 reorganization proceeding.[29] It is a common practice that the court will appoint a supervisor, as a watch-dog over the debtor. The court may appoint a trustee in an exceptional case involving gross mismanagement, depriving the debtor of the managers' rights.[30] Usually, a qualified and experienced lawyer is appointed as a supervisor or a trustee.

D. Summarized Proceedings to Verify Claims, Avoid Preferential and Fraudulent Transfers and Assess Damages of Responsible Managers

Upon the commencement of a rehabilitation proceeding, a debtor has to evaluate its assets and file a copy of the financial statements together with a written report explaining the reasons why it has fallen into financial difficulties.[31] The debtor also

---

26. See Article 33 of the Civil RL.
27. See Article 467 of the Company Law.
28. See Article 43 of the Civil RL.
29. See Article 38 of the Civil RL. *cf.*§ 1101 et seq., Chapter11, 11 USC.
30. See Articles 54 et. seq. and 64 et. seq. of the Civil RL.
31. See Articles 124 and 125 of the Civil RL.

has to report these matters orally in a meeting of creditors convened by the court. The documents filed with the court are accessible by interested parties.[32]

The creditors usually have to file their claims with the court and if the filed claim is contested by the debtor or other interested parties, the debtor and the creditor are heard at a summary hearing proceeding. The creditor whose claim is contested and denied by the court in this summary proceeding may file a plenary law suit requesting verification of the contested claim. This plenary law suit works as an appeal to the court's denial of the creditor's claim.[33]

The supervisor or a trustee (if it has been appointed) may avoid preferential and fraudulent transfers by filing a summary proceeding designed for this purpose.[34]

The debtor, a supervisor, a creditor or a trustee – if appointed – may file a summarized assessment proceeding for damages which should be compensated by managers who are responsible for the failure of the debtor company.[35]

The *above* three summary proceedings are designed to speed up the incidental processes within the civil rehabilitation proceedings and the loosing parties of the summary order are entitled to convert the proceeding to a plenary law suit.

E. SOME RESTRICTIONS ON SECURED RIGHTS

Under the Civil RL, the secured creditor is still able to enforce its secured rights, but the debtor is able to move to the court after filing a petition to commence the rehabilitation proceeding, requesting an issuance of a temporary stay order prohibiting the enforcement of secured rights during a certain period of time. The purpose of the stay order is to create a reasonable timeframe during which the debtor and the secured creditors can settle the issue between them by negotiation.[36]

According to the Japanese Civil Code, which is based on the Napoleonic Code, a secured right is not limited to the value of the collateral. In other words, a secured creditor can refuse to relinquish his/her secured right, even if a debtor has paid a part of the secured debt equivalent to the value of the collateral. The secured right cannot be extinguished without the consent of the secured creditor unless the debt has been paid in full. Under the Civil RL, however, the secured right is extinguished when the debtor pays a sufficient portion of the claim, equal to the value of the collateral. If the secured creditor does not agree with the debtor's valuation of the collateral, the court decides the amount based on the assessment made by a court-appointed appraiser.[37] Due to this provision, an under-secured creditor cannot insist on full payment even if the underlying debt exceeds the value of the collateral.

---

32. See Article 126 of the Civil RL.
33. See Article 94 et. seq. of the Civil RL.
34. See Article 127 et. seq. of the Civil RL.
35. See Article 142 et. seq. of the Civil RL.
36. See Article 31 of the Civil RL.
37. See Article 148 et. seq. of the Civil RL.

F. REHABILITATION PLAN

The debtor shall file the proposed rehabilitation plan before the deadline designated by the court, which usually occurs by the end of third months after the petition to commence the case.[38] The rehabilitation plan provides – among other alternatives – for partial debt forgiveness, rescheduling of the repayment term, debt equity swaps, etc.[39]

Upon the court's permission, the plan can provide for reverse split of stocks, change of the company's articles of incorporation in relation to the authorized amount of stock to be issued by the company, wiping-out of all or a portion of the issued stock and issuance of new stock. The court may allow a plan with these permit-required reversal provisions when the company is insolvent and stockholders have no interest in the company.[40]

The debtor is able to set off profits obtained by the debts forgiveness and/or revaluation of assets against the carried-over losses without any restrictions.

The proposed plan is accepted by the vote of the simple majority of creditors in the amount of debt and number of creditors. It is a double requirement, i.e. in number of creditors and in value of debt. Voting on the proposed plan may take place at a meeting of creditors or by post.[41]

When the proposed plan is accepted by the creditors, the court may confirm the accepted plan.[42] The court should confirm the plan if the plan meets the requirements of the best interest test[43] and the feasibility test. Usually, the confirmation of the accepted plan is made by about the end of the sixth month after filing the petition to commence the rehabilitation proceedings.

G. CLOSING THE CASE

The case is closed with a confirmation order issued by the court, when the confirmation order becomes indisputable by appeal; or, by an order to affirm the confirmation order by an appellate court. If a supervisor is appointed, the case is not closed before the consummation of the confirmed plan or three years after the confirmation order becomes final, whichever occurs first.[44] The cases which are completed by means of a M&A may be closed soon after the confirmation.

---

38. See Article 163 of the Civil RL.
39. See Article 154 et. seq. of the Civil RL.
40. See Articles 166 and 166–2 of the Civil RL.
41. See Article 169 et. seq. of the Civil RL.
42. See Article 174 et. seq. of the Civil RL.
43. By the 'best interest test' one refers to the fact that the plan must be better than liquidation to creditors.
44. See Article 188 of the Civil RL.

Japan

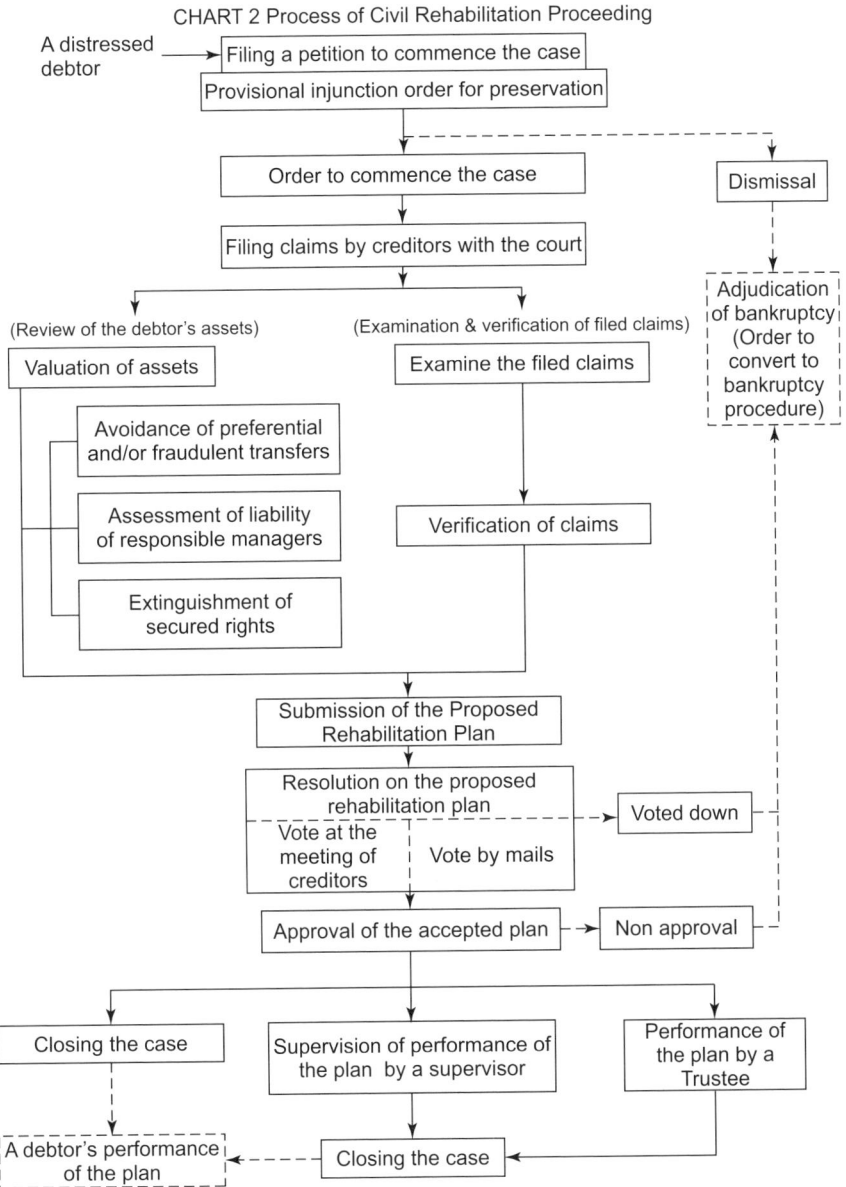

CHART 2 Process of Civil Rehabilitation Proceeding

IV. CORPORATE REORGANIZATION PROCEEDING UNDER CORPORATE REORGANIZATION LAW

As the process of a corporate reorganization proceeding under the Co. RL is roughly similar to that of a civil rehabilitation proceeding, only differences between the corporate reorganization and civil rehabilitation will be described.

A. ELIGIBILITY

While any kind of legal entity or individual is eligible to file a petition to commence a civil rehabilitation proceeding, only a stock company is eligible for a corporate reorganization proceeding.[45] While neither the Co. RL nor the Civil RL imposes limits on eligibility by size of the debtor, the use of the Co. RL is intended for larger corporations and the Civil RL for small and medium-sized enterprises. Since the Civil RL allows managers to remain in their positions as DIP, managers of larger corporations are inclined to choose the civil rehabilitation proceeding in some cases. In such circumstances, a creditor may file a petition to convert the case to a corporate reorganization proceeding aiming to deprive the managers' position in the debtor corporation that commenced a rehabilitation proceeding under the Civil RL.

B. STRONGER WEAPONS THAN CIVIL REHABILITATION

All creditors' and shareholders' rights are affected in a corporate reorganization proceeding. During a corporate reorganization proceeding all rights, i.e. not only the rights of unsecured creditors but also those of secured creditors and creditors with priority (e.g. employees' debt and tax or social security debts), are stayed.[46] Usually, these rights are also impaired by means of a reorganization plan. To balance, the rights of managers and owners of the debtor are deprived and wiped-out in the reorganization case.

The proposed reorganization plan is accepted when the majority of unsecured creditors who hold a simple majority of the aggregate amount of unsecured debts agree to the plan. The plan providing for an extension in the maturity of the claim of secured creditors will only be accepted when the secured creditors who hold two-third of secured debts in amount agree to the reorganization plan. The plan providing for impairment of the secured rights, e.g. debt for equity swap and debt forgiveness, is accepted by secured creditors when the secured creditors

---

45. See Article 1 of the Co.RL.
46. See Article 47 of the Co.RL.

who hold three-fourth of the secured debts in amount agree. No consent is required for tax and social security debts when the plan provides to extend repayment term for less than three years. No shareholder has a voting power to the plan when the debtor company is insolvent, i.e. the amount of debts exceeds assets. Most debtor corporations in reorganization cases are insolvent.[47]

When one or more classes accept the plan while others do not, the court can still confirm the plan amending it to pay the creditors of the non-accepting class/es more than they would have received in a constructive liquidation proceeding.[48]

The plan can provide for the sale of debtor's businesses, M&As of companies, wiping out of stock, issuing new stock, split of stock, consolidation of stock, split of the company, exchange of stock, transfer of stock, etc., without any resolution at a meeting of shareholders which is required by the Company Law outside the reorganization proceeding.[49]

C. CHANGE OF OWNERS AND MANAGERS

The Co. RL provides for a fair and equitable rule: when creditors' rights are impaired in any ways, the shareholders' rights must be wiped out completely.[50] Since the plan may provide for issuance of new stock, total replacement of owners of the debtor company is accomplished in almost all reorganization cases in Japan.

A trustee must be appointed in any reorganization cases at the time of the commencement of the case to deprive of the rights of the managers of the debtor company and usually an interim trustee is appointed upon filing of the petition to open the case.[51] Because the owners of the debtor who elected former managers are purged by the confirmation of the plan, there is no ways to revive the former managers.

The reformed Co. RL of 2002, however, provides that the court may appoint an incumbent manager/s as a trustee when he/she is not responsible for the failure of the debtor corporation.[52] For example, the court may appoint, as a trustee, a turnaround manager/s who has been appointed during the pre-filing workout stage to replace former managers to revitalize the debtor's business.

---

47. See Article 189 et. seq. of the Co.RL.
48. See Article 200 of the Co.RL.
49. See Article 167 et. seq. of the Co.RL.
50. See Article 199(2) of the Co.RL.
51. See Articles 42 and 30 of the Co.RL.
52. See Article 67(3) of the Co.RL.

CHART 3 Regular Time Schedule of Corporate Reorganization Proceeding (Tokyo District Court)

Timeline	Court Process	Claims Process
	Filing of a petition to commence the proceeding & provisional injunction order for preservation	
1 month	Examination of opening requirements, etc.	
	Opening order to commence a case & appointment of a Trustee	
2 months	Drafting of a Reorganization Plan to be proposed	Review of assets & debts
		Period to file claims by creditors
6 months		Completion of valuation of the debtor's assets
2 weeks		Period for examination of filed claims
10 months	Deadline to file a reorganization plan by the trustee	Verification proceedings of objected claims
	Court decision calling for voting by creditors on the proposed plan	
1 year	Voting on the proposed plan at a meeting of creditors or by mails	
	Approval order of the voted plan	
1 month / 10 years	Consummation & performance of the approved plan	
	Closing order of the proceeding	

V. CASE STUDY: THE 'X CONSTRUCTION CORPORATION CASE' (A HYPOTHETICAL OUT-OF-COURT WORKOUT CASE BASED ON THE GUIDELINE)

An analysis on a hypothetical case of an Out-of-Court Workout case based on the Guideline is provided in this section for illustration purposes. It is useful to exemplify the importance of expedited and alternative techniques in dealing with debt restructuring.

TIMELINE: MAIN EPISODES	
1889	Mr. X started his construction business as a sole proprietor.
1917	X partnership was established.
1930	X Construction Ltd. was founded.
1962	X Construction Corporation was listed in the Tokyo Stock Exchange.
2002	The first debt restructuring plan was made with four banks which had the main exposure.
2003	An Out-of-Court Workout based on the Guideline took place.

X Construction Corporation ('X') has been engaged in civil and building construction business being the 10th biggest construction company in Japan.

X was especially well-known as a well-established civil constructor and had constructed many roads, bridges, dams, power plants not only in Japan but also in foreign countries.

During the bubble economy when the property prices soared, X had been aggressively engaged in land, housing, resort and golf-course development operations, purchasing numerous real properties and incurred huge amounts of debt. The management of X encouraged their employees to initiate new development businesses such as golf courses, resort facilities, etc.

The X group was comprized of approximately 60 subsidiaries and affiliated companies. Its total amount of annual revenue reached at its peak as much as JPY 700 billion in 1992. After the burst of the bubble, the revenue declined year after year to come down to JPY 200 billion in 2002.

The total amount of debt was JPY 770 billion in 1993. It was owed to nearly 150 banks and financial institutions.

Between 1992 and 2000, X had drafted its own operational restructuring plans and implemented them five times, trying to recover its profitability. None of which was successful.

In 2001, X drafted the first debt restructuring plan assisted by its main bank which had the biggest exposure. Among other things, the draft plan requested the four major banks which had relatively big exposures to forgive portion of their debts which amounted to JPY 122 billion in total. It took nearly ten months until the four major banks consented to the plan in the absence of the Guideline. But the burden of debts was still too heavy and X could not recover its profitability.

The Guideline for Out-of-Court Workout with Multi-Creditors was enacted in September 2001 with the aim of accelerating disposal of non and poor-performing loans in Japan.

As of the end of September 2002, the total assets of X amounted to JPY 400 billion and the total amount of its debts was JPY 375 billion. The total amount of interest-bearing debts was 176 times X's annual EDITDA.

Under such circumstance, X drafted – again – a new debt and operational restructuring plan assisted by consultants and other professionals. With the consent of the main bank that had the biggest exposure to the proposed plan, X initiated an out-of-court workout proceeding based on the Guideline on 15 January 2002 and sent a notice of Standstill through fax transmissions to about 60 relevant banks and financial institutions, requesting their debt to be impaired by the proposed plan.

At the first creditors' meeting which was held on 29 January 2002 the CEO of X explained to the attending creditors the contents of the proposed plan (which was sent in advance with the standstill notice), as well as the reasons why X must be restructured. Then, he requested the creditors to accept the plan.

Three experienced lawyers and one certified public accountant, who were elected at the creditors' meeting, were appointed as 'professional advisors'. The role of the advisors was to analyze the proposed plan and report to the creditors on the fairness and the feasibility of the plan.

The plan proposed partial debt forgiveness (or haircut) totalling JPY 140 billion and debt for equity swap to the financial creditors in the amount of JPY 10 billion. Secured claims should be paid in full and most of unsecured creditors or the over-secured part of secured claims should be paid in 50 per cent of their value. In addition, repayment dates of the financial claims were to be rescheduled.

The plan also called for splitting the group of companies into good and bad companies. The good companies would continue X's core businesses such as civil and building construction that seemed profitable, while bad companies would handle non-core businesses such as land and resort developing operations which were making losses. Namely, the good companies succeeded assets and liabilities which were related to the construction businesses, while bad companies succeeded assets and liabilities which were related to the non-core businesses.

All assets of the bad companies were intended to be sold within three years and their proceeds would be used for the repayment of the succeeded debts which were mostly secured claims. When the proceeds from the assets of the bad companies become insufficient to repay the debts (the value of the assets was inferior to the amount of debt), creditors of the bad companies would had to relinquish the outstanding balance of their claims.

The bad companies were the parent companies of the good companies, owning 51 per cent of the stock of the good companies. The rest of the good companies' stock went to the shareholders of X on a *pro rata* basis.

Upon completion of the sale of all assets of the bad companies – within the three-year timeframe – they would file a petition to commence a special court-supervised liquidation under the Company Law. Subsequently, 51 per cent stock of the good company owned by bad companies would be sold in the stock markets and the proceeds were to be credited to creditors who had pledges on the stock. Afterwards, the bad companies would disappear.

The new X which was the good company continued its operation as a listed company in the Tokyo Securities Exchange.

An operational restructuring plan for the good company was developed. The plan provided for several means including reduction of redundant 1,000 employees to recover its profitability. Most of the management of X was replaced by new managers.

After intensive due diligence, the panel of professional advisors filed a report on the proposed plan with the creditors at the end of October 2002 including answers to creditors' questions which requested investigations by the advisors.

The second creditors' meeting was held on 15 November 2002 at which all relevant creditors expressed their intention to accept the proposed plan. Between mid-September and mid-November 2002, many meetings had been held between the debtor and each creditor to discuss the contents the plan.

Had unanimous consents of relevant creditors not been obtained, the debtor should have had to file a petition to commence a statutory reorganization proceeding, i.e. a civil rehabilitation or corporate reorganization proceeding, but all relevant creditors of the X ultimately consented to the proposed plan.

The bad companies were closed at the end of March 2006 and the market price of the New X's stock has doubled.

ANNEX: KEY LEGISLATION

THE GUIDELINE FOR MULTI-CREDITOR OUT-OF-COURT WORKOUTS OFFICIAL ENGLISH TRANSLATION

1. Multi-Creditor Workout subject to this guideline
   (1) A multi-creditor workout implemented under this Guideline is that aims for rehabilitation of a corporation in operational difficulties through forbearance and/or composition of debt (mainly financial debt), etc., based on an agreement between the creditors and the debtor instead of procedures in accordance with the Corporate Reorganization Law or Civil Rehabilitation Law, etc. This guideline is intended to cover only limited range of multi-creditor workout, namely those in which a number of financial institutions are involved as the Major Creditors or Relevant Creditors defined *below*.
   (2) The rehabilitation of a corporation presumed in this guideline should primary be conducted under the Corporate Reorganization Law or Civil Rehabilitation Law, etc. However, only when such legal procedures are feared to considerably erodes the enterprise value of the corporation and cause a hindrance to the rehabilitation of the corporation, and when a multi-creditor workout under with this guideline shall be implemented.
   (3) As a precondition for the debtor requesting the creditors for forbearance and/or composition, the multi-creditor workout under this guideline expects that the debtor independently exert the maximum efforts towards rehabilitation, that clarify the responsibility for mismanagement and that the shareholders (especially the controlling shareholder, if any) fulfil all of their responsibilities to the maximum extent.

2. Rules for multi-creditor workout
   (1) This guideline has been prepared by representatives of financial and other industries with consultation to neutral and fair advisors such as academics credentials and sets out rules for an implementation of the multi-creditor workout described in Article 1 *above* in fair and speedy manner. Although this guideline has no legal enforceability, it is expected that financial institutions, etc. as Major or Relevant Creditors, corporations as debtors, and other relevant stakeholders voluntarily respect and observe this guideline, In a sense, this guideline represents a general consensus among the financial and other industry regarding informal workouts for companies truly deserving to be rehabilitated,
   (2) When One of the Major Creditors (usually multiple financial institutions, including the banks with the largest credit exposure to the debtor) receives a sincere request from a debtor for the multi-creditor workout under this guideline, the Major Creditors shall deal with the request sincerely and promptly, and the Major Creditors and the debtor shall mutually cooperate

to ensure the orderly and expeditious progress of the procedures of the workout.
(3) Relevant Creditors (creditors, including major creditors, whose rights shall be affected if a rehabilitation plan is approved) shall sincerely cooperate to the multi-creditor workout in accordance with these rules.
(4) Relevant Creditors and the debtor shall mutually obligated to keep confidentiality of the information obtain in the process of the multi-creditor workout.
(5) Fairness and equity shall be observed as the principle of the multi-creditor workout in accordance with this guideline, transparency shall be respected.

3. Corporations eligible for multi-creditor workout under this guideline

A corporation can apply for the multi-creditor workout if all the conditions *below* are fulfilled.

(1) The corporation is in operational difficulty mainly due to excessive debt, and it is difficult for the corporation to rehabilitate itself through its own efforts.
(2) The possibility exists that the corporation can rehabilitated with support of creditors as the enterprise value of the company still exists (i.e. the business is profitable and promising, with a business base including technological know-how, a brand name, an established trading area and highly capable personnel) and operating profit have been posted in the major business divisions, etc.
(3) There is a concern that petition for the Corporate Reorganization Law or the Civil Rehabilitation Law, etc. may deteriorate the credibility of the debtor, considerably erodes the enterprise value of the corporation and cause a hindrance to the rehabilitation of the corporation.
(4) Rehabilitation of the corporation through the multi-creditor workout is considered more economically reasonable for creditors in recovering their credits than liquidation via bankruptcy or the procedures under the Corporate Reorganization Law or the Civil Rehabilitation Law, etc.

4. Commencement of the multi-creditor workout

(1) A debtor fulfilling the necessary conditions indicated in Article 3 *above* requests its Major Creditors for a multi-creditor workout under this guideline. Upon request, the debtor shall provide the Major Creditors with relevant information which sufficiently explain the current and past state of assets, liabilities and profit/loss, the reason for the lapse into operational difficulties and a rehabilitation plan of the corporation, etc.
(2) Major Creditors shall examine the information mentioned in (1) *above* provided by the debtor, have the debtor explain in detail, and make an examination on the points indicated *below* to decide whether it is reasonable to issue a 'Standstill Notice'. When multiple Major Creditors exist,

the, decision to issue such a notice shall be made by unanimous consent of all of Major Creditors. Items to be examined are as follows:
  (A) Whether the conditions of Article 3 are fulfilled.
  (B) Whether the Relevant Creditors are expected to agree to the rehabilitation plan.
  (C) Whether the rehabilitation plan is feasible.
(3) When the Major Creditors decide that it is reasonable to issue a Standstill Notice based on (2) *above*, the Major Creditors and the debtor shall issue the Notice in their joint name to all the Relevant Creditors.
(4) The range of Relevant Creditors is usually limited to financial institutions, but can include other creditors with large amount of credit exposures when deemed appropriate.
(5) The Standstill Notice shall be issued in writing and include a notice calling the first meeting of creditors (indicating date, time and place of the meeting). In addition, explanatory documents (debtor's financial information stating the state of assets, liabilities, profit/loss and a rehabilitation plan proposal etc.) for such meeting shall also be attached to the notice.
(6) The decision on whether a Standstill Notice is to be issued shall be made promptly. When Major Creditors have determined that the issuance of such a Notice is not appropriate, they shall inform the debtor of such fact forthwith. When it is necessary for Major Creditors to obtain additional information for determining whether to issue a Standstill, they have the right to request additional documents or further explanation from the debtor. The decision not to issue Standstill Notice means the decision that the multi-creditor workout under this guideline will not be implemented.

5. The first meeting of creditors and the creditors' committee
   (1) The debtor and Major Creditors shall convene the first meeting of creditors within two weeks from the date when the Standstill Notice was issued to the Relevant Creditors.
   (2) The debtor and Major Creditors shall convene the first meeting of creditors in joint names, In principle, a chairman of the meeting shall be elected from among the Major Creditors at the beginning of the meeting. The chairman presides over the meetings of creditors (including the second and subsequent meetings) and shall make efforts toward the orderly progress of the meeting.
   (3) The items *below* shall be implemented at the first meeting.
       (A) An explanations by the debtor regarding the current and past state of assets, liabilities, profit/loss in addition to the details of the rehabilitation plan proposal. Furthermore, questions and answers regarding the explanation as well as an exchange of opinions among the Relevant Creditors present shall also be conducted,
       (B) Discussion of whether it is necessary to assign a professional advisor such as certified public accountant, licensed tax accountant, legal attorney, real estate appraiser or other professional advisor in order to

examine the state of assets, liabilities, profit/loss and assess the accuracy and feasibility of the rehabilitation plan proposal. When such is necessary, an appropriate professional advisor shall be appointed.
- (C) Determination of the duration of the Standstill ('Standstill period').
- (D) Determination of the date/time and place of the next meeting of creditors.
- (E) Determination of whether a creditors' committee is to be established, and if such has been determined, the selection of committee members.
- (F) Determination of other necessary matters.
(4) The creditors' committee shall select the chairperson from among its members by mutual vote. The chairperson shall preside over the committee.
(5) The creditors' committee shall examine the appropriateness and feasibility of the rehabilitation plan proposal, report the results of such examination to the Relevant Creditors, carry out matters referred to the committee by the meeting of creditors, and matters necessary to facilitate the orderly processing of the multi-creditor workout under this guideline.
(6) When a creditors' committee is established by the meeting of creditors, determination on matters stipulated in Article 5(3)B or D, or Article 6(1)A or (3) may be referred to the committee.
(7) Resolution of meeting of creditors shall be made by unanimous consent of all Relevant Creditors in attendance. However, procedural matters that are related to neither rights nor obligations of the Relevant Creditors may be determined by the approval of a majority of the Relevant Creditors.

6. Standstill

(1) All Relevant Creditors and the debtor shall refrain from taking the following acts during a Standstill Period. The mere receipt of a Standstill Notice shall not constitute an cause for acceleration of payment set forth in Bank Transactions, etc.
- (A) The debtor shall not dispose of its assets or assume new liabilities except for the disposal or assumption of such that takes place in the ordinary course of business, or except for the case in which a meeting of creditors or a creditors' committee to whom decision-making power has been entrusted by the meeting of creditors permits the debtor to dispose of its assets or assume new liabilities.
- (B) The debtor shall not, for the sole benefit of a limited number of Relevant Creditors, perform any act of extinguishing its debts such as the repayment of debts (including accord and satisfaction, herein after same), or set-off, nor provide any credit enhancement such as collateral and guarantee.
- (C) Each Relevant Creditor shall maintain the outstanding credit exposure (including the credit balance or loans on notes, overdrafts, and loans on deeds) as of the date when the Standstill Notice is dispatched, and shall not improve its position against the debtor relative to other

creditors. The Relative Creditor also shall not perform any act of extinguishing debts of the debtor, such as the receipt of debt repayment or the exercise of its right of set-off, request the debtor to provide additional collateral or guarantee, exercise its security right, or file a request for compulsory execution, provisional attachment, provisional disposition, or statutory bankruptcy procedures.

(2) The Standstill Period shall commence from the date when the Standstill Notice is dispatched and end on the date when the first meeting of creditors closed. If, at the first meeting of creditors, the Standstill Period is decided to be extended to a date not exceeding three months from the date of the meeting of creditors, the Standstill Period shall be extended to such date. However, if a further extension is considered necessary, a revised extension of the Standstill Period may be determined at the second meeting of creditors or the meeting of creditors held at the continuance dated specified in Article 8(5).

7. Contents of a rehabilitation proposal

A rehabilitation plan proposal shall include the following:

(1) Business plan

A business plan shall reflect adequate self-help efforts by the debtor and include the following items in principle:

(A) Causes of operational difficulties.
(B) A detailed business restructuring plan (including solutions to causes of operational difficulties.
(C) Measures to strengthen its capital, including support through the injection of new capital and debt-equity swaps.
(D) A projection of the debtor's assets, liabilities and profits/losses for approximately the next ten years.
(E) A fund raising plan.
(F) A debt repayment plan.

(2) When the debtor's net worth is virtually negative, its rehabilitation plan proposal shall indicate that such negative net worth will be eliminate and become positive within approximately within three years from the starting date of the first fiscal year after approval of the proposed plan.

(3) When the debtor has incurred loss, its rehabilitation plan proposal shall indicate that such loss will turn to profit within approximately within three years from the starting date of the first fiscal year after approval of the proposed plan.

(4) When the debtor shall be granted composition by the Relevant Creditors, the interests the controlling shareholder of the debtor shall, in principle, be divested, and the pro-rata position of existing shareholders shall be reduced or terminated through a capital reduction and a subsequent capital increase.

(5) When the debtor shall be granted composition by the Relevant Creditors, executives of the debtor shall, in principle, retire.

(6) The adjustments of rights under a rehabilitation plan proposal shall be aimed at equal treatment among creditors, and the share bone by each creditor shall be examined individually, taking equitable treatment into consideration.
(7) Relevant Creditors shall be able to expect that the rehabilitation plan proposal be economically reasonable, such as including the certainty that a larger amount of credit will be recovered than in the case of liquidation via bankruptcy, or procedures in accordance with the Corporate Reorganization Law or the Civil Rehabilitation Law, etc.

8. Approval of a rehabilitation plan

   (1) Major Creditors (a creditors' committee if such is established) shall report the results of an examination and evaluation concerning the appropriateness and feasibility of a rehabilitation plan proposal to all Relevant Creditors prior to the second meeting of creditors.
   (2) The report mentioned in (1) *above* of this Article as well as questions and answers between creditors and the debtor, and exchanges of views among attendant Relevant Creditors regarding a rehabilitation plan proposal shall be conducted at the second meeting of creditors.
   (3) The deadline for expressing in writing whether Relevant Creditors agree to the rehabilitation plan proposal or not shall be determined at the second meeting of creditors.
   (4) When all Relevant Creditors submit written consent to a rehabilitation plan proposal, the plan will be approved. In that case, the debtor shall assume the obligation to implement the rehabilitation plan, while Relevant Creditors' rights shall be adjusted in accordance with the plan, and those creditors shall treat relevant credits in accordance with the stipulations of the rehabilitation plan, such as forbearance and/or composition.
   (5) In the case where the second meeting of creditors needs to be continued in order to change a part of a rehabilitation plan proposal or for other purposes, a continuance date (including the time and place) for the meeting may be determined. Proceedings in (2) and (3) of this Article shall also be carried out when the continued meeting is held.
   (6) In the case where all Relevant Creditor's consent to a rehabilitation plan proposal (including an amended rehabilitation plan proposal according to (5) *above* of this Article) cannot be obtained by a deadline determined according to the provisions specified in (3) and (5) of this Article, the multi-creditor workout in accordance with this guideline shall terminate, and the debtor shall take appropriate measures such as the filing for statutory bankruptcy procedures.

9. Other

   (1) When a rehabilitation plan is approved, the debtor shall disclose an outline of the plan to public in an appropriate manner. However, the debtor may be exempted from such disclosure requirement if there is a possibility that

the disclosure will cause a material adverse effect to successful rehabilitation of the debtor.
(2) After approval of a rehabilitation plan, the debtor shall report on progress in implementation of the plan to Relevant Creditors at regular meetings of creditors or other occasions in accordance with the provisions of the rehabilitation plan.
(3) In case where the debtor cannot fulfil its debt repayment obligation to Relevant Creditors in accordance with the rehabilitation plan, the debtor must take appropriate measures such as the filing for statutory bankruptcy procedures. The debtor must not leave such non-performance of the obligation unsettled. However, the debtor may be exempted from taking those measures if all Relevant Creditors give consent to an amended rehabilitation proposal.
(4) The debtor shall bear all fees and expenses incurred in connection with multi-creditor workout under this guideline, including those for professional advisors, those in connection with holding of meetings of creditors and the creditor's committee.

(September 2001)

Chapter 12
Poland

Out-of-Court Debt Restructuring in Poland

Lech Giliciński[1]

---

1. The author would like to thank Joanna Rzeźnik and Matthew Foss for their assistance in preparation of this chapter.

ACRONYMS, ABBREVIATIONS & DEFINED TERMS

Arrangement Act	Regulation of the President of the Republic of Poland dated 24 October 1934 on Arrangement Proceedings (Journal of Laws No. 93, item 836).
entrepreneurs	Natural or legal persons or organizational units without legal personality upon whom a separate legislation confers legal capacity and who in their own name pursue economic or professional activity.
EUR	Euro
Insolvency Act	Regulation of the President of the Republic of Poland dated 24 October 1934 on Insolvency Law (Journal of Laws 1991 No. 118, item 512).
Insolvency and Restructuring Law	Law on Insolvency and Restructuring dated 28 February 2003 and that entered into force on 1 October 2003 (Journal of Laws No. 60, item 535).
Restructuring Chapter	New chapter of the Insolvency and Restructuring Law on out-of-court restructuring that can be conducted by the debtor subject to the supervision of a court-appointed supervisor that requires the court approval of the arrangement reached with the creditors.

I. INTRODUCTION

Poland's traditional model of debt restructuring adopted before the Second World War and reintroduced in 1989 did not put much emphasis on debtor-initiated debt restructurings, which were conducted to a significant degree outside the court system.

Apart from certain specific restructuring statutes applicable to selected entrepreneurs (natural or legal persons or organizational units without legal personality upon whom a separate legislation confers legal capacity and who in their own name pursue economic or professional activity) or specific types of indebtedness,[2] debts could be restructured in three ways: (1) pursuant to the Regulation of the President of the Republic of Poland dated 24 October 1934 on Arrangement Proceedings (the 'Arrangement Act'),[3] whereby the debtor could file a restructuring plan with a court seeking an arrangement with creditors to be voted on under the supervision of and approved by the court, (2) under the Regulation of the President of the Republic of Poland dated 24 October 1934 on Insolvency Law[4] (the 'Insolvency Act'), whereby an already bankrupt debtor could seek an arrangement with its creditors giving it a way out of bankruptcy; or, (3) by negotiating a debt settlement with its creditors on market terms.

While the Arrangement Act proved to be a useful restructuring tool only in isolated cases (one of the drawbacks being that only certain debts could be restructured and only to a limited degree), the usefulness of arrangement proceedings under the Insolvency Act was even more limited if not non-existent. Debtors had minimal opportunities to restructure their debt since they had to negotiate on market terms with the bulk of their creditors without an opportunity to suspend the debt repayment cramdown the dissenting creditors and/or get court approval of the arrangement. A practical but risky tool for debtors was often to use the threat of filing for insolvency. This situation has changed with the advent of the new Law on Insolvency and Restructuring that entered into force on 1 October 2003[5] (the Insolvency and Restructuring Law'). The Insolvency and Restructuring Law replaced the Arrangement Act and Insolvency Act and introduced the concept of bankruptcy aimed at liquidation and bankruptcy aimed at arrangement. Under the Insolvency and Restructuring Law, the debtor can now ask the court for a declaration of bankruptcy aimed at restructuring and for an arrangement voted on within the bankruptcy proceedings. The same remedies are also available to creditors.

The Insolvency and Restructuring Law also introduced a new chapter on out-of-court restructuring that can be conducted by the debtor subject to the supervision of a court-appointed supervisor and court approval of an arrangement reached with the creditors (the 'Restructuring Chapter').

---

2. *See*, for example, the Law on Financial Restructuring of Banks and Enterprises of 3 February 1993 (Journal of Laws No. 18, item 82) and the Law on Public Aid to Enterprises of Special Importance to Labour Market of 30 October 2002 (Journal of Laws No. 213, item 1800).
3. The Arrangement Act of 24 October 1934 (Journal of Laws No. 93, item 836).
4. The Insolvency Act of 24 October 1934 (Journal of Laws 1991 No. 118, item 512).
5. The Act of 28 February 2003 – the Law on Insolvency and Restructuring (Journal of Laws No. 60, item 535).

II. SELECTED MAJOR RESTRUCTURINGS IN POLAND TO DATE.

In light of the lack of any published precedents established under the Restructuring Chapter, it is worth mentioning the major issues arising in connection with the most famous Polish restructurings that were completed before the Restructuring Chapter came into effect. These are the Netia Group and the Elektrim restructurings and they are explained *below*.

Companies from the Netia Group conducted telecom business in Poland starting from the early nineties. Acting through their Dutch affiliates, the Netia Group issued several tranches of notes from 1997 to 2000 equalling several hundred million euros whose repayment was guaranteed by the Netia Group. Unable to repay the notes and threatened with bankruptcy, the Netia Group filed for an arrangement with a Polish court under the Arrangement Act while its Dutch affiliates commenced composition proceedings in the Netherlands. The Netia Group also managed to reach an out-of-court arrangement with the noteholders and some other creditors resulting in, among others, a debt-to-equity swap and the issuance of new notes. The principal shareholders of the holding company of the Netia Group were also parties to the restructuring agreement since debt-to-equity swaps were not covered by the Arrangement Act and could not be effected without their cooperation. Netia certainly presents the most complicated and complex restructuring case in Poland to date. Given that the holding company of the Netia Group is publicly listed and the notes were reissued, various securities laws requirements had to be complied with. In addition to the successfully completed Polish and Dutch proceedings, a Section § 304 proceeding was held in New York to affirm the Polish proceedings.

Publicly listed energy and telecom conglomerate Elektrim was also a note issuer (through its Dutch affiliate). Threatened with potential bankruptcy, it managed to restructure the notes by way of an out-of-court settlement with the noteholders in late 2002. The restructuring essentially provided for the re-issuance of notes, payment deferral (of EUR 440.000.000 notes) and establishment of collateral security for the repayment, although some other measures to protect noteholders were also introduced, such as the appointment of a noteholder to the Management Board of Elektrim.[6] Elektrim was a less successful story than Netia. At the time of writing this chapter, it has still not resolved its disputes with the noteholders and is also involved in serious disputes with other shareholders of Polska Telefonia Cyfrowa Sp. z o.o., its key telecom asset. However, the 2002 restructuring only happened because the parties managed to sign a restructuring agreement in a timely manner, which could not have happened under the Arrangement Act.

---

6. This has actually turned out to be a bone of contention among the noteholders and shareholders of Elektrim.

III. RESTRUCTURING PURSUANT TO THE RESTRUCTURING CHAPTER

A. Who Can Restructure

Only entrepreneurs entered into the National Court Register, a publicly accessible record, can commence restructuring proceedings. Entities entered into local business registers are not offered such opportunity. Entrepreneurs who satisfy the *above* formal requirement can commence restructuring if they are threatened with insolvency. The Insolvency and Restructuring Law clarifies that an entrepreneur is 'threatened with insolvency' if, regardless of paying its debts, a reasonable assessment of its economic condition indicates that it will shortly become insolvent.

While the drafters of the Restructuring Chapter designed restructuring proceedings for clever, diligent debtors who seek to resolve future problems in advance, the practice to date in Poland instead shows that most debtors only think of restructuring when an insolvency test[7] has already been met and the debtor can therefore not attempt an out-of-court restructuring.

Apart from the *above* general issue, there are certain other circumstances prohibiting an entrepreneur from commencing restructuring. In particular, it cannot commence the proceedings if it was already subject to restructuring proceedings that were terminated within the last four years and/or it was already subject to an arrangement reached pursuant to the Restructuring Chapter or general proceedings under the Insolvency and Restructuring Law.

B. Commencement of Proceedings and Judicial Control.

The entrepreneur initiates restructuring proceedings by filing a statement on the commencement of proceedings, including the restructuring plan, with the court. Besides the corporate data and indication of the debtor's legal residence/corporate seat, the statement should point to the circumstances warranting the petition and credible evidence thereof.

Even though the restructuring is initiated by the entrepreneur, the court may exercise certain supervisory powers at this stage. Upon the commencement of restructuring, the court appoints a court supervisor who will supervise the restructuring and with whom the entrepreneur is bound to enter into a mandate agreement concerning the supervisor's services rendered in the course of restructuring (with the statutorily determined compensation). Failure of the entrepreneur to enter into an agreement with the court supervisor would arguably constitute a ground for the court's rejection of an arrangement. In particular, within 14 days following the

---

7. According to the insolvency test the debtor is deemed to be insolvent when he fails to perform his obligations when they have fallen due (liquidity test). Additionally, debtors having legal personality or upon whom a separate legislation confers legal capacity are deemed to be insolvent when the amount of their obligations have exceeded the value of their assets, quite irrespective of whether they timely perform their obligations (assets test).

entrepreneur's filing of a statement on the commencement of restructuring proceedings with the court, the court may prohibit the commencement of restructuring if the entrepreneur's statement was made in breach of the provisions of the Restructuring Chapter specifying the scope of statements or the information and documents required and/or if the data and/or representations contained in the statement or documents attached thereto are untrue. The court will also reject statements if the information is incomplete. It is worth noting that the documents and information required to be attached to the motion for the commencement of restructuring are almost exactly the same as in the case of debtors filing for insolvency. Therefore, the court has a chance to establish whether a particular entrepreneur is already insolvent rather than just threatened with insolvency. While the court's decision prohibiting the commencement of restructuring may be appealed, the consequences of such decision becoming final and binding are fairly harsh in that the entrepreneur will not be allowed to commence a restructuring again.

If the court does not prohibit the commencement of the restructuring or the decision prohibiting the commencement is set aside, the entrepreneur announces the commencement of restructuring proceedings in the official *Court and Business Journal*. Such announcement commences the restructuring.

C. LEGAL REPERCUSSIONS OF THE COMMENCEMENT OF RESTRUCTURING.

The commencement of restructuring carries with it certain relief for the entrepreneur and may give the entrepreneur some time to restructure. In particular:
1. payments of entrepreneur's obligations are suspended (except for certain claims, including social security contributions);
2. the calculation of interest due from the entrepreneur is suspended (except for that accruing on certain claims, including on social security contributions);
3. claims can only be set off on terms analogous to those applied in bankruptcies aimed at arrangement; and,
4. the entrepreneur's property may not be foreclosed or seized and foreclosure/seizure proceedings already initiated are stayed by operation of law.

The *above* rules do not apply to those claims which, according to the Insolvency and Restructuring Law, are not subject to an arrangement, in particular those held by secured creditors.

Upon the motion of the entrepreneur, the court may also (except with respect to the claims not covered by the arrangement) change the attachments made in order to secure monetary claims, in particular by lifting such attachments.

The *above* provisions are primarily intended to preserve the value of a business and leave the business intact to the degree possible in the course of restructuring. Debtors are further protected by the fact that entrepreneurs who enter into restructuring proceedings are prohibited from transferring and encumbering the assets of the business. An obvious exception to the *above* prohibition applies to 'the assets disposed of in the course of business activities of the entrepreneur'. While the wording of *above* exception is not entirely clear, it seems it should apply to any transactions made by the debtor in the ordinary course of business. It would be very difficult to argue that the *above* prohibition applies to the exercise of the debtor's rights in subsidiaries (such as voting rights). Even under general bankruptcy proceedings, such rights belong in principle to the debtor (unless such rights could influence the assets of the estate).

Unlike bankruptcy proceedings, restructuring proceedings do not affect non-monetary claims. Such claims are not stayed and the entrepreneur is bound to perform them.

D.   ROLE OF CREDITORS IN THE PROCESS OF CONCLUSION OF AN ARRANGEMENT

Restructuring of obligations takes place by means of an arrangement with creditors. The restructuring plan needs to be submitted in order to initiate the proceedings. Moreover, it should be focused on restoring the entrepreneur's competitiveness on the market. The plan consists of restructuring proposals of the entrepreneur which require an affirmative vote of the creditors. Once the arrangement has been approved by the creditors, the Insolvency and Restructuring Law requires the court's approval of the arrangement. The court approval takes place after having conducted a hearing. As soon as the arrangement is accepted by the court and publicly announced, its implementation will lead to the restructuring of the obligations and assets in accordance with the arrangement.

The creditors entitled to vote on the arrangement can be divided into groups for the purpose of voting, but the entrepreneur must take their respective interests into account when forming the groups:

1. creditors entitled to farmer fees under contracts for the delivery of products from their own farms;
2. secured creditors;
3. creditors being shareholders of the debtor; and,
4. the remaining creditors.

The arrangement is adopted once it has been supported by the majority of creditors in each group who jointly hold at least two thirds of the total amount of claims. As voting in groups is only optional under the Insolvency and Restructuring Law, the entrepreneur can decide that all the creditors will vote on the arrangement jointly. In such event, the arrangement is considered adopted if it is supported by the majority of creditors entitled to participate in the creditors' meeting. Additionally, this majority must hold at least two-third of the total amount of claims which give a right to vote on the arrangement. The Insolvency and Restructuring Law does not set limits on the number of creditors' meetings to decide on the restructuring proposals. The entrepreneur can convene subsequent creditors' meetings in order to present new restructuring proposals to the creditors. In order to make the entire process more efficient, the Insolvency and Restructuring Law attempts to deal with absences at subsequent creditors' meetings. In particular, a vote cast by a creditor at a creditors' meeting is still counted for the purposes of voting at a subsequent meeting (which the creditor fails to attend) as long as the new restructuring proposals are not less favourable to such creditor than the proposals he already voted on.

In practical terms, the entrepreneur's power to divide the creditors into groups may be critical for the success of a restructuring. Different results of voting en bloc and in groups may, for example, be caused by the fact that certain categories of creditors are prohibited from voting at the creditors' meeting by operation of general provisions of the Insolvency and Restructuring Law.[8]

E. COURT APPROVAL OF THE ARRANGEMENT.

Each creditor entitled to attend the creditors' meeting (as well as creditors not entitled as long as they can prove that the arrangement would impede the satisfaction of their claims) can file objections to the arrangement within the deadlines specified in the Insolvency and Restructuring Law. The court conducts a hearing concerning the approval of the arrangement, which is publicly announced in the *Court and Business Journal* and about which the creditors who filed objections are also notified.

The court will reject the arrangement in the circumstances enumerated in the Insolvency and Restructuring Law. Those circumstances are briefly discussed *below*.

1. Lack of Legal Basis to Conduct Restructuring Proceedings

According to prominent legal commentators on the Insolvency and Restructuring Law,[9] there is no legal basis when:

1. the proceedings are conducted by an entity not registered in the National Court Register;
2. the restructuring proceedings are conducted by an entrepreneur not entitled to conduct the proceedings;
3. the restructuring proceedings are conducted by an entrepreneur who could not be declared bankrupt;[10] and/or,
4. the restructuring proceedings are conducted by an entrepreneur who at the time of initiation of the proceedings was not threatened by insolvency.

---

8. *See* in particular Article 197 of the Insolvency and Restructuring Law.
9. *See* Andrzej Jakubecki, Feliks Zedler: *Prawo upadłościowe i naprawcze* on page 1198 et seq.
10. The Insolvency and Restructuring Law enumerates debtors that may not be declared bankrupt, which are: (1) the State Treasury; (2) municipal entities; (3) public hospitals and other public medical entities; (4) governmental institutions and legal persons formed pursuant to a legislative act; (5) farmers (individuals engaged in farming); and (6) universities.

2. Lack of Filing of All Relevant Documents Required in the Proceedings

All documents required to initiate the restructuring proceedings, such as the statement on commencement of the proceedings and restructuring plan, must be submitted. Failure to submit the required documents renders the creditors' control almost impossible; therefore, not filing all the required documents constitutes an absolute ground for rejection of the arrangement.[11]

In addition, in practice the majority of attempts to restructure were made by debtors who already met at least one of the two bankruptcy tests. The courts simply reject the relevant motion for restructuring from an already insolvent debtor at the initial stage, but even overlooking such circumstances should by no means prevent the court from disapproving of the arrangement after the arrangement is passed.

3. Inaccuracy of the Data in the Documents and Statements Made by the Entrepreneur

After the entrepreneur has submitted the statement on commencement of the proceedings, the court examines whether there are grounds to prohibit the initiation of the proceedings on the basis of the statements and attached documents being false. The inaccuracy of the data is an absolute ground for the rejection of an arrangement, regardless of the reasons for which the inaccuracy appeared in a statement. It seems that the commencement of restructuring proceedings by an already insolvent debtor will necessarily be based on inaccurate data since the statement on commencement of the proceedings will not come from an entrepreneur threatened with insolvency, but one that is already insolvent.

4. Lack of Notifications to All Known Creditors about the Dates of the Creditors' Meeting

The issue of informing all the creditors has far-reaching repercussions since the creditors that have not been notified are not able to participate in the creditors' meeting and consequently have no influence on the contents of the arrangement. Nor are they bound by the arrangement and their claims have to be satisfied (*see below*). This gives them an advantage over the creditors that have been notified, and, thus, are bound by the arrangement. An interesting issue arises in connection with the creditors who are owed performances from the debtor periodically, e.g., on a monthly or quarterly basis and who are therefore owed future debts that mature at specified intervals. While the debtor may arguably perform such claims with the consent of the court supervisor, there is no legal basis for excluding them from the arrangement (even though they may relate to critical economic relationships of the enterprise such as leases, security, etc.) and therefore they should be covered by the arrangement. It is conceivable that certain preferences could be

---

11. *See*: A. Jakubecki, F. Zedler, *Prawo upadłościowe i naprawcze* on page 1199.

offered to such creditors as small creditors. Even more problematic is the treatment of entities with contingent claims against the entrepreneur, e.g., on the basis of a surety. While in the previous example the entrepreneur is aware of certain creditors' claims which mature at a future date, it may be extremely difficult for it to determine whether a holder of contingent claims is indeed its creditor. In the case of a suretyship agreement, the beneficiary of the surety would only become a creditor upon the primary debt falling due. Nevertheless, it seems prudent for the entrepreneur to notify the creditors whose claims are contingent of the creditors' meeting, indicating that it is doing so in case they have become its creditors.

5. Inability of the Court Supervisor to Exercise Supervision

Restructuring is an out-of-court proceeding which is, however, subject to court supervision. The data obtained by the court by these means constitute an important source of information about the enterprise engaged in this process. The court supervisor must have the ability to control the proceedings. An example of a debtor's preventing the court supervisor from exercising control would be the entrepreneur's failure to enter into a mandate agreement with the court supervisor, as required by Article 497, item 3, of the Insolvency and Restructuring Law.

6. Infringements of Provisions of Law which could be Relevant to the Outcome of the Voting

This rule constitutes an absolute ground for rejecting an arrangement, but only if the breach was a *sine qua non* condition in relation to the result of the voting. An example of such impact is a delayed notification about the creditors meeting or alternatively having the first creditors' meeting on a date earlier than one month after initiating the restructuring proceedings. The creditors would not be in a position to become familiar with the debtor's documents, which could influence the outcome of the voting.[12]

7. Siphoning of Assets by the Entrepreneur or Granting Certain Creditors Greater Benefits in Violation of the Provisions of the Insolvency and Restructuring Law

The effectiveness of restructuring and the protection of creditors' rights during the proceedings require that the assets of the entrepreneur be frozen except for transfers of assets in the ordinary course of business. Therefore, any transfers or encumbrances outside the scope of the *above* exception constitute grounds for rejecting an arrangement. The same applies to grants of additional benefits to certain creditors constituting transfers of or encumbrances on the debtor's assets as well as waivers of an entrepreneur's claims vis-à-vis particular creditors.[13]

---

12. *See*: A. Jakubecki, F. Zedler, *Prawo upadłościowe i naprawcze* Zakamycze 2003 on page 1202.
13. *See*: A. Jakubecki, F. Zedler, *Prawo upadłościowe i naprawcze* on p. 1203.

8. Lack of Prospects for the Performance of an Arrangement

It obviously would not make sense for a court to approve an arrangement if the existing circumstances imply that the arrangement will not be performed even though the arrangement was technically passed. Such conclusion should be based on analysis of the economic situation of the entrepreneur, which should also be supported by expert opinions.

9. Detriment to Creditors who Raised Objections or Lack of a Guarantee that the Restructuring Plan will Enable the Entrepreneur to Compete in the Market

The *above* two grounds are highly subjective. In particular, it could well be argued that an arrangement always impairs creditors' rights to some extent. Therefore, the first of the *above* grounds could only be considered in limited circumstances, e.g. when the debtor could clearly satisfy the relevant creditor to a greater degree while still retaining the ability to operate in the market. The second of the *above* grounds is present when despite the restructuring of creditors' claims, there is still uncertainty whether the debtor will be capable of conducting a competitive business and generating profits.

Since the *above* two grounds are discretionary, the court will not rely on them exclusively to reject an arrangement. In fact, even in the *above* circumstances the court may approve of the arrangement if the arrangement will allow creditors to be satisfied to a degree not less than in the case of conducting bankruptcy proceedings aimed at liquidation. The *above* analysis should be based on an estimate of the level of creditor satisfaction if the business were to be liquidated, which needs to be based on expert valuations. The interested parties may submit such valuations in the course of the proceedings. The expert's valuations may well be expected to be contested in out-of-court restructurings. By way of example, valuations prepared by court appointed experts in bankruptcy proceedings tend to be excessive and the actual price obtained upon a bankruptcy sale is often much lower.

F. The Consequences of an Arrangement

When an arrangement is concluded, it is binding on all the creditors who were informed about the creditors' meeting and those who notified the court supervisor of their participation and whose claims the entrepreneur did not deny. The arrangement covers all claims entered on the list of claims acknowledged by the debtor, as well as disputed claims if the disagreement about their existence or amount was settled after the arrangement was approved. An excerpt from the list of claims together with the final decision approving the arrangement constitutes an execution title against the entrepreneur and those who secured the performance of the arrangement on the condition that the document confirming the establishment of a security for the performance was filed with the court. While securing the performance of the arrangement is not technically required for the effectiveness thereof, the need for such security appears in various cases.

The arrangement does not infringe creditors' rights with regard to the guarantor of the entrepreneur and its co-debtors. Nor are rights established by a mortgage, registered pledge or maritime mortgage affected if they were established on the assets of a third party. Arrangements do not cover the rights established by means of a mortgage, registered pledge or maritime mortgage on the assets of the entrepreneur, unless the entitled person consents to the arrangement covering those claims.

G. SETTING ASIDE AN ARRANGEMENT

According to the Insolvency and Restructuring Law, the court may set aside an arrangement if the entrepreneur fails to perform it, or alternatively if the grounds for rejecting an arrangement referred to in E *above* (except for the detriment to the rights of creditors who objected to the arrangement) became apparent in the course of performance of the arrangement. Thus, an arrangement may be set aside even if circumstances permitting rejection of the arrangement came into being after the arrangement was approved. Further, the court is entitled to set aside the arrangement if the entrepreneur fails to implement the restructuring plan. The court will set aside an arrangement based on a motion filed by a creditor or by a person authorized by the arrangement to supervise its execution. Moreover, if the debtor or its creditors file a motion for declaration of bankruptcy and the court declares the debtor bankrupt, it will also set aside the arrangement *ex officio*.

H. DISCONTINUATION

Restructuring proceedings are discontinued by operation of law if no arrangement is reached within four months from the initiation of the restructuring proceedings. This period is only three months if the entrepreneur is small or medium-sized.[14]

IV. CONCLUSIONS

Although the Restructuring Chapter was crafted like Chapter 11 of the US Bankruptcy Code[15] to be a tool for restructuring for debtors who are intelligent enough to understand that they should think ahead and not let their company approach bankruptcy, polish entrepreneurs have so far failed to take advantage

---

14. Small and mid-sized entrepreneurs are statutorily defined in Article 54 of the Law on Business Activity.
15. 11 U.S.C.

of this tool. It is too early to investigate the reasons for this phenomenon in the relatively short period from when the Insolvency and Restructuring Law came into force, but the major reasons seem to be (1) the rapid economic growth in Poland after EU accession resulting in fewer business facing the circumstances contemplated in the Restructuring Chapter; and, (2) petitioners so far misinterpreting the Restructuring Chapter and filing motions for the commencement of restructuring only after at least one of the insolvency tests has been met.

As of the time of writing this chapter, there were no reported cases of out-of-court restructurings pursuant to the Restructuring Chapter, although Polish restructuring lawyers have certainly considered such possibility. Nevertheless, the Restructuring Chapter is a much more interesting tool for forward-looking entrepreneurs willing to avoid trouble at a later stage compared to previous regulations addressing restructurings in a different or only partial manner. It remains to be seen whether a change of the economic cycle or amendments to the Restructuring Chapter (proposals of which are discussed *below*) will attract more interest in this regulation.

V. PROPOSED AMENDMENTS TO THE RESTRUCTURING CHAPTER

Shortly before completing this chapter, a legislative bill was proposed in Poland containing amendments to the Insolvency and Restructuring Law including the amendments to the Restructuring Chapter. The proposed amendments are not intended to substantially change restructuring proceedings, but their implementation could generate more interest in them. In particular, one proposal is that a debtor who is not otherwise prohibited from filing a motion to commence restructuring should now be allowed to file such motion jointly with an insolvency motion as long as a delay in the performance of its obligations is not permanent and the sum of non-performed obligations does not exceed 10 per cent of the book value of its assets. If the bankruptcy court dismisses the insolvency motion, it could at the same time allow the debtor to proceed with the restructuring. This proposal seems to address the current situation of entrepreneurs filing restructuring motions when they are already insolvent rather than only threatened with insolvency. For practical purposes, such amendment could reduce the workload of the bankruptcy courts. Another proposed amendment relates to the legal repercussions upon the commencement of restructuring.[16] The proposal would make the provisions on suspension of repayments, restrictions on set-offs, stays of enforcement, etc., apply to all claims without exceptions. This amendment is not likely to be introduced, at least in a manner limiting the rights of secured creditors, and the powerful banking lobby will almost certainly oppose it.

Apart from a number of more technical and/or clarifying amendments, one more amendment relating to the grounds for rejecting an arrangement is worthy of

---

16. *See* the discussion in point 3.3 *above*.

note. It has been proposed that if there is no legal basis for conducting restructuring proceedings or the data in the statements and documents of the entrepreneur are inaccurate – currently grounds for rejecting an arrangement – the court may nonetheless approve the arrangement if the inaccuracy in the documents or statements of the entrepreneur was due to circumstances beyond the entrepreneur's control or which had no important influence on the course of the proceedings, and if it is obvious that on the basis of the arrangement the creditors will be satisfied to a degree not less favourable than in the event of liquidating the entrepreneur. The *above* amendment would make the restructuring proceedings less formal and in addition to the already existing grounds would allow the court to approve an arrangement even if certain formal deficiencies exist when for pragmatic reasons it is pointless to conduct bankruptcy proceedings aimed at liquidation of the entrepreneur.

It is not clear whether the *above* amendments might be introduced to the Insolvency and Restructuring Law, but they would likely increase the efficiency of restructuring proceedings and could foster more interest in them.

Chapter 13

Turkey

Pre-packaged Corporate Restructuring Mechanism Under the Turkish Execution and Bankruptcy Law

Sevi Simavi[1]

---

1. The views expressed in this paper are those of the author and do not necessarily represent the views of the World Bank, its executive directors or its Member Countries.

Rodrigo Olivares-Caminal, *Expedited Debt Restructuring:
An International Comparative Analysis*, pp. 419–436.
©2007, Kluwer Law International BV, The Netherlands.

ACRONYMS, ABBREVIATIONS & DEFINED TERMS

C	Class of Creditor
D	Debtor
EBL	Turkish Execution and Bankruptcy Law as amended and restated in 2004 by Bill 5092
GNP	Gross National Product
K	Creditor
Pre-package restructuring	Pre-packaged corporate restructuring via reconciliation under the Turkish Execution and Bankruptcy Law as amended and restated in 2004 by Bill 5092
Regulations	Implementing regulations of Bill 5092 enacted by the Turkish Government

I. INTRODUCTION

Turkey's insolvency regime is governed by the Execution and Bankruptcy Law as amended and restated in 2004 (hereinafter referred as 'EBL'), which originates from the Swiss Federal Law on Debt Collection and Bankruptcy. Despite several amendments over the past seventy years, the 2001 financial crisis triggered arguably the most comprehensive reform effort to streamline debt collection, liquidation and rehabilitation schemes. The crisis particularly elicited the need for an adequate corporate restructuring mechanism to tackle with its severe impact on the real and financial sector. On February 2004 the Grand National Assembly of Turkey passed the Bill No. 5092 amending the EBL, which introduced a set of innovative provisions on pre packaged corporate restructuring by adding a new chapter entitled 'Restructuring of Corporations and Cooperatives via Reconciliation' (hereinafter referred as 'pre packaged restructuring').

This Chapter will provide a theoretical jurisdictional analysis of the new pre packaged restructuring mechanism under the EBL. Given its relatively recent adoption and the novelty of its provisions, coupled with country's rapid recovery from the crisis, the practical application of this new mechanism remains to be limited at best. To the extent available, every effort has been given to capture the intent of the law makers through the analysis of legislative history, reports released by the National Assembly as well as the working sessions the author herself has attended during the preparation of this new law.

The first section of the chapter gives a brief overview on the conditions that triggered the amendments of the EBL and the adoption of pre packaged restructure rules. The second section delves into the legal and procedural aspects.

II. BRIEF HISTORY AND THE CASE FOR REFORM

In 2001, Turkey had one of the most severe economic crises in its recent history. Its consequences were devastating: the currency devaluated by approximately 50 per cent, nominal interest rates jumped to 100 per cent and the banking sector virtually collapsed.[2] At the end of 2001, Turkey registered a 10 per cent decline in GNP, inflation was on the order of 70 per cent, and the net public debt to GNP ratio exceeded 90 per cent.[3] Corporate financial distress had reached vast amounts affecting nearly all sectors in the economy, but particularly the financial sector, with non-performing loans amounting to USD 9.6 billion.[4] In May 2001, the government of

---

2. *Country Assistance Strategy Progress Report for the Republic of Turkey for the Period of FY 2004–2007* (International Bank for Reconstruction and Development and International Finance Corporation Report No. 33995–TU, 8 November 2005) p. 4. <siteresources.worldbank.org/INTTURKEY/Resources/CAS_Progress_Report_2005.pdf> , 15 March 2006
3. Ibid.
4. 'Banking in Turkey', Republic of Turkey, Office of Prime Minister, Directorate of Press and Information, available at <www.byegm.gov.tr/REFERENCES/banking.htm>, last checked 15 March 2006.

Turkey announced a crisis response program, which included, among other measures, rapid restructuring of the banking and corporate sector.

The legal infrastructure at the time was inadequate to address this distress. It neither facilitated a swift liquidation of the non-viable firms nor provided appropriate mechanisms to rescue viable firms. Since virtually all sectors were affected by the crisis, liquidation did not offer a sustainable solution, as this would have resulted in further shrinkage of the already fragile economy. Instead, the situation required for a comprehensive corporate restructuring mechanism to deal with the vast amount of non performing loans in the system.

The only available formal restructuring mechanism as an alterative to liquidation under the EBL before the reform was the concordat ('konkordato'). However, concordat provisions were designed to facilitate restructuring of non-complex transactions of relatively small businesses and as a result were rarely used in practice. It had proven to be outmoded for addressing the needs of complex organizations and transactions of a modern economy.[5] The process was applicable for 'honest' debtors in financial difficulties and simply applied to rescheduling of or writing off a maximum of 50 per cent of unsecured debt.[6] Secured creditors were excluded from the process,[7] which made it ineffective, futile and undesired. Unsecured creditors simply met to examine the concordat proposal, and vote on whether to accept it by a majority of two-thirds. Concordat did not provide for a creditors' committee, so there was no formal participation for creditors in formulating or amending the plan. If approved, the debtor remained in control of the business under the supervision of a *concordat commissarie*, appointed by the court.

Given the limited applicability of the concordat proceeding, the primary method for restructurings was merely debt reschedulings through informal workouts.

Under these circumstances and as the first response to the legal hindrance to meaningful restructurings, a voluntary, non-judicial workout program known as the 'Istanbul Approach'[8] was adopted under the leadership of Turkish Bankers Association. The Istanbul Approach was inspired by the 'London Approach' and provided for the restructuring of debts of financially distressed companies that had credit lines with financial institutions. Despite the fact that the Istanbul Approach incorporated key aspects derived from international experience with voluntary workouts, it was backward looking since it only dealt with the restructuring of those loans that were made before the adoption of the Istanbul Approach.[9] It was primarily designed to overcome the urgency caused by the crisis and therefore did not fulfil the need for a comprehensive and permanent mechanism within the context of the

---

5. Oğuz Atalay, 'Konkordato Hukukundaki Değişiklikler' (2003), *Bankacilar Dergisi*, Sayi 47, p. 99.
6. 50 per cent requirement has been abolished by Bill No 4949 amending the EBL.
7. EBL Article 297/III.
8. Istanbul Approach is governed by Bill No 4743 on 'Restructuring of Debts to Financial Sector and Amendments To Several Laws' published in the Official Gazette No 24657 dated 31 January 2002 (Supplementary Issue No:1) and implementing regulations issued by Banking Regulatory and Supervision Agency published in the Official Gazette No 24723, dated 11 April 2002.
9. See Bill No 4743 Article 1.

Turkey

EBL.[10] To address the needs, the Government of Turkey committed to reform the EBL to allow for swift liquidation and provide a way for companies to restructure their debts on an accelerated basis.[11]

In this regard, two sets of legislative packages were enacted by the National Assembly – Bill No. 4949 and Bill No. 5092 – both amending the EBL. Bill No. 4949 dealt with issues regarding: (1) debt collection and enforcement of claims; (2) a new court supervised rehabilitation procedure called 'postponement of bankruptcy'; and, (3) streamlined the concordat procedures in conservative manner.[12] On the other hand, Bill No. 5092, introduced a set of innovative and more comprehensive provisions on pre-packaged corporate restructuring by adding a new chapter entitled 'Restructuring of Corporations and Cooperatives via Reconciliation' to the EBL.[13] The government acknowledged the fact that the country needed a new transparent and flexible turn around mechanism. The effect of liquidation would severely hamper the local, regional as well as the national economy; therefore a new rescue mechanism was needed to support restructuring of viable companies that were at the brisk of financial difficulty. This not only would benefit the enterprise itself, but also its employees facing the risk of losing their jobs and the creditors that are negatively affected by NPLs.[14]

The new rescue mechanism has been inspired by the global trend following the introduction of US Chapter 11 alike techniques in emerging markets, as well as the restructuring principles laid out by the UNCITRAL's Legislative Guide on Insolvency.[15] The following section will delve into the theoretical and procedural aspects of the new law.

III. 'RESTRUCTURING OF CORPORATIONS AND COOPERATIVES VIA RECONCILIATION' – PRE-PACKAGED RESTRUCTURING

A. AN OVERVIEW

Sections 309/m to 309/ü of the EBL (introduced by Bill No 5092) and its implementing regulations[16] are the two bodies of law that govern the pre-packaged

---

10. For detailed discussion of Istanbul Approach, see Turkey Country Economic Memorandum, (World Bank) 28 July 2003, available at <siteresources.worldbank.org/INTTURKEY/Resources/361616-1121189119378/turkey-cem-summary.pdf>, 30 June 2006.
11. Turkey – Letter of Intent, 20 November 2001, <www.imf.org/External/NP/LOI/2001/tur/05/INDEX.HTM>, 30 June 2006.
12. Mechanisms introduced under this Bill are extensive and will be the subject of a separate study.
13. This Bill was published in the Official Gazette no 25380 and entered into force on 21/02/2004.
14. *İcra ve İflâs Kanununda Değişiklik Yapılmasına Dair Kanun Tasarısı ve Adalet Komisyonu Raporu (1/718), Sayi : B.02.0.KKG.0.10/101–772/5508*, (TBMM – 12 December 2003).
15. This publication is available at <www.uncitral.org/pdf/english/texts/insolven/05-80722_Ebook.pdf>, 30 June 2006.
16. Implementing regulations were enacted by the Ministry of Justice on 17 April 2004 and published in Official Gazette No. 25,436.

corporate restructuring regime in Turkey. Pre-packaged mechanism is a novelty under the Turkish legal framework and includes several progressive principles that are found in the most advanced restructuring laws around the globe.

According to the Turkish pre-packaged restructuring provisions, a debtor that is insolvent or that is under an imminent risk of insolvency may apply to the commercial court for a fast track approval of a plan that was pre-negotiated and pre-accepted by the requisite majority of affected creditors. The provisions encourage the debtor and its creditors to reach voluntary arrangements to rehabilitate a distressed, but viable business through a wide array of options.

Three major steps should be followed to accomplish the restructuring: (1) preparation and acceptance of a restructuring plan through an out of court negotiation and voting process; (2) a fast track court approval process after the plan has been accepted by the requisite majority of affected creditors; and, (3) the implementation of the measures adopted in the plan.

As the first step, the mechanism facilitates involved parties to come up with an acceptable, amicable and equitable resolution. Such consensual and voluntary arrangement will minimize the amount of time and cost that parties would spend in a court proceeding. Detailed rules on disclosure, claims classification, voting and approval have been adopted and an ability to bind holdout creditors within the same class is also provided. Secured creditors are included in the process with balanced safeguard provisions. These will be discussed in *further* detail in Section B *below*.

Once the acceptance of the requisite majority of affected creditors is attained, the plan should to be approved by the court to render its binding effects. The court process is designed to resolve the plan objections on an accelerated basis to minimize the bankruptcy stigma and the amount of time and cost that companies spend in a formal proceeding. The court approval process also ensures that the procedure set out by the EBL is followed and that the dissenting creditors are adequately protected by the plan.

In regard to the implementation measures, the process is subject to supervision by a qualified supervisor selected by the majority of creditors. To encourage the use of the proceedings, all tax benefits and incentives granted to creditors and the debtor under the Istanbul Approach scheme have been entirely adopted under this pre-packaged restructuring mechanism.

Finally, it is worth noting that the plan can be amended upon the agreement of parties during its implementation stage. Also, if the debtor does not perform his obligations envisaged in the plan, the plan can be terminated entirely and the debtor will be liquidated.

B. THE PROCESS

1. **Eligibility for Application and the Test for Insolvency**

Only those debtors that are corporations or cooperatives may apply for a relief under the pre-packaged restructuring mechanism.[17] Unlike in the insolvency or

---
17. EBL (2004) Article 309/m.

concordat proceedings, merchants, partnerships, or so called 'personal companies' have been left outside the scope of application. The rationale behind this is that the aim of pre-packaged provisions is to prevent large failures which would hamper the economy as a whole and thus provide for the rehabilitation for troubled, but viable firms. The companies with larger economic activities are most likely to be corporations rather than merchants or small businesses operating under partnership structures. In addition, banks and insurance companies may not seek relief as debtors under these provisions, either.[18]

The EBL recognizes both the liquidity and balance sheet tests for financial distress or insolvency: (1) the debtor should either be unable to pay its mature debts when they become due (liquidity test); or, (2) the liabilities should exceed the assets of the company (balance sheet test).[19]

The liquidity test can be established in cases where the debtor has already failed to pay debts or faces a certain prospect of being unable to pay debts as they mature in the absence of a restructuring.[20]

The balance sheet test is established if the debtor can demonstrate that the liabilities of the company exceed the value of the assets. This is done by way of presenting the supporting evidence, which include an interim balance sheet, a cash flow analysis, and other valuation evidence prepared by a certified public accountant taking into account any undue or contingent liabilities.[21]

The EBL recognizes that best results for restoring the viability can be achieved when the relief is sought in a timely manner. Therefore, a third test is also provided where the debtor is under an 'imminent risk' of insolvency. The debtor is deemed to be under the 'imminent risk' if there is a substantial and real likelihood of becoming insolvent. This likelihood should clearly be demonstrated by the relevant evidence required for establishing liquidity or balance sheet tests.

The debtor may file an application for court approval if a restructuring plan has been previously negotiated and accepted by the requisite majority of affected creditors. The following section will lay out the out of court negotiation process.

2. Out of Court Negotiation Process

The EBL is not prescriptive with respect to how the out of court negotiation process should be conducted and provides flexibility to the debtor and its creditors to formulate the optimum solution for their needs. Negotiations and drafting of the plan will most likely be an ongoing process. The EBL does, however, provide for certain principles that must be followed.

The debtor must carefully analyze: (1) how a viable restructuring plan can be achieved; (2) which creditors will be affected by the proceeding; and, (3) whether more than one class of claims should be considered. Also, the debtor must prepare

---

18. EBL (2004) Article 309/t.
19. EBL (2004) Article 309/m.
20. Ibid.
21. Implementing Regulations on Restructuring of Corporations and Cooperatives Via Reconciliation (2004) (Herein after referred as 'Regulations')Article 3.

relevant financial statements for creditors' consideration, carefully craft a restructuring plan that would be supported by the majority of affected creditors and that would ultimately allow him to restore its financial viability. In addition, the debtor also must abide to the formal requirements regarding financial disclosure and solicitation of creditors' to vote on the plan before the court's approval.

In essence, the out of court negotiation process includes five steps: (1) identification of affected creditors; (2) classification of claims; (3) preparation of the plan; (4) preparation of documents and financial statements to be disclosed; and, (5) vote solicitation and voting process.

Certainly the order of the first four steps may change on a case by case basis. In any event, the debtor must demonstrate to the court during the approval process that he has duly followed and met these requirements.[22]

a.   *Identification of Affected Creditors*

Unlike in the concordat proceedings, the pre-packaged restructuring provides freedom to the debtor as to which claims should be restructured. The debtor is not required to agree on a plan with all of its creditors and has the option to negotiate with only those whose consents are critical to regain the financial viability.

In this respect, the debtor should determine the 'affected creditors' for the purpose of the restructuring. Affected creditors are defined as those creditors who will be solicited for negotiation and voting process and whose claims will potentially be affected or altered by the approved plan.[23]

To counter-balance the flexibility given to the debtor and avoid discrimination, favouritism or efforts to gerrymander the process, the debtor is required to disclose a list of its affected and unaffected creditors together with their respective classes. It may be impractical to fully disclose all of the creditors in some instances, but the disclosure statement should at least identify those unaffected creditors whose claims are substantially similar to one or more affected creditors.[24]

b.   *Classification of Claims*

Classification of claims is another novelty that pre-packaged restructuring scheme brings to the Turkish legal framework. The classification mechanism enables the debtor to group similar claims within the same class, allowing them to be subject to the same treatment under the plan.[25] It is worth noting that the principle of 'classification of claims' rather than 'classification of creditors' is clearly enshrined in the implementing regulations. A creditor may be included in more than one class based on its claims and may vote on the plan in each class separately (i.e. for each claim), where such claims are different in nature. It is the treatment of the claims that count, rather than the creditors themselves.

---

22. EBL (2004) Article 309/p.
23. EBL (2004) Article 309/m II, Regulations Article 5.
24. EBL (2004) Article 309/n, Regulations Article 7(e).
25. EBL (2004) Article 309/n II, Regulations Article 6.

The test for classification is 'substantial similarity' based on the legal nature of the claims. The meaning of 'substantial similarity' is further clarified and its principles are laid out.

The first principle comes from the very nature of the secured and unsecured claims. The plan must afford at least two separate classes, i.e. secured and unsecured claims (provided that unsecured claims are affected) and cannot bundle these two into one sole class. Bifurcation of an under-secured claim is also possible and must be based on a proper appraisal of the collateral. Accordingly, to the extent that the value of the collateral is insufficient to secure the total (secured) claim, the unsecured (or under secured) portion of may be classified as an unsecured claim.[26]

The law also offers further guidance on the classification of the various types of secured claims. Simply because the several claims are secured do not warrant them to be bundled into a same class. For instance, if one claim is secured by several assets, this claim should be treated in a separate class. Similarly, if there are a number of security interests with multiple ranks on the same package of collateral, these claims should also be treated in a separate class.[27]

While the law provides for clear guidance on classification and seems prescriptive in nature, it is important to bear in mind that if a legitimate business or economic justification exists, separate classification of similar claims may be upheld by the court.[28]

c.   *The Restructuring Plan*

Perhaps the most important aspect of the pre-packaged restructuring mechanism is the plan itself. The debtor must agree on a plan that will facilitate the company to recover its financial viability, and at the same time will provide fair and equitable treatment to all affected creditors. While the debtor and its creditors are free to enter into a wide array of arrangements to meet their individual needs, the law sets out detailed requirements with respect to the minimum content of the plan. Accordingly, the plan must contain the following information:

1. Treatment to affected creditors: The plan must clearly lay out the different classes of claims and the treatment to be provided to each class. The treatment should demonstrate how the equality among the same class of creditors is maintained and provide the dissenting/rejecting creditors at least as much as they would have gotten in a liquidation proceeding.[29] However, a creditor in a class can expressly accept a less favourable treatment than the other creditors in the same class.[30]
2. Determination of plan's effects on debtor's financials and contractual rights: The plan should specify if and how the debtor's property and

---

26. Regulations Article 6(c), (g).
27. Regulations Article 6 (d), (e), (f).
28. Regulations Article 6(a).
29. EBL (2004) Article 309/n (I), 309/p (I).
30. EBL (2004) Article 309/n (VII); Regulations Article 6.

contractual rights and obligations will be affected. It should also indicate if and how the debtor will obtain financing for restructuring purposes during the implementation stage.[31]

3. Changes on the structure of the debtor: The plan also needs to set out the way in which the debtor will restructure its debts and whether it requires any change in the form or the structure of the business. The EBL lists some alternatives by way of examples, but these are not exhaustive. For instance, the plan may provide for sale of all or any part of the debtor's business, changes in the capital structure, amendment to the debtor's charter, merger, change in the management, etc.[32]

4. Supervision of the Plan: The plan should also specify if and how the plan will be supervised after its approval. In this regard, parties to the plan may require the appointment of an independent expert to supervise the debtor's business and give periodic reports to creditors. Parties are free to agree on whom the plan supervisor will be and determine the scope of his duties, responsibilities and fees. To avoid any actual or perceived conflict of interest, the supervisors must be selected among independent third parties that are unaffiliated with any constituency.[33]

The appointment of the plan supervisor is not mandatory by law. If the plan is silent on this matter or an agreement could not be reached during the negotiations, the plan will still be valid if it is duly voted and accepted by the requisite majority. In any event, the appointment of the supervisor may be resolved during the court approval stage, where the court will have the discretion to appoint, *sua sponte*, a duly qualified plan supervisor and determine his duties.[34] However, since the overall goal of the mechanism is to uphold the autonomy and consent of the parties to the plan, the court should take into consideration the intent of the parties in this regard before rendering its decision. It will be appropriate to determine whether the parties did not need a supervisor in the first place or whether they could not reach an agreement on an impartial, qualified expert or his remuneration.

Same principles apply for the appointment of an interim supervisor, who may, as necessary, serve from the date of application for the court approval until the judgment is rendered. This issue will be elaborated in the relevant section *below*.

d. *Preparing Disclosure Documents, Financial Statements, Feasibility and Liquidation Analysis*

Another requirement under the law is that relevant disclosure documents and a thorough financial analysis must accompany the plan[35] so that the affected creditors can make an informed decision based on the debtor's past financial history

---

31. EBL (2004) Article 309/n (II), (III), (IV).
32. EBL (2004) Article 309/n (V).
33. EBL (2004) Article 309/n (VI).
34. EBL (2004) Article 309/p (II).
35. EBL (2004) Article 309/o (II), Regulations Article 7.

and best estimates for future performances. These analysis are essential for a meaningful negotiation process. The debtor, with its application to the court for plan approval, must submit a copy of these statements as well as evidence that the creditors have been provided with the said information.[36]

The law specifies what information should be included. Accordingly the debtor must disclose its financial standing by way of showing its audited financial statements for the past three years, book and market value of its assets and explain the reasons that lead to financial distress[37]. For instance, the debtor should explain whether external factors such as currency fluctuations, macroeconomic crisis or whether internal factors such as mismanagement of the company were the key determinants of the distress. The debtor should also elaborate its business strategy to overcome its distress through restructuring and lay out other potential risks that may hamper the successful implementation of the plan.[38]

In addition, these statements should be supplemented by a feasibility report from an independent audit firm assessing the viability of the proposed plan based on cash-flow and profit forecasts, availability of financing during the restructuring period and the robustness of the future projections.[39] The audit firm should also provide a liquidation analysis that will compare the treatment of affected creditors under the plan and the amount they could reasonably be expected to receive in a liquidation proceeding.[40] The debtor is required to provide the dissenting creditors with at least as much as they would have received under liquidation. This liquidity analysis is therefore critical for the court in determining whether the plan treats the dissenting creditors in fairness. It is inappropriate to allow a debtor to be rehabilitated and continue to maintain an interest in the business, when it cannot offer creditors more than what they would get if the business were liquidated. Such rehabilitation would be at the expense of the creditors with no proper allocation of risk on the debtor.

e. *Vote Solicitation and Voting Process*

The final step before having the plan approved by the court is getting it accepted by the 'requisite majority'. The requisite majority is satisfied if the plan is accepted by the absolute majority the voting creditors (more than 50 per cent) who hold at least two-thirds of the total amount of claims of such voting creditors.[41]

A critical aspect of the voting process is that the requisite majority is not calculated based on the total number of affected creditors and the amount of their claims. The final word on the plan is given by those creditors who actually take a stance on the plan by casting a vote in favour of or against it. A creditor's non-participation in

---

36. EBL (2004) Article 309/o.
37. Regulations Article 7(f), 8.
38. Regulations Article 7 (g).
39. Regulations Article 9.
40. Ibid.
41. EBL (2004) Article 309/m (III).

voting does not represent an opposition to the plan, so this will result in the exclusion of that creditor and his claim in the calculation of the requisite majority. A non-voting creditor will be bound by the decision adopted by the majority if the 'double' threshold has been achieved. This provides a means of imposing the plan on the dissenting creditors or on those uncooperative creditors that would otherwise hamper the possibility of a successful reorganization by way of non participation.

It is also important to note that if the plan contains more than one class of creditors, each class of creditors must accept the plan by a requisite majority. In this regard, the pre-packaged procedure has 'cram-down' provisions for dissenting or non participating creditors within a given class, but not among the different classes. Accordingly, the minority creditors will be bound by the treatment given to their class, but are offered protection and fair treatment in two ways: the plan should treat them equally as other creditors in the same class and they should receive at least as much as they would if the debtor were to be liquidated.[42]

The following chart contains a hypothetical scenario of a voting and the way to calculate the requisite majority with double thresholds. The facts are as follows: the debtor (D) is negotiating a restructuring plan with three different classes (Class 1, 2 and 3) of creditors (k). The claims and position of creditors towards the plan after the voting process are as follows:

	Class 1			Class 2			Class 3	
Creditor	*Claim*	*Vote*	*Creditor*	*Claim*	*Vote*	*Creditor*	*Claim*	*Vote*
C1k1*	**$100,000**	**Accept**	C2k1	$70,000	Not voted	C3k1	40,000	**Accept**
C1k2	**$20,000**	**Accept**	C2k2	$20,000	Accept	C3k2	50,000	**Accept**
C1k3	$40,000	Not voted	C2k3	$15,000	**Reject**			
C1k4	**$15,000**	**Reject**	C3k4	$15,000	Accept			
C1k5	$25,000	Not voted						
Result	***ACCEPT***		*ACCEPT*			*ACCEPT*		

* C represents the 'Class' and k represents the 'Creditor'. i.e. C1k1 means Class 1, creditor 1.

In this scenario, all three classes satisfy the requisite majority. Therefore, the plan is deemed to be accepted. In classes 1 and 2, more than half of the voting creditors (2 out of 3) representing more than two-thirds of the total claims of those voting creditors (USD) 120,000 out of USD 135,000 and USD 35,000 out of USD 50,000) have accepted the plan. Class 3 unanimously accepted the plan. For instance, If

---

42. Ibid.

C3K2 had rejected the plan, the third class would have caused the rejection of the entire plan, as each class must satisfy the requisite majority.

As the plan will ultimately be accepted by the voting creditors, it is critical to ensure a proper solicitation and voting procedure so that all affected creditors can be duly notified. Regulations clearly lay out each step that should be followed. First, the debtor should solicit the votes of each affected creditor separately with a solicitation notice in advance of the voting deadline. The solicitation notice should expressly state that those creditors that vote on the plan will make the determination on the acceptance or rejection of the plan. The effect of non voting should be explicitly stated on the solicitation notice, which should be accompanied by the proposed plan, financial statements, relevant disclosure statements and the standard ballot. The deadline should provide the affected creditors with sufficient time to make an informed decision on the plan and to timely cast their votes.[43]

The votes can be collected at a meeting convened for that purpose or by mail. If the debtor decides to conduct a meeting, its proposed venue, date and time must be selected in a manner to facilitate the participation of all affected creditors. Regardless of whether a voting meeting is convened or the ballots are collected by mail, a voting agent should be appointed with the responsibility for keeping an attendance roster to indicate those creditors that have voted the amount of their claims and classes. The Agent also supervises the voting process, tabulates the results of the vote and prepares a report describing the voting process and its outcome, which will be submitted to the court along with other documents for the approval of the plan.[44]

3. Application to the Court for Approval

After the plan is accepted by the requisite majority, it should be approved by the Commercial Court at the principal place of debtor's business.[45] There are two main reasons to get the court's approval. First is to ensure that debtor followed the procedure for disclosure and voting requirements, and that the plan provides for a fair treatment to dissenting creditors (by ensuring that they will receive at least as much as they would receive in liquidation). The second reason is to bind all parties to the terms of the plan.

a.   *Application, Procedure and Measures Taken During the Hearing*

Upon debtor's application, court should set a hearing date within 30 days to decide on the case in an expedited manner. The court may decide to hold an interim hearing (prior to the actual hearing) to facilitate – among other things – the collection of evidence and the filing of objections by the creditors. Any objections to

---

43. Regulations Article 10–11.
44. Regulations Article 12–17.
45. EBL (2004) Article 309/m.

the plan, including classification or claim disputes should be resolved during this timeframe and a decision on these matters should be made on a summary basis within 30 days from the hearing.[46]

During the hearing period and upon the request of the debtor and the creditors, the court may take all measures necessary to protect the assets (including imposing a stay on the actions pending by the affected creditors). The court may also appoint an interim supervisor, to conduct debtor's business activities until the judgment is given. The debtor and the creditors may have also agreed on an interim supervisor appointment during the plan negotiations.

The EBL also provides the debtor with the possibility of obtaining interim financing before the approval of the plan.[47] If this financing needs to be secured, unencumbered assets should be resorted as collateral.[48] In the event of debtor's default, the interim financing provider may request the debtor's liquidation.[49] Interim financing provided during the court approval stage is different from the financing being provided during the plan's implementation stage. Terms of such financing should be clearly provided in the plan.

The court will approve the plan if the following criteria has been met: (1) the plan prepared by the bona fide debtor has satisfied the content and disclosure requirements; (2) voting procedures were duly followed; and, (3) the dissenting or non-participating creditors receive as much as they would have under the liquidation proceeding. If the court decides that any of these requirements has not been satisfied, the plan will be rejected. With the judgment, the court will also resolve any disputes among the parties (e.g. on the appointment of the plan supervisor, his compensation and responsibilities).

b. *Effects of the Plan and Appeals*

Upon the court's approval, the plan will become binding on all the affected creditors and the terms of the plan will take precedence over all agreements with the affected creditors.[50]

Another critical effect of the approval of the plan relates to the debtor's relationship with unaffected creditors. It is not uncommon for agreements to regularly contain clauses or covenants that provide for default or breach of the agreement if the debtor files a proceeding under the EBL or takes certain actions that have not been approved by a counterparty. The EBL prevents the unaffected creditors from declaring a default on the basis of debtor's commencement of this proceeding or by virtue of engaging in transactions that are contained in the restructuring plan. Unaffected creditors will also be bound by the judgment to the extent that they

---

46. EBL (2004) Article 309/ö.
47. EBL (2004) Article 309/ö (III).
48. Ibid..
49. EBL (2004) Article 309/t.
50. EBL (2004) Article 309/r (I).

will not be able to challenge the judgment or declare default under their own agreements by virtue of court's approval.[51]

A further critical issue is the moment when the judgment becomes enforceable. The ability to rely on the judgment in restructurings is particularly important as the parties might need to alter their economic positions to comply with the terms of the plan. However, those parties who are obligated to change their position would face a risk in doing so if the judgment was reversed on appeal, especially if a stay pending the appeal is not granted.

The judgment may be appealed within 10 days from the date of its service. However, the law clearly recognizes that the judgment will be immediately enforceable and will not be automatically suspended until its finalization by way of appeal, notwithstanding any other general provision of the law.[52] To provide further predictability to the process, those transactions that were entered into during the appeal process will be upheld, even if the judgment is reversed as a result of the appeal.[53] Rather, the enforceability of the judgment can only be suspended by a stay of the judgment pending the appeal.

In line with this thinking, the stays and measures imposed by the court during the interim period will be released when the judgment becomes effective. In this way, the transition from the interim protective measures to full implementation of the plan will be flawless and will not create conflicts in the governance of the business in its restructured form.

4. Implementation of the Plan

During the implementation stage, the debtor will either execute the terms of the plan as agreed, or the implementation will be hindered by: (1) debtor's non performance; (2) breach of the terms and conditions of the plan; or, (3) due to unforeseen circumstances. In such cases, the plan may either be salvaged by way of amendments or it can be partially or fully terminated.

---

51. EBL (2004) Article 309/r (III).
52. EBL (2004) Article 309/r (II).
53. According to the general provisions of the Civil Procedure Code and EBL, a judgment is considered enforceable, unless its enforcement has been stayed pending the outcome of an appeal. The parties can get a stay of a judgment based on posting a bond in an amount that would compensate the successful party for any injuries or losses arising as a result of the appeal, due to the stay. There are, however, some exceptions to this rule. For instance, judgments dealing with *in rem* rights on immovable property may only be enforceable upon their finalization after the appeal process. This means that those judgments will be automatically stayed until the appeal process is finalized. In the absence of the EBL 309/r. It would not be easy to decide upon the effect of the court order in accordance with the general provisions. What would happen to a plan that deals with in rem rights on immovable property for a class of creditors, but not for other classes? What would be the nature of such a judgment? Should it be subject to automatic stay? Plans will most likely contain a number of provisions dealing with the transfer of real property or creation of other *in rem* rights. For the sake of predictability of the process, this provision clarifies the issue and prevents an automatic stay of the judgment, unless parties get a stay pending appeal by complying with the provisions of doing as such.

a.   *Amendments*

The debtor may have breached his obligations to a certain class or a particular creditor within that class. Or perhaps, an amendment to the terms of the plan may be required as a result of change of circumstances. In such cases, parties are encouraged to reach an understanding to alter their rights and obligations under the plan. The amendments should be approved by the court.

The plan may be amended without the further vote of creditors in any manner that does not materially adversely affect any party.[54] If the amendments adversely affect a particular class or classes, the debtor should solicit the creditors within that class and get their agreement on such amendment.[55] In any event, amendment should be in compliance with principle of equitable treatment and should not provide a better treatment to those whose rights are amended under the plan than the rest of the creditors.[56]

In addition, the amendment must be essential to render the plan viable and facilitate its implementation. In other words, the court should not approve the amendment if it is merely an effort for the debtor to escape from liquidation by protracting the process.[57]

b.   *Partial Termination of the Plan*

If the debtor breached his obligation to a certain class or a particular creditor within that class, another option afforded to such creditor/s is to have the plan partially terminated. In that case, those creditors will remain outside the scope of the plan and become unaffected creditors. However, all transactions until the termination of the plan will be upheld and the creditors will preserve the rights acquired under the plan.[58]

c.   *Full Termination of the Plan*

A third alternative provided in the event of the debtor's non performance is to have the plan fully terminated and request the debtor's liquidation. Unlike the two other remedies discussed *above*, the plan supervisor, any of the creditors, interim financing providers and the debtor are eligible to make a request for full termination of the plan if the debtor cannot timely fulfil its obligations under the plan and where an amendment is not feasible.[59]

Upon an application for the termination of the plan, the court should take the measures necessary to protect the assets of the debtor. The debtor will be liquidated upon determination that: (1) the debtor has failed to perform his obligations and

---

54. Regulations Article 20.
55. Ibid.
56. EBL (2004) Article 309/ş.
57. Ibid.
58. EBL (2004) Article 309/s.
59. EBL (2004) Article 309/t.

that amendments will not be viable; or, (2) the creditor providing the financing has not received his claim in part or in full.[60]

In addition, any creditor may request termination of the plan in its entirety if the plan has been proposed with dishonest motives.[61]

IV. CONCLUSION

The EBL amended by Bill 5092 introduced a new pre packaged corporate restructuring mechanism to rescue financially distressed, but viable companies. The law, introduced at the wake of the country's most recent financial crises, is inspired by the global trends and embraces several principles that are found in most advanced restructuring laws. The mechanism aims to stabilize business operations by providing an amicable forum for parties to reach a consensus out of court fosters a reorganization plan based on an objective valuation of post-reorganized enterprise and provides for equitable treatment of creditors and claims through classification. Overall, the provisions are well thought through and promising.

It is, however, too soon to determine whether the mechanism will prove to be useful in turning around financially distressed companies or the extent it will be used in practice. Lack of culture of negotiation and settling disputes out of court coupled with the novel concepts introduced for the first time may be some of the hindrances to full utilization of this new framework. Evidently, as any new piece of legislation, the mechanism needs to be further tested, applied and interpreted based on the local business and financial realities.

---

60. Ibid.
61. EBL (2004) Article 309/s.

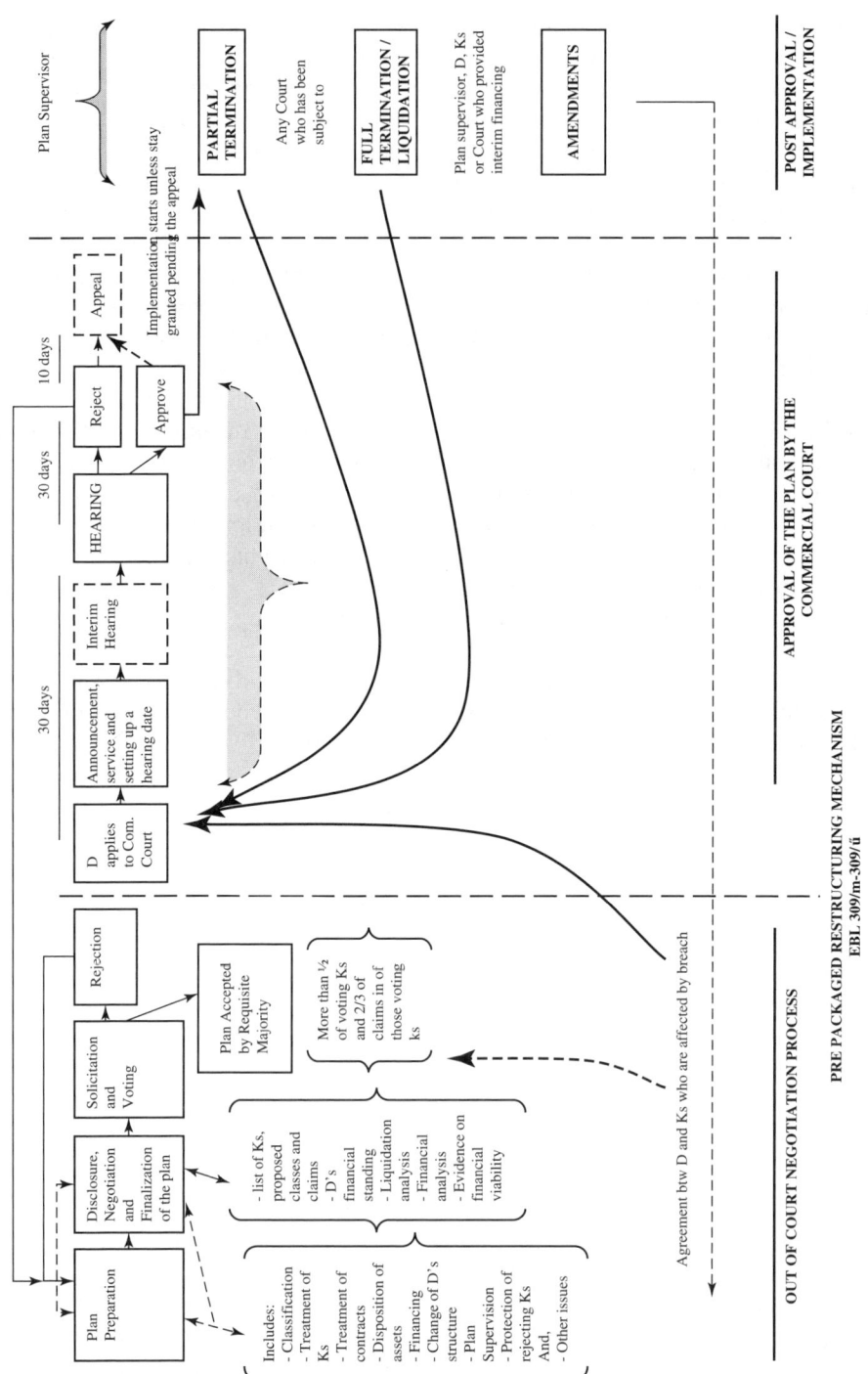

Chapter 14A
UNITED STATES – THEORY

The United States Expedited Proceedings: 'Pre-Packaged' Chapter 11 Plans

Lindsee P. Granfield and Andrés de la Cruz

ACRONYMS, ABBREVIATIONS & DEFINED TERMS

Chapter 7	A chapter 7 is a liquidation proceeding that involves the appointment of a trustee who collects the property of the debtor, liquidates it and distributes the proceeds among creditors.
Chapter 11	A chapter 11 proceeding is a court supervised reorganization of an insolvent or near insolvent business while continuing with its day to day operations.
TIA	Trust Indenture Act of 1939 (15 U.S.C. § 77aaa et seq.)
U.S.C.	United States Code
US Bankruptcy Code	Title 11 of the United States Code which governs bankruptcy cases.

In the United States, the expedited full restructuring proceeding is the so called 'pre-packaged' plan of reorganization which is a variant of a chapter 11 reorganization case.[1] To provide a picture of how pre-packaged plans allow for an expedited reorganization proceeding under US law and what the predicates of a successful pre-packaged case are, this chapter will first describe the general types of plenary bankruptcy or insolvency proceedings available to business organizations (or which may be filed against them on an involuntary basis). Then, it will describe how a pre-packaged case works, how it expedites the process and what the predicates of a successful pre-packaged chapter 11 case are.

I. GENERAL BACKGROUND: PLENARY BANKRUPTCY PROCEEDINGS UNDER THE US BANKRUPTCY CODE FOR BUSINESS ORGANIZATIONS[2]

A. CHAPTER 7 AND CHAPTER 11 IN GENERAL ENTITIES THAT CAN FILE THESE CASES IN THE US

The US Bankruptcy Code, 11 U.S.C. §§ 101 et. seq., in general, provides for two general types of bankruptcy proceedings for business organizations[3] (as opposed to natural persons)[4] – a chapter 7 liquidation proceeding[5] and a chapter 11 reorganization proceeding.[6] Both types of proceedings also include certain specialized provisions for certain special types of business organizations, such as for 'stockbroker liquidations'[7] and 'railroad reorganizations'.[8]

---

1. See 11 U.S.C. §§ 1101 to 1146.
2. In addition to the plenary bankruptcy proceedings that may be brought under chapter 7 and chapter 11, the amendments to the US Bankruptcy Code enacted in October 2005 also allow for Ancillary and other Cross-Border Cases under Chapter 15 which incorporates, with US amendments, the United Nations' Model Law on Cross-Border Insolvency. 11 U.S.C. §§ 1501 to 1532. Chapter 15 proceedings allow for a *US* Bankruptcy Court to recognize a plenary proceeding in another country as the 'main proceeding' for the particular business organization (presumptively the country under whose laws the business organization was registered), and subject to specific standards and requirements (including that there not be any matters manifestly against the public policy of the US or in breach of treaties), to give that main proceeding recognition and aid. Chapter 15 proceedings, under the right circumstances, might also be conducted on an expedited basis.
3. Section 109 of the *US* Bankruptcy Code, 11 U.S.C. § 109, generally provides that business organizations other than domestic insurance companies, banks and other similar financial institutions and foreign insurance companies engaged in business in the US may be chapter 7 or chapter 11 debtors.
4. For natural persons, in addition to chapter 7 and chapter 11, the most recent amendments to the US Bankruptcy Code under the Bankruptcy Abuse Prevention and Consumer Protection Act of 2005 that took effect in October 2005 seek to force more consumer debtors into chapter 13, which unlike chapter 7, requires future earnings of debtors to be contributed in part to paying off their creditors with debts that arose before they filed for bankruptcy.
5. See 11 U.S.C. §§ 701 to 728.
6. See 11 U.S.C. §§ 1101 to 1146.
7. See 11 U.S.C. §§ 741 to 753.
8. See 11 U.S.C. §§ 1161 to 1174.

Under the Section 1408 of the US Judiciary Code,[9] a chapter 7 or chapter 11 case may be brought in a US Bankruptcy Court in the place in the US either where the debtor (1) is incorporated or under whose laws it is organized, (2) has its principle place of business, (3) has its principle assets or (4) where a bankruptcy case is already pending for an 'affiliate'.[10] Therefore, plenary bankruptcy cases for business entities that are organized under the law of a country outside the US may be filed in the US if such business entities have a place of business in the US, assets in the US or an affiliate of theirs (e.g., any company controlled by or controlling 20 percent of the voting equity interests) has already filed a bankruptcy case in the US. This very broad grant of venue is tempered by abstention provisions under Section 1334 of the US Judiciary Code[11] and Section 305 of the US Bankruptcy Code[12] which allow US Bankruptcy Courts to abstain from hearing plenary cases based on, inter alia, comity and/or the interests of the debtor and creditors.

B. THE MAIN DIFFERENCES BETWEEN CHAPTER 7 AND CHAPTER 11 FOR BUSINESS ENTITIES

The three main differences between chapter 7 and chapter 11 cases in the US for business entities are (1) the automatic appointment of a trustee in a chapter 7 case; (2) the role of creditors committees (and in the case of chapter 11 equity committees); and, (3) the possibility of a reorganization, as opposed to liquidation, under a chapter 11 case.

In chapter 7, a trustee must be appointed to take possession and control over all of the property and business operations of the debtor business entity. Also, existing management is automatically displaced from controlling the debtor's assets and business decisions.[13]

In contrast, in a chapter 11 case, existing management (e.g., board of directors and officers) is not automatically displaced by a trustee and a trustee is appointed only at the request of a party for cause, in the interests of creditors, equity security holders and other interests of the bankruptcy estate.[14] In a chapter 11 case where existing management retains possession of the debtor's assets, it may continue to operate the debtor's business in the 'ordinary course of business' without any pre-approval or supervision from other parties in interest or the Bankruptcy Court.[15] The use of the debtor's assets 'outside the ordinary course of business', however, with respect to selling assets, entering into new business operations, or borrowing

---

9. 28 U.S.C. § 1408.
10. Definitions, such as 'affiliate', that are used throughout the US Bankruptcy Code, are found in Section 101. 11 U.S.C. § 101 (1) to (55).
11. 28 U.S.C. § 1334.
12. 11 U.S.C. § 305.
13. See, 11 U.S.C. §§ 701 to 704.
14. See, 11 U.S.C. §§ 1104 to 1107, 1112.
15. See, 11 U.S.C. § 363(b).

funds (other than ordinary unsecured trade credit) all require Bankruptcy Court approval before they can be properly undertaken.[16]

In a chapter 7 case, the only role for a committee of creditors is to vote on a trustee, if they would like to choose a trustee that is different from the 'interim' trustee that automatically gets appointed by the Office of the US Trustee (an arm of the US Department of Justice) and to designate three creditors to consult with the appointed trustee.[17] Reimbursement of counsel fees for a chapter 7 creditors committee is not provided for under the US Bankruptcy Code. In contrast, in a chapter 11 case, the US trustee is to automatically appoint a representative committee of creditors (as long as there are sufficient number of representative creditors willing to serve), whose advisors can seek reimbursement directly from the bankruptcy estate (as can the debtor's counsel and other advisors) to review and take a position on all matters in the case.[18] The US Trustee may also appoint a committee of equity security holders where it appears warranted.[19]

Certain powers and issues are applicable to both chapter 7 and chapter 11. For instance, chapter 7 trustees and debtors-in-possession in chapter 11, subject to certain exceptions, have the power, with Bankruptcy Court approval, to assume or reject executory contracts (11 U.S.C. § 365), borrow money (11 U.S.C. § 364), sell assets outside the ordinary course of business (11 U.S.C. § 363) and bring 'avoidance' actions to recover for the benefit of all creditors, preferential and fraudulent transfers (11 U.S.C. §§ 544 to 551). The 'automatic stay', a statutory injunction, protects the chapter 7 and chapter 11 debtor and its assets from collection activities and the continuation of pre-petition litigation.[20] However, the ultimate goals for which these powers may be used are different in chapter 7 and chapter 11. A chapter 7 trustee, though he or she may continue the debtor's business operations for some period of time (11 U.S.C. § 721), the duties of the trustee are in the main to 'collect and reduce to money the property of the estate for which such trustee serves, and close such estate as expeditiously as is compatible with the best interests of the parties in interest'.[21] Therefore, seeking to turn around and reorganize a business operation in order to continue the business indefinitely in the future for the benefit of its creditors and interest holders as proposed under a plan of reorganization is the purview of chapter 11.[22] Though, it should be noted that it is permissible for the plan of reorganization in chapter 11 to propose that the debtor be sold as a going concern or otherwise simply liquidated.

In addition, secured creditors (creditors whose claims are secured by liens or other pledge of assets) enjoy special protections in chapter 7 and chapter 11 cases. Secured creditors are entitled to have the value of their security be "adequately

---

16. See, 11 U.S.C. §§ 363, 364 and 549.
17. See, 11 U.S.C. §§ 702, 705.
18. See, 11 U.S.C. §§ 1102 to 1103, 1109(b).
19. See, Id.
20. See, 11 U.S.C. § 362(a).
21. See, 11 U.S.C. § 704(a)(1).
22. See, 11 U.S.C. §§ 1121 to 1141.

protected" during the pendency of a chapter 11 or chapter 7 case.[23] And they are entitled to receive the value of their collateral on their claims before all other creditors, though they cannot foreclose on their collateral without relief from the stay (permission from the Bankruptcy Court). Their collateral may be sold under certain circumstances, including if their liens continue to attach to the proceeds.[24] Adequate protection is the notion that if the value of the secured creditor's collateral is declining during the pendency of the case such that there is a threat that the creditor's fully secured claim would become unsecured in part or in full, then that value must be protected in some way (cash payments, replacement liens, etc).[25] A secured creditor may at any time in a chapter 11 or chapter 7 case move for relief from the US Bankruptcy Code's automatic stay (Section 362(a)) (which protects the debtor and its property from collection actions and interference during the bankruptcy case) for 'cause', which includes a lack of adequate protection.[26]

Though chapter 7 liquidations are supposed to be accomplished as "expeditiously" as possible, the reality is that, except for some unusual circumstances (no assets, very small known creditor group, etc.), chapter 7 cases are not expedited proceedings. In the main this is because of the time it may take for the trustee to liquidate the assets involved, but also the usually long time (in a case of any size, because of the amount of assets and number of creditors) it may take for all claims to be examined and their priority of distribution under chapter 7 determined.[27] Generally, that priority is secured claims first, claims of administration that benefited the bankruptcy estate second, priority unsecured claims third, general unsecured claims fourth and equity interests last.

C.   GENERAL PROVISIONS RELATING TO US CHAPTER 11 PLANS
       (NON-PRE-PACKAGED PLANS)

With respect to the usual, non-pre-packaged chapter 11 case, the debtor-in-possession initially has a 120-day exclusive period to propose a plan of reorganization (and 180-day period to solicit acceptances of such a plan). The exclusive period can be extended, for cause, for a total of up to 18 months to propose a plan and 20 months to solicit acceptances of that plan[28] (there are also special shorter exclusivity periods for certain types of cases, such as 'small business cases').[29]

The purpose of the plan is generally to propose how the debtor's property and business operations will be used going forward and what value is available to

---

23. See, e.g., 11 U.S.C. §§ 361, 326(d), 363(e) and 364(d)(1)(B).
24. See, e.g., 11 U.S.C. §§ 362 and 363(f).
25. See, 11 U.S.C. § 361.
26. See, 11 U.S.C. § 362(d).
27. See, 11 U.S.C. §§ 506 to 507 and 726.
28. See, 11 U.S.C. § 1121.
29. In contrast, if a chapter 11 trustee gets appointed under Section 1104, then that trustee will not enjoy an exclusive period to propose a plan of reorganization, and any party in interest may propose a plan. See, 11 U.S.C. 1121(c)(1).

distribute to creditors and equity holders, and how that value will be distributed to creditors and equity holders.[30] A creditors' committee or other party in interest may seek to end the exclusive right of a debtor-in-possession to propose and solicit acceptances of a plan or to reduce the time such debtor has to propose a plan.[31]

Creditors' claims and equity interests must be placed into classes of substantially similar claims or interests for voting on a plan.[32] Creditors and equity security holders' votes may only be solicited under a disclosure statement, which if the solicitation occurs *after a bankruptcy case has been filed*, must be a disclosure statement that has been pre-approved by the Bankruptcy Court as containing "adequate information".[33]

In order for a proposed plan of reorganization to be "confirmed" and implemented, all classes of claims and interests that are impaired[34] under the plan must vote to accept the plan by claims holding 66⅔ in amount and a majority in number of the claims and the other standards set forth in Section 1129(a) of the US Bankruptcy Code must be met.

If the all standards for confirming a plan under Section 1129(a) – including showing that creditor recoveries for creditors who have not accepted the plan are at least as good as they would receive in a chapter 7 case (the so-called 'best interests' test)[35] and that the confirmation of this reorganization plan is not likely to be followed by liquidation or the need for further reorganization (usually referred to as the 'feasibility' of the plan) – have been met, *other than* having every impaired class vote to accept the plan, then it still might be possible to confirm the plan under the 'cram-down' provisions of Section 1129(b) of the US Bankruptcy Code.

A plan may be 'crammed down' on impaired classes that have voted to reject the plan if (1) at least one impaired class (not counting the votes of 'insiders' as defined under the US Bankruptcy Code)[36] has voted to accept the plan, (2) no junior class is receiving any value under the plan if an impaired class that is senior in priority *and* rejected the plan is not receiving full value under the plan (the so-called 'absolute priority rule'); and, (3) the other standards of Section 1129(b) are met.[37]

The time it takes to be in a position in a chapter 11 case to negotiate about a plan, propose it, have a disclosure statement approved by the Bankruptcy Court,

---

30. See, 11 U.S.C. § 1123 (Contents of plan).
31. See, 11 U.S.C. § 1125(c).
32. See, 11 U.S.C. § 1122(a).
33. See, 11 U.S.C. § 1125. 'Adequate information' is defined in Section 1125(a). 11 U.S.C. § 1125(a).
34. Whether or not a claim or interest is impaired under a plan is governed by Section 1124 of the US Bankruptcy Code, which generally provides that a claim or interest is impaired, unless it is left unaltered or it is reinstated with all defaults cured and compensation for any reinstatement damages. See, 11 U.S.C. § 1124.
35. See 11 U.S.C. § 1129(a)(7).
36. See, 11 U.S.C. 101(31). In the case of corporations (11 U.S.C. 101(31)(b)), 'insider' includes: (1) director of the debtor; (2) officer of the debtor; (3) person in control of the debtor; (4) partnership in which the debtor is a general partner; (5) general partner of the debtor; or (6) relative of a general partner, director, officer, or person in control of the debtor.
37. See, 11 U.S.C. § 1129(b). The annex of this chapter includes § 1129(b).

get the plan confirmed and then implement it can vary significantly depending upon the size, complexity and issues that are dominant in any particular chapter 11 case. It would not be unusual, though, for chapter 11 cases of mid-sized or large companies (particularly where there had not been any pre-bankruptcy negotiations with creditors or negotiations had been decidedly unsuccessful) for a debtor to take the whole 18 to 20 months of exclusivity now provided in Section 1121 to propose and solicit acceptances to a plan of reorganization. Chapter 11 also contains some built in notice requirements when the debtor or another party in interest actually have a plan and disclosure statement it wishes to propose, of at least 25 days notice for a hearing on the adequacy of a proposed disclosure statement or the hearing to consider confirmation of a chapter 11 plan.[38]

II.   SPEEDY PRE-PACKAGED CHAPTER 11 PLANS

Now that the 'usual' bankruptcy processes in the US for business entities have been generally summarized *above*, this section explores *below* how the successful pre-packaged case can lead to extreme expedition, at least as to the time actually spent under the supervision of the US Bankruptcy Court.

A.   PRE-BANKRUPTCY SOLICITATION AND STREAMLINED
        POST-BANKRUPTCY PROCEDURES ARE KEY ELEMENTS

Section 1125(g) of the US Bankruptcy Code provides: "[n]otwithstanding subsection (b) [the section that requires pre-approval by the Bankruptcy Court of disclosure statements when solicitation is done *after* the commencement of the chapter 11 case], an acceptance or rejection of the plan may be solicited from a holder of a claim or interest if such solicitation complies with applicable non-bankruptcy law and if such holder was solicited *before the commencement of the case* in a manner complying with applicable non-bankruptcy law"[39] (emphasis added). This section authorizes companies that are in financial difficulty to negotiate with creditors, prepare a plan of reorganization and solicit acceptances of that plan of reorganization before actually filing a bankruptcy case, as long as the solicitation of acceptances of that plan comports with non-bankruptcy law. If they are able to successfully do that, then they can file an accepted plan with their bankruptcy petition and seek confirmation of that plan, so long as they can meet the other confirmation standards in very short order, indeed in as short a period of time as 30 to 35 days.

The fact that the post-filing phase of a successful pre-packaged bankruptcy case can be that short in duration does not mean that the pre-filing phase will be short. Again, the plan must be formulated, negotiated and acceptances of it solicited before the bankruptcy case is actually filed.

---

38. See Rule 2002(b) of the Federal Rules of Bankruptcy Procedure.
39. 11 U.S.C.§ 1125(g).

With respect to the reference in Section 1125(g) to the pre-filing solicitation being done in accordance with non-bankruptcy law, there are a few sources of that law that parties wishing to try to accomplish pre-packaged plans must review.

First, if one or more class of creditors or equity security holders that the company wishes to solicit acceptances from hold or are being offered securities of the company (as defined by the US securities laws or non-US securities laws), then the company will need to make sure that the solicitation materials used as well as the process followed in soliciting acceptances comport with federal and state securities laws and regulations. For instance, if no exemption from the registration requirements under the Securities Act of 1933[40] is available, then the solicitation may need to be registered with the Securities and Exchange Commission.[41] While a discussion of all the possible exemptions from registration that should be reviewed is beyond the scope of this chapter, suffice it to say, that this securities law analysis is a very important early step to understanding the options the company has to solicit acceptances, particularly if the company does not want to risk the delays in timing which a registered offering may impose. That analysis might also be relevant to any type of support agreement (sometimes referred to as 'lock-up' agreements) that the putative debtor might wish to seek from a group of its most important creditors (those with which it negotiated the terms of its plan) prior to starting the overall solicitation. It should also be noted, for some types of pre-packaged plans, particularly those which only seek to impair certain debt securities, while leaving all other creditors unimpaired, that it may be possible to contemplate in the registration statement or unregistered offering materials (if there is an exemption from registration available) two options: (1) simply closing a exchange offer without a bankruptcy filing if the necessary level of acceptances under the applicable indentures[42] or a very high thresholds of acceptances are met; or, (2) filing a pre-packaged plan in a chapter 11 case (if the acceptance level is

---

40. 15 U.S.C. § 77a et seq.
41. When the solicitation of votes for a plan of reorganization is done after a bankruptcy filing, then one need only comply with the provisions of Section 1125 of the Bankruptcy Code and need not seek to also comply with the US securities laws. In addition, there is an exemption from registration (with certain exceptions) of any securities of the reorganized debtor or its successor to be offered under a plan of reorganization in exchange (or principally in exchange) for creditors' claims or equity interest holders' interests. See 11 U.S.C. § 1145.
42. Under the Trust Indenture Act of 1939 (the 'TIA'), collective action clauses under bond indentures may not take away the right of an individual bondholder to collect its interest or principal when due or to extend the principal maturity date. Therefore, for bonds issued under US law and the TIA, collective non-bankruptcy compromise of these issues is not possible. Most other covenants and other protections, other than these special rights, can be affected through bondholder consents under the terms of the particular indenture by collective action. But, the unanimous consent provisions explain why transactions seeking to effect a restructuring through an exchange offer for TIA qualified bonds outside of bankruptcy will typically impose quite high acceptance threshold conditions to limit the moral hazard. The question will be what level of the old, uncompromised debt can both the company in distress and its other compromising bondholders accept. A bankruptcy or insolvency proceeding is the only way to compromise in full TIA qualified bonds without a unanimous acceptance vote. (for instance, in a chapter 11 case, the requisite vote to confirm a chapter 11 plan).

high enough for acceptance of a plan of reorganization (66⅔ per cent in amount and a majority in number), but not high enough for the desired exchange offer threshold (typically 90 to 95 per cent in amount).

Second, even if the consideration being offered is clearly not 'securities', the company soliciting acceptances will need to consider general principles of contract law as to the formation of contracts and as to the absence of fraud in the solicitation of the claimants' acceptance of the plan. In addition, though this is not specifically set forth in Section 1125(g), there is no question that the general practice is typically to have the disclosure statement upon which acceptances are solicited in a pre-packaged situation be in the form that the Bankruptcy Courts are used to reviewing when the solicitation is done with their pre-approval after a bankruptcy filing.

If a company is successful in formulating, negotiating and receiving the requisite acceptances (in accordance with non-bankruptcy law) of its pre-package plan, then it can file its plan, the disclosure document it used to gain acceptances and the evidence that it received the requisite acceptances to confirm the plan on the first day of its bankruptcy proceeding, right after it files its chapter 11 petition. It can seek the scheduling of a confirmation hearing on its plan with at least 25 days notice (as required by Rule 2002(b) of the Federal Rules of Bankruptcy Procedure), as it will not need to have an intervening disclosure statement hearing or approval of its disclosure statement by the Bankruptcy Court (at least not until the confirmation hearing). If the plan has been overwhelmingly accepted and there are no real objectors to the plan, this could mean a stay as short as 30 to 35 days under bankruptcy supervision for the debtor-in-possession company. If the debtor faces serious confirmation issues (particularly if raised by a well-funded objector), then the confirmation process can still be subject to discovery and litigation delays and uncertainties, which might take the confirmation out three to six months or longer (even if the debtor ultimately prevails in confirming the plan after litigation).

In addition to the plan confirmation process being shortened for pre-packaged plans, a number of Bankruptcy Courts will also allow many streamlined procedures to be in effect even before the pre-packaged plan has been confirmed. An example of those procedures is the Procedural Guidelines For Pre-Packaged Chapter 11 Cases in the United States Bankruptcy Court in the Southern District of New York.[43] These procedures can include extending out the date for the debtor to file the usually voluminous financial statements and schedules it usually must file within 15 days of its petition filing to a date that is after the expected confirmation of the plan, such that if the plan is confirmed, those voluminous filings (or at least the vast majority of them) never have to be made. They may also include allowing the debtor to continue paying all classes of creditors that the plan does not impair in the ordinary course of business (even their pre-petition claims). Though the US Trustee's office will typically have to ask creditors if they wish to form an official

---

43. A copy of these guidelines can be found on the website of the *US* Bankruptcy Court for the Southern District of New York under 'Procedural Orders/Guidelines' at <www.nysb.uscourts.gov>.

creditors committee, if creditors that are impaired by the plan are in the main supportive of the plan, many times (although not always), the expense of a creditors committee, its counsel and advisors can also be avoided, if not enough creditors reply to the US Trustee's office that they are willing to serve on a creditors committee. Also, if the debtor is prepared to admit to the validity and amount (at least for purposes of the pre-packaged plan) of the claims being compromised under the pre-packaged plan, then there will be no need to make creditors file proofs of claim or to undertake the usually lengthy claims reconciliation process. This can be accomplished most practically where the only creditors being affected by the plan are the holders of certain bank loan claims and/or outstanding bond debt, where usually there is not a dispute about the validity or the amount of the claims.

Of course, while there are many pre-packaged plans that companies seek to accomplish, there will always be a number that fail to achieve the time and expense savings that the successful plan achieves, either because the pre-bankruptcy negotiations or solicitation is not successful and a bankruptcy filing becomes necessary without an accepted plan or because other confirmation standards, other than the acceptance standards, are not met. With that in mind, the last section of this sub-chapter discusses the predicates of a successful pre-packaged plan and case.

III. THE PREDICATES OF A SUCCESSFUL PRE-PACKAGED PLAN

A. ONLY A WELL-DEFINED GROUP OF CREDITORS WITH COMMON INTERESTS ARE BEING AFFECTED BY THE PLAN

This typically would mean that the plan is only seeking to affect and impair a well defined group, such as the holders of bank loan claims and/or holders of bonds or notes. This is because there is usually no dispute between the parties about the validity of the debt and the amount of such debt. And, the holders of this debt are known or, as in the case of bondholders, usually can be identified through the indenture trustee or trustees for the bonds.

With other types of debt, such as trade claims or government tax or other regulatory claims, being able to quickly identify such claimants and whether or not there is a dispute as to the validity and amount of such claims is usually more problematic. Therefore, the successful pre-pack typically leaves aside all types of claims other then a few well defined classes unimpaired and has them ride through the bankruptcy case, unaffected.[44] This means that pre-packaged plans will not be

---

44. Leaving those claims unaffected does not mean admitting them. It just means that both parties, the company and the claimant can use their normal channels of reconciling claims or challenging claims, such as arbitration or non-bankruptcy litigation to resolve any disputes about the validity and amount of the claim. But it will also mean that once the validity and amount of the an unaffected claim has been agreed to or established in some other way, then the claimant will be owed 100 cents on the dollar of its claim.

practicable for some companies that either due to extent of their the financial difficulties or the complexity of the issues that cause the company to file for restructuring, need a plan of reorganization that affects all classes of its creditors, including such classes as trade and government claims. This also means that a pre-packaged plan will probably not work when the situation that induces the company to contemplate bankruptcy is large tort or other litigation problems involving many parties.[45]

There can sometimes be exceptions to these rules, like, for example, if there are some large trade claimants who must be part of the restructuring to make it feasible and are willing to accept a plan that may not treat them as well as the mass of smaller trade claimants who will remain unaffected by the plan.

B. THE PLAN IS NEGOTIATED WITH A GROUP OF CREDITORS WHOSE ACCEPTANCE GETS CLOSE TO THE AMOUNT NEEDED FOR BANKRUPTCY ACCEPTANCE

Another predicate for success of a pre-packaged plan is having the right group of creditors with which to negotiate the plan prior to seeking to solicit acceptances of that plan. This is a group that can either deliver the amount of debt needed for plan approval (or close to it) (66⅔ per cent of class of debt being affected by the proposed plan), and even more ideally, also the number of claim holders needed for plan approval as well (as majority in number). Now, in real situations, many times the creditor negotiating group will not meet these criteria completely.

However, approaching those criteria can be a very important ingredient for success, so that once the plan is negotiated both the putative debtor company and the negotiating creditor group may have some real expectation that what they have negotiated will achieve the requisite vote for plan acceptance once the plan is sent out for solicitation. Organizing a negotiating group of creditors can have its own issues, particularly with respect to confidentiality arrangements and the question of whether the company in financial difficulty will pay the expenses of legal and financial advisors for the creditor group.

C. ACHIEVING A CONSENSUS WILL LEAD TO THE MOST STREAMLINED CASES

While a pre-packaged plan of reorganization that just squeaks by with the bare requisite vote for plan acceptance might certainly be confirmed if it meets all the requirements of Section 1129 of the US Bankruptcy Code for confirmation, it probably will not be confirmed and implemented within the 30 to 35-day

---

45. It may be that there may be some streamlining benefits available through pre-bankruptcy negotiation about a plan of reorganization, but a full-blown pre-pack with pre-bankruptcy solicitation of a plan is usually very difficult in these sorts of situations, because of the numbers of claimants involved and the disputed nature of their claims.

timeframe of the most streamlined cases, where there is overwhelming acceptance of the plan by the creditor class being affected.

This is simply because if there is a group of creditors (or even one relatively large creditor) who voted against the plan who are motivated to object to and litigate any questions they can raise about the plan's confirmation, then the processes that may come into play in litigating contested issues will almost undoubtedly delay the process.

How long that delay may be will depend on a number of things, including whether there are factual (as opposed to legal) disputes, where the right to US discovery processes (document requests, depositions, etc.) can be invoked and an evidentiary hearing (as opposed to simply legal argument) must be held.

D. THE COMPANY IN FINANCIAL DIFFICULTY CAN BE 'FIXED' BY SIMPLY RESTRUCTURING OR REDUCING ITS DEBT LOAD

A pre-package plan is probably not feasible for a company with operational problems that need time to fix. The prime candidate for a pre-packaged plan is a company that has already achieved whatever operational restructuring it needs, and that has a business plan to follow that its creditors accept, which business plan shows that it will return to profitability if its debt load is either restructured (new maturities, covenants and/or interest rates) and/or reduced (debt to equity swap).

IV. CONCLUSION

With the right pre-requisites for success, a pre-packaged chapter 11 plan can lead to a very expedited restructuring process.

ANNEX: KEY LEGISLATION

Title 11. Chapter 11. Subchapter II.

§ 1125. Postpetition disclosure and solicitation

(a) In this section

(1) 'adequate information' means information of a kind, and in sufficient detail, as far as is reasonably practicable in light of the nature and history of the debtor and the condition of the debtor's books and records, including a discussion of the potential material Federal tax consequences of the plan to the debtor, any successor to the debtor, and a hypothetical investor typical of the holders of claims or interests in the case, that would enable such a hypothetical investor of the relevant class to make an informed judgment about the plan, but adequate information need not include such information about any other possible or proposed plan and in determining whether a disclosure statement provides adequate information, the court shall consider the complexity of the case, the benefit of additional information to creditors and other parties in interest, and the cost of providing additional information; and

(2) 'investor typical of holders of claims or interests of the relevant class' means investor having
   (A) a claim or interest of the relevant class;
   (B) such a relationship with the debtor as the holders of other claims or interests of such class generally have; and
   (C) such ability to obtain such information from sources other than the disclosure required by this section as holders of claims or interests in such class generally have.

(b) An acceptance or rejection of a plan may not be solicited after the commencement of the case under this title from a holder of a claim or interest with respect to such claim or interest, unless, at the time of or before such solicitation, there is transmitted to such holder the plan or a summary of the plan, and a written disclosure statement approved, after notice and a hearing, by the court as containing adequate information. The court may approve a disclosure statement without a valuation of the debtor or an appraisal of the debtor's assets.

(c) The same disclosure statement shall be transmitted to each holder of a claim or interest of a particular class, but there may be transmitted different disclosure statements, differing in amount, detail, or kind of information, as between classes.

(d) Whether a disclosure statement required under subsection (b) of this section contains adequate information is not governed by any otherwise applicable nonbankruptcy law, rule, or regulation, but an agency or official whose duty is to administer or enforce such a law, rule, or regulation may be heard on the issue of whether a disclosure statement contains adequate information. Such an agency or official may not appeal from, or otherwise seek review of, an order approving a disclosure statement.

(e) A person that solicits acceptance or rejection of a plan, in good faith and in compliance with the applicable provisions of this title, or that participates, in good faith and in compliance with the applicable provisions of this title, in the offer, issuance, sale, or purchase of a security, offered or sold under the plan, of the debtor, of an affiliate participating in a joint plan with the debtor, or of a newly organized successor to the debtor under the plan, is not liable, on account of such solicitation or participation, for violation of any applicable law, rule, or regulation governing solicitation of acceptance or rejection of a plan or the offer, issuance, sale, or purchase of securities.

(f) Notwithstanding subsection (b), in a small business case

(1) the court may determine that the plan itself provides adequate information and that a separate disclosure statement is not necessary;
(2) the court may approve a disclosure statement submitted on standard forms approved by the court or adopted under section 2075 of title 28; and
(3)
   (A) the court may conditionally approve a disclosure statement subject to final approval after notice and a hearing;
   (B) acceptances and rejections of a plan may be solicited based on a conditionally approved disclosure statement if the debtor provides adequate information to each holder of a claim or interest that is solicited, but a conditionally approved disclosure statement shall be mailed not later than 25 days before the date of the hearing on confirmation of the plan; and
   (C) the hearing on the disclosure statement may be combined with the hearing on confirmation of a plan.

(g) Notwithstanding subsection (b), an acceptance or rejection of the plan may be solicited from a holder of a claim or interest if such solicitation complies with applicable nonbankruptcy law and if such holder was solicited before the commencement of the case in a manner complying with applicable nonbankruptcy law.

§ 1129: Confirmation of plan

(a) The court shall confirm a plan only if all of the following requirements are met:

(1) The plan complies with the applicable provisions of this title.
(2) The proponent of the plan complies with the applicable provisions of this title.
(3) The plan has been proposed in good faith and not by any means forbidden by law.
(4) Any payment made or to be made by the proponent, by the debtor, or by a person issuing securities or acquiring property under the plan, for services

or for costs and expenses in or in connection with the case, or in connection with the plan and incident to the case, has been approved by, or is subject to the approval of, the court as reasonable.

(5)
- (A)
    - (i) The proponent of the plan has disclosed the identity and affiliations of any individual proposed to serve, after confirmation of the plan, as a director, officer, or voting trustee of the debtor, an affiliate of the debtor participating in a joint plan with the debtor, or a successor to the debtor under the plan; and
    - (ii) the appointment to, or continuance in, such office of such individual, is consistent with the interests of creditors and equity security holders and with public policy; and
- (B) the proponent of the plan has disclosed the identity of any insider that will be employed or retained by the reorganized debtor, and the nature of any compensation for such insider.

(6) Any governmental regulatory commission with jurisdiction, after confirmation of the plan, over the rates of the debtor has approved any rate change provided for in the plan, or such rate change is expressly conditioned on such approval.

(7) With respect to each impaired class of claims or interests
- (A) each holder of a claim or interest of such class
    - (i) has accepted the plan; or
    - (ii) will receive or retain under the plan on account of such claim or interest property of a value, as of the effective date of the plan, that is not less than the amount that such holder would so receive or retain if the debtor were liquidated under chapter 7 of this title on such date; or
- (B) if section 1111 (b)(2) of this title applies to the claims of such class, each holder of a claim of such class will receive or retain under the plan on account of such claim property of a value, as of the effective date of the plan, that is not less than the value of such holder's interest in the estate's interest in the property that secures such claims.

(8) With respect to each class of claims or interests
- (A) such class has accepted the plan; or
- (B) such class is not impaired under the plan.

(9) Except to the extent that the holder of a particular claim has agreed to a different treatment of such claim, the plan provides that
- (A) with respect to a claim of a kind specified in section 507 (a)(1) or 507 (a)(2) of this title, on the effective date of the plan, the holder of such claim will receive on account of such claim cash equal to the allowed amount of such claim;

(B) with respect to a class of claims of a kind specified in section 507 (a)(3), 507 (a)(4), 507 (a)(5), 507 (a)(6), or 507 (a)(7) of this title, each holder of a claim of such class will receive
  (i) if such class has accepted the plan, deferred cash payments of a value, as of the effective date of the plan, equal to the allowed amount of such claim; or
  (ii) if such class has not accepted the plan, cash on the effective date of the plan equal to the allowed amount of such claim; and
(C) with respect to a claim of a kind specified in section 507 (a)(8) of this title, the holder of such claim will receive on account of such claim deferred cash payments, over a period not exceeding six years after the date of assessment of such claim, of a value, as of the effective date of the plan, equal to the allowed amount of such claim.

(10) If a class of claims is impaired under the plan, at least one class of claims that is impaired under the plan has accepted the plan, determined without including any acceptance of the plan by any insider.
(11) Confirmation of the plan is not likely to be followed by the liquidation, or the need for further financial reorganization, of the debtor or any successor to the debtor under the plan, unless such liquidation or reorganization is proposed in the plan.
(12) All fees payable under section 1930 of title 28, as determined by the court at the hearing on confirmation of the plan, have been paid or the plan provides for the payment of all such fees on the effective date of the plan.
(13) The plan provides for the continuation after its effective date of payment of all retiree benefits, as that term is defined in section 1114 of this title, at the level established pursuant to subsection (e)(1)(B) or (g) of section 1114 of this title, at any time prior to confirmation of the plan, for the duration of the period the debtor has obligated itself to provide such benefits.

(b)

(1) Notwithstanding section 510 (a) of this title, if all of the applicable requirements of subsection (a) of this section other than paragraph (8) are met with respect to a plan, the court, on request of the proponent of the plan, shall confirm the plan notwithstanding the requirements of such paragraph if the plan does not discriminate unfairly, and is fair and equitable, with respect to each class of claims or interests that is impaired under, and has not accepted, the plan.
(2) For the purpose of this subsection, the condition that a plan be fair and equitable with respect to a class includes the following requirements:
  (A) With respect to a class of secured claims, the plan provides –
    (i)
      (I) that the holders of such claims retain the liens securing such claims, whether the property subject to such liens is retained

by the debtor or transferred to another entity, to the extent of the allowed amount of such claims; and

(II) that each holder of a claim of such class receive on account of such claim deferred cash payments totalling at least the allowed amount of such claim, of a value, as of the effective date of the plan, of at least the value of such holder's interest in the estate's interest in such property;

(ii) for the sale, subject to section 363 (k) of this title, of any property that is subject to the liens securing such claims, free and clear of such liens, with such liens to attach to the proceeds of such sale, and the treatment of such liens on proceeds under clause (i) or (iii) of this subparagraph; or

(iii) for the realization by such holders of the indubitable equivalent of such claims.

(B) With respect to a class of unsecured claims –

(i) the plan provides that each holder of a claim of such class receive or retain on account of such claim property of a value, as of the effective date of the plan, equal to the allowed amount of such claim; or

(ii) the holder of any claim or interest that is junior to the claims of such class will not receive or retain under the plan on account of such junior claim or interest any property.

(C) With respect to a class of interests –

(i) the plan provides that each holder of an interest of such class receive or retain on account of such interest property of a value, as of the effective date of the plan, equal to the greatest of the allowed amount of any fixed liquidation preference to which such holder is entitled, any fixed redemption price to which such holder is entitled, or the value of such interest; or

(ii) the holder of any interest that is junior to the interests of such class will not receive or retain under the plan on account of such junior interest any property.

(c) Notwithstanding subsections (a) and (b) of this section and except as provided in section 1127 (b) of this title, the court may confirm only one plan, unless the order of confirmation in the case has been revoked under section 1144 of this title. If the requirements of subsections (a) and (b) of this section are met with respect to more than one plan, the court shall consider the preferences of creditors and equity security holders in determining which plan to confirm.

(d) Notwithstanding any other provision of this section, on request of a party in interest that is a governmental unit, the court may not confirm a plan if the principal purpose of the plan is the avoidance of taxes or the avoidance of the application of section 5 of the Securities Act of 1933. In any hearing under this subsection, the governmental unit has the burden of proof on the issue of avoidance.

Title 11. Chapter 11. Subchapter III.

§ 1145. Exemption from securities laws

(a) Except with respect to an entity that is an underwriter as defined in subsection (b) of this section, section 5 of the Securities Act of 1933 and any State or local law requiring registration for offer or sale of a security or registration or licensing of an issuer of, underwriter of, or broker or dealer in, a security do not apply to

- (1) the offer or sale under a plan of a security of the debtor, of an affiliate participating in a joint plan with the debtor, or of a successor to the debtor under the plan
  - (A) in exchange for a claim against, an interest in, or a claim for an administrative expense in the case concerning, the debtor or such affiliate; or
  - (B) principally in such exchange and partly for cash or property;
- (2) the offer of a security through any warrant, option, right to subscribe, or conversion privilege that was sold in the manner specified in paragraph (1) of this subsection, or the sale of a security upon the exercise of such a warrant, option, right, or privilege;
- (3) the offer or sale, other than under a plan, of a security of an issuer other than the debtor or an affiliate, if
  - (A) such security was owned by the debtor on the date of the filing of the petition;
  - (B) the issuer of such security is
    - (i) required to file reports under section 13 or 15(d) of the Securities Exchange Act of 1934; and
    - (ii) in compliance with the disclosure and reporting provision of such applicable section; and
  - (C) such offer or sale is of securities that do not exceed
    - (i) during the two-year period immediately following the date of the filing of the petition, four percent of the securities of such class outstanding on such date; and
    - (ii) during any 180-day period following such two-year period, one percent of the securities outstanding at the beginning of such 180-day period; or
- (4) a transaction by a stockbroker in a security that is executed after a transaction of a kind specified in paragraph (1) or (2) of this subsection in such security and before the expiration of 40 days after the first date on which such security was bona fide offered to the public by the issuer or by or through an underwriter, if such stockbroker provides, at the time of or before such transaction by such stockbroker, a disclosure statement approved under section 1125 of this title, and, if the court orders, information supplementing such disclosure statement.

(b)
- (1) Except as provided in paragraph (2) of this subsection and except with respect to ordinary trading transactions of an entity that is not an issuer, an entity is an underwriter under section 2(11) of the Securities Act of 1933,[1] if such entity
  - (A) purchases a claim against, interest in, or claim for an administrative expense in the case concerning, the debtor, if such purchase is with a view to distribution of any security received or to be received in exchange for such a claim or interest;
  - (B) offers to sell securities offered or sold under the plan for the holders of such securities;
  - (C) offers to buy securities offered or sold under the plan from the holders of such securities, if such offer to buy is
    - (i) with a view to distribution of such securities; and
    - (ii) under an agreement made in connection with the plan, with the consummation of the plan, or with the offer or sale of securities under the plan; or
  - (D) is an issuer, as used in such section 2 (11), with respect to such securities.
- (2) An entity is not an underwriter under section 2(11) of the Securities Act of 1933 or under paragraph (1) of this subsection with respect to an agreement that provides only for
  - (A)
    - (i) the matching or combining of fractional interests in securities offered or sold under the plan into whole interests; or
    - (ii) the purchase or sale of such fractional interests from or to entities receiving such fractional interests under the plan; or
  - (B) the purchase or sale for such entities of such fractional or whole interests as are necessary to adjust for any remaining fractional interests after such matching.
- (3) An entity other than an entity of the kind specified in paragraph (1) of this subsection is not an underwriter under section 2(11) of the Securities Act of 1933 [1] with respect to any securities offered or sold to such entity in the manner specified in subsection (a)(1) of this section.

(c) An offer or sale of securities of the kind and in the manner specified under subsection (a)(1) of this section is deemed to be a public offering.

(d) The Trust Indenture Act of 1939 does not apply to a note issued under the plan that matures not later than one year after the effective date of the plan.

Chapter 14B
United States – Practice

American Bankruptcy Reform and Creativity Prompt the *In re Blue Bird Body Company* One-Day Pre-packaged Plan of Reorganization

Jay M. Goffman, Mark A. McDermott, and Kurt Ramlo

ACRONYMS, ABBREVIATIONS & DEFINED TERMS

BAPCPA	Bankruptcy Abuse Prevention and Consumer Protection Act of 2005, Pub. L. No. 109 – 8, 119 Stat. 23 (2005)
Blue Bird	Blue Bird Body Company, an American manufacturer of school buses and similar vehicles
Chapter 11	A chapter 11 proceeding is a court supervised reorganization of a troubled business while continuing with its day to day operations.
Prepack or Prepackaged plan	Expedited restructuring mechanism included in Chapter 11 of the US Bankruptcy Code that enables a financially troubled company to restructure its debts by proposing a restructuring plan and soliciting the required votes prior to commencement of formal Chapter 11 proceedings.
U.S.C.	United States Code
US Bankruptcy Code	Title 11 of the United States Code which governs reorganization bankruptcy cases.
USD	United States Dollar

I. INTRODUCTION

A 'prepackaged' plan of reorganization – solicited and voted on by impaired stakeholders before a bankruptcy case is filed – can drastically shorten the time a business may need to spend under bankruptcy court protection, thereby ameliorating some of the business risks caused by longer stays in bankruptcy pursuant to more traditional reorganizations. Prepackaged bankruptcies lasting just weeks have been used in the United States for over 15 years, but recent changes to the US Bankruptcy Code,[1] and the extraordinary success of Blue Bird Body Company ('Blue Bird') in its recent 'One Day Prepack', likely will prompt some companies to employ them at even greater speeds.

Blue Bird, an American manufacturer of school buses and similar vehicles that was largely owned by European investors, recently found itself in a position where a 'one-day prepack' was its last and only option for survival as a going concern. Although a one-day prepack has always been theoretically possible under American law,[2] Blue Bird was the first company to obtain bankruptcy court confirmation of a plan of reorganization in approximately one day, significantly quicker than the 16 days required in the fastest prepackaged case that preceded it.[3]

There were a number of reasons why Blue Bird could not survive a traditional reorganization proceeding under chapter 11 of the US Bankruptcy Code. One concerned the 2005 amendments to the US Bankruptcy Code. The amendments that most directly affected Blue Bird included those that created new priorities for certain classes of creditors which required that their claims be paid in full. Prior to these amendments, Blue Bird may have been able to propose a plan that compromised a significantly larger percentage of its debts. The amendments, however, largely eliminated this option.

In addition, it was clear that from a business standpoint, Blue Bird (which had already been shut down without cash for weeks) could not survive a traditional chapter 11 case. When one holdout hedge fund blocked an out of court deal, Blue Bird was left with only one possibility for survival – the proverbial one-day prepack.

This chapter tells Blue Bird's Chapter 11 story, pointing out in particular the key business considerations motivating Blue Bird's determination to limits its stay in Chapter 11 to only one day and how it was accomplished. As described below, despite the speed with which Blue Bird moved through Chapter 11, the company and its advisors nonetheless paid close attention to notice and other process requirements, thereby creating a restructuring environment that was transparent to all parties in interest. Absent observance of basic requirements of notice and due process, Blue Bird would never have succeeded in saving its business. Other companies facing similar exigent circumstances are well advised to pursue a

---

1. 11 U.S.C. §§ 101, et seq.
2. Jay M. Goffman, 'A One-Day Prepack - The Ultimate Reorganization', in 'First Annual Prepackaged Restructuring Seminars' (1996); Jay M. Goffman & Matthew P. Herenstein, 'Bankruptcy as a Business Tool: The One-Day Prepack Beckons', in 'The 1996 Bankruptcy Yearbook and Almanac' (Christopher M. McHugh, ed., May 1996).
3. The *In re Harvest Foods* Prepack in 1994 also handled by Jay M. Goffman.

campaign of maximum notice and due process if they are to have any prospect of minimizing their stay in Chapter 11 and emerging successfully.

II. BLUE BIRD BODY COMPANY

Blue Bird is one of North America's largest school bus manufacturers. The Georgia-based firm also manufactures transit and shuttle buses, touring and charter coaches, and luxury motor-homes. The company tried to address its financial problems in a 2004 out-of-court restructuring, but it nevertheless remained too highly leveraged. In late 2005, the largest shareholder of the company decided that buying the remainder of the secured debt and equity, and recapitalizing the company, was the best solution. It therefore entered into discussions with the company's lenders, who owned the secured debt and most of the balance of the equity. In early January 2006, however, on the eve of closing, the shareholder pulled out of the deal. The company faced an immediate liquidity crisis – it was basically out of cash – and was forced to furlough most of its plant workers.

Blue Bird did not believe that it could survive a traditional chapter 11 proceeding, where solicitation and voting on a plan usually occur months or years after a case is filed. The company properly feared that, in light of its financial position, its school district customers would turn to one of its two competitors. These customers needed to be assured that any seller would be viable and that warranty and repair services would remain available. In addition, the company's exclusive dealers operated under renewable one-year contracts all of which were set to expore, absent renewel a few short months after commencement of any bankruptcy. Accordingly, the company properly feared mass defections of its dealers in the event of a traditional chapter 11 bankruptcy.

The company also knew that the recent US Bankruptcy Code amendments[4] would present an additional hurdle. Before the amendments, a supplier to a Chapter 11 debtor could demand reclamation rights for goods received by the debtor while insolvent during the 10 days before the bankruptcy filing.[5] Rather than return the goods, the debtor could ask the court to grant the reclaiming seller an administrative priority expense claim in lieu of reclamation or immediate payment in full.[6] That administrative expense claim usually did not become payable for months or even years, until a confirmed plan of reorganization addressed all of the company's financial difficulties.[7] The 2005 amendments, however, extended

---

4. See Bankruptcy Abuse Prevention and Consumer Protection Act of 2005, Pub. L. No. 109–8, 119 Stat. 23 (2005) ('BAPCPA'), most provisions of which became effective in cases commenced on or after 17 October 2005.
5. Most jurisdictions within the United States have enacted a statutory reclamation right based on Uniform Commercial Code section 2–702(2), which provides that '[w]here the seller discovers that the buyer has received goods on credit while insolvent he may reclaim the goods upon demand made within ten days after the receipt'.
6. These provisions were contained in 11 U.S.C. § 546(c)(2) prior to the BAPCPA amendments.
7. The Bankruptcy Code provides that chapter 11 administrative priority expense claims must be paid on the effective date of a plan. 11 U.S.C. § 1129(a)(9)(A).

reclamation rights to any goods received during the 45 days before a bankruptcy filing.[8] For manufacturers such as Blue Bird, who operate their plants pursuant to the 'just-in-time' inventory method, i.e., who maintain almost no inventory and instead receive inventory as little as one or two days before it is needed, most of the manufacturer's inventory may be subject to reclamation rights.

Moreover, the reclaiming seller might be able to require the debtor to return or pay for the goods. Although the statute is unclear, a debtor arguably must make payment shortly after the case is filed, and can no longer satisfy the seller by grant of an administrative priority claim and payment pursuant to a subsequent plan of reorganization without the seller's consent. Additionally, the supplier can nevertheless assert administrative priority status for the value of goods sold to the debtor in the ordinary course of business and received during the 20 days before a bankruptcy filing, regardless of whether the debtor still possesses the goods or was insolvent or whether the supplier can assest a reclamation claim.[9]

Finally, some suppliers who lack the foregoing rights can nevertheless be so essential to the operation of a debtor that they are considered 'critical vendors'. Such a supplier might be the sole source for a particular component or service that the debtor must obtain to manufacture its product or to provide its services to its customers. The debtor also might constitute such a significant portion of the supplier's business that the supplier itself may be unable to remain in business without immediate payment from the debtor. Unless these vendors are already contractually bound to continue supplying the debtor, they are generally free to refuse to deal with the company after it files for bankruptcy protection. And they often do, insisting that the debtor must first pay everything it owes to the supplier as a condition to continuing shipments post-petition.

In these situations, a debtor may ask the bankruptcy court for permission to pay its 'critical vendors' during the early days of a Chapter 11 case, notwithstanding the fact that other unsecured creditors must await payment until confirmation of a plan of reorganization. Bankruptcy courts have invoked the 'doctrine of necessity' to authorize debtors to pay critical vendors,[10] reasoning that the payment to critical vendors benefits the unpaid unsecured creditors because without the critical vendors, the debtor's business will be irreparably harmed to the detriment of all stakeholders. A relatively recent Court of Appeal decision, however, has made it more challenging to obtain such permission in certain bankruptcy courts, and creating uncertainty about whether any particular debtor can obtain that relief in a traditional Chapter 11 case.[11]

---

8. 11 U.S.C. § 546(c)(1).
9. 11 U.S.C. § 503(b)(9).
10. See, e.g., *In re CoServ, L.L.C.*, 273 B.R. 487, 492–93 (Bankr. N.D. Tex. 2002).
11. See *In re Kmart Corp.*, 359 F.3d 866 (7th Cir. 2004). Critical vendor motions, however, have been granted in subsequent cases. See, e.g., *In re Birch Telecom, Inc.*, Case No. 05–12237 (Bankr. D. Del. 15 August 2005) ('Order under 11 U.S.C. §§ 105(a) and 363 Authorizing Payment of Prepetition Claims of Critical Vendors'); *In re Tropical Sportswear Int'l Corp.*, 320 B.R. 15 (Bankr. M.D. Fla. 2005).

In Blue Bird's case, approximately 86 per cent of its trade claims were held by suppliers who arguably had reclamation rights under US Bankruptcy Code section 546; held administrative priority claims under US Bankruptcy Code section 503(b)(9); and/or were critical vendors. Given these constraints, a traditional Chapter 11 would not have afforded any material relief from trade debt to Blue Bird. Moreover and since the banks already had a first lien on all of Blue Bird's assets, it was impossible for Blue Bird to obtain a debtor-in-possession financing facility without the banks' consent (which was not forthcoming). Thus, there was no conceivable benefit from a traditional Chapter 11 case and no ability to survive in Chapter 11 for more than a few hours.

Blue Bird therefore pursued an out-of-court restructuring. It quickly reached an understanding with its shareholders and all but one member of its 12-member bank group on the terms of an out-of-court restructuring. The bank group would reduce the USD 211 million balance of the secured debt to USD 100 million, while certain members of the bank group would provide a new USD 52 million revolving credit facility. In exchange, the bank group would receive all the new equity of the restructured company. All the existing shareholders, including the bank group, the shareholder who originally was interested in buying out the banks, members of management, and a European pension fund, agreed to relinquish their equity interests in the old company.

However, the existing credit agreement required unanimous consent among the banks for the out-of-court restructuring. An American hedge fund that had purchased a 7 per cent piece of the bank debt in the secondary market held out. Thus, an out-of-court restructuring was not possible.

III. A ONE-DAY PREPACKAGED CASE

The bankruptcy process enabled other creditors to outvote [this one holdout]. The Bankruptcy Code contained a lower voting requirement that trumps the voting requirements contamid in prepetition credit agreements. Specifically, a class of creditors is deemed to accept a plan if at least one-half is number of the creditors, holding at least two-thirds in amount of claims, vote in favor of the plan, careting only those creditors who actually vote and allow Blue Bird to survive.[12]

On Friday, 20 January 2006, when the hedge fund balked at the out-of-court restructuring, Blue Bird decided to attempt to obtain approval of a reorganisations plan under Chapter 11, and to attempt to do so in one day for the business reasons outlined above. Over the next four days, Blue Bird quickly negotiated with its bank group and all other interested parties a prepackaged plan of reorganization with terms virtually identical to the out-of-court restructuring described above (i.e., reduction of the bank debt and provision at a new credit facility while leaving unimpaired the claims of all other creditors).

---

12. See 11 U.S.C. § 1126(c).

At 9:30 p.m. on Tuesday, 24 January 2006, when the documents were completed, Blue Bird immediately began soliciting votes from the bank group members. When voting ended at 9:00 a.m. on Thursday, 26 January 2006, the plan had received the requisite acceptances from 90.9 per cent in number and 92.6 per cent in amount of the bank group claims. The only dissenting vote was the hedge fund, which requisite creditor acceptances in hand, beginning at 10:54 a.m., Blue Bird and five of its affiliates filed chapter 11 petitions in Reno, Nevada. By noon, the bankruptcy court had convened a telephonic hearing during which it granted Blue Bird's request to schedule the confirmation hearing for the following day, over the objection of the dissenting hedge fund. At 4:00 p.m. the next day, the court conducted a two and a half hour evidentiary hearing to consider confirmation of the plan.

After concluding that the plan met all US Bankruptcy Code requirements for confirmation; that the exigencies of the situation warranted expedited procedures; and that those expedited procedures satisfied the due process rights of the parties, the court entered an order at 7:20 p.m. on Friday night that overruled the hedge fund's objection and confirmed the plan.[13] Blue Bird drew down on its new credit facility on Monday as workers began returning to work. The 32 hours and 26 minutes between case commencement and plan confirmation (and the 7 days from start to finish) represent the shortest such span in the history of the United States bankruptcy system.[14]

IV. BANKRUPTCY ABUSE PREVENTION AND CONSUMER PROTECTION ACT OF 2005

While the BAPCPA made it more difficult for businesses to reorganize in traditional chapter 11 cases, it simultaneously made it easier to confirm a prepackaged plan. The reclamation and priority revisions discussed above can significantly increase a debtor's liquidity needs and effectively exclude those debts from discharge in bankruptcy. Other BAPCPA revisions have similar effects. For example, before BAPCPA, a debtor could often delay until plan confirmation its decision whether to assume or reject non-residential real estate leases.[15] BAPCPA now gives a debtor no more than 210 days to decide.[16] By then, a debtor must either give up the premises or assume the lease; bring current all overdue payments (whether they arose before or after the bankruptcy filing); and, if the lease is in default, provide adequate assurance of future performance.[17]

---

13. The dissenting hedge fund appealed the confirmation order. The District Court later dismissed the appeal as moot.
14. The *In re Blue Bird Body Company* model was later used to confirm a prepackaged plan of reorganization in just three days. Negotiations on a significant equity capital infusion for Davis Petroleum had broken down on 13 February 2006. Davis Petroleum then negotiated a prepackaged plan of reorganization, which it solicited over five days beginning on 2 March 2006. After filing its chapter 11 case on the same day solicitation ended, 7 March 2006, Davis Petroleum obtained court confirmation of the prepackaged plan three days later, on 10 March 2006.
15. 11 U.S.C. former § 365(d)(4).
16. 11 U.S.C. § 365(d)(4)(B)(i).
17. 11 U.S.C. § 365(b)(1).

Similarly, before BAPCPA, a debtor could provide its utilities with statutorily required 'adequate assurance of payment' for postpetition services without an outlay of cash. Debtors often persuaded the bankruptcy court that their postpetition liquidity arising from postpetition financing meant that administrative expense priority for postpetition utility service constituted adequate assurance.[18] BAPCPA prohibits this practice, effectively requiring a debtor in some courts to expend cash for security deposits, letters of credit, surety bonds and the like.[19]

BAPCPA also creates a right for a party in interest to rescind any modification of retiree health benefits that occurred during the 180 days before bankruptcy, 'unless the court finds that the balance of the equities clearly favours such modification'.[20] The priority for wage claims has been extended to those earned 180 days before bankruptcy (previously 90 days) and the cap has been raised from USD 4,000 to USD$10,950 per employee.[21] Similar revisions apply to contributions to employee benefit plans.[22] A number of provisions either increase the amount or accelerate payment of tax claims.[23] And certain debts arising from fraud owed by a corporation with respect to governmental units are now excepted from discharge under a plan of reorganization.[24]

In contrast, prepackaged bankruptcies are now somewhat easier. First, BAPCPA amended the US Bankruptcy Code to permit a debtor to continue soliciting votes on a plan of reorganization after a bankruptcy case has been filed if the debtor had commenced safication of creditors before the case filing.[25] Prior law was at best uncertain about this and a number of related issues. These issues included whether a company could continue its solicitation after a bankruptcy filing but before a court had approved the disclosure statement as containing adequate information; whether a solicitation was complete upon mailing of the plan, disclosure statement and ballots (and thus no solicitation would occur postpetition); and whether votes received prepetition could be counted if the bankruptcy court later approved the prepetition solicitation materials for continued solicitation postpetition.

By permitting solicitation to continue, this revision prevents disenchanted, holdout or ill-advised creditors from derailing the solicitation process by filing

---

18. See 11 U.S.C. § 366(b); *Virginia Elec. & Power Co. v. Caldor, Inc. (In re Caldor, Inc.)*, 117 F.3d 646, 650 (2d Cir. 1997) ('a bankruptcy court's authority to 'modify' the level of the 'deposit or other security', provided under § 366(b), includes the power to require no 'deposit or other security' where none is necessary to provide a utility with 'adequate assurance of payment''.).
19. 11 U.S.C. § 366(c).
20. 11 U.S.C. § 1114(*l*).
21. 11 U.S.C. § 507(a)(4).
22. 11 U.S.C. § 507(a)(5).
23. 11 U.S.C. § 511 (applying nonbankruptcy tax rates to payment of interest on tax claims); 11 U.S.C. § 1129(a)(9)(C) (shortening time period for payment of certain priority tax claims and increasing minimum size of installment amounts).
24. 11 U.S.C. § 1141(d)(6) (excepting from discharge (1) debts owed for fraud, false pretenses, or false representation to qui tam plaintiffs (under federal False Claims Act or similar state statute) or to government units, and (2) debts for taxes or customs duties under a fraudulent return or wilful attempt to evade them). Previously, the only debts excepted from a corporation's discharge were criminal fines and criminal restitution orders. See 18 U.S.C. § 3613(e)-(f).
25. 11 U.S.C. § 1125(g).

an involuntary bankruptcy petition against the company during the solicitation process. And the revision permits companies to file voluntary petitions if anticipated or unanticipated events make bankruptcy protection necessary or beneficial before solicitation and voting are complete.

Moreover, BAPCPA permits a bankruptcy court to dispense with the customary meeting of creditors if the debtor has filed a plan that was solicited before bankruptcy.[26] Previously, section 341 of the US Bankruptcy Code required the US Trustee to convene a meeting of creditors in every case,[27] although the local US Trustee in some prepackaged bankruptcy cases agreed not to convene such a meeting. The section 341 meeting is designed to permit creditors to examine the debtor about its financial affairs. In a prepackaged case, however, the debtor has already distributed that information as part of its disclosure statement; has negotiated with creditors that will be affected by the plan of reorganization; and has solicited acceptances of the plan. The revised section 341 recognizes that in such a case, a meeting of creditors is unnecessary and would only serve to delay confirmation of the plan.

V. CONTINUING LIMITATIONS ON PREPETITION SOLICITATION

Prepackaged bankruptcies, however, remain unavailable to some businesses that are otherwise amenable to chapter 11 relief because of various securities laws in the United States. The US Bankruptcy Code generally provides that a debtor may solicit votes on a chapter 11 plan from holders of securities, and exchange securities under a plan, regardless of whether federal, state or local law would otherwise require the debtor to obtain a valid registration statement for any securities subject to the plan.[28] Similarly, it provides a safe harbour from the securities laws to a debtor and any person that solicits a plan or that participates in the offer, issuance, sale or purchase of a security under a plan.[29]

The US Securities and Exchange Commission, however, has taken the position that these exemptions from the securities laws do *not* apply to prepackaged bankruptcies.[30] The recent amendment that permits continuation of solicitation after a case is filed is consistent with that position, as the amendment applies only if the prepetition solicitation complies with applicable nonbankruptcy law.[31] Therefore, a financially distressed debtor seeking to reorganize under a prepackaged plan by issuing mean securities must either take the very expensive

---

26. 11 U.S.C. § 341(e).
27. 11 U.S.C. § 341(a).
28. 11 U.S.C. § 1145(a).
29. 11 U.S.C. § 1125(e).
30. Jay M. Goffman, "Checkout' Time for Ch. 11 Panel's 'Prepack' Proposals', Nat'l L.J., 13 October 1997, at B11 (noting SEC positions on sections 1125(e) and 1145(a)(1)); 'A Practical Guide to Out-of-Court Restructurings and Prepackaged Plans of Reorganization' § 4.04[D], at 4–128.8 & n.311 (Nicholas P. Saggese & Alesia Ranney-Marinelli, eds., 2d ed., supp. 2000) (noting in discussion of section 1145 that SEC has not publicly announced its position).
31. See 11 U.S.C. § 1125(g).

and time consuming step of obtaining a valid registration statement or accept the limitations of negotiating and soliciting a plan that qualifies for a nonbankruptcy exemption from the securities laws.

Most commonly, debtors (such as Blue Bird) rely on the exemptions found at section 3(a)(9) or section 4(2) of the Securities Act of 1933. Section 3(a)(9)[32] exempts 'any security exchanged by the issuer with its existing security holders exclusively where no commission or other remuneration is paid or given directly or indirectly for soliciting such exchange'. Section 4(2)[33] exempts 'transactions by an issuer not involving any public offering'.

In 1997, the National Bankruptcy Review Commission proposed that the US Bankruptcy Code's standards and requirements for postpetition solicitation be applicable to solicitation of a prepackaged plan by a company that is subject to and in compliance with the reporting requirements of the Securities Exchange Act of 1934. The commission noted that 'the disclosure needs for Chapter 11 plan solicitations are the same prepetition and postpetition' and that 'the Bankruptcy Code disclosure requirements ... were designed with a financially-troubled company in mind'.[34] The US Bankruptcy Code's disclosure standard – adequate information 'in light of the nature and history of the debtor and the condition of the debtor's books and records'[35] – is quite flexible. That flexibility, however, is tempered by the requirement that a debtor provide evidence to a bankruptcy court that the disclosure standard has in fact been met.[36] The US Bankruptcy Code therefore ensures that all necessary disclosures are made, just as American securities laws are designed to require full disclosure (although without the greater level of review required by the US Bankruptcy Code). Accordingly, the commission recommended a single, uniform standard for soliciting plans of reorganization, whether prepackaged or not. Unfortunately, Congress did not include this particular proposal of the National Bankruptcy Review Commission in the 2005 amendments.

VI. LESSONS FROM BLUE BIRD – PROCESS

When a company decides to pursue a prepackaged plan, it takes the risk that a bankruptcy court will later decide that the terms of the plan of reorganization do not comply with the US Bankruptcy Code. If so, the company will likely find itself in a traditional Chapter 11 case that it may not survive. Equally important is *how* the company solicits votes on its prepackaged plan. Faulty solicitation can lead to the same unwanted traditional Chapter 11. When pursuing a one-day prepack, process therefore becomes even more important. Not only must solicitation be precisely executed, but the company must ascertain as best it can the likely hearing date for a case not yet filed, a reasonable deadline for objections to the plan, and provide timely notice of these items to all necessary parties in interest.

---

32. 15 U.S.C. § 77c(a)(9).
33. 15 U.S.C. § 77d(2).
34. 'Bankruptcy: The Next Twenty Years', National Bankruptcy Review Commission Final Report at 592, 593 (20 October 1997).
35. 11 U.S.C. § 1125(a)(1).
36. 11 U.S.C. § 1126(b).

On the day that Blue Bird decided to attempt its unprecedented one-day prepack, it knew that any judge would require a compelling explanation as to why he or she should and could do what no judge had ever done before. Blue Bird and its advisors had already completed the work necessary to show that as a substantive financial matter, a one-day prepack was its last hope. However Blue Bird also needed to conduct a solicitation and observe notice requirements with particular care in order to demonstrate to a judge that the one-day prepack had accorded due process to all affected parties. Blue Bird knew that no matter how great the need, no judge would ignore the requirements of fairness and due process.

Blue Bird began this process with a conference call with its bank group, including the holdout hedge fund, to explain that it would try to execute a one-day prepack if the hedge fund did not relent. Next, Blue Bird sent a comprehensive letter that day about the prepackaged plan process to its bank group. The letter detailed the restructuring efforts to date, confirming the information previously provided to the bank group and including a summary of the company's financial condition and how it got there. The letter then described in step-by-step detail the company's unsuccessful efforts to negotiate an out-of-court restructuring and the process it would undertake to confirm a one-day prepackaged plan. The letter (dated Friday, 20 January 2006) provided a general timeline: that Blue Bird intended to begin soliciting votes within the following four or five days; to file a chapter 11 case within the following one or two days; and to request expedited consideration of confirmation of the plan on the same day that the bankruptcy case was filed. Finally, the letter invited the holdout hedge fund and its counsel to contact Blue Bird so that Blue Bird could provide the fund with any documents or information it might need and invited the hedge fund, and its counsel, to participate in the process.

After the hedge fund's counsel contacted Blue Bird on the following business day (Monday, 24 January 2006), Blue Bird wrote the holdout hedge fund's counsel directly to memorialize the communications. The letter again invited the holdout to consent to the prepackaged plan; to submit any written alternative proposals to Blue Bird and the other bank group members; and to meet with Blue Bird so that the hedge fund could obtain any documents or information it might need to object to the plan. The letter also stated that Blue Bird intended to file its chapter case in Reno, Nevada on Thursday, 26 January 2006 and to seek confirmation at a hearing at 4:00 p.m. on Friday, 27 January 2006. The solicitation materials included this same information.

The company began its solicitation on Tuesday, 25 January 2006, at about 9:30 p.m. Pacific Standard Time, the time zone of the Reno bankruptcy court. Because of the exigencies of Blue Bird's financial condition, it set a voting deadline at just over 30 hours later (subsequently expanded to 32 hours).[37] To facilitate such a short solicitation period across multiple time zones, Blue Bird circulated the solicitation materials to each member of the bank group, and solicited their votes, by email. The bank group members were permitted to return their completed ballots by mail, facsimile, or email.

---

37. Rule 3018(b) of the Federal Rules of Bankruptcy Procedure provides that votes will not be accounted if 'an unreasonably short time was prescribed for such creditors and equity security holders to accept or reject the plan'. What constitutes an unreasonable time depends on the facts of each particular case.

Each ballot provided that its signatory certified that he or she had: (1) received the solicitation materials; (2) enough knowledge and experience to evaluate the risks and merits of the prepackaged plan; and, (3) access to the type of information he or she deemed necessary to evaluate whether to the accept the securities offered under the plan. The restructuring agreement in support of the prepackaged plan – among the company, consenting bank group members, and existing shareholders – provided that each party waived notice relating to the prepackaged plan process and expressly consented to a process under which the company would request confirmation of the prepackaged plan on the same day it filed the bankruptcy case.

As noted above, Blue Bird filed its chapter 11 case within two hours after the voting deadline. Just over an hour after the filing, the bankruptcy court convened a telephonic status conference to consider Blue Bird's request that a confirmation hearing be set for the next day. The court overruled the dissenting hedge fund's objection after considering, among other things, that (1) the dissenting hedge fund had been engaged in negotiations and discussions with Blue Bird before the prepackaged plan process had begun; (2) the hedge fund and its counsel had been apprized of all conference calls, letters and facts, (3) the 20 January 2006 letter had advised the bank group of Blue Bird's proposed schedule for the solicitation and prepackaged plan process; (4) the 24 January 2006 letter advised the hedge fund of the actual court and the actual dates and times; and, (5) the hedge fund had certified on its ballot that it had sufficient information to vote on the prepackaged plan.

These same considerations were relevant at the confirmation hearing when the court overruled the hedge fund's objection that some of the voting bank group members lacked adequate information about the plan and that Blue Bird had not complied with notice and other due process requirements for confirmation of a plan. Blue Bird clearly bore a heavy burden to prove that the bank group members had received adequate information and a sufficient opportunity to participate meaningfully in an expedited prepackaged plan process. Blue Bird's documentation of the plan process, combined with the exigencies of its financial condition, satisfied that heavy burden and permitted it to reorganize in the only manner that it could.

VII. CONCLUSION

The 2005 bankruptcy amendments have made it more difficult for companies to reorganize in a traditional Chapter 11 case. But the Blue Bird case shows that a one-day prepackaged case can work to save viable businesses otherwise unable to operate under the new US Bankruptcy Code. The mostly consensual nature of a prepackaged plan also overcame the potential uncertainty that would arise from using a traditional Chapter 11 case to bind parties outside the United States. Finally, the key to a successful one-day prepack is ensuring that the process is properly designed and executed, showing unequivocally that the process as well as the substance of the prepackaged plan fully complies with the US Bankruptcy Code and notions of due process.

ANNEX: KEY LEGISLATION

Title 11. Chapter 11. Subchapter II.

§ 1125. Postpetition disclosure and solicitation

(a) In this section

(1) 'adequate information' means information of a kind, and in sufficient detail, as far as is reasonably practicable in light of the nature and history of the debtor and the condition of the debtor's books and records, including a discussion of the potential material Federal tax consequences of the plan to the debtor, any successor to the debtor, and a hypothetical investor typical of the holders of claims or interests in the case, that would enable such a hypothetical investor of the relevant class to make an informed judgment about the plan, but adequate information need not include such information about any other possible or proposed plan and in determining whether a disclosure statement provides adequate information, the court shall consider the complexity of the case, the benefit of additional information to creditors and other parties in interest, and the cost of providing additional information; and

(2) 'investor typical of holders of claims or interests of the relevant class' means investor having
  (A) a claim or interest of the relevant class;
  (B) such a relationship with the debtor as the holders of other claims or interests of such class generally have; and
  (C) such ability to obtain such information from sources other than the disclosure required by this section as holders of claims or interests in such class generally have.

(b) An acceptance or rejection of a plan may not be solicited after the commencement of the case under this title from a holder of a claim or interest with respect to such claim or interest, unless, at the time of or before such solicitation, there is transmitted to such holder the plan or a summary of the plan, and a written disclosure statement approved, after notice and a hearing, by the court as containing adequate information. The court may approve a disclosure statement without a valuation of the debtor or an appraisal of the debtor's assets.

(c) The same disclosure statement shall be transmitted to each holder of a claim or interest of a particular class, but there may be transmitted different disclosure statements, differing in amount, detail, or kind of information, as between classes.

(d) Whether a disclosure statement required under subsection (b) of this section contains adequate information is not governed by any otherwise applicable nonbankruptcy law, rule, or regulation, but an agency or official whose duty is to administer or enforce such a law, rule, or regulation may be heard on the issue of whether a disclosure statement contains adequate information. Such an agency or official may not appeal from, or otherwise seek review of, an order approving a disclosure statement.

(e) A person that solicits acceptance or rejection of a plan, in good faith and in compliance with the applicable provisions of this title, or that participates, in good faith and in compliance with the applicable provisions of this title, in the offer, issuance, sale, or purchase of a security, offered or sold under the plan, of the debtor, of an affiliate participating in a joint plan with the debtor, or of a newly organized successor to the debtor under the plan, is not liable, on account of such solicitation or participation, for violation of any applicable law, rule, or regulation governing solicitation of acceptance or rejection of a plan or the offer, issuance, sale, or purchase of securities.

(f) Notwithstanding subsection (b), in a small business case

(1) the court may determine that the plan itself provides adequate information and that a separate disclosure statement is not necessary;
(2) the court may approve a disclosure statement submitted on standard forms approved by the court or adopted under section 2075 of title 28; and
(3)
    (A) the court may conditionally approve a disclosure statement subject to final approval after notice and a hearing;
    (B) acceptances and rejections of a plan may be solicited based on a conditionally approved disclosure statement if the debtor provides adequate information to each holder of a claim or interest that is solicited, but a conditionally approved disclosure statement shall be mailed not later than 25 days before the date of the hearing on confirmation of the plan; and
    (C) the hearing on the disclosure statement may be combined with the hearing on confirmation of a plan.

(g) Notwithstanding subsection (b), an acceptance or rejection of the plan may be solicited from a holder of a claim or interest if such solicitation complies with applicable nonbankruptcy law and if such holder was solicited before the commencement of the case in a manner complying with applicable nonbankruptcy law.

§ 1129: Confirmation of plan

(a) The court shall confirm a plan only if all of the following requirements are met:

(1) The plan complies with the applicable provisions of this title.
(2) The proponent of the plan complies with the applicable provisions of this title.
(3) The plan has been proposed in good faith and not by any means forbidden by law.
(4) Any payment made or to be made by the proponent, by the debtor, or by a person issuing securities or acquiring property under the plan, for services

or for costs and expenses in or in connection with the case, or in connection with the plan and incident to the case, has been approved by, or is subject to the approval of, the court as reasonable.

(5)
- (A)
    - (i) The proponent of the plan has disclosed the identity and affiliations of any individual proposed to serve, after confirmation of the plan, as a director, officer, or voting trustee of the debtor, an affiliate of the debtor participating in a joint plan with the debtor, or a successor to the debtor under the plan; and
    - (ii) the appointment to, or continuance in, such office of such individual, is consistent with the interests of creditors and equity security holders and with public policy; and
- (B) the proponent of the plan has disclosed the identity of any insider that will be employed or retained by the reorganized debtor, and the nature of any compensation for such insider.

(6) Any governmental regulatory commission with jurisdiction, after confirmation of the plan, over the rates of the debtor has approved any rate change provided for in the plan, or such rate change is expressly conditioned on such approval.

(7) With respect to each impaired class of claims or interests
- (A) each holder of a claim or interest of such class
    - (i) has accepted the plan; or
    - (ii) will receive or retain under the plan on account of such claim or interest property of a value, as of the effective date of the plan, that is not less than the amount that such holder would so receive or retain if the debtor were liquidated under chapter 7 of this title on such date; or
- (B) if section 1111 (b)(2) of this title applies to the claims of such class, each holder of a claim of such class will receive or retain under the plan on account of such claim property of a value, as of the effective date of the plan, that is not less than the value of such holder's interest in the estate's interest in the property that secures such claims.

(8) With respect to each class of claims or interests
- (A) such class has accepted the plan; or
- (B) such class is not impaired under the plan.

(9) Except to the extent that the holder of a particular claim has agreed to a different treatment of such claim, the plan provides that
- (A) with respect to a claim of a kind specified in section 507 (a)(1) or 507 (a)(2) of this title, on the effective date of the plan, the holder of such claim will receive on account of such claim cash equal to the allowed amount of such claim;

(B) with respect to a class of claims of a kind specified in section 507 (a)(3), 507 (a)(4), 507 (a)(5), 507 (a)(6), or 507 (a)(7) of this title, each holder of a claim of such class will receive
  (i) if such class has accepted the plan, deferred cash payments of a value, as of the effective date of the plan, equal to the allowed amount of such claim; or
  (ii) if such class has not accepted the plan, cash on the effective date of the plan equal to the allowed amount of such claim; and
(C) with respect to a claim of a kind specified in section 507 (a)(8) of this title, the holder of such claim will receive on account of such claim deferred cash payments, over a period not exceeding six years after the date of assessment of such claim, of a value, as of the effective date of the plan, equal to the allowed amount of such claim.

(10) If a class of claims is impaired under the plan, at least one class of claims that is impaired under the plan has accepted the plan, determined without including any acceptance of the plan by any insider.

(11) Confirmation of the plan is not likely to be followed by the liquidation, or the need for further financial reorganization, of the debtor or any successor to the debtor under the plan, unless such liquidation or reorganization is proposed in the plan.

(12) All fees payable under section 1930 of title 28, as determined by the court at the hearing on confirmation of the plan, have been paid or the plan provides for the payment of all such fees on the effective date of the plan.

(13) The plan provides for the continuation after its effective date of payment of all retiree benefits, as that term is defined in section 1114 of this title, at the level established pursuant to subsection (e)(1)(B) or (g) of section 1114 of this title, at any time prior to confirmation of the plan, for the duration of the period the debtor has obligated itself to provide such benefits.

(b)

(1) Notwithstanding section 510 (a) of this title, if all of the applicable requirements of subsection (a) of this section other than paragraph (8) are met with respect to a plan, the court, on request of the proponent of the plan, shall confirm the plan notwithstanding the requirements of such paragraph if the plan does not discriminate unfairly, and is fair and equitable, with respect to each class of claims or interests that is impaired under, and has not accepted, the plan.

(2) For the purpose of this subsection, the condition that a plan be fair and equitable with respect to a class includes the following requirements:
(A) With respect to a class of secured claims, the plan provides –
  (i)
    (I) that the holders of such claims retain the liens securing such claims, whether the property subject to such liens is retained

by the debtor or transferred to another entity, to the extent of the allowed amount of such claims; and

  (II) that each holder of a claim of such class receive on account of such claim deferred cash payments totalling at least the allowed amount of such claim, of a value, as of the effective date of the plan, of at least the value of such holder's interest in the estate's interest in such property;

 (ii) for the sale, subject to section 363 (k) of this title, of any property that is subject to the liens securing such claims, free and clear of such liens, with such liens to attach to the proceeds of such sale, and the treatment of such liens on proceeds under clause (i) or (iii) of this subparagraph; or

 (iii) for the realization by such holders of the indubitable equivalent of such claims.

(B) With respect to a class of unsecured claims –

 (i) the plan provides that each holder of a claim of such class receive or retain on account of such claim property of a value, as of the effective date of the plan, equal to the allowed amount of such claim; or

 (ii) the holder of any claim or interest that is junior to the claims of such class will not receive or retain under the plan on account of such junior claim or interest any property.

(C) With respect to a class of interests –

 (i) the plan provides that each holder of an interest of such class receive or retain on account of such interest property of a value, as of the effective date of the plan, equal to the greatest of the allowed amount of any fixed liquidation preference to which such holder is entitled, any fixed redemption price to which such holder is entitled, or the value of such interest; or

 (ii) the holder of any interest that is junior to the interests of such class will not receive or retain under the plan on account of such junior interest any property.

(c) Notwithstanding subsections (a) and (b) of this section and except as provided in section 1127 (b) of this title, the court may confirm only one plan, unless the order of confirmation in the case has been revoked under section 1144 of this title. If the requirements of subsections (a) and (b) of this section are met with respect to more than one plan, the court shall consider the preferences of creditors and equity security holders in determining which plan to confirm.

(d) Notwithstanding any other provision of this section, on request of a party in interest that is a governmental unit, the court may not confirm a plan if the principal purpose of the plan is the avoidance of taxes or the avoidance of the application of section 5 of the Securities Act of 1933. In any hearing under this subsection, the governmental unit has the burden of proof on the issue of avoidance.

Title 11. Chapter 11. Subchapter III.

§ 1145. Exemption from securities laws

(a) Except with respect to an entity that is an underwriter as defined in subsection (b) of this section, section 5 of the Securities Act of 1933 and any State or local law requiring registration for offer or sale of a security or registration or licensing of an issuer of, underwriter of, or broker or dealer in, a security do not apply to

  (1) the offer or sale under a plan of a security of the debtor, of an affiliate participating in a joint plan with the debtor, or of a successor to the debtor under the plan
    (A) in exchange for a claim against, an interest in, or a claim for an administrative expense in the case concerning, the debtor or such affiliate; or
    (B) principally in such exchange and partly for cash or property;
  (2) the offer of a security through any warrant, option, right to subscribe, or conversion privilege that was sold in the manner specified in paragraph (1) of this subsection, or the sale of a security upon the exercise of such a warrant, option, right, or privilege;
  (3) the offer or sale, other than under a plan, of a security of an issuer other than the debtor or an affiliate, if
    (A) such security was owned by the debtor on the date of the filing of the petition;
    (B) the issuer of such security is
      (i) required to file reports under section 13 or 15(d) of the Securities Exchange Act of 1934; and
      (ii) in compliance with the disclosure and reporting provision of such applicable section; and
    (C) such offer or sale is of securities that do not exceed
      (i) during the two-year period immediately following the date of the filing of the petition, four percent of the securities of such class outstanding on such date; and
      (ii) during any 180-day period following such two-year period, one percent of the securities outstanding at the beginning of such 180-day period; or
  (4) a transaction by a stockbroker in a security that is executed after a transaction of a kind specified in paragraph (1) or (2) of this subsection in such security and before the expiration of 40 days after the first date on which such security was bona fide offered to the public by the issuer or by or through an underwriter, if such stockbroker provides, at the time of or before such transaction by such stockbroker, a disclosure statement approved under section 1125 of this title, and, if the court orders, information supplementing such disclosure statement.

(b)
    (1) Except as provided in paragraph (2) of this subsection and except with respect to ordinary trading transactions of an entity that is not an issuer, an entity is an underwriter under section 2(11) of the Securities Act of 1933,[1] if such entity
        (A) purchases a claim against, interest in, or claim for an administrative expense in the case concerning, the debtor, if such purchase is with a view to distribution of any security received or to be received in exchange for such a claim or interest;
        (B) offers to sell securities offered or sold under the plan for the holders of such securities;
        (C) offers to buy securities offered or sold under the plan from the holders of such securities, if such offer to buy is
           (i) with a view to distribution of such securities; and
          (ii) under an agreement made in connection with the plan, with the consummation of the plan, or with the offer or sale of securities under the plan; or
        (D) is an issuer, as used in such section 2 (11), with respect to such securities.
    (2) An entity is not an underwriter under section 2(11) of the Securities Act of 1933 or under paragraph (1) of this subsection with respect to an agreement that provides only for
        (A)
           (i) the matching or combining of fractional interests in securities offered or sold under the plan into whole interests; or
          (ii) the purchase or sale of such fractional interests from or to entities receiving such fractional interests under the plan; or
        (B) the purchase or sale for such entities of such fractional or whole interests as are necessary to adjust for any remaining fractional interests after such matching.
    (3) An entity other than an entity of the kind specified in paragraph (1) of this subsection is not an underwriter under section 2(11) of the Securities Act of 1933 [1] with respect to any securities offered or sold to such entity in the manner specified in subsection (a)(1) of this section.

(c) An offer or sale of securities of the kind and in the manner specified under subsection (a)(1) of this section is deemed to be a public offering.

(d) The Trust Indenture Act of 1939 does not apply to a note issued under the plan that matures not later than one year after the effective date of the plan.

Chapter 15
Private International Law Implications of Expedited Corporate Debt Restructurings
Gerald Arends[1]

---

1. The author would like to thank Danae Vardavaki (Athens) and Daniel Dürrschmidt Munich for their instructive comments on a draft of this chapter and Rodrigo Olivares Caminal for early discussions on the topic.

Rodrigo Olivares-Caminal, *Expedited Debt Restructuring:
An International Comparative Analysis*, pp. 477–507.
©2007, Kluwer Law International BV, The Netherlands.

ACRONYMS, ABBREVIATIONS & DEFINED TERMS

APE	Argentine *Acuerdo Preventivo Extrajudicial*
Brussels Convention	Convention of 27 September 1968 on Jurisdiction and the Enforcement of Judgments in Civil and Commercial Matters
Brussels Regulation	Council Regulation (EC) No 44/2001 of 22 December 2000 on jurisdiction and the recognition and enforcement of judgments in civil and commercial matters
COMI	Centre of Main Interests
CVA	Company Voluntary Arrangements
ECDRs	Expedited Corporate Debt Restructurings
EU Insolvency Regulation	Council Regulation (EC) No 1346/2000 of 29 May 2000 on insolvency proceedings
Guide to Enactment	Guide to Enactment of the UNCITRAL Model Law on Cross-Border Insolvency
Model Law	UNCITRAL Model Law on Cross-border Insolvency
Multicanal I	In Re Board of Directors of Multicanal S.A., United States Bankruptcy Court for the Southern District of New York 12 March 2004, Case No. 04-10280 (ALG), 307 B.R. 384, 392
Multicanal II	In Re Board of Directors of Multicanal S.A., In Re Multicanal S.A., Memorandum of Decision, 27 August 2004
TIA	US Trust Indenture Act of 1939
UNCITRAL Legislative Guide	UNCITRAL, Legislative Guide on Insolvency Law
US	United States of America

The present contribution attempts to highlight some of the private international law implications of expedited corporate debt restructurings (ECDRs). It does not purport to examine exhaustively the relevant rules of the private international law of a single jurisdiction, let alone a larger number of jurisdictions. Rather, the issues will be developed on a conceptual level, drawing examples from various jurisdictions.

While the author is aware that differences exist between ECDRs in different jurisdictions, the approach taken in this chapter requires a level of generalization of some of the salient features in which ECDRs are different from other insolvency procedures. Where an actual example of an ECDR is required, recourse will be had primarily to the Argentine *acuerdo preventivo extrajudicial* (APE).[2] From the perspective of private international law, recurring themes will be (1) the entitlement to open ECDRs at a stage at which 'ordinary' insolvency proceedings are not (yet) available;[3] (2) the lack of judicial oversight and supervision over the debtor's assets and affairs; and (3) the potentially limited impact of minority creditors on the 'setting of the agenda' for the restructuring proposal and the subsequent judicial examination of the results of the majority vote.

This chapter will develop along the lines of some of the major questions arising from an ECDR in a multi-jurisdictional setting. These include the international jurisdiction of a court to administer an ECDR in respect of a specific debtor;[4] the question of the applicable law, which is intrinsically linked with the question of jurisdiction;[5] and finally the recognition of foreign ECDRs, a question that cannot be answered without recourse to the other two issues.[6] Practitioners will encounter situations where they will 'reverse-engineer' these issues in order to achieve recognition.

I.	INTERNATIONAL JURISDICTION TO ADMINISTER ECDR
A.	INTERNATIONAL JURISDICTION

1.   Qualification of ECDRs

The negotiation of ECDRs has similarities with both, privately negotiated work-outs and with insolvency proceedings. The similarity to privately negotiated

---

2. An overview of out-of-court reorganizations, pre-packaged reorganization plans and pre-arranged/pre-negotiated reorganization plans in Latin America is provided at R. Olivares Caminal, 'Corporate Debt Restructuring in Latin America: New Developments – New Opportunities?', (2005) Issue 6, International Company and Commercial Law Review 254, 255–259; a description of the APE in particular is available at R. Olivares Caminal, 'Recognition of Corporate Debt Restructuring Procedures in Latin America under US Law: Lessons from the *Multicanal* Case', (2005) 2 International Corporate Rescue 143, 145–147; A. Navarro, 'The Argentine APE as an out-of-court Restructuring Agreement', page 5, unpublished manuscript, on file with the author.
3. This issue was raised in *In re Board of Directors of Telecom Argentina S.A.*, United States Bankruptcy Court for the Southern District of New York 24 February 2006, No. 05–17811 (BRL), Slip Copy, 2006 WL 686867 (Bankr.S.D.N.Y.), para. 100.
4. See *below* I.
5. See *below* II.
6. See *below* III.

work-outs lies in that the initiative can be taken at a time when formal insolvency proceedings might not yet be available and in that there is no court compulsion until an application for ratification (homologation) is made. The similarity with formal insolvency proceedings lies in the ability to override dissenting minorities and the availability of a moratorium for the duration of the judicial proceedings.

A work-out is contractual in nature and international jurisdiction concerning the implementation of work-outs has to be determined in accordance with international jurisdiction for contractual matters. The European Court of Justice has determined in the context of Article 5(1) of the Brussels Convention[7] (now Article 5(1) of the Brussels Regulation)[8] that the decisive qualifying criterion for *'matters relating to contract'* is the voluntary assumption of obligations.[9] Due to the involuntary imposition of burdens on the dissenting minority as result of homologation granted by the court, international jurisdiction for ECDRs cannot follow the international jurisdiction for contractual matters. Accordingly, ECDRs are to be qualified as insolvency proceedings, where the imposition of burdens on dissenting parties is justified by the purpose pursued through insolvency proceedings, such as the liquidation of the debtor for the equal satisfaction of the creditors or the supervision by the courts for the purpose of rescuing the business.[10] This private international law qualification has been confirmed in *In re Board of Directors of Telecom Argentina S.A.*[11]

Although not strictly determinative for the private international law qualification, the *above* approach is mirrored by the domestic law perspective: the APE forms part of the Argentine Bankruptcy Law in its sections 69 to 76[12] (it is reported that ten first instance courts and three courts of appeal considered whether the APE forms part of insolvency law in Argentina and all courts confirmed this point).[13]

---

7. Convention of 27 September 1968 on Jurisdiction and the Enforcement of Judgments in Civil and Commercial Matters (the 'Brussels Convention'), Official Journal of the European Union OJ L 299, 31 December 1972, 32 (as amended).
8. Council Regulation (EC) No 44/2001 of 22 December 2000 on jurisdiction and the recognition and enforcement of judgments in civil and commercial matters (the 'Brussels Regulation'), Official Journal of the European Union OJ L 12, 16 January 2001, 1.
9. *Jacob Handte & Co. GmbH v. Traitements Mécano-chimiques des Surfaces SA,* European Court of Justice 8 January 1991, Case C–26/91, European Court Reports 1992, I–3967, para 15: '*15. It follows that the phrase 'matters relating to a contract', as used in Article 5(1) of the Convention, is not to be understood as covering a situation in which there is no obligation freely assumed by one party towards another*' (emphasis provided); *Réunion européenne v. Spliethoff's Bevrachtingskantoor,* European Court of Justice 28 January 1997, Case C–51/97, European Court Reports 1998, I–6511, para 17; *Fonderie Officine Meccaniche Tacconi SpA v. Heinrich Wagner Sinto Maschinenfabrik GmbH,* European Court of Justice 9 January 2000, Case C–334/00, para 23.
10. *Henri Gourdain v. Franz Nadler,* European Court of Justice 22 February 1979, Case 133/78, European Court Reports 1979, 733, para. 4.
11. *In re Board of Directors of Telecom Argentina S.A.*, United States Bankruptcy Court for the Southern District of New York 24 February 2006, No. 05–17811 (BRL), Slip Copy, 2006 WL 686867 (Bankr.S.D.N.Y.), para. 95–99.
12. Law No 24.522 as amended by, inter alia, Law No 25.589 of May 2002; an English version of the relevant provisions are on file with the author.
13. *In re Board of Directors of Telecom Argentina S.A.*, United States Bankruptcy Court for the Southern District of New York 24 February 2006, No. 05–17811 (BRL), Slip Copy, 2006 WL 686867 (Bankr.S.D.N.Y.), para. 99.

Furthermore, the US 'pre-packed' procedure is firmly based on Chapter 11 of the US Bankruptcy Code;[14] and the English CVA, which can be used for pre-arranged reorganization plans, forms Part I of the Insolvency Act 1986.[15]

2. International Jurisdiction in Insolvency Matters

There is no international consensus as to the jurisdictional basis for insolvency proceedings. A noteworthy convergence of opinion exists, however, for restructuring proceedings. Principally, the following bases for jurisdiction in insolvency matters are represented in domestic practice: (1) the place of incorporation,[16] (2) the seat of the company (defined through the main administration),[17] (3) the centre of main interests,[18] (4) the existence of an establishment,[19] (5) the presence of assets,[20] and

---

14. See *In the Matter of the Adoption of Prepackaged Chapter 11 Case Guidelines*, United States Bankruptcy Court for the Southern District of New York 2 February 1999, General Order 201, available at <http://www.nysb.uscourts.gov/orders/m201.pdf>.
15. Schemes of arrangement pursuant to section 425 of the Companies Act 1985 can also be used for pre-arranged restructuring plans. The fact that schemes of arrangement do not form part of the Insolvency Act 1986 shows that their use is broader than in pure insolvency cases. It should be noted, however, that Part XX of the Companies Act 1985 dealt with the winding up of companies until its repeal by the Insolvency Act 1986, i.e. English law did not originally distinguish between company and insolvency law.
16. See, *for example, Canada Southern Railway Co. v. Gebhard*, United States Supreme Court, 10 December 1883, (1883) 109 US 527.
17. See, *for example*, the first alternative provided for in § 3(1) of the German Insolvency Code: '*Locally competent are exclusively those insolvency courts in whose district general jurisdiction can be exercised over the debtor. If the centre of independent economic activity of the debtor is at a place in another district, the insolvency court of the district in which that place is located shall have exclusive jurisdiction*'. See also § 17(1) of the German Civil Procedure Code: '*The general jurisdictional base for claims against those [...] companies that can be sued as such, is determined by reference to their seat. The seat is deemed to be where the administration is controlled from, unless another place can be determined*'. (Translations provided by the author.) Under German law, the concepts applicable to local jurisdiction (venue) are also applied to determine international jurisdiction (the principle of double functionality).
18. See, *for example*, Article 3(1) of Council Regulation (EC) No 1346/2000 of 29 May 2000 on insolvency proceedings (the 'EU Insolvency Regulation'), Official Journal of the European Union OJ L 160, 30 June 2006, 1, for primary proceedings. See also Article 2(d) of the UNCITRAL Model Law on Cross-border Insolvency (hereinafter the 'Model Law') which imposes the concept of 'centre of main interests' through the recognition mechanism in that recognition is only obligatory (provided other conditions are met) if 'main' proceedings have been commenced in the state in which the debtor has its centre of main interests, see Article 17(2)(a) of the Model Law.
19. See, *for example*, Article 3(1) of the EU Insolvency Regulation for secondary proceedings. See also Article 2(c) and (f) of the Model Law and the recognition mechanism for non-main proceedings, Article 17(2)(b) of the Model Law.
20. See, *for example*, § 109(a) of the US Bankruptcy Code, which reads: '*Notwithstanding any other provision of this section, only a person that resides or has a domicile, a place of business, or property in the United States, or a municipality, may be a debtor under this title*'. See footnote 43 for examples of the width of the criterion 'property in the United States'.

(6) the existence of a sufficient connection.[21] It should be noted that the first three bases represent an attempt to capture the general or core presence of the company. The last two afore-mentioned bases, on the other hand, represent examples of a test of sufficient or minimum contacts. They lead, as to a common law[22] court's own finding, to extraterritorial jurisdiction.[23] This perception will assume relevance in the context of recognition of ECDRs.[24]

Given that the common law courts have a regime for establishing (and rejecting) jurisdiction that is more flexible than their civil law counterparts, they also have to deal in a more reflective way with the relevant jurisdictional issues. They will, accordingly, be addressed from the perspective of English law, with transgressions into other legal systems where these help to highlight the issues under discussion.

a.   *Winding-up Jurisdiction*

The English courts exercise jurisdiction to wind-up insolvent companies primarily on the basis of a test of incorporation[25] as it is the perspective of common law that the principal responsibility for matters of status lies with the country of the place of incorporation.[26] English courts do, however, also have statutory power to wind up

---

21. See *below* II. A. 2. (a).
22. Asset-based jurisdiction over insolvency matters is frequent in common law jurisdictions.
23. *In Re Yukos Oil Company*, United States Bankruptcy Court, Southern District of Texas, 24 February 2005, Case No. 04–47742–H3–11, 321 B.R. 396, 406.
24. See *below* III.
25. See section 73 of the UK Insolvency Act 1986. Section 73(1) reads as follows:
    '*The winding up of a company, within the meaning given to that expression by section 735 of the Companies Act, may be either voluntary (Chapters II, IV and v. in this Part), or by the court (Chapter VI)*'. (Emphasis provided.). Section 735 of the UK Company Act 1985 reads as follows: '*(1) In this Act— (a) company' means a company formed and registered under this Act, or an existing company; (b) 'existing company' means a company formed and registered under the former Companies Acts, but does not include a company registered under the Joint Stock Companies Acts, the Companies Act 1862 or the Companies (Consolidation) Act 1908 in what was then Ireland; (c) 'the former Companies Acts' means the Joint Stock Companies Acts, the Companies Act 1862, the Companies (Consolidation) Act 1908, the Companies Act 1929 and the Companies Acts 1948 to 1983. (2) 'Public company' and 'private company' have the meanings given by section 1(3). (3) 'The Joint Stock Companies Acts' means the Joint Stock Companies Act 1856, the Joint Stock Companies Acts 1856, 1857, the Joint Stock Banking Companies Act 1857 and the Act to enable Joint Stock Banking Companies to be formed on the principle of limited liability, or any one or more of those Acts (as the case may require), but does not include the Joint Stock Companies Act 1844. (4) The definitions in this section apply unless the contrary intention appears*'.
26. K. Dawson, 'The Doctrine of Forum Non Conveniens and the Winding Up of Insolvent Foreign Companies', (2005) Journal of Business Law 28, 29; *Lazard Brothers & Co. v. Midland Bank Limited*, House of Lords 28 November 1932, [1933] A.C. 289, 297 (*per* Lord Wright): '*But as the creation [of a company] depends on the act of the foreign state which created it, the annulment of the act of creation by the same power will involve the dissolution and non-existence of the corporation in the eyes of English law*'.

un-registered companies,[27] which has been consistently held to include companies which are not registered under English law.[28] Case law has developed to restrict the ambit of the wide statutory power and under the test developed in *Re Real Estate Development Limited* it is now required that '*(1) There must be a sufficient connection between the company and England, but that does not mean that assets must be situate within the jurisdiction. (2) There must be a reasonable possibility, if a winding up order is made, of benefit accruing to those applying for the winding up order. (3) One or more persons interested in the distribution of the assets must be persons over whom the court could exercise jurisdiction*' (emphasis provided).[29] The width of the power of the courts becomes apparent in *Stocznia Gdanska SA v. Latreefers Inc.* where it was stated that sufficient connections were held to exist with England so as to justify a winding up order, although there were no winding up proceedings in the country of incorporation of the company,[30] thereby risking that the company is subjected to conflicting regimes. This was despite the slightly earlier case of *Banco Nacional de Cuba v. Cosmos Trading Corp.*, where the company continued trading in its jurisdiction of incorporation. That latter case is of interest because it is an example for the proposition that jurisdiction could be declined although there were assets within the jurisdiction at the time the winding up petition was made (but subsequently removed).[31] It further highlights policy considerations that militate against the winding up of a foreign company: First, it would be undesirable to wind up a foreign company that continues trading abroad and in particular in the country of its incorporation. Secondly, any attempt of the English courts to wind up the company could not have been ancillary to foreign proceedings and would therefore have purported to have worldwide effect, as it is not possible under English law to restrict the winding up of a company to one jurisdiction only. In both instances, the English order would be unlikely to receive

---

27. Section 221 of the UK Insolvency Act 1986 reads in extracts as follows: '*(1) Subject to the provisions of this Part, any unregistered company may be wound up under this Act; [. . .]. [. . .] (5) The circumstances in which an unregistered company may be wound up are as follows – (a) if the company is dissolved, or has ceased to carry on business, or is carrying on business only for the purpose of winding up its affairs; (b) if the company is unable to pay its debts; if the court is of the opinion it is just and equitable that the company should be wound up*'.
28. Section 220 of the UK Insolvency Act 1986 defines the term 'unregistered company' only by way of express inclusion and by way of specific exclusion without addressing the point of foreign companies.
29. *Re Real Estate Development Ltd*, High Court of England & Wales (Chancery Division) 19 May 1989, [1991] BCLC 210, 216 (*per* Knox J.). For further examples of the 'sufficient connection' test see *Re A Company (No. 00359 of 1987)*, High Court of England & Wales (Chancery Division) 20 February 1987, [1988] Ch 210, 225; *Re Titan International Inc.*, Court of Appeal of England & Wales (Civil Division) 10 March 1997, [1997] EWCA Civ 1203, [1998] 1 BCLC 102, 106, which cases also stand for the proposition that assets within the jurisdiction are not required.
30. *Stocznia Gdanska SA v. Latreefers Inc.*, Court of Appeal of England & Wales 9 February 2000, [2000] EWCA Civ 36, [2001] 2 BCLC 116, 141.
31. *Banco Nacional de Cuba v. Cosmos Trading Corp.*, Court of Appeal of England & Wales 9 November 1999, [2000] 1 BCLC 813, 818.

recognition in foreign courts.[32] This consideration is not only valid for the question of winding up jurisdiction, but also for restructuring proceedings.

b.   Restructuring Jurisdiction

In England, an ECDR would be available in the form of a pre-arranged/pre-negotiated restructuring and would take the form of either a scheme of arrangement or a CVA. CVAs can be implemented in a free-standing manner or within an administration procedure. CVAs and administration procedures were, until recently,[33] limited by virtue of sections 1(1) and 8 of the Insolvency Act 1986 respectively to '*companies*', whereby that term is defined in section 735 of the Companies Act 1985, i.e. to companies registered in England, unless the '*contrary intention appears*'.[34] Administration proceedings have produced the more pronounced case law and due to the identical jurisdictional basis it is justified to have recourse to the case law on the jurisdictional scope of administration proceedings to highlight some of the policy issues arising in CVAs in a similar manner.[35]

It was held in *Re Dallhold Estates (UK) Pty Ltd* that English courts do not have original jurisdiction to make an administration order in respect of a foreign company (i.e. foreign registered company), but only if a request is made to them by a foreign court under section 426 of the Insolvency Act 1986.[36] This restrictive approach has been questioned and it has been suggested that for the purpose of administration orders the term '*company*' should include foreign incorporated companies.[37] This argument[38] receives support from the case of *Re International Bulk Commodities*, where the term '*company*' has been interpreted to include foreign companies for the purposes of administrative receivership.[39] On a policy level, the restraint (i.e. exercising jurisdiction to grant an administration order only at the request of a court of the country of incorporation) exercised by

---

32. Ibid. 818–819.
33. See *below* with regard to the implementation of the EC Insolvency Regulation.
34. Section 251 of the Insolvency Act 1986 extends the definition of 'company' in 735(1)(a) and (b) of the Companies Act 1985 to insolvency law; see also section 225 of the Insolvency Act 1986.
35. Due to the constraints of the present contribution, the subsequent discussion will focus on CVAs (and the relevant case law of administration proceedings) rather than schemes of arrangement. This seems justified not least because schemes of arrangements cannot be easily likened to ECDRs, since there is an initial involvement of the court calling a creditors' meeting, see section 425(1) of the Companies Act 1985.
36. *Re Dallhold Estates (U.K.) Pty Ltd*, High Court of Justice of England & Wales (Chancery Division) 23 February 1992, [1992] BCLC 621, 622 and 625; *Hughes v. Hannover Rückversicherungs-Aktiengesellschaft*, Court of Appeal of England & Wales (Civil Division) 28 January 1997, [1997] EWCA Civ 857, [1997] 1 BCLC 497, 511 (CA).
37. Dicey & Morris, Conflict of Laws (Sweet & Maxwell, 1999 with supplements), para 30–130. Their example, however, envisages a foreign registered company carrying on business solely in the UK.
38. For this argument see K. Baird and P. Bloxham, 'Section 426 Insolvency Act 1986 and Re Dallhold Estates Ltd', (1992) 7(9) Journal of International Banking Law 373, 376–377.
39. *Re International Bulk Commodities*, High Court of Justice of England & Wales (Chancery Division) 15 April 1992, No. 002090 of 1992, [1993] Ch 77, 83–87.

Chadwick J in *Re Dallhold Estates* is commendable. While jurisdiction in that case was based on the request of an Australian court under section 426 of the Insolvency Act 1986, it is understood that the English court could only sensibly order an administration of a foreign company due to assets being located within its jurisdiction. Accordingly, the jurisdiction exercised by the English court was in substance (though not in form) an asset-based jurisdiction. Exercise of asset-based jurisdiction is seen as an extraterritorial reach of jurisdiction and unlikely to receive recognition in foreign courts. Given that *Re Dallhold Estates* was based on a section 426 request, this issue did not, of course, arise.

Following the introduction of the EU Insolvency Regulation, the scope of sections 1 and 8 (and now in respect of the latter para. 111(1A) of schedule B1)[40] of the Insolvency Act 1986 has been extended to allow companies which are not registered in the UK to be dealt with through CVAs and arrangement proceedings, as long as they have their *'centre of main interests'* within the meaning of Article 3(1) of the EU Insolvency Regulation within the UK.[41] It was held in *In Re BRAC Rent-A-Car International Inc.* that the EU Insolvency Regulation's approach to use the jurisdictional concept of the *'centre of main interests'* applies not only to allocate jurisdiction between the EU Member States (other than Denmark), but also allowed an English court to assume jurisdiction over a non-EU registered company having its centre of main interests in England.[42] It would appear that the same reasoning, based on a textual and purposive interpretation of the EU Insolvency Regulation, would also apply to CVAs.

c.   *Policy Considerations*

Where a liquidation is conducted, asset-based jurisdiction might serve some useful purpose in that it provides the liquidator of the assets with the required powers in a jurisdiction exercising asset-based jurisdiction. The restraint exercised by the court in *Banco Nacional de Cuba v. Cosmos Trading* should, however, be noted: assets should not be liquidated in England if a liquidation is not conducted in the home jurisdiction and the recognition of an English liquidation cannot be expected in foreign courts. It is an expression of the policy that a liquidation must be either

---

40. See sections 1(4) and 8(7) of the Insolvency Act 1986 as amended by regulations 4 and 5 of the The Insolvency Act 1986 (Amendment) (No. 2) Regulations 2002 (Statutory Instrument 2002 No. 1240). Section 8 has been repealed and substituted by schedule B1 by the Enterprise Act 2002, specifically for the issue of interest here see para. 111(1A) of schedule B1 of the Insolvency Act 1986.
41. Section 1(4) of the UK Insolvency Act reads as follows: '*In this Part 'company' means – (a) a company within the meaning of section 735(1) of the Companies Act 1985, (b) a company incorporated in an EEA State other than the United Kingdom; or (c) a company not incorporated in an EEA State but having its centre of main interests in a Member State other than Denmark*'. Para. 111(1A) of schedule B1 of the Insolvency Act is worded identically, substituting reference to 'Part' with reference to 'Schedule' only.
42. *In Re BRAC Rent-A-Car International Inc.*, High Court of Justice of England & Wales (Chancery Division) 7 February 2003, [2003] EWHC 128 (Ch), [2003] 1 WLR 1421, 1426.

exercised in the jurisdiction of general jurisdiction over the debtor and any ancillary proceedings elsewhere or not at all.

The sensitivity to conflicting proceedings in various jurisdictions is even greater for reorganizations, as it is intended to maintain the company as a going concern and to allow the company to shed off its past. In *Canada Southern Railway Co v. Gebhard* it was stated in respect of a legislative scheme of arrangement (the precursor of the court-administered schemes of arrangements) that *'[u]nless all parties in interest, wherever they reside, can be bound by the arrangement which it is sought to have legalized the scheme may fail. All home creditors can be bound. What is needed is to bind those who are abroad. Under these circumstances the true spirit of international comity requires that schemes of this character, legalized at home, should be recognized in other countries'*.[43]

It is vital for a reorganization to bind all creditors and affect all assets, which can only be achieved if the jurisdiction of the court administering the reorganization is universally recognized. Such recognition might not be forthcoming, if jurisdiction is based on assets within, or a sufficient connection with, the forum.[44] Accordingly, it has long been maintained that the presence of assets only (or 'sufficient connection') is not a suitable base of jurisdiction in cases of reorganizations.[45] It should also be noted that the change to the jurisdictional scope of CVAs and administrations introduced by the advent of the EU Insolvency Regulation into English law is not a shift to a test of 'sufficient connection', but to a different type of test for the 'general presence' of a company,[46] which is likely (and within the EU certain) to receive universal recognition. The preference for jurisdiction over reorganization proceedings to be centred on a court with general jurisdiction over the debtor is also reflected in the EU Insolvency Regulation restricting secondary proceedings (i.e. proceedings outside the jurisdiction of the court where the centre of main interests of the debtor is located) to winding-up proceedings if a main proceeding has already been opened.[47]

The recognition of the need for such restraint in restructuring proceedings is, however, not universal. Most notably, the United States accept asset-based jurisdiction for its Chapter 11 reorganization proceedings. Recent cases show that only nominal amounts of assets within the US are required for a debtor to qualify as a debtor under § 109(a) of the United States Bankruptcy Code and to have access to the Chapter 11 proceedings.[48] The creditors in *In Re Board of Directors of*

---

43. *Canada Southern Railway Co. v. Gebhard*, United States Supreme Court, 10 December 1883, (1883) 109 US 527, 539.
44. See *below* III B and C.
45. UNCITRAL, Legislative Guide on Insolvency Law, New York 2005, page 43 (hereinafter 'UNCITRAL, Legislative Guide').
46. See *above* I A 2.
47. Article 3(3) of the EU Insolvency Regulation. It is, however, permissible to open secondary reorganization proceedings outside the country where the debtor has its centre of main interests if no main proceedings have been opened as yet, see D. Eickmann et al. (ed.), *Insolvenzordnung*, (C.F. Müller, Heidelberg, 2004), VIII Art. 3 EuInsVO 18a.
48. *In re Globo Comunicacoes E Participacoes S.A.*, United States District Court, Southern District of New York, 17 November 2004, No. 04 Civ. 2818(VM), 317 B.R. 235, 249; *In re Aerovias*

Multicanal S.A.[49] (Multicanal I) suggested that the Argentine debtor, rather than opening an APE and seeking recognition in the United States, should have opened Chapter 11 proceedings (based on assets within the jurisdiction) in the United States.[50] The consequences of such a potential course of action at the recognition stage will be addressed below.[51]

B.   Refusing Jurisdiction

The width of asset-based jurisdiction (or similar tests) as it is exercised in common law countries is countered by the courts discretion to decline jurisdiction. The intrinsic link between these two questions has been expressly emphasized in *In Re Yukos Oil Company*.[52] It is not entirely clear whether the doctrine of *forum non-conveniens* applies to the exercise of insolvency jurisdiction in general and jurisdiction for restructuring proceedings in particular. Typically, insolvency jurisdiction is based on statute and statutes allowing asset-based jurisdiction also provide for discretion to refuse to entertain proceedings.[53] While in one instance a judgment considered the doctrine of *forum non-conveniens* to apply to involuntary bankruptcy proceedings against an individual (though this was only an alternative ground for the decision),[54] Yukos declined to extend *forum non-conveniens* considerations to a voluntary Chapter 11 proceeding due to the availability of a statutory discretion.[55] In substance, however, the statutory exercise of discretion is similar to the common law doctrine.

Under English law, considerations akin to *forum non-conveniens* are included in the test for assumption of jurisdiction for a winding-up under the '*sufficient connection*' test of *Re Real Estate Development Limited*[56] and its subsequent application. This has been considered to be sufficient to control the potentially exorbitant exercise jurisdiction.[57] It has been argued that the test is in all but the name the doctrine of *forum non-conveniens*, and that this doctrine should be

---

    Nacionales de Colombia S.A. (In re Aviance), United States Bankruptcy Court, Southern District of New York, 23 December 2003, 303 B.R. 1, 8–9; *In re Global Ocean Carriers Ltd*, United States Bankruptcy Court, District of Delaware, 5 July 2000, 251 B.R. 31, 37–39.
49. See *further below* III A.
50. *In Re Board of Directors of Multicanal S.A.*, United States Bankruptcy Court for the Southern District of New York 12 March 2004, Case No. 04–10280 (ALG), 307 B.R. 384, 392.
51. See *further below* III B 2.
52. *In Re Yukos Oil Company*, United States Bankruptcy Court, Southern District of Texas, 24 February 2005, Case No. 04–47742–H3–11, 321 B.R. 396, 407.
53. See, for example, § 305 of the US Bankruptcy Code with respect to individual insolvencies and § 1112 of the US Bankruptcy Code with respect to restructuring proceedings.
54. *In Re Xacur*, United States Bankruptcy Court, Southern District of Texas, 18 March 1998, Bankruptcy No. 96–48539–H5–7, 219 B.R. 956, 970.
55. *In Re Yukos Oil Company*, United States Bankruptcy Court, Southern District of Texas, 24 February 2005, Case No. 04–47742–H3–11, 321 B.R. 396, 407–408.
56. See *above* I A 2 (a).
57. *Stocznia Gdanska SA v. Latreefers Inc.*, Court of Appeal of England & Wales 9 February 2000, [2000] EWCA Civ 36, [2001] 2 BCLC 116, 139–141.

acknowledged as adjunct to the *'sufficient connection'* test.[58] The power of the English courts to apply the doctrine of *forum non-conveniens* (or an equivalent statutory discretion) in insolvency matters might be affected by the decision of *Owusu v. Jackson* as that decision prevents the application of the doctrine in the relationship between English courts and non-EU courts to the extent that jurisdiction is based on the Brussels Regulation (the case is still based on the Brussels Convention of 1968 but it is generally expected that the decision applies in a similar manner).[59] Although Article 1(2)(b) of the Brussels Regulation excludes *'bankruptcy, proceedings relating to the winding-up of insolvent companies or other legal persons, judicial arrangements, compositions and analogous proceedings'* from its ambit, the same reasoning might be applied to insolvency jurisdiction exercised under Article 3(1) or (2) of the EU Insolvency Regulation. To this extent, the doctrine of *forum non-conveniens* might experience restriction in the context of insolvency jurisdictions of the United Kingdom and Ireland.

As regards ECDRs, the narrow reading of the jurisdictional test for CVAs excluding *'sufficient connection'* based jurisdiction[60] in England makes a control against exorbitant exercise of jurisdiction less pressing. But even in the context of CVAs it might be necessary or desirable to have such flexibility where different tests of general insolvency jurisdiction yield conflicting perceptions as to the appropriate court. The issue was highlighted in the case *In Re Harrods (Buenos Aires) Limited*, which concerned the winding up of a solvent company. The company was considered by the Argentine courts to be subject to the jurisdiction of the Argentine courts for the purpose of winding up as it conducted its business exclusively in Argentina and had its central control and management there. The English courts could have assumed winding up jurisdiction over the company on the basis of its incorporation in England.[61] The court found that it had the power to apply the doctrine of *forum non-conveniens*[62] (which question was contentious against the background of the Brussels Convention) and that on balance the *Spiliada* test (being the leading English case on *forum non-conveniens)*[63] led to a stay of the English proceedings in favour of the Argentine proceedings.[64] Whether English law could, if it were faced with conflicting jurisdictions for a restructuring, still apply notions of *foreign non-conveniens* is, of course, doubtful given that *Owusu v. Jackson* might have removed that flexibility.

---

58. K. Dawson, 'The Doctrine of Forum Non Conveniens and the Winding Up of Insolvent Foreign Companies', (2005) Journal of Business Law 28, 40 to 44.
59. *Owusu v. Jackson*, European Court of Justice 1 March 2005, Case C–281/02, Official Journal of the European Union OJ C 106, 30 April 2005, 2, full text of judgment available at <http://curia.europa.eu/en/content/juris/index.htm>.
60. See *above* I A 2 (b).
61. *In Re Harrods (Buenos Aires) Limited*, Court of Appeal of England & Wales (Civil Division) 13 March 1991, [1992] Ch 72, 109.
62. Ibid. 93. See also *Re A Company (No. 00359 of 1987)*, High Court of Justice of England & Wales (Chancery Division) 20 February 1987, [1988] Ch 210, 226.
63. *Spiliada Maritime Corp v. Cansulex Ltd, The Spiliada*, House of Lords 19 November 1986, [1987] AC 460.
64. Ibid. 118 to 127.

C. RESTRAINING FOREIGN PROCEEDINGS

Where an ECDR is administered in one country, there will be a concern that the moratorium imposed at the time of commencement of the court proceedings[65] will be neglected and proceedings brought abroad against the estate of the debtor attempting to restructure,[66] as happened in the case of *Multicanal I* in the preliminary stages.[67] Even if a court claims jurisdiction over the world-wide assets of a debtor,[68] a moratorium has factually a purely territorial effect unless the proceedings are recognized in the foreign courts. Foreign proceedings against the debtor can be terminated if the ECDR is recognized by foreign courts and the moratorium given effect in foreign jurisdictions.[69] If the foreign jurisdiction is a civil law country, it is likely that recognition of the ECDR will be the only viable route to prevent actions being brought against the debtor. If actions are being commenced in a common law country, or if the person commencing foreign proceedings is amenable to the jurisdiction of a common law court, it might also be feasible to restrain those proceedings by way of injunctive relief.[70]

There are several instances where it was attempted to use injunctive relief to restrain foreign proceedings against a debtor during the currency of insolvency proceedings. In *Felixstowe Dock & Railway v. United States Lines Inc.*, Chapter 11 proceedings had been commenced in the United States. Rather than seeking recognition of the US Chapter 11 proceedings and the automatic stay of proceedings produced by it[71] abroad, the US bankruptcy judge issued a restraining order to stay any proceedings worldwide against the insolvent estate.[72] The English court did not accept that such a stay has the *in rem* effect inherent in insolvency law, but only *in personam* effect[73] and allowed a *Mareva* injunction (freezing injunction) to continue so as to prevent any assets of the debtor being repatriated to the US to

---

65. E.g. see section 72 of the Argentine Bankruptcy Law, law No 24,522 as amended by law No 25,589, see *below* footnote 141.
66. The author is not aware of an incidence of foreign insolvency proceedings as such being restrained by way of injunctive relief.
67. *In Re Board of Directors of Multicanal S.A.*, United States Bankruptcy Court for the Southern District of New York 12 March 2004, Case No. 04–10280 (ALG), 307 B.R. 384, 386–387.
68. *In Re Yukos Oil Company*, United States Bankruptcy Court for the Southern District of Texas, Houston Division 24 February 2005, Case No. 04–47742–H3–11, 321 B.R. 396, 406. 28 U.S.C. § 1334(e) reads as follows: '*The district court in which a case under title 11 is commenced or is pending shall have exclusive jurisdiction of all of the property, wherever located, of the debtor as of the commencement of such case, and of property of the estate*'.
69. See *below* III.
70. See, *for example*, *In Re Board of Directors of Multicanal S.A.*, United States Bankruptcy Court for the Southern District of New York 12 March 2004, Case No. 04–10280 (ALG), 307 B.R. 384, 387.
71. See § 362 of the US Bankruptcy Code.
72. *Felixstowe Dock & Railway v. United States Lines Inc.*, High Court of England & Wales (Queen's Bench Division) 12 March 1987, [1989] 1 Q.B. 360, 370C.
73. Ibid. 375H.

the detriment of English creditors.[74] It considered the English forum to be appropriate for brining certain individual claims against the debtor.[75]

The *Felixstowe* case was seen as a low point of providing cooperation between insolvency courts in cases of cross-border insolvency proceedings.[76] The *Maxwell* litigation,[77] on the other hand, is an example of very close cooperation between the British and the US courts. On the matter discussed here, Barclays Bank was seeking an anti-suit injunction to restrain preference proceedings in the United States, where it believed such proceedings to be more difficult to resist. In *Barclays Bank plc v. Homan*, the English courts refused to issue an anti-suit injunction and considered the power of the US courts to dismiss preference proceedings on the basis of *foreign non-conveniens* sufficient and preferred not to disturb the cooperation with the US courts by an antagonizing anti-suit injunction.[78]

The danger of dissipation of assets subject to US Chapter 11 proceedings has been addressed in *In Re Yukos Oil Company, Yukos Oil Company v. Russian Federation et al.* The plaintiff was able to obtain a restraining order against the defendants (other than the Russian Federation) to participate in an auction that was to be held by the Russian Federation to execute alleged tax claims against Yukos.[79]

II.   APPLICABLE LAW

It is important to note that the question of jurisdiction to administer an ECDR goes beyond 'finding' an available court. Since ECDR procedures form part of insolvency law, the choice of a specific forum implies – to a large extent – the choice of the applicable law.

A.   LEX FORI CONCURSUS

In the *Maxwell* litigation, Barclays Bank was faced with a 'choice' of facing a preference claim under section 239 of the UK Insolvency Act 1986 or under § 547 of the US Bankruptcy Code. It considered the § 547 claim to be more difficult to defend and attempted – unsuccessfully – to enjoin the administrators to pursue

---

74. Ibid. 385 to 387.
75. Ibid. 389.
76. I.F. Fletcher, 'The Ascendence of Comity from the Ashes of Felixstowe Dock', (1993) 6(2) Insolvency Intelligence 10, 11; see also the criticism of Bankruptcy Judge *T.L. Brozman* in *In re Brierley*, United States Bankruptcy Court for the Southern District of New York 4 August 1992, Bankruptcy No. 92–B41453(TLB), 145 B.R. 151, 163.
77. See also *below* II A.
78. *Barclays Bank plc v. Homan and Others*, Court of Appeal of England & Wales 8 October 1992, Times Law Reports, 13 October 1992, 1, 2–3.
79. *In Re Yukos Oil Company, Yukos Oil Company v. Russian Federation et al.*, United States Bankruptcy Court for the Southern District of Texas (Houston Division) 16 December 2004, Case No. 04–47742–H3–11, Adv. No. 04–3952, 320 B.R. 130.

them.[80] By declining to issue an anti-suit injunction, the English court not only deferred to the US court to decide whether the latter should refuse jurisdiction over the claim on the basis of *forum non-conveniens*, but also, as Bankruptcy Judge *T.L. Brozman* noted in *In Re Brierley*, *'left to my discretion the decision whether or not to apply U.S. law to a transfer made to the creditor with a presence in New York but headquartered in England'*.[81]

It is generally accepted that the judicial or other authority assuming jurisdiction over the insolvent debtor applies its own insolvency laws as the *lex fori concursus*[82], the rationale being that insolvency law – despite its effect on substantive legal relationships – is procedural in character. A choice of insolvency laws is rarely available, with section 426 of the UK Insolvency Act 1986 providing a notable exception,[83] although being subject to the discretion of the court. Accordingly, at the present stage, since ECDRs are not universally available in all jurisdictions, only those companies that are subject to the jurisdiction of courts whose insolvency laws provide for ECDRs can avail themselves of this procedure. This in turn gives the question of the jurisdictional reach of courts in administering ECDRs a greater importance.[84]

The onset of insolvency proceedings generally marks a paradigm shift in the law otherwise applicable to the obligations of the debtor: while the law applicable to the obligations of the debtor is not altered, the 'insolvency effects' on such obligations are provided by the *lex fori concursus*. This problem is not specific to ECDRs, but rather a universal issue in insolvency law. ECDRs do, however, pose a significant problem if the procedure can be triggered at a point of time when ordinary insolvency proceedings would not yet be available. The APE, for example, may be filed by a *'debtor in default of payment or undergoing general economic or financial difficulties'*.[85] The width of that provision is understandable against the background of the Argentine economic crises and is evidence of a far-

---

80. See *above* I C.
81. *In re Brierley*, United States Bankruptcy Court for the Southern District of New York 4 August 1992, Bankruptcy No. 92–B41453(TLB), 145 B.R. 151, 164.
82. § 335 of the German Insolvency Code reads as follows: *'The insolvency procedure and its effects are governed by the laws of the state in which the procedure has been initiated, unless the contrary is expressly stipulated'* (Translation provided by the author).
83. Section 426(4) and (5) of the UK Insolvency Act 1986 read as follows: *'(4) The courts having jurisdiction in relation to insolvency law in any part of the United Kingdom shall assist the courts having the corresponding jurisdiction in any other part of the United Kingdom or any relevant country or territory. (5) For the purposes of subsection (4) a request made to a court in any part of the United Kingdom by a court in any other part of the United Kingdom or in a relevant country or territory is authority for the court to which the request is made to apply, in relation to any matters specified in the request, the insolvency law which is applicable by either court in relation to comparable matters falling within its jurisdiction. In exercising its discretion under this subsection, a court shall have regard in particular to the rules of private international law'*.
84. See *above* I.
85. Section 69 of the Argentine Bankruptcy Law; cited after Alberto Navarro, 'The Argentine APE as an out-of-court Restructuring Agreement', page 5, G. Breuer Law Firm (internal memorandum on file with the author).

reaching rescue culture. It shifts the paradigm change into an arena where it is not universally accepted and might meet with rejection at the recognition stage.

The question to what extent creditors' rights under New York law could be affected by the 'insolvency effects' of an APE was argued in *Multicanal I*[86] (although it did not address the afore-mentioned ECDR specific issue that could arise in an APE). On trial of the preliminary points the US bondholders contended that their US federal law rights under the trust indenture could not be overridden by the APE. They argued that the constitutional protection from impairment of contractual rights pursuant to state law[87] (which applies via the due process clause equally to federal law)[88] prevents recognition of the APE under § 304 Bankruptcy Code[89] purporting to override contractual entitlements. The court had recourse[90] to the following passage of *Canada Southern Railway Co v. Gebhard*:[91] '*[E]very person who deals with a foreign corporation impliedly subjects himself to such laws of the foreign government, affecting the powers and obligations of the corporation with which he voluntarily contracts, as the known and established policy of that government authorizes. To all intents and purposes, he submits his contract with the corporation to such a policy of the foreign government, and whatever is done by that government in furtherance of that policy which binds those in like situation with himself, who are subjects of the government, in respect to the operation and effect of their contracts with the corporation, will necessarily bind him*'. In that case a Canadian type of legislative 'scheme of arrangement' stood in question. Such a statute would have fallen foul of the express provision of the US Constitution were it a US law, but was nevertheless entitled to recognition, on the basis that it fell within the powers of the home jurisdiction of a corporation to enact laws that modify the obligations of a company, even if such obligations are governed by foreign (New York) law (such as the law of the court in which the foreign proceedings are recognized).

It is submitted that *Multicanal I* could have been distinguished from *Canada Southern Railway* on the facts in that the latter case emphasized[92] the strong public

---

86. *In Re Board of Directors of Multicanal S.A.*, United States Bankruptcy Court for the Southern District of New York 12 March 2004, Case No. 04–10280 (ALG), 307 B.R. 384, 386–387.
87. US Constitution, Article 1, Section 10, Clause 1 reads as follows: '*No State shall enter into any Treaty, Alliance, or Confederation; grant Letters of Marque and Reprisal; coin Money; emit Bills of Credit; make any Thing but gold and silver Coin a Tender in Payment of Debts; pass any Bill of Attainder, ex post facto Law, or Law impairing the Obligation of Contracts, or grant any Title of Nobility*' (emphasis in bold provided).
88. See the *Sinking-Fund Cases, United Pacific Railroad Company v. United States*, United States Supreme Court October Term 1878, 99 U.S. 700.
89. 11 U.S.C. § 304 – now repealed, see *below*.
90. *In Re Board of Directors of Multicanal S.A.*, United States Bankruptcy Court for the Southern District of New York 12 March 2004, Case No. 04–10280 (ALG), 307 B.R. 384; 2004 Bankr. LEXIS 308, 11–12.
91. *Canada Southern Railway Co v. Gebhard*, United States Supreme Court 10 December 1883, (1883) 109 US 527.
92. *In Re Board of Directors of Multicanal S.A., In Re Multicanal S.A.*, United States Bankruptcy Court for the Southern District of New York 27 August 2004, Case No. 04–10523 (ALG), 2004 Bankr. LEXIS 1356, 32.

interest (consideration of provincial transportation) involved in passing the purportedly offending Canadian act and in that in *Multicanal I* a court decision and not a foreign act of parliament stood in question. In *In Re Board of Directors of Multicanal S.A., In Re Multicanal S.A.* (*Multicanal II*) it was made clear that the choice of law exercised by private parties has its limitations: '*[i]n contracting with a foreign entity, a person subjects himself to those laws of the foreign government "affecting the powers and obligations of the corporation with which he voluntarily contracts"*'.[93]. *Cunard S.S. Co. v. Salen Reefer Services AB*, considered to be one of the leading cases in the recognition of foreign insolvency proceedings, emphasized the underlying reason for the need to recognize foreign insolvency proceedings, as such recognition '*enables the assets of a debtor to be dispersed in an equitable, orderly and systematic manner, rather than in a haphazard, erratic or piecemeal fashion*'.[94] *Cunard* also approved[95] of the following passage of the *Canada Southern Railway* case dealing specifically with reorganization proceedings: '*Unless all parties in interest, wherever they reside, can be bound by the arrangement which it is sought to have legalized the scheme may fail. All home creditors can be bound. What is needed is to bind those who are abroad. Under these circumstances the true spirit of international comity requires that schemes of this character, legalized at home, should be recognized in other countries*'.[96] An orderly reorganization is not possible in international insolvencies if insolvency effects are denied in countries other than the one administering the insolvency proceedings.

It has been identified as a potential problem that ECDRs might be triggered in the pre-insolvency arena where a consensus as to the application of insolvency regimes does not exist. The general policy considerations for recognition of foreign restructuring proceedings expressed in *Canada Southern Railway* do, of course, apply. It is particularly noteworthy that *In re Board of Directors of Telecom Argentina S.A.* held for the US perspective that a pre-insolvency APE is capable of recognition as much as the US Bankruptcy Code does not contain a requirement of formal insolvency.[97] It is also instructive to note that *Canada Southern Railway* refers in general terms to the expectations somebody is deemed to have when contracting with a foreign company. There is no specific mention of insolvency

---

93. *In Re Board of Directors of Multicanal S.A., In Re Multicanal S.A.*, Memorandum of Decision, 27 August 2004, available at <http://siteresources.worldbank.org/GILD/Resources/Multicanal-DecisionAug2004.pdf> (last visited 30 October 2005), 21.
94. *Cunard S.S. Co. v. Salen Reefer Services AB*, United States Court of Appeals (Second Circuit) 19 September 1985, No. 85–7365, 773 F.2d 452, 458 (2d Cir 1985). See also *In Re Koreag, Controle et Revision S.A.*, United States Court of Appeals (Second Circuit) 9 April 1992, No. 651, Docket 91–5061, 961 F.2d 341, 348: '*The purpose of a § 304 petition is to prevent the piecemeal distribution of assets in the United States by means of legal proceedings initiated in domestic courts by local creditors*'.
95. Ibid.
96. *Canada Southern Railway Co v. Gebhard*, United States Supreme Court 10 December 1883, (1883) 109 US 527, 539.
97. *In re Board of Directors of Telecom Argentina S.A.*, United States Bankruptcy Court for the Southern District of New York 24 February 2006, No. 05–17811 (BRL), Slip Copy, 2006 WL 686867 (Bankr.S.D.N.Y.), para. 100, 205–206.

laws in the relevant passage, but only a general reference to such person subjecting himself to the effects of the laws of the state of incorporation of that foreign entity. This might suggest that deference is owed to the 'home jurisdiction' of a company even outside the scope of strict insolvency cases, advocating deference also to foreign ECDR legislation operating at the pre-insolvency stage. To the extent that this proposition is accepted the conflicting perceptions as to which jurisdiction is to be considered the proper 'home jurisdiction' will gain additional importance.

B. CHOICE OF FORUM – CHOICE OF LAW?

The effect of the applicability of the *lex fori concursus* principle and the unavailability of ECDR procedures in some countries increases the incentive to 'forum shop' in order to obtain access to ECDR proceedings, as is evidenced by the general concern about forum shopping expressed in the preamble to the EU Insolvency Regulation[98]. The ability to influence the applicable law by choosing an adequate forum is well demonstrated by the cases of *Barclays Bank plc v. Homan* and *In Re Brierley*.[99] It has been noted that the creditors of Multicanal argued in *Multicanal I*, after having abandoned the argument that their rights under the TIA[100] could not be compromised by bankruptcy laws, that Multicanal could and should have subjected itself to Chapter 11 proceedings, as only US bankruptcy law could compromise their TIA rights (an argument that equally failed in front of the court).[101] This is yet another example for the ability to choose between different fora for the conduct of ECDRs, and also for the diverging motivations and interests of the debtor and the creditors in choosing one or the other forum.

The opportunity for forum shopping in cases of reorganization proceedings is more limited than in liquidation proceedings, as jurisdiction for reorganization proceedings is more rarely based on assets within the jurisdiction (with the notable exception of the US), but rather on a test allocating the corporate presence to a single country. More traditional, formulaic tests, such as the place of incorporation might today seem ill-suited for a highly interconnected, globalized of business world, but provided more certainty, as they are harder to manipulate.

Nevertheless, differences in jurisdictional tests still leave scope for reorganizing companies under different laws as is well evidenced by in *In Re Harrods (Buenos Aires) Ltd.*[102] The current trend for establishing the general presence of a company is towards more factual tests, such as the 'centre of main interests' (*COMI*) in

---

97. Preamble (4) of the EU Insolvency Regulation reads as follows: '*It is necessary for the proper functioning of the internal market to avoid incentives for the parties to transfer assets or judicial proceedings from one Member State to another, seeking to obtain a more favourable legal position (forum shopping)*'.
98. See *above* I. C. and II. A.
99. 15 U.S.C. § 77aaa et seq.
101. *In Re Board of Directors of Multicanal S.A.*, United States Bankruptcy Court for the Southern District of New York 12 March 2004, Case No. 04–10280 (ALG), 307 B.R. 384, 392.
102. See *above* I. C.

the EU Insolvency Regulation,[103] the Model Law[104] and Chapter 15 of the US Bankruptcy Code (implementing the Model Law).[105] The COMI test is better capable of addressing the interrelationship between a company's activities within its host society and the policies of the host country as expressed in its insolvency laws. The COMI test does, however, compared with the test of place of incorporation, lead to increased uncertainty: even where courts apply the same test, they might reach at different conclusions as to where the COMI is located. This has happened in the *Parmalat* litigation, which has been referred to the ECJ in the case of *Eurofood IFCS Limited*.[106] It should also be noted that within the EU the ability to forum shop in insolvency matters by moving the COMI has been curtailed by *Susanne Staubitz-Schreiber*, whereby the COMI has to be determined by reference to the facts at the time of the opening of the insolvency proceedings.[107]

The situation is further complicated by several developments in company law and private international law affecting companies in Europe. Developments in company law especially in the European Union allow companies to 'migrate' their seat between jurisdictions and thereby between applicable insolvency laws. It should be noted that seat and COMI are not identical, but frequently coincide. The cases of *Centros*,[108] *Überseering*[109], and *Inspire Art*[110] have established that companies established under the law of one EU Member State may move there centre of activity (their 'seat') to another Member State without the need for re-incorporation. Thereby, an increasing number of English private companies limited by shares (often referred to as 'Limiteds') are being used in other EU Member States having corporate activities exclusively outside their country of incorporation.[111] Under the COMI test of the EU Insolvency Regulation they thereby come under the insolvency jurisdiction of the host jurisdiction. Further,

---

103. Article 3(1) of the EU Insolvency Regulation.
104. Article 2(b) of the Model Law.
105. § 1502(4) of the US Bankruptcy Code.
106. *Eurofood IFCS Limited*, European Court of Justice 2 May 2006, Case C–341/04, Official Journal of the European Union OJ C 143, 17 June 2006, 11, full text of judgment available at <http://www.curia.europa.eu/en/content/juris/index_form.htm>.
107. *Susanne Staubitz-Schreiber*, European Court of Justice 17 January 2006, Case C–1/04, full text of judgment available at <http://www.curia.europe.eu/en/content/juris/index_form.htm>.
108. *Centros Ltd v. Erhvervs- og Selskabsstyrelsen*, European Court of Justice 9 March 1999, Case C–212/97, European Court Reports 1999, I–1459.
109. *Überseering BV v. Nordic Construction Company Baumanagement GmbH (NCC)*, European Court of Justice 5 November 2002, Case C–208/00, European Court Reports 2002, I–9919, also available at <http://www.curia.europa.eu/en/content/juris/index_form.htm>.
110. *Kamer van Koophandel en Fabrieken voor Amsterdam v. Inspire Art Ltd*, European Court of Justice 30 September 2003, Case C–167/01, European Court Reports 2003 I–10155.
111. From the voluminous literature on the question of the applicable law see, for example, D.G. Lawlor, 'Die Anwendbarkeit englischen Gesellschaftsrechts bei Insolvenz einer englischen Limited in Deutschland' (2005) 8 Neue Zeitschrift für für das Recht der Insolvenz und Sanierung 432; T. Kuntz, 'Die Insolvenz der Limited mit deutschem Verwaltungssitz – EU-Kapitalgesellschaften in Deutschland nach 'Inspire Art'' (2005) 8 Neue Zeitschrift für das Recht der Insolvenz und Sanierung 424; J. Walterscheid, 'Die englische Limited im Insolvenzverfahren' (2006) 16 Deutsche Zeitschrift für Wirtschafts- und Insolvenzrecht 95.

case law such as the *SEVIC Systems* judgment of the European Court of Justice[112] and legislative developments such as the Tenth Company Law Directive promote statutory mergers across borders,[113] which might trigger cross-boundary relocations of the COMI.

It has been argued that the extension of ECDRs into the pre-insolvency arena is acceptable under the rationale of *Canada Southern Railway*[114] as the applicable insolvency regime, even if more extensive than others, should be determinable from the outset. The company law developments addressed *above* call the rationale of *Canada Southern Railway* into question and thereby threaten to invalidate the argument made in favour of recognition of ECDRs, in that the applicable insolvency law is less ascertainable and less invariable. This can be of considerable practical importance. It is likely that these questions will become a matter for lender legal due diligence and appropriate undertakings were lending is envisaged to a debtor who is or might become subject to the jurisdiction of a court that administers ECDRs.

III. RECOGNITION OF FOREIGN ECDR

During the negotiation of an ECDR, the debtor is exposed to creditor action. It does not have the protection available that is normally part of full insolvency proceedings, such as a moratorium which is only available – in some cases – as of the presentation for homologation. Equally, only once the debtor applies to court, does the ECDR enter a formal proceeding that is capable of recognition and enforcement in foreign courts.

A. MULTICANAL

The question of recognition of an APE was central to the case of *Multicanal I* and *Multicanal II*[115]. The case was dealt with under the then § 304 of the US Bankruptcy Code[116], which has been repealed by the US Bankruptcy Abuse Prevention and Consumer Protection Act of 2005, which introduced a new Chapter 15 into the

---

112. *SEVIC Systems AG*, European Court of Justice 13 December 2005, Case C–411/03, Official Journal of the European Union OJ C 36, 11 February 2006, 5, full text of judgment available at <http://www.curia.europa.eu/en/content/juris/index.htm>.
113. See *further* E.-M. Kieninger, 'Grenzüberschreitende Verschmelzungen in der EU – das SEVIC-Urteil des EuGH' (2006) 17 Europäisches Wirtschafts und Steuerrecht 49; M. Frischhut, 'Grenzüberschreitende Verschmelzungen von Kapitalgesellschaften – ein Überblick über die Zehnte gesellschaftsrechtliche Richtlinie' (2006) 17 Europäisches Wirtschafts- und Steuerrecht 55.
114. See *above* II A.
115. See *above* I C, II A and II B.
116. § 304 of the US Bankruptcy Code read as follows: '*§ 304. Cases ancillary to foreign proceedings. (a) A case ancillary to foreign proceedings is commenced by the filing with the bankruptcy court of a petition under this section by a foreign representative. (b) Subject to the provisions of subsection (c) of this section, if a party in interest does not timely controvert the petition, or after trial, the court may— (1) enjoin the commencement of continuation of (A) any*

US Bankruptcy Code dealing with '*Ancillary and other Cross-border Cases*' with effect from 17 October 2005. *Multicanal* still merits detailed analysis in the present context, though a re-evaluation under the new Chapter 15 will be required.[117]

Multicanal II raised – to the extent relevant for the present purposes – the following questions of law: (1) whether Multicanal's board of directors qualify as '*foreign representative*', (2) whether the APE qualifies as a '*foreign proceeding*', and (3) whether on balance the factors in § 304(c) weigh in favour of recognition. As regards the first issue, it was argued that the board of directors of Multicanal did not qualify as '*trustee*' or other independent fiduciary under the definition of '*foreign representative*'.[118] The Bankruptcy Court, inspired by the similarity of the Argentine and the US position, held that '*[a] board of directors may be an appropriate representative in a § 304 case [. . .] if it plays a role similar to that of a debtor-in-possession under the U.S. Bankruptcy Code, where management remains in control of the reorganizing debtor and an independent trustee is not ordinarily appointed*'.[119] This conclusion was helped by *In re Board of Directors of Hopewell International Ins. Ltd.* according to which the relevant test is whether the relevant person is charged with the obligation of carrying out the provisions of the foreign proceeding;[120] the question was answered in the affirmative, as the directors took the initiative to propose the scheme of arrangement, decided to file those proceedings and proposed that they would implement the reorganization plan if approved. Regarding the second issue, the court held that Multicanal's APE clearly comes within the very broad definition of '*foreign proceedings*' in § 101(23) of the US Bankruptcy Code as it then was.[121]

---

     action against (i) a debtor with respect to property involved in such foreign proceeding; or (ii) such property; or (B) the enforcement of any judgment against the debtor with respect to such property, or any act or the commencement or continuation of any judicial proceeding to create or enforce a lien against the property of such estate; (2) order turnover of the property of such estate, or the proceeds of such property, to such foreign representative; or (3) order other appropriate relief. (c) In determining whether to grant relief under subsection (b) of this section, the court shall be guided by what will best assure an economical and expeditious administration of such estate, consistent with— (1) just treatment of all holders of claims against or interests in such estate; (2) protection of claim holders in the United Sates against prejudice and inconvenience in the processing of claims in such foreign proceedings; (3) prevention of preferential or fraudulent dispositions of property of such estate; (4) distribution of proceeds of such estate substantially in accordance with the order prescribed by this title; (5) comity; and (6) if appropriate, the provision of an opportunity for a fresh start for the individual that such foreign proceeding concerns'.

117. See *below* III B.
118. At the time, § 101(24) of the US Bankruptcy Code read as follows: ''*foreign representative*' *means duly selected trustee, administrator, or other representative of an estate in a foreign proceeding*'.
119. *In Re Board of Directors of Multicanal S.A., In Re Multicanal S.A.*, United States Bankruptcy Court for the Southern District of New York 27 August 2004, Case No. 04–10523 (ALG), 2004 Bankr. LEXIS 1356, 34.
120. *In re Board of Directors of Hopewell International Ins. Ltd.*, United States Bankruptcy Court for the Southern District of New York 19 August 1999, Bankruptcy No. 98 B 45440(TLB), 238 BR 53–54.
121. § 101(23) of the US Bankruptcy Code read as follows: ''*foreign proceeding*' *means proceeding, whether judicial or administrative and whether or not under bankruptcy law, in a foreign country*

The question whether the weighing of the factors under § 304(c) militated in favour of recognition was used by the creditors to challenge Multicanal's APE on various grounds. One of the creditors contended that *'the APE is a form of private insolvency regime not subject to adequate judicial control and not entitled to recognition under the general standards of § 304(c)'*.[122] The court maintained, however, that not the APE per se, but only its application to Multicanal is subject of the investigation[123]. In *Multicanal I* it was held that § 304 *'does not require that the foreign proceeding be identical to the U.S. proceeding [...]'*[124] and *Multicanal II* held that, in particular, the foreign proceeding does not need to satisfy the requirements under § 1129 of the US Bankruptcy Code for the confirmation of a US chapter 11 proceeding (though some of the factors such as good faith would be taken into account in the evaluation of the factors under § 304(c)).[125] Despite maintaining the position that the foreign proceeding needs to be evaluated on a stand-alone basis, the judge took great comfort in the procedural similarity between the APE and the US chapter 11 pre-pack. This allowed him to deal with most of the objections of the creditors, providing the judge with a familiar benchmark for the evaluation of the factors in § 304(c). While the judge appears to contradict himself on this point, it is not suggested to criticize him for doing so. To the contrary, for the further discussion it should be noted that recognition of an ECDR might be more likely in a jurisdiction that is familiar with its structure due to having similar proceedings.

B.   RECOGNITION OF FOREIGN ECDRs IN A MODEL LAW COUNTRY

It is doubtful whether US courts, which to-date provided with *Multicanal* a key case on recognition of foreign ECDRs, would be able to decide this case similarly after the new Chapter 15 of the US Bankruptcy Code came into effect. The scheme of Chapter 15 allows a *'foreign representative'* to apply for recognition of a *'foreign proceeding'*.[126] Such recognition (as either main or non-main proceeding)[127] is, provided certain formalities are fulfilled, automatic unless the public policy

---

        in which the debtor's domicile, residence, principal place of business, or principal assets were located at the commencement of such proceeding, for the purpose of liquidating an estate, adjusting debts by composition, extension or discharge, or effecting a reorganization'.

122. *In Re Board of Directors of Multicanal S.A., In Re Multicanal S.A.*, United States Bankruptcy Court for the Southern District of New York 27 August 2004, Case No. 04–10523 (ALG), 2004 Bankr. LEXIS 1356, 40.
123. Ibid. 42.
124. *In Re Board of Directors of Multicanal S.A.*, United States Bankruptcy Court for the Southern District of New York 12 March 2004, Case No. 04–10280 (ALG), 307 B.R. 384, 391.
125. *In Re Board of Directors of Multicanal S.A., In Re Multicanal S.A.*, United States Bankruptcy Court for the Southern District of New York 27 August 2004, Case No. 04–10523 (ALG), 2004 Bankr. LEXIS 1356, 42.
126. See § 1515 of the US Bankruptcy Code.
127. See § 1517(2) of the US Bankruptcy Code.

exception applies.[128] The wide discretion and balancing of various factors under § 304 of the Bankruptcy Code (as it was) no longer applies. The difficulties arising for foreign ECDRs are primarily due to the modifications of the definitions of *'foreign proceeding'* and *'foreign representative'* deriving from the implementation of the Model Law.

The Guide to Enactment of the UNCITRAL Model Law on Cross-Border Insolvency (the 'Guide to Enactment') does not provide much clarity on the pertinent points as it states, on the one hand, that the requirements of the definitions are meant to narrow the scope of application of the Model Law,[129] and, on the other hand, it explains that the terminology is meant to be descriptive from a functional perspective rather than using technical meanings, as this might lead to too narrow a reading of the provision.[130] The question of ECDRs is not expressly addressed in the Guide to Enactment.

1. Foreign Proceeding

The definitions for Chapter 15 of the US Bankruptcy Code now closely mirror the provisions of the Model Law[131] (similar issues arise under the UK Cross-Border Insolvency Regulation 2007).[132] For a better understanding recourse should be had to the case law under the pre-Chapter 15 definitions.[133] Case law under the previous definition of 'foreign proceeding' has shown a liberal, although not boundless, attitude towards foreign insolvency proceedings.

According to *In re Board of Directors of Hopewell International Ins. Ltd* it is essential to analyze the level of involvement of the foreign court and the degree to which creditors can have access to the courts. The case concerned a Bermudan

---

128. See § 1506 of the US Bankruptcy Code.
129. Para. 68 of the Guide to Enactment.
130. Para. 71 of the Guide to Enactment.
131. Article 2 of the Model Law defines 'foreign proceeding' and 'foreign representative' as follows: *'(a) 'Foreign proceeding' means a collective judicial or administrative proceeding in a foreign State, including an interim proceeding, pursuant to a law relating to insolvency in which proceeding the assets and affairs of the debtor are subject to control or supervision by a foreign court, for the purpose of reorganization or liquidation; [. . .] (d) 'Foreign representative' means a person or body, including one appointed on an interim basis, authorized in a foreign proceeding to administer the reorganization or the liquidation of the debtor's assets or affairs or to act as a representative of the foreign proceeding '.*
132. Article 2(i) of the schedule of The Cross-Border Insolvency Regulations 2006 (Statutory Instrument 2006 No. 1030) reads as follows: *'(i) 'foreign proceeding' means a collective judicial or administrative proceeding in a foreign State, including an interim proceeding, pursuant to a law relating to insolvency in which proceeding the assets and affairs of the debtor are subject to control or supervision by a foreign court, for the purpose of reorganization or liquidation; (j) 'foreign representative' means a person, including one appointed on an interim basis, authorized in a foreign proceeding to administer the reorganization or the liquidation of the debtor's assets or affairs or to act as a representative of the foreign proceeding'.* The Cross-Border Insolvency Regulations 2006 implement the UNCITRAL Model Law in the UK under section 14 of the Insolvency Act 2000.
133. See III A.

scheme of arrangement that had already closed. The court held that this was no obstacle to recognition, as the courts remained available to the creditors.[134] It also considered the level of court involvement in the course of approving and sanctioning the scheme to suffice, as there were court appearances to authorize the calling of the creditors' and members' meeting and to sanction the scheme and that the members had these two and other opportunities to seek redress in the court against the scheme and against its implementation. It analogized the scheme with a US Chapter 11 pre-pack and considered that the Bermudan scheme provided an even higher level of judicial involvement and access to the courts.[135] *Hopewell* built on *In Re Ward*, where the judicial involvement and oversight over the actions of the company-selected liquidator in a Zambian creditors' voluntary winding-up was examined in detail and where sufficient opportunities for aggrieved creditors were found to exist and a sufficient level of court control was considered to be exercised and accessibility of the court given.[136] The Zambian proceedings, accordingly, were considered to be '*foreign proceedings*' under the US Bankruptcy Code. *In Re Ward* itself distinguished the earlier case of *In Re Tam*, concerning a Cayman Islands creditors' voluntary winding-up where no court supervision existed and no access to the courts was provided, and in which case the Cayman Islands proceedings were considered not to be '*foreign proceedings*'.[137]

The ease with which *Multicanal* accepted the APE to constitute a '*foreign proceeding*' within the meaning of the Bankruptcy Code is testimony to the flexible attitude of the US case law. *Multicanal* also recurred onto *In Re Netia Holdings S.A.* in which a Polish administration procedure was considered to constitute a '*foreign proceeding*' even in the initial stages between filing an application to the court and the actual opening of the administration procedure, although the automatic stay of individual creditor action and appointment of a court supervisor would not come into effect until the actual opening.[138] The intermittent period provided for a sufficient level of court involvement through the granting of interim relief, the taking of evidence and the dealing with objections.[139] *In Re Netia Holding* distinguished[140] *In Re Master Home Furniture Co.* in which Taiwanese reorganization proceedings were not considered to be '*foreign proceedings*' since a

---

134. *In re Board of Directors of Hopewell International Ins. Ltd.*, United States Bankruptcy Court for the Southern District of New York, 19 August 1999, Bankruptcy No. 98 B 45440(TLB), 238 BR 49.
135. Ibid. 52.
136. *In Re Ward*, United States Bankruptcy Court for the Southern District of New York 3 October 1996 (corrected 10 October 1996), Bankruptcy No. 96 B 44240 (JLG), 201 B.R. 357, 359–360, 362.
137. *In re Tam*, United States Bankruptcy Court for the Southern District of New York 22 August 1994, Bankruptcy No. 94 B 40991 (JLG), 170 B.R. 838, 844.
138. *In Re Netia Holdings S.A.*, United States Bankruptcy Court for the Southern District of New York 29 April 2002, No. 02–10744 (REG), 277 B.R. 571, 576–577.
139. Ibid. 582.
140. Ibid. 583.

stay of proceedings applied in a prolonged period between filing and opening of proceedings, during which funds could be dispersed and the Taiwanese court did not exercise any supervision or oversight.[141] *In Re Master Homes* was, of course, decided in another district and is therefore not binding precedent on the Bankruptcy Court of the Southern District of New York, which could hold that '*[t]he cases in this district have never disqualified a proceeding from section 304(a) status based on the lack of an automatic stay, or because the foreign court would not supervise or administer the business operation of the company. Section 304(a) makes no mention of those as requirements; under those circumstances, this Court believes it to be inappropriate to judicially craft such requirements now*'.[142]

The implementation of the Model Law has now created the second such requirement, in that only those proceedings qualify as a '*foreign proceeding*' in which '*assets and affairs of the debtor are subject to control or supervision by a foreign court*'.[143] It has been doubted whether CVAs and schemes of arrangements – which could both be used as English pre-arranged ECDRs – would still qualify as '*foreign proceedings*'.[144] The US courts do, however, appear to continue to take a liberal approach, in that they have already recognized an English scheme of arrangement[145] an approach which can be supported on the existing case law.[146]

The Guide to Enactment indicates that it is intended that debtor-in-possession proceedings should come within the definition of '*foreign proceedings*', as long as a level court supervision (such as suspension of payments) is maintained.[147] ECDRs are typically debtor-in-possession proceedings, which raises the question whether there is sufficient judicial supervision. The problem is aggravated by the fact that the court is not involved at the initial stage of negotiation of a reorganization plan between debtor and creditors, but only for a limited period between filing of the plan and sanctioning. '*Foreign proceedings*' cannot exist prior to the point of filing, as there is no judicial or other authority involved.

---

141. *In Re Master Home Furniture Co.*, United States Bankruptcy Court for the Central District of California 24 April 2001, No. RS 01–10638 MJ, 261 B.R. 671, 676–677.
142. *In Re Netia Holdings S.A.*, United States Bankruptcy Court for the Southern District of New York 29 April 2002, No. 02–10744 (REG), 277 B.R. 571, 586.
143. § 101(23) of the US Bankruptcy Code reads in its version amended by the Bankruptcy Abuse Prevention and Consumer Protection Act 2005 as follows: '*The term 'foreign proceeding' means a collective judicial or administrative proceeding in a foreign country, including an interim proceeding, under a law relating to insolvency or adjustment of debt in which proceeding the assets and affairs of the debtor are subject to control or supervision by a foreign court, for the purpose of reorganization or liquidation*'.
144. B. Bell and B. Ziegler, 'Chapter 15 of the US Bankruptcy Code: Some Observations from a UK perspective', (2005) 2 International Corporate Rescue 216, 217.
145. In *Re United Kingdom Marine Insurance Account known as the MMA Account*, United States Bankruptcy Court for the Southern District of New York 7 December 2005, Case No. 05–60100 (BRL), Slip Copy, 2005 WL 3764946 (Bkrtcy.S.D.N.Y., 2005).
146. For more detail see G. Arends, 'Chapter 15 of the US Bankruptcy Code: Better than its Reputation?', International Corporate Rescue, Volume 3, Issue 4, 2006, 240–244.
147. Para. 24 of the Guide to Enactment.

If the APE is used as an example, it is at least doubtful whether *'foreign proceedings'* can be presumed to exist after filing for homologation. The filing creates a stay of proceedings against the debtor (moratorium)[148] pending the decision on homologation. The assets of the debtor are, however, not attached; the debtor can continue to make payments and there is no court supervision of its assets or affairs. On the basis of the previous case law, a similarity with *In Re Tam* and *In Re Master Homes* cannot be denied. Creditors can, however, seek to challenge the APE in the approval phase and can challenge any action of the directors that is not in accordance with the approved plan, which would appear analogous with the period between filing and opening of the arrangement procedure in *In Re Netia* (where, of course, the opening of the arrangement procedure marked the beginning of a heavier involvement of the court) and *In Re Hopewell* where the court remained available to the creditors for challenges to debtor's action after the scheme was closed (i.e. during the implementation phase). The author is of the opinion that, while the scales are finely balanced, there with some likelihood that the US courts would consider the APE to constitute *'foreign proceedings'* under the amended definition.

The Model Law's restrictive definition of *'foreign proceedings'* can be attributed to the fact that it provides for automatic recognition (subject only to a public policy exception) and therefore requires a higher level of trust in (and appearance of) fairness and impartiality of the supervision of any foreign proceeding. Indeed, the perception of retail creditors in Argentina is that APEs are often abused by the debtor. This dovetails to an extent with the criticism levied by the minority opinion of *Harlan J.* in *Canada Southern Railways*: He argued that the Canadian scheme of arrangement could not be recognized in the United States, since the creditors did not *'have their day in court'*,[149] as it was a parliament-sanctioned scheme of arrangement. While ECDRs are, of course, sanctioned/homologated by courts, there is a difference between ex post confirmation of fairness and ex ante involvement in the drawing-up of the restructuring plan. If the court is involved throughout, it and minority creditors can influence the 'agenda' for any restructuring and the macrostructure of any proposal, rather than examining whether the resulting structure is unfair. There is also a distinction to be drawn between refusing approval of an unfair proposal and supervising of a fair proposal.

2. Foreign Representative

Slightly less problematic is the question whether the directors of a company undergoing an ECDR can be considered to be *'foreign representatives'* under its new

---

148. Section 72 of the Argentine Bankruptcy Law reads as follows: *'Section 72. Homologation requirements. [...] Effects of the presentation. As from the time the application for homologation of the out-of court composition has been filed, all legal action against debtor, of a financial nature, are suspended in accordance with the terms set in Section 21, points 2 and 3. [sic]'* (an English translation is on file with the author)
149. *Canada Southern Railway Co v. Gebhard*, United States Supreme Court 10 December 1883, (1883) 109 US 527, 543–544.

definition.[150] The definition hinges, first, upon an understanding of *'foreign proceeding'* and, secondly, requires that the person be *'authorized [...] to administer the reorganization or the liquidation of the debtor's assets or affairs'*. In respect of the previous definition, *In Re Board of Directors of Hopewell International Ins. Ltd.* held that the wording of the relevant definition was wide and that *'absolutely nothing in the statute requires the foreign representative to be appointed by a court'*.[151] While not as unproblematic, it is submitted that there is no obstacle in the foreign court appointing a person as a 'foreign representative' for the purposes of the ECDR who is also otherwise authorized to act for the company. *In Re Kingscroft Insurance Company Ltd.* held that while normally *'foreign representatives'* would be court appointed provisional liquidators and administrators, there is no obstacle to recognize as a *'foreign representative'* a director retaining his authority in an English or Bermudan voluntary winding-up. The case expressly pointed out the similarity to a US debtor-in-possession proceeding.[152] Given that ECDRs are typically debtor-in-possession restructurings, this will be the most sensible course of conduct. It will be recalled that in *In Re Ward* the court considered that Zambian court's approval of dealings of the company-selected liquidator to constitute an approval of that liquidator, although there was no express appointment by the court.[153] Similarly, the approval by a court of an ECDR plan implicitly assumes that the directors of the company would effect the implementation and should be seen as sufficient authorization for the purposes of the definition of *'foreign representative'*. It is therefore submitted, that – as long as the precondition of a foreign proceeding can be met (as this is one of the criteria for a foreign representative) – it will not constitute an insurmountable obstacle to recognition of foreign ECDRs that the directors applying to court and giving effect to the reorganization plan have not been appointed by a court.

If Chapter 15 were to preclude the recognition of foreign ECDRs, South American companies having raised substantial amounts of capital on the US capital markets will be negatively affected. Directors would face a choice between conducting an ECDR in their home jurisdiction, risking that such proceeding will not bind US creditors, and filing a pre-packaged Chapter 11 proceeding in the US based on assets within that jurisdiction, but always risking that a Chapter 11 plan will not be recognized in other countries (including the home

---

150. § 101 (24) of the US Bankruptcy Code reads in its version amended by the Bankruptcy Abuse Prevention and Consumer Protection Act 2005 as follows: *'The term 'foreign representative' means a person or body, including a person or body appointed on an interim basis, authorized in a foreign proceeding to administer the reorganization or the liquidation of the debtor's assets or affairs or to act as a representative of such foreign proceeding'*.
151. *In Re Board of Directors of Hopewell International Ins. Ltd.*, United States Bankruptcy Court for the Southern District of New York, 19 August 1999, Bankruptcy No. 98 B 45440 (TLB), 238 BR 53.
152. *In Re Kingscroft Insurance Company Ltd.*, United States Bankruptcy Court for the Southern District of Florida 30 January 1992, No. 91–22065–BKC-AJC, 138 B.R. 121, 124.
153. *In Re Ward*, United States Bankruptcy Court for the Southern District of New York 3 October 1996 (corrected 10 October 1996), Bankruptcy No. 96 B 44240 (JLG), 201 B.R. 357, 360–361.

jurisdiction of the debtor) for reason of being based on an unacceptable base of jurisdiction. It is hoped that this adverse position will be avoided by a sufficiently liberal interpretation of the requirements of *'foreign proceeding'* and *'foreign representative'*. It should be kept in mind that individual proceedings that prove to be unfair on specific creditors can always be challenged under the public policy exception.

C. RECOGNITION OF FOREIGN ECDRS IN A CIVIL LAW COUNTRY

Civil law countries follow in many instances a recognition regime[154] that allows for automatic recognition if certain threshold criteria are met and the public policy (*ordre public*) of the recognizing jurisdiction is not violated. By way of example, pursuant to the German Insolvency Code (which applies in respect of ECDRs originating in non-EU countries), recognition of a foreign ECDR will have to meet three requirements: (1) the ECDR must be classifiable as insolvency proceeding; (2) the foreign court must have had jurisdiction; and (3) the German procedural *ordre public* must not be violated.[155]

Whether the ECDR in question is considered to constitute an insolvency proceeding has to be determined by way of qualification of the foreign proceedings. If they regulate the consequences of the insufficiency of the debtor's assets in a situation where there is no reasonable prospect that the debtor will meet its obligations and the foreign proceedings thereby react to the financial melt-down of the debtor they are to be classified as insolvency proceedings.[156] A foreign ECDR would not be able to meet this requirement to the extent it is used in a situation where the debtor only faces general economic or financial difficulties, as might be the case under an APE. Some writers want to have recourse to the criteria of the EU Insolvency Regulation, the Brussels Regulation and the Model Law and its Guide to Enactment "determining whether *the solvency proceedings*" are given.[157] The EU Insolvency Regulation requires that proceedings be collective,

---

154. The analysis of the recognition regime shall be restricted to an exemplary analysis of the 'autonomous' regimes applicable in the EU Member States in the case of recognition of non-EU insolvency proceedings. A civil law country within the EU might need to have recourse to the EU Insolvency Regulation if an ECDR originating within the EU had to be recognized.
155. § 343 of the German Insolvency Code provides: *'(1) The opening of foreign insolvency proceedings is to be recognized. This does not apply to 1. the courts of the state of the opening of the insolvency proceedings would not have had jurisdiction under German law; 2. the extent that the recognition would lead to results obviously incompatible with fundamental principles of German law, and in particular to the extent that the results are incompatible with fundamental rights. (2) Paragraph 1 equally applies to the recognition of protective measures that have been made after the application for the opening of insolvency proceedings, as well as for decisions required for the conduct or the conclusion of recognized insolvency proceedings'* (Translation provided by the author).
156. D. Eickmann et al. (ed.), *Insolvenzordnung*, (C.F. Müller, Heidelberg, 2004), I InsO § 343, 6 (commentary by G. Stephan).
157. S. Smid, *Deutsches und Europäisches Internationales Insolvenzrecht* (W. Kohlhammer GmbH, Stuttgart, 2004) § 343 InsO, 5 (commentary by S. Smid).

entail the divestment of the debtor of its assets and the appointment of a liquidator[158] (which term includes administrators).[158, 159] On this test the APE would fail as it does not provide for the divestment of the debtor which would otherwise protect the creditors. It is therefore likely that the criterion of '*insolvency proceeding*' will, if cases arise, restrict the range of ECDRs capable of recognition.

The second requirement for recognition of an ECDR under German law is that the foreign court had international competence in insolvency matters, which the recognizing German court will assess using the German rules on international jurisdiction in insolvency matters (the mirror principle).[161] The German autonomous rules on international jurisdiction in insolvency matters follow the rules on local jurisdiction (venue) (the principle of double functionality).[162] From a German law perspective, the international jurisdiction over companies having an economic activity is exclusively exercised at the centre of independent economic activity.[163] It will be noted that the autonomous German rules on international jurisdiction in insolvency matters do not accept jurisdiction based on assets within the jurisdiction. It follows that an ECDR which is founded on asset-based jurisdiction would not be capable of recognition. If the introduction of Chapter 15 of the US Bankruptcy Code were to force Latin American companies to file pre-packaged Chapter 11 proceedings based on assets within the US rather than their local ECDR proceedings, these proceedings would not be recognizable in countries such as Germany.

Finally, the *ordre public* reservation might be raised if the recognition of the foreign ECDR were to obviously violate fundamental principles of German law and the understanding of justice embedded within it. Such unacceptability might derive from the substantive order made or the procedure by which the foreign court arrived at its conclusion. In either case, however, it is essential that the foreign ECDR procedure is not examined in abstract, but that the recognition of a specific ECDR would have to violate such fundamental notions of German law.[164] It is also essential that a sufficient connection to Germany (such as presence of creditors)

---

158. The importance of a court-appointed liquidator or supervisor was stressed also in a case concerning the determination of the 'insolvency exception' from the scope of Article 1(2) of the Brussels Convention (now Article 1(2)(b) of the Brussels Regulation), see *Henri Gourdain v. Franz Nadler*, European Court of Justice 22 February 1979, Case 133/78, European Court Reports 1979, 733, para. 4.
159. Article 2(b) of the EU Insolvency Regulation.
160. Article 1(1) of the EU Insolvency Regulation.
161. D. Eickmann et al. (ed.), *Insolvenzordnung*, (C.F. Müller, Heidelberg, 2004), I InsO § 343, 8 (commentary by G. Stephan).
162. D. Eickmann et al. (ed.), *Insolvenzordnung*, (C.F. Müller, Heidelberg, 2004), I InsO § 343, 6 (commentary by G. Stephan).
163. § 3 I 2 of the German Insolvency Code; if the company does conduct any economic activity, international jurisdiction over insolvency matters follows the place of general jurisdiction, which refers to the seat of the company (which in turn is presumed to be at the centre of its administration), see § 3 II 1 of the German Insolvency Code in connection with § 17 I 1 and 2 of the German Civil Procedure Code.
164. D. Eickmann et al. (ed.), *Insolvenzordnung*, (C.F. Müller, Heidelberg, 2004), I InsO § 343, 11 (commentary by G. Stephan).

exists to justify the operation of the reservation.[165] A particular important aspect are the fundamental rights (human rights) and in particular the right of access to the courts and the right to be heard.[166] The right to be heard has been considered violated if decisions have been made without an affected person being heard at all. It is also a violation of fundamental rights if an affected person has no opportunity to actively influence the proceedings.[167] Against this backdrop ECDRs might cause difficulties where the debtor tries to agree a reorganization plan with the majority creditors only without active and sincere engagement with the minority creditors. The subsequent approval process in the court approving the ECDR might not be sufficient to provide the minority creditors with their '*day in court*' (to use the language of the *Canada Southern Railways* case). The subsequent sanctioning of an ECDR does not allow the minority creditors to actively influence the content of the reorganization plan, but only assesses its fairness. When this issue is revisited in the recognizing German court, the court might be convinced that the lack of ability to influence the reorganization plan should be considered to violate the German *ordre public* when recognizing the effects of the ECDR decision. The answer to this question cannot be found in abstract and it would be hoped that the directors of a debtor are alerted to this issue when negotiating the reorganization plan and that the powers of the approving court are sufficient to deny approval of ECDRs that would violate the *ordre public* in a recognizing court. The development of best practice for the negotiation of ECDRs and the interaction with (minority) creditors might go some way in alleviating these risks.

IV. CONCLUSION

The emergence of ECDRs, but also the existence of pre-packaged Chapter 11 proceedings in the US has not yet lead to a settled body of case law on the private international law implications of ECDRs. Challenges to the effective recognition of ECDRs in foreign courts derive from three areas: the exercise of asset-based jurisdiction (predominantly in the US), the application of ECDRs in the pre-insolvency arena, and the threshold requirements for recognition, most notably the public policy/*ordre public* exception.

This contribution has highlighted the interplay between jurisdictional questions, the applicable law and the recognition of foreign ECDRs. Where the debtor tries to treat minority creditors unfairly, where ECDRs are invoked without the financial situation of the debtor requiring such course of action and where courts assume jurisdiction on the basis of a flimsy test, recognition is in grave danger.

---

165. S. Smid, Deutsches und Europäisches Internationales Insolvenzrecht (W. Kohlhammer GmbH, Stuttgart, 2004) § 343 InsO, 7 (commentary by S. Smid).
166. Articles 103 I of the Basic Law (Constitution) of Germany.
167. Staudinger, Internationales Verfahrensrecht in Ehesachen (A.L. Sellier, Berlin, 13th ed., 2005), § 328 ZPO 565 (commentary by U. Spellenberg); H.-J. Musielak, Kommentar zur Zivilprozessordnung (C.H. Beck, München, 4th ed., 2004) § 328 ZPO 26.

Private International Law

Further risks arise from the uncertainty of the legislative framework, in particular due to the implementation of the UNCITRAL Model Law. It is hoped that more clarity can be achieved in those countries that are still to implement it. The lesson to be learnt in the meantime should be that a sensible and fair approach towards proposing and implementing an ECDR provides the best safeguard to it being internationally recognized.

Chapter 16

The Tax Consequences of Corporate Debt Restructuring

Daniel Dürrschmidt[1]

---

1. The author wishes to thank Professor Wolfram Reiß and Nina Schneider, both University of Erlangen-Nuremberg, and Gerald Arends, Ashurst London, for their assistance. All errors and omissions remain the sole responsibility of the author.

Rodrigo Olivares-Caminal, *Expedited Debt Restructuring:*
An International Comparative Analysis, pp. 509–542.
©2007, Kluwer Law International BV, The Netherlands.

ACRONYMS, ABBREVIATIONS & DEFINED TERMS

AO	*Abgabenordnung* (German Fiscal Code)
BFH	*Bundesfinanzhof* (German Federal Fiscal Court)
BFHE	*Sammlung der Entscheidungen des Bundesfinanzhofs* (German BFH reports)
EC	European Community
EStG	*Einkommensteuergesetz* (German Income Tax Act)
InsO	*Insolvenzordnung* (German Insolvency Act)
IRC	Inland Revenue Code (US)
ITA	Income Tax Act (Canada)
KStG	*Körperschaftsteuergesetz* (German Corporation Tax Act)
M&A	Mergers and Acquisitions
UStG	*Umsatzsteuergesetz* (German Turnover Tax Act)
VAT	Value Added Tax

I. INTRODUCTION

Corporate debt restructuring procedures serve important societal objectives. They prevent business closures harmful to the economy, and protect the creditors, employees and intermediaries.[2] Like any other business transaction, corporate debt restructuring procedures are subject to tax consequences,[3] both positive and – despite the positive effects

---

2. See, e.g., E. Warren and J. Lawrence Westbrook, 'The law of Debtors and Creditors: Text, Cases and Problems', Third Edition, Little Brown and Company, 1996, pages 470–471.
3. See in particular International Fiscal Association, *Cahiers de droit fiscal international, Volume 91a, The tax consequences of restructuring of indebtedness (debt work-outs)* (Amersfoort, Sdu Fiscale & Financiële Uitgevers, 2006) which includes a general report and 30 country reports; further A. Hibben, 'Umschuldungs- und Rekapitalisierungsmaßnahmen – Steuerliche Konsequenzen bei grenzüberschreitenden Sanierungen' (2006) 15 *Internationales Steuerrecht* 542–545 and the following articles focusing on specific jurisdictions S. Caveggia, C. Aquila and A. Gustavo Consoli, 'Tax Treatment and Consequences of Debt Restructuring and Workouts', (2006) 8 *Derivatives & Financial Instruments* 143–150 (Argentina); R. Schneider, 'Austria: Tax Treatment and Consequences of Debt Restructurings and Workouts', (2005) 7 *Derivatives & Financial Instruments* 263–270 (Austria); H. Lamon and M. Chalot, 'Belgium: Tax Treatment and Consequences of Debt Restructurings and Workouts', (2005) 7 *Derivatives & Financial Instruments* 277–295 (Belgium); G. Lian Haddad, R. Ferreira Bolan and A. Trevisan Neto, 'Tax Treatment and Consequences of Debt Restructuring and Workouts', (2006) 8 *Derivatives & Financial Instruments* 151–157 (Brazil); J. Bernstein, K. Leung and H. Chong, 'Canada: Tax Treatment and Consequences of Debt Restructurings and Workouts', (2005) 7 *Derivatives & Financial Instruments* 176–184; J. Niederhoffer and R. Keilty, 'Canada: Tax planning for debt restructuring', (2004) *Tax Planning International Review* 15–22 (both Canada); C. Gaw, 'Measures for the Income Tax Treatment of Enterprise Debt Restructuring', (2003) 31 *Intertax* 384–385 (China); S. Marciniak, 'France: Tax Treatment and Consequences of Debt Restructurings and Workouts', (2005) 7 *Derivatives & Financial Instruments* 216–221 (France); A. Born, 'Germany: Tax Treatment and Consequences of Debt Restructurings and Workouts', (2006) 8 *Derivatives & Financial Instruments* 25–36; G. Hölzle, 'Besteuerung der Unternehmenssanierung – Die steuerlichen Folgen gängiger Sanierungsinstrumente', (2004) 86 *Finanz-Rundschau* 1193–1210 (both Germany); P. Flora, 'Italy: Tax Treatment and Consequences of Debt Restructurings and Workouts', (2005) 7 *Derivatives & Financial Instruments* 222–227 (Italy); E. de Gunst and J. Kin, 'Netherlands: Tax Treatment and Consequences of Debt Restructurings and Workouts', (2005) 7 *Derivatives & Financial Instruments* 228–236 (The Netherlands); F. Carreño, R. Rodríguez and C. Mayo, 'Tax Treatment and Consequences of Debt Restructuring and Workouts', (2006) 8 *Derivatives & Financial Instruments* 193–198 (Spain); D. U. Lehmann, 'Tax Treatment and Consequences of Debt Restructurings and Workouts', (2006) 8 *Derivatives & Financial Instruments* 199–206 (Switzerland); J. Lindsay, 'United Kingdom: Tax Treatment and Consequences of Debt Restructurings and Workouts', (2006) 8 *Derivatives & Financial Instruments* 37–45 (United Kingdom); D. R. Hardy, 'The Restructuring of a Troubled Multinational Company', (2004) 5(4) *Corporate Business Taxation Monthly* 1–17; P. C. Lau, N. Stapleton and S. Soltis, 'Work out the best tax consequences for debt workouts', (2002) 69 *Practical Tax Strategies* 68–85; M. Hirschfeld, 'Unexpected Tax Surprises for the Creditor in Debt Restructurings', (1998) 12(4) *The Practical Tax Lawyer* 17–23; R. C. Maiorano and L. P. Tunnell, 'Debt Restructuring Alternatives for the Financially Troubled Corporation: Possible Risks and Benefits', (1992) 44 *Tax Executive* 187–200; R. C. Ricketts, 'Troubled Debt Transactions', (1994) 25 *Accounting & Tax Periodicals* 131–140; H. I. Sniderman, M. A.Gallagher and J. H Joshowitz, 'A Tax Overview of Troubled Company Debt Restructuring', (1990) 21 *Accounting & Tax Periodicals* 199–213 (all United States).

of such procedures – adverse.[4] Examples of these will be addressed in the course of the analysis. At this stage, it is important to note that tax planning must be an essential part of any corporate debt restructuring due to the implications of corporate debt restructurings on the tax position and the liquidity of the debtor company and other parties.[5] The tax consequences may even have the effect that the parties involved abstain from commencing a corporate debt restructuring procedure at all or from closing such a procedure successfully (i.e. with a corporate debt restructuring agreement).[6] As will be shown, expedited corporate debt restructuring procedures should not raise any tax issues different from those of ordinary corporate debt restructuring procedures.[7]

Since this chapter takes a multi-jurisdictional approach, it does not examine the tax issues of corporate debt restructurings arising in all jurisdictions covered in the previous chapters, but deals with the issues at an abstract level describing general issues and possible solutions. It would be beyond the scope of this chapter to analyze the tax treatment of corporate debt restructurings in any given jurisdiction. It merely shall name the relevant issues and address general principles which may provide a first approach as to the legal position in the individual jurisdictions.[8]

The rescue of a company may not only be affected by way of corporate debt restructurings but also by way of M&A transactions[9] or by state aid assistance. Particularly M&A transactions give rise to a number of tax issues[10] which

---

4. See R. H. Herz, E. J. Abahoonie and L. Krule, 'Restructuring Corporate Debt', (1992) 94(8) *Business Credit* 10 at 10.
5. See B. Bringewat and T. Waza, *Insolvenzen und Steuern* (Herne, NWB, 6th ed, 2004), paras 157–173.
6. See K. H. Maus, 'Die Besteuerung von Sanierungsgewinnen als Problem in der Unternehmensinsolvenz', (2000) 3 *Neue Zeitschrift für das Recht der Insolvenz und Sanierung* 449 at 453 regarding the German *Insolvenzplanverfahren* (Insolvency Plan Procedure; ss.217–269 of the *Insolvenzordnung* (Insolvency Act; hereinafter 'InsO')) which is – as far as tax issues are concerned – comparable to expedited procedures (see *below* II.B.).
7. See *below* 2.B.
8. It is important to note that tax legislators often do not comply with such principles to avoid revenue losses.
9. The term M&A transaction in this context particularly refers to the transfer of the entire business to a third party to use the proceeds for the satisfaction of the creditors. This way of dealing with a difficult financial situation must not be confused with the transfer of assets to a creditor to settle debts. See *below* III.A.4.d.
10. See on the tax consequences of M&A transactions, particularly in an international context, International Fiscal Association, *Cahiers de droit fiscal international, Volume 90b, Tax treatment of international acquisitions of businesses* (Amersfoort, Sdu Fiscale & Financiële Uitgevers, 2005); D. J. Piltz, 'Cross-Border Mergers and Acquisitions: Tax Considerations' in N. Horn (ed.), *Cross-Border Mergers and Acquisitions and the Law* (The Hague/London/New York, Kluwer Law International, 2001), pp. 305–330; further particularly on VAT issues from the French perspective, G. Bernier, D. Colin and L. Chetcuti, 'VAT Treatment of 'European Mergers' under French Law' (2005) 16 *International VAT Monitor* 339–341, and from the German perspective, W. Reiß, 'Umsatzsteuer und Grunderwerbsteuer beim Unternehmens(ver)kauf', in: H. Schaumburg (ed), *Unternehmenskauf im Steuerrecht* (Stuttgart, Schäffer-Poeschel, 3rd ed, 2004), pp. 241–287; further specifically on M&A transactions in the context of corporate rescue from the German perspective G. Hölzle, 'Unternehmensumwandlung in Krize, Sanierung und Insolvenz' (2006) 88 *Finanz-Rundschau* 447–461.

significantly differ from those arising as regards corporate debt restructurings. Given the focus of the book on corporate debt restructurings in the classic meaning, the alternative forms of corporate rescue (i.e. M&A transactions and state aid assistance) shall not be considered any further.

In this chapter, after some general comments (see II *below*), attention will only be drawn to the tax consequences of corporate debt restructurings by way of cancellation of indebtedness and other forms of debt modifications (see III and IV *below*). In addition, the treatment of tax liabilities accrued before the corporate debt restructuring agreement was concluded will be discussed (see V *below*). The chapter will close with some conclusions (see VI *below*).

II. GENERAL COMMENTS

A. Relationship between Insolvency Laws and Tax Laws

Corporate debt restructurings are regularly – but not necessarily – conducted at a time when a company is undergoing a liquidity crisis, which might lead to an insolvency crisis. The resulting interaction between insolvency and tax law merits more detailed analysis than can be achieved in the present setting.[11] It is submitted, however, that it is preferable to seek solutions which retain the integrity of the core principles of both areas of law. Accordingly, no area of law shall prevail over the other.

The issue of the relationship between insolvency law and tax law is of greater relevance in the context of the liquidation of an insolvent company. In this regard, one must decide how tax liabilities which had been incurred before and those which were incurred after the company became insolvent are treated. In this context, the crucial point is whether the *pari passu* principle[12] (i.e. equal treatment of all creditors) also applies to tax liabilities[13] and whether tax authorities

---

11. See on this issue from the German perspective G. Frotscher, *Besteuerung bei Insolvenz* (Heidelberg, Verlag Recht und Wirtschaft, 6th ed, 2005), pp. 17–20; S. Kling in H.-P. Kirchhof, *Münchener Kommentar zur Insolvenzordnung Band 3* (München, C.H.Beck, 2003), Insolvenzsteuerrecht, para.1.
12. See on this basic principle underlying the insolvency laws of many jurisdictions A. Keay and A. Braine, 'The Distribution of Assets of Companies in Insolvent Liquidation: An Australian-South African Comparative Study', (2002) 4 *International and Comparative Corporate Law Journal* 1 at 5–6 with further references in note 13.
13. Tax liabilities accrued after the commencement of the insolvency proceedings are regularly subject to priority treatment. See, e.g. from the German perspective, §§ 53 and 55(1)(1) of the InsO. By contrast, tax liabilities accrued before the commencement of the insolvency proceedings enjoy priority treatment only in some countries. See B. K. Morgan, 'Should the Sovereign be Paid First? A Comparative International Analysis of the Priority for Tax Claims in Bankruptcy', (2000) 74 *American Bankruptcy Law Journal* 461–506 and Keay and Braine, *above* note 11 at 1–36 on tax priorities in general with a comparative analysis of particular jurisdictions; further, particularly from the Australian perspective, B. Rätke, 'Die Rangrücktrittsvereinbarung zwischen Insolvenzrecht und Steuerrecht', (2005) *Buchführung Bilanzierung Kostenrechnung* Fach 12, pp. 4811–4820; and particularly from the German perspective,

must collect tax claims according to the rules provided for by the applicable insolvency law.[14]

The liquidation of a company is aimed at the final settlement of claims against that company which by necessity must include tax liabilities. Therefore, the issue of the treatment of tax liabilities does usually not arise in this form in the context of corporate debt restructurings. By contrast, corporate debt restructurings do not automatically result in a (total) settlement of the debts (including tax liabilities) of the debtor company. The fate of individual debts (including tax liabilities) in the course of corporate rescue transactions principally depends on what the parties to the corporate debt restructuring agreement (i.e. the debtor company and the creditors) agree. Debts remain unaffected if the parties exclude these debts from their agreement. Therefore, the issue of the relationship between insolvency law and tax law is irrelevant if the parties to the corporate debt restructuring agreement do not include tax liabilities. This is particularly the case if tax authorities do not allow doing so, or do not agree to the restructuring.

Matters may be different with regard to corporate debt restructuring procedures which enable the conclusion of a corporate debt restructuring agreement by way of majority decisions which individual creditors cannot escape from.[15] In the absence of any special provision excluding tax liabilities from majority decisions, tax liabilities are also affected by such agreements resulting in a total or partial involuntary cancellation of those liabilities regardless of the consent of the tax authorities. In such a case, insolvency law prevails over tax law. However, the primacy of insolvency law in this regard only affects the continuity of tax liabilities not to the accrual of such liabilities. The latter is in every case governed by the tax law. In the end, both the insolvency and the tax law apply simultaneously honouring the principles underlying both areas of law.

B.   CONNECTING FACTORS OF TAX LAWS REGARDING CORPORATE DEBT RESTRUCTURINGS

Tax law shall enable tax authorities to raise the funds necessary to finance the budgets.[16] The tax legislator should, however, comply with the superior principle

---

    D. Dürrschmidt, 'Abolition of Tax Priorities in Germany: A Myth?', (2005) 2 *International Corporate Rescue* 227–233; H. Kroth, ''Steuerrecht versus Insolvenzrecht' oder: '(Wider) die Auferstehung des Fiskalprivilegs?', (2004) 7 *Neue Zeitschrift für das Recht der Insolvenz und Sanierung* 345–351.

14. In Germany, e.g., tax authorities must collect tax claims according to the insolvency law; see § 251(2)(1) of the *Abgabenordnung* (Fiscal Code; hereinafter 'AO') and §§ 174–186 of the InsO; further, e.g., *Bundesfinanzhof* (Federal Fiscal Court; hereinafter 'BFH'), Judgment of 24.8.2004, VIII R 14/02, (2005) 207 *Sammlung der Entscheidungen des Bundesfinanzhofs* (*BFH reports*; hereinafter 'BFHE') 10 at 12 = (2005) *Bundessteuerblatt II* (hereinafter: BStBl. II) 246–248.
15. Majority decisions may not only be available in expedited corporate debt restructuring procedures but also in ordinary corporate debt restructuring procedures. See, e.g. from the German perspective, § 243(1) of the InsO.
16. See *generally* V. Thuronyi, *Comparative Tax Law* (The Hague/London/New York, Kluwer Law International, 2003), pp. 45–59; further from the German perspective, J. Lang in K. Tipke and

of equal treatment[17] according to which comparable situations must entail the same (tax) consequences. The decisive issue in this respect is what is understood as 'comparable situations'. According to the fundamental principle of 'ability-to-pay' – which is acknowledged worldwide –[18] the legal circumstances must not play a predominant role determining the comparability of two situations as far as the application of the principle of equal treatment to tax law is concerned. One must rather take an economic view. Therefore, tax law must provide for the same tax consequences if taxpayers are in a comparable economic situation. The economic comparability of different taxpayers is determined by their comparable ability-to-pay, i.e. their ability to contribute to public revenue.[19] Accordingly, the tax law must affect all taxpayers' ability-to-pay to the same extent to conform to the superior principle of equal treatment.

Applying these basic principles to corporate debt restructuring procedures, one may state that the specific development of such procedures may not be decisive for the tax consequences.[20] Features like: (1) the extent of court involvement; (2) the moment of involvement of the court; or, (3) the threshold for the votes necessary to close a procedure successfully, do not impact on the ability-to-pay of the persons involved, in particular the debtor company. Therefore, these specifics are not relevant from the tax perspective. Accordingly, expedited corporate debt restructuring procedures forming the subject matter of this book do not present tax issues which cannot arise in the context of ordinary corporate debt restructuring procedures such as the German *Insolvenzplanverfahren* (Insolvency Plan Procedure)[21] lacking the features of their expedited equivalents. The connecting factors for tax law are the economic effects of the corporate debt restructuring procedures which are independent from the development of the procedure. In the case of corporate debt restructuring procedures, the economic effects are, generally

---

J. Lang (eds), *Steuerrecht* (Cologne, Otto Schmidt, 18th ed, 2005), § 1, paras 1–9, and § 3, paras 9–27.

17. The principle of equal treatment is constitutional law in many jurisdictions which limits the legislators' powers. It particularly applies to the field of tax law. See *generally* G. T. K. Meussen (ed.), *The Principle of Equality in European Taxation* (The Hague, Kluwer Law International, 1999); Thuronyi, *above* note 15 at 64–70 and 82–92; further, particularly from the German perspective, J. Lang in Tipke and Lang (eds), *above* note 15, § 4, paras. 70–132.

18. See, e.g., R. A. de Mooij and L. G. M. Stevens, 'Exploring the future of the ability to pay in Europe', (2005) 14 *EC Tax Review* 9–15; J. Lang in Tipke and Lang (eds), *above* note 15, § 4, paras. 81–123. It is important to note in the context of this book that the ability-to-pay principle is also relevant for companies. See J. Lang in Tipke and Lang (eds), *above* note 15, § 4, para. 90.

19. See, e.g., K. Tipke, *Die Steuerrechtsordnung Band 1* (Cologne, Otto Schmidt, 2nd, 2000), p. 480. This not only holds true for the application of the general principle of equal treatment but also for the application of the non-discrimination clauses of the Fundamental Freedoms within the European Community (hereinafter: EC). See, e.g., D. Dürrschmidt, 'Tax Treaties and Most-Favoured-Nation Treatment, particularly within the European Union', (2006) 60 *Bulletin for International Taxation* 202 at 208.

20. It should be noted that for the same reason, the tax consequences of corporate debt restructuring procedures as outlined in this chapter in principle also apply in the event of private debt-workouts.

21. See §§ 217–269 of the InsO.

speaking, the cancellation of indebtedness resulting in positive income at the debtor level and negative income at the creditor level. These effects may have implications on direct taxes, in particular on income and corporation tax, and on indirect taxes, in particular value added tax (hereinafter 'VAT') and transfer taxes.

Because of this legal position, the tax law of countries which do not have an expedited corporate debt restructuring procedure may also be considered to illustrate the basic tax issues of expedited corporate debt restructuring procedures. Conversely, (general) conclusions reached considering tax issues of expedited corporate debt restructuring procedures may also apply to corporate debt restructuring procedures not qualifying as expedited procedures. This is so, because the outcome of an 'ordinary' and 'expedited' restructuring procedure will be the same, the only difference will be the pace in which it takes place.

III. ISSUES REGARDING DIRECT TAXES (INCOME AND CORPORATION TAX)

A. DEBTOR

1. General Comments

The most obvious tax consequence of a corporate debt restructuring agreement concerns the implications of a cancellation of indebtedness on the corporation tax[22] at the debtor level which will be addressed *below*. In respect of the cancellation of indebtedness, one must distinguish between different motivations for the transaction. The creditor might be motivated by the intention to rescue the debtor company's business (see 2 *below*) or by other reasons which is particularly the case if the creditor is a person related to the debtor company (see 3 *below*). Creditors do not necessarily need to discharge the debtor company from debts to facilitate its business' rescue. It may suffice that the creditors (or some of them) and the debtor company agree on other ways of debt modifications such as a deferral or subordination of a debt (see 4 *below*). The tax consequences of a cancellation of indebtedness may be different if the debt does not result from a loan but from the delivery of goods (see 5 *below*).

---

22. It is important to note that corporation tax may be levied on businesses at different levels. E.g. in the US, businesses may be subject to corporation tax at the federal, at the state and at the local level; in Germany, corporation tax is levied at the federal and at the local (so-called *Gewerbesteuer* (trade tax)) level. The tax consequences of corporate debt restructuring procedures both at the debtor and at the creditor level discussed in this chapter may principally occur at all levels so that one does not need to distinguish between the different levels.

2. Cancellation of Indebtedness Intended to Rescue the Debtor

a. Cancellation of Indebtedness Income

The cancellation of indebtedness as result of the rescue of the company[23] results in positive income at the debtor level amounting to the debt cancelled.[24] The taxable income of a business is usually calculated as the difference between the equity at the beginning and at the end of the fiscal year.[25] The equity in turn is calculated as the difference between the value of the assets and the value of the liabilities as specified in the tax balance sheet. Cancellation of indebtedness effects a reduction of the liabilities which results in an increase of equity.[26] One arrives at the same outcome if a business is allowed to calculate its taxable profit as the difference between the revenues and the expenditures.[27] It should be noted, however, that companies must normally calculate their taxable income in the first way.[28] In such a case, the cancellation of indebtedness is treated as revenue amounting to the debt cancelled.[29]

By contrast to the approach of the general principles of tax law, the applicable tax law in a restructuring may expressly provide a special regime for the taxability of cancellation of indebtedness income.[30] The applicable tax law may also categorize the cancellation of indebtedness income providing a special tax treatment for such income.[31]

The time when the cancellation of indebtedness income accrues may differ between jurisdictions. Conceivable effective dates are the date when the

---

23. See Thuronyi, *above* note 15 at 266 who rightly points out that the cancellation of indebtedness may not be a taxable event if the debt cancelled is private and the applicable tax law does not attribute the 'cancellation of indebtedness income' to a specific 'schedule' of income. In the context of this book, this aspect is, however, irrelevant since companies do not have a private sphere.
24. See Hardy, *above* note 2 at 2 and A. Hibben, 'Generalthema I des IFA-Kongresses 2006 in Amsterdam: Die steuerlichen Folgen der Umschuldung und Rekapitalisierung', (2005) 14 *Internationales Steuerrecht* 615 at 616 pointing out that this tax consequence may arise worldwide.
25. See, e.g. from the German perspective, § 4(1)(1) of the *Einkommensteuergesetz* (Income Tax Act; hereinafter 'EStG'). It is important to note that the provisions of the German EStG providing for the calculation of the taxable income also apply to companies subject to corporation tax. See § 8(1) the *Körperschaftsteuergesetz* (Corporation Tax Act; hereinafter 'KStG').
26. See, e.g. from the Chinese perspective, Gaw, *above* note 2 at 385.
27. See, e.g. from the German perspective, § 4(3)(1) of the EStG.
28. See, e.g. from the German perspective, § 4(1) of the EStG and § 140 of the AO.
29. See, e.g. from the German perspective, G. Crezelius in P. Kirchhof, *EStG KompaktKommentar* (Heidelberg, C.F.Müller, 6th ed., 2006), § 4, para. 134.
30. See, e.g. from the Canadian perspective, s.80(13) of the Income Tax Act (hereinafter 'ITA (Canada)'); and from the US perspective, s.61(a)(12) of the Internal Revenue Code (hereinafter 'IRC'); further, from the UK perspective, Lindsay, *above* note 2 at 37–40 on the so-called 'loan relationship legislation'.
31. See, e.g. from the Italian perspective, Flora, *above* note 2 at 225. In Italy, cancellation of indebtedness income constitutes 'extraordinary income' which is only subject to corporation tax but not to the regional tax.

cancellation of indebtedness becomes effective, i.e. in the context of this book, the effective date of the corporate debt restructuring agreement, or the performance of such agreement.[32]

The taxability of cancellation of indebtedness income may be counterproductive since the debtor company is relieved from a debt (i.e. the debts cancelled) just in order to become liable to corporation tax (i.e. the tax liability resulting from the cancellation of indebtedness income). Such result could prompt creditors to refrain from participating in the rescue of the debtor company's business by way of a debt restructuring. It is an unattractive proposition to cancel a debt for the benefit of the entire economy (e.g. maintenance of jobs or future prospects) if tax authorities raise revenue at the same time.[33] The creditor's unwillingness to agree on a corporate debt restructuring agreement could increase if respective tax claims enjoy priority treatment in case the rescue fails.[34] Even if the creditors nevertheless enter into a corporate debt restructuring agreement, the debtor's financial crisis may not have been overcome. Although the tax liability does not equal the debts cancelled,[35] the tax liabilities replacing the debts cancelled may (partly) burden the debtor company in a way which either perpetuates an existing illiquidity situation or results in an insolvency situation shortly after the corporate debt restructuring agreement came into effect.[36]

The negative impact of the taxation of cancellation of indebtedness income may be reduced if the debtor company is entitled to 'loss carry forwards'. Loss carry forwards may be utilized to reduce the tax base which after the conclusion of a corporate debt restructuring agreement often solely consists of cancellation of indebtedness income. If such income can be offset against losses carried forward by the company from previous fiscal years, no tax liability arises. Also, the debtor company is not burdened by new debts which might lead the debtor company into a new crisis. The critical point in this regard is, however, that a loss carry forward is an important factor impacting on the value of the debtor company's business.[37] The loss of a loss carry forward may, on the one hand, reduce the debtor company's chances to

---

32. See, e.g. from the German perspective, Maus, *above* note 5 at 451.
33. See, e.g., H.-G. Fritsche, 'Die Streichung von § 3 Nr. 66 EStG als Sanierungshindernis und die Sicherung des Sanierungserfolgs mittels Erlass nach §§ 163, 227 AO', (2000) 38 *Deutsches Steuerrecht* 2171 at 2171.
34. E.g. in Germany, a tax liability resulting from cancellation of indebtedness income would constitute a so-called *Masseverbindlichkeit* which would be settled before liabilities accrued before the commencement of the insolvency proceedings (so-called *Insolvenzforderung*). See, e.g., Maus, *above* note 5 at 451; A. Vögeli, 'Sanierungsgewinn – Gewinn oder Grund erneuter Insolvenz?', (2000) 3 *Zeitschrift für das gesamte Insolvenzrecht* 144 at 145.
35. The reason is that the debt cancelled itself does not constitute the tax liability, but only increases the tax base to that extent. The amount of the tax liability depends on the applicable tax rate.
36. See for a practical example from Germany Georg, *above* note 47 at 94–95.
37. See for the importance of loss compensation in general E. Breuninger, 'Postakquisitorische Verlustnutzung', in: H. Schaumburg (ed), *Unternehmenskauf im Steuerrecht* (Stuttgart, Schäffer-Poeschel, 3rd ed., 2004), pp. 221–239; M. Lehner, 'Verfassungsrechtliche Vorgaben für die Verlustberücksichtigung', in: M. Lehner (ed), *Verluste im nationalen und Internationalen Steuerrecht* (München, C.H. Beck, 2004), pp. 1–22.

The Tax Consequences of Corporate Debt Restructuring 519

attract new investors and new potential creditors which might be an important aspect for the successful rescue of the business. On the other hand, one may argue that such a result would comply with basic principles of tax law according to which the overall income of a business shall be subject to tax. The 'ability-to-pay' principle[38] as a sub-principle of the principle of equal treatment requires that one takes into account the taxpayer's lifetime income.[39] This income comprises both the cancellation of indebtedness income and the losses carried forward. Only this composition of the debtor company's income would consider its real lifetime ability-to-pay.[40] From this perspective, it would be consistent to compensate cancellation of indebtedness income with losses carried forward. Therefore, the loss of loss carry forwards is an economically undesirable event but sound as a matter of principle.

b.   *Relief*

i.   General Comments

Tax law or tax authorities may provide for relief of the debtor company from the taxability of cancellation of indebtedness income to prevent creditors to refrain from entering into a corporate debt restructuring agreement or that unfavourable effects for the debtor company (e.g. a new liquidity problem or the decrease of its business value) frustrates a corporate debt restructuring procedure.

ii.   General Exemption

The first way to achieve relief is to adopt a provision in the tax law exempting cancellation of indebtedness income from taxation. Such provision may be found in a number of countries.[41] The requirements of such provisions usually comprise the need for the rescue of the debtor company, the suitability of the cancellation of indebtedness for the rescue and the intention to rescue the debtor company.[42] Some jurisdictions apply a rather formal approach. Accordingly, the exemption applies if the cancellation of indebtedness occurs in a corporate debt restructuring procedure, if the debtor company is insolvent or if the debt cancelled results from particular

---

38. See *above* II.B. on the principle of equal treatment and the 'ability-to-pay' principle as one of its sub-principles relevant for taxation.
39. The division of the total period into assessment periods serves enforcement purposes which shall not suspend basic principles of substantive tax law such as the 'ability-to-pay' principle. Therefore, the division of the total period into assessment periods is irrelevant for the application of the 'ability-to-pay' principle. See, e.g. from the German perspective, J. Lang in Tipke and Lang (eds), *above* note 15, § 4, paras 44–47.
40. See, e.g. from the German perspective, J. Lang in Tipke and Lang (eds), *above* note 15, § 9, para.60 whose comments are not restricted to the cancellation of indebtedness income.
41. E.g. in the US, s.108 of the IRC provides for an exemption of cancellation of indebtedness income under particular circumstances. In Germany, § 3(66) of the EStG provided for a reconstruction relief (*Sanierungsprivileg*) regarding cancellation of indebtedness income (*Sanierungsgewinn*) until 1998 (see Art.1(1) of the *Gesetz zur Fortsetzung der Unternehmenssteuerreform* (Company Taxation Reform Continuation Act 1997)).
42. See, e.g., Fritsche, *above* note 32 at 2171 on the former German tax exemption in § 3(66) of the EStG.

forms of transactions.[43] In case of such formal requirements for the exemption of cancellation of indebtedness income, tax authorities do not need to consider whether there is a need for the rescue of the debtor company. The tax law typifies the situations in which the need for the rescue of the debtor company can be presumed.

The effect of such a provision is that the cancellation of indebtedness income is not taxed. The tax exemption of such income may, however, come along with negative implications on the tax attributes of the debtor company such as loss carry forwards.[44] In such case, loss carry forwards cannot reduce the taxable income of the debtor in the future to the extent that cancellation of indebtedness income was tax exempted. Therefore, tax authorities do usually not lose revenue because of the tax exemption of cancellation of indebtedness income. Only the remaining cancellation of indebtedness income, i.e. the cancellation of indebtedness income which cannot be offset against loss carry forwards, is tax exempt.

The tax exemption of cancellation of indebtedness income may be problematic in case of a so-called 'reinstatement agreement'. Under such an agreement, the debtor company is obliged to pay the debts 'cancelled' in case its financial situation improves. Accordingly, the debts are not 'cancelled' finally. Usually, payments of the debtor company to the creditors based on such an agreement constitute negative income at the debtor level which may be deducted from the tax base.[45] If the cancellation of indebtedness income was, however, tax exempt, the payments must not be deductible since otherwise the debtor company could benefit twice from the tax exemption which is obviously not the intention.[46]

The justification of a tax exemption of cancellation of indebtedness income is subject to fundamental criticism.[47] On the one hand, one may argue in favour of such relief that in case of the liquidation of the debtor company, the tax authorities would not have been able to levy taxes on the debtor company although the liquidation of a company results in a discharge of the debtor company from all debts. Such event, however, does usually not result in taxable cancellation of indebtedness income.[48]

---

43. See, e.g. from the US perspective, s.108(a)(1) of the IRC. It is noteworthy that s.108(a)(1)(A) of the IRC explicitly includes chapter 11 proceedings. See Lindsay, *above* note 2 at 44 on the similar legal position in the UK.
44. See, e.g. from the Canadian perspective, s.80 of the ITA (Canada), and from the US perspective, s.108(b) of the IRC. This is also the German approach. See *Bundesministerium der Finanzen* (Federal Ministry of Finance) circular of 27.3.2003, IV A 6–S 2140–8/03, (2003) *Bundessteuerblatt I* 240–243. It is worth mentioning that German tax authorities generously grant relief on a case-by-case basis (see *below* iii.) in case cancellation of indebtedness income has been offset against loss carry forwards.
45. See, e.g. from the German perspective, Fritsche, *above* note 32 at 2172; A. M. Nolte, 'Ertragsteuerliche Behandlung von Sanierungsmaßnahmen. Steuerstundung und Steuererlass aus sachlichen Billigkeitsgründen', (2005) *Neue Wirtschafts-Briefe* Fach 3, p. 13735 at 13740.
46. See, e.g. from the German perspective, Fritsche, *above* note 32 at 2172; Nolte, *above* note 44 at 13740.
47. See Maus, *above* note 5 at 450 with an overview of the arguments in favour and against such relief.
48. See, e.g. from the German perspective, § 11(2)to(4) of the KStG which provides for the calculation of the taxable income arising in the course of the liquidation of a company. It only

In this respect, tax authorities do not take part in the distribution of the company's assets in the course of the liquidation.[49] Therefore, the exemption of cancellation of indebtedness income from taxation does not result in a loss of revenue compared to the scenario in which the debtor company is liquidated. One may also argue that the rescue of the debtor company is in the public interest, in particular because of the fact that without the rescue, jobs and the debtor company as a taxpayer could be lost.[50] On the other hand, one may also take the opposite view and consider the tax exemption of cancellation of indebtedness income unjustified. In principle, one may apply the same arguments as to the role of loss carry forwards.[51] Accordingly, the principle of equal treatment and the 'ability-to-pay' principle[52] require the consideration of the total period with all profits and losses. The tax exemption of cancellation of indebtedness income would be inconsistent with this principle. Supporters of such a position point out that a debtor company is usually entitled to loss carry forwards since a business is usually loss making before the need for a rescue occurs.[53] This argument is, however, not valid in every case since the need for a rescue of a debtor company by way of a corporate debt restructuring procedure may also result from a mere illiquidity which does not usually accompany losses or loss carry forwards which might be used to compensate cancellation of indebtedness income.[54] Even in such case, however, the exemption of cancellation of indebtedness income from taxation would not be justified against the background of the 'ability-to-pay' principle.

iii.   Exemption on a Case-By-Case Basis
The second type of relief from the taxability of cancellation of indebtedness income is the cancellation of a respective tax liability on a case-by-case basis. Relief in such a case may depend on an application of the debtor company. Such decision is discretionary which enables the tax authorities to consider the circumstances of the individual case. The tax authorities may make such a decision both at the assessment[55] and at the enforcement level.[56] It is important to note that

---

considers assets, equity and liabilities which exist at the time the liquidation of the company commences; liabilities which arise in the course of the liquidation are irrelevant. See *further* T. Georg, 'Insolvenzplanverfahren: Erste Erfahrungen', (2000) 3 *Zeitschrift für das gesamte Insolvenzrecht* 93 at 94.
49. It is important to note that this comment does not affect tax liabilities accrued before the commencement of the insolvency proceedings.
50. See Fritsche, *above* note 32 at 2171.
51. See *above* a.
52. See *above* II.B. on the principle of equal treatment and the 'ability-to-pay' principle as one of its sub-principles relevant for taxation.
53. See, e.g., Marciniak, *above* note 2 at 217; M. Groh, 'Abschaffung des Sanierungsprivilegs?', (1996) 49 *Der Betrieb* 1890 at 1890.
54. See Fritsche, *above* note 32 at 2172.
55. See, e.g. from the German perspective, § 163 of the AO.
56. See, e.g. from the German perspective, § 227 of the AO. Fritsche, *above* note 32 at 2173 points out that tax authorities should cancel a respective tax liability already at the assessment level since waiting until the enforcement level would be time consuming and cause uncertainty in particular for the creditors.

such provisions are usually general and not specifically targeted at tax liabilities resulting from cancellation of indebtedness income.

Discretionary powers of tax authorities to make decisions based on a case-by-case basis may be a way to close gaps contained in the law. Two fundamental approaches can be discerned. If the tax law does not contain an exemption for cancellation of indebtedness income, it could be assumed that the legislator deliberately abstained from providing for a tax exemption, particularly if there had been such an exemption in the law before.[57] Therefore, the gap in the tax law must not be closed by way of decisions based on a case-by-case basis.[58] Taking such a view, the negative effects of a failure of a corporate rescue on the economy could not be employed as reasoning for a decision granting relief on a case-by-case basis. As an alternative approach, one may take the position that it is one of the strengths of provisions enabling decisions on a case-by-case basis that they allow tax authorities to consider the specific situation of the debtor company, in particular the need for its rescue and the suitability of the debt restructuring for its rescue.

The crucial aspect regarding the cancellation of tax liabilities resulting from cancellation of indebtedness income on a case-by-case basis is, however, that tax authorities must – alike the tax legislator – observe the principle of equal treatment, i.e. all taxpayers must be treated according to their individual 'ability-to-pay'.[59] Therefore, one may bring forward the same reservations as applicable to a general tax exemption of cancellation of indebtedness income.[60] Accordingly, the total period must be considered determining the taxpayer's ability-to-pay. Disregarding the cancellation of indebtedness income would result in an overall income not reflecting the debtor company's overall ability-to-pay. Thus, the tax exemption of tax liabilities resulting from cancellation of indebtedness income on a case-by-case basis would be unjustified against the background of the superior 'ability-to-pay' principle.

Despite these concerns regarding the principle of equal treatment, tax authorities must also consider a range of further aspects, in particular the intention of corporate debt restructuring procedures. Considering such aspects may result in the discharge from a tax liability resulting from cancellation of indebtedness income.[61] Corporate debt restructuring procedures – irrespective of whether they may be characterized as expedited as those subject to this book – are intended to rescue the debtor company's business not only for the benefit of the debtor company but also, e.g., for the maintenance of jobs.[62] The need for the

---

57. Germany is a good example (see *above* ii.).
58. See Maus, *above* note 5 at 453.
59. See *above* II.B. on the principle of equal treatment and the 'ability-to-pay' principle as one of its sub-principles relevant for taxation; further Fritsche, *above* note 32 at 2173 on the 'ability-to-pay' principle in the context of discretionary decisions of tax authorities.
60. See *above* ii.
61. See M. Take and R. Schmid-Sperber, 'Steuerliche Behandlung der Sanierungsgewinne im Insolvenzplanverfahren', (2000) 3 *Zeitschrift für das gesamte Insolvenzrecht* 374 at 375–376 and Vögeli, *above* note 33 at 145–146 on this and other aspects which might play a role in the decision-making process.
62. This is why German tax authorities handle the option for a discharge from tax claims on a case-by-case basis generously in insolvency situations. See the above mentioned (*above* note 43) circular.

consideration of the intention of corporate debt restructuring procedures forces tax authorities to take into account the entire legal order and balance its different purposes.[63] Such approach has some merits although it should be subject to an assessment of the individual case whether the rescue of the debtor company's business should prevail over the principle of equal treatment. In every case, one may state that the discharge from a tax liability may only justify a breach of the principle of equal treatment if the tax liability results from cancellation of indebtedness income in case the cancellation is conducted for the purpose of the rescue of the debtor company's business. Conversely, the discharge from a tax liability resulting from cancellation of indebtedness income cannot prevail over the principle of equal treatment if the creditors discharge the debtor company from a debt for reasons other than the rescue of the debtor company's business. Accordingly, one must rather consider the creditors and their motivation instead of the debtor company.[64] After all, relief on a case-by-case basis could produce better results as general exemptions provided for by law since the individual case can be considered comprehensively.

Though this way of providing relief for debt restructurings may remove the tax liability resulting from the cancellation of indebtedness income, it is problematic since it is in the discretion of the tax authorities to grant such relief. Even if tax authorities are in principle bound by their own practice,[65] there remains uncertainty as to the availability of relief in the individual case.[66] Uncertainty may exist whether relief is available at all and, if so, to what extent tax authorities grant relief. The background of the latter aspect is that options to grant relief on a case-by-case basis usually enable a total or a partial discharge from tax liabilities[67] since this way ensures that tax authorities can best consider the circumstances of the individual case.[68] The uncertainty may cause creditors to abstain from agreeing on a corporate debt restructuring to prevent that they are bound by such agreement in case tax authorities do not discharge the debtor company from tax liabilities resulting from cancellation of indebtedness income. The creditors' reservations may not only concern the replacement of their claims by tax claims, but also the fact that the financial consequences may not be predicted since the amount of taxes to be paid cannot be determined before the final assessment. In case of progressive or gradual corporation tax rates, the applicable tax rate depends on the tax base which cannot be determined before the end of the assessment period.[69] In such a case, a corporate debt restructuring agreement may be concluded subject to the condition that the tax authorities grant relief. This does not, however, remove uncertainty. Though, it prevents creditors from being bound by an agreement that they would not have

---

63. See Take and Schmid-Sperber, *above* note 60 at 375.
64. See Nolte, *above* note 44 at 13735–13748 on the German approach as set in out in the *above* mentioned (*above* note 43) circular.
65. The practice may be documented establishing a position which taxpayers may rely on; see e.g. the German circular mentioned *above* note 43.
66. See, e.g., Maus, *above* note 5 at 453.
67. See, e.g. from the German perspective, §§ 163, 227 of the AO; see *further* Fritsche, *above* note 32 at 2174.
68. See, e.g., Take and Schmid-Sperber, *above* note 60 at 375–376.
69. See, e.g., Maus, *above* note 5 at 453; Maus, *above* note 5 at 451–452.

concluded if they had known that the tax authorities do not grant relief. Another option might be to apply to tax authorities for a binding opinion on the tax treatment of tax liabilities resulting from cancellation of indebtedness income.[70]

A special issue may arise if the country whose tax authorities discharge the debtor company from a tax liability resulting from cancellation of indebtedness income is a Member State of the European Community (hereinafter 'EC'). The EC Treaty[71] contains the prohibition of State aid distorting the competition among the market players within the EC.[72] Favourable tax provisions or favourable tax treatment is not in every case State aid incompatible with the EC Treaty. According to a notice issued by the European Commission, the competent authority for the administration of State aid law,[73] only tax measures which are selective or specific in the sense that they favour 'certain undertakings or the production of certain goods' are prohibited by the EC Treaty.[74] The cancellation of tax liabilities related to the rescue of a business may be regarded as State aid since not all businesses may benefit from such favourable tax treatment.[75] The critical issue in this context is whether general rules – regardless of whether they are contained in the law or in administrative regulations – may rule out the selective character of a favourable tax treatment since such measures are available to all businesses which face a crisis.[76] Because of the limited territorial scope of application of EC law, the State aid issue shall not be considered further.

The comments so far concerned the tax exemption of cancellation of indebtedness income on a case-by-case basis and the discharge from tax liabilities resulting

---

70. See, e.g., Georg, *above* note 47 at 94–95. S. Kling Kirchhof, *above* note 10, Insolvenzsteuerrecht, para.244 suggests the negotiation of a discharge from respective tax liabilities before the conclusion of the corporate debt restructuring agreement. Such solution, however, may fail if the uncertainties mentioned *above* (e.g. applicable tax rate) cannot be classified in the course of the negotiations.
71. Treaty Establishing the European Community of 25 March 1957, OJ C 325, 24.12.2002, pp.33–183 (consolidated version).
72. Art.87(1) of the EC Treaty.
73. Art.88 of the EC Treaty.
74. See European Commission, Notice on the application of State aid rules to measures relating to direct business taxation, OJ C 384, 10.12.1998, pp. 3–9.
75. See *generally Industrie Aeronautiche e Meccaniche Rinaldo Piaggio SpA v. International Factors Italia SpA (Ifitalia), Dornier Luftfahrt GmbH, Ministerio della Difesa*, European Court of Justice, Judgment of 17 June 1999, Case C-295/97, European Court Reports, I–3735 (also available at: <http://europa.eu.int/smartapi/cgi/sga_doc?smartapi!celexplus!prod!CELEXnumdoc&lg=en&numdoc=61997J0295>); further P. Taylor, 'Competition Law Issues in Insolvency and Restructuring', (2006) *International Corporate Rescue* 90 at 90–91; and, in particular from the German perspective, Nolte, *above* note 44 at 13746; further generally on the relationship between EC State aid law and tax law C. H. J. I. Panayi, 'State Aid and Tax: the Third Way', (2004) 32 *Intertax* 283–306; P. Rossi-Maccanico, 'State Aid Review of Member States' Measures Relating to Direct Business Taxation', (2004) 3 *European State Aid Quarterly* 229–251; W. Schön, 'Taxation and State Aid Law in the European Union', (1999) 36 *Common Market Law Review* 911–936; K.-J. Visser, 'Commission expresses its view on the relation between state aid and tax law', (1999) 8 *EC Tax Review* 224–228.
76. Nolte, *above* note 44 at 13746 regards the *above* mentioned (note 43) circular of German tax authorities as sufficient to prevent incompatibility with the EC Treaty.

from cancellation of indebtedness income. The discharge of the debtor company from a tax liability is not the only measure of tax authorities which may provide relief for the debtor company regarding taxable cancellation of indebtedness income on a case-by-case basis. Tax authorities may provide for a deferral of a relevant tax liability.[77] This option would avoid conflicts with the principle of equal treatment and the 'ability-to-pay' principle[78] since the tax liability itself remains unchanged and may be enforced after the debtor company has overcome its crisis. However, the suitability of a deferral of tax liabilities to provide for relief is limited.[79] Firstly, the option of a deferral of tax liabilities often depends on the fact that the enforceability of the tax liabilities is not at risk. This, however, cannot be ensured in a financial crisis. Secondly, irrespective of the potential risk for the enforceability of the respective tax liabilities, the deferral of tax liabilities is often subject to the provision of security by the taxpayer. Security may not only be provided in cash but also in the form of liens, mortgages, etc. on the taxpayer's assets. In an insolvency situation, however, most of the debtor company's assets might already be burdened by such security. Thirdly, a deferral of tax liabilities does not remove debts which may maintain the poor financial standing of the company.

iv.   Alternative Forms of Relief

There are further options to provide for relief from tax liabilities resulting from cancellation of indebtedness income.[80] One option might be to allow the debtor company to set aside in the tax balance sheet a reserve representing the tax liability resulting from cancellation of indebtedness income. In such case, the debtor company would have to release the reserve over a certain period.[81] The release would increase the debtor company's taxable income in the fiscal years following the fiscal year in which the cancellation of indebtedness income accrued. Such reserve prevents the debtor company from the obligation to pay taxes on the entire cancellation of indebtedness income in the fiscal year in which the corporate debt restructuring came into effect. This form of relief is a standardized form of a deferral of tax liabilities which makes the handling of the 'deferral' independent from the individual case. The availability of a reserve representing the cancellation of indebtedness income may be made subject to the approval of the tax authorities.[82]

A liquidity aid would be another option for relief.[83] In such case, the debtor company is granted an amount of money equalling the amount of the tax liability

---

77. See, e.g. from the German perspective, § 222 of the AO.
78. See *above* II.B. on the principle of equal treatment and the 'ability-to-pay' principle as one of its sub-principles relevant for taxation.
79. See, e.g. from the German perspective, J. Kroschel, 'Rechtskritische Anmerkungen zur steuerlichen Behandlung von Sanierungsgewinnen', (1999) 37 *Deutsches Steuerrecht* 1383 at 1387–1388; Take and Schmid-Sperber, *above* note 60 at 376.
80. See, e.g., Maus, *above* note 5 at 453–454 on such options.
81. See, e.g. from the Chinese perspective, Gaw, *above* note 2 at 384; and Kroschel, *above* note 78 at 1388 for a proposal regarding German tax law.
82. See, e.g. from the Chinese perspective, Gaw, *above* note 2 at 384.
83. See, e.g., F. Trompeter, 'Die Sanierungsbeihilfe als Alternative zur steuerlichen Sonderbehandlung von Sanierungsgewinnen', (2000) 55 *Betriebs-Berater* 433 at 436.

resulting from the cancellation of indebtedness income. The liquidity aid would be a repayable debt with the status of a subordinated debt. Regardless of concerns regarding the compatibility with EC State aid law,[84] the decision on the liquidity aid would be time consuming and, because of the fact that it would be in the discretion of the competent authorities, uncertain to consider when planning the corporate debt restructuring.

3. Cancellation of Indebtedness by a Related Person

a. General Comments

The tax consequences of the cancellation of indebtedness may be different if it is not motivated by the intention to rescue the debtor company but by personal reasons. This might particularly be the case if the discharge traces back to the relationship between the debtor company and the creditor. In the context of corporate debt restructurings, a relationship may particularly be constituted by the fact that the creditor is also a shareholder[85] of the debtor company and vice versa. The critical question in this respect is when a cancellation of indebtedness is motivated by the intention to rescue the debtor company and when by the personal relationship between the debtor company and the creditor. Therefore, the relation between the discharge by a creditor related to the debtor company and the discharge by unrelated creditors might be a guideline. If a creditor related to the debtor company discharges the debtor company from a debt at a higher ratio than the unrelated creditors, one may consider the discharge by the related creditor – at least to the extent that it exceeds the discharge by unrelated creditors – as motivated by the relationship between the debtor company and the creditor.[86] An unrelated creditor would presumably not be willing to be treated less favourably in a corporate debt restructuring procedure than the creditors related to the debtor company so that the assumption is justified.

b. Creditor Shareholder of the Debtor

If the shareholder creditor discharges the debtor company from a debt motivated by the relationship between the debtor company and the shareholder creditor, the discharge would be treated as a capital contribution at the debtor level.[87] A capital contribution usually does not trigger tax consequences.[88] It does not constitute an

---

84. See *above* iii.
85. See, e.g. from the German perspective, G. Förster and J. Wendland, 'Steuerliche Folgen von Gesellschafterdarlehen in der Krise der GmbH', (2006) 97 *GmbH-Rundschau* 169–178.
86. See, e.g. from the Chinese perspective, Gaw, *above* note 2 at 385; and from the German perspective, Hölzle, *above* note 2 at 1205–1206.
87. If the creditor is not a shareholder of the debtor company, the discharge must be qualified as gift revenue. See, e.g. from the Chinese perspective, Gaw, *above* note 2 at 385; and from the US perspective, D. V. Buckel and Z. W. Daughtrey, 'Hidden Tax Consequences of Restructuring Debt', (1992) 174 *Journal of Accountancy* 37 at 37. A gift revenue may trigger gift tax.
88. See, e.g. from the German perspective, Hibben, *above* note 23 at 616.

increase of the capital of the company in the ordinary course of business so that it is irrelevant for corporation tax purposes. Treating the discharge of the debtor company from a debt as capital contribution, tax authorities may distinguish between recoverable and irrecoverable debts. In such case, only the discharge from recoverable debts may be regarded as capital contribution, i.e., the discharge from such debts would not have any tax consequences.[89] Conversely, the irrecoverable part of the debt discharged would constitute cancellation of indebtedness income,[90] i.e., it would increase the taxable income.

c. *Debtor Shareholder of the Creditor*

In the opposite case (i.e. the debtor is a shareholder of the creditor), the cancellation of indebtedness income may be treated as distribution at the debtor level to the extent that the cancellation is motivated by the relationship between the shareholder debtor and the creditor company.[91] The shareholder debtor receives dividends. Unlike cancellation of indebtedness income,[92] dividends do usually not qualify for relief.

4. Alternative Forms of Debt Restructuring

a. *Modification of Debts*

The cancellation of indebtedness is the classic form of corporate debt restructuring. The cancellation of indebtedness is disadvantageous for the creditors since they lose their claim. Therefore, creditors seek ways which keep the debts in existence. The most obvious way to relieve the debtor company and to save the creditors' claims is the deferral of the debts. It does not change the amount of the debt itself; it only affects the maturity of the debt.[93] The mere deferral of debts usually has no corporation tax consequences.

Deferral of debts might have tax consequences if the deferral is granted for a (taxable) consideration. In such case, the consideration would be treated as expenditure at the debtor level. The deferral would also have tax consequences if the deferral results in a significant[94] decrease of the value of the debt deferred. This may be the case if the deferral constitutes significant cash flow advantages for the debtor and respective disadvantages for the creditor. In such case, the debtor

---

89. See, e.g. from the German perspective, Hibben, *above* note 23 at 616.
90. It is important to note that the debtor company may be relieved from tax liabilities resulting from cancellation of indebtedness income (see *above* 3.b.).
91. See, e.g. from the Chinese perspective, Gaw, *above* note 2 at 385.
92. See *above* 3.b. on relief possibly available for cancellation of indebtedness income.
93. See, e.g. from the Austrian perspective, Schneider, *above* note 2 at 271; and from the Italian perspective, Flora, *above* note 2 at 222–223.
94. See, e.g. from the US perspective, Hardy, *above* note 2 at 4–5; H. Klumpp, 'Mapping the dangers of debt restructuring', (2002) 13(10) *International Tax Review* 27 at 27–28; Lau, Stapleton and Soltis, *above* note 2 at 72–74; M. A. Melone, 'Restructuring LLC Debt to Minimize Adverse Tax Consequences for Borrowers', (1997) 12 *Accounting & Tax Periodicals* 50–56.

company recognizes cancellation of indebtedness income[95] to the extent that the value of the debt decreases.

There is a wide range of further debt modification options which may lead to cancellation of indebtedness income if they establish a significant modification,[96] e.g., debts may be modified by a change of the interest payable[97] or by an addition, alteration or elimination of a premium. The crucial point is to determine the threshold for a debt modification being significant. A general guideline cannot be given in this chapter since the individual jurisdictions vary significantly.

b.   *Subordination of Debts*

The subordination of a debt does not result in the total and automatic loss of a debt. The main effect of the subordination of a debt is that the creditor is treated similar to a shareholder as regards the subordinated debts. Accordingly, the creditors' claims may only be settled in the course of the liquidation of the company if all un-subordinated creditors' claims have been settled. The subordination of a debt is intended to prevent over-indebtedness which usually requires the debtor company to file for insolvency.[98]

The removal or prevention of over-indebtedness within the meaning of the insolvency law does not, however, necessarily affect the trade and the tax balance sheet since the debt as such remains in existence.[99] If the applicable tax law does not provide for implications of the debt subordination on the debtor company's tax balance sheet, the subordination of a debt does not have any tax consequences at the debtor level. In particular, the subordination does not result in taxable cancellation of indebtedness income. In case the applicable tax law follows the insolvency law, i.e. the debt does no longer exist for tax purposes after the subordination, the tax consequences are the same as in the case of a cancellation of indebtedness. Consequently as set out *above*,[100] one would have to distinguish between creditors related to the debtor company, in particular shareholders, and such unrelated to the debtor company.

---

95. It is important to note that the debtor company may be relieved from tax liabilities resulting from cancellation of indebtedness income (see *above* 3.b.).
96. See, e.g. from the Canadian perspective, Bernstein, Leung and Chong, *above* note 2 at 179.
97. It is important to note that the valuation of a liability may depend on the interest payable. E.g. in Germany, liabilities must be discounted by 5.5 per cent if the liability runs for more than 12 months or if it is non-interest bearing (see § 6(1)(3) of the EStG). Accordingly, if the debt modification relieves the debtor company from an obligation to pay interest, the liability must be discounted in the tax balance sheet which results in taxable income.
98. See, e.g. from the German perspective, § 19 of the InsO.
99. See, e.g. Hibben, *above* note 23 at 616; and G. Hölzle, 'Der qualifizierte Rangrücktritt als Sanierungsmittel – und Steuerfalle?', (2005) 96 *GmbH-Rundschau* 852–859 on the legal position in Germany.
100. See *above* 2. and 3.

c. *Debt-for-Debt and Debt-for-Equity Transactions*

The debtor company may also be relieved from debts by debt-for-debt and debt-for equity transactions.[101] In the former case, a creditor grants a new loan to the debtor company replacing an old one.[102] Such transaction is tax neutral if the value of the new debt equals the value of the debt replaced. A debt-for-debt transaction, however, results in cancellation of indebtedness income[103] if the book value of the debt replaced is lower than the fair market value of the new debt.

This is principally the same with debt-for-equity transactions in which the debt is converted into equity.[104] The debtor company must recognize cancellation of indebtedness income to the extent that the fair market value of the equity received by the creditor (shares in the debtor company) is lower than the book value of the debt replaced. Only in case the value of the equity equals the debt replaced, the transaction may be tax neutral.

It is noteworthy that debt-for-debt or debt-for-equity transactions might not trigger corporation tax resulting from cancellation of indebtedness income if such transaction is not motivated by the rescue of the debtor company's business but by the relationship between the creditor and the debtor company. In the latter case, the comments regarding the cancellation of indebtedness by creditors related to the debtor company apply.[105]

As regards debt-for-equity transactions, it should be borne in mind that loss carry forwards may be lost if the transaction results in a 'change of control'. Many jurisdictions provide that a change of control results in a loss of loss carry forwards.[106] The idea of such limitation is that the company having incurred the losses has changed its economic identity. Such restrictions shall frustrate transactions which are mainly operated to utilize loss carry forwards (loss trafficking).[107] Loss trafficking transactions usually comprise the acquisition of so-called 'shell companies,' i.e. companies without any operative unit but with other favourable attributes such as loss carry forwards.[108] In case the change of control results from a debt-for-equity transaction serving the rescue of the debtor company's business, there is no loss trafficking which would justify restrictions as described above. Therefore, the applicable tax law may provide for relief in such cases.[109]

---

101. See, e.g. from the Canadian perspective, Bernstein, Leung and Chong, *above* note 2 at 182–184, and from the US perspective, Hardy, *above* note 2 at 3–12.
102. See, e.g. from the German perspective, Hibben, *above* note 23 at 616.
103. It is important to note that the debtor company may be relieved from tax liabilities resulting from cancellation of indebtedness income (see *above* 3.b.).
104. See Lindsay, *above* note 2 at 43 for the different approach in the UK.
105. See *above* 3.
106. See, e.g. from the German perspective, § 8(4)(1) of the KStG; and from the US perspective, s.382 of the IRC.
107. See, e.g., D. Kluger and D. Löhr, 'Internationaler Mantelkauf', (2005) 58 *Der Betrieb* 791 at 791 on this intention of respective limitations.
108. See, e.g., P. Brendt in B. Erle and T. Sauter (eds), *Körperschaftsteuergesetz* (Heidelberg, C.F. Müller, 2003), § 8, paras 379–385, in particular 384.
109. The German reconstruction relief in § 8(4)(3) of the KStG does not refer to the change of control but just to the contribution of capital which is one of two features characterizing a change of the economic identity under German law.

d. *Transfer of Assets*

The debtor company and the creditors may also agree on a transfer of assets from the debtor company to the creditors[110] to settle the creditors' claims. The transfer of assets shall replace the settlement of the debts in cash. The crucial point in this regard is that the assets transferred may contain built-in gains, i.e. the book value of the assets is lower than the fair market value.[111] If the transaction results in a settlement of debts higher than the book value of the assets transferred, built-in gains are realized which constitutes taxable income or capital gains.[112] Unlike transactions such as the exchange of shares or the transfer of assets in the sense of the transfer of branches, the transfer of assets not forming a branch is usually not subject to relief by the reorganization tax law. The purpose of a reorganization tax law is that a transaction shall not have tax consequences if the group of persons engaged in the reorganizing companies does not change in the course of the transaction, continuing its business activities just in another legal form.[113] Accordingly, built-in gains shall only be realized in the event of assets with built-in gains being disposed of. Therefore, the transfer of assets not forming a branch to a creditor is treated as a disposal resulting in the realization and taxation of built-in gains since in such case the business is not continued in its initial form.

The transfer of assets to creditors serving the settlement of the creditors' claims may be combined with a cancellation of indebtedness resulting in cancellation of indebtedness income. In such case, one must determine to what extent the debts were settled through the transfer of assets and to what extent they were discharged through the cancellation of indebtedness. Principally, both are taxable events. However, relief[114] may only be available for the cancellation of indebtedness part but not for the transfer of assets part.

5. Debts Resulting from Delivery of Goods

The comments thus far have only dealt with debts resulting from loans. Debts as shown in the tax balance sheet may, however, also result from the delivery of goods.[115] Such debts may also be ground for the over-indebtedness which shall be overcome by a corporate debt restructuring procedure. Therefore, one must

---

110. See, e.g. from the US perspective, Lau, Stapleton and Soltis, *above* note 2 at 69–72.
111. See, e.g., J. Hey in Tipke and Lang (eds), *above* note 15, § 17, para. 210.
112. The taxation of capital gains differs across the world. There are countries like Germany in which capital gains are subjet to the ordinary income and corporation tax, and countries like the UK in which capital gains are subjects to a separate capital gains tax. See Thuronyi, *above* note 15 at 260–266. The differences do not matter for the purposes of this chapter.
113. See on this basic idea of all reorganization tax laws Y. Brauner, 'A Good Old Habit, or Just an Old One? Preferential Tax Treatment for Reorganizations', (2004) *Brigham Young University Law Review* 1–68; C. H. Johnson, 'A Full and Faithful Marriage: The Substantially-All-The-Properties Requirement in a Corporate Reorganization', (1997) 50 *The Tax Lawyer* 319–380.
114. See *above* 3.b.
115. In the following, the term 'goods' shall comprise both fixed and floating assets.

discuss the tax consequences if deliverers of goods participate in corporate debt restructuring procedures.

At the debtor level, the delivery of goods affects two positions in the tax balance sheet, namely assets and liabilities. Both the assets and the liabilities are valued at the purchase prize.[116] Principally in the case of a change of the purchase prize, the acquisition costs relevant for tax purposes need to be readjusted, i.e. the value of the assets must be written off.[117] At the same time, the liabilities must be reduced. In the end, the cancellation of indebtedness resulting from the delivery of goods results just in a contraction of the tax balance sheet, i.e. both the assets and the liabilities are reduced while the equity remains unchanged. Accordingly, no taxable income arises so that a corporate debt restructuring procedure has no negative effects on the financial situation of the debtor company.

This outcome does not apply, however, if the goods do no longer form business assets of the debtor. In such a case, the comments regarding cancellation of indebtedness income[118] apply.[119]

B. CREDITOR

1. **General Comments**

The tax consequences at the debtor level as set out *above*[120] correspond with the tax consequences at the creditor level. Analogous to the situation at the debtor level, one must distinguish between different constellations, i.e. the cancellation of indebtedness by an unrelated creditor (see 2 *below*); and, by a creditor related to the debtor company (see 3 *below*). Further, one should consider the tax consequences of debt modifications (see 4 *below*) and the discharge from debts resulting from the delivery of goods (see 5 *below*).

2. **Cancellation of Indebtedness Intended to Rescue the Debtor**

As regards the discharge of the debtor company from debts by an unrelated creditor – mainly such creditors can be assumed to intend the rescue of the debtor – one must distinguish between commercial and private loans.

In case of private loans, the cancellation of indebtedness cannot be treated as expenditure amounting to the debt discharged[121] since losses in the private sphere

---
116. See, e.g. from the German perspective, § 6(1)(1)(1) of the EStG.
117. See, e.g. from the German perspective, P. Fischer in Kirchhof, *above* note 28, § 6 para. 44.
118. It is important to note that the debtor company may be relieved from tax liabilities resulting from cancellation of indebtedness income (see *above* 3.b.).
119. See *above* 2. and 3.
120. See *above* A.
121. See, e.g. from the German perspective, G. Crezelius in Kirchhof, *above* note 28, § 4, para. 134.

of a taxpayer are usually not relevant for tax purposes.[122] However, it is unlikely that a private person grants a loan to a business if that person is unrelated to the debtor company so that this scenario shall not be considered any further.

In the case of commercial loans, the cancellation of indebtedness is treated as negative income in the amount of the debt cancelled.[123] The cancellation of indebtedness decreases the equity of the creditor which results in negative income relevant for tax purposes or at least in a decrease of the taxable income. The recognition of negative income requires, however, that the discharge is motivated by business reasons. In case the creditor is a company, the cancellation of indebtedness is in every case 'motivated' by business/commercial reasons since a company has no private sphere. If the creditor is a natural person, the cancellation of indebtedness may be triggered by business/commercial or private[124] reasons. In the latter case, the cancellation may be treated as a withdrawal which does not decrease the taxable income.[125]

3. Cancellation of Indebtedness by a Related Person

a. General Comments

The tax consequences of the cancellation of indebtedness are more complicated if the creditor and the debtor are related. The most important case of such a relationship is that the creditor is a shareholder of the debtor and vice versa. Therefore, one must consider whether the cancellation of indebtedness is motivated by business reasons or by the relationship between the creditor and the debtor company.

b. Creditor Shareholder of the Debtor

If the creditor discharges the debtor company from a debt for business/commercial reasons, the comments on cancellation of indebtedness by an unrelated creditor who discharges the debtor company from a debt for business reasons apply.[126] Accordingly, the discharge must be treated as negative income at the creditor level.

In case the cancellation of indebtedness is motivated by the fact that the creditor is a shareholder of the debtor, i.e. the relationship between the debtor company and the creditor, one must distinguish whether the interest in the debtor company constitutes business/commercial or private assets.

---

122. See *below* 3.b. for exceptions.
123. See, e.g. from the German perspective, G. Crezelius in Kirchhof, *above* note 28, § 4, para. 119; S. Kling, 'Steuerrechtliche Auswirkungen der neuen Insolvenzordnung', (1998) 36 *Deutsches Steuerrecht* 1813 at 1817; and from the US perspective, Hirschfeld, *above* note 2 at 18–19. Hibben, *above* note 23 at 616 points out that this effect occurs worldwide.
124. E.g., the creditor discharges the debt to do the debtor – possibly a related person – a favour.
125. See, e.g. from the Chinese perspective, Gaw, *above* note 2 at 385; and from the German perspective, G. Crezelius in Kirchhof, *above* note 28, § 4, para. 119.
126. See *above* 2.

In the first case, the cancellation of indebtedness must be treated as a capital contribution.[127] Such transaction results in an increase of the acquisition costs and a write off of the claim against the debtor. Both aspects concern the assets of the creditor's tax balance sheet. Therefore, the transaction does not affect the equity and, therefore, the taxable income. It is important to note that the increase of the acquisition costs may be subject to the fact that the debt is recoverable. If the debt is irrecoverable, the negative income is relevant for tax purposes since one cannot consider the discharge from a (worthless) irrecoverable debt as capital contribution.[128]

In case the interest in the debtor company constitutes private assets, the tax consequences of the cancellation of indebtedness depend on the taxability of capital gains arising from the disposal of the interest. Similar to the discharge of the debtor company from non-business loans by unrelated creditors,[129] the discharge of the debtor company from a debt is principally irrelevant for tax purposes at the creditor level since capital gains arising from the disposal of the interest are not taxable in many jurisdictions.[130] Therefore, the increase of the acquisition costs for the interest in the debtor company through the discharge of the debtor company from the debt has no tax consequences at the creditor level. Only in case the disposal of the interest forming private assets constitutes a taxable event, the increase of the acquisition costs is relevant for tax purposes at the creditor level. Accordingly, the increase of the acquisition coststhrough the cancellation of indebtedness decreases the taxable capital gain in the event of the disposal of the shares in the debtor company. The taxability of capital gains arising from the disposal of an interest in a company may be based on a general capital gains tax covering respective capital gains[131] or on rules making respective capital gains taxable under particular circumstances. Such circumstances may be an interest exceeding a particular threshold or interest which is held for a period of time shorter than specified in the applicable tax law.[132] It is noteworthy that the applicable tax law may provide that the discharge of the debtor company from a debt may increase the acquisition costs only to the extent that the debt discharged was recoverable.[133]

c.   *Debtor Shareholder of the Creditor*

If the debtor is a shareholder of the creditor, the cancellation of indebtedness constitutes a distribution to the shareholder which does not reduce the creditor

---

127. See, e.g. from the German perspective, Hölzle, *above* note 2 at 1206.
128. See, e.g. from the German perspective, Hölzle, *above* note 2 at 1206.
129. See *above* 2.
130. See, e.g., Thuronyi, *above* note 15 at 260.
131. E.g., Australia or the UK apply such a capital gains tax. In Germany, the legislator wants to introduce a capital gains tax (included in the ITA) covering all disposals of shares in companies and land.
132. See, e.g. from the German perspective, § 17(1)(1) of the EStG (interest of one percent or more at any time within the last five years) and §§ 22(2) and 23(1)(1)(2) of the EStG (interest held not longer than one year).
133. See, e.g. from the German perspective, Hölzle, *above* note 2 at 1207.

company's profit in case the cancellation is motivated by personal reasons. Only if the cancellation is motivated by business reasons, the creditor company recognizes negative income relevant for tax purposes.

4. Alternative Forms of Debt Restructuring

a. Modification of Debts

The deferral of a debt has no tax consequences at the creditor level if the deferral does not have tax consequences at the debtor level.[134] Accordingly, only in case the deferral constitutes cancellation of indebtedness income at the debtor level, the creditor recognizes negative income relevant for tax purposes. This is particularly the case if the deferral results in a significant decrease of the value of the creditor's claim. The applicable tax law may provide for current-value depreciation if the value of the loan has decreased permanently[135] in case the loan forms a business asset.

In case the deferral of the debt is granted for a consideration, the consideration constitutes ordinary income at the creditor level.

Other forms of debt modification[136] have tax consequences at the creditor level if the modification results in cancellation of indebtedness income at the debtor level, i.e. if the modification is significant.[137] In such a case, the creditor recognizes negative income relevant for tax purposes.

b. Subordination of Debts

The subordination of a debt usually does not have tax consequences at the creditor level as long as the rescue of the debtor company does not fail. It may be different, however, if the subordination of the debt results in the cancellation of the debt not also for the purposes of insolvency law but also for tax purposes. In such case, the creditor recognizes negative income for tax purposes.

In case the rescue of the debtor company fails, the debtor company must be liquidated and the creditor loses his claim. Such loss of a claim is usually treated as cancellation of indebtedness since it does not matter from an economic point of view – which is decisive for tax law[138] – whether the creditor loses its claim voluntarily (by way of a cancellation indebtedness) or involuntarily (by way of the liquidation of the debtor company).[139] Accordingly, the comments *above*[140] on the cancellation of indebtedness by unrelated creditors (seldom in the case of a

---

134. See *above* A.4.a.
135. See, e.g. from the German perspective, § 6(1)(2)(2) of the EStG; further Hölzle, *above* note 2 at 1197.
136. See *above* A.4.a. on the other forms of debt modification.
137. E.g., if the debtor company must discount the debt (see *above* note 96), the creditor normally must write-off the claim.
138. See *above* II.B. on the connecting factors of tax law.
139. See, e.g. from the German perspective, Hölzle, *above* note 2 at 1207.
140. See *above* B.2.

subordination of debts) and by creditors related to the debtor company, in particular shareholders, apply.[141]

c. Debt-for-Debt and Debt-for-Equity Transactions

Debt-for-debt and debt-for-equity transactions may result in negative income relevant for tax purposes at the creditor level if the book value of the claim replaced by another claim or by equity is higher than the fair market value of the claim or equity received. If the value of the claim replaced equals the equity or the new claim, the transaction is tax neutral at the creditor level.

d. Transfer of Assets

The transfer of assets from the debtor company to the creditor raises the question at which value the assets transferred must be entered in the creditor's books. Since such a transaction results in a realization of built-in gains at the debtor level, there is no risk that built-in gains could be lost for taxation purposes. Therefore, the assets transferred may be entered in the books at the fair market value of the assets.[142]

If the transfer of assets is combined with a cancellation of indebtedness, the extent of the transfer of assets and of the cancellation of indebtedness must be determined. The cancellation of indebtedness component is more advantageous for the creditor since the creditor recognizes negative income relevant for tax purposes (only) to the extent that the transaction qualifies as cancellation of indebtedness.

5. Debts Resulting from Delivery of Goods

The cancellation of indebtedness resulting from the delivery of goods does not present any specifics compared with the cancellation of indebtedness resulting from loans at the creditor level. Therefore, the comments on the latter constellation also apply in this regard.[143]

C. INTERNATIONAL ASPECTS

The comments *above* have shown that the tax treatment of debt restructurings at the debtor level often corresponds to that at the creditor level. Incongruencies might occur if the debtor company and the creditor are subject to different jurisdictions.[144] Principally, each person involved is treated according to the provisions of the tax law of the jurisdiction that it is subject to. Such approach may bear

---

141. See *above* 2. and 3.
142. See, e.g. from the German perspective, § 6(1)(2)(1) of the EStG.
143. See *above* 2. and 3.
144. See, e.g. from the French perspective, Marciniak, *above* note 2 at 219–221; and from the German perspective, Hibben, *above* note 23 at 615–617.

chances and risks for the persons involved since the tax systems are developed in many different ways. This may result in double-dip situations, i.e. all the persons involved may benefit from favourable provisions in the countries in which they are resident, but also in situations in which the persons involved face disadvantageous provisions in all jurisdictions.

IV. ISSUES REGARDING INDIRECT TAXES

A. GENERAL COMMENTS

Thus far, only issues regarding direct taxation, i.e. taxes on income (and capital gains), have been discussed. Direct taxation issues evidently play a key role in the context of corporate debt restructuring procedures. As shown *above*,[145] the tax consequences do not depend on the nature of the business (i.e. loan or trade debts). It is different with indirect taxes.[146] However, only the cancellation of debts resulting from the delivery of goods is of major relevance as to indirect taxes in the course of corporate debt restructuring procedures.[147] The taxes concerned may particularly be the VAT (see B *below*) but also other forms of indirect taxes such as transfer taxes (see C *below*).

B. VALUE ADDED TAX (VAT)

1. Debtor

The most important form of indirect taxes is VAT.[148] VAT taxes the supply of goods and services as such without taking into account the personal situation of any person involved. Therefore, the debtor company has to pay VAT on all supplies of goods and services received. However, most VAT systems provide that only the

---

145. See *above* III.
146. See *above* III.A.5 on the direct tax consequences of the delivery of the cancellation of debts resulting from the delivery of goods.
147. See *below* B.1. for the reason.
148. The terminology for this form of indirect taxes differs across the world, but also within English-speaking countries having such form of tax. E.g., the UK has a VAT, Australia a Goods and Services Tax (GST). Interestingly, the US has no equivalent to the VAT at the Federal level, but knows Sales Taxes at the state level. The Austrian and the German *Umsatzsteuer* substantially is a value added tax although the name – literally translated – implies that the tax is a turnover tax. Alike within the English language, the German language has different terms for this form of tax. The German edition of the Sixth Directive (Sixth Directive 77/388/EEC of 17 May 1977 on the harmonization of the laws of the Member States relating to turnover taxes – Common system of value added tax: uniform basis of assessment, OJ L 145, 13.6.1977, p. 1–40) uses the term *Mehrwertsteuer* which is the literal translation of 'value added tax'.

end-consumer but not a taxpayer running a business must bear VAT.[149] Therefore, a taxpayer running a business must be disburdened from VAT which is usually achieved by allowing such tax payer to deduct input tax, i.e. the VAT that it had to pay on supplies to it, from VAT that it had to charge on supplies provided by it.[150] In case the input tax exceeds the VAT to be charged for supplies carried out by the entrepreneur, the entrepreneur must be refunded the exceeding input tax.

The input tax deduction may be a critical aspect with regard to corporate debt restructurings. If the creditor discharges the debtor company (totally or partly) from the debt resulting from the supply of goods or services, the debtor company might have deducted input tax which it would not have been allowed to if the debtor company and its supplier had initially agreed on a smaller consideration. Accordingly, tax authorities may lose revenue. Therefore, the VAT laws usually provide for an obligation to refund input tax deducted in case the tax base, i.e. the consideration,[151] is reduced after the input tax was deducted.[152] In the end, the debtor company is (partly) discharged from a debt, but becomes liable to an obligation to refund input tax deducted. Although this is consistent since a taxpayer running a business shall not benefit from an input tax deduction without a VAT payment, it burdens the financial situation of the debtor company since it is subject to a new liability in a financial crisis.

VAT usually is not an issue with regard to loans, i.e. the allocation of money in return for interest, since financial services are usually VAT exempt.[153] Accordingly, the debtor does not have to pay VAT on the allocation of money by the creditor and on the payment of interest (i.e. the consideration). Therefore, there is no need for a refund of input tax in the event of a discharge from a debt resulting from a loan.

2. Creditor

From the comments on the VAT consequences of a discharge from a debt resulting from the delivery of goods at the debtor level,[154] one may directly deduce that the discharge from a debt must also have VAT consequences at the creditor level. If the

---

149. See, e.g., H. Friedrich-Vache, *Verbrauchsteuerkonforme Umsatzbesteuerung von Finanzdienstleistungen Plädoyer für die Abschaffung unechter Steuerbefreiungen* (Köln, Dr. Otto Schmidt, 2005), pp.19–21; Thuronyi, *above* note 15 at 305–312; W. Reiß in Tipke and Lang (eds), *above* note 15, § 14, paras1–5. VAT law may also affect the restructuring of debts resulting from loans in case securities for the loans are also subject to the restructuring. See on such issues from the Italian perspective Flora, *above* note 2 at 223–227. See *generally* on the role of indirect taxes in debt restructurings from the Austrian perspective Schneider, *above* note 2 at 270–271.
150. See, e.g. from the German perspective, § 15(1)(1) of the *Umsatzsteuergesetz* (Turnover Tax Act; hereinafter 'UStG').
151. See, e.g. from the German perspective, § 10(1) of the UStG.
152. See, e.g. from the German perspective, § 17(1)(2) of the UStG.
153. See Friedrich-Vache, *above* note 151 at 1; Thuronyi, *above* note 15 at 322–324; further, e.g. from the German perspective, § 4(8)(a) of the UStG which is based on the Sixth Directive.
154. See *above* 1.

creditor discharges the debtor company from a debt resulting from the delivery of goods, the consideration for the goods (i.e. the purchase prize) establishing the tax base for VAT purposes is reduced. Therefore, if VAT to be charged has already been remitted to tax authorities by the creditor, VAT accounting for the debt discharged must be refunded.[155] This is consistent since VAT shall only be charged on the actual supplies. Therefore, the actual consideration must constitute the tax base so that retroactive changes, in particular reductions of the consideration by way of a discharge from a debt, must be taken into account. Unlike the debtor company, the VAT consequences of the discharge from a debt improve the financial situation of the creditor since he receives liquidity.[156]

Similar to the legal position at the debtor level,[157] a discharge from a debt may only have VAT consequences in case the debt cancelled results from a delivery of goods. In case the debt discharged results from a loan, the granting of a loan and the payment of interest as consideration usually is VAT exempt. Accordingly, there is no need for a refund of input tax in the event of a discharge from a debt.

C.   TRANSFER TAXES

Although VAT is a consumption tax, i.e. the connecting factor for the tax is not the supply of goods or services as such but the consumption by the consumer,[158] it technically ties in with the supply of goods or services (i.e. a transaction) for administrative purposes. By contrast, original transfer taxes legally and economically charge all relevant transfers, not only those in relation to consumers.[159] Prominent examples for transfer taxes are land transfer taxes or generally stamp duties for the transfer of land or shares.[160] If the debtor company is partly discharged from the debt, the consideration which usually establishes the tax base of the transfer tax/stamp duty is reduced. If the transfer tax has already been paid, the overpaid transfer taxes must be refunded to ensure that only the actual transaction is subject to the transfer tax.[161]

The tax consequences for the debtor company and the creditors are principally the same as those occurring in respect of VAT. One must, however, consider the

---

155. See, e.g. from the German perspective, § 17(1)(1) of the UStG.
156. Though this is a positive effect, it does not contribute to the rescue of the debtor's business since only the creditor benefits from an improvement of the financial situation.
157. See *above* 1.
158. See *above* B.
159. If a transaction is covered by a transfer tax, it usually is exempt from VAT to avoid double taxation. See, e.g., G. Arends and D. Dürrschmidt, 'Stamp Duty Land Tax (Grunderwerbsteuer) im Vereinigten Königreich – Die Perspektive des deutschen Investors –', (2005) 51 *Recht der Internationalen Wirtschaft* 198 at 202 regarding the UK Stamp Duty Land Tax and the German *Grunderwerbsteuer* (Land Transfer Tax).
160. See, e.g., Thuronyi, *above* note 15 at 332–335.
161. See, e.g., Arends and Dürrschmidt, *above* note 161 at 202 regarding the UK Stamp Duty Land Tax and the German *Grunderwerbsteuer* (Land Transfer Tax).

difference between original transfer taxes and VAT, namely the missing input tax deduction. Therefore, there must only be a refund of the overpaid transfer tax. Depending on which party had paid the transfer tax, either the debtor company, the creditor or both are entitled to the refund of the overpaid transfer taxes.[162] The refund in every case improves the financial situation of whoever receives the refund.

V. TAX LIABILITIES SUBJECT TO DEBT RESTRUCTURING AGREEMENTS

A. GENERAL COMMENTS

The comments so far addressed tax issues which the outcome of corporate debt restructuring procedures may present. Accordingly, a corporate debt restructuring agreement may result in tax liabilities, in particular against the debtor company that actually should be discharged from debts. Tax liabilities may, however, also be of relevance in another respect. The debtor company facing a financial crisis which gave rise to the corporate debt restructuring procedure may also be subject to tax liabilities which have accrued before the corporate debt restructuring procedure was commenced. Tax liabilities of the debtor company may amount to a significant share in the debtor company's overall debts. This may particularly be true since the debtor company might have tried to rescue his business by paying creditors other than tax authorities in order to avoid that these creditors stop providing supplies and services necessary to run the business.[163] Therefore, the issue arises how tax liabilities accrued before the corporate debt restructuring procedure was commenced are treated.

The crucial point as regards tax liabilities is that tax law must comply with superior principles such as the principle of equal treatment. According to this principle, tax authorities must not arbitrarily discharge a taxpayer from tax liabilities. Such behaviour would unlawfully discriminate other taxpayers. With regard to tax liabilities subject to corporate debt restructuring procedures, there are four separate issues which are of relevance. Firstly, one must address the issue of whether tax liabilities should be subject to corporate debt restructuring procedures at all (see B *below*). Secondly, one must consider whether tax authorities should be bound by superior principles agreeing on/voting for a corporate debt restructuring agreement (see C *below*). Thirdly, one may wonder what happens to tax liabilities in the event of a corporate debt restructuring agreement comes into existence (see D *below*). Finally, one must think of the way how tax authorities may collect and execute taxes after a corporate debt restructuring procedure has been commenced (see E *below*).

---

162. In many cases, all persons who are party to a relevant transfer are jointly and severally liable to transfer taxes. In practice, however, in most of the cases, the debtor company is obliged by the contract governing the transaction to pay the transfer tax.
163. It is important to note in this context that in such case, the directors of the company may be liable in addition to the company in case tax authorities cannot cover the taxes. See, e.g. from the German perspective, § 69 of the AO.

B. TAX LIABILITIES AND CORPORATE DEBT
RESTRUCTURING PROCEDURES

Concerning the first issue, one must maintain that the exemption of tax liabilities from corporate debt restructuring procedures would significantly reduce the chances of the rescue of the debtor company's business. Creditors other than tax authorities might be reluctant to contribute to the rescue of the debtor's business if tax liabilities resulting from cancellation of indebtedness income remain unchanged or even increase while these creditors lose their claims.[164] A *pari passu* principle orientated treatment of tax liabilities in corporate debt restructuring procedures (i.e. tax liabilities are settled at the same ratio as all the other debts) would, however, be acceptable to the creditors other than tax authorities. Therefore, it should be preferred to other options.

Exempting tax liabilities from corporate debt restructuring procedures would be inconsistent in case the applicable tax or insolvency law does not provide for a tax priority in insolvency proceedings, in particular in the liquidation of a company. In such case, tax authorities would be better off in a corporate debt restructuring procedure.[165] Therefore, it might be advantageous for creditors other than tax authorities to abstain from participating in the rescue of the debtor company's business instead of contributing to the rescue of the company by way of a corporate debt restructuring agreement. In case the relevant jurisdiction provides both for a tax priority and an exemption of tax liabilities from corporate debt restructurings, tax authorities are in every case in a better position. Nevertheless, the exemption of tax liabilities from corporate debt restructuring procedures may make creditors reluctant towards the rescue of the debtor's business, particularly if the cancellation of indebtedness by creditors other than tax authorities results in taxable cancellation of indebtedness income. It might be different if tax liabilities are subject to corporate debt restructuring procedures whereas tax authorities enjoy priority treatment in insolvency proceedings. In such case, tax authorities might be averse to corporate debt restructuring procedures since they would be better off in the event of the liquidation.

C. REQUIREMENTS FOR THE PARTICIPATION OF TAX AUTHORITIES
IN CORPORATE DEBT RESTRUCTURING PROCEDURES

Assuming that tax liabilities are subject to corporate debt restructuring procedures, the secondary issue is whether tax authorities must meet the requirements of provisions allowing the discharge of a taxpayer from tax liabilities on a case-by-case basis[166] if they participate in a corporate debt restructuring procedure. Such provisions usually require tax authorities to exercise discretion. Thereby

---

164. See *above* III.A.2.
165. See, e.g. from the German perspective, Loose, *above* note 65 at 22.
166. See *above* III.A.2.

they must adequately consider superior principles such as the principle of equal treatment. Principally, tax authorities may not avoid their obligation to apply tax law equally to all taxpayers, i.e., they must not arbitrarily favour a taxpayer through a discharge from tax liabilities. However, provisions allowing the discharge from tax liabilities on a case-by-case basis are intended to consider the circumstances of the individual case which include public interests such as chances to save jobs. This intention should also play a vital role in respect of the tax authorities' conduct in a corporate debt restructuring procedure. Accordingly, the tax authorities should take into account everything that would be taken into account while making a decision on a case-by-case basis.[167]

In this regard, it should be noted that the insolvency law governing the corporate debt restructuring procedure may prohibit the obstruction of the conclusion of a corporate debt restructuring agreement.[168] Such a prohibition applies, if available in the applicable insolvency law, in case creditors (including tax authorities) obstruct the conclusion of a corporate debt restructuring agreement although such agreement would not put them in a worse position compared to the liquidation of the debtor company's business. In such case, the competent court usually replaces the creditor's consent to the conclusion of the agreement. Particularly in case the law governing a corporate debt restructuring procedure contains a respective provision, tax authorities cannot be hindered to enter into a corporate debt restructuring agreement by principles such as the principle of equal treatment and the 'ability-to-pay' principle as one of its sub-principles relevant for taxation.[169] Therefore, it should be in the interest of all parties involved to allow tax authorities to agree on or vote for such an agreement.

D.   EFFECTS OF CORPORATE DEBT RESTRUCTURING PROCEDURES ON TAX LIABILITIES

The third issue concerns the implications of a corporate debt restructuring agreement on tax liabilities. Principally, the law governing such procedures must provide for the effects of such agreement. If corporate debt restructuring procedures enable majority decisions, corporate debt restructuring agreements come into effect irrespective of the consent of the individual creditors (including tax authorities).[170] The creditors only need to implement the corporate debt restructuring agreement.[171] The actual effects of corporate debt restructuring agreements on tax liabilities may vary. In the end, it depends on the conduct of tax authorities. If they agree on a cancellation of tax

---

167. See, e.g. from the German perspective, Bringewat and Waza, *above* note 4, para.455; S. Kling in Kirchhof, *above* note 10, Insolvenzsteuerrecht, para.240; further Fett and Barten, *above* note 166 at 888, and Loose, *above* note 166 at 27 and 30 who do not apply §§ 163 and 227 of the AO but nevertheless arrive at the same result.
168. See, e.g. from the German perspective, § 245 of the InsO (so-called *Obstruktionsverbot*).
169. See *above* II.B. on these principles.
170. See, e.g. from the German perspective, § 251(1)(1) of the InsO.
171. See, e.g. from the German perspective, Fett and Barten, *above* note 166 at 886.

liabilities, the tax liabilities cease to exist. In case tax authorities are outvoted by a majority of creditors, it depends on the law governing corporate debt restructuring agreements whether (tax) liabilities cease to exist or remain unchanged.[172] In the latter case, only the tax authorities' power to enforce (tax) claims is limited. If the corporate debt restructuring agreement is terminated, creditors (including tax authorities) retrieve their power to collect and execute (tax) claims.

E. COLLECTION AND EXECUTION OF TAX LIABILITIES

The final issue is how tax authorities may collect and execute tax claims subject to a corporate debt restructuring agreement. In an insolvency situation, tax authorities may be bound by the insolvency law when it comes to the collection and execution of tax claims. Accordingly, tax authorities must collect and execute tax claims alike ordinary creditors[173] provided the applicable tax or insolvency law does not contain a tax priority. This rule applies both to the liquidation of a company and to the rescue of a company by way of a corporate debt restructuring procedure. Thereby, tax authorities must not apply the normal rules for the collection and the execution of tax claims (i.e. in particular the assessment of taxes by way of a notice of assessment which constitutes the basis for the execution of the tax claims by tax authorities).[174] Alike all creditors, tax authorities may benefit from the fact that a corporate debt restructuring approved by the competent court may serve as basis for the execution.[175] Accordingly, tax authorities do not asses the taxes by way of a notice of assessment.

VI. CONCLUSION

The comments *above* have shown that a corporate debt restructuring procedure – irrespective of whether or not it is an expedited procedure – raises tax issues in almost every case. Therefore, tax law must be taken into account in the course of a corporate debt restructuring procedure to avoid, or at least to lessen, unfavourable tax consequences. The tax consequences may contradict the aim of a corporate debt restructuring procedure in a way that a corporate debt restructuring procedure may fail or is not even commenced. The effects would outreach the area of tax law since a failure of a corporate debt restructuring procedure may result in the liquidation of the debtor company. The economic consequences, in particular the loss of jobs, would be an undesirable result.

---

172. In Germany, e.g., an *Insolvenzplan* does not result in the discharge of the tax liabilities. See, e.g., Bringewat and Waza, *above* note 4, paras 460–461; Fett and Barten, *above* note 166 at 886–887; Loose, *above* note 166 at 27.
173. See, e.g. from the German perspective, § 251(2)(1) of the AO; further Loose, *above* note 166 at 21. In this context, it is important to remind that insolvency law only impacts the coverage of tax claims, not the accrual of such (see *above* II.A.).
174. See, e.g. from the German perspective, Dürrschmidt, *above* note 12 at 228–229.
175. See, e.g. from the German perspective, § 251(2)(2) of the AO and § 201(2) of the InsO.

Chapter 17
Implications of Merger Legislation for Corporate Restructuring

Ioannis Kokkoris[1]

---

1. The views expressed in this chapter are those of the author and not of the UK Office of Fair Trading. The author thanks Professor Richard Whish for his helpful comments.

ACRONYMS, ABBREVIATIONS & DEFINED TERMS

4064/89	Council Regulation (EEC) 4064/89 of 21 December 1989 on the control of concentrations between undertakings
Aerospatialle	Aerospatiale SNI
Alenia	Alenia-Aeritalia e Selenia Spa
Andersen UK	Arthur Andersen in the United Kingdom
ATR	Avions de Transport Régional
BASF	BASF Aktiengesellschaft
Bertelsmann	Bertelsmann AG
BetaDigital	BetaDigital Gesellschaft fl'Or digitale Fernsehdienste mbH
BetaResearch	BetaResearch Gesellschaft fl'Or Entwicklung und Vermarktung digitaler Infrastrukturen mbH
Blokker	Blokker Holding BV
Boeing	Boeing, US
Citizen	Citizen Publishing Co.
Clayton Act	1914 Clayton Antitrust Act
CLT-UFA	CLT-UFA SA
Commission	European Commission
Congress	US Congress
Council	European Council
Council of Ministers	Council of Ministers of the EU
DAC	Douglas Aircraft Company
DF 1	DF 1 GmbH & Co. KG
DOJ	US Department of Justice
EC Merger Regulation	Council Regulation (EC) No 139/2004 of 20 January 2004 on the control of concentrations between undertakings
EC Treaty	Treaty of Rome 1957
ECJ	European Court of Justice
ECMR	Council Regulation (EC) No 139/2004 of 20 January 2004 on the control of concentrations between undertakings

EMC	EMC Group
ESK	Elektroschmelzwerk Kempten
EU	European Union
EU Guidelines	Guidelines on the assessment of horizontal mergers under the Council Regulation on the control of concentrations between undertakings
Eurodiol	Eurodiol SA
FTC	Federal Trade Commission
HHI	Herfindahl-Hirschmann Index
HSR	Hart-Scott-Rodino Antitrust Improvements Act of 1976
Kali	Kali
Kirch	Kirch Group
MDC	McDonnell Douglas Co.
MdK	a state owned company of the former German Democratic Republicf
Meinl	Julius Meinl AG
NCAs	National Competition Authorities of the European Union
Newscorp	News Corporation Limited, Australia
Nom	a private investment and development company for the northern provinces of the Netherlands
OECD	Organization for Economic Co-operation and Development
Pantochim	Pantochim SA
Premiere	Premiere Medien GmbH & Co. KG
R&D	Research and Development
Rewe	Rewe Group
Saint-Gobain	Saint-Gobain Group
Salz	Salz
SCPA	Société Commerciale des Potasses et de l'Azote
SEPR	Société Européenne des Produits Réfractaires
SIEC	Significant Impediment to Effective Competition
SLC	Substantial Lessening of Competition

Star	Star
Stream	Stream Spa
Taurus	Taurus Beteiligungs-GmbH & Co. KG
Telepiù	Telepiù Spa
Toys 'R' Us	Toys 'R' Us Inc.
Treuhand	Treuhandanstalt
Tribunal de Commerce	Commercial Court of Charleroi (Belgium)
US	United States of America
US Guidelines	1992 Horizontal Merger Guidelines
USBC	Title 11 of the United States Code (Bankruptcy Code)
Wacker-Chemie	Wacker-Chemie Group

I. INTRODUCTION

Nowadays we face global restructuring of industries that may be the most significant economic change of the last decades. Fierce competition from imports, severe overcapacity in some industries and technological advancements are only some of the features that characterize markets nowadays. Distressed companies on the verge of bankruptcy are a common phenomenon that is observed in both developed and developing economies. Companies that are in distressed financial conditions may choose to embark on a restructuring process in order to ensure their viability and profitability.

Restructuring is often done as part of bankruptcy procedures. Restructuring is the term for the act of fully/partially dismantling and reorganizing a company. It might involve the selling of sectors/units of the company and severe job losses. Restructuring of the liability and stockholders equity components of a financial balance sheet is normally undertaken because the issuer does not generate enough cash flow to service its debt and other liabilities. Restructuring may include deferral of principal or interest payments on debt, equalization of debt or other liabilities, and, in bankruptcy, modification or termination of burdensome contractual commitments. Restructuring is normally done with reference to the outcome that would ensue in a bankruptcy proceeding even where no such proceeding occurs.[2]

Debt restructuring aims at enabling the company to continue business operation without danger from debt. One of the costs associated with a business debt restructuring is the time required to negotiate with bankers, creditors, tax authorities and suppliers. According to Norton,[3] if a company decides to restructure its debt, it will be faced, inter alia, with three alternatives that are negotiated and implemented out-of-court, out-of-court reorganization, pre-packaged reorganization plans and pre-negotiated reorganization plans. An 'out-of-court reorganization' is the financial restructuring of the debt of the company by means of a contractual voluntary agreement without the intervention of any court or regulatory authority. According to the 'pre-packaged reorganization plan' the company designs and negotiates a settlement with its creditors without having the need to file a full court-supervised reorganization procedure. Then, the approved plan is filed with the court for homologation in order to make it binding to the dissenting minority. A 'pre-negotiated' plan is negotiated between the debtor and its creditors on an out-of-court basis and then is filed with a court who will summon a creditors' meeting to obtain their consent and approval. If the plan is adopted by the required majority, the court will approve it and it will become mandatory to all comprised parties.[4]

---

2. <www.cmra.com/html/body_glossary.html>.
3. Norton W. L. Jr., 'Norton Bankruptcy Law and Practice', (2nd ed.), § 86:1, also available online at <www.westlaw.co.uk>.
4. Olivares-Caminal R., 'Recognition of Corporate Debt Restructuring Procedures in Latin America under US Law: Lessons from the Multicanal Case', International Corporate Rescue, Volume 2, Issue 3, 2005, pages 143–150. Also see Kokkoris I. 'Weak-Form Tests of Market Efficiency in Corporate Debt Restructuring', (2005), vol. 2, issue 6, pp. 337–343.

A strategic response for struggling firms and one of the means of implementing a successful debt restructuring process is to combine in order to achieve competitively necessary efficiencies.[5] Either a failing firm within a booming industry or firms in a distressed industry will choose to merge/acquire/be acquired, or choose to sell loss-making divisions in order to enhance the firm's viability and profitability. Given these wrenching transformations, the applicability and importance of the failing firm defence and failing division defence[6] might be crucial.

As this chapter will illustrate, a merger/acquisition[7] is one of the means by which a company may wish to implement a restructuring procedure. Merger control has a significant role in today's economies, a fact which is underlined by the ever increasing number of mergers that are completed. The purpose of merger legislation is to capture mergers that may have anti-competitive effects on the market structure.

There are several reasons for firms to engage in mergers. A merger or an acquisition is a common method that firms choose in order to be profitable and sustain their viability and profitability through time. Mergers consolidate the ownership and control of business assets, including physical assets (e.g. plant) and intangibles (e.g. brand reputation). They can enhance corporate – and wider economic – performance by improving the efficiency with which business assets are used. Further reasons for firms to engage in mergers and acquisitions include economies of scale and economies of scope[8] that firms benefit from as well as efficiencies stemming from the tendency of some countries to endorse the concept of 'national champions'.[9] In addition, mergers provide means to a firm to exit the industry and at the same time reap monetary reward or compensation for the risks and the initial investments. Furthermore, mergers may also satisfy the ambitions of executives for more power and greater control.[10]

---

5. Valentine D. 'Horizontal Issues: What's Happening and What's on the Horizon'. <www.ftc.gov/speeches/other/dvhorizontalissues.htm>. 8 December 1995.
6. An equivalent term is failing company defence.
7. For the purposes of this chapter, the terms 'merger' and 'acquisition' will be used interchangeably and will refer to the term 'concentration'.
8. Economies of scale refer to the situation where long run average costs of production decrease as output rises. See *further*: Begg D., Fischer S. and Dornbusch R. (1997), '*Economics*' 5th ed., McGraw-Hill, UK. Page 109. Economies of scope refer to the situation where the joint output of a single firm is greater than the output that could be achieved by two different firms each producing a single product (with equivalent production inputs allocated between the two firms). See *further*: Pindyck R. and Rubinfeld D. (1998), '*Microeconomics*', 4th ed., Prentice Hall International, New Jersey. Page 227. Economies of scope are conceptually similar to economies of scale. Economies of scale apply to efficiencies associated with increasing or decreasing the scale of production and refer to changes in the output of a single product type. Economies of scope refer to efficiencies associated with increasing or deceasing the scope of marketing and distribution and refer to changes in the number of different types of products. In addition, economies of scale refer primarily to supply-side changes (such as level of production) whereas economies of scope refer to demand-side changes (such as marketing and distribution).
9. The concept 'national champion' refers to domestic firms that post-merger are able to successfully compete in international markets.
10. Managers may be interested in the size, growth or risk diversification of the company they run. Owners of firms may sometimes give managers incentives in their contracts to achieve some of

The importance of mergers (and thus of the failing firm defence) for the restructuring process is indicated, *inter alia*, by the US Supreme Court in the case *United States v. General Dynamics Corp.*[11] The Court upheld that three groups of private parties, shareholders, creditors benefit from the merger of a failing firm. The shareholders are unlikely to lose the investment and are likely to reap benefits if the merger proves profitable. The creditors will benefit as a result of retaining their rights against the debtor and are likely to be reimbursed for the credit they have provided to the firm. On the contrary, in insolvency proceedings they are not as likely to be fully reimbursed.

The restructuring process can thus be used as a tool to determine if a division of the firm or the whole firm must be merged or acquired by another undertaking in order to maintain its viability and its future prospects for profitability. In such a case the only possible means of restructuring is through a successful merger/acquisition. This merger may need to be assessed by the relevant competition[12] authorities. If the authorities consider that the merger will have anticompetitive effects, they may block it, resulting thus in the unsuccessful completion of the restructuring procedure.

This chapter will address the interaction of debt restructuring and competition law. Particularly, it will deal with the implications of the failing firm defence on corporate debt restructuring in the European Union (EU) and the United States of America (US).

The reason for choosing these jurisdictions is that both the EU and the US have developed merger legislation and an extensive practice on the topic.

Each of the *above mentioned* jurisdictions has its own criteria for assessing the failing firm defence argument. The satisfaction of these criteria is an essential factor for a merger which is likely to have anticompetitive effects, to be allowed to proceed. In addition each of the *above* jurisdictions has its own legislation regarding merger assessment. It would be necessary for the purposes of this chapter and for a complete understanding of the implications of merger legislation, as they are identified through the failing firm defence, to provide a brief analysis of the legislation concerning the assessment of mergers in these jurisdictions. Thus, for each of the *above* jurisdictions an analysis of the relevant legislation will be provided. It is imperative to tie the analysis of the relevant legislation with its actual application in cases where the failing firm defence has been invoked. For each jurisdiction the landmark cases related to failing firm defence will be analyzed in order to evaluate how the competition authorities and the courts have assessed the failing firm defence.

This multi jurisdictional volume deals with the issue of expedited corporate debt restructuring. This chapter will provide insights on the implications of merger

---

these targets (i.e. increasing the firm's size in the marketplace). See *further*: Motta M. (2004), '*Competition Policy-Theory and Practice*', Cambridge University Press, Cambridge. Page 243.
11. *United States v. General Dynamics Corp.*, (1974) 415 U.S. 486.
12. This chapter will mainly use the term 'competition' which is interchangeable with 'antitrust' as used in the US for the law or authorities that protect trade and commerce from restraints, monopolies, price-fixing and price discrimination. See Black's Law Dictionary for the definition of antitrust law (8th ed. 2004), page 92.

legislation on corporate debt restructuring. Thus, apart from the analysis of competition legislation surrounding mergers, this chapter should also include a brief analysis of the restructuring process during which the failing firm defence may be invoked if it is decided that the means of viability of the firm are through a merger/acquisition. Therefore, an analysis of the basic concepts surrounding corporate debt restructuring is imperative.

This chapter will be comprised of five parts. It will begin with a brief analysis of the main issues that surround corporate debt restructuring. Then, the notion of failing firm defence will be analyzed in general terms, since more details will be provided in the relevant part of the chapter dealing with each jurisdiction. Subsequently, the next two parts will deal with the concepts of failing firm defence and failing division defence as these two have been developed in the legislation and case law of the EU and US. The fifth part will expose some of the controversial issues surrounding the success of the failing firm defence. Finally, concluding remarks regarding failing firm defence and failing division defence will be presented.

II. CORPORATE DEBT RESTRUCTURING

In the analysis of companies with financial difficulties or that are on the verge of bankruptcy, it is essential to assess the plan of reorganization and the prospects of the reorganized company as regards profitability and viability. Changes in the market conditions which may affect the future prospects of the company's viability should also be taken into account.

According to Norton,[13] if a corporation is financially troubled and decides to restructure its debt to find its way to recovery it will be faced with three alternatives that, for the most part, are negotiated and implemented out-of-court. These alternatives include out-of-court reorganization or non-bankruptcy workouts, pre-packaged reorganization plans and pre-arranged or pre-negotiated reorganization plans.[14]

An 'out-of-court reorganization' or 'non-bankruptcy workout' is a financial restructuring of a company by means of an understanding between the debtor and its creditors without the intervention of any court or regulatory authority. It is a contractual voluntary agreement where the terms and conditions are agreed between the parties.[15]

A 'pre-packaged reorganization plan' or simply 'pre-pack', is the procedure that companies can recourse if it is either in default or has general economic or financial difficulties to design and negotiate a settlement with its creditors without having the need to file a full court-supervised reorganization procedure. The aim of these plans or procedures is to enhance the efficiency of the insolvency procedures by permitting a fast recovery from a situation that might lead to bankruptcy and its implications. Upon the filing of the agreement reached by the parties, the court or

---

13. William L. Norton Jr., Norton Bankruptcy Law and Practice, 2nd Edition, § 86:1.
14. William L. Norton Jr., Norton Bankruptcy Law and Practice, 2nd Edition, § 86:1.
15. Olivares-Caminal R., 'Recognition of Corporate Debt Restructuring Procedures in Latin America under US Law: Lessons from the Multicanal Case', International Corporate Rescue, Volume 2, Issue 3, 2005, pages 143–150.

regulatory authority depending on the jurisdiction reviews that it fulfils the minimum requirements set-forth by law and proceeds to homologate it. The main effects of the homologation of the agreement are the novation of all the obligations having an origin or cause prior to the agreement and the homologated agreement produces effects with respect to all general creditors whose claims had been included in the agreement, even if they have not participated in the restructuring or if they have opposed. Even though the homologation of the agreement was obtained, the bankruptcy of the debtor can be adjudicated. For the bankruptcy to proceed, the agreement shall be declared null and void on the existence of fraud used to exaggerate the liabilities, acknowledge or simulate non-existing or fraudulently created preferences, and conceal or exaggerate assets.[16] If the agreement is approved by the court it becomes binding to all creditors affected by the agreement even though they have rejected or abstained to vote.[17]

A 'pre-arranged' or 'pre-negotiated' plan (pre-negotiated agreement) is similar to the pre-packaged reorganization plan since it is also negotiated between the debtor and its creditors on an out-of-court basis and then is filed with a court to obtain the benefits of its approval. Although the parties have conducted substantial negotiations prior to the filing, there is no formal solicitation of votes. As Jacoby[18] argues, the difference between the 'pre-packaged reorganization plan' and the 'pre-arranged' or 'pre-negotiated plan' is if it is 'pre-voted' or 'post-voted'.

A related concept to that of corporate debt restructuring is the concept of insolvency which consists in a debtor's ultimate inability to meet his financial commitments.[19] The liabilities exceed the assets with the consequence that it is impossible for all the liabilities to be discharged in full. Insolvency as such is not a condition to which legal consequences can be attached. These occur only after there has been some formal proceeding, such as winding up or the appointment of an administrator or administrative receiver. A formal insolvency proceeding is necessary, at which point transactions entered into by the company at a time when it was insolvent will in certain conditions be void or liable to be set aside. A winding up or administration order gives retroactive legal significance to an earlier state of insolvency which at the time it first arose had no impact in law.[20]

Significant adjustments are often made to the assets and liabilities by the time a company completes its reorganization process. These adjustments are noticeable when assets are sold during the reorganization process and also when the asset values are compared with estimates of the liquidation value of the assets. In planning the reorganization, a failing firm with one or more subsidiaries must decide if the plan will incorporate substantive consolidation of the subsidiaries. Under substantive consolidation, all of the assets and liabilities of the entities in question

---

16. Olivares-Caminal R., 'Recognition of Corporate Debt Restructuring Procedures in Latin America under US Law: Lessons from the Multicanal Case', International Corporate Rescue, Volume 2, Issue 3, 2005, pages 143–150.
17. Olivares-Caminal R. 'Corporate Debt Restructuring in Latin America: New Developments – New Opportunities?' (2005), *ICCLR*, issue 6, 254.
18. Melissa B. Jacoby, 'Prepacks and the Deal-litigation Tension', (2004), 23–2 *ABIJ* 34.
19. Fletcher I. '*The Law of Insolvency*', (1990), Sweet and Maxwell. Page 1.
20. Goode R.M. '*Principles Of Corporate Insolvency Law*', (1997), 2nd ed., Sweet and Maxwell. Page 65.

are pooled and used collectively to pay debts. In order for substantive consolidation to be granted by court, proponents must prove that the parent and the subsidiaries in question operated as a single unit. This can be proved by such means as inter-company guarantees and transfers of assets.[21]

In general, there are different approaches that can be used to invest in the distressed market. Large and aggressive investors may buy a substantial block of the debtor's bonds and try to become a significant player in the reorganization plan. Moreover, investors may pool their resources in 'vulture funds', which invest in the securities of bankrupt companies. Such funds often operate by acquiring large blocks of a particular class of securities and use their leverage in the reorganization process to formulate a plan favourable to their position. In addition, individual investors may buy specific securities in a bankrupt company. Not all such strategies are profitable.[22]

The analysis of companies in bankruptcy that have filed plans of reorganization should be approached in a systematic way. The analysis must place more emphasis on *pro formas* and less on historical results. Often the relative rates of return among old securities are substantially reordered under the reorganization plans. The analysis must therefore value all securities of debtors and purchase those that offer the highest potential returns.[23]

As mentioned *above*, significant adjustments are often made to the assets and liabilities by the time a company completes its reorganization process which *inter alia*, concern assets that are sold during the reorganization process. In such a case, the success of failing firm defence may prove invaluable. The concept of failing firm defence is the focus of the next part of this chapter.

III.   FAILING FIRM DEFENCE

> *'Acquisition of a failing firm is always efficient'*
>
> McChesney, F. S.,
> 'Defending the Failing Firm Defence'
> 65 *Nebraska Law Review* 1986, page 1.

The failing firm defence refers to the supposedly neutral effect on competition of concentrations where one (or both) of the merging parties (the acquirer and/or the target) are failing or will fail, due to poor financial performance.[24]

---

21. Fabozzi F. *'The Handbook of Fixed Income Securities'*, (1991), 3rd ed., Business One Irwin. Page 399.
22. Fabozzi F. *'The Handbook of Fixed Income Securities'*, (1991), 3rd ed., Business One Irwin. Page 401.
23. Fabozzi F. *'The Handbook of Fixed Income Securities'*, (1991), 3rd ed., Business One Irwin. Page 406.
24. Baccaro V. (2004), 'Failing Firm Defence and Lack of Causality: Doctrine and Practice in Europe of Two Closely Related Concepts', *ECLR*, issue 1, pp. 11–24. At page 11.

Implications of Merger Legislation

As mentioned *above*, a significant and frequent, in certain economies, reason for engaging in mergers is the restructuring of debt of a company which is on the verge of bankruptcy. There is a growing literature on the effect of bankruptcy procedures on ex ante decisions by firms and shareholders. The restructuring of the debt may entail the sale of a loss making division and if the company has subsidiaries, the sale of the subsidiary/ies as a whole. Thus, failing firm defence and failing division defence can be invoked in cases where this sale is assessed by the relevant competition authorities. However, the failing division defence has not been given much acceptance and accreditation by the *above mentioned* competition authorities and courts.

Weeds and Mason[25] argue that the policy towards failing firms that competition authorities may adopt affects entry decisions. A firm entering a market also considers its ease of exit, foreseeing that it may later wish to leave should market conditions deteriorate. A way of entering in a market is the acquisition/merger with an incumbent. Such a merger/acquisition will allow the entrant to benefit from the infrastructure, expertise and customer base of the incumbent in the market. In addition, by facilitating exit in times of financial distress, the failing firm defence can encourage entry so as welfare to increase overall. Even if welfare is decreased when the firm enters the market by merging with or acquiring an incumbent, the increase in welfare resulting from earlier entry may more than offset this loss.

Apart from the importance and implications of entry in a merger involving a failing firm, in the assessment of a merger in a failing industry the competition authorities should also pay attention to potential dynamic or innovative efficiencies. Dynamic or innovative efficiencies may make a particularly powerful contribution to competitive dynamics, R&D ('Research and Development'), and welfare but are not readily verifiable and quantifiable because they tend to focus on future products. Merger analysis should give efficiencies more weight if the profitability of a failing industry can be improved by the merger (e.g., by lowering fixed costs) even if the price effects are not immediate. Thus, there is a trade off between the viability of the failing firm and the positive impact that it may have on competition due to the existence of one additional competitor in the market and the further consolidation in the market (if a competitor merges with/acquires the failing firm) due to the merger, which may also result though from the exit of the failing firm from the market.

Competition authorities have recognized the importance of a merger/acquisition in avoiding bankruptcy as well as the impact of the failing firm defence on entry in the market and the role of potential dynamic or innovative efficiencies and have taken into account the financial distress in which a company may be in the assessment of mergers involving the said company. Both in the EU and US the 'failing firm defence' is addressed in the merger guidelines. The case-law has provided further impetus to the development of the defence in both jurisdictions.

In order to accomplish the target of sustaining the competitive structure of the post-merger market, the competition authority must apply a legal substantive test in order to determine the likelihood of the anti-competitive impact of the merger, as well as to determine the level and quality of evidence it needs in its assessment of whether the merger should be prohibited.

After having analyzed the fundamentals and the rationale behind 'corporate debt restructuring', in the next parts of the chapter the 'failing firm defence' argument and how it can be taken into account and influence the assessment of a merger will be addressed. We will analyze the criteria that need to be satisfied in order for such a defence to be acceptable and examine how the defence has been invoked in practice in the assessment of merger cases and whether it has been successful. The merger legislation analysis provided in this chapter will focus on EU and US laws.

In order to acquire a complete understanding of the implications of merger legislation for corporate debt restructuring, a brief background on the competition legislation and the implementing structure of the competition legislation of the EU, USA are necessary. After briefly examining these issues, the chapter will analyze cases where the failing firm defence has been invoked and assess the criteria that need to be satisfied in order for such a defence to be successful.

IV. THE EUROPEAN UNION PERSPECTIVE

'For the achievement of the aims of the Treaty, Article 3(1)(g) gives the Community the objective of instituting a system ensuring that competition in the internal market is not distorted. Article 4(1) of the Treaty provides that the activities of the Member States and the Community are to be conducted in accordance with the principle of an open market economy with free competition. These principles are essential for the further development of the internal market.

The completion of the internal market and of economic and monetary union, the enlargement of the European Union and the lowering of international barriers to trade and investment will continue to result in major corporate reorganizations, particularly in the form of concentrations'.[26] 'Council Regulation (EC) No 139/2004 of 20 January 2004 on the control of concentrations between undertakings (the EC Merger Regulation)'.[27]

A. LEGISLATION

1. The European Community Merger Regulation

The Treaty of Rome of 25 March 1957 (EC Treaty)[28] did not provide any specific provision for the control of mergers. Articles 81 and 82 of the EC Treaty focus

---

25. Mason R., Weeds H. (2003), 'The Failing Firm Defence: Merger Policy and Entry', repec.org/res2003/Mason.pdf.
26. Recitals 2 and 3 of the preamble of Council Regulation (EC) No 139/2004 of 20 January 2004 on the control of concentrations between undertakings (the EC Merger Regulation), Official Journal L 24, 29.01.2004, pages 1–22.
27. Official Journal L 24, 29.01.2004, pages 1–22.
28. The Treaty of Rome established the European Economic Community (EEC) and was signed by France, West Germany, Italy, Belgium, the Netherlands and Luxembourg (the latter three as part of the Benelux) on 25 March 1957.

Implications of Merger Legislation 555

on controlling the behaviour of undertakings rather than dealing with mergers. The European Commission (Commission)[29] steered by such omission sought to persuade the European Council (Council)[30] to enact a merger control provision, while at the same time attempted in some instances to apply Articles 81 and 82 to prevent the anti-competitive conduct arising from some mergers.

The application of Articles 81 and 82 on mergers entail certain drawbacks. Motivated by such shortcomings the Council of Ministers of the EU (Council of Ministers),[31] on 21 December 1989, adopted Council Regulation 4064/89[32] (4064/89), which came into force on 21 September 1990. The 4064/89 is based both on Article 83 which provides for the making of Council Regulations to implement the provisions of Articles 81 and 82 and on Article 232 which grants the Council the residual power to take appropriate measures where action proves necessary in order to attain one of the Commission's objectives and the EC Treaty has not provided the necessary powers.[33] The main aim of the 4064/89 is to provide means for the prevention of anti-competitive concentrations as well as to provide a single framework within which such transactions can be assessed ('one-stop shop' principle).[34]

According to Article 2(3) of the 4064/89, 'a concentration which creates or strengthens a dominant position as a result of which effective competition would be significantly impeded in the common market or in a substantial part of it shall be declared incompatible with the common market'. A merger may lead either to unilateral effects or non-coordinated effects. These two effects are mutually

---

29. The European Commission is the executive body of the European Union. Alongside the European Parliament and the Council of the European Union, it is one of the three main institutions governing the Union. Its primary roles are to propose and implement legislation, and to act as 'guardian of the treaties' which provide the legal basis for the EU. The Commission consists of 25 Commissioners, one from each Member State of the EU, heading the General Directorates.
30. The European Council is a meeting of the heads of state or government of the European Union, and the President of the European Commission. On average four European Councils are held each year. Discussion and decisions take place on the matters of key issues and direction of the EU.
31. The Council of the European Union forms, along with the European Parliament, the legislative arm of the European Union. The Council of the European Union contains ministers of the governments of each of the European Union Member States.
32. Council Regulation (EEC) 4064/89 of 21 December 1989 on the control of concentrations between undertakings, [1989] OJ L395/1, corrigendum [1990] OJ LL257/14. Council Regulation (EC) No 1310/97 (OJ L 180, 9/7/97) amended the 4064/89 on the control of concentrations between undertakings, focusing mainly on issues such as multiple notifications, joint ventures, remedies and referrals to Member States.
33. Articles 81, 82, 83 and 232 of the EC Treaty (ex 85, 86, 87 and 235 of the EC Treaty prior to the Treaty of Amsterdam which came into force on the 1 May 1999 – note that Article 12 of the Treaty of Amsterdam provided for the renumbering of the EC Treaty Articles).
34. The Commission will consider whether the adverse effect of the transaction on effective competition is transitory or permanent and will only initiate an investigation in the latter case, as the approach in Aerospatiale indicated. See *further*: Case No. IV/M53, *Aerospatiale-Alenia/de Havilland*, OJ [1991] L 334/42, [1992] 4 *CMLR* M2. This case was the first prohibition decision concerning single dominance. See *further*: Livingston D. and Scott J. (1995), '*Competition Law and Practice*', FT Law & Tax, Great Britain. Page 768.

inconsistent[35] since non-coordinated effects arise when the merged group enjoys market power without depending for its success and profitability on coordinated interaction with other the firms in the market, whereas coordinated effects depend on the successful coordinated interaction of the merged entity with the other firms in the market. A merger may either lead to the post-merger firm unilaterally engaging in anti-competitive conduct or may lead the remaining firms after the merger to collectively coordinate their behaviour.

Article 1(4) of the 4064/89 required the Commission to report to the Council before 1 July 2000 on the operation of the thresholds and on the criteria for determining whether a concentration has a community dimension. The Commission submitted a report which considered several jurisdictional, procedural and substantive issues that needed to be addressed. The Commission published these issues in a 'Green Paper'[36] in December 2001. In December 2002 the Commission published its proposals for reform of the 4064/89[37] together with a draft Notice on the appraisal of horizontal mergers,[38] as well as draft 'Best practices on the conduct of EC merger control proceedings'.[39] The draft Notice was the response of the Commission to a widespread demand for enhanced legal certainty surrounding the Commission's merger decisions. The reforms aimed at clarifying the criteria applied by the Commission in the appraisal of concentrations in situations where the undertakings concerned are active sellers in the same relevant market or potential competitors in that market (horizontal mergers).[39,40]

The analysis continues with the reforms proposed in the Green Paper and adopted in the '*Council Regulation (EC) No 139/2004 of 20 January 2004 on the control of concentrations between undertakings (the EC Merger Regulation)*'[42] (ECMR). The new Regulation entered into force in May 2004 coinciding with the expansion of the EU from 15 to 25 Member States. The reform aimed at improving the parties' rights of defence and the Commission's decision

---

35. Europe Economics (2001), 'Study on Assessment Criteria for Distinguishing between Competitive and Dominant Oligopolies in Merger Control'. europa.eu.int/comm/enterprize/library/lib-competition/libr-competition.html. At pages vi, 62, 63.
36. See *further*: Green Paper on the Review of Council Regulation (EEC) No. 4064/89, COM(2001) 745/6, 11/12/2001. It should be noted that the Commission issued a Green Paper rather than a White Paper. Green Papers are typically issued at an early stage in the legislative process, setting out the various options for change under discussion and establishing the overall framework of debate.
37. Proposal for a Council Regulation on the control of Concentrations Between Undertakings, COM/2002/0711 final – CNS 2002/0296. Official Journal C 020, 28/01/2003 P. 0004 – 0057.
38. Commission Notice on the appraisal of horizontal mergers under the Council Regulation on the control of concentration between undertakings, COM/2002, 11/12/2002.
39. *See*: DG Competition Best Practices on the conduct of EC merger control proceedings, available from the DG Competition website: <europa.eu.int/comm/competition/index_en.html>.
40. For a definition of the concept of horizontal as well as of vertical and conglomerate mergers *see* below the relevant section of this chapter on the Horizontal Merger Guidelines.
41. For further details on the history of the debate concerning the change of the legal substantive test, see *further*: Fountoukakos K., Ryan S. (2005), 'A New Substantive Test for EU Merger Control', *ECLR*, issue 5, pp. 277–296.
42. Official Journal L 24, 29.01.2004, pages 1–22, 'recast ECMR'.

making process,[43] both essential for the application of the ECMR especially in an enlarged EU of 25 Member States. The ECMR reform further aimed at minimizing transaction costs for firms through the 'one-stop-shop'[44] principle and at augmenting the transparency and the speediness of the assessment procedure of concentrations, leading thus to enhanced legal certainty.

The adopted reforms concerned procedural, jurisdictional and substantive issues. This part of the chapter will deal with the substantive reforms and will only briefly address the jurisdictional and procedural reforms. The substantive proposed reforms concerned the change from the dominance test to the 'Substantial Lessening of Competition' (SLC) test. The Commission proposed and the Council accepted an altered version of the dominance test in the ECMR[45] as the substantive legal standard for assessing mergers. The Commission considered that the aim of improving legal certainty and enhancing transparency regarding the scope of the dominance test is best served by clarifying the ECMR itself. The new test is outlined in Article 2(3) of the ECMR which states that 'a concentration which would significantly impede effective competition, in the common market or in a substantial part of it, in particular as a result of the creation or strengthening of a dominant position, shall be declared incompatible with the common market'.[46] Thus, the creation or strengthening of a dominant position is only one example, although the principal example, of a significant impediment to effective competition. The significant impediment to effective competition ('SIEC') test is a hybrid of the dominance test and the SLC test. The new legal substantive test is regarded as a compromise between the two tests.[47]

There was considerable debate in the Council, with Germany, Italy and the Netherlands being in favour of the current dominance test whereas the United Kingdom, Ireland and Sweden preferred a move to SLC. Denmark and Portugal supported the Commission's proposal, while France and Spain suggested a compromise wording based on their own domestic tests. Finally, the Franco-Spanish compromise prevailed, supplemented by a last-minute German addition to a recital[48] which provided

---

43. William, Cutler and Pickering (2002), 'The European Commission Adopts Merger Control Reform Package'. <www.wilmer.com/docs/frameset.cfm?SECTION=practice&PAGE=index>.
44. According to the 'one-stop shop' principle, a single authority, this being the Commission, assesses mergers having a Community dimension within a strict and short timetable and has exclusive Community-wide competence.
45. Official Journal L 24, 29.01.2004, pages 1–22, 139/2004.
46. Article 2(3), Council Regulation (EC) No 139/2004 of 20 January 2004 on the control of concentrations between undertakings (the EC Merger Regulation), (139/2004), Official Journal L 24, 29.01.2004, pages 1–22.
47. For a fuller analysis of the reforms as well as of the debate between the 'dominance test' and the 'substantially lessening of competition' test that the Green Paper induced see: Kokkoris I. 'The reform of the European Control Merger Regulation in the aftermath of the Airtours case. The eagerly expected debate: SLC v Dominance test', (2005), *ECLR*, volume 26, Issue 1, pp. 37–47.
48. When interpreting provisions of regulations and directives, the European courts look at the aim of the provision and frequently examine recitals to elicit that aim. It is therefore likely that the German amendment will have the effect of narrowing the plain meaning of the SIEC test. See *further*: <www.internationallawoffice.com/ld.cfm?Newsletters_Ref=7850#substantive>.

that SIEC will only be applied to non-dominance situations for the purpose of catching non-collusive oligopolies. Since, most EU Member States adhere to the dominance test it would have been unreasonable for the Commission to switch to the SLC test, since such a move would inhibit the harmonization of national competition laws and would enhance legal uncertainty.

The legal substantive test in the ECMR, the SIEC test, is intended to fill the perceived 'gap' in the dominance test which was illustrated by cases such as *Airtours*[49] and *Heinz*.[50] The 'gap' corresponds to the situation where the post-merger entity's market share falls below the level required for dominance but the merger may lead to unilateral effects. Recital 25 of the ECMR states that the notion of SIEC 'should be interpreted as extending, beyond the concept of dominance, only to the anti-competitive effects of a concentration resulting from the non-coordinated behaviour of undertakings which would not have a dominant position in the market concerned'.[51] According to this Recital, the SIEC extends, in a disciplined way, beyond dominance, and makes clear that the new test covers non-coordinated effects, thus rectifying the problem of the 'gap'. In the formulation of Recital 25, the Commission has attempted to enhance legal certainty by creating the impression that the interpretation of the SIEC test is compatible with former court judgments.[52]

Even though the new wording of the legal substantive test rectifies the 'gap', the application of the SIEC test may be quite wide and allow increased scrutiny of smaller transactions between smaller firms in concentrated markets, where the reduction in the number of players may lead to a possible reduction in competition due to the loss of competitive constraints on the remaining firms in the post-merger market. Although, the wording used in the new provision[53] could be read as extending the reach of the ECMR further than the SLC test would have, Voigt and Schmidt argue the SIEC in rectifying the 'gap' does not make the European merger policy more restrictive, however, gives the Commission more discretion in its assessment of concentrations. According to the authors, the enhancement of the restrictiveness of the European merger policy due to the introduction of the new substantive test is mitigated and balanced by the explicit introduction of the efficiency defence,[54] including the failing firm defence. However, both the new test

---

49. Case T–342/99 *Airtours v. Commission* [2002] 5 *CMLR*317.
50. US District Court, Columbia, *FTC v HF Heinz Company et al.*, 00–5362a, (2000).
51. Recital 25 of Council Regulation (EC) No 139/2004 of 20 January 2004 on the control of concentrations between undertakings (the EC Merger Regulation), (139/2004), OJ L 24, 29.01.2004, pages 1–22.
52. Voigt S., Schmidt A. (2004), 'Switching to Substantial Impediments to Competition (SIC) can have substantial costs', *ECLR*, 25(9), pp. 584–590. At page 587.
53. Wording such as 'appreciable' rather than 'substantial' as well as the reference to foreclosure of competitors. See *further*: See *further*: William, Cutler and Pickering (2002), 'The European Commission Adopts Merger Control Reform Package'. <www.wilmerhale.com/files/Publication/7178d077-068a-4bd2-9976-cb2dcf73db4d/Presentation/PublicationAttachment/bef3d442-7bcc-48a2-99a9-50a85b9c7490/ACFD854.pdf>.
54. See *further*: Voigt S., Schmidt A. (2004), 'Switching to Substantial Impediments to Competition (SIC) can have substantial costs', *ECLR*, 25(9), pp. 584–590. At page 589.

and the efficiency defence increase the Commission's discretion and, hence, make merger policy less predictable.

Apart from substantive reforms there were also procedural and jurisdictional reforms adopted in the ECMR. An extensive account of these reforms is outside the scope of this chapter. Procedural changes included enhanced flexibility for companies in deciding when to file merger notifications, allowing firms to better organize their transactions without being obliged to fit their planning around unnecessary regulatory rigidities and deadlines for Commission decisions. In addition, amendments to the time schedule provide more time to the Commission, to consider remedies proposed by firms (this 'stop-the-clock' provision will operate at the parties' request). In combination with the new Regulation[55] for the enforcement of Articles 81 and 82 i.e. the Council Regulation 1/2003, the procedural and jurisdictional reforms to the ECMR strengthen the Commission's enforcement powers.

Regarding jurisdictional issues, a pre-notification process will determine the allocation of jurisdiction between the Commission and national competition authorities (NCAs), will tackle the phenomenon of intra-EU multi-jurisdictional filings, whilst at the same time enhance the effectiveness of the 'one-stop-shop' principle according to which parties may request the Commission to take jurisdiction in cases where the turnover thresholds are not met but the merger needs to be notified to at least three Member States. The 'one-stop-shop' principle[56] is essential for the efficient application of the ECMR, especially in the enlarged EU.

Apart from substantive procedural and jurisdictional reforms, the Commission published Guidelines on the assessment of horizontal mergers under the Council Regulation on the control of concentrations between undertakings ('EU Guidelines')[57] as well. The Commission, with its EU Guidelines, aims to clarify the criteria it would apply in the assessment of concentrations under the ECMR. the next section will provide a detailed analysis on the EU Guidelines.

2. The Horizontal Merger Guidelines[58]

In a world of multiple sovereign jurisdictions there is no guarantee that all jurisdictions will adopt the same approach in the assessment of a concentration. The EU Guidelines help expose similarities and differences such as diverse approaches to market definition and entry conditions, various analyzes of co-ordinated and

---

55. Council Regulation (EC) No 1/2003 of 16 December 2002 on the implementation of the rules on competition laid down in Articles 81 and 82 of the Treaty, Official Journal L 1, 04.01.2003, pages 1–25.
56. See *further*: William, Cutler and Pickering (2002), 'The European Commission Adopts Merger Control Reform Package'. <www.wilmerhale.com/files/Publication/7178d077-068a-4bd2-9976-cb2dcf73db4d/Presentation/PublicationAttachment/bef3d442-7bcc-48a2-99a9-50a85b9c7490/ACFD8 54.pdf>.
57. Guidelines on the assessment of horizontal mergers under the Council Regulation on the control of concentrations between undertakings, Official Journal C 31, 05.02.2004, pages 5–18.
58. Guidelines on the assessment of horizontal mergers under the Council Regulation on the control of concentrations between undertakings, Official Journal C 31, 05.02.2004, pages 5–18.

non-coordinated effects, and different treatment of efficiencies. Such an exposure is a first step towards harmonization of merger legislation across different jurisdictions.

The Commission issued the EU Guidelines setting out the Commission's approach to transactions commonly known as horizontal mergers, clarifying the applicability of the ECMR and explaining the economic rationale the Commission employs in assessing horizontal mergers. Before analyzing the EU Guidelines, it is useful to briefly define the concepts of horizontal, vertical and conglomerate mergers[59] that will be used throughout in this chapter.

Horizontal mergers are mergers between parties that operate in the same relevant market. Such mergers can increase the market power of the merging firms so that they could unilaterally impose a profitable post-merger price increase. Other firms in the market might raise their prices in response, also unilaterally. Thus, rivalry might weaken. Moreover, a horizontal merger may increase the likelihood of (and/or stability and sustainability of) collusion, either tacit or explicit, between the remaining firms in the market.

Vertical mergers are mergers between parties which operate at different levels of an industry. Such mergers, though often pro-competitive, may in some circumstances reduce competitive constraints faced by the merged firm as a result of increased barriers to entry, raising rivals costs, substantial market foreclosure or increased likelihood of collusion. This risk is, however, unlikely to arise except in the presence of existing market power or in markets where there is already significant vertical integration as well as vertical restraints.

Conglomerate mergers are mergers between firms in apparently unrelated markets which would rarely significantly impede effective competition. However, in some jurisdictions, mergers of this type have been found to create competition problems, e.g. through the exercise of 'portfolio power'.

The EU Guidelines[60] describe both the theoretical basis and the analytical methodology for evaluating the potential for anticompetitive effects resulting from a horizontal merger. More importantly, in line with the desire to improve economic reasoning, the EU Guidelines focus on the nature of the analysis needed to identify the competitive constraints that each of the merging parties currently poses on the other. The aim is to provide greater predictability with a view to increase legal certainty for all parties concerned.

The EU Guidelines explore the possible anti-competitive effects of horizontal mergers and consider the main ways in which a horizontal merger may significantly

---

59. For the respective definitions, see *further*: ICN Merger Working Group, Analytical Framework Sub-group 'The Analytical Framework for Merger Control', Final paper for ICN annual conference on 28 and 29 September 2002, Office of Fair Trading, London. <www.internationalcompetitionnetwork.org/afsguk.pdf>.
60. 'Guidelines on the assessment of horizontal mergers under the Council Regulation on the control of concentrations between undertakings', OJ C 31, 05.02.2004, pages 5–18. Commission's Notices and Guidelines are not legally binding. However, they strongly indicate the Commission's position on a variety of important issues. In this chapter we will analyze the failing firm defence as regards the horizontal mergers. We can argue though that the same principles that apply for failing firm defence in horizontal mergers apply for vertical and conglomerate mergers.

impede competition. By eliminating the competitive constraints between the parties, a horizontal merger may allow the merged firm to increase its prices regardless of the response of its remaining competitors, and thus may lead to non-coordinated effects. In addition, a horizontal merger may lead to coordinated effects by creating an environment favourable to sustainable tacit collusion, reducing thus the effectiveness of competition and consequently leading to price increases.

The Commission will, in line with European Court of Justice ('ECJ') case law,[61] consider the 'failing firm defence'. In vigorously competitive markets, mergers involving failing firms may often enhance general welfare either through increasing the efficiency of existing capacity, redeploying that capacity to socially more valued uses, or preserving jobs and having other socially beneficial advantages.[62] Moreover, there might be, on economic grounds beneficial effects resulting from, *inter alia*, economies of scale, economies of scope, or other efficiencies, so that prohibiting the deal would add new detrimental economic and social effects to the effect on competition which would exist in any case. The burden of proof of such welfare benefits lies with the party that claims the defence. If one of the companies in the merger is a 'failing firm' and would leave the market anyway, then the merger may be deemed not to significantly impede effective competition. The basic requirement is that the deterioration of the competitive structure that follows the merger cannot be said to be caused by the merger.[63]

The 'lack of causality' between the merger and the possible worsening of the competitive structure due to the merger plays a major role in assessing the acceptability of the failing firm defence. The analysis of the counterfactual, a comparison between the competitive conditions occurring due to the merger and the conditions that would prevail if the merger is blocked, are crucial in assessing the acceptance of failing firm defence.

The Commission considers the following three criteria[64] as relevant for the application of a 'failing firm defence'. First, the allegedly failing firm would in the near future be forced out of the market because of financial difficulties if not taken over by another undertaking. Second, there is no less anti-competitive alternative purchase than the notified merger. There may be the case that buyers may be interested in buying the failing firm's assets after the firm exits the market. A firm's exit may also provide the means for new entry in the market. In addition, it may be more beneficial for competition for more than one firm to acquire the assets of the failing firm rather than a single firm acquiring the total of the failing firm's assets. Third, in the absence of a merger, the assets of the failing firm would inevitably exit the market. Once the conditions for the application of the failing firm defence are fulfilled the merger would not be considered to cause a significant

---

61. Applied in IV/M308 *Kali und Salz/MdK/Treuhand* [1994] OJ L186/30; on appeal Cases C–68/94 and C–30/95 *France v. Commission, Societe Commerciale es Potasses et de l'Azore (SCPA) v. Commission* [1998] ECR I–1375, [1998] 4 *CMLR* 829.
62. Hewitt G. (1999), 'The Failing Firm Defence', *OECD Journal of Competition Law and Policy*, vol. 1, issue 2, pp. 113–133. Page 115.
63. Guidelines § 89.
64. Guidelines § 90.

impediment to effective competition in the common market. The three criteria outlined in the EU Guidelines appear to be the cumulative requirements in order to prove lack of causality between the merger and the worsening of the competitive structure that it would otherwise create.[65]

Thus, if one of the parties is financially failing, the EU Guidelines would permit an otherwise anti-competitive merger.[66] The rationale is that the competitive structure would deteriorate equally absent the merger. The future market structure would be equally detrimental to competition irrespective of whether the deal is cleared or blocked. Thus, there is no link of causality between the merger and the negative effects on competition and therefore no legal ground for prohibiting the merger. The Commission made it clear in the *Kali und Salz*[67] decision that the acceptance of the failing firm defence is an exceptional situation. Normally, there would be a presumption that a concentration which results in a significant impediment to effective competition is the cause of this deterioration in the competitive structure. The burden of proof that the requirements of the failing firm defence are fulfilled and that there is no causal link between the merger and the deterioration of the competitive structure is upon the parties.

Firms on the verge of administration may not meet the criterion of exit of the firm in the near future. Firms in liquidation though, are more likely to satisfy the criterion. Decisions by a parent company which is profitable to shut down its loss making subsidiaries are not likely to be accepted as a credible failing firm defence.

It has been argued that the new substantive test and the accompanying EU Guidelines are an indication of the Commission's likely intention to adopt a more interventionist approach towards mergers. The EU Guidelines widen the potential scope of the ECMR below the traditional threshold associated with findings of single firm dominance. By removing the safe harbour previously implicit in the definition of single firm dominance, the EU Guidelines may be regarded as implying that the Commission will intervene in a significantly large number of transactions.

The purpose of the ECMR is to sustain an effective and well-functioning internal market by effectively ensuring that reorganizations in the market will not have any anti-competitive impact on markets. Mergers eliminate any competition that exists between the merging parties and reduce the number of firms competing in the market. Where this reduction has a substantial effect on overall market competition, the market will be less oriented to consumer and efficiency goals, even in the absence of breaches of competition law.

In order to assess the impact of a merger on the structure of competition, a number of elements are taken into account, including the market position of the merging companies, the existence and degree of actual and potential competition,

---

65. Baccaro V. (2004), 'Failing Firm Defence and Lack of Causality: Doctrine and Practice in Europe of Two Closely Related Concepts', *ECLR*, issue 1, pp. 11–24. At page 23.
66. Firms on the verge of administration may not meet the criterion of exit of the firm in the near future. Firms in liquidation though, are more likely to satisfy the criterion. It should be noted that decisions by a parent company which is profitable to shut down its loss making subsidiaries are not likely to be accepted as a credible failing firm defence.
67. IV/M308 *Kali und Salz/MdK/Treuhand* [1994] OJ L186/30.

demand and supply trends, barriers to entry, buying power of the customers of the relevant goods and services, the interests of the intermediate and ultimate consumers, and the development of technical and economic progress provided that it is to consumers' advantage and does not form an obstacle to competition.[68] In addition, efficiencies resulting from the merger and the existence of failing firms among the merging parties will also be taken into account.

After reviewing the legislation applicable to mergers in the EU, and the inclusion of the failing firm defence in the EU Guidelines, merger cases in which the failing firm defence has been invoked will be addressed.

B. APPLICATION OF THE FAILING FIRM DEFENCE

Even before the previous 4064/89 came into force,[69] the Commission dealt with companies acquiring bankrupt companies. In 1989, the Commission authorized Mannesmannröhrenwerke AG, Klöckner Stahl GmbH, Krupp Stahl AG, Lech Stahlwerke GmbH, Thyssen Stahl AG, Thyssen Edelstahlwerke AG and the Land of Bavaria to form a new company under the name of 'Neue Maxhütte Stahlwerke Gmbh'. The new company would take over part of the facilities and workforce of Eizenwerk Gesellschaft Maximilianschütte mbH, which was declared bankrupt on 16 April 1987. The Land of Bavaria would hold 45 per cent of the shares in the new company with the remaining 55 per cent being divided among the other companies that formed the Neue Maxhütte Stahlwerke Gmbh. A restructuring plan was devised that provided for production cuts and closure of the Haidhof works. The plan was expected to help the company return to viability as well as to contribute to the restructuring of the Community (i.e. European Community) steel industry.[70]

Also, the Commission's approach to situations where the failure of a firm is imminent unless the merger is put into effect will be analyzed. In such cases, the parties can request derogation under Article 7.3 of the ECMR, as is indicated by the *Kelt/American Express* case, analyzed *below*.

The previous ECMR, i.e. 4064/89 did not include any reference to the failing firm defence. However, the defence had been invoked and dealt with in a number of Commission's decisions, the most important of which are analyzed *below*.

1. Aerospatiale-Alenia/de Havilland[71]

Initially the failing firm defence was invoked in *Aerospatiale*. Alenia-Aeritalia e Selenia Spa ('Alenia') and Aerospatiale SNI ('Aerospatiale') would have acquired De Havilland, Boeing's regional aircraft division ('Havilland'). Aérospatiale and Alenia were already active through ATR in the relevant markets for regional

---

68. Article 2(1)b of 139/2004.
69. 4064/89 entered into force on 21 September 1990.
70. Nineteenth Report on Competition Policy, 1990, page 86. <europa.eu.int/comm/competition/publications/publications/#PORTS>.
71. Case IV/M.053 *Aerospatiale- Alenia/de Havilland*, [1991], OJ L334/42.

turbo-prop aircrafts (three different markets were defined according to the size of the aircrafts). The activities of Avions de Transport Régional ('ATR') and De Havilland were overlapping in the market for medium-size turbo-prop where the new entity would have reached a 64 per cent market share worldwide. The parties invoking the failing firm defence argued that Boeing would shut down de Havilland. The Commission questioned the relevance, for the assessment of dominance under the 4064/89, of de Havilland facing liquidation if it were not taken over by Aerospatiale-Alenia. The Commission argued that such elimination was not probable.[72] In addition, the Commission argued that even if de Havilland exited the market, the parties were not the only potential purchasers.

In assessing the likelihood of De Havilland leaving the market in the absence of the merger, the Commission took into account a number of factors including that de Havilland produced good quality, well known and highly respected products the net selling price of its aircrafts had increased and the production costs had decreased while there was still room for further increase of the productivity.[73] Although the Commission did not expressly mention this aspect, the burden of proof is heavier for the merging firms in the case of a 'failing division' than in the case of a 'failing firm'.

2. Kali und Salz[74]

The concept and the condition of the failing firm defence were discussed at length in the Commission's decision in *Kali und Salz*. The case concerned the joint venture between Kali (Kali) and Salz (Salz) and Treuhandanstalt (Treuhand) and the concentration of the rock-salt and potash activities of Kali and Salz, a subsidiary of the German chemical company BASF Aktiengesellschaft (BASF) and a state owned company of the former German Democratic Republic (MdK), a state owned company of the former German Democratic Republic. The *above*-mentioned concentration would create a monopoly on the market (98 per cent in the market for potash products).

The economic situation of MdK was critical and the firm was on the verge of bankruptcy. MdK's current economic situation was mainly a result of the firm's operating structure and a crisis in sales attributable primarily to the collapse of markets in Eastern Europe. In addition, MdK's sales on the German market had fallen quite substantially, and MdK would not be able to dispose of an efficient distribution system. The undertaking could not continue to operate without the Treuhandanstalt which had been covering the losses.

Hence, the Commission in its appraisal of the notified proposal of merger examined whether the requirements of the failing firm defence were met. The parties argued that, without the merger, MdK would soon be forced out of the market and that the market shares that would become available would be acquired by Kali and Salz.

---

72. Case IV/M.053 *Aerospatiale- Alenia/de Havilland*, [1991], OJ L334/42, para 31.
73. OECD, 'Failing firm defence', (1996), page 93. <www.oecd.org/dataoecd/35/6/1920253.pdf>.
74. IV/M308 *Kali und Salz/MdK/Treuhand* [1994] OJ L186/30.

Without an acquisition by a private industrial partner with the necessary management expertise and in the absence of synergies, a rescue of MdK appeared to be unlikely. The Commission stated that the costs of restructuring would be higher than the aid provided for the merger. An administration charged with privatization cannot be expected to rescue with extraordinary high aid one of its own undertakings that cannot be expected to survive and to hold it in the long term as a State-owned company. The Commission concluded thus, that there was sufficient proof that MdK would withdraw from the market if it was not taken over by a private undertaking.

In addition, due to the fact that the structural factors of the German potash market had isolated it from competitors from other countries, the Commission accepted that MdK's share of the German potash market would accrue to Kali and Salz since the latter could increase its potash production without any further expenditure and become the sole supplier in the German market.

The Commission further accepted that a purchase of all or a substantial part of MdK by companies other than Kali and Salz could be discounted. The Commission concluded that Goldman Sachs made a substantial effort to interest as many firms as possible in purchasing MdK. According to the Commission, the lack of alternative buyers was objectively justified by a number of factors, i.e. the operating structure of MdK, the existence of over-capacities, the generally depressed state of the potash market and the absence of significant synergies as a result of the acquisition.

The Commission stated that a merger which should normally be considered to lead to the creation or reinforcement of a dominant position on the part of the acquiring firm can be regarded as not causing such a position in the market if, even in the event of the merger being prohibited, the acquirer would inevitably achieve or reinforce a dominant position.

Thus, there is a lack of causality between the concentration and the deterioration of the competitive structure if:[75]

1. the acquired undertaking would in the near future be forced out of the market if not taken over by another undertaking,
2. the acquiring undertaking would take over the market share of the acquired undertaking if it were forced out of the market,
3. there is no less anticompetitive alternative purchase.

As regards the first criterion, the criterion reveals an exclusive focus on the failing firm's market. If the failing firm's assets exit the market, there will be a tendency for the supply in that market to be decreased. Such reductions and the welfare reducing price increases they entail are very likely where there was little or no excess capacity in the pre-merger situation. Furthermore, the negative effects of decreased supply may not be quickly reversed through the addition and use of new capacity.[76]

---

75. This chapter refers to these three criteria as: the *Kali und Salz* criteria.
76. See *further*: OECD, 'Failing firm defence' (1996) <www.oecd.org/dataoecd/35/6/1920253.pdf>. Page 19.

The lack of causality implies that it is the disappearance of the failing company, which would be unavoidable even in the event of the concentration being prohibited, and not the concentration itself, which creates or strengthens the dominant position. The burden of proof for a missing link of causality lies with the merging undertakings.

In assessing the merger the Commission concluded that after the proposed merger a dominant position in the German market for agricultural potash would be strengthened. However, it also concluded that Kali and Salz' dominant position would be reinforced even in the absence of the merger, because MdK would withdraw from the market in the foreseeable future if it was not acquired by another undertaking and its market share would then accrue to Kali and Salz. Furthermore, it could be practically ruled out that an undertaking other than Kali and Salz would acquire all or a substantial part of MdK. The Commission concluded that the merger was not therefore the cause of the reinforcement of a dominant position in the German market and cleared the merger.[77]

The Commission further stated,

> bearing in mind the causality considerations outlined above, a merger leading to the creation or reinforcement of a dominant position must take place in such a way as to cause the least possible damage to competition. This means that any alternative partial disposal of the target company which will reduce the deterioration of the competitive structure must as a rule be carried out if the rest of the merger is to be accepted under merger law.[78]

The Commission's decision was appealed by the French Government and Société Commerciale des Potasses et de l'Azote (SCPA), subsidiary of EMC Group ('EMC') and by EMC *French Republic v. Commission*.[79] The French Government, SCPA and EMC applied for the annulment of the Commission's decision to the ECJ on the grounds that it is incompatible with the common market, the way the Commission examined the merger in highly concentrated markets, that

---

77. Recital 23 to the Merger Regulation (139/2004, or Recital 13 of 4064/89) mentions the objective of strengthening the Community's economic and social cohesion. Recital 23 states that it is necessary to establish whether or not concentrations with a Community dimension are compatible with the common market in terms of the need to maintain and develop effective competition in the common market. In so doing, the Commission must place its appraisal within the general framework of the achievement of the fundamental objectives referred to in Article 2 of the Treaty establishing the European Community and Article 2 of the Treaty on European Union. In the *Kali und Salz* decision, after concluding that the 'rescue merger' (or 'failing firm defence') principle applied, the Commission stated that given the severe structural weakness of the regions in East Germany which were affected by the merger and the likelihood of serious consequences for them of the closure of MdK, this conclusion would also be in line with the objective mentioned in Recital 23. Again this was not a criterion for the application of the 'failing firm defence', whose requirements were anyway met in the *Kali und Salz*, but an additional factor pointing in the same direction. See *further*: OECD, 'Failing firm defence', (1996), <www.oecd.org/dataoecd/35/6/1920253.pdf>. Page 93.
78. IV/M308 *Kali und Salz/MdK/Treuhand* [1994] OJ L186/30. Para 87.
79. Cases C–68/94 and C–30/95 *France v. Commission, Societe Commerciale es Potasses et de l'Azore (SCPA) v. Commission* [1998] ECR I–1375, [1998] 4 *CMLR* 829.

the Merger Regulation has been applied incorrectly and also the concept of the failing company defence was used incorrectly.

The French Government stated *inter alia* that the Commission had wrongly applied the failing firm defence, without taking into account all the requirements used in US antitrust law. The Commission stated that in the contested decision did not adopt the American failing firm defence in its entirety. Nevertheless, the ECJ stated that it is not apparent how that could have affected the lawfulness of Commission's decision. The ECJ confirmed that the failing firm defence was relevant for the assessment of whether the concentration was compatible with the common market. The discrepancy in the requirements between the Commission and the US antitrust divisions did not in itself constitute the ground of invalidity of the contested decision. According to the ECJ, the Commission proved that MdK was very likely to close down in the near future if not taken over by a private undertaking and the failing firm defence was applied correctly.

The French Government challenged the Commission's inclusion of the criterion that the acquiring party need absorb all the market share of the target if the latter exited the market. The ECJ held that the *above*mentioned criterion intended to ensure the existence of a causal link between the concentration and the deterioration of the competitive structure of the market. According to the ECJ, a failing firm defence could be accepted if the competitive structure resulting from the concentration would deteriorate in a similar fashion even if the concentration did not proceed. The ECJ further stated that

> the criterion of absorption of market shares, although not considered by the Commission as sufficient in itself to preclude any adverse effect of the concentration on competition, therefore helps to ensure the neutral effects of the concentration as regards the deterioration of the competitive structure of the market. This is consistent with the concept of causal connection set out in Article 2(2) of the Regulation.[80]

Thus, the approach taken by the ECJ was wider than the conditions set out in Commission's *Kali und Salz* decision. The ECJ's reasoning seems unduly restrictive since it could permit the approval of a monopoly but block transactions that give rise to less concentrated markets.[81]

3. Saint Gobain[82]

The case concerned the creation of a joint venture in the silicon carbide sector between Société Européenne des Produits Réfractaires (SEPR), which belonged to the Saint-Gobain group from France (Saint-Gobain), Elektroschmelzwerk

---

80. See *further*: Cases C–68/94 and C–30/95 *France v. Commission, Societe Commerciale es Potasses et de l'Azore (SCPA) v. Commission* [1998] ECR I–1375, [1998] 4 *CMLR* 829, para 116. The ECJ annulled the Commission's decision due to erroneous findings concerning the collective dominant position on the non-German markets within the Community.
81. Levy N. 'The Control of Concentrations Between Undertakings', in Korah V. '*Cases and Materials on EC Competition Law*', (2001), 2nd ed., Hart Publishing, page 614.
82. Case No IV/M.774, *Saint-Gobain/Wacker-Chemie/NOM*, [1997] OJ L247/1.

Kempten (ESK), which belonged to the Wacker-Chemie group from Germany (Wacker-Chemie), and Nom a private investment and development company for the northern provinces of the Netherlands (Nom) (owned by the Dutch State). The operation would have brought together the two largest producers of silicon carbide and would have enabled them to secure market shares of more than 60 per cent in the markets for silicon carbide for abrasive applications and for silicon carbide for heat-resistant applications.

The Commission rejected the failing firm defence since it considered that the *Kali und Salz* criteria were not satisfied. The Commission did not expect the financial difficulties of Wacker-Chemie to lead to the exit of the firm from the market. In addition, it claimed that Saint Gobain would not have acquired Wacker-Chemie's market share if the latter exited the market. Thus, the competitive structure after the merger was likely to be worse than the competitive structure if the merger was blocked. Finally, the Commission claimed that there were alternative purchasers for Wacker-Chemie than Saint Gobain and less anti-competitive solutions such as the sale of one of the most advanced processing plants in the world (belonging to Wacker-Chemie), whose processing capacities though would remain in the market competing with Saint-Gobain.

The Commission could not establish a lack of causality between the merger and its effects on the market. According to the *Kali und Salz* criteria, there has to be no causal link between the merger and the deterioration of the competitive market structure. It can be argued that the *Kali und Salz* criteria that the Commission has defined as necessary for a successful failing firm defence are defined very narrowly and thus cannot easily be met in practice.

4. Blokker/Toys 'R' Us[83]

In *Blokker/Toys 'R' Us* the Commission adopted the ECJ approach in *Kali und Salz* in the necessity for lack of causation between the concentration and the creation or strengthening of a dominant position (under the 4064/89) or of the significant impediment to competition (under the ECMR). An increase of 4 per cent was sufficient to cause the Commission to block the concentration outright. In this case, the Commission argued that the undertaking would go out of business in the near future.

However, the lack of causality was not established as the total market share of Toys 'R' Us Inc. ('Toys 'R' Us') was not likely to be obtained by Blokker Holding BV ('Blokker'), and alternative more pro-competitive solutions compared to the merger could be found. It is essential for the acquirer to obtain the market share of the target firm even in the absence of the acquisition.[84] Thus, the failing firm defence was not accepted. As mentioned *above*, the 'failing company' doctrine is based on the lack of causality between the concentration and the creation or strengthening of a dominant position. As Baccaro mentions, the defence was

---

83. Case No IV/M.890 – *Blokker/Toys 'R' Us*, OJ [1998] L 316/1.
84. Cook C.J. and Kersey C.S., '*E.C. Merger Control*', (2000), 3rd ed., Sweet and Maxwell, London. Page 279.

technically a 'failing division defence', but was assessed by the Commission according to the *Kali und Salz* criteria.[85]

5. Boeing[86]

The Boeing/McDonnell Douglas case had both a US antitrust law and a Community dimension. The parties invoked the failing firm defence in order to have the merger approved by the US Federal Trade Commission (FTC) and the EU Commission.

Boeing US ('Boeing') operates in two principal areas, commercial aircraft as well as defence and space. Commercial aircraft operations involve development, production and marketing of commercial jet aircraft and providing related support services to the commercial airline industry worldwide. McDonnell Douglas Co (MDC) is a US corporation which operates in four principal areas, military aircraft, missiles, space and electronic systems, commercial aircraft and financial services. In 1996, Boeing and MDC entered into an agreement by which the corporation would merge and MDC would become a wholly owned subsidiary of Boeing.

The market shares of Boeing in the relevant product market would increase from 64 per cent to 70 per cent. By acquiring MDC, Boeing would be faced with only one competitor in the relevant market and its capacity in commercial aircraft, particularly the skilled work force, would also be increased. The notified merger would also strengthen the ability of Boeing to induce airlines to enter into exclusivity deals, thereby further foreclosing the market. The Commission concluded that Boeing already enjoyed a dominant position on the overall market for large commercial aircraft. The proposed concentration would lead to the strengthening of this dominant position through which effective competition would be significantly impeded in the common market.

According to Boeing, MDC was a failing firm, regarding its civil section, Douglas Aircraft Company (DAC). Failure of a competitive recovery research and development programme as well as a threefold fall of its market shares caused the company's weakness. Due to the fact that at the time of the merger notification, MDC held of 6 per cent of the global large civil aircraft orders, these production and revenues from its aircraft servicing operation kept DAC profitable. This profitability clearly precluded the application of the failing firm defence. The Commission accepted that no existing aircraft manufacturer was interested in acquiring DAC and was unable to prove the existence of a potential entrant who could use DAC as a means of entering the market.[87] Thus, the failing firm defence argument was not accepted.

---

85. Baccaro V. (2004), 'Failing Firm Defence and Lack of Causality: Doctrine and Practice in Europe of Two Closely Related Concepts', *ECLR*, issue 1, pp. 11–24. At note 22, page 15.
86. Case No IV/M.877 – *Boeing/McDonnell Douglas*, [1997] OJ L336/16.
87. Bishop S. and Walker M. (2002), '*The Economics of EC Competition Law: Concepts, Application and Measurement*', Sweet & Maxwell, London. Page 308.

The FTC, taking into account the consumer welfare evaluation, approved the merger. In its view, the decision prohibiting the proposed merger could harm important US defence interests.[88]

6. Bertelsmann[89]

CLT-UFA SA (CLT-UFA) and Taurus Beteiligungs-GmbH & Co. KG (Taurus) would acquire joint control of Premiere Medien GmbH & Co. KG (Premiere), BetaDigital Gesellschaft fΓ Or digitale Fernsehdienste mbH (BetaDigital) and BetaResearch Gesellschaft fΓ Or Entwicklung und Vermarktung digitaler Infrastrukturen mbH (BetaResearch). The proposed concentration was to be effected through the purchase of shares.

Bertelsmann AG (Bertelsmann) was the common parent company of the leading German media group. The Bertelsmann group had activities primarily in book and magazine publishing, book clubs, printing, music publishing and sound recording, and had holdings in commercial television. CLT-UFA was a joint venture between Bertelsmann and Audiofina SA, in which the parent companies had merged their European television interests. These included the shareholding in Premiere. Taurus was a holding company belonging to the Kirch group (Kirch). Kirch was the leading German supplier of feature films and entertainment programmes for television and was also active in commercial television.[90]

The merger between the two German pay-TV platforms was prohibited as it would have led to a near monopolistic structure of the German pay-TV market.

Unlike *Kali und Salz*, this case did not involve a whole company being on the verge of exiting the market. In fact, DF 1 GmbH & Co. KG ('DF 1') formed only part of Kirch's pay-TV business. A closure by Kirch of its pay-TV business would not imply that Kirch as a whole would be dissolved. Kirch's decision to shut down the pay-TV market was simply a management decision to give up an area of its business that had not performed as expected. As the Commission emphasized,

> Where the 'failing division defence' and not the 'failing company defence' is invoked, particularly high standards must be set for establishing that the conditions for a defence on the grounds of lack of a causal link have been met. If this were not so, any concentration involving the disposal of an allegedly unprofitable area of a business could be justified for merger-control purposes by a declaration on the part of the seller that, without the merger, it would be necessary to close down the seller's business in that area.[91]

The Commission claimed that the parties' arguments do not suffice to establish the defence of lack of a causal link. The parties had failed to provide evidence that the division DF 1 was likely to exit the market. Even if Kirch were to decide that it

---

88. See for example para 12 of Case No IV/M.877 – *Boeing/McDonnell Douglas*, [1997] OJ L336/16.
89. Case No IV/M.993 – *Bertelsmann/Kirch/Premiere* [1999] OJ L 053/1.
90. Case No IV/M.993 – *Bertelsmann/Kirch/Premiere* [1999] OJ L 053/1. para 7.
91. Case No IV/M.993 – *Bertelsmann/Kirch/Premiere* [1999] OJ L 053/1, para 71.

would close down DF 1 in view of the high initial losses and failure to live up to expected growth rates for subscribers, its withdrawal from the pay-TV market would not automatically follow, since DF 1 is merely the marketing platform for Kirch's digital bouquet. In the Commission's view, the parties' arguments that the market shares relinquished by DF 1 would in any case fall to Premiere, were inconclusive. The competitive situation which would arise, with or without the proposed concentration, was not the same. In addition, the parties' arguments were insufficient to establish that the failing firm/failing division criteria requirements had been fulfilled. They had not proved that the acquisition of DF 1, in its entirety or of significant parts, by businesses other than Premiere can be excluded.

Even if Kirch terminated the operations of DF 1 the negative effects on competition would be less severe than if the merger was allowed, since DF 1's assets and all of its pay-TV distribution rights would not be transferred to Premiere allowing competing pay-TV organizations to acquire Kirch's pay-TV distribution rights and enter the pay-TV market in competition with Premiere. Accordingly the parties did not fulfil any of the *Kali und Salz* criteria in order to establish a defence on the ground of lack of a causal link.

The Commission's rationale was that if the criteria for a successful failing division defence were not stricter than the ones for failing firm defence, then any merger/acquisition involving the disposal of an allegedly unprofitable business could be justified by a declaration that the division in question would be closed.[92]

The European Commission might have considered being less restrictive to a merger involving division of a firm. However, some assurance that the division's failing status is not merely a reflection of creative accounting as regards issues like transfer payments and the allocation of common costs should have been necessary.

7.   Rewe/Meinl[93]

In this case the German company Rewe ('Rewe') wanted to acquire all the shares of the Austrian company Julius Meinl AG ('Meinl'). The concentration would cause the creation or strengthening of a dominant position and thus was cleared after commitments were accepted by the Commission.

The parties, in invoking failing division defence, argued that Meinl was experiencing severe competitive disadvantages vis-à-vis larger competitors. Similar to *Bertelsmann*,[94] the decision to sell Meinl was a management decision to give up an area of its business that had not performed as expected. It was not based on the grounds of Meinl's quasi insolvency. The parties' arguments were not such as to justify applying the defence based on lack of causality. The parties had not proved that, in the absence of a takeover by another firm, Meinl would in any event withdraw from the market in the near future and in such a case, its market

---

92. Extract from Levy N. 'The Control of Concentrations Between Undertakings', in Korah V. '*Cases and Materials on EC Competition Law*', (2001), 2nd ed., Hart Publishing, page 614.
93. Case No IV M.1221 *Rewe/Meinl*, [1999] OJ L 274/1.
94. Case No IV/M.993 – *Bertelsmann/Kirch/Premiere* [1999] OJ L 053/1.

share would accrue mainly to Rewe. The parties' contention that there was no less anti-competitive alternative to the sale to Rewe/Billa, Spar being ineligible owing to its market position, was unsubstantiated. Therefore, the competitive situation which would arise with or without the proposed operation was not the same.

The parties therefore satisfied none of the *Kali und Salz* criteria for sustaining the defence of lack of causality. The Commission concluded that the proposed operation gave rise for this reason to the creation of a dominant position. Similar to the *Bertelsmann* merger, the European Commission might have considered being less restrictive to a merger involving division of a firm.

8. BASF[95]

A fundamental step in the development of the failing firm defence for the Commission was the case *BASF/Eurodiol/Pantochim*. The case was decided before the publication of the EU Guidelines.

BASF Aktiengesellschaft (BASF) would acquire control of Pantochim SA (Pantochim), Eurodiol SA (Eurodiol) and ProvironFtal NV by purchase of assets from the parent company SISAS. Although BASF would have a market share of 70 per cent, the Commission took into account that the acquiring companies were facing financial difficulties and allowed the merger on the basis that the merger would have less harmful impact on the market than the counterfactual of the undertakings exiting the market.

BASF stated that Eurodiol and Pantochim were on the verge of bankruptcy and would have been forced out of the market if they had not been acquired. On 18 September 2000, Eurodiol and Pantochim were placed under a pre-bankruptcy regime (*concordat judiciaire*) by the Commercial Court of Charleroi (*Tribunal de Commerce*) in Belgium. In the same judgment, the Court nominated four Court Commissioners (*Commissaires au sursis*) to supervise the management of Eurodiol and Pantochim during the period of pre-bankruptcy proceedings. In addition, the Italian parent company SISAS SPA, was in bankruptcy proceedings as well.[96]

During the observation period (*période d'observation*) under this pre-bankruptcy regime (*concordat judiciaire*), the *Tribunal de Commerce* ordered the provisional postponement of debts (*sursis provisoire*), that is a preliminary suspension of the rights of the creditors. Due to the lack of liquidity and the significant amount of the companies' debts, a restructuring plan (*plan de redressement*) which would theoretically have allowed the *Tribunal de Commerce* to prolong the *concordat judiciaire* and the suspension of the rights of the creditors by means of a *sursis définitif* was not proposed in this case. Therefore, the danger of bankruptcy of both Eurodiol and Pantochim was obvious. The *Tribunal de commerce* of Charleroi, responsible for the pre-bankruptcy proceedings, had confirmed to the Commission that both undertakings would have to be declared bankrupt if a buyer

---

95. Case COMP/M.2314 *BASF/Pantochem/Eurodial*, [2002] OJ L132/45.
96. Case COMP/M.2314 *BASF/Pantochem/Eurodial*, [2002] OJ L132/45, para 5.

for Eurodiol and Pantochim were not approved before the expiry of the observation period. Once BASF had terminated financial support they would have inevitably been forced out of the market.[97] Thus, the first *Kali und Salz* criterion was satisfied.

BASF argued that there is no alternative buyer of Eurodiol and Pantochim. Since a restructuring plan could be excluded, the Tribunal de commerce of Charleroi authorized the Commissaires au sursis to find a suitable buyer. Subsequently, a number of competitors were contacted. Apart from BASF, no other company approached by the Court Commissioners was ready to submit a viable offer for these companies. The Commission decided to further inquire as to the possibility of an acquisition by an alternative purchaser and concluded that, no less anti-competitive solution was available. Thus, the second condition identified in the *Kali und Salz* decision was met.

BASF argued that as far as the third condition of the *Kali und Salz* decision, namely the accrual to the acquiring company of the entire market share of the acquired undertaking, was concerned, it is sufficient that only a part of the market share is accrued to the acquiring company. The Commission recognized that the assets of the failing firm would definitely exit the market. This exit would most probably have led to a considerable deterioration of market conditions, to the disadvantage of the customers. The Commission argued that an immediate take-over of Eurodiol and Pantochim, after bankruptcy, by a third party seemed unlikely. In addition, a restart of the plants at a later stage, after the expiry of six months, would be relatively expensive compared with an immediate takeover since *inter alia*, the shutdown of production would cause additional costs for new catalysts when the plant would be restarted. Finally, it was not likely that a third party would buy specific assets of the two companies after their shutdown following a bankruptcy judgment. The Commission concluded that it was very likely that the assets of Eurodiol, as well as those of Pantochim, would definitely exit the market. However, in slightly departing from the *Kali und Salz* criteria, the Commission mentioned

> Nor can it be expected that BASF would absorb merely all of Eurodiol's market share since their main competitors are likely to gain significant parts of this share as well. However, the Commission recognizes that the assets of the failing firm would definitely exit from the market in this case. This exit would most probably lead to a considerable deterioration of market conditions, to the disadvantage of the customers. The Commission considers that these elements are equally relevant for the application of the rescue merger concept.[98]

The Commission in clearing the merger which nominally gave BASF a market share of around 70 per cent in certain markets placed importance to a series of factors. It took into account the particular and exceptional circumstances of the case, which were characterized by the imminent bankruptcy of the failing companies in the absence of the merger, the absence of a timely alternative offer under

---

97. Case COMP/M.2314 *BASF/Pantochem/Eurodial*, [2002] OJ L132/45, para 144.
98. Case COMP/M.2314 *BASF/Pantochem/Eurodial*, [2002] OJ L132/45, para 151.

the Belgian bankruptcy proceedings, and the inevitable exit from the market of the assets to be acquired, combined with capital intensive plants, tight capacity constraints in the industry and demand inelasticity.[99] In its decision the Commission stated that the exit of assets and the production capacities of the failing companies would cause 'a significant capacity shortage for products, which were already offered on the market under very tight capacity constraints'. Given this reduction in capacity, at least for a considerable transitional period of time, market conditions would be adversely affected as a direct consequence of the exit of Eurodiol's capacity. As *above*mentioned, if the failing firm's assets exit the market, there will be a tendency for the supply in that market to be decreased inducing price increases which are very likely where there was little or no excess capacity in the pre-merger situation.[100] The Commission concluded that the deterioration of the competitive structure resulting from the notified operation will be less significant than in the absence of the merger and the market conditions could be expected to be more favourable than in case of the market exit of the assets to be acquired.

In *BASF* the Commission refined the *Kali und Salz* criteria. The Commission indicated that the approach taken by the Court of Justice in *Kali und Salz* is wider than the criteria set out in the Commission's decision. According to the Court of Justice, the existence of a causal link between the concentration and the deterioration of the competitive structure of the market can be excluded and so a merger can be regarded as a rescue merger[101] only if the competitive structure resulting from the concentration is expected to deteriorate in similar fashion even if the concentration were not allowed to proceed, that is to say, even if the concentration were prohibited.[102]

Although the Commission left the first two *Kali und Salz* criteria unaltered, it argued that it was not necessary for BASF to obtain the total market shares of Eurodiol and Pantochim, contrary to the *Kali und Salz* requirement that the acquirer would acquire the market share of the acquired undertaking if the latter exited the market. The approach in *Kali und Salz* is not suitable in a situation where post bankruptcy a monopoly situation would not be created as was the case in the *Kali und Salz*. Thus, the third *Kali und Salz* criterion was changed from the requirement of the acquirer to gain the whole market share to the requirement that the assets of the acquired are likely to exit the market. The Commission stated that for the application of the rescue merger, two conditions must be satisfied:

1. the acquired undertaking would in the near future be forced out of the market if not taken over by another undertaking; and
2. there is no less anti-competitive alternative purchase.

---

99. Case COMP/M.2314 *BASF/Pantochem/Eurodial*, [2002] OJ L132/45, para 163.
100. See *further*: OECD, 'Failing firm defence' (1996) <www.oecd.org/dataoecd/35/6/1920253.pdf>. Page 19.
101. i.e. application of the failing firm defence.
102. Case COMP/M.2876 – *Newscorp/Telepiù*, [2004], OJ L110/73, para 207.

Implications of Merger Legislation

In *BASF* decided that, in addition to the first two criteria, it was necessary to establish that:

1. (c) the assets to be purchased would inevitably disappear or exit from the market in the absence of the merger.[103]

The Commission cleared the merger after comparing the level of competition likely to result from the merger with the level of competition likely to result from the exit of the failing firm and not with the *status quo*.[104] The Commission once more stated that the application of the concept of the 'rescue merger' requires that the deterioration of the competitive structure through the merger is at least no worse than in the absence of the merger.[105]

9. The Arthur Andersen Cases[106]

These merger cases were a result of the disintegration of the Andersen network in the aftermath of the Enron scandal. These cases can be argued were decided based on 'failing firm defence' doctrine. However, the failing firm defence issue was not addressed and the assessment was focussed on the 'causality' issue.[107] The Commission's investigation showed that Andersen Worldwide was no longer able to discharge its core contractual obligations of co-ordinating the global development of the member firms. In these mergers there were significant overlaps in the market for audit and accounting services to listed and large companies at national level.

In *Deloitte & Touche/Andersen UK*[108] the Commission stated that no conceivable alternative to the proposed merger would be less harmful for competition and thus there was no causal link between the proposed operation and any possible deterioration of the competitive structure in the market resulting from the present operation. The parties argued that Arthur Andersen in the United Kingdom (Andersen UK) was no longer an effective top-tier audit competitor and, hence, that the reduction in the number of top-tier suppliers of audit services would inevitably be reduced from five to four, irrespective of the merger. The rapid disintegration of Andersen's world-wide network had compounded the difficulty of any possibility of reversal of Andersen's demise or for another organization to use the individual Andersen units to recreate a fifth force for the provision of audit and accounting services. The Commission argued that even if Andersen UK could continue as an independent audit and accounting services firm, the market

---

103. Case COMP/M.2876 – *Newscorp/Telepiù*, [2004], OJ L110/73, paras 207–208.
104. Bishop S. and Walker M. (2002), '*The Economics of EC Competition Law: Concepts, Application and Measurement*', Sweet & Maxwell, London, page 309.
105. Case COMP/M.2314 *BASF/Pantochem/Eurodial*, [2002] OJ L132/45, para 143.
106. COMP/M.2810 *Deloitte & Touche/Andersen UK*, COMP/M.2824 *Ernst & Young/Andersen Germany*, COMP/M.2816 *Ernst & Young/Andersen France*.
107. Baccaro V. (2004), 'Failing Firm Defence and Lack of Causality: Doctrine and Practice in Europe of Two Closely Related Concepts', *ECLR*, Issue 1, pp. 11–24. Page 19.
108. COMP/M.2810 *Deloitte & Touche/Andersen UK*. At para 61.

investigation had shown that Andersen UK could no longer exist as a viable competitor in the market for audit and accounting services to quoted and large companies.[109]

The Commission in *Ernst & Young/Andersen France* argued that there is no causal link between the proposed operation and the possible situation of collective dominance.[110] As the Commission already found in *Deloitte Touche Tohmatsu/ Andersen UK*, the reasons for excluding this causal link were:

1. the reduction from five to four global accounting networks was inevitable;
2. the proposed merger was not more harmful for competition than other possible scenarios as regards the risk for collective dominance on the market for audit and accounting services to large and quoted companies.

In addition the Commission argued that if the transaction proposed did not take place for any conceivable reasons (such as withdrawal of the notification or regulatory prohibition), only two possible alternative scenarios to the proposed transaction could be established. These two scenarios were:

1. the take-over of Andersen France by one of the other remaining Big Four audit and accounting firms;
2. no take-over would take place and the existing clients would be dispersed between the remaining Big Four firms (with two sub-scenarios for the attribution of shares)[111]

Therefore the Commission concluded that there is no causal link between the proposed operation and a risk of collective dominance that would result from it. In addition, the Commission considered all the alternative scenarios and concluded that the mergers did not lead to a more harmful outcome than the alternative scenarios.

Although there was no firm in clear financial hardship, the Commission took into account the Kali und Salz criterion ('lack of causality') and the counterfactual to the mergers and cleared all the mergers.

10. Newscorp[112]

This case was a combination of a change from joint to sole control of Stream ('Stream') by one of its parent companies, Newscorp ('Newscorp'), and its merger with another company, i.e. Telepiù ('Telepiù'). As Stream was a separate division of one company, Newscorp, this merger raised the question whether the 'failing firm defence' applied when the acquiring firm was financially healthy but one of its divisions, which was failing, was merging with another entity. Thus, it referred to whether the failing division defence can be accepted.

---

109. COMP/M.2810 *Deloitte & Touche/Andersen UK*. At paras 45, 46.
110. COMP/M.2816 *Ernst & Young/Andersen France*, para 75.
111. COMP/M.2816 *Ernst & Young/Andersen France*, para 80.
112. Case COMP/M.2876 – *Newscorp/Telepiù*, [2004], OJ L110/73.

Newscorp argued that Stream was currently a 'failing firm' which would exit the market in the absence of the merger because there were no realistic prospects of Stream becoming profitable as a stand alone entity. The acquirer of sole control of the failing company was one of its parent companies, which was also acquiring sole control of Telepiù. The whole firm (i.e. Newscorp) was not likely to exit the market. Stream's withdrawal from the Italian pay-TV market would accordingly take the form of a management decision to abandon a business activity whose development had not lived up to the expectations of the firm's managing board.[113]

Newscorp further argued that in the absence of substantial synergies, there was no realistic prospect of a less anti-competitive purchaser emerging because it was very difficult to imagine somebody having synergies large enough to substantially change the financial outlook for Stream. Newscorp had neither indicated the potential buyers with which Newscorp and the Vivendi group have entered into negotiations to sell their respective companies in Italy nor the reasons for which the negotiations had failed. According to the information available to the Commission, neither Newscorp nor Telecom Italia had ever put Stream on public offer.

According to Newscorp, the assets to be acquired would inevitably exit the market. As regards Stream's premium rights, Newscorp argued that they would most likely be acquired by Telepiù. Following Stream's bankruptcy, the rights would be returned to the right holders that would be able to put them up for sale again. Newscorp further stated that there was no causal link between the merger and the deterioration of the competitive structure of the market as a result of the transaction.

The Commission considered that Newscorp had not been able to demonstrate that there is no causal link between the concentration and the effect on competition, because conditions of competition could be expected to deteriorate to a similar or identical extent even without the concentration in question. However, the Commission took into account that allowing the merger subject to appropriate conditions will be more beneficial to consumers than a disruption caused by a potential closure of Stream. Thus, the Commission took into account the overall market conditions (i.e. chronic financial difficulties of both companies, specific features of Italian market) in clearing the merger. In this case, the European Commission adopted a more lenient approach in this merger involving a division of a firm. It took into account the specific conditions and features of the market in clearing the merger.

The lack of causality between the merger and the adverse impact on the competitive situation in the market was not substantiated, thus the failing division defence was not successful. Baccaro (2004) suggests that an additional criterion to the criteria for failing firm defence i.e. the lack of causality as regards the deterioration of the competitive structure of the market should be satisfied if a failing division defence is invoked.[114] The importance of proving lack of causality is even

---

113. The Commission took also into account the fact that the parties have raised this argument at a very late stage which crated further doubts on the probative value of their claim as nothing has fundamentally changed since the notification.
114. Baccaro V. (2004), 'Failing Firm Defence and Lack of Causality: Doctrine and Practice in Europe of Two Closely Related Concepts', *ECLR*, issue 1, pp. 11–24. Page 16.

greater in the case of a claimed 'failing division', which is actually the acquiring company.[115] Otherwise, every merger involving an allegedly unprofitable division could be justified under merger control law by the declaration that, without the merger, the division would cease to operate.

11. Kelt[116]

There may be particular circumstances regarding the financial viability of the merging parties that may constitute a quick assessment of the merger a necessity. If that is the case, then derogation may be granted according to Article 7.3 of the ECMR. Until March 2006 there were 90 Article 7.3 derogation from suspension.[117]

In deciding on the request, the Commission shall take into account *inter alia* the effects of the suspension on one or more undertakings concerned by the concentration or on a third party and the threat to competition posed by the concentration. Such derogation may be made subject to conditions and obligations in order to ensure conditions of effective competition. Derogation may be applied for and granted at any time, be it before notification or after the transaction.[118] If derogation is granted, the concentration will be put into effect before the decision of the Commission regarding its compatibility with the Common Market.

The Commission has granted such derogation in *Kelt/American Express*. The Commission examined the latest annual accounts and was satisfied of the very serious nature of the undertaking's financial position. Given the specific circumstances of the case it was convinced of the need to swiftly effect the restructuring operation in order to prevent serious damage to one or more undertakings concerned by the concentration. For this reason it granted, on being requested, a derogation in accordance with the terms of Article 7(4) of the 4064/89 allowing the concentration to be put into effect.

As the case law analysis indicates, arguments such as that the target company will exit the market if it becomes independent, that jobs will be lost will not provide reasons for clearance of the concentration. However, as Ritter *et. al* argued revitalization of the target company to operate more efficiently may constitute a reason for the concentration to be assessed under Article 1(b), which calls for an evaluation of the 'development of technical and economic progress' possibly in the light of 'economic and social cohesion' as referred to in recital 13 of Regulation 4064/89 and Article 158 (ex 130a).[119]

---

115. Case COMP/M.2876 – *Newscorp/Telepiù*, [2004], OJ L110/73, para 212.
116. Case No IV/M.116 – *Kelt/American Express*, [1991], OJ L223/0.
117. Including derogations according to article 7(4) (under 4064/89). An article 7(4) derogation was allowed in COMP/M.2621 *SEB/Moulinex* (the equivalent of article 7(3) under 139/2004 is article 7(4) under 4064/89).
118. See *further*: article 7.3 of the 139/2004.
119. Ritter L., Braun D. '*European Competition Law: A Practitioner's Guide*', (2004), 3rd ed., Kluwer Law International, page 597.

IV. UNITED STATES OF AMERICA

> *'Shortly stated, the evidence establishes the case of a corporation in failing circumstances, the recovery of which to a normal condition was, to say the least, in gravest doubt, selling its capital to the only available purchaser in order to avoid what its officers fairly concluded was a more disastrous fate'.*
>
> *International Shoe Co. v. Federal Trade Comm'n*, 280 U.S. 291 (1930), at 301.

A. LEGISLATION

The assessment whether the planned merger would significantly increase concentration in the market and whether the merger, in the light of concentration, raises concern about potential harmful competitive effects, is based on the SLC test. The 1992 Horizontal Merger Guidelines (US Guidelines)[120] reflect the analytical framework of analysis of horizontal mergers under US merger law. Section 7 of the 1914 Clayton Antitrust Act (Clayton Act)[121] (15 U.S.C. § 18) prohibits mergers and acquisitions that may substantially lessen competition or tend to create a monopoly. The government gains its authority to review mergers and acquisitions before the parties are allowed to consummate the transaction under Section 7A of the Clayton Act (15 U.S.C. § 18a), or the Hart-Scott-Rodino Antitrust Improvements Act of 1976 (HSR).[122] Although Section 7 of the Clayton Act refers to mergers that may 'lessen' competition, mergers that worsen the competitive situation of markets that already exhibit weak competition and mergers that, while preserving the status quo, forestall future competition, will also be prohibited.[123] Under the wording of section 7, it is not necessary to prove that the competition has been restrained. It is enough that it 'may' tend to substantially lessen competition. A transaction could also be challenged on the basis that it is an agreement in restraint of trade (Section 1 of the 1890 Sherman Antitrust Act)[124] or alternatively that it is an 'unfair method of competition' (Section 5 of the Federal Trade Act).[125]

---

120. 1992 Horizontal Merger Guidelines. <www.usdoj.gov/atr/public/guidelines/horiz_book/toc.html>.
121. The Clayton Antitrust Act is comprised of §§ 12, 13, 14–19, 20, 21, 22–27 of Title 15 of the U.S.C. Some sections have been edited or eliminated because of space concerns.
122. <profs.lp.findlaw.com/mergers>.
123. OECD 'Substantive Criteria Used for the Assessment of Mergers'. <http://www.oecd.org/dataoecd/54/3/2500227.pdf>, page 295.
124. 15 U.S.C. § 1 through 15 U.S.C. § 7.
125. Global Legal Group, 'The European and US Merger Control Rules: Issues for Private Equity Investors' (2006), <www.sjberwin.com/media/pdf/publications/eu/mergercontrol2006.pdf>.

The US Congress (Congress) recognized a failing firm exemption in the legislative history to the 1950 amendments to Section 7. Some have suggested that Congress intended to exempt failing firms from Section 7 merger analysis in order to protect private interests, such as shareholders and employees, when firms are failing, while others argue that while Congress was perhaps concerned about private interests in the failing firm situation, it did not intend to override the primary concern of antitrust which is competition.[126]

The US Guidelines provide guidance on how mergers are to be evaluated for potential anticompetitive effect. The review of a proposed merger is typically conducted according to the US Guidelines.

The analytical framework of the US Guidelines that is employed in determining whether to challenge a horizontal merger involves the following:

1. Defining the relevant product market and geographic market and identifying the firms that compete in these relevant markets.
2. Whether the merger, in light of market concentration and other factors that characterize the market, raises concern about potential adverse competitive effects. For market concentration the Herfindahl-Hirschmann Index ('HHI') is used.
3. Assessing the likelihood of entry by new firms into the markets.
4. Assessing the likely competitive effects of the merger in light of the market concentration and other factors that characterize the markets.
5. Considering any significant efficiencies resulting from the merger that could not be achieved by other means.

In order the antitrust authorities to assess the anticompetitive impact of a merger they must determine the products that belong in the same market as the products of the merging firms. Market definition and the evaluation of market shares and concentration provide the starting framework for analyzing the competitive impact of a proposed merger.

When determining whether a product can be substituted for another product, the agencies will consider evidence of whether the buyers perceive the products as substitutes, the price movements in the products involved, similarities or differences in design and use of the products, consumer preferences, the seller's perception of the substitutability of the products, as well as barriers and costs associated with switching demand to potential substitutes. For each product market, the enforcement agencies must identify the geographic markets in which the firms sell their products. When determining whether geographic substitutability exists, the agencies will consider diversion of orders to other areas, basic demand characteristics, views of customers and competitors, the shipment patterns of the merging firms and competitors as well as barriers and switching

---

126. Federal Trade Commission (FTC), 'Competition Policy in the New High-Tech, Global Marketplace' 1996, volume 1, Chapter 3. <www.ftc.gov/opp/global/report/gc_v1.pdf>. Page 4.

Implications of Merger Legislation

costs associated to divert orders to companies located in other areas and the excess capacity of firms outside the location of the merging firm.

Market power for a seller is the ability profitably to maintain prices above competitive levels for a significant period of time.[127] Once the product and geographic markets have been established, the individual market shares of the merging firms are examined. Market concentration is a function of the number of firms in a market and their respective market shares. The HHI is used for the calculation of market concentration. The HHI is calculated by summing the squares of the individual market shares of all the participants. Thus, a market with only one participant (a pure monopoly) will have the HHI of 10,000 while a market with ten equal participants will have the HHI of 1,000. If there were only four firms in a particular market, each with 25 per cent of the market, the HHI would be 2,500 ($25^2 \times 4$). Any market with an HHI over 1,800 is considered highly concentrated, between 1,800 and 1,000 the market is considered moderately concentrated and below 1,000, the market is considered to be un-concentrated.

Mergers producing an increase in the HHI of more than 50 points in highly concentrated markets will raise significant antitrust concerns. A merger that increases the HHI by more than 100 points in highly concentrated markets is considered to create market power and is likely to be challenged by the enforcement agencies.[128]

In addition, a merger is unlikely to create or enhance market power if entry into the relevant market is relatively easy. For entry to be considered a sufficient competitive constraint on the merging parties it must be shown to be likely, timely (within two years) and sufficient to deter or defeat any potential anti-competitive effects of the merger. Under the US Guidelines, the enforcement agencies will also examine whether a lessening of competition through either 'coordinated interaction' or 'unilateral effects' exists. If a merger does not pose a serious threat to competition, it is unlikely to be challenged. If a substantial threat is present, however, the enforcement agencies will assess whether net efficiencies (e.g., economies of scale, cost reductions and/or technological advancements) outweigh the likely adverse impact on competition.

In the US, the agencies take an economically driven, consumer welfare approach to merger review whereby the agencies evaluate the likely net effect of a transaction on price and output. The agencies assess whether the merger, in light of market concentration and other factors that characterize the market, raises concern about potential adverse competitive effects. A merger may diminish competition by enabling the incumbents firms more successfully and more completely to engage in co-ordinated interaction that harms consumers.[129]

---

127. OECD 'Substantive Criteria Used for the Assessment of Mergers'. <www.oecd.org/dataoecd/54/3/2500227.pdf>, page 293.
128. <profs.lp.findlaw.com/mergers>.
129. OECD 'Substantive Criteria Used for the Assessment of Mergers'. <www.oecd.org/dataoecd/54/3/2500227.pdf>, page 293.

The US Guidelines contain a specific section on the issues of failing firm defence and failing division defence. The antitrust authorities assess whether, either party to the transaction would be likely to fail, causing its assets to exit the market if the merger is blocked. The theory is that '[a] *merger is not likely to create or enhance market power or to facilitate its exercise, if imminent failure of one of the merging firms would cause the assets of that firm to exit the relevant market. In such circumstances, post-merger performance in the relevant market may be no worse than market performance had the merger been blocked and the assets left the market*'.[130]

A merger is not likely to create or enhance market power or facilitate its exercise if the following circumstances are met:[131]

1. the allegedly failing firm would be unable to meet its financial obligations in the near future;
2. it would not be able to reorganize successfully under Chapter 11 of Title 11 of the US Code ('Bankruptcy Code' or 'USBC');
3. it has made unsuccessful good-faith efforts to elicit reasonable alternative offers of acquisition of the assets of the failing firm that would both keep its tangible and intangible assets in the relevant market and pose a less severe danger to competition than does the proposed merger; and,
4. absent the acquisition, the assets of the failing firm would exit the relevant market.

These criteria are less stringent than the equivalent criteria under EU legislation (ECMR), since they do not require that the target company's market share must be obtained by the acquirer if the failing firm exits the market.

A similar argument to the one made for the failing firm, can be made for a failing division of a firm. The antitrust authorities will allow the acquisition of a failing corporate division if the division has a negative cash flow on an operating basis, there is evidence that, absent the acquisition, the assets of the division would exit the market in the near future and the owner of the failing division has made unsuccessful good-faith efforts to elicit reasonable alternative offers of acquisition of the assets of the failing division and have complied with the competitively preferable purchaser requirements of Section 5.1 of the US Guidelines.[132]

Although the US Guidelines do not recognize a distressed industry defence, they suggest that distressed industry conditions may be considered when assessing the degree to which a merger would create or enhance market power.[133]

It is worth noting that bankrupt entities are subject to the standard pre-merger notification thresholds under the HSR Act. However, Section 363(b) of the USBC

---

130. US Guidelines, Section 5.0.
131. US Guidelines, Section 5.1.
132. Section 5.2 of US Guidelines.
133. Para 1.521 of the US Guidelines. See *further*: Nigro, 'The Effect of Market Conditions on Merger Review – Distressed Industries, Failing Firms, and Mergers with Bankrupt Companies'. <www.abanet.org/antitrust/committees/communication/distressedindustry.pdf>.

provides for special treatment when the target company is in bankruptcy. The USBC alters the HSR Act filing requirements as regards who and when to file the notification form as well as the waiting periods before the closure of the transaction.[134]

One exemption for the violation of the Section 7 of Clayton Act is the failing firm defence. A merger is not deemed to substantially lessen competition if one of the merging firms is failing and absent the merger the assets would exit the market. The rejection of the proposed merger when the target is failing might lead to the liquidation of the productive assets. The failing firm defence was created by the case law rather than by statute. The US Supreme Court first recognized this defence in 1930 in the leading case *International Shoe Co. v. Federal Trade Commission*. The Court allowed the merger of two firms, one of which was facing grave financial difficulties. This judgment has laid down the cornerstone for the failing company defence. The Court aimed at a broad analysis of the competitive and the anti-competitive effect of the acquisition of the company on the edge of the bankruptcy.

The legislative history of revision of the Clayton Act by the Celler-Kefauver Act of 1950 eliminated any doubts concerning the validity of the failing firm defence. The *International Shoe* case was the base for the *above*mentioned amendment. The US Supreme Court subsequently reaffirmed the validity of the defence in the case law.

A failing company claim presents a large number of variables for consideration as well as uncertainty about the allegedly failing firm's future viability. The possibility of failure may be likely but not imminent, reorganization cannot be ruled out and thus the eventual viability of the company may be very uncertain. Furthermore, there may be an alternative purchaser but the price to be offered may be so low that it is arguably unfair or inconsistent with the goal of preserving competition.[135]

In order to invoke the failing firm defence, the failing company should be genuinely failing. This means that the company must be insolvent, on the verge of insolvency, or in imminent danger of financial collapse. The Courts have applied this requirement very strictly. The fact that the company's hopes for recovery are dim or non-existent has to be proved.[136] Furthermore, the failing company should not receive a significant share of the gains from merger, if it does, this is the indication that the firm is not failing.

---

134. See *further*: Nigro, 'The Effect of Market Conditions on Merger Review – Distressed Industries, Failing Firms, and Mergers with Bankrupt Companies'. <www.abanet.org/antitrust/committees/communication/distressedindustry.pdf>.
135. Correia E. 'The Failing Company Defence', <www.ftc.gov/opp/global/final.htm>. 14 November 1995.
136. Correia (1995) argues that it is inconsistent with the goals of Section 7 to preclude consideration of a failing firm claim unless the risks of failure are close to 100 per cent. Even based on output considerations alone, the risk of failure in the 75 per cent and up range can be shown to result in higher expected costs than merger. In addition, the relative desirability of the acquiring competing firm and the out-of-market acquirer needs to be reassessed. See *further*: Correia E. 'The Failing Company Defence', <www.ftc.gov/opp/global/final.htm>. 14 November 1995.

The company, if allowed to fail, can act in accordance with Chapter 11 of the USBC and still be present in the market. The reorganization process is not costless and shareholders as well as creditors suffer losses. The companies can be reorganized and fail, ceasing the capacity and liquidating the assets. Thus, causing competitive loss based on the lost output and loss of jobs. The second element of the failing firm defence requires the firm to prove that 'it would not be able to reorganize successfully'. This ensures that the firm does not only face the short-term difficulties, but is also not viable in the long-term.

An additional criterion for the acceptance of the failing firm defence is that there must be no other prospective purchaser. In other words, this condition refers to an alternative buyer that would pose less severe danger to competition. Furthermore, this buyer must make a reasonable offer. This offer is defined as 'any offer to purchase the assets of the failing firm for a price above the liquidation value of those assets – the highest valued use outside the relevant market or equivalent offer to purchase the stock of the failing firm – will be regarded as a reasonable alternative offer'.[137] Thus, the alternative buyer needs only offer more than the liquidation value and be able to keep the assets operating in the markets, even though the alternative purchaser may have less to offer in the way of improving the efficiency of the failing firm than the prospective competitor purchaser. The competition authorities should consider whether the alternative purchaser has the capability to run the failing firm as a competitive, on-going business, including infusions of capital that will ensure the viability of the failing firm.[138]

By rating the least anticompetitive alternative in liquidation value terms, the satisfaction of the failing firm defence criteria is biased in favour of non-market participants. Any efficiency that a potential competitor-purchaser might generate from the merger may be unnecessarily sacrificed. Furthermore, a non-market participant may simply seek a revenue stream rather than seek to operate as an effective competitor by making long term investment plans.[139] Many firms that purchase a distressed business may intend to ensure a revenue stream and not to compete vigorously.

The question arises why the competitor is willing to pay substantially more than the out-of-market firm. An acquiring competitor's offer is higher due to the fact that it includes a market power premium – a payment for expected increase in the market power. The competitor-purchaser's willingness to pay more than the outsider more likely reflects an efficiency premium than a market power premium.[140] The reason for purchasing an unprofitable firm is the possibility of profits from increased concentration through oligopolistic interdependence. By

---

137. Footnote 39, US Guidelines.
138. McDavid J. 'Efficiencies, Failing Firms and the *General Dynamics* Defence', 5 December 1995. <http://www.ftc.gov/opp/global/194817.htm>.
139. Valentine D. 'Horizontal Issues: What's Happening and What's on the Horizon'. <www.ftc.gov/speeches/other/dvhorizontalissues.htm>. 8 December 1995.
140. Federal Trade Commission (FTC), 'Competition Policy in the New High-Tech, Global Marketplace' 1996, volume 1, Chapter 3. <www.ftc.gov/opp/global/report/gc_v1.pdf>. Page 13.

Implications of Merger Legislation 585

making an unprofitable company a good investment, the acquiring company believes that it can reduce its costs and/or improve product lines.

The lack of an alternative purchaser must be established by good faith efforts to find another purchaser. It is required that the failing firm has made a good faith effort to obtain offers from other firms that would keep the failing firm in the market while making a less serious threat to competition. Thus, the failing firm must explore the alternative merger possibilities and seek out the *bona fide* offers. Current policy towards failing firm defence may prefer systematically alternative purchasers that are unlikely to offer the same efficiencies that a competitor purchaser may offer. In addition, the defence may induce companies to be in a severe state of decline before they qualify for the defence.

Thus, the requirement to make a good faith effort to find an alternative purchaser safeguards against a loss in competition. However, the alternative purchaser may have much less to offer in the way of improving the efficiency of the acquired firm than the prospective competitor-purchaser. In addition, there is concern that the competitor's offer is higher because it includes a market power premium, a payment for anticipated gains in market power. There could be a market power premium, or an efficiency premium or both. The problem is that it is difficult to separate them. Overestimating the market power premium means underestimating the efficiency premium. The willingness of the acquirer to buy a company that is headed toward failure justifies giving its efficiency claims some additional credence.[141] The US Supreme Court interpretation of the alternative buyer condition was presented in the case of *Citizen Publishing Co. v. United States*.

Failing company claims indicate a trade-off between two scenarios that need to be considered, the company exiting the market and an anticompetitive merger. The first scenario is of a great importance if the costs of the merger are balanced against the costs of blocking this merger, where there is a probability that the failing firm will survive and remain competitive. If blocking the merger implies that the failing firm's assets will exit the market and therefore the output of this firm will be lost, the allowance of the merger seems to be the only sensible solution. The loss to stockholders, and community where the business operates would be less severe if the merger was allowed rather than if the firm exited the market.

Looking from an economic perspective, the capacity is a good predictor of likely output and lost output is a good measure of the competitive harm. In the case of a merger increasing concentration, it is very unlikely that the output will be reduced through the interdependence. More output is reduced if the acquired firm's assets exit the market thus the merger is the preferred option.[142] However, it should

---

141. Correia E. 'The Failing Company Defence', <www.ftc.gov/opp/global/final.htm>. 14 November 1995.
142. A number of authors have estimated the loss in output from a firm exiting the market with the loss in output stemming from increased concentration. This literature points toward the conclusion that a certain loss in output by virtue of a firm's assets leaving the market will exceed the loss in output from a merger under any realistic set of assumptions. *See* Kwoka & Warren-Boulton, 'Efficiencies, Failing Firms, and Alternatives to Merger: A Policy Synthesis', 31 *Antitrust Bull.* 431, 445 (1986), Friedman, 'Untangling the Failing Company Defence', 64 *Tex.*

be noted that the current market share of the failing firm may overstate its future competitive significance as well as the anticompetitive effects of a merger. What would be of importance is whether the merged entity can unilaterally or collectively affect prices and/or output.

The failing firm defence might also be applied when only a part of the company is failing. Refusal of such defence would force the parent company either to end a subsidiary or to keep it going at a loss. This requirement was widely discussed by the US Supreme Court in the case of *International Shoe Co. v. Federal Trade Commission*.

The *General Dynamics* case[143] provided the definition of the 'flailing', 'quasi-failing', or 'weak competitor' defence which was first applied by the lower courts in *U.S. v. International Harvester Co.*[144] The Court held that the acquisition did not violate Section 7 because the acquired company did not have sufficient financial resources to compete effectively. The claim that the firm to be acquired is a weak competitor is made in order to show that the merger is less troubling than the combined market shares. A 'weak competitor claim' can be made in the circumstances that are difficult to evaluate. In the case of *United States v. International Harvester Co.* the acquired company's 'weak competitor claim' arose from its difficulty in borrowing the capital. The court allowed the acquisition because the acquired company lacked financial resources necessary to operate competitively. Nevertheless, a 'weak competitor claim' does not circumvent the requirement of the alternative purchaser. In *FTC v. Warner Communications Inc.*[145] the Court noted that a weak company defence would expand the strict limits of the failing company doctrine.

The spirit of the *General Dynamics* decision has been incorporated into the US Guidelines by language acknowledging that 'recent or ongoing changes in the market may indicate that the current market share of a particular firm either understates or overstates the firm's competitive significance' and committing to take into consideration 'reasonably predictable effects of recent or ongoing changes in market conditions in interpreting market concentration and market share data'.[146]

In *United States v. General Dynamics Corp.* although the US Supreme Court rejected a distressed industry defence, it emphasized the importance of considering all relevant facts, especially in cases where the relevant market or industry exhibits fluctuations as well as dynamic features.[147] Antitrust authorities could also consider industry conditions as an argument in favour of approving a transaction.

L.Rev. 1375 (1986), McChesney, 'Defending the Failing-Firm Defence', 65 *Nebraska L.Rev.* 1 (1986). See *further*: Correia E. 'The Failing Company Defence', <www.ftc.gov/opp/global/final.htm>. 14 November 1995. Note 4.
143. *United States v. General Dynamics Corp.*, (1974) 415 U.S. 486.
144. *United States v. International Harvester Co.*, 564 F.2d 769 (7th Cir. 1977).
145. 742 F.2d 1156 (9th Cir. 1984) (per curiam). See *further*: Correia E. 'The Failing Company Defence', <www.ftc.gov/opp/global/final.htm>. 14 November 1995.
146. Nigro, 'The Effect of Market Conditions on Merger Review – Distressed Industries, Failing Firms, and Mergers with Bankrupt Companies'. <www.abanet.org/antitrust/committees/communication/distressedindustry.pdf>.
147. *United States v. General Dynamics Corp.*, (1974) 415 U.S. 486, at 504–506.

However, distressed industry conditions could lead to increased entry barriers and, therefore, make it more difficult for a transaction to obtain approval. In spite of that, antitrust authorities take into account the impact of economic conditions on the ability of firms to raise capital and make investments, which are needed to be more effective competitors.

The presence of distressed industry conditions could also affect the speed of the investigation as a prolonged merger review may harm the firm to be acquired and could weaken it to a point that the merger no longer makes sense to the purchaser.[148] The US Supreme Court rejected the failing industry defence in *Socony-Vacuum*.[149] However, the US Department of Justice (DOJ) in *United States v. LTV Corp.*[150] considered the weakened state of the companies and the efficiencies that would result from the transaction.

Accepting the distressed industry arguments could help revitalize failing industries by lowering their overall costs and enabling them to compete more efficiently. In moderately concentrated industries exhibiting excess capacity, the ease of entry in combination with the increased threat of import competition would render any anticompetitive impact of the merger unlikely. However, difficulty in the identification of a distressed industry and the distinction between a distressed industry and an industry experiencing a downturn may constitute putting crucial weight on the consideration of the distressed industry circumstances unlikely. In the distressed industry defence there is a consensus that mergers are strong candidates to achieve efficiencies.[151] Thus, efficiencies which may not be credible in booming industries may be applicable when the distressed industry defence is invoked.

The failing firm defence has mostly been rejected in the contested proceedings in which it was raised. Some of these cases will be analyzed in more detail in order to see how the defence has been invoked and applied.

B. APPLICATION OF THE FAILING FIRM DEFENCE

1. International Shoe[152]

The US Supreme Court first recognized the failing firm defence in *International Shoe Co. v. FTC*, which involved an FTC challenge to the merger of two shoe manufacturers. The US Supreme Court reversed a lower court decision upholding

---

148. Nigro, 'The Effect of Market Conditions on Merger Review – Distressed Industries, Failing Firms, and Mergers with Bankrupt Companies'. <www.abanet.org/antitrust/committees/communication/distressedindustry.pdf>.
149. *U.S. v. Socony-Vacuum Oil Co.*, 310 U.S. 150 (1940) 310 U.S. 150. See *further*: Valentine D. 'Horizontal Issues: What's Happening and What's on the Horizon'. <www.ftc.gov/speeches/other/dvhorizontalissues.htm>. 8 December 1995.
150. 1984–2 Trade Cas. (CCH) 66,133 (D.D.C.) appeal dismissed, 746 F.2d 51 (D.C.Cir.1984).
151. Federal Trade Commission (FTC), 'Competition Policy in the New High-Tech, Global Marketplace' 1996, volume 1, Chapter 3. <www.ftc.gov/opp/global/report/gc_v1.pdf>.
152. *International Shoe Co. v. Federal Trade Comm'n*, 280 U.S. 291 (1930).

the challenge on the grounds that the acquired company faced 'financial ruin' and argued that the anticompetitive effect that would result if the acquisition was allowed would be greater than if the failing firm exited the market.

According to the FTC the effect of such acquisition was to substantially lessen competition between the two companies, to restrain commerce in the shoe business and to tend to create monopoly. At the time of acquisition the financial condition of the acquired company was such as to necessitate liquidation or sale, thus the prospect for future competition or restrain was entirely eliminated. The Court also upheld that the acquired company was faced with financial ruin and that the only alternative was liquidation. The company had reached the point where it could no longer pay its debts as they became due. In this case the requirement of failure of the failing firm defence was defined.

The Court considered the alternatives for the failing company. The company might have obtained further financial help from the banks, with a resulting increased load of indebtedness which the company might have carried and finally paid. Even it might have availed itself of a receivership no predictions can be made whether such a course would have meant ultimate recovery or final and complete collapse. If it had proceeded, or been proceeded against, under the USBC, holders of the preferred stock might have paid or assumed the debts and gone forward with the business, or they might have considered it more prudent and less risky to accept whatever could be salvaged from the failing firm.[153] The Court concluded that between the alternatives of proceeding under the USBC, and the sale to the only available purchaser, the officers, stockholders, and creditors, thoroughly familiar with the factors of a critical situation and more able than commission or court to foresee future contingencies, after much consideration, felt compelled to choose the latter alternative.

The Court took into consideration the fact that the corporation's resources were so depleted and the prospect of rehabilitation was so remote in conjunction with the fact that it was very likely to fail, with resulting loss to its stockholders and injury to the communities where its plants were operated. It held that the purchase of its capital stock by a competitor (the only available purchaser), with the purpose of facilitating the accumulated business of the purchaser and with the effect of mitigating seriously injurious consequences otherwise probable rather than lessening competition, neither substantially lessens competition nor is contrary to the law prejudicial to the public.

Thus, according to the Court, the failing-company defence presupposes that the effect on competition and the loss to the company's stockholders as well as injury to the communities where its plants were operated, will be less if a company continues to exist even as a party to a merger than if it exits the market. It is, in a sense, a 'lesser of two evils' approach, in which the possible threat to competition resulting from an acquisition is deemed preferable to the adverse impact on competition if the company exits the market.

---

153. *International Shoe Co. v. Federal Trade Commission*, 280 U.S. 291 (1930), at 302.

2. United States v. General Dynamics Corp[154]

The significance of this case lies on the fact that the Court made a realistic evaluation of the probable anticompetitive effects of the merger of a firm which was neither failing nor a strong competitor. The Court upheld that the recent market shares of the acquired firm overstated its long-term market shares since its non-renewable assets were relatively low to other competitors. The claim was made that the future combined market shares would be smaller than the current combined market shares. The Court further argued that the combined market share figure did not accurately reflect the firm's future competitive weakness.

No claim was made that the merger would strengthen the acquired firm. The possibility of the failing firm defence was justified on the ground that one of the firms was at least in a position of financial weakness. In addition, the company's coal reserves were depleted or committed under long-term contracts. The court further found that the acquired entity, standing alone, would not contribute meaningfully to further competition since virtually all its economically mineable strip reserves were committed under long-term contracts and it possessed neither the capability to obtain more strip reserves nor the expertise to develop its deep reserves.[155]

The US Supreme Court allowed the acquisition of a coal mining company which resulted in a company with a large market share in a concentrated industry. The profitability of the acquired company was declining but was not in immediate danger of bankruptcy. This raised the possibility of flailing firm defence, i.e. of justifying a merger on the grounds that one of the firms, while not in imminent danger, is at least in a position financial weakness.

The court further stated since the rationale of the failing-company defence is the lack of anticompetitive consequence if one of the combining companies was about to disappear from the market at any rate, the viability of the 'failing company' must be assessed as of the time of the merger.

The Court in *United States v. General Dynamics Corp.* upheld that three groups of private parties benefit from the merger of a failing firm: shareholders, creditors and employees. Major shareholder losses occur mainly in the case of liquidation. The shareholders are unlikely to lose the investment and are likely to reap benefits in case the merger is profitable. The creditors will benefit as a result of retaining their rights against the debtor and are likely to be reimbursed for the credit they have provided to the firm. On the contrary, in insolvency full reimbursement is not likely.

As McDavid states, the US Guidelines retained the *General Dynamics* concept by recognizing that '*recent or ongoing changes in the market may indicate that the current market share of a particular firm either understates or overstates the firm's competitive significance... . The Agency will consider reasonably*

---

154. *United States v. General Dynamics Corp.*, (1974) 415 U.S. 486.
155. At 523, *United States v General Dynamics Corp.*, (1974) 415 U.S. 486.

predictable effects of recent or ongoing changes in market conditions in interpreting market concentration and market share data'.[156]

3. Citizen Publishing Co. v. United States[157]

The owners of the Star (Star) and the Citizen Publishing Co. (Citizen) negotiated a joint operating agreement between the two newspapers for the period of 25 years from March 1940 that was extended in 1953 until 1990. By its terms the agreement may be terminated only by mutual consent of the parties. The agreement provided, amongst others, for the formation of Tucson Newspapers, Inc. owned in equal shares by the Star and the Citizen. The only real defence of the appellants was the failing firm defence. The Court rejected this argument and set up the strict conditions under which the defence would be accepted. The Court also stated that no effort was made to sell the newspaper. The Court added that the burden of proving that the conditions of the failing firm defence have been satisfied is on those who seek protection under it, but that burden had not been satisfied in this case.

The requirements of the failing company doctrine were not met. As the Court stated:[158]

1. There is no indication that the Citizen's owners were thinking of liquidating the company or selling the newspaper, and there is no evidence that the agreement was the last straw at which the Citizen grasped.
2. The failing company doctrine can be applied only if it is established that the acquiring company is the only available purchaser.
3. The prospects for the failing company of reorganization through receivership or through Chapter 10 or Chapter 11 of the USBC would have to be dim or nonexistent to make the failing company doctrine applicable.
4. The burden of proving that the requirements of the doctrine are met is on those who seek refuge under it, and that burden had not been satisfied in this case.

The Court in *Citizen Publishing Co. v. United States* stated a three part-test for the applicability of the failing-company defence. The defence should be stringent and the defence is one of 'narrow scope' and that the burden of proving the defence is 'on those who seek refuge under it'. The prospects of continued independent existence must be 'dim or nonexistent' and it must be established that the acquiring company is the only available purchaser. The failing company doctrine plainly cannot be applied in a merger or in any other case unless it is established that the company that acquires the failing company or brings it under dominion is the only available purchaser. If another person or group could be interested, a unit in the

---

156. McDavid J. 'Efficiencies, Failing Firms and the *General Dynamics* Defence', 5 December 1995. <http://www.ftc.gov/opp/global/194817.htm>.
157. *Citizen Publishing Co. v. United States*, 394 U.S. 131, 138–139 (1969).
158. *Citizen Publishing Co. v. United States*, 394 U.S. 131, 138–139 (1969). At 132.

competitive system would be preserved and not lost to monopoly power.[159] The Court restricted merging companies' abilities to invoke the failing firm defence.

In *Citizen Publishing Co. v. U.S.*[160] the US Supreme Court adopted a formal test for the failing firm defence that was similar, to the test that was adopted by the FTC and the DOJ as part of the US Guidelines. The Court held that an otherwise unlawful acquisition of a failing firm could be permitted if three general requirements were met:

1. the acquiring company must show that the target is in imminent danger of failure
2. the failing firm must have no realistic prospect for successful reorganization and
3. the failing firm must show that it has made a reasonable, good faith attempt to locate an alternative buyer and there is no viable alternative purchaser that poses less anticompetitive risk.

4. Other Cases

The failing company defence in the banking sector was mentioned in the case of *United States v. Philadelphia National Bank*.[161] The case involved a horizontal merger of the second and third largest of the 42 commercial banks in the metropolitan area consisting of Philadelphia and its three contiguous counties. The US Supreme Court rejected the failing firm defence but upheld that the failing company doctrine applied to the banking sector due to the greater public impact of a bank failure compared with ordinary business failure.[162] In addition, the Court rejected the position that commercial banking is subject to a high degree of governmental regulation or because it deals in the intangibles of credit and services rather than in the manufacture or sale of tangible commodities, is somehow immune from the anticompetitive effects of undue concentration.[163]

As the Court argued in *United States v. Third National Bank*,[164] the Congress was concerned about banks in danger of collapse – banks not so deeply in trouble as to call forth the traditional 'failing company' defence, but nonetheless in danger of becoming before long financially unsound institutions. The Congress seemed to have felt that a bank failure is a much greater community catastrophe than the failure of an industrial or retail enterprise, and that a much smaller risk of failure than that required by the failing company doctrine should be sufficient to justify the rather radical preventive step of an anticompetitive merger.[165] The failing firm defence was not accepted. As the Court further argued, if the gains in better service

---

159. *Citizen Publishing Co. v. United States*, 394 U.S. 131, 138–139 (1969). At 138.
160. *Citizen Publishing Co. v. United States*, 394 U.S. 131, 138–139 (1969).
161. *United States v. Philadelphia National Bank*, 374 U.S. 321, (1963).
162. At 369, *United States v. Philadelphia National Bank*, 374 U.S. 321, (1963).
163. At 368 of *International Shoe Co. v. Federal Trade Commission*, 280 U.S. 291 (1930).
164. *United States v. Third National Bank*, 390 U.S. 171, (1968).
165. *United States v. Third National Bank*, 390 U.S. 171, (1968). At 187.

outweighed the anticompetitive detriment and the merger was essential to secure this net gain to the public interest, the merger should be approved.

In the beer brewing industry the failing firm defence was applicable under the condition that all requirements are fulfilled.[166] The defence was invoked in several cases, *inter alia* in the case of *United States v. Pabst Brewing Co.*[167] The facts indicated a thirty year decline in the number of brewers and a sharp rise in the market share controlled by the leading brewers.[168] The US Supreme Court rejected the Pabst's failing company defence due to the fact that the party failed to prove the elements of this defence.

In the *United States v. Diebold Inc.*[169] the US Supreme Court argued that it was improper for the District Court to decide the applicability of that doctrine and dismiss the case on a motion for summary judgment. The failing firm defence was not accepted.

The failing firm defence was also held to justify the merger in *United States v. Maryland & Virginia Milk Producers Assn.*[170] In this case an agricultural co-operative association acquired the capital stock of Embassy Dairy, the largest milk dealer in the area which competed with the association's dealers. Finally, the failing firm defence justified allowing the merger in *Union Leader Corp. v. Newspapers of New England.*[171]

V. REFLECTIONS FROM THEORY AND PRACTICE

This chapter deals with the issues that surround corporate debt restructuring methods which may involve the sale/merger of a whole firm or of the loss making division of a firm. Both the US and the EU have devised criteria against which the failing firm defence can be assessed. In US, *inter alia*, the firm would not be able to reorganize successfully under Chapter 11 of the USBC and absent the acquisition, the assets of the failing firm would exit the relevant market. In EU, *inter alia*, the allegedly failing firm would in the near future be forced out of the market because of financial difficulties if not taken over by another undertaking. Furthermore, in the absence of a merger the assets of the failing firm would inevitably exit the market. Thus, for the failing firm to apply, a merger/acquisition and/or sale should be the only viable method of corporate restructuring. Otherwise, the failing firm defence cannot be applicable. A tentative conclusion can be made that lack of alternative means of reorganization is a vital criterion for the success of the failing firm defence. As Correia states, if the reorganized firm does not survive

---

166. In the case of *United States v. Pennzoil Co.*, 252 F Supp 962 (1965) the failing firm defence argumentation was invoked in oil refining industry.
167. *United States v. Pabst Brewing Co.*, 384 U.S. 546, (1966).
168. *United States v. Pabst Brewing Co.*, 384 U.S. 546, (1966). At 551.
169. *United States v. Diebold, Inc.*, 369 U.S. 654 (1962).
170. *United States v. Maryland & Virginia Milk Producers Assn.*, 167 F. Supp. 799, aff'd, 362 U.S. 458, (1968).
171. *Union Leader Corp. v. Newspapers of New England*, 284 F.2d 582.

reorganization or if it does so with substantially reduced capacity, then there has been a competitive loss based on the output that will be lost.[172] However, there is substantial uncertainty surrounding the reorganization scenario. Thus, a central problem in applying the reorganization criterion is that it may be impossible to make reliable predictions at the time of assessing the merger as regards the likelihood that alternative restructuring methods will be successful.

The Organization for Economic Co-operation and Development (OECD) has produced a detailed report on failing firm defence.[173] The report states that business failure can be traced to managerial inefficiency (broadly defined), market-wide excess capacity,[174] or some mixture of the two. Inefficiency should be dealt with by a reorganization or takeover designed to improve the firm's management. Redeployment is the optimal solution however if a firm is failing because of a market-wide excess capacity situation.

In case the reason for failure is managerial inefficiency the merger should be reviewed by analyzing and comparing all available alternatives including liquidation, and the proposed merger should be blocked only if it is inferior to one or more of the assessed alternatives. It would not be sufficient that a management decision is said to be made, but in order for the failing firm defence to apply, the decision to close down must be inevitable in view of economic and financial factors. The efficiencies may be more significant and verifiable if the merger enhances the managerial capacities of the failing firm. Though liquidation will change the relative market shares of incumbent firms less than various mergers would, the surviving incumbents' shares will tend to rise, and they will increase most for the enterprises whose products are the closest substitutes for those of the failing firm.

In case the acquired firm is failing because of adverse conditions in the market relating to market-wide excess capacity, with the acquirer not being an actual or potential competitor of the failing firm, and after the merger all acquired assets being redeployed outside the failing firm's current market, competition authorities should consider the effects in both markets rather than exclusively concentrate on the market the failing firm currently operates.

In case the acquired firm is failing because of market-wide excess capacity, but the proposed merger involves no immediate redeployment of capacity outside the market where the failing firm operates, competition authorities should consider the effects in both markets rather than exclusively concentrate on the failing firm's market. The main rationale for the merger will usually be to facilitate a more cost effective redeployment of excess capacity than would occur without the merger. In this case the acquiring firm may have no intention of using or giving access to the failing firm's assets. Furthermore, the assets may be acquired merely to

---

172. Correia E. 'The Failing Company Defence', <www.ftc.gov/opp/global/final.htm>. 14 November 1995.
173. OECD, 'Failing firm defence', (1996) <www.oecd.org/dataoecd/35/6/1920253.pdf>.
174. This refers to a situation in which total installed capacity (the sum of outputs assuming each supplier produces at the minimum point of its average cost curve) exceeds the quantity demanded at the equilibrium competitive price.

substantiate a threat of a likely increase in output as a means to deter new entrants or discipline rivals. Such likely motives should be taken into account by competition authorities to the extent possible.

Furthermore, if the merger/acquisition of a failing firm is not allowed and the failing firm exits the market any technical or productive achievements of the failing firm will be lost. Hence, there may be adverse welfare implications. However, exit of the failing firm may be preferable from a competition perspective since the remaining firms may compete more aggressively to counteract the decrease in supply due to the loss of the failing firm's capacity and to win the failing firm's customers.

The failing firm defence carries most weight when it can be shown that the merger enables productive assets to continue in productive use. The exit of the failing firm will lead to an increase in demand and an ensuing increase in production costs and prices (unless the firm is the least competitive in a declining market). If the failing firm merges or is acquired by a dominant firm, the latter will obtain assets and know-how that allow an increase in productivity, enhancing thus its competitive position. Hence, such a merger/acquisition may lead to lower production costs and prices.

However, the takeover of a failing firm by a dominant competitor may weaken the competitive position of the remaining smaller competitors and may induce them to seek merging counterparts leading thus to further consolidation of the market. A dominant firm should be a permissible acquirer only where there is an imminent danger of liquidation of the failing firm and no other less anticompetitive purchaser is available.[175] If a non-dominant firm acquires or merges with the failing firm and becomes dominant there is high probability that the non-dominant firm's market power would increase in any case once the failing firm exits the market. In such a case, the merger is not the cause of the adverse impact on competition. Thus, the difference between allowing and blocking the merger is trivial as far as the anticompetitive effects of the merger are concerned.

In certain jurisdictions a failing firm defence/exception is not provided for in the law or regulations. Competition authorities should take into account the fact that the merger involves a failing firm in the estimation of the market shares pre and post the merger. This approach is of great importance when the failing firm's market share appears to be in long term decline. Furthermore, the competition authority may grant particularly generous treatment to claimed efficiencies when a failing firm is involved in a merger. Finally, the requirement for causation between a merger involving a failing firm and a significant reduction in competition (as is required for mergers involving failing firms that are assessed according to the European Community Merger Regulation) may be relaxed implying that the competition authority is prone to accept a failing firm defence/exception.

In general, in the absence of any other benefits (such as avoiding exit costs), mergers involving failing firms should not be allowed if they increase market

---

175. Ritter L., Braun D. '*European Competition Law: A Practitioner's Guide*', (2004), 3rd ed., Kluwer Law International, page 594.

power. The failing firm should be genuinely failing, and not merely 'ailing' ('flailing firm defence'). Thus, the merger should be allowed only when the alternative is immediate bankruptcy, and the failing firm should not receive a significant share of the gains from the merger. If it does, this should be interpreted as a signal that the firm is not failing. Finally, the greater the weight on consumer welfare and the greater the adverse effects on competition, the less likely to be blocked is a merger involving a failing firm.

The assessment of a merger involving a failing firm should not be assessed in the same way as a merger which does not involve failing firms. Where a merging firm is failing pre-merger competitive conditions should not be used as a benchmark. If the competition authorities reject one or more mergers falling below an unsustainable benchmark, the result could well be a liquidation expected to produce greater harm to competition than is predicted to result from one or more of the rejected mergers. As the Office of Fair Trading guidelines state, if one of the parties to a merger is failing, pre-merger conditions of competition might not prevail even if the merger were prohibited. In such case, the counterfactual might need to be adjusted to reflect the likely failure of one of the parties and the resulting loss of rivalry.[176]

A merger that would be blocked due to its adverse effect on competition is permitted when the firm to be acquired is a failing firm and a less detrimental merger is unavailable. Blocking the merger will cause the loss of jobs and assets from the market and thus possible economic and social benefits will be foregone. Therefore, the merger with the failing firm leading to high concentration may be accepted under the failing firm defence. In the assessment of a merger involving a failing firm defence, competition authorities should take into account the conditions in the industry, potential efficiencies and the counterfactual to blocking the merger.

As *above mentioned* one of the criteria to successfully invoke the failing firm defence in the EU and the US requires that the assets will exit the market in the absence of the merger involving a failing firm. This criterion reveals an exclusive focus on the failing firm's market. However, as the OECD report indicates there is another aspect to it that merits further probing. If the failing firm's assets exit the market, there will be a tendency for supply in that market to be decreased.[177] The decrease in supply resulting from the failing firm exiting the market may not always be greater than the decrease in supply after an anticompetitive merger involving the failing firm.

In addition, the assessment of the failing firm defence in merger cases should take into account the effect of the policy rule on the incentives for entry (and ex

---

176. OFT, 'Mergers, Substantive Assessment Guidance', available from www.oft.gov.uk. At page 34.
177. Such reductions and the welfare reducing price increases they normally entail are virtually certain where there was little or no excess capacity in the pre-merger situation. See *further*: OECD, 'Failing firm defence' (1996) <www.oecd.org/dataoecd/35/6/1920253.pdf>. Page 19.

ante investment decisions in general).[178] A lenient approach towards mergers involving failing and financially distressed firms can balance the losses from increasing concentration post merger with the gains from hastening entry and competition. However, the beneficial effect of a more permissive merger policy on entry is reduced if the share given to the failing firm is small. If the failing firm defence is less likely to be accepted in cases where the share given to the failing firm is reasonably significant, the wider benefits of the policy will not be realized. In addition, a failing firm that has greater bargaining power, perhaps because it is a division of a large corporate group, gains a greater share of the surplus from merger and its entry decision will be more sensitive to the merger rule.[179] According to research conducted by Mason and Weeds, the failing firm defence can generate greater welfare gains in cases where the target gains a substantial share of the surplus than in those where the failing firm has little bargaining power.

An argument can be made in favour of a more lenient policy which could be characterized as permitting the defence to be used by severely distressed as well as by imminently failing firms and may yield social benefits through its beneficial impact on entry, resulting in more effective competition in the long run. Thus, competition authorities might consider being less restrictive not only to mergers involving failing firms, but also to mergers involving divisions of failing firms, as well as failing divisions of firms. However, some assurance may be needed that the division's failing status is not merely a reflection of creative accounting as regards issues like transfer payments and the allocation of common costs.

The economic and social benefits should be taken into consideration in the assessment of the failing firm defence. There is difficulty in determining the extent of social costs/benefits in a failing firm context and how to account for them. The burden is borne in the form of higher prices and lost consumer surplus, while the relevant benefits relate to the failing company's workers and shareholders and the community in which the failing company's assets are located. According to Posner[180] the failing firm defence is 'one of the clearest examples in antitrust law of a desire to subordinate competition to other values'.[181] The social policy consideration regarding the merger works alongside the impact of the merger on competition. The relevant public policy consideration regards the protection of

---

178. Mason R., Weeds H. (2003), 'The Failing Firm Defence: Merger Policy and Entry', repec.org/res2003/Mason.pdf. Page 33.
179. The outcome of the *ICI-Kemira Oy* case (<http://www.competition-commission.org.uk/rep_pub/reports/1991/293kemira.htm#full>), assessed by the MMC (UK), in which a failing division was judged more harshly than may have been the case for a stand-alone firm in a similar financial position, also threatens to undermine the benefit of the policy. See *further*: Mason R., Weeds H. (2003), 'The Failing Firm Defence: Merger Policy and Entry', repec.org/res2003/Mason.pdf. Page 3.
180. Richard Posner was an assistant to the Federal Trade Commission, assistant to the solicitor general of the United States, in 1981 appointed as a judge of the U.S. Court of Appeals for the Seventh Circuit. He was the chief judge of the court from 1993 to 2000.
181. Posner, R A, '*Antitrust: cases, economic notes and other materials*', West Publishing, 2nd ed., 1981, p. 472.

private parties whose future depends on the existence of the failing firm as well as the welfare of the locality of the failing firm. Social costs could be considered as a policy matter, since neither the legislative history to the Cellar-Kefauver amendment to Section 7 in 1950 nor US Supreme Court precedent precluded expressly do so.[182] According to Correia, competition authorities should take social costs into account in adopting some general formulation of the failing company defence, rather than taking social costs into account in individual cases.

As Fox stated, in relation to the failing firm defence invoked in *Citizen Publishing*,[183] failing firm defence as a matter of US Supreme Court case law (Citizen Publishing), is devised in the interests of stockholders and communities (e.g., jobs).[184] In addition, as was mentioned earlier in this chapter, the US Supreme Court in the case *United States v. General Dynamics Corp.*[185] upheld that three groups of private parties, shareholders, creditors benefit from the merger of a failing firm. Major shareholder losses occur only in the case of liquidation. The shareholders are unlikely to lose the investment and are likely to reap benefits in case where the merger is profitable. The creditors will benefit as a result of retaining their rights against the debtor and are likely to be reimbursed for the credit they have provided to the firm. On the contrary, in insolvency proceedings they are not as likely to be fully reimbursed.

Fox stressed that the case law may seem of questionable wisdom to those who believe that the job of antitrust is antitrust. Shareholders by definition take risks of losing an investment and employment policy is not best handled by antitrust exemptions. Allowing mergers can result in job losses as may also be the case in prohibiting mergers. If a merger is not allowed and the failing firm exits the market, the lost jobs originate from plant closure. If an anticompetitive merger is allowed, jobs may be lost when the industry raises prices and reduces output. When the failing firm disappears from the market, the employment resources of this firm are likely to be devoted to the manufacture of a completely different product or provide totally different services, perhaps not as efficiently. The likelihood of job losses, inefficient use of labour force and the political/social ramifications that such issues may have should not determine the assessment of mergers under the antitrust law.

Competition authorities (e.g. US and EU) are unwilling to extend the failing firm defence/exception to firms which have not yet failed but are less efficient competitors. If a flailing firm defence/exception exists, parties to competition reducing (and thus likely profitable) mergers would have a strong tendency to claim that they are flailing even if their situation is not as severe as the one of a failing firm in order to invoke the defence and be treated more leniently than they should. In addition as the OECD report states, even if flailing firms could be

---

182. Federal Trade Commission (FTC), 'Competition Policy in the New High-Tech, Global Marketplace' 1996, volume 1, Chapter 3. <www.ftc.gov/opp/global/report/gc_v1.pdf>. Page 14.
183. *Citizen Publishing Co. v. United States*, 394 U.S. 131, 138–139 (1969).
184. 'Antitrust and Competitiveness: Efficiencies, Failing Firms, and the World Arena', statement of Eleanor Fox, December 13, 1994. <http://www.ftc.gov/opp/global/fox.htm>.
185. *United States v. General Dynamics Corp.*, (1974) 415 U.S. 486.

reliably identified, competition authorities may take the view that the competition such firms provide, albeit weak, benefits consumers and should be allowed to continue as long as possible. A merger involving a flailing firm might foster a considerably better competitive environment than a similar merger involving a failing firm.[186] Similar arguments can be put forward for the unwillingness of competition authorities to accept declining industry arguments. However, what should be taken into consideration is that in declining industry situations it is more likely that firms which may be currently flailing may continue to be in an adverse situation and may not be viable at all in the near future.

As the *above* analysis has illustrated, the application of the failing firm defence is highly controversial. The role of antitrust legislation in taking into consideration the phenomenon and consequences of failing firms in assessing transactions involving such firms is important in safeguarding and advancing the aims of competition law.

VI. CONCLUDING REMARKS

Mergers and joint ventures in impacted industries are a necessary part of this world, and if the antitrust laws are perceived to be an undue barrier to such combinations, then a legislative affirmation that this it is not the case would be desirable. This chapter has analyzed the implications of the failing firm defence on the restructuring process that financially distressed companies may be involved in.

Firms in financially distressed conditions may face the prospect of illiquidity and may embark on a restructuring process in order to ensure their viability and profitability. Restructuring is the term for the act of converting a debt into another debt that is repayable at a later time.[187] In this process of restructuring the companies may be involved in acquisitions and/or mergers. In such cases, the implications of competition legislation on the restructuring process may be severe. There may be instances where the negotiations leading to a restructuring plan may have been completed successfully and the proposed solution i.e. merger/acquisition to be blocked by the competition authorities. A safe harbour for such cases is the concept of failing firm defence/failing division defence.

Each jurisdiction has its own formulated criteria that need to be satisfied in order for the failing firm defence to be acceptable. In general, the criteria that need to be satisfied include, *inter alia*, that the allegedly failing firm would in the near future be forced out of the market because of financial difficulties if not taken over by another undertaking. Thus, the firm must be insolvent, on the verge of insolvency or in imminent danger of financial collapse. In addition, there must be no less anti-competitive alternative purchase than the notified merger and in the absence of a merger the assets of the failing firm would inevitably exit the market. Once these conditions are fulfilled the merger would not be considered to cause the deterioration of the competitive structure that follows the merger.

---

186. OECD, 'Failing firm defence', (1996) <www.oecd.org/dataoecd/35/6/1920253.pdf>. Page 21.
187. Oxford English Dictionary, available online at http://www.askoxford.com.

Implications of Merger Legislation

Hence, to qualify for the failing firm defence, the merging undertakings must show that one of the undertakings is a failing firm and that therefore the merger itself does not bring about any anticompetitive effects. The logic in the defence is that the deterioration in the competitive structure of the market would have occurred even in the absence of the merger through the exit of the failing firm.[188]

Considering the merger with the failing firm, the economic aspects of allowing and blocking this merger, such as the loss of jobs, benefit to consumers, price maintenance, should also be born in mind. Social costs must be taken into account in adopting some general formulation of the failing company defence, rather than taking social costs into account in individual cases.[189]

The courts, mainly in the EU, have in most instances been negative towards the failing firm defence.[190] However, there have been some landmark cases in the two *above*mentioned jurisdictions that are analyzed in this chapter which have formulated the development of the concepts of failing firm defence and failing division defence. These decisions by the competition authorities and courts along with the guidelines issued by the competition authorities have provided the framework within which the request for such a defence must be assessed.

Deciding when and how to apply the defence is difficult in part because the facts underlying the failing company claim may be closely intertwined with other claims, which are analytically distinct. For example it may seem that current policy benefits alternative purchasers that are unlikely to offer the same efficiencies that a competitor purchaser may offer. In addition, the failing firm defence can be assumed to constitute an efficiency claim, since the acquiring company argues that it can ensure the viability and profitability of the failing company. As Correia argues, a failing company claim may also occur in the context of a declining industry where capacity is certain to exit the market. If that is the case, a merger may be justified both on efficiency grounds as well as on failing firm defence grounds, which must be analyzed separately. In general, only if the merger risks substantial harm to competition must the failing firm defence be assessed.[191]

As this chapter has indicated, the failing firm defence as well as the failing division defence are parts of competition law jurisprudence. With increased globalization of the marketplace and the increased competitive pressures placed on firms as a result of it, failing firm defence will arise more frequently. Competition authorities should take into account the viability and profitability of the merging firms and assess the transaction accordingly. The rigorous competitive effects analysis undertaken by the enforcement authorities is sufficient to ensure that valid claims of failure and changing market conditions are carefully considered and evaluated.[192]

---

188. MacCulloch A., Rodger B. '*Competition Law and Policy in the EC and UK*', (2004), 3rd ed., Cavendish Publishing, page 221.
189. Correia E. 'The Failing Company Defence', <www.ftc.gov/opp/global/final.htm>. 14 November 1995.
190. Albeit a small number of cases where the defence has been invoked.
191. Correia E. 'The Failing Company Defence', <www.ftc.gov/opp/global/final.htm>. 14 November 1995.
192. Leeds L. 'The Failing Firm Defence', Federal Trade Commission Hearings on Changing Nature of Competition in a Global and Innovation-Drive Age. <www.ftc.gov/opp/global/GC111495.htm>. 14 November 1995.

ANNEX

This annex will present the legal substantive test for the assessment of mergers in the two jurisdictions analyzed in this chapter as well as the relative parts of the legislation (where applicable) that refers to the failing firm defence/failing division defence.

A. EUROPEAN UNION

Council Regulation (EC) No 139/2004 of 20 January 2004 on the control of concentrations between undertakings (the EC Merger Regulation)

Article 2 (3)

A concentration which would significantly impede effective competition, in the common market or in a substantial part of it, in particular as a result of the creation or strengthening of a dominant position, shall be declared incompatible with the common market.

Guidelines on the assessment of horizontal mergers under the Council Regulation on the control of concentrations between undertakings

VIII. FAILING FIRM

89. The Commission may decide that an otherwise problematic merger is nevertheless compatible with the common market if one of the merging parties is a failing firm. The basic requirement is that the deterioration of the competitive structure that follows the merger cannot be said to be caused by the merger.[193] This will arise where the competitive structure of the market would deteriorate to at least the same extent in the absence of the merger.[194]

90. The Commission considers the following three criteria to be especially relevant for the application of a 'failing firm defence'. First, the allegedly failing firm would in the near future be forced out of the market because of financial difficulties if not taken over by another undertaking. Second, there is no less anti-competitive alternative purchase than the notified merger. Third, in the absence of a merger, the assets of the failing firm would inevitably exit the market.[195]

---

193. Cases C–68/94 and C–30/95 *France v. Commission, Societe Commerciale es Potasses et de l'Azore (SCPA) v. Commission* [1998] ECR I–1375, [1998] 4 *CMLR* 829, para 110.
194. Cases C–68/94 and C–30/95 *France v. Commission, Societe Commerciale es Potasses et de l'Azore (SCPA) v. Commission* [1998] ECR I–1375, [1998] 4 *CMLR* 829, para 114. See also Commission Decision 2002/365/EC in Case COMP/M.2314 *BASF/Pantochem/Eurodial*, [2002] OJ L132/45, points 157–160. This requirement is linked to the general principle set out in paragraph 9 of this Notice.
195. The inevitability of the assets of the failing firm leaving the market in question may, in particular in a case of merger to monopoly, underlie a finding that the market share of the

91. It is for the notifying parties to provide in due time all the relevant information necessary to demonstrate that the deterioration of the competitive structure that follows the merger is not caused by the merger.

B.   UNITED STATES OF AMERICA

Clayton Act

§ 7 (Acquisition by one corporation of stock of another)

No person engaged in commerce or in any activity affecting commerce shall acquire, directly or indirectly, the whole or any part of the stock or other share capital and no person subject to the jurisdiction of the FTC shall acquire the whole or any part of the assets of another person engaged also in commerce or in any activity affecting commerce, where in any line of commerce or in any activity affecting commerce in any section of the country, the effect of such acquisition may be substantially to lessen competition, or to tend to create a monopoly.

No person shall acquire, directly or indirectly, the whole or any part of the stock or other share capital and no person subject to the jurisdiction of the FTC shall acquire the whole or any part of the assets of one or more persons engaged in commerce or in any activity affecting commerce, where in any line of commerce or in any activity affecting commerce in any section of the country, the effect of such acquisition, of such stocks or assets, or of the use of such stock by the voting or granting of proxies or otherwise, may be substantially to lessen competition, or to tend to create a monopoly.

This section shall not apply to persons purchasing such stock solely for investment and not using the same by voting or otherwise to bring about, or in attempting to bring about, the substantial lessening of competition. Nor shall anything contained in this section prevent a corporation engaged in commerce or in any activity affecting commerce from causing the formation of subsidiary corporations for the actual carrying on of their immediate lawful business, or the natural and legitimate branches or extensions thereof, or from owning and holding all or a part of the stock of such subsidiary corporations, when the effect of such formation is not to substantially lessen competition.

Nor shall anything herein contained be construed to prohibit any common carrier subject to the laws to regulate commerce from aiding in the construction of branches or short lines so located as to become feeders to the main line of the company so aiding in such construction or from acquiring or owning all or any part of the stock of such branch lines, nor to prevent any such common carrier from acquiring and owning all or any part of the stock of a branch or short line constructed by an independent company where there is no substantial competition

---

failing firm would in any event accrue to the other merging party. *See* Cases C–68/94 and C–30/95 *France v. Commission, Societe Commerciale es Potasses et de l'Azore (SCPA) v. Commission* [1998] ECR I–1375, [1998] 4 *CMLR* 829, paragraphs 115–116.

between the company owning the branch line so constructed and the company owning the main line acquiring the property or an interest therein, nor to prevent such common carrier from extending any of its lines through the medium of the acquisition of stock or otherwise of any other common carrier where there is no substantial competition between the company extending its lines and the company whose stock, property, or an interest therein is so acquired.

1992 Horizontal Merger Guidelines

5. Failure and Exiting Assets

5.0 Overview

Notwithstanding the analysis of Sections 1–4 of the Guidelines, a merger is not likely to create or enhance market power or to facilitate its exercise, if imminent failure, as defined *below*, of one of the merging firms would cause the assets of that firm to exit the relevant market. In such circumstances, post-merger performance in the relevant market may be no worse than market performance had the merger been blocked and the assets left the market.

5.1 Failing Firm

A merger is not likely to create or enhance market power or facilitate its exercise if the following circumstances are met: 1) the allegedly failing firm would be unable to meet its financial obligations in the near future; 2) it would not be able to reorganize successfully under Chapter 11 of the USBC[196]) it has made unsuccessful good-faith efforts to elicit reasonable alternative offers of acquisition of the assets of the failing firm[197] that would both keep its tangible and intangible assets in the relevant market and pose a less severe danger to competition than does the proposed merger; and 4) absent the acquisition, the assets of the failing firm would exit the relevant market.

5.2 Failing Division

A similar argument can be made for 'failing' divisions as for failing firms. First, upon applying appropriate cost allocation rules, the division must have a negative cash flow on an operating basis. Second, absent the acquisition, it must be that the assets of the division would exit the relevant market in the near future if not sold. Due to the ability of the parent firm to allocate costs, revenues, and intracompany transactions among itself and its subsidiaries and divisions, the Agency will require evidence, not based solely on management plans that could be prepared solely for the purpose of demonstrating negative cash flow or the prospect of exit from the relevant market. Third, the owner of the failing division also must have complied with the competitively-preferable purchaser requirement of Section 5.1.

---

196. 11 U.S.C. Sections 1101–1174 (1988).
197. Any offer to purchase the assets of the failing firm for a price above the liquidation value of those assets – the highest valued use outside the relevant market or equivalent offer to purchase the stock of the failing firm – will be regarded as a reasonable alternative offer.

Index

A

Ability-to-pay 515, 519, 521, 522, 525, 541
ABL 21, 24–28, 30, 31, 33, 38, 40, 44, 48–51
Acceptance 6, 12, 16, 24, 25, 103, 106, 107, 143, 144, 148, 270, 271, 387, 424, 444–446, 448–451, 469, 470, 561, 562
  solicit 442–445, 448
Account Holders 158, 242, 251
ACLC 69, 71–74, 76, 79, 80, 82, 87, 309
Acquisition 81, 83, 84, 86, 326, 327, 350, 512, 548–550, 552, 553, 565, 571, 579, 582, 583, 586, 588, 589, 601, 602
  costs 531, 533
ACSR 64, 65, 67–76, 79–83, 87
Action Letter 38, 39
Ad hoc receiver 265–268, 281
Adequate information 443, 450, 451, 464, 466, 468–470
Adhesion 122, 123, 362, 363, 365, 367
Adjournment 184, 220, 222
Adjustments 103, 123, 124, 211, 403, 501, 551, 552
Administration 32, 57–62, 64–76, 78, 79, 81–84, 88–90, 92, 116, 165, 166, 223, 226, 227, 244, 252–254, 481, 485, 486

  order 173, 227, 244, 253, 484, 551
  period 62, 67, 68, 74
  procedures 484, 500
    extraordinary 359, 366
  proceedings 195, 253, 484
  voluntary 57–59, 61, 63
Administrator 58–80, 82–86, 88–92, 165, 171, 195, 196, 198, 213, 227, 228, 262, 278–280, 282, 284–287, 293, 294, 318
  judicial 261, 262, 266, 270, 271, 279–281, 283–285
  of Spyglass Management Group Pty Ltd 73, 74
  approval 79
  votes 63
Administrator Appointed 74
Administrators Appointed 71–73
Advisors, professional 133, 148, 149, 151, 229, 314, 387, 396, 397, 400, 401, 404
Affected
  classes of creditors 14, 15, 132
  creditors 10, 15, 16, 104, 135, 140, 143, 144, 147, 218, 426–429, 431, 432
  identification of 426
  requisite majority of 424, 425
Affiliate 440, 451, 452, 455, 463, 470, 471, 474

Agreement 12–16, 24–27, 51, 103–105,
	107–109, 186, 196, 267–273,
	275–277, 310, 311, 359, 360,
	369–372, 432–434, 541, 550, 551
  binding 186, 348
  credit 462
  debtor-creditor 336, 347, 348
  enforcement of 99, 101, 102, 105–107,
	113–116, 120–124
  memorandum of 290
  outof-court 310
  plan 101
  prepetition credit 462
  preventive 20, 21, 115
  prior 104, 106, 114, 115
  procedure, enforcement of 104
  process 119
Air Canada 131
ALG 21, 42, 478, 487, 489, 492, 494,
	497, 498
ALR 69, 70, 73, 75, 76, 78, 79, 87
Alternatives, out-of-court reorganization 121
Amalgamation 194, 337
Andersen France 575, 576
Andersen UK 575, 576
Anor 67, 69–75, 78, 79
Ansett Australia Limited 64, 72, 73, 79
Ansett Australia Ltd 79, 80
Anticompetitive effects 549, 560, 586, 588,
	589, 591, 594, 599
Antitrust 549, 580–583, 586, 587, 596, 597
  authorities 580, 582, 586, 587
AO 514, 517, 518, 521, 523, 525, 539, 541,
	542
APE 21, 22, 25–35, 39–42, 44–52, 102, 479,
	487, 491, 492, 496–498, 500, 502,
	504, 505
  agreement 28, 46, 47
  approval order 49
Appellants 38–40, 42, 590
Appellate court 307, 308, 390
Applicant 178, 179, 181, 182, 185, 191, 192,
	224, 225, 228, 277
Approval
  judicial 6, 26, 52, 53
  procedure, supervised 48
  processes, fast track court 424
  unanimous 141

Argentina 20–25, 27–29, 31, 33, 35, 37,
	39–41, 43–45, 47, 49, 51, 53, 103,
	480, 488
Argentine Court 26, 32, 35, 38, 40, 41, 46–49
Argentinian Recovery Company 20, 21, 29,
	31, 38
Argentinian Recovery Company Argo 20,
	47–49
ARP 22–24, 28, 29, 43, 45, 46
Arrangement 57, 87, 166–169, 171, 172,
	174–178, 193–196, 207, 208,
	213–217, 224–226, 228–238,
	298–300, 306–308, 322, 406–418,
	500–502
  contractual 140, 196
  court insolvency 170
  creditors 236
  linked 180
  out-of-court 408
  plan of 132, 143, 155
  power 237
  procedure 299, 300, 302, 305, 317, 502
	voluntary 162, 195, 205, 295
  proceedings 406, 407, 485
  process 300
	voluntary 295
  restructuring 141, 142
  voluntary 162, 195, 202, 203, 205–207,
	210, 212, 216–219, 221, 223, 224,
	228, 229, 231, 233, 235–237, 301,
	424
Arrangement Act 407, 408
ASIC 75, 78, 81, 82, 84, 92, 93
Asset-based jurisdiction 482, 485–487, 505
  exercise of 485, 506
Asset classification 324, 338, 339, 352–354
  category 349, 354
  norms 349
  status 349, 351, 353
Assets
  personal 294
  principle 440
  private 532, 533
  productive 327, 328, 583, 594
  repossession of 110
  restructured 349, 354
  secured 331
  shared 140

Index 605

standard 340, 349, 352–355
subject 11, 136, 490
succeeded 396
transfer of 414, 512, 530, 535, 552
AUD 59, 73, 83, 84, 86
Australia 57, 59, 61, 63–65, 67–69, 71, 73, 75–79, 81, 83, 85, 87, 89, 91, 93
Australian Chartered Bank 183, 184, 187, 188
Azore 561, 566, 567, 600, 601

B

Balance sheet 312, 313, 332, 339, 340, 354, 381
  tests 425
Bank 10–12, 26, 290–293, 310, 311, 330, 333–336, 339, 340, 342–347, 349, 350, 353–355, 360–363, 371, 372, 381–386, 395, 396, 462
  deposits 22, 23
  group 462, 463, 467, 468
    members 463, 467, 468
Bank Loans 30, 447
Bank National Association 47, 49
Banking Companies 326, 327
Bankrupt Companies 552, 563, 582, 583, 586, 587
Bankruptcy 20, 21, 31–36, 39–43, 47–49, 99, 100, 103, 105–113, 115, 117, 118, 131, 132, 134, 139,166, 167, 253, 368, 369, 407, 408, 439–445, 448, 458–460,, 464–466, 468, 463–465, 481, 487, 489, 490, 495–501,547, 550–552, 573
  section 462
Bankruptcy, company approach 416
Bankruptcy Court 31
  case 42, 48, 160, 166, 438, 440, 442–444, 447, 459, 464, 467, 468
  court
    approval 441
    claiming 49
    confirmation 459
    dismisses 417
  courts 417, 440, 446, 461
  decree of 117, 118, 125
  estate 112, 117, 370, 440–442

judge 278–281, 284, 288, 489–491
law 20, 24, 32, 49, 99, 100, 108, 380, 420, 421, 494, 497
order 142, 231, 233
petition 99, 118, 236, 444
prepackaged 459, 464, 465
procedures, statutory 402–404
proceedings 101, 111, 359, 407, 411, 415, 439, 572
  plenary 439
restrictions orders 204
sale processes 134
BAPCPA 42, 460, 463–465
Bar date 162, 163, 250
Barclays Bank 490, 494
Bari, court of 364, 365, 367
BASF 564, 572–575, 600
BCC 172–174, 179–182, 184–189, 193, 196, 203, 205, 206, 211–214, 218, 221, 222, 224, 225, 229, 231, 232, 234–236
BCLC 171, 172, 175–182, 184, 185, 187–191, 193, 198, 203, 204, 207, 209, 213, 215, 216, 223–225, 227, 230, 483, 484
Bertelsmann 570, 571
BIA 130, 132, 135, 139, 142–144, 146, 147, 154
Blokker 568
Blue Bird Company 459–463, 466–468
Board 59, 107, 146, 149, 192, 199, 328, 329, 336, 345
Boeing 563, 564, 569, 570
Bond 24, 26, 32, 145, 189, 190, 238, 239, 242, 245, 246, 250, 354, 365, 368, 433, 445, 447
  issues 239, 240, 242, 248, 249, 251, 252
  series 26
  trustee 239, 240, 242
Bondholders 48, 190, 191, 239–242, 245, 250–252, 445, 447, 492
  meetings of 240, 251
Borrowers 74, 325, 330, 331, 338, 343, 345–351, 353, 527
BPIR 203, 210–213, 216, 221, 224, 230, 232–234, 236, 318

BRA 358–360
Branches 117, 118, 126, 127, 173, 281, 530, 601
Brazil 99–101, 103–105, 107, 109, 111–113, 115, 117, 119, 121, 123, 125–127, 511
Brazilian Out-of-court Reorganization 102
British Aviation Insurance Company 163
BRL 122, 479, 480, 493, 501
Brussels Convention 480, 488, 505
Brussels Regulation 480, 488, 504, 505
Business
 activities 106, 131, 365, 366, 370, 411, 416, 432, 530, 577
 assets 133, 153, 155, 534, 548
 competitive 415
 corporations 383, 386
 days 59, 60, 62, 67, 69, 70, 216, 218, 222, 467
 decisions 72, 440
 enterprises 143, 151
 entities 440, 444
 judgment rule 151
 judgments 151
 non-core 396
 operations 279, 313, 382, 383, 440–442, 501, 547
 organizations 439
 pay-TV 570
 plan 44, 49, 122, 144, 145, 148, 149, 402, 449
  focused 145
  rational 147
 problems 144, 154
 reasons 462, 532, 534
 reorganization plan 384
 solutions 144, 145
 transaction 511
 value 519
Business Credit 512
Business Journal 410, 412
Business Recovery Professionals 203, 205, 206
Businessman 3, 105, 106

C

CA 56–70, 73–77, 79–81, 84, 176, 484
Canada 131, 133–139, 141–147, 149–151, 153, 155, 167, 168, 510, 511, 517, 520

Canadian
 court supervised sale procedures 134
 courts 133–135, 148, 152, 155, 167
Cancellation
 of Debts Resulting 536
 of indebtedness income 517–531, 534, 540
Capital
 contribution 526, 527, 533
 gains 530, 533, 536
 tax 530, 533
Case-by-case basis 116, 345, 520–525, 540, 541
Case COMP 572–576, 578, 600
Cash Option 29, 30, 34, 35
Cash payments, deferred 453, 472
Categories, standard 340, 353–355
Causality 552, 561, 562, 565, 566, 568, 569, 571, 572, 575–577
CCAA 131–133, 135, 143, 146, 147, 151, 152, 154, 155
 proceedings 131, 135, 154
CDR 342, 345–347, 351, 352, 355
 CDR Cell 343–346, 349, 355
 CDR Core Group 344, 347, 351
 CDR Empowered Group 343–346, 350
 CDR mechanism 342, 346–348, 350–352
 CDR Standing Forum 343–346
 CDR system 342–349, 351, 352
Cent
 market share 564
 notes 28
Century 3, 83–86, 99
Chairman 184–186, 212–215, 222–224, 227, 243, 318, 333, 334, 342, 343, 400
Chairperson 64, 342, 387, 401
Challenges 111, 254, 255, 332, 368, 502, 506
Chancery Division 483–485, 488
Charge 3, 59, 62, 67, 90, 91, 117, 201, 205, 207, 210, 218, 222, 228, 229, 302, 537, 538
Chargee 67, 90
Chinese perspective 517, 525–527, 532
Citizen Publishing Co 585, 590, 591, 597
Civil Court 263, 278
Civil Rehabilitation Law 379, 380, 387–390, 392, 398, 399, 403
Claim 15, 16, 52, 53, 138, 139, 148, 163–167, 211–216, 229, 230, 241, 242, 389, 426, 427, 443, 444, 447, 450–456, 469–475, 533–535

Index 607

  agreement 244
  property 452, 454, 471, 473
Claimants 446–448
Class
  action claim 247
  meetings 178, 179, 183, 184, 188
    single 182
    special 386
  members 132, 185
  post 216
  rights 5
Classes 112–115, 132, 133, 147–150, 171, 172, 176–184, 186–190, 300, 317–319, 322, 332, 424–427, 430, 431, 433, 434, 452–455, 471–474
  asset 340
  composition of 181, 318
  constitution of 165, 183, 317, 318
  created 386
  of creditors 112, 165, 318
  designated 386
  distinct 179, 180
  impaired 443, 452, 471
  relevant 161, 450, 469
  single 178–181, 303
  subordinate 153
  unsecured 145, 146, 148
Classification 41, 112, 119, 132, 144, 312, 347, 354, 424, 426, 427, 432, 435, 436
Claw 103, 371
Clayton Act 544, 579, 583, 601
CLR 67–70, 73
CMH 320
CMLR 558, 561, 566, 567, 600, 601
Co 44, 379, 380, 386, 392, 393, 480, 482, 493, 544–546, 570
CO 298–301, 305, 313
  CO Hong Kong Companies Ordinance 298
  CO section 299, 300
Code 101, 102, 125, 160, 166, 358, 360–363, 462, 497, 582
Codified provisional liquidation scheme 321
Collateral 112, 126, 135–137, 153, 276, 389, 401, 402, 427, 432, 442
Combined Options 29, 30, 34, 35
COMI 169, 173, 174, 258, 288, 494–496
  COMI Centre of main interests 158, 478

Commencement 5, 13–16, 31, 32, 41, 61, 388, 409, 410, 413, 417, 444, 450, 451, 469, 470, 489, 496–498, 513
Commerce 260, 263, 278, 288, 546, 549, 572, 601
Commercial
  production 351, 352
  protests 107, 108
  Commercial Code 259, 262, 264, 265, 268–270, 272–278, 280, 283–285, 288, 293, 386
  Commercial Court 35, 258, 260–265, 268, 270–272, 274, 275, 278, 424, 431, 436
Commission 36, 37, 176, 466, 588
Commission's
  decision 556, 563, 564, 566, 567, 574
  merger decisions 556
Committee 9, 49, 60, 141, 142, 192, 216, 278, 279, 282, 283, 362, 382–385, 387, 400, 401, 403, 404, 582, 583, 586, 587
  of creditors 60, 75, 85, 440, 441, 447
Community 124, 153, 554, 563, 566, 567, 585, 588, 596, 597
COMP 575, 576, 578
Companies
  Companies Act 158, 161, 167, 168, 170–179, 182, 183, 186, 187, 189, 191–195, 202, 206, 224, 329, 330, 332, 481, 482, 484, 485
  Companies Court 158, 181, 182, 332
  Companies Ordinance 299, 301, 322
  Companies subject 517
Company
  acquired 383, 586, 588, 589
  acquiring 572, 573, 578, 585, 590, 591, 599
  actions of 93, 94
  applications 286
  arrangement 56–58, 60, 61, 63–66, 68, 72, 74–83, 85, 88, 91, 92
    deeds of 58, 76–78, 85, 86
  assisted 382
  bad 396, 397
  bankrupt housing loan 381
  core 158, 165, 249
  creditor 527, 534

Company debt
  debtor-in-possession 446
  Corporate Debt Restructuring Mechanism 325, 333, 335
  Corporate Debt Restructuring Procedures 479, 540, 547, 550, 551
  Corporate Debt Restructuring Standing Forum 333–335
  Corporate Debt Restructuring 333, 342, 479, 511–515, 517, 519, 521, 523, 525–527, 529, 531, 533, 535, 537, 539–541
  Corporate Debt Restructuring Cell 333–335, 348
  Corporate Debt Restructuring Empowered Group 334, 335
  debts 277, 315
  directors 261
  distressed debtor 381
  eligible 195
  failing 236
  foreign 172, 173, 176, 177, 196, 483–485, 493
  good 396, 397
  holding 75, 94, 158, 164, 165, 238, 247, 248, 250, 251, 291, 305, 358, 372, 408, 570
  information 174
  insolvency 8
  insolvent Canadian 132
  key 165, 249
  law 202, 380, 388, 393, 397, 495
  medium-sized 258, 285, 286, 360
  meetings 198, 202
  moratorium 225
  new 175, 188, 194, 563
  officials 263, 264
  operating 159, 247, 248, 251
  owning 602
  personal 425
  power 248
  property 284
  putative debtor 448
  reorganization 8
  rescue 295
  subsidiary 164, 358, 372
  target 566, 578, 582, 583
  transferee 177, 194
  transferor 194
  treasury 74, 85
  troubled 22, 28, 50, 131, 244, 302, 361, 370, 458
  unregistered 172, 173, 176, 483
Company Rescue Act 258, 259, 261, 263, 269, 270, 272, 274, 276, 279, 283–285, 295
  new 263, 265, 269, 270, 285, 286
Company rescue proceedings 285
Company-selected liquidator 500, 503
Company Voluntary Arrangements 158, 161, 179, 195, 247
Company's
  assets 366
  obligations 372
Company's Affairs Administrator 88
Comparator 181, 182, 190
Competition 152, 524, 545, 547, 549, 552–554, 556, 558, 559, 561–563, 566–568, 571, 575–585, 588, 589, 594–599, 601, 602
  authorities 549, 553, 584, 593–599
  effective 545, 555, 557, 560–562, 566, 569, 578, 596, 600
  law 549, 555, 561, 562, 598, 599
  legislation 550, 554, 598
  level of 575
Competitive effects 580, 581
Composition 27, 32, 52, 53, 76, 161, 168, 181, 182, 195, 196, 334, 337, 359, 380, 398, 403, 488
Compromise 131, 132, 139–143, 145, 147–149, 151, 164, 171, 174, 175, 191–195, 248, 249, 253, 254, 293, 322, 330, 332, 333
  of creditors 76, 138, 151
Concentrations 163, 548, 552, 554–559, 562, 564–571, 574, 577–580, 600
  control of 544, 545, 554–560, 567, 571, 600
Conciliation 266–272, 274–278, 281, 287, 290, 291
Conciliation Agreements 274–277
Conciliator 270–273, 281, 290
Concordato preventivo 364–367, 371
Concurso preventivo 25, 26
Conducting Creditors Meetings 64
Confidentiality agreements 133, 142

Index

Confirmation 6, 15, 16, 124, 242, 246, 372, 390, 393, 443, 444, 446, 448, 449, 451–454, 463, 467, 468, 470–473
  hearing 446, 463, 468
  order 390, 463
Congress 23, 105, 466, 544, 580, 591
Connection, sufficient 172–174, 176, 482, 483, 486–488, 505
Consensus 99, 101–107, 113, 114, 116, 121, 147–149, 171, 398, 435, 448, 493, 587
Constituents 137, 139, 145–147, 149, 252
Constitution of classes of creditors 165, 317
Constraints, competitive 558, 560, 561, 581
Construction
  businesses 395, 396
  company 312–314, 320, 395
    insolvent 299, 311, 312, 321
Consultation Paper 301, 302, 304
Contract price 140, 141
Contractor 140, 316
Contracts 10, 12, 102, 110, 140, 179, 196, 268, 283, 284, 312, 314–316, 320, 321, 369, 480, 492, 493
Control 58, 65, 75, 90, 91, 143, 169, 170, 274, 278, 279, 329, 413, 414, 443, 487, 488, 499, 501, 576, 577
Controllers 278, 280
Cooperation 42, 140, 141, 270, 331, 361, 362, 408, 490
Cooperatives 421, 423–425
Core Group 333, 334, 336, 343, 344, 346, 347
Corp Scheme 239, 245
Corporate debt 299, 325, 333–344, 346, 351, 355, 379, 511–516, 518, 519, 521–527, 530, 531, 536, 539–542, 549–551, 554
  expedited 57, 295, 512, 514–516, 549
Corporate Reorganization
  Corporate Reorganization Law 392, 398, 399, 403
  Corporate Reorganization Proceeding 380, 381, 386, 394
Corporation 6, 24, 43, 65, 68, 69, 150, 151, 326, 327, 330, 392, 398, 399, 423–425, 464, 492, 493, 569, 601
  tax 516–518, 529, 530

Corporations Act 56, 57, 59, 61, 63, 65, 68–70, 73, 75, 78, 79, 81–84, 87
Corporations Regulations 63, 64, 77
Costs 67, 68, 136, 137, 145, 188, 191, 205, 209, 222, 223, 228, 229, 246, 247, 254, 291, 292, 314, 335, 336, 585
  order 176
  pre-emptive 191
  social 596, 597, 599
Council 261, 555–557
  of ministers 544, 555
Counsel 441, 447, 467, 468
Court
  administrator 117
  of appeal of England 483, 484, 487, 488, 490
  application 232
  approval
    motions 152
    process 424
    stage 134, 428, 432
  auction 134
  of Brescia 364, 365, 368
  claim 118
  competent 25, 98, 118, 281, 364, 367, 541, 542
  decision 123, 228, 394, 493
  file 218
  hearing 166, 254, 255, 281
  intervention 330, 333
  involvement 255, 303, 500, 515
  jurisdiction 26
  negotiation process 425, 426, 436
  officer 133, 144, 152, 154
  order sanctioning 168
  orders 94, 132, 162, 168, 185, 187, 228, 232, 319, 330, 433, 455, 474
  power 232
  procedure 165
  proceedings 131, 136, 294, 489
  process 424
    slow 330
  sanctions 166, 168, 177, 186, 246
  secured creditor opposition 153
  supervising 151
  supervision 134, 152, 278, 287, 414, 500, 502
  supervisor 409, 413–415, 500

Index

Court-appointed liquidator 505
Court approval 25, 87, 132, 149, 154, 155, 165, 288, 386, 406, 407, 411, 412, 425, 428
Court-approval 276
Court Commissioners 572, 573
Court Estate Limited 176, 177
Court-ordered Receivership 291
Court-supervised liquidation, special 397
Court Supervised Sale Proceedings 133
Court's Power 69
CP 359, 363, 364, 366, 367, 369, 370
Credit
   contracts, rural 109
   exposures 400, 401
     largest 381, 383, 398
   facility 340, 352, 353, 462, 463
   instrument 107
   obligations 116
   subject 118
Creditor
   approval 77
   bank, main 381–384
   claim 241
     agreement 241
     contingent 252
   claiming 47
   classes 149, 153, 449
     subordinate 153
     unsecured 145–149
   committees 15, 16, 145, 279, 280, 287
   constituents 145
   discharges 532, 537, 538
   groups 145–147, 180, 225, 250, 251, 442, 448
     businesses approach 147
   interests 137
     balance legitimate 137
   issues 182, 183, 188, 249
   level 516, 531–535, 537
   profile 239
   proxy-holder 222
   Creditor Agreements 339
   Creditor Rights Systems 2, 3, 5
   Creditor Shareholder 526, 532
   Creditor subject 27
   Creditors
     best interests of 40
     bondholder 188
     cent 351
     connected 214, 215
     execution 210
     existing 338, 349–351
     external 158, 165, 249, 359, 365–367, 369, 370, 372, 375
     file 416
     first 123, 124, 396, 414
       meeting of 59, 85, 220, 384, 400, 402
     holdout 21, 28, 424
     identification of 239, 241, 250
     individual 16, 148, 183, 300, 514, 541
     labour-law 112
     list of 25, 52, 109, 119, 227, 366
     main 189, 224, 270, 271, 276, 278, 290
     meeting, final 72
     non-bank 311
     non-consenting 47
     participating 140–142, 430
     petitioning 209, 308
     post-arrangement 234
     potential 163, 519
     preferential 195, 209
     proceedings 358, 359
     relevant 2, 9, 172, 185, 189, 191, 214, 384, 385, 387, 397–404, 415
     second 69, 70, 85, 123, 124, 397
       meeting of 60, 61, 69, 70, 85, 402, 403
     selection of 114
     shareholder 526
     subject 25, 46, 98, 103, 104, 107, 119
     transaction defrauding 198
     trusts 78
     unaffected 15, 16, 147, 426, 432, 434
     unknown 239–241, 246, 250
     unrelated 526, 531–534
     unsophisticated 42
     veto 148, 155
     voting 370, 429–431
Creditors, aggrieved 166, 225, 226, 500
Creditors Arrangement Act 130, 131
Credits 23, 25, 47, 98, 99, 102–105, 107, 110–118, 122–124, 201, 226, 276, 325, 338, 360, 403
   agreement 107
   simulation of 120
   subject 107, 113

Index

Criminal Code 89, 95
Crisis 3, 11, 22–24, 28, 43, 100, 151, 301, 325, 326, 358, 362, 364, 368, 421, 422, 524, 525
Cross-Border Insolvency 42, 160, 170, 439, 478, 481, 499
  Cross-border insolvency issues 170
  Cross-Border Insolvency Regulations 158, 170, 499
Cross-Border Mergers 512
Cross Border Regulations 170
CVA 158, 161, 162, 164–166, 169–171, 195–198, 201–203, 205, 207–216, 218–220, 222, 225–233, 236–238, 240, 241, 243–255, 484–486

D

DAC 569
Date 25, 26, 29, 32, 52, 84, 200–202, 209, 216, 229, 275–277, 337–340, 352–355, 400–402, 455, 474
  of approval 34, 349
  effective 242, 245, 246, 452–454, 456, 460, 471–473, 475, 518
  maturity 365, 367, 445
  of suspension of payments 265, 276, 277
Days, clear 185, 216, 217
Deadlock 63, 64, 79
Debentures 24, 145, 181, 192, 194, 339, 340, 354
  Debenture holders 179, 181, 186, 188, 192, 193, 201
Debiti 364, 365, 367, 371
Debt forms, proof of 241, 242, 245, 246
Debt Restructuring Agreements 358, 359, 375, 539
Debt Restructurings, consequences of 511
Debtor
  bankrupt 407
  company 24, 26, 106, 107, 135, 138, 144, 147, 148, 206, 210, 305, 382, 388, 389, 393, 514–516, 518–542
    discharges 526
  corporations 381, 383, 385, 392, 393
    troubled 381
  enterprise 336
  files 103, 432

  level 516, 517, 520, 526–528, 531, 534, 535, 537, 538
  shareholder 527
  subject 406, 407
  trusts 266
Debtor Creditor Agreement 339
Debtor-in-possession 283, 442, 443, 497, 503
Debtor Shareholder 527, 533
Debts 9–12, 66–68, 73–77, 89–91, 93–95, 141, 142, 212–216, 330–332, 342–348, 381–387, 392–397, 447–449, 516–520, 525–540, 547–550
  bank 30, 32, 239, 462
  conversion of 109, 243, 337, 350
  excessive 379, 381, 382, 385, 387, 399
  intercompany 79
  interest-bearing 396
  legal term of 117
  new 244, 245, 396, 518, 529
  out-of-court 361, 363, 366
  partial 81, 82
  payments of 6, 120, 492
  preferential 209
  proof of 207, 239, 241
  repayment of 325, 401
  restructured 339, 349, 352, 382
  secured 136, 359, 389, 392, 393, 460, 462
  social security 103, 387, 392, 393
  uncompromised 445
  unliquidated 212
  unsecured 66, 67, 90, 392, 422
  votes 64
Decision
  informed 15, 16, 78, 243, 244, 311, 428, 431
  recent 301, 365, 367, 368, 371
  scheme administration 192
Decree 22, 23, 107, 115, 259–261, 263, 265, 266, 272, 280, 284, 359, 364, 365, 367, 368, 375
Deed administrators 72, 73, 76, 77, 79, 80, 82
Default 22, 43, 50, 110, 135, 172, 198, 203, 208, 209, 227, 228, 233–237, 276, 322, 332, 432
Defence 60, 117, 139, 151, 553, 554, 556, 561, 563, 568–572, 583, 585–587, 590–592, 596, 597, 599

failing-company 588–590
Deferral 141, 142, 274, 285, 516, 525, 527, 534, 547
  of debts 527
Deloitte 575, 576
Derivatives 511
Derogation 578
Deterioration 328, 349, 381, 388, 561, 562, 565–568, 574, 575, 577, 598–601
DF 544, 570, 571
Directors 35–42, 47–49, 58, 65, 66, 81–83, 88, 89, 149–151, 193, 196–207, 220, 221, 233–237, 478–480, 492–494, 497–500, 502, 503
  board of 119, 149, 151, 219, 262, 326, 328, 336, 349, 440, 497
Disadvantages 80, 187, 268, 274, 275, 277, 283, 284, 360, 573
Discharge 32, 100, 182, 183, 196, 215, 231, 277, 283, 285, 331, 463, 464, 498, 522–527, 531–533, 537–542
  post-arrangement liabilities 235
Disclosure statement 15, 426, 431, 443, 444, 446, 450, 451, 455, 464, 465, 469, 470, 474
  approved 451, 470
Discrimination 33, 35–37, 76, 426
Disposition 136, 236, 277
Dissenting
  creditors 10, 13, 14, 132, 187, 254, 300, 311, 379, 381, 386, 407, 424, 429–431
  hedge fund 463, 468
Distressed companies 13, 112, 121, 261, 285, 295, 312, 313, 328, 329, 359–363, 370–374, 382, 422, 435, 547, 598
Distressed Industries 582, 583, 586, 587
Distribution 32, 34, 35, 49, 75–77, 79, 112, 122, 123, 125, 126, 151, 152, 236, 244, 246–249, 456, 475, 548
District 41, 481, 487, 498, 501, 503
District Court 36–39, 47, 48, 387, 463, 489, 558, 592
Divestment 75, 505
Dividends 93, 162, 205, 206, 208, 209, 212, 214, 216, 220, 222, 227, 229, 231, 232, 236, 527

Division 88, 89, 91–93, 95, 115, 172, 178, 281, 282, 322, 519, 549, 571, 572, 576–578, 582, 596, 602
Dominance 558, 562, 564
  test 557, 558
Dominant position 555, 557, 558, 565, 566, 568, 569, 571, 572, 600
DRA 359, 360, 363–374
Dues 341, 345, 346, 350
Duties 58, 65, 68, 71, 75, 100, 133, 146, 150, 151, 203, 208, 234, 263, 264, 280, 281, 428

E

EBL 421–429, 431–436
EC 158, 168, 478, 480, 481, 515, 524, 544, 554–559, 599, 600
  EC Council Regulation Directive 168, 173, 174
  EC Insolvency Regulation 168, 170, 172–174, 223, 228, 484
  EC merger control proceedings 556
  EC Merger Regulation 544, 554, 556–558, 600
  EC Treaty 524, 555
ECDRs 479, 480, 482, 484, 488–491, 493, 494, 496, 498, 499, 501–507
ECJ 495, 561, 566, 567
ECMR 556–560, 562, 563, 568, 578, 582
ECR 561, 566, 567, 600, 601
EEA insurer 173, 174
Effective Court Supervised Reorganization Procedures 143
Effective Insolvency 2, 3, 5
Efficiencies 134, 226, 418, 548, 550, 553, 560, 561, 563, 580, 584, 585, 587, 590, 593, 597, 599
Eickmann 486, 504, 505
Employees 17, 58, 76, 85, 109, 111, 112, 137, 148, 175, 176, 262, 263, 279–281, 286, 294, 303, 304, 315
Empowered Group 334, 335, 345, 346, 349, 350
Enforcement
  agencies 580, 581
  proceedings 104, 125, 369–371

Index 613

English
  court 163, 167, 168, 179, 482–485, 488–491
    order sanctioning 168
    courts exercise jurisdiction 482
  English Scheme 167, 172, 174, 179, 501
  English scheme subject 169
Enterprises 4, 6, 10, 11, 305, 335, 336, 345, 382, 407, 413, 414, 423, 593
Entities 7, 8, 24, 29, 32, 36, 42, 78, 85, 178, 275, 278, 329, 454–456, 473–475, 576, 577
  debtor business 440
Entrepreneur 364, 368, 406, 409–418, 537
Entry 82, 122, 285, 328, 373, 553, 554, 560, 561, 563, 580, 581, 587, 595, 596
Equal treatment, principles of 361, 515, 519, 521–523, 525, 539, 541
Equitable Life Assurance Society 176, 177, 179, 180, 184, 185, 187
Equity 6, 86, 243, 245, 246, 337, 339, 340, 350, 354, 382, 385, 460, 517, 529, 531–533, 535
  holders 6, 16, 443
  interest holders 445
Estate 24, 31, 32, 35, 233, 248, 253, 254, 294, 411, 441, 452, 454, 471, 473, 489, 497, 498
EStG 517–519, 528, 531, 533–535
EU 169, 173, 486, 495, 496, 504, 544, 549, 550, 553–556, 563, 592, 595, 597, 599
  EU Guidelines 559, 560, 562, 563, 572
  EU Insolvency Regulation 481, 485, 486, 488, 494, 495, 504, 505
EUR 45, 48, 238, 249, 263, 279, 281, 285, 292, 359, 361, 364, 408
Eurodial 572–575, 600
European Commission 524, 555, 571, 572, 577
European Court of Justice 169, 480, 488, 495, 496, 505, 524, 561
European Court Reports 480, 495, 505, 524
European merger policy 558
Eurotunnel 282, 285
Excess capacity, market-wide 593
Exchange 29, 34, 37–39, 46, 81, 103, 177, 187, 189, 191, 229, 360, 361, 445, 446, 455, 456, 474, 475

Execution 52, 117, 201, 210, 282, 363, 367, 369–371, 416, 421, 542
Exemption 33, 35, 37, 38, 40, 81, 82, 367, 445, 455, 465, 466, 474, 519, 521, 522, 580, 583
Exercise, restructuring 333, 335, 336, 347, 348, 350
Exigencies 151, 152, 463, 467, 468
Exit procedures 77, 131, 165, 166, 252, 350, 548, 553, 561, 573–575, 577, 578, 582, 583, 592, 594, 595, 597–600, 602, 247, 248
Expedited Creditor Compromises 138
Expedited debt 20–22, 27, 28, 50, 264
Expenses, administrative 455, 456, 474, 475
Expert 45, 189, 264, 270, 281, 291, 292, 335, 346, 358, 359, 363, 364, 366, 367, 370, 372, 375, 415
Expiry 339, 365, 367, 573
Exposure 2, 9, 11, 238, 334, 335, 343, 344, 347–350, 384, 387, 395, 396, 560
Extortionate credit transactions 230

F

Failing 94, 142, 150, 312, 548–554, 558, 560–569, 571–577, 580, 582–602
  company 566, 568, 573, 574, 577, 583, 585, 586, 588–591, 596, 599
    claim 583, 599
    defence 548, 567, 570, 583, 585, 586, 591, 593, 597, 599
    doctrine 586, 590, 591
  credible 562
  division 564, 578, 582, 596, 602
    defence 548, 550, 553, 569–571, 576, 577, 582, 598–600
  firm defence 552, 554, 561–566, 569, 574, 575, 577, 587, 593, 595, 596, 598, 599
  firms 553, 563, 582–585, 590, 595–598, 602
    involving 561, 594, 596
  industry 553
  pre-merger 595
  Failing-Firm Defence 586
Fairness 28, 34, 37–40, 46, 48, 144, 146, 147, 149, 163, 190, 193, 224, 254, 361–363, 502

hearing 38–41
procedural 137
FCR 72, 73, 76, 79
Federal Rules of Bankruptcy Procedure 444, 446, 467
Federal Trade Commission 569, 580, 583, 584, 586–588, 591, 596, 597
Fees 53, 192, 202, 205, 208, 209, 217, 220, 222, 228, 230, 232, 271, 315, 316, 453, 472
File objections 46, 47, 53, 412
Finance, additional 338, 349, 350
Financial
  circumstances 60, 88, 89, 91
  creditors 137, 242, 315, 379, 381–384, 396
  information, disclosure of 142, 143
  institutions 11, 12, 44, 110, 112, 158, 242, 266, 325–328, 330, 331, 333–336, 339, 343–347, 381–384, 396, 398
Financial Instruments 354, 368, 511
Financial Reconstruction 328, 329, 336
Financiers 12, 73, 74, 84, 289
Financing 5, 37, 365, 428, 429, 432, 435, 436
Firm defence 548–550, 552–554, 558, 560–564, 566–569, 571, 572, 574–577, 582–600
Firms 146, 232, 422, 425, 548, 553, 556–560, 562, 565, 576, 580, 581, 583–587, 589, 594, 596–599
First day distributions 239, 246, 247
Fiscal year 119, 382, 402, 517, 518, 525
Floating charge 66, 67, 73, 90, 202, 302
Foreign
  courts 38, 166, 167, 169, 170, 484, 485, 489, 496, 499, 501, 504–506
  creditors 10, 12, 43, 48, 119, 120, 167, 179
  jurisdiction 168, 489
  proceedings 31, 169, 253, 483, 489, 492, 496, 497, 500–502, 504
Foreign ECDRs 479, 498, 499, 503–506
Forfeiture 206, 210
Form business assets 531
Formal proceedings 131, 149, 151
Forum non-conveniens, doctrine of 487, 488
Forwards 518–521, 529

France 259–261, 263, 265, 267, 269, 271, 273, 275, 277, 283–285, 291–293, 295, 511, 566, 567, 600, 601
Fritsche 518–523
FTC 558, 569, 570, 580, 584, 586–588, 591, 597, 601
Fulfilment 105, 106, 368, 369, 372
Funds
  flows 246, 249
  hedge 462, 463, 467, 468
  sufficient 199, 204, 206, 283, 284, 303, 304

G

Gains, built-in 530, 535
GBP 159, 190, 201, 206, 212, 213, 226, 238, 240, 241, 247–249
  bondholders 189, 190
General Dynamics Corp 549, 586, 589, 597
General Insurance Ltd 87, 317
General Trust Company 175
German
  market 564–566
  perspective 512–515, 517–521, 523–529, 531–535, 537–542
  potash market 565
German court 505, 506
German Insolvency Code 481, 491, 504, 505
Goods 66, 89, 103, 109, 226, 276, 279, 460, 461, 524, 530, 531, 536–538, 563
  delivery of 516, 530, 531, 535–538
Government 24, 57, 99, 150, 259, 260, 301–303, 312, 314–316, 321, 326, 327, 332, 333, 340, 423, 492, 555
Governmental
  entity, authorized 38
  unit 454, 464, 473
Green Paper 556, 557
Group 73, 74, 77, 84, 85, 107, 111, 112, 174, 238, 239, 241, 242, 244, 247–249, 290, 305, 329, 411, 412, 589, 590
  of creditors 87, 107, 114, 115, 124, 125, 142, 165, 179, 186, 217, 248, 293, 448, 449
  subject 104, 107

Index

Guide 2–8, 12–14, 17, 78, 478, 499, 501, 504
Guideline-based reorganization plans 385
Guidelines 2, 3, 5, 8, 205, 333–335, 342–346, 378, 379, 383–385, 395, 396, 398–401, 403, 404, 446, 559–561, 579–582, 599, 600

H

Handbook of Fixed Income Securities 552
Harmer Report 57
Havilland 555, 563, 564
Hawk Insurance Co Limited 177, 178, 180, 188
Hearing 16, 34, 37–39, 176, 182, 192, 212, 281, 411, 412, 431, 432, 444, 450, 451, 453, 454, 469, 470, 472, 473
Heavy Industries Co 301, 317–319
HHI 580, 581
High Court 38, 69, 329, 330
  of England 483, 489
  of Justice of England 484, 485, 488
HIH Casualty 87, 317
HKAB 298, 299, 309–311
HKD 303, 304, 312
HKLRD 298, 301, 305–307, 318
HKMA Guidelines 298, 310, 311
HoldCo 358, 372
Holders 29, 30, 32, 35, 41, 45, 46, 112, 125, 239, 240, 250, 251, 444, 447, 450–454, 456, 469–473, 475
Homologation 25–27, 30, 46, 50, 98, 101–104, 107, 108, 110, 115–118, 120, 124, 480, 496, 502, 551
  of consensus 99, 101–106, 113, 114, 116, 121
Hong Kong 298, 299, 301–315, 317–319, 321
  Hong Kong Court 311, 317
  Hong Kong Government Gazette 298, 302
Horizontal Merger Guidelines 546, 556, 559, 579, 602
Horizontal mergers 556, 560, 561, 579, 580, 591
  appraisal of 556
  assessment of 545, 559, 560, 600

I

IBL 358–360, 363–371, 373, 374
Income 6, 28, 43, 316, 321, 340, 354, 516–520, 522, 536
  negative 516, 520, 532–535
  taxable 517, 520, 525, 527, 528, 530–533
Incorporation 109, 119, 173, 174, 177, 202, 227, 279, 289, 332, 386, 390, 481–484, 488, 494, 495
Indebtedness 5, 9, 28, 43, 73, 74, 361, 363, 407, 511, 513, 516–519, 526–530, 588
  cancellation of 513, 516–519, 526–535, 540
  income 517–531, 534, 540
    exemption of cancellation of 519–521
    tax exemption of cancellation of 520–522, 524
Indemnity 66–68, 73, 74, 89–91, 181
Index 495, 556, 557
India 324–329, 331–333, 335, 337, 339, 341–345, 347, 349, 351, 353, 355
Indian Banks 343, 344
Industrial company 328, 329, 331
Industrial Development Bank of India Ltd 343, 344, 346
Industries, construction 312, 316, 320
Information 9, 10, 13, 15, 16, 78, 79, 146, 147, 193, 199, 203, 204, 243, 244, 262, 263, 361, 362, 399, 400, 410, 450, 467–469
Injunction order, provisional 391, 394
Input tax 537
INR 335, 337, 338, 340
Insider 443, 452, 453, 471, 472
InsO 504–506, 512–515, 528, 541, 542
INSOL 9, 379, 383, 384
Insolvency 2–5, 17, 81, 82, 143, 144, 169, 170, 203, 204, 288–291, 301, 302, 367–369, 406, 407, 409–414, 416–418, 423–425, 504, 505, 551
  accredited 135
  courts 481, 490
  cross-border 42
  effects 491–493
  insurance 162, 163
  jurisdiction 487, 488, 495

law 3, 4, 8, 10, 12, 14–17, 195, 288, 380, 406, 478, 480, 481, 489–491, 513, 514, 528, 540–542
liquidation 3, 7
practitioners 162, 163, 199, 203, 218, 220, 221, 227, 229, 237, 280, 282, 286, 291, 295
procedures 199, 293, 373, 374, 479, 491, 550
proceedings 3, 10, 17, 100, 142, 150, 260, 261, 263, 264, 288, 289, 360, 478–481, 495, 496, 504, 513, 540
  cross-border 490
  foreign 380, 489, 493, 499, 504
  formal 7, 14, 131, 137, 139, 223, 360, 370, 480
  process 131, 133, 138, 142, 146, 152, 206, 217, 238, 245, 252
    formal 137, 247
professionals, accredited 133
provision 299
reorganization 5, 14
  international 21, 28
Insolvency Act 130, 132, 162, 170, 172–175, 195–204, 206, 207, 209–211, 217–228, 230–237, 248–251, 253, 254, 407, 481, 484, 485
Insolvency Partnerships Order 196
Insolvency, personal 64, 162, 220, 221, 301
Insolvency Plan Procedure 512, 515
Insolvency Practice 159, 203, 228
Insolvency Rule 197, 199, 200, 205, 206, 211–223, 225–233, 235, 237, 251
Insolvency systems 5, 7, 17
Insolvent
  business, near 158, 169, 438
  companies 3, 4, 8, 17, 57, 61, 75, 76, 80, 82, 88, 93, 154, 250, 299, 300, 359, 360, 364
    large 359
      restructuring 57
  debtor 8, 139, 143, 151, 152, 371, 413, 491
  Insolvent Foreign Companies 482, 488
  Insolvent Scheme sheltering 169
Insolvenz 495, 512–514
Insolvenzforderung 518
Insolvenzordnung 486, 504, 505, 512
Insolvenzplan 542

Insolvenzrecht 495, 513, 514, 518, 521, 522
Institutions 29, 202, 210, 211, 264, 326–328, 333, 335, 338, 343–346, 555
Insurance
  companies 24, 161–163, 176, 180, 425
  undertakings 158, 168, 173, 174
Insurers 163, 168, 173–175, 326
Inter-company balances 164, 165, 249
Inter-Corporate Contractual Agreement 333
Inter-Creditor Agreement 347, 348
Inter-creditor differences 11
Intercompany transaction matrices 240
Interest
  element 352, 353
  holders 441
  income 349, 352, 354
  payments 44, 340, 352, 547
  property 452, 454, 471, 473
  rates, nominal 421
  sacrifice 353
Interests 42–45, 79–82, 133–137, 150, 151, 186–188, 192–195, 224, 225, 252, 253, 291–294, 337–340, 352–354, 440–445, 450–456, 469–475, 532, 533
  best 48, 64, 141, 150, 201, 233, 300, 306, 441, 443
  collateral 166, 185, 252, 253, 255
  common 140, 178, 180, 181, 190, 317
  conversion of 354
  of creditors 6, 78, 81, 150, 262, 321, 440, 452, 471
  elements of 352, 353
  equity 442, 443, 462
  fractional 456, 475
  low 337
  material 193
  multiple 111
  payments of 339, 353, 355, 464, 537, 538
  private 317, 580
  public 80, 204, 521, 541, 592
  statutory trust 140
Interlocking CVAs 165, 225, 247, 249
International Company of Mexico 175
Investors 41, 86, 112, 293, 312, 314–316, 320, 321, 329, 341, 361, 373, 374, 450, 469, 519, 552
  hypothetical 450, 469

Index 617

IPO 86
IRCJ 381, 382, 385
ISIN 44
Issue securities 34, 37
Issuer 29, 36, 38, 40, 238, 408, 455, 456, 466, 474, 475, 547
Istanbul Approach 422–424
Italian
   insolvency legislation 359, 373
   market 374, 577
   Italian Civil Code 363, 367, 369, 370
ITL 48

J

Japan 378, 379, 381–383, 385–387, 389, 391, 393, 395–397, 399, 401, 403
Japanese
   banks 383
   courts 380, 381
Jeopardy 305, 307–309, 321
Joint Stock Companies Acts 482
JPY 45, 46, 382, 383, 395, 396
JRH Group 289–291
Judge 27, 31, 52, 53, 100, 115, 117–120, 124, 126, 127, 182, 260, 261, 280, 281, 306, 307, 318, 319, 467, 498
   elected 260, 261
Judgment, enforcement of 158, 167, 168, 478, 480
Judicial
   auxiliary officers 261, 278, 279
   liquidator 278, 279, 281, 294
   reorganization 100, 101, 103, 105, 107–109, 111–113, 115, 117, 120, 121, 123–125, 272, 273, 275, 276, 279, 282, 283, 293, 294
Juris 488, 495, 496
Jurisdictional 491, 556, 557
   bases 167, 481, 484
Jurisdictions 39, 68, 69, 118, 119, 167, 168, 173, 174, 244–246, 328–330, 478–491, 494–496, 503–506, 512, 513, 535, 536, 549, 550, 559, 560, 598–601
   of foreign creditors 10, 12
   home 485, 492, 494, 503
   international 479–481, 505
Justice, court of 495, 574

K

Kali 561, 562, 564–566, 568–574, 576
Keview 298, 305, 306
Key Holding Companies 248
Kind 103, 109, 115, 117, 121, 125, 126, 174, 386, 392, 450, 452, 453, 455, 456, 469, 471, 472, 474, 475
Kirch 570, 571
Ks 436

L

Landlord 206, 207, 210, 212, 229
Lang 514, 515, 519, 530
Large companies 145, 444, 575, 576
Latin America 41, 479, 547, 550, 551
Law
   antitrust 549, 567, 569, 596–598
   applicable nonbankruptcy 450, 451, 465, 469, 470
   reorganization tax 530
Legal rights 141, 142, 145, 149, 188, 317
   Legal Supplement 298, 302
   Legal tools 100, 262, 373
Legend 298, 299, 307–309, 314
Legge fallimentare 365, 367–369, 371
Legislative Guide 2–4, 423, 478, 486
Lenders 73, 141, 302, 310, 311, 331, 334, 340, 348, 350, 360, 460
   secured 153
Letter 36, 119, 120, 126, 234, 242, 243, 245, 251, 255, 267, 280, 423, 464, 467, 468
   account holder 245
   no-action 36–39, 41
Level
   of court involvement 500
   court supervision 501
Liabilities 8, 9, 27, 65, 66, 68, 75, 76, 78, 79, 194, 195, 207, 213–216, 399–402, 517, 518, 528, 531, 547, 551, 552
   contingent 213, 425
Licences 232, 312–316, 320, 321
Liens 31, 66–68, 73, 91, 117, 153, 210, 441, 442, 453, 454, 462, 472, 473, 497, 525
   equitable 67, 68, 73
Lieu 303, 304, 337, 338, 460

Life Insurance Corporation of India 326, 327, 333
Link, causal 562, 567, 568, 570, 571, 574–577
Liquidation
  analysis 428, 429, 436
  corporate 301
  insolvent 190, 304, 513
  judicial 273, 276, 283, 288, 293
  out-of-court 290
  proceedings 7, 8, 173, 216, 328, 494
  value 47, 551, 584, 602
    terms 584
  voluntary 199, 221, 222, 229, 231, 236
Liquidator 65, 67, 68, 87, 139, 171, 188, 189, 191, 192, 205, 206, 225–229, 234–237, 260–262, 280–283, 285, 293–295, 322
Loan assets 340, 355, 381, 382
Loans 43, 44, 293, 325, 327, 330, 334, 336–340, 351–354, 371, 381, 382, 385, 386, 401, 422, 529, 530, 534–538
Loi 258, 259, 289, 290, 423
Lord Millett 178, 317, 319
Loss 11, 68, 137, 181, 209, 210, 232, 329, 399–402, 518–521, 529, 553, 562, 584–586, 588, 594–596
Lower court decision upholding 587
LRC 301–303, 308
LRC Sub-Committee 301, 302

M

Main
  interests, centre of 169, 481, 485, 486, 494
  section hereof 126, 127
Major creditors 199, 245, 255, 300, 310, 335, 360, 381, 383, 387, 398–400, 403
Majority decisions 82, 514, 541
Management 6, 24, 68, 78, 92, 145, 204, 205, 259, 261–264, 266, 271, 272, 279, 280, 288, 289, 313, 320, 321
Managers 26, 71, 76, 107, 108, 119, 133, 136, 262–264, 274, 294, 379, 382, 383, 388, 389, 392, 393, 397
Managing Directors 86, 266, 333, 343
Mandat ad hoc 264–269, 281, 288, 289, 295

Marconi 166, 238, 239, 241, 244, 245, 251
Market 6, 11, 22, 82, 85, 86, 243, 331, 332, 415, 553, 554, 556, 560–562, 564–586, 588, 589, 592–595, 597–600
  common 555, 557, 562, 566, 567, 569, 578, 600
  competition 562
  competitive 561
  competitiveness 372
  concentrated 558, 566, 567, 581
  concentration 580, 581
  conditions 275, 550, 573, 574, 577, 582, 583, 586, 587, 590
  geographic 580, 581
  pay-TV 570, 571
  post-merger 553, 558
  power 556, 560, 581, 582, 584, 585, 594, 602
    premium 584, 585
  product 569, 580
  relevant 556, 560, 563, 569, 580–582, 584, 586, 592, 602
  shares 558, 564–569, 571–574, 580–582, 586, 589, 592, 594, 600
    combined 586, 589
  structure, competitive 568
  terms 407
  value 354, 429
    fair 529, 530, 535
    real 11
Marketing 133, 134, 137, 152–154, 371, 548, 569
process
  extended insolvency 152
  supervised 154
Mason 553, 554, 596
Matching 456, 475
Material irregularity 166, 219, 224, 225, 254, 255
Maus 512, 518, 520, 522, 523, 525
MDC 569
MdK 545, 561, 562, 564–567
Medium Term Notes 44
Meetings 30, 63, 64, 70, 71, 161–168, 181–190, 192, 193, 196–202, 211–228, 248–251, 254, 317–319, 344, 396, 397, 400, 411–415
  adjourned 220

Index 619

bondholder 240, 251, 252
of creditors 59, 63, 64, 79, 122, 181–183,
    212, 220, 244, 245, 316, 318, 387,
    389–391, 394, 400–402, 465
order 182, 185, 186
relevant 186, 202, 223, 300, 317
second 60, 251, 384
separate 178, 180, 188, 190, 300, 317
variation 230, 231
Meinl 571
Member States 170, 173, 485, 494, 495, 524,
    536, 554–557, 559
Mentha 72–74, 76, 78, 79
Mercantile Investment 175, 185, 192
Merger 83, 109, 207, 370, 378, 428, 510,
    548–550, 553–566, 568–590,
    592–602
  anti-competitive 562
  anticompetitive 585, 591, 595, 597
  assessment of 549, 553, 579, 581,
      597, 600
  conglomerate 556, 560
  control provision 555
  guidelines 553
  notified 561, 569, 598, 600
  planned 579
  Merger Legislation 548, 549, 560
    implications of 545, 547, 549, 551,
        553–555, 557, 559, 561, 563, 565,
        567, 569, 571, 573, 575
  Merger Mines Corp 40
  Merger Policy 554, 559, 596
  Merger Regulation 566, 567
  Merger Review 581–583, 586, 587
  Merger subject 577
  Mergers consolidate 548
Merging companies, court restricted 591
Milano 364–367, 371
Ministers 261, 544, 555
Minority creditors 14, 430, 479, 502, 506
  reticent 386
Model 246, 249, 333
Model Law 42, 160, 170, 439, 478, 481, 495,
    499, 501, 502, 504
Modifications 111, 192, 205, 208, 222–224,
    346, 464, 499, 528, 534, 547
Monitor 130, 135, 144, 146–148, 152, 154,
    155

Moratorium 50, 58, 61, 62, 77, 162, 195–197,
    199–202, 206, 207, 210, 211, 226,
    227, 300, 302, 303, 339, 340, 352,
    489
  period 201, 352
  statutory 61–63, 68, 162
Mortgages Act 136
Most debtor corporations 393
Motion 47, 123, 124, 184, 266, 268, 410, 413,
    416, 417, 592
Multi-Creditor Out-of-court Workouts
    Official English 398
Multi-creditor workout 398–401, 403, 404
Multi-Creditor Workouts 9, 379
Multicanal 21, 22, 28–38, 40–42, 51, 478,
    487, 489, 492–494, 496–498, 500
  board of directors of 21, 35–39, 41, 42, 497
Multicanal's assets 32
Multicanal's Class 29

N

National Bankruptcy Review Commission
    466
National Commercial Court of appeal 25
National Council of Commercial Court 261
NBLR 99, 100, 108, 109, 115–117
NBRL 99–117, 120–124
Negotiating reorganization schemes 99
Negotiation process 10, 12, 13, 429
Negotiations 4, 5, 8, 13, 99, 100, 111, 148,
    268, 272–275, 278, 279, 287, 290–
    294, 425, 426, 435, 436, 524, 577
  voluntary 8, 11–14, 17
Netia Group 408
New Company Law 380, 386
New money 273, 276, 295, 360, 362, 363, 382
Newscorp 574–578
Nigro 582, 583, 586, 587
Nolte 520, 523, 524
Nominee 197, 199–208, 212, 216, 217, 219,
    220, 222, 223, 226–228, 232, 344
Non-compliance, certificate of 228, 233, 235
Non-coordinated effects 555, 556, 558, 560,
    561
Non-QIBs 29, 30, 33–39
Noteholders 29–34, 36, 46, 48, 50, 408
  meeting 46

Notes 26, 28–32, 35, 44, 45, 47, 48, 265, 278, 355, 401, 408, 447
Notification 163, 165, 200, 226, 239, 241, 249, 250, 330, 413, 576–578
file merger 559
Novation 27, 109, 110, 116–118, 183, 551
NPA 346, 347, 353, 354
NPLs 381, 383, 423
NSWSC 71, 72, 87, 317

O

Objections 14, 16, 27, 47, 48, 53, 82, 176, 184, 188, 191, 308, 367, 368, 431, 463, 468
OECD 564–566, 574, 579, 581, 593, 595, 598
Office-holders 223, 225, 232, 251, 252, 254, 255
Official Journal 168, 480, 481, 488, 554, 556, 557, 559
Official Receiver 159, 208, 237
One-day prepack 459, 466–468
Ongoing Group 85, 86, 245
Opp 580, 583–587, 590, 593, 597, 599
Option 29, 35, 45, 46, 94, 152, 165, 212, 294, 310, 311, 315, 316, 349, 350, 455, 459, 474, 524, 525
Order subject 208
Ordre 504–506
Ors 72, 73, 76, 78, 79, 82, 83
Out-of-court 103, 108, 109, 111, 113, 115, 360, 370, 406, 409, 414, 460, 462, 467
  agreements 360
    private 363
  restructurings 415, 417, 465
  workout 378, 379, 381, 383, 385–387, 395, 396
  Out-of-court Reorganization 99–112, 114, 116–118, 120–123, 125, 479, 547, 550
    chapter 102
    plan 101, 103, 106, 108–111, 113, 115–117, 119–122, 125–127
    procedures 101–103, 105, 114
    proceedings 110
  Out-of-court Reorganization, process of 110, 116
  Out-of-court rescue guidelines 299
  Out-of-court Restructuring Agreement 491

Out-of-Court Workout 379, 383
  processes 384–386
  scheme 379
Out-of-court workout, multi-creditor 383
Out-of-Court Workout Process 386
Output 548, 581, 585, 586, 593, 594, 597
Outstanding debt 21, 28, 29, 44–46, 109
Owners 6, 28, 58, 62, 65–67, 110, 113, 140, 155, 240, 242, 243, 251, 295, 382, 392, 393

P

Pabst's failing company defence 592
Package 41, 225, 335–338, 347, 349–351, 427
  restructuring 334, 335, 343, 345, 348–352, 354, 355
Pantochem 572–575, 600
Pantochim 572–574
Par 34, 35, 274
Par Option 29, 30, 34, 35
Paragraph 25, 94, 95, 108, 125–127, 198–202, 206, 219–221, 224–226, 359, 360, 363, 368–370, 453, 455, 456, 472, 474, 475
Parallel Schemes 168
Parent companies 107, 291, 397, 562, 570, 576, 577, 586
Paris Commercial Court 260, 263, 265, 282, 285, 291
Part 5.3A 57, 58, 61–63, 66–70, 72, 73, 75, 76, 78, 80, 81, 83, 313
  administrations 57–59, 61, 69
Participants 5, 10, 13, 137, 138, 140, 141, 146, 266, 269, 279, 291, 312, 316, 348, 361, 581
  non-market 584
Partners 24, 26, 107, 109, 292, 443
Pasminco 73, 74, 81–86
Pasminco Group 57, 72–74, 77, 83, 85, 86
Pasminco Group Administrators 83, 84
Payment conditions 114, 115, 125
Payments 29, 102, 103, 106, 107, 109–115, 117, 118, 122, 138–140, 207–209, 214, 276, 277, 283, 284, 338–340, 365–367, 369, 370, 460, 461
  of creditors 105, 112, 122, 372
  regular 359, 365, 367, 372, 375
  severance 303, 304

Index 621

suspension of 269, 273, 275, 278, 281, 282, 285, 501
Pendency 349, 351, 442
Performance, satisfactory 353, 355
Period
  180-day 442, 455, 474
  convening 60, 61, 69–72, 85
  observation 7, 276, 281–283, 572, 573
  specified 346, 353
  total 346, 519, 521, 522
  two-year 455, 474
Person 34, 37–39, 59, 62–65, 89–95, 171, 172, 182–184, 194, 195, 218–223, 225–228, 366, 503, 532, 535, 536, 601
  connected 215
  single 26, 30
  subjects 493, 601
Personal liability 58, 59, 63, 66, 68, 69, 73, 74, 85, 210, 293
Perspective 78, 359, 373, 479, 482, 493, 517, 519, 520, 526, 527, 529, 530, 532
Petition 31–33, 47, 49, 50, 108, 109, 118–120, 122, 125–127, 200, 201, 233–237, 369–371, 387–394, 397, 446, 455, 474
Philippines 307
Plan 5, 6, 13–17, 101–120, 122–127, 132, 143–149, 153, 282–285, 384–387, 390–394, 396, 397, 402–404, 424–436, 442–456, 462–475
  accepted 6, 390, 391, 444, 447
  company rescue 286
  complies 451, 470
  confirmation
    of 451, 463, 470
    process 446
  court-approved 386
  debt repayment 402
  filed 552
  financial 370–372
  focused 143, 146
  joint 451, 452, 455, 470, 471, 474
  out-of-court 108, 125
  outline 146, 147, 149
  payment 111
  process
    expedited prepackaged 468
    pre-packaged 468
    prepackaged 467, 468
  rescue 278, 280, 282–284, 302, 303, 306, 308
  supervisor 428, 432, 434, 436
    qualified 428
  voted 394
Plan Supervision 436
Plants 207, 315, 320, 334, 461, 548, 573, 588
  advanced processing 568
Plc 188, 238, 239, 242–247
Plc Schemes 239, 243
Poland 407–409, 411, 413, 415, 417
  Republic of Poland 406, 407
Policies 163, 164, 181, 183, 194, 287, 308, 310, 326, 331, 334, 335, 343–346, 485, 492, 495, 596
Policyholders 163, 164, 176, 181, 182, 326
Pooling 77, 79, 80
Possession 62, 65, 67, 88, 90, 91, 143, 187, 282, 330, 331, 380, 440
Power plants 395
Powers 64–67, 69, 70, 72, 79, 80, 82, 83, 89, 90, 92, 188, 189, 191, 192, 208, 228–232, 305, 306, 441, 492, 493, 595, 596
  normal 305, 306
  statutory 307, 308, 482, 483
PPSA legislation 136
Practice Statement 158, 178, 181–183, 188, 318
Pre-packaged plans 21, 102, 284, 287, 439, 445–449
Predicates 439, 447, 448
Preference shares, redeemable 94, 176, 177
Premiere 570, 571
Premium, credit risk 352
Prepackaged plan 458, 463, 465–468
President 23, 262–268, 270–272, 274, 275, 281, 406, 407, 555
President-approved 270, 272, 274, 275
Preventive concordata 99, 100, 105–108, 111–113, 122, 123
Previous Law 99, 100, 104, 106, 107, 111, 112, 123
Principles 2–6, 8–12, 99, 100, 105, 108, 113–115, 379, 380, 383–385, 402, 425–428, 519, 521–523, 539–541, 554, 555, 559, 560

basic 99, 111, 513, 515, 519
condicio creditorum 361
pari passu 208, 211, 513
of procedural economy 123, 124
superior 514, 515, 539, 541
Procedural Orders 446
Procedures
   conciliation 264, 266, 268, 269, 272, 273, 275, 276, 295
   preventive 258, 264, 268, 270, 277
Proceedings 5–7, 14, 15, 39, 103, 104, 166–170, 254, 255, 267–270, 274–276, 278, 279, 282–284, 411–415, 439, 486–490, 501, 502, 504–506
   debtor-in-possession 501
   expedited 14–16, 442
   out-of-court 121
      workout 379
   pre-bankruptcy 572
Process 5, 9–12, 77, 78, 109–112, 134, 135, 137, 138, 151, 152, 154, 155, 162, 240–243, 249–251, 266–269, 291, 292, 424–426, 466–468
   comparative 244
   court-driven 161
Professions 261, 262, 277, 278
Profitability 206, 208, 372, 381, 383, 387, 396, 397, 449, 547–550, 553, 556, 569, 589, 598, 599
Prolan 121–124
Promoters 331, 336, 337, 339, 343, 351, 352
Proof, creditors file 447
Property 31, 32, 59–62, 65–68, 77, 88–92, 135, 136, 194, 289, 440–442, 451, 452, 454, 455, 470, 471, 473, 474, 481, 497
   development company 181
   interests 38, 39
   receiver of 90
Proponent 451–453, 470–472, 552
Prospective Trustee 146, 147
Protection, bankruptcy court 459
Providers 349, 367
Provisional
   liquidation 299, 305, 306, 308, 309, 311, 315, 321
      adapting 299
   liquidators 300, 305–309, 312–316, 319–321

   appointed 67, 503
   appointment of 306–309
   Provisional Supervision Procedure 301, 302
Provisions
   applicable 451, 470
   general 412, 433, 442
   of law 371–373, 414
   legal 120, 123, 208, 293
   operative 244
   set 361–363
   takeovers 81, 82
Proxies 46, 171, 184–186, 202, 217, 218, 221, 222, 228, 241, 245, 247, 322, 601
Prudential norms 324, 338, 354
Public Prosecutor 261, 265, 270, 273, 280, 281, 286
Purchase business assets 134
Purchaser 130, 133–135, 152, 350, 585, 587, 588
   alternative 568, 573, 583–586, 591, 599
   available 579, 588, 590
PWIF 303, 304

Q

QIBs 29, 30, 35, 42

R

Rate change 452, 471
Ratification 102, 125–127, 480
RBI 333, 334, 338–343, 350, 351
RCC 381, 385
In re Board of directors of
   Hopewell International Ins 497, 499, 500, 503
   Multicanal 21, 478, 487, 489, 492–494, 497, 498
   Multicanal SA 39–42
   Telecom Argentina 44, 45, 47–49, 479, 480, 493
In Re Kingscroft Insurance Company Ltd 503
In Re Multicanal 478, 492, 493, 497, 498
In Re Ward 500, 503
In Re Yukos Oil Company 482, 487, 489, 490
Receiver 67, 71, 72, 76, 90, 130, 133–137, 152, 154, 155, 201, 266, 268, 285, 307

Index 623

Receivership
  proceedings, court supervised 133
  sale processes 134
Recital 558, 566
Recognition 8, 21, 31, 33, 35, 48, 167–170, 313, 478–482, 484–487, 489, 492, 493, 496, 498, 504–506
Recommendations 5, 12, 14–17, 57, 85, 154, 243, 261, 272, 302, 303, 308, 330, 342, 363
Reference 33, 47, 57, 71, 75, 169, 213, 214, 328, 329, 335, 336, 345–350, 359, 360, 366, 367, 369, 370, 372, 494, 495
Reforms 70, 164, 195, 259–261, 290, 379, 421–423, 556, 557, 559
  jurisdictional 559
Refund 539
Register 34, 35, 38, 41, 172, 272, 293, 359, 364–366, 368, 369, 371, 372, 375
Registered company, foreign 484
Registrar of company 159, 174, 189, 200, 201, 223, 225, 226, 228–230, 232, 245, 319
Registration 33, 34, 40–42, 117, 171, 174, 319, 322, 445, 455, 474
  statement 40, 44, 45, 445
Regulations 11, 36, 37, 44, 63, 78, 158, 168, 173, 174, 280, 407, 417, 450, 451, 469, 470, 485, 556, 557
  Regulations Article 426–429, 431, 434
  Regulations, implementing 422, 423, 425, 426
Rehabilitation 4, 307, 329, 335, 345, 346, 380, 387–389, 392, 398, 399, 404, 425, 429, 588
  civil 379–381, 387, 392, 397
  plan 345, 346, 387, 388, 390, 391, 399, 400, 403, 404
    proposal 400–403
Rejection 26, 30, 127, 146, 214, 221, 222, 409, 413, 431, 436, 444, 450, 451, 469, 470, 492, 583
Relief 10, 12, 32, 41, 74, 82, 84, 107, 253, 424, 425, 442, 519–523, 525, 527, 529, 530
In rem
  guarantees 112–115
  rights 112, 117, 433

Remuneration 66, 67, 89, 91, 188, 208, 223, 228, 231, 244, 266, 267, 270, 271, 280, 428, 466
Reno bankruptcy court 467
Reorganization 3–8, 12, 13, 15–17, 32, 33, 100–106, 109–113, 121, 123, 124, 168, 169, 172–175, 439–446, 459–466, 486, 498, 499, 590–593
  agreement 13, 359, 368, 370, 375
    preventive 368
  cases 32, 380, 392, 393, 439
    corporate 380
  corporate 8, 161, 359, 373, 379–381, 392, 397, 530, 554
  expedited 13, 14, 439
  of insolvent companies 3, 17, 299
  plan 4, 5, 14, 15, 102, 109, 111–113, 118, 121–123, 384, 387, 392, 394, 441–446, 459–461, 464–466, 506
    corporate 380
    formal 14
    grant 384
    pre-arranged 481
    pre-negotiated 479, 547, 550
    pre-packaged 24, 479, 547, 550, 551
    prepackaged 462, 463
    ratified out-of-court 127
  procedure
    court-supervised 25, 385, 547, 550
    renewed Out-of-court 108
    statutory 380, 387
    supervised 25
  proceedings 4, 5, 11, 17, 121, 169, 381, 486, 493, 494
    expedited 13–15
    full 14–16
    outof-court 112
    statutory 379–381, 383
  process 99, 105, 110, 111, 551, 552, 584
  traditional 4, 459
Reorganization Court 121, 123
Rep 21, 35–39
Repayment 9, 74, 109, 330, 336, 350, 351, 353, 355, 360, 387, 396, 408, 417
Reported creditors 53
Request 25, 27, 253, 269, 387, 398–400, 402, 432, 434, 453, 454, 467, 468, 472, 473, 484, 485, 491, 559
Rescheduling of interest element 352, 353

Rescue 4, 6, 9, 42, 276–278, 282–287, 302, 303, 311–314, 516–524, 526, 529, 531, 534, 538–540, 565
  companies 309, 321
  corporate 298, 301–304, 306–308, 321, 513, 522
  merger 566, 574, 575
    concept 573
  procedure, corporate 299, 305
  proceedings 258, 261, 266, 275, 277–280, 282–288
Reserves 211, 215, 242, 246, 247, 525, 589
Resolution 11, 12, 22, 23, 31, 32, 35, 36, 49, 59, 61, 63, 64, 91, 131, 192, 193, 227, 319, 381, 386
  of inter-creditor differences 11
Responsive Business Plan 144
Restrictions 72, 102, 106, 114–116, 174, 179, 195, 201, 230, 245, 246, 265, 266, 326, 331, 389, 390, 529
Restructure 5, 10, 12, 28, 44, 63, 76, 78, 79, 81, 82, 85, 86, 99, 100, 132, 137, 138, 140, 141, 407–410
Restructured accounts 353, 354
Restructuring
  negotiations, voluntary 8, 10, 12–16
  plan 10, 133, 146–149, 151, 155, 268, 305, 343, 346, 372, 382, 395, 396, 415, 416, 424–427, 572, 573
    focused 144, 149, 155
    operational 387, 396, 397
  procedures 20, 21, 28, 41, 98, 99, 264, 511, 512, 514–516, 519, 521, 522, 526, 530, 531, 536, 539–542, 548, 549
    intention of Corporate Debt 522, 523
    recognition of Corporate Debt 479, 547, 550, 551
    tax consequences of Corporate Debt 515, 516
  proceedings 131–133, 135, 144, 409–414, 416–418, 481, 484, 486, 487
  process 49, 57, 132, 133, 138, 144, 145, 148, 149, 151, 153, 171, 243, 248, 360–362, 371, 372, 547–550, 598
    formal 138, 143, 146
Restructuring agreements 10, 13, 17, 27, 358–361, 363, 365, 366, 370, 408, 468, 512–514, 516, 518, 519, 523, 524, 539–542

outof-court 479
voluntary 13
Restructuring Chapter 407–410, 416, 417
Restructuring Law 155, 406, 407, 409–412, 414, 416–418
Retail holders 34, 35, 41
Rewe 571, 572
Rights 15–17, 27, 32, 64, 65, 109, 110, 117, 118, 177–181, 190–193, 214–216, 379–382, 386–388, 392, 393, 411, 414–416, 434
  contractual 141, 427, 428, 492
  of creditors 175, 180, 416
  fundamental 504, 506
  reclamation 460–462
  secured 384, 387, 389, 391, 392
Ristrutturazione 364–367, 371
RL 379, 380, 386, 392, 393
Rogers VP 307–309
Rs 346, 347, 501
Rupee debt 338
Russian Federation 490

S

Sacrifice 335–337, 339, 340, 343–345, 352, 353, 355
Sale 75–77, 85, 86, 112, 116, 117, 130, 131, 133–138, 152–155, 281, 282, 289, 325, 330, 331, 454–456, 473–475, 553, 591, 592
  agreement 154
  asset 11
  of assets 76, 103, 112, 152
  proceedings 131, 133, 134
    ordered 152
  process 85, 133–135, 152
    court receivership 133
    expedited 134
    extended 134
    supervised 152
Salz 561, 562, 564–566, 568, 570, 574
  criteria 565, 568, 569, 571–574, 576
  decision 566, 567, 573
Sanction 10, 12, 132, 161, 163, 164, 166, 168, 174, 176, 178, 179, 183, 184, 186–189, 191–194, 253, 254, 316–319
  hearing 187–192, 241, 245, 253, 254, 319

Index

Scale, economies of 548, 561, 581
Schedule A1 199–202, 210, 211, 217, 219, 220, 225
   paragraph 200
Schedule B1 485
Scheme 87, 159, 161–169, 171–194, 196, 225, 238–248, 250–255, 300, 308, 309, 312–320, 379, 380, 486, 493, 500
   of arrangement 57, 63, 81, 87, 161, 168, 169, 171, 174, 196, 299, 300, 306–308, 311, 312, 481, 484, 500, 501
      procedure 299, 300, 302, 305, 317
   companies 163, 182, 189, 241, 242
   court-administered 486
   creditor 182, 239, 241, 245
   creditors committing 242
   documentation 164, 244, 316, 318
   information 318
   meetings 87, 242
   procedure 313
   process 163, 246
   proposals 241
   supervisors 244, 245, 247
      prospective 240
   unreported 190
Scheme Administrators 318, 319
Scope, economies of 548, 561
SCPA 561, 566, 567, 600, 601
Sec 21, 35–39
   staff 36, 37
Sectors, financial 11, 325, 421, 422
Secured
   creditor voting 64
   creditors 64, 65, 67, 112–115, 133, 135, 136, 140–142, 153, 154, 179, 207, 208, 210, 211, 302, 330, 331, 389, 392, 441, 442
      rights of 380, 387, 417
      uncooperative 300
   party 135, 136
Securities 29, 30, 33, 34, 36–42, 65, 67, 73, 136, 139, 210, 211, 242, 330–332, 455, 456, 464–466, 474, 475, 552
   issuance of 34, 109
   laws 30, 33, 35, 40, 41, 445, 455, 465, 466, 474
      federal 36

marketable 339
   new 33, 35, 41
   registered 36, 39, 41, 136
   sale of 41, 456, 475
   subject 465
   unregistered 41
   value of 64, 210
Security
   Securities Act 20, 34–41, 445, 454–456, 466, 473–475
   Securities, exchange of 36, 39
   Securities Interest Act 347
Security interest 106, 117, 136, 141, 179, 331, 427
Seller 239, 460, 461, 570, 580, 581
Senate 23, 102, 103, 259
Separate classes 133, 178, 179, 181, 182, 186, 190, 252, 255, 300, 427
Services, accounting 575, 576
Settlement 138, 140–143, 158, 164, 175, 242, 248, 251, 255, 332, 360, 362, 514, 530, 547
Shareholder
   creditor discharges 526
   issues 243
Shareholders 81–83, 150, 175, 183, 184, 276, 316–318, 385, 386, 388, 392, 393, 397, 398, 408, 462, 526–528, 532, 533, 596, 597
   ordinary 178, 184
Sick Industrial Companies Act 324, 328, 329
SIEC 557, 558
   test 557, 558
SIP 203, 205, 216, 218, 221–223
Slip Copy 49, 479, 480, 493, 501
SME Turnaround Committees 382, 385
SMEs 378, 380, 385
Smid 504, 506
Societe Commerciale 561, 566, 567, 600, 601
Solicitation 44, 426, 431, 436, 443–448, 450, 451, 460, 464–470
Solicitors 205, 217, 218, 268, 596
Solvent companies 181, 182, 488
Southern District 21, 32, 42, 446, 478–481, 486, 487, 489–494, 497, 498, 500, 501, 503
   of Texas 482, 487, 489, 490
Spyglass Management Group Pty Ltd 69, 73, 74

Stakeholders 133, 135, 137, 138, 144, 145, 147, 148, 150, 151, 155, 259, 343, 346, 360, 373, 398, 461
  Stakeholder groups 150, 151
Standing Forum 334, 344–346, 348, 351
Standstill Notice 387, 399–402
Standstill Period 2, 9, 387, 401, 402
State aid 274, 524
State Bank of India 327, 334, 343, 344
Statement 10, 16, 25, 52, 64, 91, 126, 127, 193, 199, 200, 206, 217, 409, 410, 413, 418, 429
  of affairs 197, 199, 200, 206, 217, 233
  of Insolvency Practice 203, 228
Statutory proceedings, court-supervised 381
Steuerrecht 496, 513–515, 518
Stock 21, 24, 386, 387, 390, 393, 397, 584, 601, 602
  designated class of 386
Stockbroker 455, 474
Stockholders 107, 108, 119, 387, 390, 585, 588, 597
Structure, competitive 553, 561, 562, 565–568, 574, 575, 577, 598–601
Sub-principles 519, 521, 522, 525, 541
Sub-standard 339, 340, 342, 346, 349, 351–354
Subcontractors 76, 140, 141, 315
Subject-matter jurisdiction 261
Subordination 516, 528, 534
  of debts 528, 534, 535
Subsection 32, 52, 53, 89–92, 94, 95, 194, 195, 322, 450, 451, 453–456, 469, 470, 472–475, 491, 497
  provisions of 31, 496
Successor 445, 450, 452, 453, 455, 469, 471, 472, 474
Sums 94, 196, 208, 209, 251, 304, 305, 326, 417, 593
Supervision 5, 25, 92, 103, 135, 144, 169, 284, 391, 406, 407, 422, 424, 479, 480, 499, 501, 502
  of French courts 258, 277
  provisional 299, 302–305, 321
Supervisor 130, 135, 146, 197, 202, 203, 205–209, 211, 213, 216, 217, 220, 222–237, 244, 388–391, 409, 428

court-appointed 406, 407
  provisional 302, 303
Supplies 536–539
Supreme Court 23, 31, 150, 151, 549, 583, 586, 587, 589, 591, 592, 597
  of India 327, 328
Synergies 565, 577
System, restructuring 333, 335–338, 340, 343

T

Takeover 81, 83, 84, 330, 571, 573, 593, 594
Tax 22, 58, 103, 112, 125, 274, 392, 393, 464, 513–516, 519, 520, 522–525, 529, 535, 536, 538, 539, 541, 542
  authorities 207, 263, 291, 513, 514, 518–525, 527, 537–542, 547
  balance sheet 517, 525, 528, 530, 531, 533
  base 518, 520, 523, 537, 538
  consequences 248, 511, 512, 515, 516, 526–528, 530–534, 538, 542
    of Corporate Debt Restructuring 511, 513, 515, 517, 519, 521, 523, 525, 527, 529, 531, 533, 535, 537, 539
  exemption 520, 522
  indirect 516, 536
  issues 512, 515, 516, 542
  law 513–517, 519, 522, 524, 534, 535, 539, 541, 542
    applicable 517, 528, 529, 533, 534
  liabilities 513, 514, 518, 521–525, 527–529, 531, 539–542
    deferral of 525
    exemption of 540
    respective 521, 524, 525
    subject 539
  planning 511, 512
  priorities 513, 514, 540, 542
  purposes 528, 531–535
Tax Treatment 511, 512, 524, 535
Taxation 518, 519, 521, 522, 524, 525, 530, 541
  direct business 524
Taxpayers 515, 519, 521–523, 525, 532, 537, 539–541
Telecom 22, 28, 43–51
  liquidation value of 47, 49
Telepiù 574–578

Index 627

Termination 65, 78, 80, 91, 148, 232–234, 273, 274, 279, 284, 313, 369, 434, 436, 547
Test 40, 133, 165, 173, 184, 189, 224, 233, 240, 317, 327, 482, 483, 486–488, 494, 495, 557, 558
  best interest 390
Third parties 2, 6, 8, 9, 68, 75, 124, 178, 209, 249, 268, 270, 272–275, 277, 287, 288, 573
Three-fifths, least 104, 105, 107, 108, 115
Thuronyi 514, 515, 517, 530, 533, 537, 538
TIA 29, 31, 47, 48, 445, 478, 494
Time debts 93, 94
Tipke 514, 515, 519, 530
Tonne 84
Totality 105–107, 114, 115
Touche 575, 576
Toys 546, 568
Trade creditors 81, 137, 212, 381, 384, 385
Trading 77, 78, 84, 86, 199, 234, 235, 239, 245, 271, 272, 483
  insolvent 58, 75, 301–303
Transactions 38, 40, 139, 155, 230, 432–434, 455, 474, 512, 513, 529, 530, 538, 539, 558–560, 576–579, 581–583, 586, 587
  debt-for-equity 529, 535
  intracompany 602
Transfer taxes 516, 536, 538, 539
Treatment 13, 32, 34, 35, 48, 49, 100–102, 105, 109, 111, 115, 119, 147, 148, 352, 353, 426, 427, 429, 430, 436
  of assets 5, 339
  unfavourable 114, 115, 120, 125
Treuhand 561, 562, 564, 566
Tribunal 260, 332, 546, 572, 573
Trust 77–80, 207, 236, 237, 251, 259, 502
  account 303, 304
Trust Account Arrangement 298, 304
Trust assets 236
Trustee 26, 78, 130, 135, 139, 144, 146–148, 154, 155, 251, 252, 368, 380, 388, 389, 393, 394, 440–442, 465
Turkey 421–425, 427, 429, 431, 433, 435

TXU Europe group 158, 159, 240, 247, 250–252
TXU Holding Company CVAs 251, 254
Types 4, 14, 30, 33, 37, 76, 100–110, 112, 114–116, 140, 141, 177–181, 260–262, 439, 445, 447

U

UDL Argos Engineering 180, 301, 317–319
UK Companies Act 158, 161
UK Cross-Border Insolvency Regulation 499
UK Insolvency Act 162, 482, 483, 485, 490, 491
Unanimous consent 384, 385, 387, 400, 401
UNCITRAL 2–4, 42, 160, 423, 478, 486
Undertakings 204, 380, 496, 524, 544, 545, 554–560, 565, 567, 571, 572, 578, 599, 600
Undervalue 230
Underwriter 455, 456, 474, 475
Unfair prejudice 165, 212, 224, 225, 253–255
United States 22, 34, 35, 439, 459–461, 463, 465, 467–469, 481, 486, 487, 489, 490, 492, 493, 501, 502, 585–587, 589–592, 596, 597
  United States Bankruptcy 497, 498
  United States Bankruptcy Court 32, 446, 478–482, 487, 489–494, 497, 498, 500, 501, 503
  United States Code 160, 438, 458, 546
  United States Court of appeal 493
  United States District Court 486
  United States Supreme Court 481, 486, 492, 493, 502
Unsecured creditors 26, 30, 49, 51, 52, 62, 64, 68, 148, 149, 209, 211, 212, 217, 241, 242, 252, 392, 461
  connected 209
  ordinary 243
  unconnected 209, 214
USBC 582–584, 588, 590, 592, 602
USD 21–24, 28–30, 43–46, 48, 50, 84, 158, 189, 190, 238, 239, 248, 249, 298, 303, 304, 430, 462, 464
UStG 537, 538

V

Validity 102, 161, 199, 215, 447, 583
Value 4, 112, 113, 153, 211–214, 240, 312, 340, 346–348, 387–390, 441–443, 452–454, 471–473, 516–518, 527–531, 534–536
  asset 551
  break-up 340, 354
  of creditors 183, 216
  enterprise 381, 387, 398, 399
  quoted 340
  vote 63
VAT 229, 516, 536–539
  consequences 537, 538
Vendors, critical 461, 462
Vesting Order 135
Viability 144, 149, 151, 200, 209, 210, 335, 339, 345, 351, 383, 425, 429, 547–550, 583, 584, 598, 599
Vice President 23
Vote 26, 29–31, 33, 41, 42, 63–65, 147–149, 184–186, 211–213, 215, 216, 218, 219, 222–225, 240, 242, 243, 250–255, 431
  casting 63, 64, 79
  company solicits 466
  creditor class 149
  of creditors 37, 243, 253, 303, 434
  favourable creditor 132
  five 30, 31
  impaired class 443
  secured creditor 64
  soliciting 35, 37, 463, 464, 467
  subject 213, 215

Voting
  process 250, 424, 426, 429–431
  purposes 163, 164, 182, 209, 211, 213, 214, 216, 241

W

Wacker-Chemie 567, 568
Wages 58, 298, 303, 304, 309, 315, 464
Warrant 427, 455, 474
Weak competitor claim 586
Weeds 553, 554, 596
Winding-up 139, 171–174, 187, 190, 225, 250, 306, 308, 487, 488
  of insurance undertakings 158, 168, 173, 174
  order 173, 300, 305, 307–309
Winding-Up Provisions 301
WLR 175–179, 181, 186–188, 190, 191, 194, 213, 216, 219, 223, 224, 233, 318, 485
Workers 105, 112, 301, 303, 304, 309, 321, 331, 463, 596
Workforce 275, 277, 280, 281, 563
Workouts 9–11, 82, 310, 383, 385, 386, 399, 511
Works Bureau 298, 314, 320
Wound 58, 60–62, 80, 82, 88, 172–174, 305, 306, 312, 322, 332, 483
WRH-ARC 31–33

Y

Yukos Oil Company 490

Z

Zinifex 86